THE WORLD OF THE NEW TESTAMENT

THE WORLD OF THE NEW TESTAMENT

ENCOUNTERING TEXTS IN CONTEXT

DAVID CIELONTKO,
TOBIAS NICKLAS,
LILY C. VUONG,
PREDRAG DRAGUTINOVIĆ
EDITORS

FORTRESS PRESS
Minneapolis

THE WORLD OF THE NEW TESTAMENT
Encountering Texts in Context

30 29 28 27 26 25 1 2 3 4 5 6 7 8 9

Library of Congress Control Number: 2025944255 (print)

Cover image: Israel, Lower Galilee, Zippori National Park The city of Zippori (Sepphoris) A Roman Byzantine period city with an abundance of mosaics Mosaic floor in the Cardo, from PhotoStock-Israel / Alamy Stock Photo
Cover design: Ashley Muehlbauer

Print ISBN: 979-8-8898-3449-6
eBook ISBN: 979-8-8898-3450-2

CONTENTS

PREFACE

The idea for this book dates back to a June evening in 2023, when two of us, David Cielontko and Tobias Nicklas, were sitting together in a nice pub in Prague and discussing many things, including some future projects. One topic that came up was teaching resources, particularly for a seminar introducing the world of the New Testament. Of course, there are many introductions to the New Testament, volumes on the history of early Judaism and the New Testament period, and collections of interesting source material. However, it proved challenging to find a recent book that was comprehensive and up to date, yet concise and accessible for students.

Even today, it is unclear whether our solution was the result of an insufficient search for better options, our enthusiasm for specific ideas about creating such a book, or simply the pleasant atmosphere we enjoyed in the pub. In any case, the idea was born to create a new volume. Our goal was to put together a book that would combine solid, fundamental knowledge with an emphasis on the importance of working with sources. The result is now in your hands. However, this would not have been possible without the help of two friends: Lily C. Vuong and Predrag Dragutinović, who agreed to collaborate with us on this project.

This book is the result of our efforts, which would not have been possible without the close cooperation of our editorial team and our excellent team of contributors from around the world. Our contributors come from eleven countries spanning four continents. Since not all contributors are native English speakers, Jacob Cerone and Michael Scott Robertson translated or proofread some chapters; Lily C. Vuong performed a final language review of the entire volume; and finally, Tomáš Blažek assisted with formatting. We are incredibly grateful to all of them.

Last but certainly not least, it is always a pleasure and an honor to work with Fortress Press. We are especially grateful to Carey Newman and his team for their consistently friendly and professional collaboration.

David Cielontko, Tobias Nicklas, Lily C. Vuong,
and Predrag Dragutinović
Prague; Regensburg; Eugene, Oregon;
and Belgrade on June 1, 2025

LIST OF FIGURES

Introduction to the World of the New Testament: A Few Words About This Book

Tobias Nicklas and David Cielontko,
in collaboration with Lily C. Vuong and Predrag Dragutinović

A Word to Our Reader

Possibilities, Facets and Limits of Historical Approaches

An important prerequisite for appropriate study of the writings of the New Testament is to *understand* them as documents written in concrete historical times and contexts. For anyone able to read the New Testament text in its original language, this is a very basic experience. The Greek New Testament is foreign to us. It uses different language, syntax, images, metaphors, and cultural, social, and religious references. To understand it, we must find out what its words meant to their original readers. We must also understand how they perceived the places where the stories took place and how they imagined people would behave, dress, or think. This is by no means an easy task, and it is the fundamental aim of this book. While it is impossible to provide an encyclopedia of all the aspects of the rich and broad historical context in which the New Testament texts were written, we hope this volume can serve as an introduction for anyone who is interested.

The interpretation of the New Testament is not simply a matter of reconstructing the original meaning of the texts. All texts—and especially writings that have shaped cultures over the centuries—can grow and open new possibilities for interpretation. Historically oriented exegesis can help to answer a variety of questions that arise from the very fact that the writings of the New Testament are almost two thousand years old and thus refer to realities of a time and a culture about one hundred generations removed from our own. When one considers how much we seem to take for granted today, that what we encounter every day was completely unthinkable to our grandparents' generation (from cell phones to hot showers), and what things we barely know today that our grandparents took for granted (from telegraphs to poor medical care), then one can get some idea of what it might mean to bridge a hundred generations. It is important to stress this point, since we may not always be able to notice how *different* the New Testament world is; the living tradition we are part of is continually adapting our perception of it to the changing culture and society. It is not easy to perceive these changes when we are part of them. This is usually only possible from a certain distance, and through this book, we would like to provide at least some experience of this distance. For example, delving into other ancient texts from the period of the New Testament can easily show us that people back then not only talked and thought differently but also laughed at or valued different things than we do.

Engaging with the historical context of the biblical texts does not mean proving the historicity of the Bible—that is, that the events recounted in the text have happened in exactly the form in which it is told. This is clearly not possible because the writings of the Bible—and also those of the New Testament—repeatedly contradict each other in various details. The Gospels, for example, report different last words of the dying Jesus on the cross. The words of institution of the Eucharist reported in the three synoptic Gospels and in Paul differ in theologically important details. The Gospel of Matthew and the Gospel of Luke pass on a different family tree of Jesus of Nazareth and these family trees cannot be harmonized simply. This all points to the important aspect that the claim to truth of a narrative (or of a text in general) does not have to be fulfilled in every historical detail in order to be truthful. Even stories that might have happened still require interpretation. For example, John 2:18–22 provides an interesting insight into this process of interpretation. When Jesus responds to the Jews' request for a sign proving his authority by saying he will raise the temple in three days after its destruction, everyone present logically assumed he was talking about the Jerusalem temple where the episode took place. However, the author of the Gospel tells us that "after he was raised from the dead, his disciples recalled what he had said. Then they believed the scripture and the words that Jesus had spoken" (John 2:22). Clearly, Jesus never rebuilt the Jerusalem temple in three days. However, the true meaning of his words was only recognized later when his disciples reflected on the event and the scriptures.

Therefore, we need to understand what narratives do, and we need to differentiate between the terms "historically accurate" and "true." The ability to tell stories is one of the most important characteristics that make people human. In this context, we speak of *homo narrans*—that is, the being that only becomes human through the ability to narrate.[1] If people want to understand something about themselves—as individuals or as a group—they have to tell stories about their origins; about their plans and hopes; about significant events and decisions in their lives; about other people who are important to them, who have shaped them; and much more. Being able to encounter oneself at all in such stories, to *construct* oneself, is what makes us human. However, whether a story is true or not does not necessarily depend on whether every detail really happened as reported. A story about a relationship with another person is about something deeper than historically tangible details; it is about things that *cannot be* counted, measured, weighed, or even photographed by simple means. It is about friendship, love, perhaps even a deep-seated enmity. However, a story about great love can be true even if details are not historically accurate, cannot be proven, or are contradictory. Whether one of the two lovers was wearing a blue or a green sweater when they first met, or had forgotten his wristwatch (or not), may be completely irrelevant to the veracity of the narrative. Such a story may not be historically trustworthy in every detail, but it is true if it makes clear that two lovers met here—and if these two really loved each other.

Additionally, the story may change depending on the context. For example, when we tell the story to the police as a witness to an accident, we emphasize different aspects than when we tell the same story to our friends or family. The context in which a story is told shapes its function, content, and meaning. This is particularly relevant for stories told in retrospect.

The same applies to the writings of the Bible: Their claim to truth is so profound that it does not have to fail because of historical details. The Gospels, for example, can be read as origin stories—that is, stories that allow us to understand the roots of what Christians understand as the *good news* (*euangelion*, Mark 1:1–3). The Gospel of Mark is not trying to inform us primarily about Jesus's life. Its truth claim is to demonstrate that Jesus of Nazareth is the crucified Christ and the Son of God who was raised from the dead by God. Whether or not this truth claim can be accepted is not primarily a problem of historical details, but a question of belief, or trust (*pistis*), in the good news proclaimed by this text (Mark 1:15) and thus the view of the world that it conveys.

Nevertheless, and precisely for this reason, it is necessary to not only be historically informed, but also to have a *critical historical approach*. Since the New Testament writings were composed by specific individuals in particular historical contexts, they contain problematic statements that reflect their historical contexts more than anything else. Sometimes texts from the New Testament have led to terrible interpretations that despise people: Biblical arguments were used to feed Christian antisemitism, to defend racism and slavery, and to discriminate against women and other marginalized groups. They played and still play a role in structures of spiritual and sexual abuse in the churches.

To know that the Jewish authorities at the time of Jesus had no legal power to pass a death sentence and that the crucifixion penalty at that time was applied by the Roman occupation to people who did not have Roman citizenship can help to speak out against such horrific statements as "The Jews killed our Lord Jesus." We should always be aware that countless Jewish people were killed on the basis of sentences like these.[2] Many other examples, some of which can also be found in this book, could be cited here. In other words, the New Testament is a wonderful book but in the wrong hands, it can become a dangerous book. This is actually something that the New Testament itself thematizes. For example, in the passages in which the devil himself quotes Scripture (cf. Matt 4:6), we can see how easily the biblical word of God can become a diabolical and destructive lie.

Ultimately, however, it is also necessary to be aware of the limits of what can be known historically. History does not equate with the past; it is an image of the past captured in a narrative.[3] Such a narrative is based on the interpretation of the extant sources about the past that are preserved, and these sources are extremely fragmentary, especially for antiquity. Much of what we would like to know is lost because there are no adequate sources. There are actually thousands of ancient texts that only exist in the form of their titles because the texts themselves did not survive—and even they covered only aspects of the past, as many events were never documented at all.

For example, in the Jewish history of the first and second centuries CE, we are best informed about parts of the first century and especially about the Jewish War of 66–70 CE because here we have the documents of a Jewish historian, Josephus (ca. 37–100 CE), who in many cases was an eyewitness to what he reported. For later events such as the devastating diaspora revolt of 115–17 CE or the Bar Kokhba War (132–35 CE), however, such sources are almost completely lacking. Moreover, these events relate to what we call political history. Sources on the everyday lives of ordinary people, among whom Jesus spent most of his time, are much more limited.

Historiography of antiquity therefore always has to do with highly fragmentary knowledge. It is only reliable when it reveals its methods and constantly reflects on its limitations. Historiography, like any kind of human narrative, can never be completely objective. Academic historiography reveals the sources and methods used, as well as the perspectives employed to distinguish between historical facts, interpretations, and hypotheses. Facts alone do not constitute history. First, they must be placed in a meaningful context. This is only possible with the help of interpretations that lead to hypotheses. Therefore, in addition to the dimensions of historically informed and critical historical exegesis, there is also the need to critically scrutinize the constructions of history that we reconstruct. Do they really incorporate all available sources properly? How strong are their arguments? What are their limitations and omissions? How well are they historically validated? In a world where the phrase *fake news* seems to be omnipresent, this dimension of critical thinking when dealing with history is urgently needed. People who want to remain free must constantly rethink the narratives we construct about history in an appropriately critical way.

A Preface for Christian Readers

Christianity considers itself to be a religion of revelation—that is, it claims to represent truths that can be traced back to God himself. This idea continues to represent an indispensable theological basis for all Christian denominations. In our book, this is evident from the fact that the authors of the individual chapters come from different confessions and beliefs. At the same time, it was an important rediscovery of the Age of Enlightenment that Christianity has developed historically. This ultimately applies to all its institutions and accomplishments, its theological insights, and its Holy Scriptures—the Bible of the Old and New Testaments. Jesus of Nazareth was also a person, whose life can at least be roughly determined within history. The realization that Christianity (or rather the various forms in which Christianity is encountered today) is subject to a historical development is complementary to the claim that Christianity is a religion of revelation. The important conclusion is that God reveals himself in human history through and with the help of specific people. In other words, the word of God is encountered through the words of humans.

That this is indeed the case is shown most profoundly in the incarnation—that is, in the fact that the living Word of God, which was begotten by God before all time, became a person in Jesus of Nazareth (John 1:14). Christians believe that God came into the world in the most intense way possible in the concrete, historical, Jewish man, Jesus of Nazareth. Similarly, Jesus's resurrection was a historical event witnessed by specific people who expressed their experiences through the language and ideas they knew. This means that the Christian gospel is not primarily about some philosophical wisdom but about a historical event and its meaning within history. But this idea can be taken even further: The entire Bible is a testimony to how God has shown himself again and again within history—or, to quote a biblical passage, how God has spoken (and continues to speak) "in many and various ways" (Heb 1:1).[4]

To read the Bible as a part of history is therefore inherent to understanding the revelation of God throughout history. In other words, to assert that Christianity is a historical religion means that to understand its history is a *theological enterprise*. Coming to terms with the historical Jesus, Paul, or any of Jesus's other early followers means seeing them differently. Most likely, it involves recognizing that in their everyday life, they had more in common with other Jews of their time than with us today.[5]

Interpreting the writings of the Bible with the help of historical approaches does not mean that they can no longer be read as inspired by God.[6] However, it must always be borne in mind that the human authors of Scripture, as well as their readers, were and remain people of their time. This begins already on a level of language: Jesus spoke in Aramaic; the authors of the New Testament wrote in the Greek of their time, and we modern readers tend to read the New Testament in our modern vernacular languages. This process already involves movement through various cultures and epochs, each represented by different ideas and notions about the world. The first Christian communities read the writings which came to be the New Testament through the lenses of their own culture, society, and religious ideas. And we do the same. It is not possible to avoid this, which means we have to do it responsibly.

This, however, does not necessarily mean that Christianity cannot represent timeless truths. But these are always communicated in historically determined conditions so that we can understand them in our own language and culture. In this book, we take these fundamental considerations seriously, and we invite you to come closer to the richness of what constitutes the writings of the New Testament within the broad historical contexts of their origins. As it should now be clear, reading these writings as historical documents does not mean underestimating or neglecting their theological claims. It means understanding them as human testimonies about confrontation with God.

World of the New Testament

To read the writings of the New Testament in a historically responsible manner means to understand the world of the New Testament as comprehensively as possible. What is meant by *world of the New Testament* is actually the world of the ancient Mediterranean region as seen through the lenses of useful history for understanding of the New Testament. In other words, it is a particular perspective that selects some aspects of a much larger and complex world of the selected historical period, which seem to be relevant for interpreting the New Testament texts and the histories behind them.

At the same time, we should avoid speaking of the "background" (Ger. *Umwelt*) of the New Testament. This would create the false impression that the New Testament writings (and the people who wrote and received them) represent a special, isolated entity, not fully belonging to the world around them. This is clearly not the case. The serious consequences of such prejudices can already be seen from the fact that the Greek of the New Testament was long treated as a kind of "special language" that differed in important respects from the usual Greek of the time. This is flawed, yet it is still evident today when examining lexicons that define specific meanings for significant words in the New Testament. For example, the word *ekklēsia* is often considered to have the special meaning of "church" in the New Testament, while it simply means "assembly." Similarly, *metanoia* is often considered to have the special meaning of "repentance," while its standard meaning is "to change one's mind, rethink."

When we speak of the world of the New Testament, we are interested in the *life-world* (Ger. *Lebenswelt*) of its authors and original readers. By *life-world* we mean the universe of meaning and understanding that shaped the world as experienced by these individuals in their everyday lives This can include diverse circumstances such as spatial and temporal structures, the organization of daily life, food production and consumption, clothing, engagement with nature, religious beliefs, political and economic circumstances, daily habits, social and cultural codes, knowledge of nature and the cosmos, cultural stereotypes, and hopes and fears. To understand these, one must understand the basic contours of the history of the time in which they developed.

The aim of this book is to relate the life-world of the authors and addressees of these writings to their textual world. By *textual world*, we mean the world that these writings presuppose in order for what they speak or argue about to function plausibly. Anyone who loves science fiction or fantasy novels knows that life-worlds and textual worlds can differ significantly. However, even in these genres, these worlds are not entirely separate from one another. A spaceship in a 1970s science fiction novel differs significantly from one in a more recently written novel. This is simply because our knowledge and perception have changed in today's world compared to earlier times, which in turn changes our imagination. The life-world of the author of the Acts of the Apostles may largely coincide with the textual world he constructs in his writing. However, the situation is very different for the Apocalypse of John, since it is highly unlikely that its author ever encountered a fiery red dragon in everyday life (cf. Rev 12:3). Nevertheless, he interprets his life-world in such a way that he is able to construct a textual world in which aspects of his life are meaningfully interpreted through the fall of the dragon to earth (Rev 12:12).

Finally, speaking of the world of the *New Testament* is also a simplification. The writings that comprise the New Testament were written in the first and second centuries CE. However, the collection known as the New Testament developed from these writings in a lengthy, complex process which today can only be reconstructed in its main lines.[7]

On the Structure and Use of This Book

This book contains twenty-three chapters offering a selection of the topics we believe to be the most important for accessing the exciting world of the New Testament. Many more chapters could be added, but we hope that this selection will provide solid basics for anyone interested in understanding the New Testament texts in more depth. This book can be, of course, read cover to cover, but individual chapters can be also read on their own, or in thematical clusters. Every chapter is self-contained and can be read separately.

All chapters follow the same structure with a certain didactic purpose in mind. It always starts with an overview of the topic by a renowned expert. This overview provides some important information about the topic in a concise form. Naturally, this format does not allow us to dive into complex discussions or polemics; the goal here is plain: to convey certain knowledge. In order to be curious about more complex and deeper questions, we always need to have some basic scope of knowledge. Therefore, it is important to start somewhere, and this section seeks to offer that starting point.

This is followed by the second part devoted to the primary texts. Any overview or synthesis of knowledge is a result of previous interpretations of the sources. It is very important for us to emphasize that in order to construct bigger ideas and concepts about the world of the New Testament, we must always start with the sources. While our overviews do not allow us to delve much into the sources, this second part is reserved for that purpose. It offers a small selection of primary texts in English translation that form the basis of our knowledge of the given topic. Of course, this selection provides only a tiny fraction of the sources we use to build our synthesis and theories in scholarship. However, we believe that it is crucial to go back to the sources and to discuss their interpretations and implications for our understanding of the ancient world. Without sources and their interpretation, there is no knowledge. This is an important truth that we hope this section can illustrate.

After the selection of the primary texts from the world of the New Testament, the final section focuses on selected passages of the New Testament. Since we believe that knowledge of the historical context is important to the interpretation of the New Testament texts, this final section provides some examples of how our understanding can be broadened when we are historically informed. Of course, our brief examples can only give a small sample, but our intention is to encourage you to discover and explore more. If the topic caught your attention, you can find more information in the chapter endnotes and in the suggested further reading at the end of each chapter.

We see this book as a useful tool in a variety of contexts. It can be used as a textbook in the classroom for New Testament studies, where individual chapters can be selected for a seminar or course. These chapters could be assigned for home reading, with further discussion of the primary text examples in class, possibly supplemented by many other examples. They can also be selected as introductions for more specialized courses focusing only on historical, social, or religious contexts. We encourage you to use this book as a toolkit, supplemented in various ways by other resources.

However, this book can also be fruitfully used as a handbook for individual study. We believe that the reader will benefit from the breadth of perspectives and topics covered, as well as from good recommendations for further reading, which provide ample opportunity for deeper engagement.

Notes

1 For basic information on this, see Albert Koschorke, *Wahrheit und Erfindung: Grundzüge einer allgemeinen Erzähltheorie* (Fischer, 2017), 9–12.

2 See, for example, Sarah Rollens, Eric M. Vanden Eykel, and Meredith J. C. Warren, eds., *Judeophobia and the New Testament: Texts and Contexts* (Eerdmans, 2025).

3 See Hayden White, *Metahistory: The Historical Imagination in Nineteenth-Century Europe* (The Johns Hopkins University Press, 1973).

4 On the importance of the role of testimony for history and theology, see Paul Ricœur, "The Hermeneutics of Testimony," in *Essays on Biblical Interpretation* (Fortress, 1980), 119–54.

5 Franz Mussner, "Der 'Jude' Jesus (1971)," in: *Jesus von Nazareth im Umfeld Israels und der Urkirche*, Wissenschaftliche Untersuchungen zum Neuen Testament 111 (Mohr Siebeck, 1999), 89–97. A case such as this very fundamental contribution, which ends in an in-depth reflection on statements of the creed, is a clear sign of how historical work and theological reflection based on faith can go hand in hand.

6 However, naive and dangerous forms of pure verbal inspiration must be overcome. Important insights for this can be found, for example, in Stefan Alkier, Christos Karakolis, and Tobias Nicklas, *The Promise of Ecumenical Interpretation* (Fortress, 2024).

7 The exact process is still a matter of debate on many levels. For an overview see, Stefan Alkier and David M. Moffitt, *New Testament Basics: A Guide for Reading and Interpreting the Text* (Fortress, 2022) 21–44.

CHAPTER ONE

A Short History of the Hellenistic and Roman Periods in the Mediterranean

Stefan Pfeiffer
(Martin-Luther-Universität Halle-Wittenberg)

Historical Awareness

"THE NAME ALEXANDER (the Great) marks the end of one world era and the beginning of another."[1] With these words, Johann Gustav Droysen (1808–84) "invented" the Hellenistic period, which began with the conquests of Alexander the Great in 334 BCE and led to Greek-Macedonian rule over large parts of the Middle East and Egypt. During this period, a cultural and religious fusion took place across the world, led by Greek elements, which ultimately prepared the ground for Christianity. The origin of the word *Hellenism* can be traced back to the Bible. In 2 Maccabees 4:13, *hellēnismos* refers to the adoption of the Greek way of life, and in Acts 6:1, the fledgling Christian community is divided into *hellēnistai* (Greek-speaking Jews) and *hebraioi* (Aramaic speaking Jews).

The fact that many ancient contemporaries saw Alexander as heralding a new era is evident in Daniel, which describes a vision of a ram and a goat: The goat represents the rule of the Greeks, which destroys the ram, symbolizing the rule of the Persians (Dan 8: 20–26). During the second century BCE, it became increasingly clear that a new superpower was shaping the world: Rome. The Greek historian Polybius (ca. 200–120 BCE) highlights this in his universal history: Within only fifty-three years, between 220 and 167 BCE, almost the entire world had fallen under the sole rule of the Romans.[2] Before that time, there had been no connection between Italy and Africa on the one hand and Greece and Asia on the other, but the Romans brought about an "intertwining" (*symplokē*), so that since then history has been a whole, as it were a single body.[3]

Modern historiography considers Augustus's victory over Cleopatra's kingdom in 30 BCE to be the end of the Hellenistic era. This was indeed a decisive turning point in ancient history. For Christians, the birth of Christ under Augustus marked the beginning of a new era. However, if we look at the social and cultural developments triggered by Greek and Macedonian rule over a vast part of Asia, it is entirely justified to extend the Hellenistic period well into the

Roman era. The reign of Emperor Hadrian provides a good turning point. When Hadrian ascended the throne, almost half a millennium after Alexander, much of the known world was under the rule of an emperor who considered himself to be the great unifier of all Greeks.[4] By this time, even the Greeks began to identify with the Roman Empire.[5] Since Alexander's conquests, a globalized world had developed, largely pacified by Rome, where people could communicate throughout in Latin or Greek. Within this Pax Romana, people could travel safely and interact with one another.

The travel routes of the bilingual empire simultaneously became the channels for spreading the word of God because it was only against the backdrop of the empire's high degree of connectivity, urban lifestyle, and linguistic unity that the Great Commission—"Go into all the world and proclaim the good news to the whole creation," (Mark 16:15)—could be fulfilled.

The Successors of Alexander the Great

After the death of Alexander the Great (323 BCE), his generals succeeded his rule over the empire.[6] We call them "successors" or, using the Greek term, the *Diadochi*. They divided the satrapies (provinces) of Alexander's empire among themselves and fought countless wars against each other over the next forty years. In the fog of these wars, several successor empires emerged by 281 BCE, named after the founders of their respective dynasties: the Seleucid Empire (primarily in Asia), the Ptolemaic Empire (primarily in Egypt, Cyrene, and Cyprus), and the Antigonid Empire (Macedonia). Later, smaller kingdoms emerged, such as that of the Attalids in Western Asia Minor, and even a Greek kingdom formed in Bactria in the Hindu Kush. Alongside these kingdoms were the trading powers of Rhodes and various independent Greek cities, which joined together to form city leagues (*koina*). From the Mediterranean to the Hindu Kush and Ethiopia, Greeks and Macedonians now determined the political conditions, and Greek became the lingua franca of the known world. Greek cultural techniques and ways of life also frequently merged with local practices, the aforementioned *hellēnismos* criticized in 2 Maccabees.

The Greeks' longing for peace in this age of wars—and the entire Hellenistic period was marked by such conflict—is expressed in a hymn by the Athenians to Demetrius Poliorcetes, one of the Diadochi: "The other gods are so far away or have no ears or do not exist or are not turned toward us. But we see you present, not wooden or stone, but real. Therefore, we pray to you, 'First, bring us peace, beloved!'"[7] From then on, it was good Greek practice to honor the living king as a god, savior, and benefactor with temples, altars, and priests.[8] Many Indigenous peoples also established cults for their kings from Macedonia, partly in the tradition of the ancient monarchies, and partly in the adaptation of Greek cultic elements.

1 Maccabees, however, shows that these Greek-Macedonian kings were not loved by all their subjects. On the contrary, it states that Alexander's successor dynasties increased "wickedness on earth" (1 Macc 1:9). In fact, many of the foreign kings eventually established exploitative laws in the regions they had subjugated.

In some regions, unexpectedly long periods of peace led to a flourishing of art and culture. This is particularly evident in the longest-lasting dynasty, that of the Ptolemies in Egypt (306–330 BCE). The library and museum in its capital, Alexandria, made the city a symbol of Greek education and science that still shines today. It was also here that the Pentateuch was translated into Greek, known as the Septuagint (abbreviated as LXX) after the seventy-two scholars who accomplished the work, and it was home to the largest Jewish diaspora community in the ancient world.

The arrival of the Celts—whom the Greeks at the time called *Galatai*—in 279 BCE came as a shock to the new "Greek" world. They pillaged their way to Egypt, either as mercenaries for Hellenistic kings or as raiders. Eventually, the Galatians settled in the center of Asia Minor in the region named after them, Galatia. Although they remained Celts, over time they adopted the Greek cultural forms of expression. It was to these Galatians, a Celtic people, that Paul addressed his only letter not directed either to Greeks, Romans, or a city.

The Seleucid Empire is a prime example of Greek rule over foreign cultures, as its kings ruled over numerous peoples. There were petty kings and dynasts, temple rulers, and Greek cities to which the Seleucids granted partial autonomy, as well as ethnic groups that were subject to a Seleucid governor.

Like every Hellenistic king, Seleucids did not see themselves as the kings of a particular people but used the term *king* (*basileus*) in an absolute sense. Their kingdom and people were their *affairs* (*pragmata*), which they administered together with their advisory staff and their friends (*philoi*) of Greek and Macedonian origin. Like every Hellenistic king, it was important for the Seleucids to appear victorious and to gain military glory: Their charisma legitimized their position of authority.

However, the victorious Antiochus IV Epiphanes was forced to bow to the new power of Rome on the "Day of Eleusis" in 168 BCE: Although he had conquered Egypt, he did not submit to the legions arrayed against him, but instead simply obeyed the will of an embassy that demanded he renounce Egypt. Rome was now the only remaining superpower in the ancient world. Antiochus IV Epiphanes was also the king against whom the Maccabees dared to revolt in Judea. The uprising, which began in 167 BCE and whose success in 165 BCE is still commemorated today by the festival of Hanukkah, led to the establishment of the Hasmonean kingdom in Judea.

The Seleucids quickly lost their holding in Asia, leaving them with only a small empire in Syria. The Roman general Pompey dissolved what was once Alexander's largest successor empire in 63 BCE. When Cleopatra died by suicide thirty-three years later, Egypt also became a province. The Hellenistic states on the shores of the Mediterranean had been absorbed into the Roman Empire. Of course, Rome did not rule directly everywhere because in principle it was sufficient for the Romans to install loyal kings in neighboring empires, as the example of Herod in Judea shows. After the death of Cleopatra, the Romans ruled in this way, either directly or indirectly, over the entire Mediterranean region.

A New "Golden" Age
The Prince of Peace and His Successors

Parallel to Rome's rise to world power, numerous bloody conflicts arose within the Roman elite from the end of the second century BCE. The last of these civil wars resulted from the disputes over succession that followed the assassination of Gaius Julius Caesar in 44 BCE.[9] His son Gaius Octavius (Octavian), who was adopted in his will and subsequently took the name Gaius Julius Caesar, prevailed in a comprehensive war against Mark Antony and Cleopatra. His victory in 30 BCE brought in a new era of peace to the entire Mediterranean region. Three years later, he was awarded the honorary title of Augustus by the Senate. Honored in this way, he transformed the Roman Republic into a military autocracy tailored entirely to meet his own personal needs. However, he was a master of political communication because he avoided presenting himself as a monarch to his Roman subjects. After all, a monarchy was incompatible with Roman ideas of freedom (*libertas*). For this reason, Augustus, as the "first man" of the republic (*princeps*), wanted to gain acceptance for his rule among the decisive political actors. He therefore proclaimed the "restoration of the republic" (*res publica restituta*) to the Senate, the army, and the urban population. The Roman historian Tacitus later wrote that Augustus had "under the style of 'Prince,' gathered beneath his empire a world outworn by civil broils."[10] Now, with respect to the Roman Empire from Augustus to Diocletian, we refer to the "first man in the state" as the principate.

The Pax Romana

The poets praised Augustus as the destined ruler of Rome, chosen by providence, and the founder of a new golden age. He fulfilled Jupiter's early prophecy of giving the Romans an *imperium sine fine*[11] (command without

Emperor	Reign	Events
Julio–Claudian dynasty		
Imperator Caesar Augustus	27 BCE–14 CE	birth of Jesus
Tiberius Caesar Augustus	14–37	crucifixion of Jesus
Gaius Caesar Augustus Germanicus (Caligula)	37–41	
Tiberius Claudius Caesar Augustus Germancius	41–54	47 start of Paul's mission journeys 48/50 Jerusalem Council ca. 50 start of Paul's letters
Nero Claudius Caesar Augustus Germanicus	54–68	56 end of Paul's third mission journey 60 death of Paul 64/67 death of Peter (in Rome?)
Year of the Four Emperors	69	
Flavian dynasty		
Imperator Caesar Vespasianus Augustus	69–79	70 destruction of Jerusalem ca. 70 Gospel of Mark
Imperator Titus Caesar Vespasianus Augustus	79–81	
Imperator Caesar Domitianus Augustus Germanicus	81–96	ca. 80/90 Gospel of Matthew ca. 90 Gospel of Luke
Nerva–Antonine dynasty		
Imperator Nerva Caesar Augustus	96–98	
Imperator Caesar Nerva Traianus Augustus	98–117	100/110 Gospel of John 112 Rescript of Trajan to Pliny concerning Christians
Imperator Caesar Traianus Hadrianus Augustus	117–38	
Imperator Caesar Titus Aelius Hadrianus Antoninus Augustus Pius	138–61	
Imperator Caesar Marcus Aurelius Antoninus Augustus	161–80	
Imperator Caesar Marcus Aurelius Commodus Antoninus Augustus	180–92	

Figure 1.1. Roman emperors and events during the early Jesus movement.

end). In the account of his deeds, Augustus proclaims that Rome's power extends to the ends of the earth, for even the Indians begged for the friendship (*amicitia*) of the Romans.[12] The *orbis terarrum* had now become an *orbis Romanus*.

Subjects of this rule also welcomed this new era of peace, at least outwardly. The cities of Asia Minor announced a competition to see who could best honor Augustus. It was certainly no coincidence that the Roman proconsul won this competition by "suggesting" that the cities' calendars be aligned with the birth of Augustus. This was done on the following grounds: "for the world, the beginning of the good news (euangelia) brought by him [Augustus] was the birthday of the god [Augustus]."[13] Although Augustus was not a god in Rome itself, but rather the son of god (*divi filius*), the Greeks and inhabitants of the East naturally elevated him to the status of their formerly deified kings. The provincials established cults for him, some out of inner conviction, others for political reasons—such as the hope of gaining Rome's favor—and still others as a form of lip service. The aforementioned calendar reform, for example, which the cities carried out at the "suggestion" of a governor, indicates that coercion may also have been at work here. What remains astonishing, however, is that over time, more and more subjects came to identify with Rome and sought to become Romans. A hundred years later, with an awareness of the empire's attractiveness, Pliny the Elder summed up Rome's "manifest destiny," saying that the city was "chosen by the providence of the Gods to render even heaven itself more glorious, to unite the scattered empires of the earth, to bestow a polish upon men's manners, to unite the discordant and uncouth dialects of so many different nations by the powerful ties of one common language, to confer the enjoyments of discourse and of civilization upon mankind, to become, in short, the mother country of all nations of the Earth."[14] Rome, of course, did not see itself as an oppressor, but as the protector of all people.[15]

The Augustan ideology of peace provides the political and social backdrop against which Jesus of Nazareth was born in Bethlehem (Luke 2:1–21). His "good news" (euangelion) can, in turn, be interpreted on a social level as competing with Rome's "good news." The uprisings in Judea, in particular, show that for many subjects, Roman peace was nothing more than graveyard peace: Those people who refused to accept the blessings Rome bestowed on civilization were mercilessly destroyed by the legions, as demonstrated by the Jewish War and the suppression of the Bar Kokhba Revolt. Although the New Testament is largely a very "Rome friendly" text (cf. Matt 22:21; Matt 27; Rom 13:1–7), in part because its mission was to convert Romans to Christianity, it can also be read indirectly as a form of "liberation theology" that addresses the exploitation of the rural population by Rome's tax collectors and reveals the people's longing for salvation (cf. Luke 4:18–19).

Nevertheless, uprisings among the provincial population were rare, and explicitly anti-Roman texts are certainly nonexistent, since it was the victors who "wrote the history." Criticism of Rome could therefore only be expressed indirectly, for example in prophecy, whether in the book of Revelation or the Sibylline Oracles. Due to the plight of the people, Jesus's good news fell on fertile ground, not only because it promised salvation in a hopeless situation (Rom 5:8; 1 Cor 15:3–5), but also because his followers practiced Jesus's "works of mercy" (Matt 25:34–36) in an extremely merciless world.[16]

The Julio–Claudian and Flavian Dynasties and the Survival of Hellenism

Augustus founded the ruling family known today as the Julio–Claudian dynasty. The modern name is composed of the familial name of Augustus and that of his successor, Tiberius (14–37 CE). The first *princeps* became a member of the Julian family after his adoption by Gaius *Julius* Caesar. His adopted successor, Tiberius Julius Caesar, was originally named Tiberius *Claudius* Nero and thus came from the Claudian family. Tiberius was the emperor whose image Jesus and his contemporaries would have seen on coins (cf. Matt 22:15–21); he was also the ruler under whom Pontius Pilate, the prefect of Judea,[17] executed Jesus as a traitor.

Tiberius's successor, Gaius (37–41 CE), is known as Caligula (which means "the little soldier's boot"). He renounced the practice established by Augustus of an autocracy disguised as a republic, openly showing his contempt for the senators. Among other things, it is said that he wanted to make his horse consul and

Figure 1.2. A coin of Tiberius the emperor from Utica, 27/28 CE. (Reinhard Saczewski, Wikimedia Commons. Used under the Creative Commons Public Domain Mark 1.0.)

have himself worshipped as a god in Rome. He also turned the Jews against him because he planned to erect an image of himself—an "abomination of desolation" (cf. Mark 13:14)—in the Temple of Jerusalem. Before he could do so, however, he was assassinated. In Roman historiography, Caligula is considered a madman because the history of these events were written by senators or circles close to the Senate. Thus, those emperors who did not seek to establish a consensus with the Senate were considered bad emperors.

Compared to Caligula, Claudius (41–54 CE) was relatively harmless. He reigned before his adopted son Nero (54–68 CE) ascended the throne. Nero, however, was described in the worst possible terms by the aforementioned senatorial historians. If his later critics are to be believed, Nero, the last representative of the Julio–Claudian dynasty, transformed his rule into an open monarchy based on the Hellenistic model. He ruthlessly abused senators and was not interested in state affairs. Instead, he wished to be an artist. He is known for his performances as a musician, his tour of Greece, and above all, the great fire of Rome in 64 CE. Christians appear for the first time in pagan tradition within this context. The Roman historian Tacitus reports that Nero had Christians executed en masse as scapegoats for the fire.[18] Perhaps, as Christian tradition would have it, Peter and Paul also experienced martyrdom in Rome because of Nero's execution of Christians (1 Clem 5–6). Nero then rebuilt the city center, which had been destroyed by the fire, into a magnificent and extensive palace complex, the Golden House (*domus aurea*). Shortly afterward, the Senate declared Nero an enemy of the state, and a slave helped him in his suicide in 68 CE.

With Claudius and Nero, we have entered the period when the first written records of Christianity emerged—most notably through Paul, who not only preached in the eastern Mediterranean between 47 and 56 CE but also wrote his letters during this time.

Two years before Nero's death, an initially successful uprising had broken out in Judea, but the empire struck back in the form of General Vespasian. Legions from the East finally succeeded in establishing him as emperor during the conflicts of the so-called Year of the Four Emperors in 68/69 CE. To secure the throne in Rome, he left the suppression of the Jewish revolt to his son Titus, who razed Jerusalem to the ground. This brings us to the period when the Gospel of Mark was probably written as Jesus's prophecy of the destruction of the temple (Mark 13:1–2) is commonly regarded as *vaticinium ex eventu*—that is, a prediction made after the event. Thus, it was not Jesus himself who predicted this event, but rather that the author of the Gospel attributed the prediction to him based on his direct experience of it.

All that remains today of the artificial plateau on which the temple once stood is the Wailing Wall. This event marked the beginning of almost 2,000 years of Jewish diaspora. The triumphal procession celebrating the victory over the Jews is depicted on the inside of the Arch of Titus in the Roman forum, and the spoils brought back from the temple helped finance the construction of the Colosseum in Rome. The victory over the Jews provided military legitimacy for an emperor who did not come from an ancient noble family. Additionally, before Vespasian was proclaimed emperor, he had performed two healing miracles in Alexandria. On behalf of the god Serapis, he had restored sight to a blind man and enabled a lame man to walk again (cf. Matt 11:5).[19] This clearly demonstrated the emperor's claim to lead the people back to an Augustan Age after the Roman civil war.

Vespasian was succeeded by his two sons, one after the other. First came Titus (79–81 CE), during whose reign Mount Vesuvius buried Pompeii in volcanic ash, and then Domitian (81–96 CE) succeeded his brother. Whereas Vespasian and Titus are regarded as good emperors in senatorial historiography, Domitian is portrayed in similarly grim terms to Caligula and Nero. He also shared their fate and was assassinated. Later, Christian historians would attempt to prove that these "bad emperors" were also "persecutors of Christians." In doing so, Christians wanted to demonstrate that Christian values and senatorial ideals were compatible, and that Christianity and the rule of Rome were not at odds: "Such are ever our persecutors—men unjust, impious, foul—men whom you yourselves are accustomed to condemn; and those whom they condemn you have become accustomed to restore. But from among so many emperors down to today, men wise in things divine and human, pick me out one who warred against the Christians!"[20]

The Adopted Emperors and the Transformation of Hellenism

With the death of the "tyrant" Domitian, the senators decided that the *princeps* should no longer be determined based on dynastic origin but rather that the most suitable candidate should be adopted as successor.[21] The Senator-Emperor Nerva, who ruled for only two years, adopted Trajan (98–117 CE), who acted as *optimus princeps* and expanded the empire as far as Mesopotamia with his military campaigns. It was also he who, in his rescript to Pliny the Younger around 110 CE, laid down the state's policy toward Christians, stating that they should not be "searched out." In the same rescript, the Christians' self-identification is expressed for the first time in their statement "I am a Christian" (*Christianus sum*).[22]

Trajan was succeeded by the second adopted emperor, Hadrian (117–38 CE). Just as Hadrian identified with the Greeks, his *philhellenism*, or love of all things Greek, was intended to help Greek elites identify with Rome, even though many intellectuals remained critical of Roman rule.[23] Under his successor, Antoninus Pius, the empire also experienced a period of prosperity (138–61 CE), which lasted until the plague and the Marcomannic Wars under Marcus Aurelius's reign (161–80 CE).

It is interesting to note that despite Rome's high regard for Greek culture and the Greeks' acceptance of Rome, a change in the meaning of the word "Hellene" itself can be observed in the course of the second century CE. Hellenists (*hellēnistai*) were, as mentioned at the beginning, initially simply Greek-speaking Christians. However, by the time of Tatian's *Address to the Greeks* (170 CE), the word *Hellene* had become a (pejorative) term for polytheistic non-Christians in Christian usage.[24] Over time, *Hellenism* developed into a term denoting paganism.[25]

TAKING A CLOSER LOOK: SOURCES

Sources from the World of the New Testament

The Assimilation Politics of Rome in Tacitus

> "For, to accustom to rest and repose through the charms of luxury a population scattered and barbarous and therefore inclined to war, Agricola gave private encouragement and public aid to the building of temples, courts of justice and dwelling-houses, praising the energetic, and reproving the indolent. Thus, an honorable rivalry took the place of compulsion. He likewise provided a liberal education for the sons of the chiefs and showed such a preference for the natural powers of the Britons over the industry of the Gauls that they who lately disdained the tongue of Rome now coveted its eloquence. Hence, too, a liking sprang up for our style of dress, and the "toga" became fashionable. Step by step they were led to things which dispose to vice, the lounge, the bath, the elegant banquet. All this in their ignorance, they called civilization, when it was but a part of their servitude." (Tacitus, *Agricola* 21)[26]

The question of what the Romans brought to their subjects can be answered in a way similar to the claims of modern colonial powers, which asserted that they brought civilization ("the white man's burden"): aqueducts, sanitary facilities, roads, and above all peace. The so-called benefits that Roman civilization was said to have brought to its subjects were by no means intended to make them happy. Rather, as the present text clearly states from a Roman perspective, they were designed to enslave and exploit the provincials.

The account of the departure itself comes from Tacitus's biography of his father-in-law, Agricola (ca. 58–120 CE). The author praises this governor of Britain for his achievements in pacifying the province. It is clear that Rome was particularly keen on turning the tribal inhabitants who lived in the countryside into controllable and tax-paying subjects by building cities. As can be inferred, Rome wanted to win the hearts and minds of the subjugated, primarily by binding the local elites to Roman interests, often by granting them citizenship, in order to transform them into promoters of Roman rule. In addition to the "urbanization" of the subjugated, Rome aimed to avoid placing an excessive burden on the rural population. For this reason, the tax system was designed to ensure, as Rome believed, that the population could lead to productive lives in the interests of Rome's growth. A paradigmatic example of this is the remark made by Emperor Tiberius when a governor from Egypt once sent him a higher amount than expected: "I want my sheep shorn, not shaven."[27]

Rome's Rule as Protector of the People

> Roman generals and Emperors entered your territory, as they did the rest of Gaul, with no ambitious purposes, but at the solicitation of your ancestors, who were wearied to the last extremity by intestine strife, while the Germans, whom they had summoned to their help, had imposed their yoke alike on friend and foe. How many battles we have fought against the Cimbri and Teutones, at the cost of what hardships to our armies, and with what result we have waged our German wars, is perfectly well known. It was not to defend Italy that we occupied the borders of the Rhine, but to insure that no second [German] Ariovistus should seize the empire of Gaul. . . . There have ever been the same causes at work to make the Germans cross over into Gaul, lust, avarice, and the longing for a new home, prompting them to leave their own marshes and deserts, and to possess themselves of this most fertile soil and of you its inhabitants. Liberty, indeed, and the like specious names are their pretexts; but never did any man seek to enslave his fellows and secure dominion for himself without using the very same words.
>
> Gaul always had its petty kingdoms and intestine wars, till you submitted to our authority. We, though so often provoked, have used the right of conquest to burden you only with the cost of maintaining peace. For the tranquility of nations cannot be preserved without armies; armies cannot exist without pay; pay cannot be furnished without tribute; all else is common between us. You often command our legions. You rule these and other provinces. There is no privilege, no exclusion. From worthy Emperors you derive equal advantage, though you dwell so far away, while cruel rulers are most formidable to their neighbors. Endure the passions and rapacity of your masters, just as you bear barren seasons and excessive rains and other natural evils. There

> will be vices as long as there are men. But they are not perpetual, and they are compensated by the occurrence of better things. (Tacitus, *Hist.* 4.73–74)[28]

Ancient historians often put words into the mouths of historical figures in their works. In this case, Tacitus has the Roman general Petilius Cerialis deliver a speech to the Treveri and Lingones, Gallic tribes that were brought back to reason after a rebellion in 69 CE. It provides insight into the Roman concept of rule: In this sense, Rome does not wage wars of conquest but only goes to war when called upon to help (*bellum iustum*). Territories are not made provinces in order to exploit them but to protect the people living there from attackers or internal unrest. The only difference between the provincials and the Romans is that the former must pay tribute to Rome, in exchange for which they share in the benefits guaranteed by Roman rule.

The problems of Roman rule and the cause of uprisings did not lie in the fact that the system was inherently flawed, but rather that there were good and bad emperors. The latter behaved unjustly, not only toward the provincials, but even more so toward Romans citizens. According to Cerialis, however, such cases are merely exceptions to the rule that occur from time to time. Josephus also sees the cause of conflicts between Romans and Jews not in Roman rule per se, but in the poor administration of specific Roman rulers (Josephus, *J.W.* 2.277–79).

Praise of Rome

Speech of Aelius Aristides

> For of all who have ever gained empire you alone rule over men who are free. Caria has not been given to Tissaphernes, nor Phrygia to Pharnabazus, nor Egypt to someone else; nor is the country said to be enslaved, as household of so-and-so, to whomsoever it has been turned over, a man himself not free. But just as those in states of one city appoint the magistrates to protect and care for the governed, so you, who conduct public business in the whole civilized world exactly as if it were one city state, appoint the governors, as is natural after elections, to protect and care for the governed, not to be slave masters over them. Therefore, governor makes way for governor unobtrusively, when his time is up, and far from staying too long and disputing the land with his successor, he might easily not stay long enough even to meet him. (Aristid. *Or.* 14.36)[29]

The Greek orator Aelius Aristides (117–81 CE) from Asia Minor, who was likely granted Roman citizenship by Emperor Hadrian, shows us the tension faced by Greeks who had become Romans. Although being now a Roman citizen himself,

Aristides nevertheless praises Rome as a *foreign* power that had (allegedly) brought peace and freedom to the people.

From the orator's detailed praise of Rome, only a short excerpt has been selected here to illustrate the brave new world in which the inhabitants of the Greek East of the empire in particular were now supposed to find themselves. Now, at last, the people of Asia Minor and Egypt, previously oppressed by kings and slavery, were living in freedom. The people, therefore, obeyed voluntarily and in return the governors of Rome took care of them.

Praise for rulers is, of course, a double-edged sword, and Aristides praises Rome with an exuberance that may have puzzled even his ancient audience, for he almost certainly had a different lived reality. However, in a world where open criticism is not expedient, praise of a ruler offered a way to indirectly express criticism and to morally encourage the ruler to act in accordance with the wishes of the one who praises him. When Aristides effusively praises the good governors and the procedure of their appointment by Rome, he indirectly points out that it was often the governors themselves who caused unrest among the provincial population through unfair and unjust measures.

Reading the New Testament Texts

The Trial of Jesus

> Now Jesus stood before the governor; and the governor asked him, "Are you the King of the Jews?" Jesus said, "You say so." . . .
>
> Now at the festival the governor was accustomed to release a prisoner for the crowd, anyone whom they wanted. At that time they had a notorious prisoner, called Jesus Barabbas. So after they had gathered, Pilate said to them, "Whom do you want me to release for you, Jesus Barabbas or Jesus who is called the Messiah?" For he realized that it was out of jealousy that they had handed him over. While he was sitting on the judgment seat, his wife sent word to him, "Have nothing to do with that innocent man, for today I have suffered a great deal because of a dream about him." Now the chief priests and the elders persuaded the crowds to ask for Barabbas and to have Jesus killed. The governor again said to them, "Which of the two do you want me to release for you?" And they said, "Barabbas." Pilate said to them, "Then what should I do with Jesus who is called the Messiah?" All of them said, "Let him be crucified!" Then he asked, "Why, what evil has he done?" But they shouted all the more, "Let him be crucified!"
>
> So when Pilate saw that he could do nothing, but rather that a riot was beginning, he took some water and washed his hands before the

> crowd, saying, "I am innocent of this man's blood; see to it yourselves." Then the people as a whole answered, "His blood be on us and on our children!" . . .
>
> And when they had crucified him, they divided his clothes among themselves by casting lots; then they sat down there and kept watch over him. Over his head they put the charge against him, which read, "This is Jesus, the King of the Jews." (Matt 27:11–37)

Jesus's good news about the coming kingdom of God, which is "not of this world," is essentially a countermessage to the kingdom of the Roman emperor "in this world."[30] Rome ultimately claimed to have brought a new golden age to humanity, and the birth of Augustus was to be regarded by all as the ultimate good news. Jesus's good news, on the other hand, was that the kingdom of God was near and that repentance was necessary. The numerous uprisings, not only in Judea but also in other provinces of the empire, show how little the bitter reality of the rural population matched the ideas of a golden age. Not only charismatic men but also women, as the example of Boudicca in Britain (60/61 CE) shows, were able to rise to the forefront of rebellious movements.[31] In Judea, on the other hand, the oppressed hoped for a future leader who would restore the kingdom of David. In Roman eyes, such a person declaring himself king (*basileus*) called Roman rule into question. The claim to be king, confirmed during Jesus's trial, is also attested to by his entry into Jerusalem modeled on a royal appearance (*parousia*) (Matt 21:1–11; Mark 11:1–11; Luke 19:28–44; John 12:12–19). This made Jesus a traitor in the eyes of Rome, and capital punishment became imperative if Rome was to avoid losing face.

What really happened during Jesus's trial remains unclear because the Gospels do not present an eyewitness account but rather a narrative shaped by the later Christian community and infused with theological significance, which also serves to protect the Roman governor Pontius Pilate: Rome should not be blamed for Jesus's death. The governor merely responds to the pressure of the Jews as a whole or to the pressure of the religious elites. This idea is expressed in the statement attributed to Pilate when he declares that he is washing his hands of the matter.

What could well be historical, however, is the inscription above the cross, which in three languages describes the crime that earned Jesus the death penalty in the form of Roman crucifixion: "Jesus of Nazareth, King of the Jews" (*Iesus Nazarenus rex Iudaeorum*), as it was written on a plaque according to John 19:19. By adding "of Nazareth," the inscription affixed by the state authorities also makes clear that Jesus's claim as a descendant of David is unfounded. This, in turn, is addressed in the nativity story, which asserts that Jesus was born in Bethlehem and descended from the line of David (Matt 2:5–6; Luke 2:4, 15; Luke 3; Rom 1:3).

The Whore of Babylon

> Then one of the seven angels who had the seven bowls came and said to me, "Come, I will show you the judgment of the great whore who is seated on many waters, with whom the kings of the earth have committed fornication, and with the wine of whose fornication the inhabitants of the earth have become drunk." So he carried me away in the spirit into a wilderness, and I saw a woman sitting on a scarlet beast that was full of blasphemous names, and it had seven heads and ten horns. The woman was clothed in purple and scarlet, and adorned with gold and jewels and pearls, holding in her hand a golden cup full of abominations and the impurities of her fornication; and on her forehead was written a name, a mystery: "Babylon the great, mother of whores and of earth's abominations." And I saw that the woman was drunk with the blood of the saints and the blood of the witnesses to Jesus.
>
> When I saw her, I was greatly amazed. But the angel said to me, "Why are you so amazed? . . .
>
> "This calls for a mind that has wisdom: the seven heads are seven mountains on which the woman is seated; also, they are seven kings . . ."
>
> And he said to me, "The waters that you saw, where the whore is seated, are peoples and multitudes and nations and languages. . . . The woman you saw is the great city that rules over the kings of the earth." (Rev 17:1–18)

In addition to the many positive statements about Rome in the New Testament, its final book, Revelation, offers a strikingly contrasting view. The seer finds himself in a time of "tribulation" on the island of Patmos and writes a letter to seven churches in Asia Minor about what Jesus tells him concerning his imminent return. Jesus had already announced this in his discourse about the end of times (cf. Matt 24). The ongoing persecution of Christians is also described in the text, but despite numerous efforts, the book of Revelation cannot be dated precisely; scholars commonly suggest it was written during the reign of Domitian or Hadrian, but neither can be confirmed.

In his description of the horrors and destruction that will occur before the millennial kingdom and the arrival of the heavenly Jerusalem, the seer essentially presents a vision of the globalized world of antiquity, as the text draws upon biblical, Greek, Roman, and Egyptian imagery. Whether the main audience of the "letter" were Jewish followers of Jesus, as some believe, or Christians from other nations, as others argue, it could certainly have been understood by contemporary non-Christians. Today, however, the images are difficult for us to decipher, resulting in numerous interpretations of the text's multilayered symbolism. Often, there are representations that can be understood in both

Jewish and Greek contexts. This is evident, for example, in the passage about the whore of Babylon. In addition to the many allusions to biblical history—such as the city of Babylon itself or Jezebel—a non-Jewish interpretation is also possible, which was immediately understandable to the audience. The seer hints at which city Babylon actually refers to in verse 9, where he writes, "the seven heads are seven mountains on which the woman is seated."

Babylon is therefore likely to be a code name for Rome, the city that, as Propertius writes, "sits enthroned on seven hills."[32] Roman coins also depict Rome being personified, resting on seven hills. The she-wolf, Rome's symbolic animal, also depicted on these coins suckling Romulus and Remus, is called *lupa* in Latin. This is an ambiguous term that can refer to a wolf but was also used colloquially to refer to a "whore." This is precisely how anti-Roman literature of the Hellenistic period interpreted the birth story of Romulus and Remus, who were thus considered the children of a prostitute.[33] If the author of Revelation equates Rome with a prostitute, then Greek and Roman readers could also make this connection. The image of the ostentatious, drunken, and immoderate woman is also accessible not only to non-Jews but also to conservative Romans who lamented the moral decline of their time. This complaint is summarized in Juvenal's famous verses: "The Syrian Orontes has long since flowed into the Tiber and brought with it its language, morals, and the crooked harps with the flute player, and its national tambourines, and girls made to stand for hire at the Circus. Go thither, ye who fancy a barbarian harlot [*lupa*] with embroidered turban."[34] Thus, not only every Christian, but also every traditionally minded Roman would have understood and shared the criticism of Rome in Revelation.

FURTHER READING

Boardman, John, ed. *The Cambridge Ancient History*. Vol. 11, *The High Empire, A.D. 70–192*. Cambridge University Press, 2000.

Bowman, Alan K., ed. *The Cambridge Ancient History*. Vol. 10: *The Augustan Empire*. Cambridge University Press, 1996.

Erskine, Andrew, ed. *A Companion to the Hellenistic World*. Wiley, 2008.

Green, Peter. *Alexander to Actium: The Historical Evolution of the Hellenistic Age*. University of California Press, 1990.

Potter, David S., ed. *A Companion to the Roman Empire*. Blackwell, 2006.

Notes

1 Johann G. Droysen, *Geschichte des Hellenismus*, vol. 1, *Geschichte der Nachfolger Alexanders* (Friedrich Perthes, 1836), 3.

2 Polybius, *Histories* 1.5.

3 Polybius, *Histories* 1.4.11.

4 See Angelos Chaniotis, *Age of Conquests: The Greek World from Alexander to Hadrian 336 BC–AD 138* (Profile Books, 2018). This book, written in essay form, provides an excellent overview of the period covered.

5 Clifford Ando, *Imperial Ideology and Provincial Loyalty in the Roman Empire* (University of California Press, 2000), 278–332.

6 On the history of Hellenism, see most recently Peter F. Mittag, *Geschichte des Hellenismus* (de Gruyter, 2023).

7 Duris FGrH 76 F 13 = Ath. 6,253b–f; translation by Victor Ehrenberg, "Athenischer Hymnus auf Demetrios Poliorketes," *Die Antike* 7 (1931): 279–97.

8 On the Greek imperial cult, see Christian Habicht, *Divine Honors for Mortal Men in Greek Cities: The Early Cases* (Michigan Classical, 2017).

9 On the history of the Roman imperial age, see Hartwin Brandt, *Die Kaiserzeit: Römische Geschichte von Octavian bis Diocletian, 31 v. Chr.–284 n. Chr.* (C. H. Beck, 2021).

10 Tacitus, *The Annals,* trans. John Jackson (Harvard University Press, 1931–37) 1.1.

11 Virgil, *Aeneid* 1.279.

12 *Res Gestae Divi Augusti* 26–31.

13 Merkelbach, Reinhold, and Wolfgang Blümel, eds., *Inschriften der Städte Kleinasiens*, trans. Stefan Pfeiffer, vol. 69 (Habelt, 2014), 14, 11.40–41.

14 Pliny the Elder, *Naturalis Historia*, trans. Henry T. Riley (H. G. Bohn, 1855) 3.39.

15 See Tacitus, *Historiae*, 4.73–74, cited in the "Taking a Closer Look: Source" section of this chapter.

16 On the ultimately unanswerable question of why Christianity was able to prevail, see the recent and very critical work by Éric Rebillard, "Why Did People Become Christians in the Pre-Constantinian World? Reframing the Question," in *The Cambridge History of Ancient Christianity*, ed. Bruce W. Longenecker and David E. Wilhite (Cambridge University Press, 2023), 80–106.

17 Corpus Inscriptionum Iudaeae/Palaestinae II, 1277.

18 Tacitus, *Ann.* 15.38–44.

19 For possible connections between the two events, see Tobias Nicklas, "Jesus und Vespasian? Das Markusevangelium als politisch interessiertes 'Anti-Evangelium' zum Aufstieg der Flavier?," in *Reading the Political in Jewish and Christian Texts*, ed. Julia A. Snyder and Korinna Zamfir (Peeters, 2020), 159–78. See also the chapter on "Magic, Miracles, and Healing" by Janet Spittler in the present volume.

20 Tertullian, *Apologeticum*, in *Tertullian's Apology and de Spectaculis*, trans. T. R. Glover and Gerald H. Rendall (Harvard University Press, 1931), 5.4–5.

21 See Tacitus, *Ann.* 1.16.2.

22 Pliny the Younger, *Epistulae* 10.96–97. The authenticity of the correspondence has recently been questioned, albeit unconvincingly, in Enrico Tuccinardi, "An Application of a Profile-based Method for Authorship Verification: Investigating the Authenticity of Pliny the Younger's Letter to Trajan Concerning the Christians," in *DSH* 32, no. 2 (2017): 435–47.

23 Cf. Caroline Vout, "What's in a Beard? Rethinking Hadrian's Hellenism," in *Rethinking Revolutions Through Ancient Greece*, ed. Simon Goldhill (Cambridge University Press, 2006), 96–123.

24 Tatianus, *Oratio ad Graecos*; R. Klein, s.v. "Hellenen. (Teil A.II–IV.B.)," *Das Reallexikon für Antike und Christentum* 14 (1988): 389–445.

25 Bonifatius Kotter, *Die Schriften des Johannes von Damaskus IV: Liber de haeresibus, Opera polemica*, Patristische Texte und Studien 22 (de Gruyter, 1981), 19–21.

26 *Complete Works of Tacitus*, trans. Alfred J. Church and William Jackson Brodribb (Random House 1942), 21.

27 Dio Cassius, *Roman History*, trans. Earnest Cary, based on the version of Herbert Baldwin Foster, vol. 7, *Books LVI–LX*, Loeb Classical Library 175 (Harvard University Press, 1924), 57.10.5.

28 Tacitus, *Historiae*, in *The Complete Works of Tacitus*, trans. Alfred J. Church and William J. Brodribb (Random House, 1942), 4.73–74.

29 "The Ruling Power. A Study of the Roman Empire in the Second Century after Christ through the Roman Oration of Aelius Aristides," trans. James H. Oliver, *Transactions of the American Philosophical Society* 43, no. 4 (1953), 871–1003.

30 On the Gospel of Matthew in particular see Tobias Nicklas, "Der matthäische Davidssohn und das Römische Reich," in *Christ and the Emperor: The Gospel Evidence*, ed. G. Van Belle and J. Verheyden, Biblical Tools and Studies 20 (Peeters, 2014), 229–48.

31 Tacitus, *Ann.* 14.29–39; Tacitus, *Agr.* 14–16.

32 Propertius, *Elegies* 3.11. For text, see Proertius, *Elegies*. Edited and translated by G. P. Goold. Loeb Classical Library 18, (Harvard University Press, 1990).

33 For example, Dionysius Halicarnassus, *Antiquitates Romanae* 1.84.4.

34 Juvenal, *Satires*, 3.62-66, in *The Satires of Juvenal, Persius, Sulpicia, and Lucilius*, trans. Lewis Evans, (Henry G. Bohn, 1857), 3.62–66.

CHAPTER TWO

A Short History of the Jews in the Hellenistic and Roman Period

Viktor Kókai-Nagy
(Debrecen Reformed Theological University)

History is not simply the past; rather, it offers a narrative, a story that makes as much sense as possible, formed from the information that has been handed down from the past. Ancient historians in particular were not only concerned with painting as accurate a picture of the past as possible but also with offering a memorable narrative about the past. This is why, especially when dealing with ancient historiography, it is crucial to take into account the specific perspectives and evaluations that can be discerned in the mostly fragmentary sources. For this reason, we can only gain an approximate picture of what really happened in the past.

The Hasmonean Period

According to 1 Maccabees, which praises the glory of the Jewish dynasty of the Hasmoneans, the incorporation of Palestine into the rule of Antiochus III (223–187 BCE), a ruler of the Seleucids Empire,[1] did not bode well for the region. The Seleucids had their center of power in Antioch on the Orontes. Despite being ruled by the Seleucids, however, the Jews (or the inhabitants of Judea), were guaranteed a constitution (*politeia*)—that is, the right to live according to the laws of their ancestors (Josephus, *Ant.* 12.138–46). In fact, the Hellenistic rulers, including the Seleucids, generally tolerated the traditions of their subjects, but there is no doubt that the monotheistic faith of Judaism was strange to them, particularly the fact that Judaism could not accept the worship of other gods. With the accession of Antiochus IV Epiphanes in 175 BCE, however, there was a significant change in the situation of the Jews. It is difficult, though, to determine exactly what happened. This is partly because the Jewish sources available to us describe the ruler as the personification of evil, who wanted to force the Hellenistic culture and way of life on his Jewish subjects by force (1 Macc 1:44–53; 2 Macc 6:1–11; cf. Dan 11:31; 12:11). The Greek historian Polybius, however, paints a very different picture of him: "King Antiochus was both energetic, daring in design, and worthy of the royal dignity."[2] Jewish sources also indicate that it was not only the Seleucid king who was responsible for the deterioration of the situation, but that internal conflicts among the Jewish people also contributed to it. On the one hand, we can assume that there was serious rivalry within the Jewish aristocracy; on the other hand, we can surmise that there was a divide in society between the urban aristocracy and the rural population. The Hellenization of the former was much faster and more intense, but that does not mean that this intellectual movement that had prevailed in Palestine since the fourth century BCE did not influence all the people living there. Nevertheless, the lives of the rural population were much more strongly influenced by traditions on which not only religious life but also the social order was based.

It was common practice among Hellenistic rulers to establish new Greek cities (*poleis*) or to give old non-Greek cities a Greek constitution. This was probably the background to Antiochus IV's actions when he partnered with the Jewish high priests he had appointed during his campaign. A sure sign of Jerusalem's development into a Hellenistic *polis* is the construction of an *ephēbeion* and *gymnasium*—that is, educational and training facilities for young athletes in the city (2 Macc 4:12). This was followed a few years later by a fortress, the Acra, which not only served military purposes but also became the financial, economic, and cultural center of the Hellenistic city. When the temple became part of the Hellenistic city, it was considered unclean in the eyes of conservative Jews. However, whether the king actually issued a decree prohibiting Jewish worship and uniting the peoples of the kingdom (1 Macc 1:41–50) is not historically verifiable and is, at the very least, controversial.[3] The fact that many among the Jewish people supported the process of progressive Hellenization suggests that the uprising that broke out in 167 BCE was as much a civil war triggered by internal disputes as it was a struggle against the regime of Antiochus IV and his religious policies.

The revolt was led by the Maccabees, or as Josephus calls them, the Hasmoneans (see Josephus, *Ant.* 12.265; *J.W.* 1.36), whom 1 Maccabees describes as a priestly family from Modein (1 Macc 2:1). Judas Maccabeus (d. 160 BCE), one of the sons of Mattathias, who had initiated the uprising according to 1 Maccabees, led the rebels to their first successes. Under his leadership, the Jews were able to freely practice their religion from 162 BCE onwards. In 152 BCE, his brother Jonathan was given the title of high priest; the third brother, Simon, finally achieved tax-exempt status in 142 BCE and thus practical independence from Seleucid rule. This picture is complicated, however, by the emergence of numerous Jewish groups that defined their identity in opposition to the Hasmoneans.[4] One reason for sharply criticizing the Hasmonean high priests and their rule was that the Maccabees (Hasmoneans) did not descend from the high priestly family of the Zadokites, and their high priesthood was therefore considered illegitimate by many Jews (see 4Q175; 11Q19 lvii 5–21; Pss. Sol 17:5–7, 20, 22, 33; Jub. 31; Josephus, *Ant.* 13.288–92). Despite internal conflicts, however, the new ruling dynasty can be considered successful. Over the following decades, it not only gained new territories (Samaria, Idumea, Galilee), bringing the Hasmonean Empire to roughly the size of the Davidic Empire, but also enforced observance of Jewish law in these regions (Josephus, *Ant.* 13.254–58, 267–87).

Within Judaism, we know of at least three important, often competing political groups: the members of the priestly aristocracy, the Sadducees, and finally the Pharisees, who were also very popular in rural areas.[5] The rulers managed to keep these groups in check through appropriate policies, alliances, intimidation, and occasionally violence (Josephus, *Ant.* 13.380). The fate of the royal family was sealed by internal rivalries. The conflict between Hyrcanus II, who had attained the title of high priest in 76 BCE, and his brother Aristobulus II (ca. 100–49 BCE) led to a civil war. Since, in the meantime, Rome had defeated the Seleucid Empire and had thus become the dominant power in the region, both brothers turned to Pompey, the Roman governor and later ally of Caesar and Crassus in the First Triumvirate, to settle their dispute. However, Pompey, who at the time was settled in Damascus, was approached not only by them but also by a third delegation demanding an end to the Hasmonean monarchy. This group advocated for a governing system ruled solely by priests.

The Reign of Herod

Pompey settled the internal dispute between the Hasmonean brothers in Roman fashion: He marched into Judea with his army and conquered Jerusalem in 63 BCE. Although Hyrcanus II was able to remain high priest, now with Rome's support, he had to pay a high price: His power was limited to Jerusalem and Judea, and the territory was incorporated into the Roman province of Syria. Simultaneously, the Greek cities occupied by the Hasmoneans regained their independence. Thus, it is not at all surprising that the high priest became an ally of Julius Caesar when he conquered Pompey. In Judea, Hyrcanus's most important political supporter was Antipater, the father of the later King Herod (37–4 BCE), who enjoyed the trust not only of the high priest but also of Rome. Since Jewish soldiers and the Jews in Alexandria had supported Caesar's Egyptian campaign and victory, Caesar promoted Hyrcanus to the rank of ethnarch and appointed Antipater as procurator. After the time of the Hasmoneans, Caesar once again separated religious from secular authority. In so doing, he granted the Jews many privileges that determined their status in the Roman Empire even at the time of the events recounted in the New Testament: freedom from taxes to the Romans, from military occupation, and from conscription into the Roman army, and freedom to practice their religion and life according to their laws. These rights were granted to Jews not only in their homeland but also in the diaspora (Josephus, *Ant.* 14.190–217).[6]

Both of Antipater's sons were appointed as generals (*stratēgoi*): Phasael became *strategos* of Judea and Herod was given command of Galilee. They held these positions even after the assassination of their father in 43 BCE. Although they sided with Cassius, who was involved in the assassination of Caesar on March 15, 44 BCE, they managed to gain the support of Mark Antony, who defeated Cassius. Anthony, who was a member of the Second Triumvirate along with Octavian (later Emperor Augustus), and Lepidus, took control of the eastern provinces. Despite all efforts by their opponents, he appointed the brothers Phasael and Herod as tetrarchs, while Hyrcanus II remained high priest. Antigonus, the son of Hyrcanus II's deposed brother, refused to accept Antony's decision and seized the throne with the help of the Parthian king. The latter, in turn, gladly seized the opportunity to support a new ally against Rome. Thus, another Hasmonean king, Antigonus II, was able to rule in Judea, although his reign was short lived (40–37 BCE). He mutilated his uncle Hyrcanus II so that he could no longer exercise the office of high priest and took Phasael prisoner. Phasael took his own life in captivity, and Herod fled to Rome. There, with the support of Antony and Octavian, the Senate appointed him king of Judea, but he still had to conquer his kingdom.

This was an enormous challenge, for Herod had to prevail on two fronts: against his royal rival Antigonus II, who was supported by the Jewish aristocracy and the Sadducees; and against radical groups who saw him as a symbol of foreign, Roman power. He accomplished the task in three years and conquered Jerusalem in 37 BCE, Antigonus was executed by Antony, and Herod's revenge fell upon his internal enemies. His marriage to Mariamne, who came from the Hasmonean house, in the same year is often interpreted as a move by Herod to secure his power. However, it cannot be ruled out that he was actually in love. The marriage was also in the interests of the Hasmoneans, as it was their last chance to continue to share power.

After Antony's defeat at the Battle of Actium in 31 BCE, Octavian, who saw Herod as a strong governor of the region and a guarantor of peace, confirmed him in his position and even added new territories to his empire. As a friend of Rome and of the emperor, Herod helped his client kingdom to prosperity. The middle period of his reign (27–13 BCE) was marked by economic prosperity and investment. The taxes levied were tolerable and trade flourished, which also had a positive effect on the rural economy, where a more prosperous class also emerged. Throughout the empire, huge construction projects were carried out (Josephus, *Ant.* 15.267–341, 380–425). His greatest achievement, however, was the rebuilding of the temple. Jerusalem became a central pilgrimage site, connecting Jews around the world with each other and with their religious center in an unprecedented way. Despite his political stability and economic success, he was criticized by many and was depicted by posterity as a bloodthirsty tyrant—a reputation certainly due to the Gospel of Matthew's account, which claims he ordered the deaths of all boys in Bethlehem from infancy up to two years old in order to ensure the death of the newborn Jesus (Matt 2:16–18). In truth, his style of ruling probably differed little from that of his contemporaries. Ultimately, there is no doubt that the last years of his reign were marked by his ruthless treatment of even members of his closest family.

Judea and Galilee After Herod

Herod appointed his three sons as his heirs: Philip, Antipas (who is often referred to as Herod in the New Testament), and Archelaus. After his death in 4 BCE, conflict broke out. Some wanted to get rid of Herod's successors, whereas others wanted to end Roman rule. The Syrian governor had to intervene in order to quell the unrest. One center of resistance was Galilee (Josephus, *J.W.* 2.5–79; *Ant.* 17.206–99), where the resistance was closely linked to messianic expectations. Octavian, now Emperor Augustus, ultimately approved the substance of Herod's will. Philip was appointed tetrarch (one of four princes) of Iturea, Golan, and Trachonitis (in the north). His reign was largely peaceful. Since there were no successors, the territory fell back to the province of Syria after his death in 34 CE and was handed over by the Roman emperor Caligula (37–41 CE) to his friend Agrippa I, Herod's grandson.

Herod Antipas, the second son of Herod, ruled Galilee, the homeland of Jesus and most of his disciples, as well as Perea. He supported Hellenistic culture but also promoted Jewish piety, supporting the Pharisees who were active in the countryside. The same search for balance characterized his relationship with Roman power. His private life, however, was not as successful. He divorced his wife for his sister-in-law, but since her husband was still alive, he was deemed an adulterer by Jewish standards. Because of this, he was criticized by pious Jews such as John the Baptist. The New Testament reports on this conflict, which ended with the execution of the Baptist (Mark 6:14–29; see also Josephus, *Ant.* 18.116–19). To make matters worse, the divorced woman was a Nabataean princess. This led to the revenge of the Nabataean king, who successfully attacked Antipas. Antipas was only able to save himself with Roman help. In 39 CE, however, Emperor Caligula exiled him on charges of conspiracy; in 40 CE, his territory was handed over to Agrippa I.

Herod's third son, Archelaus, was only able to hang on to power for a short period of time. However, his inheritance, the territories of Judea, Idumea, and Samaria, was a real hornet's nest. Archelaus was attacked by his own family[7] and also found himself in conflict with the Jewish aristocracy, which preferred to be directly subordinate to Rome.[8] Finally, the Jews, together with their archenemies the Samaritans,[9] complained to Augustus, who in turn banished Archelaus in the interest of peace. As desired by the aristocracy, the territories of Archelaus were now placed under direct Roman administration, and a prefect appointed by the emperor took over the administration of the territory. The local aristocracy, however, had probably conceived of the new system differently, as the emperor divided power among three parties. This threefold division destabilized the administration of the region, made it more difficult to maintain order, and became a source of conflict: (1) Under the leadership of the high priest, the Jews were primarily responsible for religious matters; (2) Rome was represented locally by a prefect who had only limited military power; (3) The region was under the jurisdiction of the province of Syria whose head was responsible for other affairs. For example, he controlled the tax census that became necessary because of the new status.[10] Although this census only affected the former region controlled by Archelaus, it provoked a sharp reaction from Jewish radicals in Galilee (Acts 5:37; Josephus, *Ant.* 18.3–10; *J.W.* 2.117–18). This was also possible because Antipas was more lenient toward these radical groups in order to maintain his popularity, and Roman legionaries were not constantly present in the region.

Augustus chose prefects from among the equestrian order who were ambitious but also loyal to him. Although the prefect was the representative of the law and, unlike the Jewish authorities, could also impose death sentences, he primarily performed administrative tasks, the most important of which was the collection of taxes and duties. This task was carried out by his subcontractors, the tax collectors, who were despised by the population as collaborators of Rome. Due to his duties, the prefect had no significant military forces at his disposal, and most of what he did have were stationed in the center of the Roman administration, Caesarea Maritima. In addition, there was a permanent military presence in Jerusalem, which was reinforced on major holidays (such as Passover).

The new high priest appointed by Rome, Hannas I (6–15 CE), reorganized the Sanhedrin (the Jewish council) and remained highly influential, even after his dismissal, until his death. Although his son-in-law Caiaphas (18–36 CE) was the high priest at the time of Jesus's trial, his father-in-law probably had an influence in the decision (John 18:12–24). The high priest, who had the support of the aristocracy, became influential both as the religious and the political leader of the Jewish people. Although his real political power did not extend to the Jews of the diaspora, he nevertheless represented the entire Jewish people before the emperor, at least symbolically. In religious matters, his word also counted in the diaspora (Acts 9:2). The highest Jewish legislative body was the Sanhedrin, which was made up of high priests, elders, and scribes. The elders were originally the representatives of the most distinguished families. Their political clout, however,

<table>
<tr><th>Roman ruler</th><th colspan="3">Local Ruler in Judea and other regions</th></tr>
<tr><td rowspan="2">The Second Triumvirate
Mark Antony
Octavian (Augustus)
Lepidus
(43–36 BCE)</td><td colspan="2">Roman Judea
Antigonus II (40–37 BCE)</td><td></td></tr>
<tr><td colspan="3">Herodian Judea</td></tr>
<tr><td rowspan="3">Augustus (31 BCE–14 CE)</td><td colspan="3">Herod the Great (37–4 BCE)</td></tr>
<tr><td>Judea, Idumea, Samaria</td><td>Galilee, Perea</td><td>Iturea, Batanaea, Trachonitis etc.</td></tr>
<tr><td>Archelaos
(4 BCE–6 CE)</td><td>Antipas
(4 BCE–39 CE)</td><td>Philip
(4 BCE–34 CE)</td></tr>
<tr><td>Tiberius (14–37 CE)</td><td>Roman Prefects
(6–41 CE)</td><td></td><td></td></tr>
<tr><td>Caligula (37–41 CE)</td><td>[Pontius Pilatus,
(26–36 CE)]</td><td></td><td>(After 34 CE = Province Syria)</td></tr>
<tr><td rowspan="2">Claudius (41–54 CE)</td><td>Herod Agrippa I
41–44 CE</td><td>40–44 CE</td><td>37–44 CE</td></tr>
<tr><td colspan="2">Roman Procurators
[Marcus Antonius Felix, 52–60 CE]</td><td rowspan="4">Herod Agrippa II
(53–100 CE)</td></tr>
<tr><td>Nero (54–68 CE)</td><td colspan="2">[Porcius Festus, 59–62 CE]
[Gessius Florus, 64–66 CE]</td></tr>
<tr><td>Year of Four Caesars
(68–69 CE)</td><td colspan="2">Jewish War
66–70 CE</td></tr>
<tr><td>Flavian Dynasty
(69–96 CE)</td><td colspan="2">Imperial Roman Province Governed by Legate</td></tr>
</table>

Figure 2.1. Political rule in Herod's kingdom and after his death.

was taken over in New Testament times by the group of scribes who were experts in interpreting the Torah (the Jewish law). Among them were officials, judges, and teachers. The Sadducees were primarily limited to Jerusalem and were closely connected to the aristocracy. The Pharisees were mostly representatives of the Jewish bourgeoisie and had a strong base in the countryside. The high priest therefore needed the support of all three groups. The Jewish people were represented by a "council of high priests" (cf. 1 Macc 12:6–18).

Due to the unusual monotheism of Judaism and the religious commandments associated with it, Rome had to take into account the sensitivities of the Jews. With regard to the privileges granted to the Jews by Caesar, it was up to the current emperor to decide whether they should remain in force. However, it was also the responsibility of local authorities to decide how they wanted to enforce them.

Augustus's successor, Tiberius (14–37 CE), did not change the administration of Palestine, but extended the term of office for prefects in order to reduce their greed. At the same time, the ban on foreign cults in Rome (19 CE)[11] including that of the Jews, and the anti-Jewish attitude of Sejanus (the leader of the equestrian order), also had an impact on the behavior of the prefects. The most famous prefect from this time is Pontius Pilatus (26–36 CE), who clashed with the Jews on several occasions, but whose ten years of service attests to his success in the position. The description of the trial against Jesus makes it probable that he and the high priest worked well together. In the eyes of those with power, Jesus was a self-proclaimed messiah who had to be eliminated as quickly as possible in order to maintain peace in the country. Their actions were probably considered a success because there were no riots after the death of the prophet from Galilee.[12] Some years later, when Pilate brutally crushed a similar movement on Mt. Gerizim (in Samaria), he was removed from office by the emperor because of his cruelty (Josephus, *Ant.* 18.85–89).

The Pre-War Period

The new emperor Caligula (37–41 CE) did not change the prefectural system but transferred the former territories of Herod's sons (Philip and later the sons of Antipas) to his friend Agrippa I. In connection with the ascent of Agrippa, we must point out an event that illustrates the precarious political situation of the Jewish people. When Agrippa was appointed king in 37 CE, he made a stop in Alexandria on his way from Rome to Palestine, where a considerable number of Jews had lived for centuries. The Jews of Alexandria enjoyed important privileges, which helped make the city into one of the major centers of Jewish culture.[13] With the arrival of Agrippa, which was perceived as a provocation by the city's Greek population, the tensions between the Greek and Roman communities escalated. Agrippa complained to Caligula, and Jews and Greeks also sent a delegation to the emperor, who ultimately favored the Greeks. The conflict dragged on for a long time and it was not until the next emperor, Claudius (41–54 CE), that order was restored. The incident in Alexandria, however, was not an isolated event during Caligula's reign, as similar unrest broke out elsewhere (Josephus, *Ant.* 18.310–79). The conflict in Palestine also escalated, and the emperor added fuel to the fire when he ordered his statue to be erected in the temple in Jerusalem. Thanks to Agrippa's intercession and the tactics of the Syrian legate, it was possible to gain time; the execution of the order, which contradicted all the rules of the Jewish religion and would certainly have led to a bitter uprising, was prevented because Caligula was assassinated in 41 CE. Caligula's successor Claudius, whose election was actively supported by his friend Agrippa, annexed the territories of Judea and Samaria to Agrippa's former kingdom. This allowed Herod's grandson to rule the kingdom for several years (41–44 CE).

This was a decisive time for Jesus's disciples. There is no question that after the death of Jesus they saw their lives and future in Judaism. Their gospel was successfully oriented toward the Jews in Jerusalem, including those who had returned from the diaspora (Acts 2:1–41), who were not only familiar with Hellenistic culture but whose mother language was Greek. This fact certainly contributed to the rapid translation of Jesus's teaching into Greek. During the rule of Agrippa, the execution of James the son of Zebedee (ca. 42 BCE) took place, as well as the arrest of Peter, who was forced to flee Jerusalem as reported in Acts 12. James the brother of the Lord became the new leader of the Jerusalem congregation. He probably stood for a conservative theology that saw the future of Christ's followers entirely within the framework of Judaism. The Hellenistic-Jewish followers of Christ, who—because of the persecutions starting with the death of Stephen (Acts 8:1–4; 11:9–21)—fled from Jerusalem to Antioch (on the Orontes), became the foundation for a new form of Christianity that was also open to other peoples.

When Agrippa I died (Acts 12:19–23; Josephus, *Ant.* 19.343–50), his son did not succeed him to the throne. Instead of placing the seventeen-year-old Agrippa II on his father's throne, the emperor returned to the Augustan system of administration, with one change: He added Galilee to the former prefecture consisting of Judea, Samaria, and Idumea and appointed a procurator at its head. Agrippa II (27–100 CE), whom we encounter in the New Testament during the interrogation of Paul (Acts 25:11–26:32), was appointed as king and overseer of the temple in 50 CE. His kingdom, however, was smaller than his father's. It encompassed mainly the territory of Philip and later expanded to include additional areas. Nevertheless, the death of Agrippa I meant the virtual end of Jewish kingship. This reawakened the desire for freedom which was linked to an idyllic image of the old kingdom, the hope of defending the religion of their ancestors, and the expectation of the arrival of the Messiah promised in the Holy Scriptures. Rebellions broke out immediately under the first procurator and were brutally suppressed. But it was not only the rise of nationalist sentiments and radical groups that remained a persistent problem; the procurators appointed by Rome were incompetent and are generally described in our sources as oppressors of the people. Here we can trace the beginning of the spiral of violence that ultimately led to the outbreak of the so-called Jewish War.

The expulsion of the Jews from Rome by Emperor Claudius in 49 CE[14] (Acts 18:2) did not exactly improve the perception of Jews in the empire. In Alexandria, the conflict between Greeks and Jews intensified once again. Following the intervention of Agrippa II, the emperor finally sided with the Jews. At the same time, tensions also increased in the mother country, and new radical groups such as the zealots and *sicarii* (men of the dagger) emerged. Increasing social insecurity led to the uprooting of many people, which created an increase in gang activity. This, of course, resulted in the deterioration of public security; time and again we hear of the appearance of false messiahs.[15] The attacks, which were rooted in national self-consciousness, apocalyptic beliefs, and messianic hopes—and were ideologized by these factors—affected not only the Romans but also many Jews, and the situation became increasingly worse (Josephus, *J.W.* 2.250–70). This growing radicalism may have been the situation that James warned Paul about when he arrived in Jerusalem at that time (Acts 21:24–26). The Jews apparently denounced Paul to the governor, Mark Antony Felix (52–60 CE), who arrested him but took no further action. If we follow the account in Acts, only his successor, Porcius Festus (60–62 CE) decided to send the apostle to Rome.

The Jewish War (66–70 CE)

The outbreak of the Jewish War had several causes: the incompetence of the Roman prefects and procurators (Josephus, *J.W.* 2.277–332 especially emphasizes the responsibility of the last governor, Gessius Florus [64–66 CE]), the weakening of the Jewish aristocracy, the rivalry between the priestly groups, the incompetence of the governors of Syria, and the accumulated tensions in society (conflicts between Judeans, Galileans, Samaritans, and Greeks living in the Hellenistic cities of Palestine). The country joined the uprisings that began in Jerusalem. Only Samaria and the Hellenistic cities did not participate. In Judea, however, it was possible to build up a reasonably unified resistance. None of the various Jewish groups involved in the uprising managed to take the lead. At least in the early stages, the differences were repeatedly overcome by the enthusiasm to fight a common enemy. When Emperor Nero learned of the initial successes of the Jewish rebels, he commissioned the proven General Vespasian to suppress the uprising, who involved his son Titus in the preparations for the operations. At the beginning of 67 CE, he arrived in Galilee with an army of sixty thousand men. Vespasian kept his army together and marched victoriously from city to city, and from fortress to fortress. By the spring of 68 CE, only the area around Jerusalem and the Dead Sea remained in the hands of the rebels, partly because many had fled Jerusalem.

The political events in Rome, however, prompted Vespasian to wait and see what would happen next. The Senate stripped Nero of his power. The emperor, who died by suicide in June 68 CE, died without an heir, leading to turmoil over his succession. In just over a year, three candidates for the Roman throne

Figure 2.2. The Arch of Titus in Rome depicting the triumph in Judaea. (Paolo Villa, Wikimedia Commons. Used under the Creative Commons Attribution-Share Alike 4.0 International license.)

failed (68–69 CE). The civil war that broke out in the West as a result was merely observed by the legions and their commanders in the East. Eventually, Vespasian was proclaimed as emperor. As the new emperor, who first had to secure his rule in the West, Vespasian entrusted the completion of the Jewish War to his son. Titus conquered Jerusalem in 70 CE, and in 71 CE, father and son celebrated their glorious victory in Rome, even though the last stronghold of resistance, Masada, did not fall until 73 or 74 CE. The number of Jewish casualties of the war is difficult to determine; a large number of Jews were taken into slavery. With the conquest of Jerusalem by the Romans in August 70 CE, the Temple of Jerusalem, which had been magnificently rebuilt by Herod, was also destroyed. This was a catastrophe for Judaism, which had not only lost a center, but the place where, according to Jewish belief, God had taken up residence in a special way and—on the annual Day of Atonement (Yom Kippur)—granted reconciliation to his people time and again. From then on, God's covenant with his people was deeply endangered, and the surviving Jewish groups had to try to find a new direction. It was during this period that the foundations of later rabbinic Judaism, which was particularly devoted to the study of the Torah, were laid. For many Jewish followers of Christ, the memory of Jesus of Nazareth, the Messiah and Son of God, became the central focus of their belief.

After the War

Although Agrippa II fought alongside Vespasian and was a loyal ally of the Flavians, the newly founded imperial family, the Jews lost their former rights after the war. Palestine to the west of the Jordan became an imperial province with no place for an autonomous nation. All central institutions of the Jewish people lost their official status. The Sanhedrin was abolished, and thus the political influence of the Sadducees diminished. While imperial propaganda exploited the victory in the Jewish War to the fullest, the rights of the Jews living in the diaspora were not fundamentally curtailed under the Flavians. The extent to which the tax previously payable to the Jerusalem temple was replaced by a new tax, the *fiscus Iudaicus*, which initially served to rebuild the Temple of Jupiter Optimus Maximus in Rome, is still disputed today.

The death of Emperor Nerva marked the beginning of the era of adopted emperors (98–180 CE). The new practice of the emperor adopting his successor allowed him to choose the new emperor based on his outstanding abilities rather than his ancestry—a shift that led to a golden age for the Roman Empire. During the reign of Emperor Trajan (98–117 CE), the Roman Empire reached its greatest extent: Trajan conquered parts of Armenia and Mesopotamia as well as the Dacian Empire in present-day Romania. However, successful wars disrupted peace in the hinterland. It was particularly important to Trajan that the front in the East was not endangered by unrest. In 115, however, a revolt of Jews in the diaspora broke out in several places at once. Mesopotamia and Egypt, Cyrene (in North Africa), and Cyprus were particularly affected. Whether the diaspora revolt[16] of the years 115–17 CE was a single revolution or several conflicts that broke out simultaneously cannot be determined with certainty today due to a lack of reliable sources. An important center of the rebellion was in Cyrene and Egypt, where many (radical) Jews had fled after the Jewish War. From there, it spread to other areas, breaking out in Mesopotamia after its conquest by Trajan. The result of this war was devastating for Judaism. The diverse Jewish diaspora, which had flourished in large parts of the Roman Empire up until then, lost its significance for centuries. Important Jewish communities (such as in Alexandria) were almost completely wiped out.

Decades after the destruction of the Jerusalem temple, there was still hope that it would soon be rebuilt. This, however, was not in the interests of the Flavian dynasty founded by Vespasian and Titus, as it would have weakened the imperial propaganda based on victory in the Jewish War. In Palestine itself, the unrest did not cease with the end of the Jewish War in 70 CE. It is certainly no coincidence that a legion was stationed in Palestine after the war and that an additional legion had to be sent to the region around 120 CE. The tensions that preceded the Jewish War were apparently still present in society, reinforced by escalating eschatological expectations and the hope that God would intervene in the history of his people.[17] According to the Roman historian Cassius Dio,[18] Emperor Hadrian, who had been ruling since 117 CE, decided in 130 CE to build a new colony called Aelia Capitolina on the ruins of Jerusalem. A sanctuary for Jupiter, the god of the new city, was to be built on the site of the destroyed temple. With the founding of the city, Hadrian wanted to promote Greek culture and secure the favor of the Greek upper class living there. The reaction of the Jews living in the land of Judea was similar to what had happened centuries earlier under the rule of Antiochus IV Epiphanes. Probably in 132 CE, a new uprising broke out, which was probably concentrated in Judea. It is unknown how many people from Galilee joined. Since the uprising, unlike the Jewish War of 66–70 CE, is poorly documented, many questions remain unanswered: Was there only one leader of the uprising, known to posterity as Bar Kokhba (or Bar Kosiba), or did several territorial lords fight against the Romans? Did the rebels succeed in taking Jerusalem, or was it an intense guerrilla war confined to a small area? After all, the rebels' successes are evidenced by the fact that the Romans deployed a large army in the area, commanded by their best generals. What is certain is that the goal of the rebels was to restore the house of Israel and that they fought for the Torah and the temple. The suppression of this second revolt, whose last major battle took place in 135/136 CE at Betar, was a severe blow to Judaism, not only because of the many victims, but above all because Judaism lost its right to the land of its ancestors. According to the account of Eusebius of Caesarea, Hadrian now forbade Jews from entering the area around Jerusalem.[19] The province of Judea was renamed Syria-Palestine, the Jewish population was expelled from the area, and their presence in Judea was reduced to almost zero.

TAKING A CLOSER LOOK: SOURCES

Sources from the World of the New Testament

Josephus's Foreword in *Jewish War*

> The war of the Jews against the Romans—the greatest not only of the wars of our own time, but, so far as accounts have reached us, well nigh of all that ever broke out between cities or nations—has not lacked its historians. Of these, however, some, having taken no part in the action, have collected from hearsay casual and contradictory stories which they have then edited in a rhetorical style; while others, who witnessed the events, have, either from flattery of the Romans or from hatred of the Jews, misrepresented the facts, their writings exhibiting

> alternatively invective and encomium, but nowhere historical accuracy. In these circumstances, I—Josephus, son of Matthias, a Hebrew by race, a native of Jerusalem and a priest, who at the opening of the war myself fought against the Romans and in the sequel was perforce an onlooker—propose to provide the subjects of the Roman Empire with a narrative of the facts, by translating into Greek the account which I previously composed in my vernacular tongue and sent to the barbarians in the interior. (Josephus, *J.W.* 1 [H. St. J. Thackeray])

Very similar thoughts are expressed in Luke 1:1–4.[20] Both authors have the same goal: They want to convince their readers why they should choose their writings. Both are familiar with other texts that have already dealt with their subject, but they do not consider them reliable. For them, reliability rests on two pillars. The first is authenticity, which is guaranteed by eyewitnesses. Josephus is himself an eyewitness, and Luke processes the memories of eyewitnesses and has "carefully investigated everything from the beginning." The second pillar, in contrast to confusion, is order. Both Josephus and Luke treat historical events according to their own ideas, in good order. However, neither author speaks of an objective, impartial account. The opposite is true: They consciously strive to describe events from their own perspective, as authentically as possible.

Talmud on the Hanukkah Miracle

> The Sages taught in *Megillat Ta'anit*: On the twenty-fifth of Kislev, the days of Hanukkah are eight. One may not eulogize on them and one may not fast on them. What is the reason? When the Greeks entered the Sanctuary they defiled all the oils that were in the Sanctuary by touching them. And when the Hasmonean monarchy overcame them and emerged victorious over them, they searched and found only one cruse of oil that was placed with the seal of the High Priest, undisturbed by the Greeks. And there was sufficient oil there to light the candelabrum for only one day. A miracle occurred and they lit the candelabrum from it eight days. The next year the Sages instituted those days and made them holidays with recitation of *hallel* and special thanksgiving in prayer and blessings. (b. Šabb 21b [Koren—Steinsaltz])

Both 1 and 2 Maccabees tell the story of the cleansing of the temple (1 Macc 4:36–59; 2 Macc 10:1–6) and point out that this took place on the same day as the desecration of the temple by pagans years earlier. According to both reports, it was celebrated for eight days and became an annual festival for the Jews (cf. John 10:22). What makes the Talmudic text really fascinating is the fact that the Maccabean books are not part of the Hebrew canon, so we find no quotations from them by the rabbis, and the name Maccabees is not mentioned in these texts. Josephus does report on the event, but since he was considered a traitor by the Jews, his works were not popular. Apart from Josephus's description, only one version of 1 Maccabees 1–9 is known from the Middle Ages (*Megillat Antiochus*): "and its origin probably goes back to the need to give more prominence to the festival of Hanukkah."[21] But in this Talmudic text, we read about the miracle of the oil, which is an essential part of today's Hanukkah celebration.

A Letter of Pliny the Younger

> I have never been present at any legal examination of the Christians, and I do not know, therefore, what are the usual penalties passed upon them, or the limits of those penalties, or how searching an inquiry should be made. I have hesitated a great deal in considering whether any distinctions should be drawn according to the ages of the accused; whether the weak should be punished as severely as the more robust; whether if they renounce their faith they should be pardoned, or whether the man who has once been a Christian should gain nothing by recanting; whether the name itself, even though otherwise innocent of crime, should be punished, or only the crimes that gather round it. (*Letters* 10.96, [J. B. Firth])[22]

Pliny's perplexity is understandable: Even in Trajan's time, there was no routine procedure for dealing with Christians, and it is unlikely that there had been widespread persecution of Christians in the Roman Empire prior to that time. The imperial governor of Bithynia Pliny cannot accept that there are people who, despite all threats, are prepared to profess their faith in Christ and sacrifice their lives for their beliefs. In his letter, he describes his method for finding out who is truly a Christian and who is not. Two further facts become clear: First, at the time of Trajan, the authorities no longer considered Christians to be part of Judaism. Second, Christians certainly deserve to be punished for their stubbornness and unyielding obstinacy. The letter also reveals a certain admiration on the part of the author, who nevertheless considers Christianity to be "nothing but a wild, excessive superstition."[23]

Reading the New Testament Texts

The End of the Jerusalem Temple

Chapter 13 of the Gospel of Mark offers a detailed speech by Jesus about the end of times, which the text apparently expects in the very near future (cf. parallels in Matt 24 and Luke 21). Before the actual speech, Jesus is addressed by one of his disciples, who is enthusiastic about the Herodian Temple, which was already shining in splendor at the time:

> As he came out of the temple, one of his disciples said to him, "Look, Teacher, what large stones and what large buildings!" Then Jesus asked him, "Do you see these great buildings? Not one stone will be left here upon another; all will be thrown down." (Mark 13:1–2)

The passage plays a key role for the dating of the Mark's Gospel: It can be understood as a *vaticinium ex eventu*, that is a prophecy which was composed only *after* the event and put into the mouth of Jesus. In this case, the Gospel of Mark including this passage must have been composed (maybe shortly) after the destruction of the Jerusalem temple in the year 70 CE. It is, however, also not excluded that the text is a real prophecy: Even Jesus himself may have been remembered to speak about the end of the temple. This was probably remembered shortly before the destruction when the catastrophe was already unavoidable. It seems, however, that the Greek verb *katalyō*, which is translated here as "will be thrown down" (v. 2) can be understood as a technical term referring to how the Roman used machines to tear out the heavy stones of the temple from below. All this seems to suggest that the writer of this sentence had at least a very clear image in mind of how the temple was destroyed. A bit later, we read again from Jesus's mouth, "But when you see the desolating sacrilege set up where it ought not to be (let the reader understand), then those in Judea must flee to the mountains" (Mark 13:14).

It is unclear what is meant with the term "the desolating sacrilege." It may again refer to the Roman army and their actions in destroying the temple and the holy of holies within—that it, according to Jewish belief, God's dwelling place on earth. It was, however, also understood as a possible reference to Emperor Caligula's attempt to erect his statue in the temple, which was only prevented by the emperor's unexpected death in the year 41 CE. The nature of the apocalyptic language used here,[24] however, makes it impossible to decide with certainty to which event this passage refers.

Jesus's Passion According to John

Knowledge of the legal situation in Judea at the time of Jesus is important for understanding many of the scenes from the passion stories in the Gospels. John 18:28–31, for example, is an interesting passage in which the representatives of the Jewish authorities hand over Jesus, after having already been arrested by them (John 18:1–11), to the jurisdiction of the Roman prefect, Pontius Pilate:

> Then they took Jesus from Caiaphas to Pilate's headquarters. It was early in the morning. They themselves did not enter the headquarters, so as to avoid ritual defilement and to be able to eat the Passover. So Pilate went out to them and said, "What accusation do you bring against this man?" They answered, "If this man were not a criminal, we would not have handed him over to you." Pilate said to them, "Take him yourselves and judge him according to your law." The Jews replied, "We are not permitted to put anyone to death." (John 18:28–31).

According to John 11:45–53, it is Caiaphas himself who told the Sanhedrin that it would better if Jesus died for (or instead of) "the people than to have the whole nation destroyed" (John 11:45), a sentence which John understands as an unconscious prophecy by the high priest (John 11:46).[25] After his arrest Jesus is first led to Hannas (John 18:12–13), still the decisive Jewish authority in the background; after the trial in front of Hannas, Jesus is handed over to the official Jewish representative, Caiaphas (John 18:24). Caiaphas, however, has to deal with the problem: According to John, the Jewish authorities had already decided to kill Jesus, but they were not permitted to carry out the death sentence. In the case of Jesus (who, unlike Paul, did not have Roman citizenship), Pilate was the person to address. The highly artificial story plays with the high priest's dilemma: He is unable to present a clear accusation against Jesus while also trying to convince Pilate to sentence him to death. The following dialogue between Jesus and Pilate (18:33–38) probably also reveals the historical reason for Jesus's final execution: Jesus was most likely executed as an insurrectionist who was accused of claiming the royal throne of Israel, a clear lèse-majesté crime. This also clarifies what pressure the Jewish representatives put on Pilate when they cry out "If you release this man [Jesus], you [Pilate] are no friend of Caesar. Everyone who claims to be a king sets himself against Caesar" (John 19:12). There is, however, another aspect of the scene that is highly important: The stories about Jesus's passion differ in many details; while all of them remember that some members of the Jewish elite played a role in Jesus's sentence to death, it must have been the Roman authorities who made the final decision and the Roman soldiers in particular who tortured and killed Jesus. Anything else would have been legally impossible and highly improbable: Jews typically dreaded the punishment of crucifixion, which was a common Roman form of execution for enslaved people and rebels in the provinces.

The Death of Herod Agrippa

When the New Testament mentions the name *Herod*, it is important to look more closely at precisely which Herod is meant: The Judean king who seeks to kill the newborn Jesus by ordering the massacre in Bethlehem (Matt 2:13, 16–18) is Herod the Great. The fact that the Gospel of Matthew relates the time of Jesus's birth to a reign suggests that Jesus could have been born before the turn of the era, possibly around 6 BCE. However, most gospel references likely refer to Herod Antipas, the tetrarch of Galilee and Perea, who is reported, among other things, to have imprisoned John the Baptist and ultimately had him beheaded (Mark 6:17–29). Despite Herod's interest in Jesus (Mark 6:14–16.), there is only one known encounter between them, which is reported in Luke's passion narrative (23:6–12): Pilate, seeking to avoid responsibility for Jesus, sends him as a captive to his sovereign, Herod Antipas, who coincidently is also staying in Jerusalem at this time (23:7). Herod Agrippa I, who was reinstated as king due to his relationship with Caligula, is simply referred to as Herod in the Acts of the Apostles. Acts presents him as a persecutor of the early church who, at the same time, was attempting to secure support from part of the Jewish population that had not joined the new movement (12:3). When he became the new ruler of Judea, he had James the son of Zebedee executed (Acts 12:2) and Peter imprisoned—Peter was freed only because of a miraculous intervention (Acts 12:6–19a).

Acts goes on to recount a strange scene that can only be interpreted in light of this information:

> When Herod had searched for him [Peter] and could not find him, he examined the guards and ordered them to be put to death. Then he went down from Judea to Caesarea and stayed there. . . . On an appointed day Herod put on his royal robes, took his seat on the platform, and delivered a public address to them. The people kept shouting, "The voice of a god and not of a mortal!" And immediately, because he had not given the glory to God, an angel of the Lord struck him down, and he was eaten by worms and died. (Acts 12:19b–23)

The cruelty and the associated hubris of the Jewish ruler are only briefly described: The guards who were unable to prevent Peter from escaping prison are themselves condemned to death. Herod moves from Jerusalem, the traditional residency of Jewish kings, to Caesarea, Pilate's former official residence. There, Agrippa allows himself to be celebrated like a god, a clear case of blasphemy that is also immediately punished by an angel of God. The description of his death is reminiscent of king Antiochus IV Epiphanies (2 Macc 9:9), whose reign also falls because of his excessive self-aggrandizement.

FURTHER READING

Grabbe, Lester L. *A History of the Jews and Judaism in the Second Temple Period*. Vols. 3–4. T&T Clark, 2020–21.

Regev, Eyal. *The Hasmoneans: Ideology, Archaeology, Identity*. Vandenhoeck & Ruprecht, 2013.

Marshak, Adam Kolman. *The Many Faces of Herod the Great*. Eerdmans, 2015.

Mason, Steve. *A History of the Jewish War*. Cambridge University Press, 2016.

Mor, Menahem. *The Second Jewish Revolt: The Bar Kokhba War, 132–136 CE*. Brill, 2016.

Schwartz, Seth. *The Ancient Jews from Alexander to Muhammad*. Cambridge University Press, 2015.

Notes

1 See the chapter "A Short History of the Hellenistic and Roman Period in the Mediterranean" by Stefan Pfeiffer in the present volume.

2 Polybius, *The Histories*, trans. William Roger Paton, Loeb Classical Library (Harvard 1922), 28.18.1.

3 For possible interpretations of the events, see Daniel R. Schwartz, *1 Maccabees* (Yale University Press, 2022), 54–58.

4 For more information on the origins and characteristics of Jewish groups, see Albert I. Baumgarten, *The Flourishing of Jewish Sects in the Maccabean Era* (Brill, 1997).

5 For more on this group, see Josephus, *J.W.* 2.128–64. See also Seth Schwartz, *The Ancient Jews from Alexander to Muhammad* (Cambridge University Press, 2015), 67–69.

6 Suetonius, *Julius Caesar* 84.2.

7 Dio, *Roman History* 55.27.6.

8 Jesus may also be referring to this in Luke 19:11–27.

9 See the chapter on "Samaritans" by József Zsengellér in the present volume.

10 Luke 2:1–2 may refer to this census, although the Gospel of Luke places it too early, i.e., at the time of Jesus's birth.

11 See Suetonius, *Tiberius* 36.

12 According to Luke 23:6–12, Antipas was ruler over Jesus and thus also involved in his trial. Whether this note is historically accurate must remain open.

13 See the chapter on "Living as a Jew in Diaspora" by Ruben Bühner in the present volume.

14 Suetonius, *Claudius* 25.

15 See also the chapter on "Early Jewish Messianism" by Thomas Hatina in the present volume.

16 For details, see Lester L. Grabbe, *A History of the Jews and Judaism in the Second Temple Period*, vol. 4, *The Jews Under the Roman Shadow (4 BCE–150 CE)*, (T&T Clark, 2021), 458–61.

17 This is evident from documents such as 4 Ezra and 2 Baruch, which are believed to have been written shortly before the Bar Kokhba revolt.

18 Dio Cassius, *Roman History* 49.12.
19 Eusebius, *Ecclesiastical History* 4.6.3.
20 Steve Mason, *Josephus and the New Testament*, 2nd ed. (Hendrickson, 2003), 252–56.
21 Michael Tilly, *1 Makkabäer* (Herder, 2015), 51.
22 Pliny the Younger, *The Letters of the Younger Pliny*, trans. John Benjamin Firth (Walter Scott, 1910), 10.96.
23 Pliny, *Letters* 10.96.
24 See also the chapter on "Apocalypticism" by Jörg Frey in the present volume.
25 For a discussion of the irony in this story see Tobias Nicklas, "Die Prophetie des Kajaphas. Im Netz johanneischer Ironie," *New Testament Studies* 46, no. 4 (2000): 589–94.

CHAPTER THREE

Documentary Sources

Peter Arzt-Grabner
(University of Salzburg)

THE CLASSIFICATION OF documentary sources is not as simple as it might seem at first glance. To begin with, there are two specialized disciplines: epigraphy and papyrology. Epigraphy traditionally deals with texts that have been incised into writing material: stone, walls, wax, ceramics, and various metals. Papyrology is concerned with ancient texts written in ink, which only came to light again through purchases on the antiquities market or scientific excavations from the late nineteenth century onwards:[1] papyri, parchments, potsherds, and wooden tablets. In terms of language, context, and genre, contracts or school exercises incised on wax tablets and curse tablets incised in lead lamellae, for example, have a whole lot in common with inscribed papyri but very little with stone inscriptions. A more useful classification, therefore, is the distinction between texts on *immobile material* and those on *mobile media*. The former are usually characterized by their general accessibility and the intention of being on public display, while the latter belong to the private, business, or administrative sphere and were primarily intended to be handed over or transmitted and read by specific addressees.

A further distinction can be made between documentary and semiliterary texts. The first category includes texts that document everyday life across a wide variety of contexts, while semiliterary texts reveal a certain proximity to literary texts but do not yet constitute genuine literature. Among these semiliterary or subliterary texts are extensive magical handbooks, instructions in religious methods, prayers, amulets, oracle questions, binding spells, curse tablets, horoscopes, nonliterary medical manuals, recipes, lists of ingredients, doctors' reports, and texts related to ancient education. In this context, it should not be forgotten that, unlike today, *magic* was not the counterpart to institutionalized religion but a part of it, especially in areas of popular religion. There is also an overlap between magical and medical treatments. Usually, semiliterary texts are preserved on mobile writing materials. In a broader sense, coins can also be seen and studied as documentary sources.

Documentary sources are not only abundant but also remarkably diverse. They include documents relating to commerce, administration, and legislation

Editions of Greek Inscriptions:
List of Abbreviations of Editions and Works of Reference for Alphabetic Greek Epigraphy (GrEpiAbbr): https://aiegl.org/grepiabbr.html
Supplementum Epigraphicum Graecum (SEG): https://scholarlyeditions.brill.com/sego/abbreviations
Editions of Greek, Latin, Demotic, and Coptic Papyri, Ostraca, and Tablets:
So-called Checklist: https://papyri.info/docs/checklist

Figure 3.1. Standard lists of epigraphic and papyrological editions.

as well as to all areas of private life—among them, extensive personnel lists or accounts, various contracts, minutes, private letters, honorary inscriptions, decrees, orders within the military or administrative chain of command, and much more.[2] The documentary material attests to genres that are otherwise very poorly represented.

Private and official letters, for example, are known from Plato, Cicero, Seneca, Pliny the Younger and others, whose letters have survived in edited anthologies, from which some of the original epistolary features and formulas may have been stripped during the editorial process. Papyrus and ostracon letters, however, have been preserved in the original form and thus provide direct access to the real world of Greco-Roman epistolography. Discoveries and studies in recent decades have shown that the wide range of papyrus letters contains not only short and simple messages, but also evidence of high education, sophisticated language, and extensive conception, even if such artifacts are the exception. One example is the private letter of a certain Aurelius Ammon, a scholar and lawyer in the Roman province of Egypt, to his mother.[3] Its length is perfectly comparable to Paul's letter to the Christ groups in Galatia (Galatians). Ammon's letter deals with rather unpleasant family matters, but like Paul, he not only mentions his current situation and that of his addressee but also comments on them at length with philosophical and religious thoughts that carry value regardless of the specific occasion. Even short papyrus letters from Greco-Roman antiquity provide significant parallels to the structure and formulas of New Testament letters.

To give just one other selected example: The reports on tax collectors and descriptions of Roman food laws known from ancient literature concern the provincial level of the Roman Empire. Documentary texts, however, provide information on the Roman tax system at the level of the village or town detailing the variety of taxes levied and the rates applied to individuals, trades, crafts, land, and certain crops. Furthermore, these sources provide us with interesting details about the methods of tax collection and the personnel involved in the revenue system. Several archives of local tax agents found in situ contain not only receipts, declarations, accounts, and other documents relevant to the tax system, but also private letters that allow us to reconstruct the personal and administrative networks of the agents and their numerous activities that were not related to tax collection. In some cases, these archives even contain literary texts that show that tax agents were also active as collectors and readers of literature.

The great importance of scientific excavations can be illustrated by the example of the ostracon archive of a certain Philocles,[4] a Greek-speaking Egyptian who earned his living by selling vegetables and procuring women for Roman soldiers in the military camps of Krokodilo and Didymoi in the Eastern Desert of Egypt. As a result of systematic excavations, it was possible to reconstruct the chronology of circumstances during the late first and early second centuries CE, the commercial and private networks of the involved individuals, and the sometimes highly dramatic relationships of pimps, prostitutes, and their clients.

Immobile Materials

Stone Inscriptions and Graffiti

The majority of documentary texts preserved on immobile material are represented by stone inscriptions. The text genres are manifold, including decrees, catalogs, honorary inscriptions, vows, funerary inscriptions, donations to gods, dedicatory, votive, and commemorative inscriptions. In absolute numbers, most of the inscriptions are very short. The more extensive examples include edicts and decrees that were displayed in public areas like squares, arenas, theaters, and temple precincts. Stone inscriptions were rarely set up in enclosed, purely private spaces, as they were usually made for long-term display and intended to be read and perceived by as many people as possible. To a limited extent, this also applies

- Database with metadata of inscriptions, papyri, and related material: https://www.trismegistos.org
- Searchable Greek Inscriptions (provided by the Packard Humanities Institute): https://epigraphy.packhum.org
- The Ashmolean Latin Inscriptions Project: https://latininscriptions.ashmus.ox.ac.uk
- Epigraphik-Datenbank Clauss/Slaby (EDCS): https://db.edcs.eu
- Epigraphic Database Heidelberg (EDH): https://edh.ub.uni-heidelberg.de
- Epigraphic Database Roma (EDR): http://www.edr-edr.it
- Epigraphic Database Bari, Inscriptions by Christians in Rome: https://www.edb.uniba.it
- The Ancient Graffiti Project (AGP): http://ancientgraffiti.org

Figure 3.2. Online databases for epigraphy.

- Corpus Inscriptionum Latinarum (CIL): https://cil.bbaw.de
- Inscriptiones Graecae (IG): http://telota.bbaw.de/ig/
- Inscriptions grecques et latines de la Syrie (IGLS): https://www.persee.fr/collection/bah
- Roman Inscriptions of Britain (RIB) Online: https://romaninscriptionsofbritain.org
- Supplementum Epigraphicum Graecum (SEG) Online: https://scholarlyeditions.brill.com/sego/

Figure 3.3. Selected epigraphic online editions.

to graffiti,[5] scratched into the outer or inner walls of prayer houses, temples, dining halls, baths, or latrines. Due to their durability even under extreme conditions, and in contrast to papyri and related materials, stone inscriptions have been preserved from all areas of the Roman Empire.

Mobile Materials

Papyri, Parchments, Ostraca, and Tablets

Documentary texts provide a body of evidence that is always limited to what has thus far surfaced and been edited. This applies even more to papyri, ostraca, and tablets than to stone inscriptions because the former mostly come from the garbage dumps of antiquity—artifacts that, once discarded, were never meant to matter again. Only comparatively few have been found in situ in houses or, to name another notorious possibility, in the caves of the Judean Desert.

Papyrus, in particular, could only survive in conditions where it was protected from moisture. This explains why the most extensive finds come from the arid regions of Egypt, Israel, and Syria, including papyrus documents found in Egypt but originally written elsewhere. That papyrus can be regarded as *the* stationery of Greco-Roman antiquity is also evidenced by the numerous depictions of papyrus scrolls on vases, frescoes, mosaics, or in the hands of statues from all regions of the Roman Empire. A further indication of its widespread use are the hundreds of thousands of clay seals with papyrus imprints on the reverse that have been found in areas where the papyrus documents themselves have not survived.

The term *papyrus* refers to both the plant and the writing material made from it. In ancient times, the papyrus plant grew in Egypt, the Levant, Babylonia, and Sicily; but it was only in Egypt that papyrus was processed into a writing material. From there, papyrus rolls were exported to the entire Mediterranean world. In fact, the roll was the standard format available for purchase in shops.[6]

The idea that ancient scribes bought individual sheets, glued them together as needed, and then wrote on them is a misconception that is disproved by documentary and material evidence.[7] Depending on their needs, scribes used an entire roll(for the continuous and multiyear accounts of a large company, for example), or cut off smaller pieces of various sizes for receipts, tax returns, petitions, or letters. Alternatively, one could also write one or more columns at the beginning of a roll and then cut the written piece off the roll afterward. As a result, the glued joints are still visible on many documents, and in many cases, the writing simply runs across them.[8]

Leather seems to have been the preferred writing material in the ancient Middle East and Asia for centuries, as most Qumran scrolls and documents from Avroman and Bactria show.[9] Unlike parchment, leather was always tanned and, above all, not stretched and dried while wet. Such documents are inscribed on one side only, probably because the flesh side of leather is too uneven and can absorb too much of the writing fluid.

The claim that parchment was invented by Eumenes II (197–159 BCE) in Pergamon (and therefore named *pergamena*) because of a halt to papyrus exports from Egypt is historically unlikely,[10] but its original production may still be connected to Hellenistic Pergamon. The writing material is made from animal hides, usually those of sheep, calves, or goats. Its manufacture required many individual steps and was very time-consuming: pickling, scraping off the hairs, liming, stretching and simultaneous drying, and smoothing.[11] The high value of parchment is reflected in its frequent reuse through reinscription (palimpsest or codex rescriptus).

Especially in a humid climate, parchment is much more durable than papyrus, but beyond durability, the fact that animal skins did not have to be imported must have also been relevant for the transition from papyrus to parchment.

For a long time, documentary ostraca were considered less valuable than papyri and parchments. More recently, however, it has been recognized that they represent a rich source of data on Roman finance and taxation, as well as social and economic affairs.[12] Ostraca are potsherds incised with a sharp tool (*stilus*), usually of metal, bone, or ivory. They were used in all periods of Greco-Roman antiquity in different regions and for different genres such as simple petitions and letters. The evidence for this type as well as for ostraca inscribed with a reed pen (*kalamos*) or with a brush and ink, suggests that both were used simultaneously for many centuries. Among the earliest ink-written ostraca are two thousand in Aramaic originating from Idumea,[13] the oldest dating to the early sixth century BCE. In addition to thousands of ink-written ostraca from Egypt, the ostraca found at Bu Njem in Libya, at Chersonesos in Crete, and in the central cemetery of Rhodes also belong to this type.

Due to the typical small size of the potsherds, ostraca usually contain short texts and were primarily used for receipts and letters, or for semiliterary texts related to medicine, magic, worship, and education.

One thing that wax tablets (*tabulae ceratae*) and metal tablets have in common with incised ostraca is that the text was engraved into the surface of the tablet with a stylus. Wax tablets are therefore also called stylus tablets. The tablets of a "double-leaf" diptych or a polyptych, which consists of more than two tablets, were first made of wood and only subsequently covered with a layer of wax on the inside. The term *wooden tablet* refers to a wooden board or a thin wooden sheet (*tilia*) inscribed with ink. Also, *tiliae* were frequently used in the form of diptychs. In general, only the inner pages of diptychs and polyptychs were inscribed or incised; the outer pages served as covers to protect the inner text from damage. Unlike wooden tablets, *tabulae ceratae* could be reused several times. For this purpose, the stylus was flattened on one side so that it could be used to smooth the wax and prepare the tablet for another incision. In most cases, the text to be deciphered is the last engraved on the tablet. The fact that most *tiliae* were found in Britain could indicate that this format was used more frequently in these northern regions, likely because papyrus exports from Egypt hardly reached them.

A typical Egyptian use of wooden tags is evidenced by the several thousand mummy labels found to date. The names and short notes carved or written in ink were intended to ensure that the corpses were not misidentified during the lengthy embalming process or during transportation.

The most common material used for metal tablets was lead. The earliest private letters are preserved on lead tablets found in the Black Sea region, Athens,[14] other parts of Greece, and the Iberian Peninsula.[15] The number of lead letters, however, is far larger than the seventeen hundred lead curse tablets that have been found to date,[16] indicating that lead was the preferred material for this text genre. Simple lead tags with engraved names, on the other hand, were used in the textile industry.[17]

- Trismegistos Texts (database with metadata of inscriptions, papyri, and related material, including links to open access editions): https://www.trismegistos.org
- Papyrological Navigator (database with papyrological texts and metadata, including data from APIS, HGV, Trismegistos): https://papyri.info
- Thesaurus Defixionum (database of Greek and Latin curse tablets): https://heurist.fdm.uni-hamburg.de/html/heurist/?db=The_dema&website
- Kyprianos Database of Ancient Ritual Texts (coptic magical papyri): https://www.coptic-magic.phil.uni-wuerzburg.de/index.php/manuscripts-search/

Figure 3.4. Online databases for papyrology.

- Online Coins of the Roman Empire: https://numismatics.org/ocre/
- Roman Provincial Coinage Online: https://rpc.ashmus.ox.ac.uk

Figure 3.5. Online databases for numismatics.

Discharge from military service was confirmed by the issue of a military diploma, many of which have been preserved on bronze plates throughout the Roman Empire. Materials rarely used for tablets due to their high value include ivory, silver, and gold, with gold and silver lamellae occasionally used for precious amulets.[18]

Coins

Ancient coins were minted by order of the state and served not only as a means of payment and value but also as a medium for propaganda. Both the iconography and the inscriptions on coins were an expression of the ideology of those in power. Whenever this ideology was changed or realigned, it could be communicated relatively quickly and widely by minting new types of coins. As documentary sources, coins therefore also shed light on the political, economic, and social conditions of the time and area of their circulation. In the everyday life of ordinary people, copper and silver coins were predominantly used. This is why copper and silver coins hold greater documentary value than gold coins. The often-abbreviated inscriptions also contribute to the lexicography and semantics of the vocabulary of their time.[19]

TAKING A CLOSER LOOK: SOURCES

Sources from the World of the New Testament

Contract of Apprenticeship

Greek papyrus from Oxyrhynchos, Egypt; September 25, 36 CE.

> [Agreeing with each other are Thamounion daughter of Onnophris, with her] son Tryphon son of Dionysios [as guardian], and Abaros son of Didymos, weaver, inhabitant of the city of |[5] Oxyrhynchos: Thamounion, on the one hand, that she has apprenticed (literally: handed out) to Abaros her son Onnophris, the brother of Tryphon and son of the same Dionysios, who is still a minor, for two years |[10] from the first of Phaophi of the current twenty-third year of Tiberius

Caesar Augustus, in order that he may serve (*diakoneō*) and perform all the works ordered to him by Abaros in respect of the weaver's craft, and Abaros, on the other hand, that he will teach the boy the weaver's craft as he knows it for the agreed period of time, in which [Abaros] will furnish four silver drachmas a month to Thamounion for the boy's food [and clothe] the boy for the same [amount of time], and furthermore he will pay the trade-tax requested for the boy for the same amount of time . . . drachmas for the poll-tax and dike-tax and pig-tax requested for the boy shall be incumbent on Thamounion. But for as many days the boy does not work, Thamounion will deliver him for an equal number of days to Abaros after the period, or she has to pay to him a penalty of one silver drachma for each day, but if he is withdrawn before the period is up, a fine of sixty silver drachmas and the same sum to the State. And if Abaros for his part does not teach ⟨. . .⟩* The contract of apprenticeship is valid. Year 23 of Tiberius Caesar Augustus, month Augustus 28.

(Hand 2) I, Abaros son of Didymos, will teach the boy as written above. I, Didymos, have written for my father for he does not know how to write.

Year 23 of Tiberius Caesar Augustus, month Augustus 28. (SB 10.10236 [TM 16675])[20]

* The sentence was not completed; the scribe probably simply omitted a line from his template. By analogy with comparable contracts, the continuation likely should have read: "the boy, he shall be liable to the same fine."

Documentary papyri are an excellent source for shedding light on ancient crafts, especially weaving. Two archives from first-century Oxyrhynchos allow us to trace the private, business, and social lives of two families who ran their weaving workshops over several generations. The family archive of Tryphon, son of Dionysios, currently comprises forty-four texts in forty-one published documents; that of Pausiris, son of Pausiris, consists of twenty-three texts, of which only nine have been edited so far.[21]

The apprenticeship contract presented above is part of the Tryphon archive and was agreed upon by Tryphon's mother, Thamounion, and the master weaver, Abaros. Tryphon himself acts as the legal guardian (*kyrios*)[22] of his mother, who concludes this contract on behalf of her other son Onnophris. A similar contract from the archive is P.Oxy. 2.275 with BL 9:179, which was concluded on September 18, 66 CE between Tryphon himself, who—as we know from his archive—at this time ran the family workshop as master weaver, and another master weaver, Ptolemaios son of Pausirion. Another similar apprenticeship contract from the family archive of Pausiris is P.Wisc. 1.4 with BL 6:69 (August 29–September 27, 53 CE), concluded between the master weaver Pausiris and another master weaver, Apollonios son of Apollonios, to have the son of Pausiris trained in the workshop of Apollonios.

In general,[23] such a contract could be concluded by an adult relative, in most cases a father or mother, or by the master of a slave, who would send the boy or girl to a master weaver to learn the craft of weaving. The contract specified the duration of the apprenticeship, who was responsible for providing food and clothing and for paying any taxes due, and that the apprentice was required to remain with the master weaver for the entire time and could not be removed. In this way, it was ensured that the master weaver had the agreed-upon time available to provide the thorough training to which he had committed himself. These agreements were followed by penalty clauses, a validity formula, the date, and the signatures.

After specifying the contracting parties, the apprentice, and the duration of the apprenticeship, such a contract included a clause whereby the parent or slave owner confirms that the apprentice will do everything that the master weaver instructs according to his craft. In the three contracts mentioned above, this clause is preceded by the confirmation that the apprentice will also "serve" (*diakoneō*) the master weaver. What distinguishes these contracts from other apprenticeship contracts is the fact that both parties are master weavers, or in the case of the contract presented here, the wife of the presumably deceased owner of the workshop. The likely reason for this was that a master weaver did not want his son to learn the craft exclusively in his own workshop, but to have his skills refined in another workshop and perhaps even learn a different technique. The *diakoneō* clause thus serves to emphasize that the son, who had already "served" his father in his own workshop, was formally obliged to "serve" another master weaver as soon as the contract took effect.

In addition to the examples mentioned above, the clause is also preserved in another contract from Oxyrhynchos, SB 24.16253 (98–103 CE). The two parties filing this contract were brothers, but only one of them is explicitly identified as a weaver, namely—as is customary in these contracts—the one who is to train the apprentice. However, the *diakoneō* clause in line 7 of this contract indicates—by analogy with what we know from the family archives of Tryphon and Pausiris—that both brothers were weavers, as was the case with Tryphon and his brother as well as with Pausiris and his two brothers.[24]

A striking analogy to the *diakoneō* clause is found in Paul's letter to Philemon (Phlm 13). The similarity is so strong that we can conclude Paul was thoroughly familiar with this clause from apprenticeship contracts, and here indicates in his own words that he was a weaver, or—as a tentmaker (cf. Acts 18:3)—at least a member of the ancient textile industry. As a citizen of Tarsus, a metropolis of Greco-Roman weaving that was famous for its distinctive art,[25] it is plausible that Paul was a master of his craft who ran the family workshop after his father's death and had at least once signed an apprenticeship contract with another master in Tarsus for a brother or nephew. It is possible that Philemon also ran a weaving workshop and therefore immediately understood the intent behind Paul's language, which may well have been Paul's intention anyway: By analogy to weaving, Paul would be only too willing to train Onesimus in the art of spreading the gospel, if only a contract were drawn up between Philemon and Paul (cf. Phlm 14). And since Paul had so much confidence in this slave, why should not Onesimus's master also entrust him with a responsible task as well? (cf. vv. 11, 15–17).

Letter of Recommendation

Latin wooden tablet (diptych) from Vindolanda, (northern) Britannia; ca. 97–103 CE.

[Claud]ius Karus to his C[e]r[ialis], g[reetings].

. . . Brigionus (?) has asked me, lord, to recommend him to you. I therefore ask you, lord, if you are willing to support him in what he has requested of you. I ask that you think fit to commend him to Annius Equester, (centurion) *regionarius* at Luguvalium, [by doing which] you will, both in [his?] and [my own] name, place me in debt [to you]. I pray that you have the best of fortune and are in good health.

(Hand 2) Farewell, brother.

(Back, hand 1) To Cerialis, pref(ect). (T.Vindol. 2.250 [TM 114893])[26]

The recommended person's name in line 3 is either Brigionus, preceded by a short (or abbreviated) *gentilicium*, or only the second part of his name (-brigionus) is preserved. The addressee is Flavius Cerialis, the prefect of the ninth cohort of Batavians, stationed in the Roman fort of Vindolanda where he lived, together with his family around 100 CE. Also, his wife Sulpicia Lepidina is known from the Vindolanda tablets.[27]

By sending Brigionus with this tablet to the prefect of Vindolanda, Claudius Karus fufills the soldier's request to recommend him to Cerialis. The perfect tense in "what he has requested of you," refers to the soldier's option to inform Cerialis personally and orally about his wishes, but also to the possibility that Cerialis might prefer to hear the letter carrier's request before reading the letter. In any case, the main request is also explicitly mentioned in the letter by Karus: Cerialis should send and commend Brigionus to Annius Equester, the centurion of the region at Luguvalium (modern Carlisle).

Letters of recommendation are also preserved on papyri from Egypt and from Masada in Israel.[28] These letters provide us with valuable background information on Paul's letter to Philemon as well as other Pauline passages (Rom 16:1–2; 1 Cor 16:3, 15–18; 2 Cor 3:1, 8–9; Phil 2:25–30).[29]

Bylaws of a Greco-Roman Association

Stone inscription from Liopesi, Attica; second century CE.

> The law [*nomos*] of the *eranistai.*
>
> It is not lawful for anyone to enter this most holy assembly [*synodos*] of *eranistai* without being first examined as to whether he is pure and pious and good. Let the president [*prostatēs*] and the *archeranistēs*, and the secretary, and the treasurers and the syndics examine (the candidate). And except for the president [*prostatēs*], let these be chosen by lot each year. The one who has been entrusted with (the tomb of) the hero shall be the liturgist for his lifetime. May the club [*eranos*] increase because of the zealousness (of its members). But if anyone of those should be seen where fighting or disturbances occur, he shall be expelled from the club [*eranos*], being fined twenty-five Attic drachmas or being punished with double the blows in addition to judgment (?). (IG II^2.1369.30–44)[30]

Presumably most, if not all, Greco-Roman associations had bylaws like the one quoted above, by which membership, conduct, and responsibilities were regulated. Similar early bylaws, some of them much more detailed, are preserved as stone inscriptions from Lydia, Cilicia, Attica, Locris, Samnium, and Campania, or on papyri from Egypt.[31] These regulations only came into effect once they had been ratified by the members, on which noncompliance could also be punished.

One purpose of the bylaws was presumably to present the association as a group of individuals of integrity, thus preventing or minimizing the sometimes restrictive interventions of the state. Perhaps this is why violations of behavioral norms were punished with particularly harsh penalties. What all bylaws have in common is that the members were evidently committed to integrity and an ethically responsible lifestyle and attitude. In this sense, the ancient associations can be seen as "trust networks," as joining an association signaled both internally and externally that the members were trustworthy and shared the core values of the association.[32]

Numerous studies have already demonstrated that comparing ancient associations with the structures of early Christ groups can be very fruitful.[33] This comparison applies to the functionaries (the title *prostatēs*, often used for the president of an association, is also used by Paul for Phoebe in Rom 16:2) but also to the internal jurisdiction (cf. 1 Cor 5–6; 2 Cor 7:9–11) and the banquets that were regularly organized and held with mandatory attendance (cf. 1 Cor 11:17–34).[34] In the passage quoted above, it is the reference to fights and fines that suggests that a banquet was held by this *eranos* at regular intervals. According to P.Mich. 5.243.1–2 (14–37 CE), a guild of sheep and donkey rearers at Tebtynis in Egypt regulated that all members "shall hold a banquet each month on the 12th, each one [of the members] contributing for his monthly dues the twelve silver drachmas assigned equally to each," and that "anyone who, at the banquets, falls on another person's place at the table has to pay an extra three obols for his own seat" (lines 6–7). P.Lond. 7.2193.15–16 (69–58 BCE?) regulates that "no one should speak badly of others at the symposium."

Reading the New Testament Texts

Thanksgiving Reports in Romans

> First, I thank my God through Jesus Christ for all of you, because your faith is proclaimed throughout the world. (Rom 1:8)

By analogy with many papyrus letters, the thanksgiving passages in most of the authentic Pauline letters (Rom 1:8; 1 Cor 1:4–8; Phil 1:3–5; 1 Thess 1:2–5; Phlm 4–6) and elsewhere in the New Testament (Eph 1:15–16; Col 1:3–6, 11–12; 2 Thess 1:3–10; 2 Tim 1:3–5) should not be interpreted simply as a formula of the letter opening, but rather they can be recognized as a widespread convention in the introductory part of the letter body.[35] It is not a formula that could be used in every letter, like the formulas of the letter opening, but depends on the prior arrival of good news from the current addressee, conveyed orally or by letter through a messenger. Since such a thanksgiving phrase reports the letter author's reaction to receiving good news, it is not a "thanksgiving" in the proper sense but rather the report of a thanksgiving, already performed as a religious act or prayer before a god. As such, the thanksgiving was performed *before* the letter in which it is mentioned was written.

The examples preserved in papyrus letters from the second century BCE to the third century CE show a great variety in their forms. A certain Aline, for instance, writes in one of her letters to her husband, "We thank all the gods for the health of you that . . .";[36] the context is fragmentary, but the reference to "your letter" in the following line likely refers to Aline's source of good news about her husband. A rather long and very personal thanksgiving is reported by Aurelius Apollonios in PSI 12.1261.3–13 (212–17 CE):

> "We rejoiced greatly and in many ways when Gorgias came to us and informed us that you are well and live, according to our prayers, safely and in reputation, as it is befitting you; very many thanks therefore to the gods and to the Fortune of our lord, the invincible Severus Antoninus,[37] which preserved you, and of which we, in our longing for you, wish to benefit with our own eyes and no longer only by letters—since we already have seen you once in your home staying well."

Another example is preserved in P.Oxy. 77.5113.3–6 (third cent. CE), where a Dorion reports to his "child" Phanias that he rejoiced and thanked the god Sarapis after learning that the god had restored his health. In SB 16.12589.4–5 (second cent. CE), Plousia writes to her brother: "When I learned that you fare well, I thanked all the gods."

Sometimes a received message is not explicitly mentioned but can be assumed based on the context. For example, the female servant Taus mentions in P.Giss. 1.17.5–7 (113–20 CE): "I was very anxious, my lord, as I heard that you were indisposed, but thanks to all the gods that they guard you carefully, free from harm." Thus, after receiving bad news about the health of her addressee, Taus must have been informed of his improved condition, which prompted her thanksgiving.

As the corresponding passages in the letters sent by Paul confirm, his thanksgiving reports are also motivated by the receipt of written or oral news about the well-being of his addressees. In Paul's case, however, the news is not about the health or physical well-being of his followers, but concerns their spiritual well-being, their faith in God, their fellowship with Jesus Christ, and their imitation of the apostle in their daily lives.

The most amazing form of a thanksgiving is reported by Paul in Romans 1:8. At the time of writing the letter, Paul had not yet been to Rome, and there is nothing to indicate that he had received a letter or oral news from a Roman Christ group. Nevertheless, he insinuates to have heard good news about the spiritual welfare of these Roman communities, testifying that "your faith is spoken of throughout the whole world," which was reason enough for him to perform an act of thanksgiving before God and to tell his addressees about it.

The Roman Census in Luke

> In those days a decree went out from Caesar Augustus that all the world should be registered. This was the first registration and was taken while

> Quirinius was governor of Syria. All went to their own towns to be registered. Joseph also went from the town of Nazareth in Galilee to Judea, to the city of David called Bethlehem, because he was descended from the house and family of David. He went to be registered with Mary, to whom he was engaged and who was expecting a child. (Luke 2:1–5)

The basic type of tax collected by the Roman authorities was the poll tax, which had to be paid by every man, including slaves, between the ages of 14 and 60. All women and privileged persons such as Roman citizens were exempt from the poll tax. To calculate the tax revenue in advance, a census was carried out every fourteen years. In this way, the authorities knew in advance when a young man would reach the taxable age of 14.

Luke 2:1–2 refers to such a census—namely "the first registration while Quirinius was governor of Syria." As we now know from papyrus evidence, what Luke does not describe correctly is that the census to register the taxable population was not an imperial census, but a provincial census; that is, it was not carried out in the same year for the entire empire, but conducted, for example, for Syria in 6/7 CE but for Egypt in 4/5 CE. Other details provided by Luke are, however, correct, such as the Greek term *apographē* for registering the population or the remark that this *apographē* was carried out for the first time for Syria and Judea under Quirinius. In the year 6 CE, Augustus had formed the Roman province of Judea by uniting Judea, Samaria, and Idumea, and he had placed the new province directly under the control of the legate of Syria, Publius Sulpicius Quirinius. Due to its great importance, conducting a census was one of the first tasks to be carried out in a new province.

Luke introduces this *apographē* to explain why Joseph and Mary went from the town of Nazareth in Galilee to Judea, to the city of David called Bethlehem. According to Luke, they had to do so because all the people were ordered to go to their own towns to be registered, and since Joseph was descended from the house and family of David, he had to go to Bethlehem (cf. Luke 2:3–4). Luke's account is supported by the papyrus P.Lond. 3.904, col. 2 (p. 124).[38] By this edict, issued in 104 CE, the *praefectus Aegypti* Gaius Vibius Maximus ordered that, in preparation for the upcoming census, all those who, for whatever reason, were not residing in their place of origin but were staying in Alexandria must return to their own homes in order to register there and to cultivate the fields for which they were responsible. A comparison of the relevant texts suggests that Luke was looking for a historically plausible reason to explain the already established tradition that Jesus of Nazareth was born in Bethlehem. But in the end, Luke's attempt at an explanation fails for three main reasons: First, Galilee was not part of the province of Judea and, therefore, not under Quirinius's control. There was definitely no census order which would have required someone living in Nazareth to travel to Judea to be registered. Second, someone born during the census of 6/7 CE could not have been thirty years old in the fifteenth year of Tiberius, that is, in 28/29 CE, which would have applied to Jesus according to Luke 3:1, 23.[39] And third, the edict of the prefect of Egypt attests to a reintegration order issued for the residents of the urban and administratively important Egyptian capital Alexandria—whereas Nazareth was a small and largely unknown village, and it is unlikely it would have been subject to such orders.

The Coins of Herod Antipas in Matthew

> As they went away, Jesus began to speak to the crowds about John: "What did you go out into the wilderness to look at? A reed shaken by the wind? What, then, did you go out to see? Someone dressed in soft robes? Look, those who wear soft robes are in royal palaces. What, then, did you go out to see? A prophet? Yes, I tell you, and more than a prophet. This is the one about whom it is written, 'See, I am sending my messenger ahead of you, who will prepare your way before you.' "Truly I tell you, among those born of women no one has arisen greater than John the Baptist, yet the least in the kingdom of heaven is greater than he." (Matt 11:7–11)

In Matthew 11:7–11, the crowd is first offered three rhetorical questions, each offering a metaphorical figure whom they could have gone out into the desert to see. The prophet mentioned in the third metaphor is identified with John the Baptist and as the intended target (vv. 9–11), which implicitly excludes the first two: "a reed shaken by the wind" (v. 7) and "a man dressed in soft robes" (v. 8). While "those wearing soft robes" are immediately identified with the officials in royal palaces, the identity of the "reed shaken by the wind" remains open.

Gerd Theissen has proposed a numismatic interpretation of Matthew 11:7. He argued that the "reed shaken by the wind" has its direct counterpart on coins struck in 20/21 CE to commemorate the founding of Tiberias in 19 CE,[40] and that the reed on the obverse of these coins and the reference in Matthew 11:7 must be a symbol for Herod Antipas himself.[41] The metaphor, Theissen continues, can be interpreted in two ways: positively, as an advantageous adaptation; or negatively, as a symbol of opportunistic instability. In reality, both interpretations were likely at play: Antipas probably intended the reed to symbolize positive qualities akin to the founding of Tiberias, while the local population may have viewed it negatively, as a sign of Antipas's own weakness. This negative view likely prevailed, which may explain the change in iconography, with the palm branch replacing the reed on later coins.[42]

FURTHER READING

Arzt-Grabner, Peter. *Letters and Letter Writing.* Papyri and the New Testament 2. Brill Schöningh, 2023.

Arzt-Grabner, Peter, John S. Kloppenborg, and Christina M. Kreinecker. *More Light from the Ancient East: Understanding the New Testament through Papyri.* Papyri and the New Testament 1. With a contribution by Gregg Schwendner. Brill Schöningh, 2023.

Ascough, Richard S., Philip A. Harland, and John S. Kloppenborg, eds. *Associations in the Greco-Roman World: A Sourcebook.* Baylor University Press, 2012.

Corsten, Thomas, Markus Öhler, and Joseph Verheyden, eds. *Epigraphik und Neues Testament.* Wissenschaftliche Untersuchungen zum Neuen Testament 365. Mohr Siebeck, 2016.

Kloppenborg, John S. *Christ's Associations: Connecting and Belonging to the Ancient City.* Yale University Press, 2019.

Theophilos, Michael P. *Numismatics and Greek Lexicography.* T&T Clark, 2019.

Notes

1 Apart from a few specimens that had previously attracted attention and, of course, the discovery of an entire library of carbonized papyrus scrolls in Herculaneum in 1752–54.

2 See also the chapter on "Social Status and Relations in Private Life" by Michael Sommer and Isabel Kraus in the present volume.

3 P.Ammon 1.3, written between 324 and 330 CE.

4 So far, the ostraca from this archive have been published as Ostraca Didymoi (O.Did.) and Ostraca Krokodilo (O.Krok.) 2.

5 For graffiti in general, see Peter Keegan, *Graffiti in Antiquity* (Routledge, 2014).

6 A standard size was a roll of twenty sheets; for example, P.Oxy. 75.5063.19–20 (late third cent. CE). This example also shows that the Greek term *chartē* or (as here) *chartarion* does not denote the leaf made from strips of the pith of papyrus, but the "piece" in the sense of a whole roll.

7 For example, the letter authors of BGU 3.822.28–29 (after May 5, 105 CE?) and P.Flor. 3.367.6–10 (third cent. CE) refer to "papyrus for writing letters" or "uninscribed papyrus" because the only remaining roll is nearly used up; they do not refer to a single sheet of papyrus.

8 For example, SB 5.8754 (February 5, 77 BCE); for a digital image see http://www.papyrology.uw.edu.pl/papyri/pberlin16876.htm; P.Fay. 109 (June 19, 10 BCE or 34 CE); P.Oxy. 42.3057 (first or second cent. CE); 55.3810 (second or third cent. CE); cf. P.Oxy. 55, pp. 191–92.

9 Two Greek contracts for the sale of a vineyard on leather have been found in a stone jar in Avroman, Iran (ancient Kopanis): Jur.Pap. 36 (October 20–November 18, 88 BCE) and TM 97890 (22/21 BCE). A Greek tax receipt on leather, SB 22.15765 (second cent. BCE), originates from ancient Bactria.

10 Pliny the Elder (*Naturalis historia* 13.21 [70]) does not mention the alleged connection, but only reports—referring to Varro—that *membranae* (sic, not *pergamenae*) were

invented in Pergamon due to an absence of papyrus exports from Egypt. The explicit association between the city name Pergamum and *pergamena* is referred to by Isidore of Seville (560–636) in *Etymologiae* 6.11.1.

11 See Ronald Reed, *Ancient Skins, Parchments and Leathers*, Studies in Archaeological Science (Seminar Press, 1972).

12 Cf. Clementina Caputo, "Looking at the Material: One Hundred Years of Studying Ostraca from Egypt," in *Antike Texte und ihre Materialität: Alltägliche Präsenz, mediale Semantik, literarische Reflexion*, ed. Cornelia Ritter-Schmalz and Raphael Schwitter, Materiale Textkulturen 27 (de Gruyter, 2019), 93–117; Francesca Maltomini, "Greek *Ostraca*: An Overview," *Manuscript Cultures* 5 (2014): 33–41.

13 Bezalel Porten and Ada Yardeni, eds., *Textbook of Aramaic Ostraca from Idumea*, 5 vols. (Eisenbrauns, 2014–23).

14 For example, SEG 50.276 and Syll.[3] 3.1259, both early fourth cent. BCE.

15 See Esther Eidinow and Claire Taylor, "Lead-Letter Days: Writing, Communication and Crisis in the Ancient Greek World," *The Classical Quarterly* 60 (2010): 30–62; Paola Ceccarelli, *Ancient Greek Letter Writing: A Cultural History (600 BC–150 BC)* (Oxford University Press, 2013), 27–47, 334–38, 340–56.

16 See "*Thesaurus Defixionum* (TheDefix)," Universität Hamburg, updated August 2021, https://heurist.fdm.uni-hamburg.de/html/heurist/?db=The_dema&website&id=41774&pageid=48841.

17 See Ivan Radman-Livaja, "Craftspeople, Merchants or Clients? The Evidence of Personal Names on the Commercial Lead Tags from Siscia," in *Making Textiles in Pre-Roman and Roman Times: People, Places, Identities*, ed. Margarita Gleba and Judit Pásztókai-Szeőke, Ancient Textiles Series 13 (Oxbow, 2013), 87–108.

18 See Roy Kotansky, *Published Texts of Known Provenance*, vol. 1 of *Greek Magical Amulets: The Inscribed Gold, Silver, Copper, and Bronze Lamellae*, Papyrologica Coloniensia 22/1 (Westdeutscher Verlag, 1994).

19 See Michael P. Theophilos, *Numismatics and Greek Lexicography* (T&T Clark, 2019).

20 Addenda/Corrigenda in BL 7:216–217. Cf. Maria Valentina Biscottini, "L'archivio di Tryphon, tessitore di Oxyrhynchos," *Aegyptus* 46 (1966): 60–90, 186–292, here 209–13 no. 14. Online image: https://digital.bodleian.ox.ac.uk/objects/aa999e97-a7ad-49f8-97ad-27b99e8b2ec5/. TM and the added number refer to the dataset in the Trismegistos Texts database (see fig. 3.4). You can access the data records of this and the following examples by entering the URL of Trismegistos Texts (https://www.trismegistos.org) + "/text/" + number (for SB 10.10236 this would be https://www.trismegistos.org/text/16674). Unless otherwise stated, all translations in this section are the author's.

21 See the lists in Peter Arzt-Grabner, "Three Weavers of the First Century CE: Tryphon of Oxyrhynchus, Pausiris of Oxyrhynchus, and Paul of Tarsus," *Early Christianity* 10 (2019): 72–86, here 74–79. Information on papyrological archives (i.e., compilations of texts that can be related to a particular person, family, or group) is also provided by Trismegistos Archives, a subsection of the Trismegistos Database (see fig. 3.4). The archive of Tryphon is identified there as "TM Arch id: 249" (see https://www.trismegistos.org/archive/249) and that of Pausiris as "TM Arch id: 176" (see https://www.trismegistos.org/archive/176).

22 In Greco-Roman antiquity, a woman needed an adult male as her legal guardian to do business. Usually, the closest male relative (husband, father, or son) served this purpose. However, several papyrus documents provide evidence that the guardian did not have to be present in person when legal acts were performed; it was sufficient for the woman to present a document naming the authorized guardian.

23 Further contracts are listed by Arzt-Grabner, "Three Weavers," 76–77, numbers 10–12.

24 See the family trees in Arzt-Grabner, "Three Weavers," 73, 80.

25 A weaver specialized in producing his textiles according to the art of Tarsus. The *tarsikarios* is known from Egyptian papyri from the second century CE onwards (cf. P.Bodl. 1.27).

26 Addenda and Corrigenda: T.Vindol. 3, p. 157; C.Epist.Lat. 3, p. 197. Cf. P. Cugusi 1992 (C.Epist.Lat. 90); PNT 2.95 (= Peter Arzt-Grabner, *Letters and Letter Writing* [Brill Schöningh, 2023] 276–78 no. 2.95). Online information and image: https://romaninscriptionsofbritain.org/inscriptions/TabVindol250.

27 Cf. T.Vindol. 2.291, the fully preserved birthday invitation from Claudia Severa to Lepidina, which is also the earliest known example of Latin writing by a woman preserved in its original form.

28 Cf. Arzt-Grabner, *Letters and Letter Writing*, 38n10.

29 For more on this see Arzt-Grabner, *Letters and Letter Writing*, 36–42.

30 The inscription is no longer extant. Cf. John S. Kloppenborg and Richard S. Ascough, *Attica, Central Greece, Macedonia, Thrace*, vol. 1 of *Greco-Roman Associations: Texts, Translations, and Commentary*, Beihefte zur Zeitschrift für die neutestamentliche Wissenschaft 181 (de Gruyter, 2011), 229–34 no. 1.49 (= GRA 1.49).

31 Stone inscriptions are: TAM 5.1539 (Philadelphia, Lydia; ca. 100 BCE; cf. GRA 2.117); LSAM 80 (Elaiussa Sebaste, Cilicia; ca. 27 BCE–14 CE; cf. GRA 2.152); AE 1929.161 (Trebula Mutuesca, Samnium, today's Monteleone Sabino; 60 CE); SEG 31.122 (Liopesi, Attica, modern Paiania; early second cent. CE; cf. GRA 1.50); CIL 14.2112 (Lanuvium, Latium et Campania; May 9, 136 CE); IG 9.12.670 (Physkos, Locris; ca. mid second cent. CE; cf. GRA 1.61); IG II^2.1368 (Athens, Attica; 164/165 CE; cf. GRA 1.51).

Four selected early Greek bylaws preserved on papyri from first-century Egypt, all from the Arsinoite nome, are: P.Lond. 7.2193 (Philadelphia; 69–58? BCE; cf. GRA 3.199); P.Mich. 5.243 (Tebtynis; 14–37 CE; cf. GRA 3.206); 244 (Tebtynis; August 26, 43 CE; cf. GRA 3.212); 245 (Tebtynis; August 18, 47 CE; cf. GRA 3.219).

GRA 2 = Kloppenborg and Ascough, *Attica, Central Greece, Macedonia, Thrace*; Philipp A. Harland, *North Coast of the Black Sea, Asia Minor*, vol. 2 of *Greco-Roman Associations: Texts, Translations, and Commentary*, Beihefte zur Zeitschrift für die neutestamentliche Wissenschaft 204 (de Gruyter, 2011); GRA 3 = John S. Kloppenborg, *Ptolemaic and Early Roman Egypt*, vol. 3 of *Greco-Roman Associations: Texts, Translations, and Commentary*, Beihefte zur Zeitschrift für die neutestamentliche Wissenschaft 246 (de Gruyter, 2020).

See also the index of bylaws in Kloppenborg, *Ptolemaic and Early Roman Egypt*, 403.

32 Cf. Andrew Monson, "The Ethics and Economics of Ptolemaic Religious Associations," *Ancient Society* 36 (2006): 221–38. This is based on Charles Tilly, *Trust and Rule* , Cambridge Studies in Comparative Politics (Cambridge University Press, 2005).

33 See especially John S. Kloppenborg, *Christ's Associations: Connecting and Belonging to the Ancient City* (Yale University Press, 2019).

34 On the nature and procedure of these banquets, see Eva Ebel, *Die Attraktivität früher christlicher Gemeinden: Die Gemeinde von Korinth im Spiegel griechisch-römischer Vereine*, Wissenschaftliche Untersuchungen zum Neuen Testament 2/178 (Mohr Siebeck, 2004), 152–76.

35 See Peter Arzt-Grabner, "The 'Epistolary Introductory Thanksgiving' in the Papyri and in Paul," *Novum Testamentum* 36, no. 1 (1994): 29–46; Peter Arzt-Grabner, "Paul's Letter Thanksgiving," in *Paul and the Ancient Letter Form*, ed. Stanley E. Porter and Sean A. Adams, Pauline Studies 6 (Brill, 2010), 129–58; Arzt-Grabner, *Letters and Letter Writing*, 123–28; Christina M. Kreinecker, *2. Thessaloniker*, Papyrologische Kommentare zum Neuen Testament 3 (Vandenhoeck & Ruprecht, 2010), 108–13.

36 P.Giss. 1.20.3–4; ca. 117–18 CE.

37 Referring to the Emperor Caracalla.

38 Corrections in BL 2.2:83; 3:94; 5:541.

39 On Luke's chronology regarding the age of Jesus in 28/29 CE and the calculation of Jesus's year of birth based on this, see Peter Arzt-Grabner, John S. Kloppenborg, and Christina M. Kreinecker, *More Light from the Ancient East: Understanding the New Testament through Papyri*, with a contribution by Gregg Schwendner, Papyri and the New Testament 1 (Brill Schöningh, 2023), XXV–XXXIII.

40 Cf. Gerd Theissen, *Lokalkolorit und Zeitgeschichte in den Evangelien: Ein Beitrag zur Geschichte der synoptischen Tradition*, Novum Testamentum et Orbox Antiquus 8 (Universitätsverlag Fribourg; Vandenhoeck & Ruprecht, 1989), 26–34; Aaron J. Kogon and Jean-Philippe Fontanille, *The Coinage of Herod Antipas: A Study and Die Classification of the Earliest Coins of Galilee*, Ancient Judaism and Early Christianity 102 (Brill, 2018), esp. 10, 45–46. For examples, see "Search Results," Roman Provincial Coinage Online, British Museum Press and Bibliothèque Nationale de France, https://rpc.ashmus.ox.ac.uk/search/browse?q=herod+antipas+reed.

41 Cf. Theissen, *Lokalkolorit*, 34–41.

42 Cf. Kogon and Fontanille, *The Coinage of Herod Antipas*, 10, 46–47.

CHAPTER FOUR

Early Jewish Literature

David Cielontko
(Charles University)

FEW THINGS HAVE changed New Testament studies in recent decades as much as the intensive research and scholarly engagement with early Jewish literature. After the horrors of World War II and the devastating consequences of abhorrent antisemitism, the postwar era has seen a necessary and urgent revision of historical and theological perspectives on ancient Judaism, which has so often been caricatured as so-called *Spätjudentum* (Late Judaism), a dead religion characterized by ethnic particularism and the mindless legalism of Mosaic law observance. The emphasis on *lateness* was set in contrast to the religion of the prophets of Israel who, in the texts of the Old Testament, set the stage for the universalistic perspective of Jesus of Nazareth, which emphasized grace from a merciful God over adherence to the Torah. This caricature of both early Judaism and Christianity was largely the result of projecting a particular interpretation of the New Testament texts and their perspectives onto the complex historical reality of the first century, when Jesus's polemics with the Pharisees (whose "Judaism" was anachronistically drawn from rabbinic literature) provided one such basis for entrenched antagonisms.[1]

This process of reassessment and critical reflection was complemented by another significant stimulus in the form of new manuscript finds, among which the unearthing of the Dead Sea Scrolls has a special place. Other important texts were discovered in genizoth (repositories for unused manuscripts in synagogues) and monastic libraries, where most of them survived unnoticed or unstudied for centuries, preserved in ancient and medieval translations in languages such as Greek, Syriac, Coptic, Ethiopic, Armenian, Georgian, Old Slavonic and Latin.[2] The extent to which Christianity is based on its Jewish roots became very clear in the light of these texts. They have greatly enriched our knowledge of early Judaism, leading to a fundamental change in its scholarly perception. Since Jesus, Paul, and most, if not all, of the New Testament writers were themselves Jewish, this naturally led to similar changes in the study of emerging early Christianity.

Moreover, many of the themes of Jewish religious belief and practice that New Testament texts presume, such as the apocalyptic worldview, messianic expectations, interest in cosmology, demons, angels, resurrection, and specific forms of cultic and ritual observance, are virtually absent from the Hebrew Bible and their development can only be traced in early Jewish literature.[3]

This chapter surveys the rich corpus of Jewish texts written over several centuries in different languages (Hebrew, Aramaic, and Greek). There are various names for this corpus: It has been referred to as Intertestamental, Second Temple, Early or Middle Jewish Literature, or, with a chronological emphasis, Jewish literature of the Hellenistic and Roman periods, or Jewish literature between the Bible and the Mishnah. Each of the proposed labels has its own advantages and disadvantages. Some are confessional, others are based on canonical considerations, and still others are rooted in historical or theological concerns.[4] Most of them are not problematic per se if we understand their origin and what they imply. In this chapter, however, the corpus will be referred to as early Jewish literature, a label derived from the term "early Judaism" as a historical phenomenon of the Hellenistic and Roman periods. This designation follows some recent literary and archaeological research that traces important developments in the religious and social practice of ethnic Jews (or Judeans) in this historical period, especially in relation to Torah observance in ordinary Jewish society, which can be seen as constitutive of Jewish identity.[5]

In order to provide an overview of this vast corpus, it will be further subdivided into the following categories: Apocrypha, Pseudepigrapha, Dead Sea Scrolls, and individual authors, Philo and Josephus. There are other ways to organize this material—for example, based on chronology, genre, or group ideology—but any such presentation comes with its own problems. The decision to use these categorizations here is a pragmatic one that follows many published anthologies and thus allows the reader easier access to the texts under discussion.

Apocrypha

The name *Apocrypha* comes from the Greek *apokryphos* (hidden, concealed). In late antiquity, the term increasingly took on the meaning of "doubtful" or even "heretical," which was developed in close relation to the polemics over the New Testament Apocrypha.

The "Old Testament Apocrypha" were, in ancient and medieval times, an integral part of the Bible in most of the Greek and Latin Christian manuscripts. This changed when Martin Luther, in his 1534 German translation of the Bible, set the Apocrypha apart as a separate unit, which he described as useful and good to read, but not equal to the Holy Scriptures. In response, the Council of Trent (1545–63) reaffirmed their canonical status for the Catholic Church, which in turn led to the new term *deuterocanonical* books. Similarly, the Eastern

Codex Alexandrinus	**Vulgate +(*appendix in Clementina*)**	**Luther's Apocrypha**	**Deuterocanonical Books**	**Eastern Orthodox Deuterocanonical Books**
• Baruch as a part of Jeremiah	• Tobit	• Judith	• Tobit	• Tobit
• Esther with additions	• Judith	• Wisdom	• Judith	• Judith
• Daniel with additions	• Esther with additions	• Tobit	• Esther with additions	• Baruch
• Tobit	• Wisdom	• Sirach	• Wisdom	• Sirach
• Judith	• Sirach	• Baruch	• Sirach	• 1 Maccabees
• 1 Esdras	• Baruch	• 1 Maccabees	• Baruch as a part of Jeremiah	• 2 Maccabees
• 1 Maccabees	• Daniel with additions	• 2 Maccabees	• Daniel with additions	• Wisdom
• 2 Maccabees	• 1 Maccabees	• Additions to Esther	• 1 Maccabees	• Esther with additions
• 3 Maccabees	• 2 Maccabees	• Additions to Daniel	• 2 Maccabees	• Daniel with additions
• 4 Maccabees	• (*Prayer of Manasseh*	• Prayer of Manasseh		• Prayer of Manasseh
• Psalm 151	• *1 Esdras*			• 1 Esdras
• Prayer of Manasseh	• *2 Esdras*)			• 2 Esdras
• Wisdom				• 3 Maccabees
• Sirach				• 4 Maccabees
• Psalms of Solomon				• Psalm 151

Figure 4.1. Various forms of the Apocrypha including their order.

Orthodox Church rejected the shorter Protestant canon at the Synod of Jerusalem (1672).[6]

However, the exact delineation of which texts are part of this category is a tricky endeavor. The content of the early Greek biblical manuscripts often varies. Some contain texts that were not later included in the Latin Vulgate, which, in its turn, adds others. Moreover, the Apocrypha in the Vulgate do not align exactly with Luther's Apocrypha or the deuterocanonical books of the Catholic Bible. Nevertheless, modern textbooks and editions tend to include all texts that at least at some point belonged to the Apocrypha.

Although these texts are derived from the Greek biblical manuscripts transmitted by Christians, not all of them were originally written in Greek. Some were translated from Hebrew or Aramaic, such as Tobit, Sirach, and 1 Maccabees. Apart from their common "canonical" history, the Apocrypha have little in common. They consist of very different literary genres from various historical periods.

1 and 2 Maccabees are historiographical works that provide insights into the Maccabean revolt against the Seleucid king Antiochus IV Epiphanes and the origins of the Hasmonean dynasty. 4 Maccabees retells the story of the heroic martyrdom of 2 Maccabees 6–7 in the form of a philosophical treatise promoting the Jewish way of life as the best embodiment of virtue. Unexpectedly, 3 Maccabees is not set in the Maccabean period, but in Ptolemaic Egypt in the third century BCE, and is connected to this tradition only by a common focus on the adherence to ancestral traditions amid persecution.

1 Esdras is also a historiographical work, providing the history of Judah from king Josiah to the Persian period, following the narrative of 2 Chronicles 35–36, as well as Ezra and Nehemiah. 2 Esdras (or 4 Ezra) is an apocalyptic text reflecting on the tragedy of the fall of Jerusalem and its temple in the year 70 CE, and the Prayer of Manasseh provides the words of the prayer of the imprisoned King Manasseh, only hinted at in 2 Chronicles 33.

The books of Tobit and Judith are literary novels that promote Jewish values in a diasporic context. The book of Tobit tells the story of Tobias, son of Tobit, who is sent by his blind father to his relative in Media to collect the family money entrusted to him. Tobias and Azariah, his guardian angel in disguise, embark on a journey full of challenges, including fighting a big fish and a jealous demon. Along the way, they also find a wife for Tobias, solving all family problems, and they return with blessings and wealth. The book of Judith recounts the story of a heroine of the same name who, through her devotion to God, saves her people from the Assyrian general Holofernes and his armies.

The books of Sirach and Wisdom belong to the genre of wisdom literature. Sirach offers an interesting glimpse into Torah-oriented Jewish education in practical wisdom. Wisdom shows much influence from both the Septuagint and Greek rhetorical training and is an invaluable source of Hellenistic-Jewish philosophical and theological thought.

Another category is made up of the so-called additions to various biblical books. The Greek versions of Jeremiah, Daniel, and Esther are longer and contain additional stories not found in the original Hebrew (or Aramaic) versions. Until Luther, these additions were transmitted as part of the biblical books. However, following the principle of *Hebraica Veritas*, Luther's translation of Jeremiah, Daniel, and Esther did not include these additions. Instead, he collected them separately in the section with the Apocrypha, as is the case in many modern Bibles. The Greek Jeremiah is grouped together with the canonical Lamentations and the apocryphal Epistle of Jeremiah and book of Baruch. The additions to Daniel include the stories of Susanna, Bel and the Dragon, and the Prayer of Azariah. Finally, the additions to Esther represent more of a new Greek redaction of the book, resulting in a significant change in the tone and emphasis on the whole book.

Pseudepigrapha or Other Early Jewish Texts Preserved (Mostly) in Christian Manuscripts

The name *pseudepigrapha* comes from Greek *pseudēs* and *epigraphē*, meaning "falsely attributed texts." In this literal sense, it was already used by the Church Fathers for certain apocryphal gospels that were rejected because of their dubious authorship. The modern use of the category is much broader and refers to all extracanonical (Jewish) texts that do not belong to the Apocrypha, or other clearly identified corpora of texts (the Dead Sea Scrolls or rabbinic texts).[7] Similarly to the Apocrypha, some Pseudepigrapha are considered canonical in certain church traditions, such as the Book of Jubilees and 1 Enoch, which are canonical in the Ethiopic Orthodox Church.

One of the most controversial issues with regard to the Pseudepigrapha is their original provenance. Since these texts have survived only in later copies in Christian manuscripts (and often in translation), it is not always easy to determine whether Christian scribes were merely transmitters, editors, or actual authors. Only in some cases do we have pre-Christian manuscripts that clearly prove their Jewish origin. In other cases, it is necessary to provide a plausible case for it.[8] As the Jewish provenance of many Pseudepigrapha has been challenged in recent decades, the category came to be used more broadly and descriptively to encompass all the extracanonical texts attributed to characters from the Old Testament, regardless of whether they were written in a Jewish or Christian context.[9] To complicate matters further, recent scholarship has also questioned the sharp separation between Jewish and Christian identities in late antiquity, since the split between these two groups was historically more of a process (the "parting of the ways") than an event, with varying manifestations across different geographical regions.[10]

The manuscripts discovered in Ethiopian monasteries in the early nineteenth century made several early Jewish apocalyptic texts available through a text known as 1 (Ethiopic) Enoch, which is actually a collection of several originally separate works written several hundred years apart:

- Chapters 1–36: The Book of the Watchers (third cent. BCE).
- Chapters 37–71: The Book of Parables (40 BCE–70 CE).
- Chapters 72–82: The Astronomical Book (third cent. BCE).
- Chapters 83–90: The Book of Dream Visions (mid-second cent. BCE).
- Chapters 91–105: The Epistle of Enoch (mid-second cent. BCE).
- Chapters 106–8: The Birth of Noah and additional conclusion (first cent. BCE–first cent. CE).

Figure 4.2. Individual Texts of 1 Enoch.

The most influential of these was the Book of the Watchers, which was well known and read in antiquity, and is even explicitly quoted in the Epistle of Jude.[11] It tells the mythological story of the origin of evil, in which the angels of heaven descend to earth, where they mate with the daughters of men, to whom they also reveal the secrets of heaven, and thus bring evil to earth. This expanded version of the perplexing story of Genesis 6:1–4 describes the consequences of this heavenly rebellion on human affairs.

Another influential text preserved in the Ethiopian manuscripts is the Book of Jubilees. Written in the second century BCE, it offers an interpretive retelling of Genesis and Exodus 1–24 in the form of a revelation to Moses. Fragments of both parts of 1 Enoch and the Book of Jubilees have survived among the Dead Sea Scrolls.

Other texts that have survived both inside and outside the Dead Sea Scrolls include two texts known from the medieval genizah of the Ben Ezra Synagogue in Cairo: the Damascus Document and the Aramaic Levi Document. The former is written in Hebrew and describes the history of the origins and rules of an ancient Jewish group, most likely related to the Essenes in the Second Temple era. The latter, written in Aramaic, deals with the origins of the Levitical priesthood and conveys the testament of the Patriarch Levi. It may have originated somewhere between the fourth and second centuries BCE.

Other important early Jewish texts have come down to us through Church Slavonic manuscripts. The second Book of Enoch (or Slavonic Enoch) is an apocalypse, probably originally written in Greek in the Egyptian diaspora in the first century CE. The Apocalypse of Abraham is also an apocalyptic text extant only in Church Slavonic. It reflects the fall of Jerusalem and the temple in 70 CE. It shares the focus of this ultimate tragedy with another Jewish apocalypse called 2 Baruch, which is incidentally known only from a single Syriac manuscript. Both texts date from the early second century CE.

In Latin manuscripts, we have the text of the Assumption of Moses (or Testament of Moses), which contains the final speech of Moses in the form of future prophecies about the history of Israel and eschatological predictions. It probably dates from the early first century CE. Another surviving Latin text is the Liber antiquitatum biblicarum (LAB), which was transmitted with the work of Philo, leading scholars to refer to the author as the Pseudo-Philo. It takes the form of a rewritten biblical text, covering the period from Adam to the reign of King David.

The most extensive corpus of pseudepigraphic texts is preserved in Greek manuscripts, which, unlike the Ethiopic, Slavonic, Syriac or Latin, is often their original language. The Letter of Aristeas recounts the story of the translation of the Torah from Hebrew into Greek at the request of the Egyptian king Ptolemy II Philadelphus, who sought to obtain a book of Jewish laws for his library in

Alexandria. This letter is attributed to an official of the royal court, Aristeas, but in fact was written by some (Alexandrian) Jew during the second century BCE. Similarly pseudonymous are the Sentences of Pseudo-Phocylides, a collection of poetic wisdom verses attributed to the famous Greek poet from Miletus of the sixth century BCE. In fact, they are the work of a Greek-speaking Jew of the Roman period.

Among the texts that creatively elaborate on biblical narrative, Joseph and Aseneth tells the story of the patriarch Joseph and his wife, the daughter of the Egyptian priest Potiphar, from Genesis 39. The story depicts Aseneth's renunciation of idols, which is recognized as her conversion to the true God of Israel. Life of Adam and Eve elaborates on Genesis 4–5, describing the implications of the original couple's fall in relation to the themes of suffering and evil. The Lives of the Prophets adopts a quasi-biographical genre, providing brief (but legendary) information on the biblical prophets, including their places of birth, death, and burial. Finally, the Testament of Job retells the famous story of the archetypal biblical sufferer, here presented as the pagan Egyptian king Jobab who converts to the worship of the Jewish God.

Other texts that survived in Greek are the apocalypses and prophetic and eschatological works such as 3 Baruch and books 3–5 of the Sibylline Oracles. The origins of both are believed to be in Greek-speaking Egypt. The Sibylline Oracles imitate the traditional Greek oracular tradition of the pagan Sibyl from fifth century BCE Ionia, appropriating this genre into a Jewish context in a form

Apocalypses and Eschatological Writings	Expansions and Legends	Wisdom and Poetic Texts
• The Book of the Watchers (1 En. 1–36) • Parables of Enoch (1 En. 37–71) • Astronomical Book (1 En. 72–82) • Book of Dream Visions (1 En. 83–90) • Epistle of Enoch (1 En. 91–105) • 2 Enoch • 2 Baruch • 3 Baruch • Apocalypse of Zephaniah • Apocalypse of Abraham • Assumption of Moses • Sibylline Oracles, books III–V	• The Letter of Aristeas • The Book of Jubilees • Joseph and Aseneth • Life of Adam and Eve • Pseudo-Philo (LAB) • Testament of Job • Lives of the Prophets • The Birth of Noah (1 En. 106–7)	• Apocryphal Psalms • Hellenistic Synagogal Prayers • Pseudo-Phocylides

Figure 4.3. Pseudepigrapha.

Historical works	Poetic and Philosophical works
• Demetrius • Eupolemus • Pseudo-Eupolemus • Artapanus • Cleodemus Malchus • Aristeas • Pseudo-Hecateus • Theophilus • Thallus • Justus of Tiberias	• Theodotus • Philo the Epic Poet • Ezekiel the Tragedian • Aristobulus • Pseudo-Orpheus

Figure 4.4. Fragmentary Hellenistic-Jewish authors.

similar to the prophetic tradition of the Hebrew Bible. 3 Baruch provides another apocalyptic text, composed in response to the fall of the Jerusalem temple. There is also the Apocalypse of Zephaniah, which survives only in fragments in two Coptic manuscripts and a fragment by Clement of Alexandria. Its theme, like that of many other apocalypses, is the question of divine justice.

The Hellenistic context of Roman Egypt, and Alexandria in particular, profoundly influenced many other Jewish works, most of which have survived only in small fragments quoted in the works of later Christian authors such as Eusebius or Clement of Alexandria. Through these fragments, we know that various Jewish authors experimented with literary genres and styles from a wider Hellenistic cultural context, such as tragedy, epic, history, or poetry. They also adopted critical methods of working with the Hebrew Bible from Alexandrian scholarship that non-Jewish authors had applied to Homer.[12]

Dead Sea Scrolls

Between 1947 and 1962, thousands of fragments of scrolls were discovered near the Dead Sea and became known as the Dead Sea Scrolls. Most of them came from eleven caves near the settlement of Khirbet Qumran and are thought to be part of an ancient collection of texts that may have had some connection with the Jewish inhabitants of the site in the Roman period. The standard interpretation identifies them as belonging to an Essene community which called itself *ha-Yaḥad* ("the community"; "unity") and which was part of a wider movement with settlements in various locations.[13] It is argued that the discovered Scrolls, particularly those from the caves four to ten, may have formed the library of this Qumran community, or the library of the wider Essene movement, deposited here only in the wake of the Jewish War.[14]

Figure 4.5. Caves near Khirbet Qumran. (David Cielontko, used by permission.)

This extraordinary discovery has provided us with dozens of hitherto unknown early Jewish texts, manuscript evidence in the original languages of many others known only from late Christian translations, and the earliest manuscript evidence for the texts of the Hebrew Bible.

The approximately nine hundred fragmentary manuscripts discovered at Qumran can be divided into three main groups according to their content:

- about 40 percent are manuscripts of texts known from the Hebrew Bible (in Hebrew, Aramaic, and Greek copies).
- about 35 percent are manuscripts of early Jewish noncanonical texts not directly produced by the Qumran community.
- about 25 percent are "sectarian texts"—that is, texts containing terminology, beliefs, worldview, or rules of the Qumran community.[15]

Figure 4.6. The Dead Sea Scrolls manuscripts.

Among the early Jewish texts known from elsewhere (mostly apocrypha and pseudepigrapha), parts of 1 Enoch, Jubilees, Tobit, Sirach, Psalms 152–55, and the Aramaic Levi Document have survived. These manuscripts are invaluable resources for understanding the textual history of these texts, which otherwise exist only in various ancient and medieval languages. In addition, previously unknown texts such as the Temple Scroll, the Genesis Apocryphon, the Book of the Giants, the New Jerusalem Text, the Targum of Job, the Melchizedek Document, the Songs of the Sabbath Sacrifices, the Visions of Amram, the Prayer of Nabonidus, and the Testament of Qahat have been discovered.

Among the sectarian texts are various genres such as rules (e.g., the Rule of the Community, the Rule of the Congregation), liturgical texts (Hodayot), eschatological texts (the War Scroll), scriptural interpretations or Pesharim (the Pesher Habakkuk), halachic texts (4QMMT [the Halachic Letter]), and calendrical texts or Mishmarot (4QOtot). These texts offer insight into the origins of this community associated with the person named as the Teacher of Righteousness, their self-conception, including various conflicts with other Jewish groups over halachic issues, as well as their interpretation of the scriptures, rules for self-organization, communal dining, teaching, ritual and liturgical conduct, and various eschatological ideas.[16]

In addition to the manuscripts discovered in the eleven caves around Qumran, several hundred more manuscripts have been discovered around the Dead Sea at sites Wadi Daliyeh, Wadi Sdeir, Nahal Hever, Nahal Seiyal, and Masada.[17]

Philo of Alexandria

Unlike many anonymous or pseudepigraphic early Jewish works, there are at least some Jewish texts written by known authors. Among these, Philo and Josephus are the most significant. Philo of Alexandria (ca. 20 BCE–50 CE) was a prominent, wealthy, and powerful member of the large Jewish community of Alexandria. He was well educated in the typical Greek fashion as well as in the Jewish tradition of his ancestors. He was a Torah-observant Jew in a diasporic context, but also an enthusiast of Hellenistic delights such as athletics and theater. His extensive literary work shows his close affinity with the Greek philosophical tradition, especially Plato, and with the critical scholarship fostered in Alexandria. Not much is known about his life except that he was the head of the Jewish embassy to Caligula in Rome after the massacre of the Jews in Alexandria in 38 CE. Philo's texts were well received and transmitted by Christians from antiquity. Some Christian authors made Philo a convert to Christianity or even a bishop.[18]

Forty-nine complete or nearly complete texts of Philo have survived, about two-thirds of what he wrote according to the list in Eusebius and his own references, most of them in the original Greek, but some only in Georgian or Latin translations.

At the heart of his writings are three series of biblical commentaries: the Questions and Answers on Genesis and Exodus, the Allegorical Commentary, and the Exposition of the Law. They were all written at different stages in his career and for different audiences.[19] The Allegorical Commentary belongs to the early phase of his career and is addressed to highly educated members of the Jewish community in Alexandria. In this work, he quotes biblical texts, engages with complex textual problems and provides allegorical interpretations deeply influenced by Platonic philosophy. The Questions and Answers are much more accessible and do not delve into complex textual issues. It may have been written as a handbook for students. However, the method is similar to the previous series in citing the biblical passages followed by a commentary. Finally, in the Exposition of the Law, Philo does not quote long biblical passages but rather retells the biblical stories. He also does not presume knowledge of the texts or even Jewish customs, which suggests a non-Jewish audience. This series also engages with Roman Stoicism and its values, suggesting it was probably produced in Rome during his embassy.

The Allegorical Commentary	The Questions and Answers	The Exposition of the Law
• Allegorical Interpretation 1–3 • On the Cherubim • On the Sacrifices of Cain and Abel • That the Worse Attacks the Better • On the Posterity of Cain • On Giants • That God is Unchangeable • On Agriculture • On Planting • On Drunkenness • On Sobriety • On the Confusion of Tongues • On the Migration of Abraham • Who is the Heir? • On the Preliminary Studies • On Flight and Finding • On the Change of Names • On God • On Dreams 1–2	• Questions and Answers on Genesis 1–4 • Questions and Answers on Exodus 1–2	• On the Creation of the World • On the Life of Abraham • On the Life of Joseph • On the Decalogue • On the Special Laws 1–4 • On the Virtues • On Rewards and Punishments

Figure 4.7. Philo's commentaries.

Historical Writings	Philosophical Writings
• On the Embassy to Gaius • Against Flaccus	• On the Rationality of Animals • An Apology on Behalf of the Jews • Every Good Man Is Free • On Providence 1–2 • On the Eternity of the World • On the Contemplative Life

Figure 4.8. Philo's other works.

Philo's other works consist of historical and philosophical treatises, all most likely written during the Roman part of his career. The historical writings report directly on events related to his Roman anabasis and the philosophical texts are aimed at a wider Greco-Roman audience, which fits better with this later period.

Josephus

Josephus came from an elite Jerusalem priestly family and, like Philo, was sent on a diplomatic mission to Rome. His mission was to Emperor Nero because Felix, the procurator of Judea, unjustly imprisoned local priests and sent them to Rome. In Josephus's own account, he was successful in securing their release with the help of the emperor's wife Poppaea Sabina. He later became actively involved in the resistance during the Jewish War (67–70 CE), taking part in the defense of the town of Jotapata against Roman armies. However, they were eventually defeated, and Josephus was captured. He then fell into the service of the general of the campaign, Vespasian. He was an eyewitness to the conquest of Jerusalem and the destruction of its temple, and after the war, he lived in Rome, where he also wrote all his works.

His first writing is the seven-volume *Jewish War* (written between 76–79 CE), in which he explores the background, course, and immediate consequences of this tragic war in his native land. As an eyewitness, Josephus puts himself in the role of a credible person who can provide a reliable account of the events. He argues that he is well qualified to do so because, as a Judean, he has a unique understanding of the situation. *Jewish War* is an invaluable source concerning both the course of the war and the situation in Judea and Galilee at the time of Jesus and his followers.

His second writing is the extensive *Jewish Antiquities* in twenty books, which he completed around 93 or 94 CE. *Antiquities* covers the Jewish history from the creation of the world to the present day. Books 1–11 are based on the Hebrew Bible, which is paraphrased and interpreted. From book 12 onwards, it describes the Hellenistic-Roman period, including the history of the Hasmonean kingdom, Herod the Great, and up to contemporary events in the first century CE. It shows the antiquity of the Jewish nation as well as its superior constitution revealed to Moses by God.

After that, Josephus wrote his autobiography *Life of Josephus*, which offers a thorough account of the events of 66 and 67 CE, during which he was stationed in Jotapata. This account is surprisingly different from the early one in the *Jewish War*. Josephus attempts to explain his actions and challenges the reader to judge his character. His last work, *Against Apion*, returns to the subject of the antiquity of the Jewish people, over which he polemicizes with some Alexandrian scholars, led by a certain Apion.

TAKING A CLOSER LOOK: SOURCES

There are numerous examples of how early Jewish texts can help shed light on New Testament texts, many of which are found in other chapters. The following examples are intended to provide a variety of ways in which early Jewish and New Testament texts intersect.

Sources from the World of the New Testament

The Origin of Evil Spirits

> Why have you forsaken the high heaven, the eternal sanctuary; and lain with women, and defiled yourselves with the daughters of men; and taken for yourselves wives, and done as the sons of earth; and begotten for yourselves sons, giants? You were holy ones and spirits, living forever. With the blood of women, you have defiled yourselves, and with the blood of flesh you have begotten, and with the blood of men you have lusted, and you have done as they do—flesh and blood, who die and perish. Therefore I gave them women, that they might cast seed into them, and thus beget children by them, that nothing fail them on the earth. But you originally existed as spirits, living forever, and not dying for all the generations of eternity; therefore I did not make women among you. The spirits of heaven, in heaven is their dwelling; But now the giants who were begotten by the spirits and flesh—they will call them evil spirits on the earth, for their dwelling will be on the earth. The spirits that have gone forth from the body of their flesh are evil spirits, for from above they came into being, and from the holy watchers was the origin of their creation. Evil spirits they will be on the earth, and evil spirits they will be called. The spirits of heaven, in

> heaven is their dwelling; but the spirits begotten on the earth, on the earth is their dwelling. And the spirits of the giants <lead astray>, do violence, make desolate, and attack and wrestle and hurl upon the earth and <cause illnesses>. They eat nothing but abstain from food and are thirsty and smite. These spirits (will) rise up against the sons of men and against the women, for they have come forth from them. (1 En. 15:3–12 [Nickelsburg])[20]

In the New Testament, we repeatedly encounter unclean spirits (*to pneuma to akatharton*) or demons (*daimonion*) who cause much evil and terrorize people through possession. Throughout the Gospels, Jesus expels them (e.g., Mark 1:21–28; 5:1–13), but he also debates with the scribes and teachers of the law about the power by which he is able to do so (Mark 3:20–27). The apostle Paul refers to the deities of other nations as demons (1 Cor 10:19–21). Yet the New Testament nowhere explains the origin of these evil spirits, and its demonology is rather implicit.

The story of their origin is developed in the quoted text from the Book of the Watchers, which had a significant influence on Jewish apocalyptic and New Testament texts. According to this story, some heavenly angels rebelled against God by descending to earth to mate with the daughters of men. As a result of this unholy union, great giants were born who created chaos and ravaged the earth. It was through this rebellion that evil entered the human world. In response, God ordered the flood to cleanse the earth of all evil, the giants and all humankind, except the righteous Noah and his family. However, because the giants were the children of heavenly angels and earthly women, they had both a fleshly and a spiritual nature. After their physical destruction by the flood, their evil spirits remained on earth and sought to inflict evil upon people.

Testamentary Discourse as a Literary Form

> The book of the words of Job. . . . Now on the day when, having fallen ill, he began to settle his affairs, he called his seven sons and his three daughters. . . . And when he called his children, he said: "Gather around, my children, gather round me so that I may show you the things which the Lord did with me and all the things which have happened to me." (T. Job 1:1–4 [Spittler])[21]

> And now, my son Methuselah, call to me all your brothers, and gather to me all the children of your mother. For a voice is calling me, and a spirit is poured out upon me, so that I may show you everything that will happen to you forever. (1 En. 91:1 [Nickelsburg])[22]

These are just two of many early Jewish texts that attest to the existence of a literary form of testamentary discourse (as part of larger literary units) or even testamentary literature. This discourse shares similar themes and aims to pass on a body of knowledge and instruction from an important close-to-death figure to his children and descendants. Significant models were the farewell speeches of the biblical patriarchs Moses (Deut 31–34), Joshua (Josh 23–24), and Samuel (1 Sam 12). Early Jewish literature testifies to an evolution from these biblical prototypes, and certain established formal stylistic criteria of the genre can be discerned, including a common framework, vocabulary, and motifs.[23] The famous Johannine farewell discourse of Jesus in John 13–17 fits well into this genre:

> Little children, I am with you only a little longer. You will look for me; and as I said to the Jews so now I say to you, 'Where I am going, you cannot come.' I give you a new commandment, that you love one another. Just as I have loved you, you also should love one another. By this everyone will know that you are my disciples, if you have love for one another." (John 13:33–35)

This genre was successfully adopted by the emerging Christianity not only for this well-known Johannine farewell discourse but also for the composition of the Testaments of the Twelve Patriarchs, which drew extensively on earlier Jewish traditions, and many others.

Reading the New Testament Texts

The Matthean Beatitudes

> Blessed are the poor in spirit, for theirs is the kingdom of heaven. Blessed are those who mourn, for they will be comforted. Blessed are the meek, for they will inherit the earth. Blessed are those who hunger and thirst for righteousness, for they will be filled. Blessed are the merciful, for they will receive mercy. Blessed are the pure in heart, for they will see God. Blessed are the peacemakers, for they will be called children of God. Blessed are those who are persecuted for the sake of righteousness, for theirs is the kingdom of heaven. Blessed are you when people revile you and persecute you and utter all kinds of evil against you falsely on my account. 12 Rejoice and be glad, for your reward is great in heaven, for in the same way they persecuted the prophets who were before you (Matt 5:3–11).

The famous Sermon on the Mount begins with a series of Beatitudes (or blessings) in which Jesus offers comfort and promises the reward of the kingdom of heaven to those who are mournful, meek, merciful, pure in heart, or persecuted. This form of blessing is also known from the Hebrew Bible, where it usually takes the form of a proverbial saying which praises someone for their pious state, attainment of wisdom, or closeness to God (Ps 32:1, 84:4; Prov 3:13). The gospel form, which contrasts the present (grim) state with the future promise of change, is considered rather unusual within this tradition. However, it has some antecedents in early Jewish texts. For example, in Tobit, we read: "Blessed are those who grieved over all your [Jerusalem's] afflictions, *for they will rejoice for you upon seeing all your glory, and they will be made glad forever*" (Tob 13:14, emphasis added). The Parables of Enoch even uses the beatitude in connection with the eschatological promise (cf. 1 En. 58:2–3).

Its form as a repetitive list ending with a longer blessing is another supposed idiosyncrasy of the Beatitudes. Nevertheless, this structure is also known from the fragmentary Jewish wisdom Qumran text (4Q525), where we read:

> [Blessed is he who speaks] with a pure heart and does not slander with his tongue.
> Blessed are those who hold fast to its statutes and do not hold fast to the ways of injustice.
> Ble[ssed] are those who rejoice in it, and do not exult in paths of folly.
> Blessed are those who seek it with pure hands, and do not search for it with a deceitful [hea]rt.
> Blessed is the man who attains wisdom, and walks in the law of the Most High: establishes his heart in its ways, restrains himself by its corrections, is continually satisfied with its punishments, does not forsake it in the face of [his] trials, at the time of distress he does not abandon it, does not forget it [in the day of] terror, and in the humility of his soul he does not abhor [it.] But he meditates on it continually, and in his trial he reflects [on it, and with all] his being [he gains understanding] in it, [and he establishes it] before his eyes so as not to walk in the ways [of wickedness]. (4Q525 II, 1–7 [Wise et al.])[24]

The Sermon on the Mount has long been read in a polemical and anti-Jewish way, mostly based on the problematic reading of the so-called antitheses (Matt 5:21–48).[25] These parallels show us that the Beatitudes are thoroughly Jewish in their form of expression and structure.[26] This should come as no surprise, since Jesus himself, and most likely the author of Matthew's Gospel, were both Jews.

Biblical Villains in the Epistle of Jude

> But these people slander whatever they do not understand, and they are destroyed by those things that, like irrational animals, they know by instinct. Woe to them! For they go the way of Cain and abandon themselves to Balaam's error for the sake of gain and perish in Korah's rebellion. These are blots on your love feasts, while they feast with you without fear, feeding themselves. They are waterless clouds carried along by the winds; autumn trees without fruit, twice dead, uprooted; wild waves of the sea, casting up the foam of their own shame; wandering stars, for whom the deepest darkness has been reserved forever (Jude 10–13).

The Epistle of Jude offers a sharp polemic against certain false teachers, whom it compares to negative paradigmatic figures from both biblical and extrabiblical Jewish texts. In the second series of these negative figures, the author likens them to Cain, Balaam, and Korah, with some surprising remarks. Within this controversy, false teachers are accused of showing contempt for authority, spreading false teachings, blasphemy, seduction, and engaging in sexual immorality. However, the accusation of "going in the way of Cain" seems misplaced, since they are nowhere accused of murder or jealousy, for which the biblical Cain is known. Similarly, "Balaam's error for the sake of gain" does not seem accurate, as the biblical Balaam refused to curse Israel for the money offered by Balak and instead blessed Israel (Num 22–24). Only with Korah does the reference to rebellion have a clear origin in biblical history (Num 16), although this rebellion is expressed with a peculiar Greek word *antilogia*, emphasizing more a verbal dispute or quarrel.

However, it appears that the author of Jude is not drawing these examples directly from the Hebrew Bible, but from the interpretation of these stories that can be found in the early Jewish texts. While the biblical Cain was the first murderer, the interpretation of his story in the first century CE saw him more as a villain *who taught others* his sinful ways (Josephus, *Ant.* 1.52–62; Philo, *Post.* 38–39). The Targums even portray him as an apostate and heretic. Similarly, Balaam's portrayal as the one who cursed Israel for his own gain appears in Philo (*Migr.* 113–14, *Conf.* 159), and he is seen as a tempter to idolatry in Pseudo-Philo, LAB (18:13). This image of Balaam also appears in Revelation 2:14. Finally, Korah was seen as the prototypical antinomian instigator even in early Jewish texts.[27] This example shows the importance of studying early Jewish texts and their authors as representations of biblical interpretation in the time of the New Testament writers.

FURTHER READING

Brooke, George J. and Charlotte Hempel, eds. *T&T Clark Companion to the Dead Sea Scrolls*. Bloomsbury, 2019.

Chapman, Honora H. and Zuleika Rodgers, eds. *A Companion to Josephus*. Wiley-Blackwell, 2016.

DeSilva, David A. *Introducing the Apocrypha: Message, Context, and Significance*. 2nd ed. Baker Academic, 2018.

Gurtner, Daniel M. *Introducing the Pseudepigrapha of Second Temple Judaism: Message, Context, and Significance*. Baker Academic, 2020.

Niehoff, Maren R. *Philo of Alexandria: An Intellectual Biography*. Yale University Press, 2018.

Oegema, Gerbern S., ed. *The Oxford Handbook of the Apocrypha*. Oxford University Press, 2021.

Xeravits. Géza G., and Peter Porzig. *Einführung in die Qumranliteratur: Die Handschriften vom Toten Meer*. De Gruyter, 2015.

Notes

1 See Konrad Schmid, "The Interpretation of Second Temple Judaism as "Spätjudentum" in Christian Biblical Scholarship," in *Confronting Antisemitism from the Perspectives of Christianity, Islam, and Judaism*, ed. Armin Lange et al. (de Gruyter, 2020), 141–54. On the history of the perception of Jews and Judaism in modern biblical scholarship, see Anders Gerdmar, *Roots of Theological Anti-Semitism: German Biblical Interpretation and the Jews, from Herder and Semler to Kittel and Bultmann* (Brill, 2009).

2 On these discoveries, see Malka Simkovich, *Discovering Second Temple Literature: The Scriptures and Stories that Shaped Early Judaism* (Jewish Publication Society, 2018).

3 See Matthias Henze, *Mind the Gap: How the Jewish Writings between the Old and New Testament Help Us Understand Jesus* (Fortress, 2017).

4 For critical evaluation and discussion of the different labels, see *WiBiLex*, "Pseudepigraphen (AT)," by Christfried Böttrich, last updated December 3, 2018, https://bibelwissenschaft.de/stichwort/31588/.

5 See John J. Collins, *Invention of Judaism: Torah and Jewish Identity from Deuteronomy to Paul* (University of California Press, 2017); Jonathan Adler, *The Origins of Judaism: An Archaeological-Historical Reappraisal* (Yale University Press, 2022).

6 The overall situation of the Old Testament apocrypha in the Orthodox churches is, however, still highly complex and in many cases a matter of debate.

7 See the discussion in James H. Charlesworth, ed., *The Old Testament Pseudepigrapha*, vol. 1, *Apocalyptic Literature and Testaments* (Doubleday, 1983), xxiv–xxv.

8 See James Davila, *The Provenance of the Pseudepigrapha: Jewish, Christian, or Other?* (Brill, 2005).

9 Thus, for example, Charlesworth's *Old Testament Pseudepigrapha* in two volumes.

10 See Adam H. Becker and Annette Yoshiko Reed, eds., *The Ways that Never Parted: Jews and Christians in Late Antiquity and the Early Middle Ages* (Mohr Siebeck, 2003);

Tobias Nicklas, *Jews and Christians? Second Century 'Christian' Perspectives on the 'Parting of the Ways'* (Mohr Siebeck, 2014).

11 For the reception, see Annette Yoshiko Reed, *Fallen Angels and the History of Judaism and Christianity: The Reception of Enochic Literature* (Cambridge University Press, 2005).

12 See Maren R. Niehoff, *Jewish Exegesis and Homeric Scholarship in Alexandria* (Cambridge University Press, 2011).

13 On the history of *Yahad*, see John J. Collins, *Beyond the Qumran Community: The Sectarian Movement of the Dead Sea Scrolls* (Eerdmans, 2010).

14 For the discussion, see Sidnie White Crawford and Cecilia Wassen, eds., *The Dead Sea Scrolls at Qumran and the Concept of a Library* (Brill, 2015).

15 For classification and description of this category, see Devorah Dimant, "The Vocabulary of the Qumran Sectarian Texts," in *History, Ideology, and Bible Interpretation in the Dead Sea Scrolls: Collected Studies* (Mohr Siebeck, 2014), 57–100.

16 See Daniel Stökl Ben Ezra, *Qumran: Die Texte vom Toten Meer und das antike Judentum* (Mohr Siebeck, 2016), 237–316.

17 See Mladen Popovic, "The Manuscript Collections: An Overview," in *T&T Clark Companion to the Dead Sea Scrolls*, ed. George J. Brooke and Charlotte Hempel (Bloomsbury, 2019), 37–50.

18 David T. Runia, "Philo and the Early Christian Fathers," in *The Cambridge Companion to Philo*, ed. Adam Kamesar (Cambridge University Press, 2009) 210–30.

19 See Maren R. Niehoff, *Philo of Alexandria: An Intellectual Biography* (Yale University Press, 2018).

20 George W. E. Nickelsburg and James C. VanderKam, *1 Enoch: The Hermeneia Translation* (Fortress, 2012).

21 R. P. Spittler, "Testament of Job," in *The Old Testament Pseudepigrapha*, vol. 1, *Apocalyptic Literature and Testaments*, ed. James H. Charlesworth (Doubleday, 1983), 839.

22 Nickelsburg and VanderKam, *1 Enoch*.

23 See Jürgen Becker, "Die Gattung des literarischen Testaments," in *Das Evangelium nach Johannes. Kapitel 11–21*, Ökumenischer Taschenbuchkommentar zum Neuen Testament 4/2, 3rd ed. (Gerd Mohn, 1991), 523–29.

24 Michael O. Wise, Martin Abbeg and Edward M. Cook, "4Q525 (4QBeatitudes)," in *The Dead Sea Scrolls Reader: Calendrical and Sapiential Texts*, ed. Donald W. Perry and Emanuel Tov (Brill, 2004), 247–49.

25 See Ulrich Luz, *Das Evangelium nach Matthäus (Mt 1–7)*, Evangelisch-Katholischer Kommentar zum Neuen Testament I/1, 5th ed. (Benziger Verlag, 2002), 328–31.

26 For discussion, see James H. Charlesworth, "The Qumran Beatitudes (4Q525) and the New Testament (Mt 5:3–11, Lk 6:20–26)," *Revue d'Histoire et de Philosophie religieuses* 80, no. 1 (2000): 13–35.

27 See Peter H. Davids, "The Use of Second Temple Traditions in 1 and 2 Peter and Jude," in *The Catholic Epistles and the Tradition*, ed. J. Schlosser (Peeters, 2004), 418–22; Jörg Frey, *Der Brief des Judas und der zweite Brief des Petrus*, Theologischer Handkommentar zum Neuen Testament 15/2 (Evangelische Verlagsanstalt, 2015), 88–92.

CHAPTER FIVE

Greco-Roman Literature

Thomas Tops
(Universität Regensburg)

THE PRESENT OVERVIEW adopts a broad definition of Greco-Roman literature, referring to all literary works written in Greek or Latin in the Archaic, the Classical, the Hellenistic, and the Roman periods.[1] Although the NT writings were composed in the Roman period, this does not mean that the writings of the previous three periods are not helpful for interpreting and contextualizing them. Given that the Greco-Roman writings of the Archaic, Classical, and Hellenistic periods were formative of the Roman period, they are essential for examining the Greco-Roman context of the NT. They have shaped the historical horizon of both the authors and the addressees of the NT writings and should therefore be given proper attention, alongside the Greco-Roman literature of the Roman period. Only writings composed after the NT, in the later second century CE and beyond, are excluded from this overview because they self-evidently could not have influenced the first readers of the NT.[2]

The Archaic Period

After the introduction of the Greek alphabet around 800 BCE, the Archaic period gave birth to the epic genre (800–600 BCE). The great poet Homer set the literary standards for the following centuries with the *Iliad* and the *Odyssey*. Almost nothing is known about him and doubt has been cast upon his existence. Scholarship was divided on questions about the artistic integrity of the Homeric poems and the unicity of their author. Regardless of these questions, which even challenged ancient readers, the language of Homer became the norm for later literary developments. For instance, the *Iliad* is not only an epic narration of the anger of the heroic Achilles but is also dramatic and contains principles of the later genre of tragedy. The dramatic character of the *Iliad* is also attested by the fact that the fall of Troy and the death of Achilles and Hector are all repeatedly announced from the beginning, and that fate hangs heavily over the whole poem. Plato, therefore, correctly calls Homer the father of tragedy.[3] After Homer, there are many other epic poems, including for instance, Panyassis, Arctinus of Miletus, and Lesches of Pyrrha, but their works are nonextant and are

Epic poets	Lyric poets	Pre-Socratic philosophers
Homer: *Iliad, Odyssey* Hesiod: *Theogony, Works and Days*	Alcaeus Sappho Anacreon Alcman Stesichorus Ibycus Simonides Bacchylides Pindar	Thales Pythagoras Xenophanes of Colophon Heraclitus Parmenides Anaximander Anaximenes Empedocles Anaxagoras Democritus

Figure 5.1. Poetry and philosophy.

only known to us through the summaries of the compilers and scholiasts of the Roman period.

The other important poet of the Archaic period is Hesiod, who was often depicted as being a competitor of Homer.[4] His *Theogony* and *Works and Days* are highly autobiographical and have a strongly theological content. The latter work combines various literary forms such as the maxim, fable, myth, and admonition, which became popular in later literary writings. Hesiod strongly praises justice in a world that is characterized by conflict and disorder.

The Archaic period further created the lyric genre (650–450 BCE). Unlike the epic poems, the lyric poems are short, flexible, and direct. They were sung and usually accompanied by the lyre (hence, the name *lyric*). Most of the lyric poems are lost today. Except for Pindar's, we have almost no complete poems. The themes and the rhythms of the poems are known for their diversity. Unlike epic poems, they all engage with conflicts of the present and are spoken in the first person. The lyric genre is subdivided in five subgenres: iambic and elegiac poetry, monody, choral lyric, and epinician odes.

Philosophy, too, originated in the Archaic period in the sixth century BCE. The pre-Socratic philosophers attempted to explain the origin and nature of the universe without using mythology or anthropomorphic images. For instance, Thales thought water was the principal material of the cosmos. Heraclitus opted for fire, whereas Anaximenes considered it to be air. Essential is their assumption that the cosmos has a rational order that can be articulated by human reason.

The Classical Period

The classical age of the fifth to the fourth centuries BCE is generally associated with the flowering of Athens and Athenian democracy. The Athenian assembly required new literary and intellectual traditions. The Sophists taught the arts of speaking well and right thinking. On the one hand, there was Gorgias, who extolled the power of speech and attempted to seize hold of the listener's soul through poetic expressions, as seen for instance in his *Encomium of Helen*. On the other hand, there was Protagoras, who was more interested in dialectic and introduced the practice of antilogy—that is, providing two contradictory arguments on the same subject, as demonstrated in his *Antilogiae*. This literary technique required the use of arguments based on probability—that is, arguments based on what public opinion believes to be possible in order to deal with contradictions. Protagoras is famous for his claim that human beings are the measure of all things.[5]

With the rise of Athens came the popularity of the Athenian theater in the fifth century BCE. The most important literary genres created in Athens were tragedy and comedy. Greek tragedy is usually composed of a spoken prologue, songs by the chorus, and spoken episodes. The three great tragedians are Aeschylus, Sophocles, and Euripides.[6] They shared the desire to regularly depict heroic figures as unconsciously moving toward a gruesome death (most famously Oedipus).

The genre of comedy came into being at the beginning of the fifth century BCE, with Aristophanes as one of its major proponents, nine of whose forty-four plays have survived. Both the origins of tragedy and of comedy are linked with the cult of Dionysus. The word *comedy* is derived from the Greek word *kōmos*, which refers to a group of drunken followers of Dionysus. The oldest nine plays

Aeschylus	**Sophocles**	**Euripides**
Persians	*Ajax*	*Alcestis*
Oresteia	*Antigone*	*Medea*
Suppliant Maidens	*Women of Trachis*	*Heracleidae*
Prometheus	*Oedipus the King*	*Hippolytus*
Seven Against Thebes	*Philoctetes*	*Andromache*
	Oedipus at Colunus	*Hecuba*
		Suppliant Maidens
		Ion
		Electra
		Heracles
		Trojan Women
		Iphigenia in Tauris
		Phoenician Women
		Orestes
		Iphigenia in Aulis
		Bacchae

Figure 5.2. Tragedy.

Old Comedy	Middle Comedy	New Comedy
Aristophanes: *Acharnians* *Knights* *Clouds* *Wasps* *Peace* *Birds* *Lysistrata* *Thesmophoriazusae* *Frogs*	Aristophanes: *Assembly of Women* *Plutus*	Menander: *The Shield* *The Grouch* *The Arbitration* *The Hated Man* *The Girl with her Hair Cut* *The Girl from Samos*

Figure 5.3. Comedy.

of Aristophanes are labeled as Old Comedy. Middle Comedy is illustrated by Aristophanes's *Assembly of Women* and *Plutus*. The chief representative of New Comedy is Menander. Comedy was used to deride well-known characters and could have a political message. In this genre, women, rulers, and celebrities were often the object of mockery.

The Classical period also gave birth to the genre of historiography. No longer satisfied with the epic as history, Hecetaeus wrote rational chronologies of mythology and epic legends in prose form at the turn of the sixth and fifth centuries BCE. For the "Father of History," however, we must turn to Herodotus in the fifth century BCE. His *Histories* extensively reports about the people (Lydians, Egyptians, Babylonians, etc.) he met on his travels. He focuses both on their customs (eating and sexual habits, religious beliefs, rites, political organization) and their countries (climate, soil, vegetation, fauna). His work was greatly influenced by the advent of the Persian wars: He established its facts and analyzed the causes and events. The motifs of revenge and divine causality play an important role in his interpretation. Another historian of the time is Thucydides, whose *History of the Peloponnesian War* analyzes the causes of the war and attempts to relate the facts as accurately as possible. Instead of giving a role to the gods, Thucydides gives much attention to chance and psychology to explain series of events. Although not as grand as his predecessors, Xenophon later continued Thucydides's history in his *Hellenica*.

Hecataeus	Herodotus	Thucydides
Peregesis *Genealogies*	*Histories*	*History of the Peloponnesian War*

Figure 5.4. Historiography.

Also important in the Classical period is the further development of the genre of philosophy. Although he never wrote anything himself, Socrates and his dialogues became the object of the writings of Plato. Plato (428–347 BCE) wrote thirty-five dialogues. We also have thirteen Platonic letters of which the authenticity is uncertain. Plato's dialogues are usually divided into five groups. The first group of dialogues are the Socratic dialogues, which echo the conversations of Socrates. They are aporetic in the sense that they give no answer to the questions they raise. Their topics are the nature of truth and falsehood, wisdom, courage, friendship, beauty, and piety. The second group of dialogues are a transition to the third group of dialogues from Plato's maturity after the foundation of his school, the Academy. The fourth group are the metaphysical dialogues. The last group comprises of the dialogues written at the end of his life. Of all his dialogues, the most famous are likely *Republic* and *Laws*, where Plato examines the necessary conditions for the establishment of a just city.[7]

Less literary than his teacher Plato, Aristotle (383–322 BCE) was more interested in the empirical and the natural: see, for instance, his biological treatises *Parts of Animals* and *On Generation and Corruption*, his study of the general principles of movement in the *Physics*, and his cosmology in *On the Heavens*. Additionally, Aristotle wrote *Metaphysics* (lit. "what comes after physics") and more practical writings on ethics and politics: *Eudemean Ethics*, *Nicomachean Ethics*, and *Politics*. His *Rhetoric* and *Poetics* were the most influential on later literature.[8]

The Classical period was also beneficial for the development of the genre of rhetoric. According to Athenian law, defendants had to defend themselves in court. Many Athenian citizens hired professional speech writers (*logographoi*) to write defenses for their cause. The most famous example of such a speech writer

Socratic dialogues	Second group	Mature dialogues	Metaphysical dialogues	Final group
Apology *Crito* *Hippias Minor* *Charmenides* *Laches* *Lysis* *Euthyphro* Perhaps also: *Hippias Major* *Alcibiades* *Ion*	*Protagoras* *Gorgias* *Meno* *Euthydemus* *Cratylus* *Menexus*	*Symposium* *Phaedo* *Republic* *Phaedrus*	*Parmenides* *Theaetetus* *Sophist* *Politicus*	*Timaeus* *Critias* *Hermocrates* *Laws*

Figure 5.5. Plato's writings.

Lysias	Isocrates	Demosthenes
Against Eratosthenes	*Panegyricus* *Encomium of Helen*	*On the Crown* *First Philippic*

Figure 5.6. Rhetoric.

is Lysias, the father of judicial oratory. Of his 233 speeches we have only 30 at our disposal, with the most famous one being *Against Eratosthenes*. Lysias was renowned for his simple style and pure Attic Greek. Probably due to the plainness of his style, most people consider Lysias to be overshadowed by the later Isocrates and Demosthenes. The language of Isocrates is more elevated and contains more imagery than that of Lysias. Major orations of his include, for instance, the *Panegyricus* and *Encomium of Helen*. In general, his orations have a civilizing power and exemplify not only good speech but also good thinking. Only Demosthenes can be said to have a more elevated style. Like a burst of thunder, Demosthenes is famous for his pathos, variety, abundancy of metaphors and similes, paradoxes, interjections, proverbs, and more. His oration *On the Crown* is probably one of the finest speeches of all times. Also very popular is his *First Philippic*.

The Hellenistic Period

After the conquests of Alexander, new territories opened for Greek culture, resulting in new forms of literature and marking the start of the Hellenistic period (323–32 BCE). Due to the diffusion of a common language (the koine), Greek culture became more homogeneous and widespread. Additionally, writers focused more on readers than on hearers. Whereas the writings of archaic lyric poetry and classical theater were read aloud for the entire body of citizens, Hellenistic writings were read by a cultivated elite. Writing became a scholarly endeavor, often conducted at the library of Alexandria, the largest library in the world at that time. Art was made for art's sake, as can be seen for instance in the Hellenistic poetry of Callimachus in his *Hymn to Delos* or his *Hymn to Athena*, in the *Idyll* of Theocritus, and in the *Argonautica* of Apollonius of Rhodos.

The nature of philosophical literature drastically changed in the Hellenistic period.[9] No longer was the focus of philosophy on nature or the problems of the city-state. The representatives of Epicureanism and Stoicism, the two biggest philosophical schools of this period, were searching more for "the good life." Epicurus (341–271 BCE) was the founder of the Epicurean school. We have fragments, aphorisms, and three letters of his work through *Lives and Opinions of Eminent Philosophers* by Diogenes Laertius. Additionally, several fragments from his *On Nature* are preserved on papyri from the Herculaneum library. For the reconstruction of his ideas, we are, furthermore, dependent on Lucretius's *De rerum*

On Flattery, On Arrogance, On Household Economics, On Greed, On Slander, On Beauty, On Eros, On Piety, On Frank Speech, On Gratitude, On Wealth, On Conversation, On Anger, On Death, On the Good King According to Homer, On Sensations, On Signs.

Figure 5.7. Selected writings of Philodemus.

natura (ca. 54 BCE). After Epicurus, Philodemus (ca. 110–40 BCE) played a major role in the popularization of Epicureanism in Rome. Many fragments of his works have been preserved through the papyri of the Herculaneum library.[10]

Compared to the Epicureans, the Stoics progressively developed their teaching through representatives of the Early Stoa (Zeno of Citium, Cleanthes of Assos, Chrysippus of Soloi) and the Middle Stoa (Panaetius of Rhodes, Posidonius of Apamea). Again, Diogenes Laertius is our most important source for reconstructing their ideas. For both the Epicureans and the Stoics, ethics and moral instruction became more important than physics. The ideal was a life in control of emotions and without disturbances. In addition to the philosophical schools, there were the Cynics, a group of philosophers who propagated a return to nature and criticized all societal conventions. They were characterized by a way of life rather than ideas and doctrine. They never wrote anything, and we only know their way of life through the writings of Diogenes Laertius and the Stoics. The most famous Cynic was Diogenes of Sinope (413–327 BCE).[11]

As for the literary genre of historiography during the Hellenistic period, worthy of special mention are the universal histories by Polybius and Diodorus of Sicily. The *History* of Polybius of Megalopolis (208–126 BCE) discusses the conquest of the inhabited world by the Romans. Influenced by Thucydides, he emphasizes the importance of fortune for explaining events and the usefulness of historiography. Polybius not only describes the Roman expansion but also explains and justifies it. The *Universal History* of Diodorus of Sicily (first century BCE), on the other hand, does not focus on the history of one state, but blends the histories of various states into a single narrative. It imitates the descriptions of Herodotus but also introduces contemporary ideas in his narrative. His idea of historiography is one of critical judgment: Only after testing the stories of previous historians can one adequately write history.

The Roman Period

The Roman period was initiated by Octavian's victory at the Battle of Actium (31 BCE) after which the whole Hellenistic world was under Roman dominion. Yet this did not result in the acculturation of the Greeks, but the opposite: the Hellenization of the Romans. Although Latin became the political and legal language, Greek remained the language of culture. As in the Hellenistic period, literature was written for the cultured elite and was characterized by classicism instead of the previous Hellenistic preciosity.

This interest in the writings of the Classical period is perfectly illustrated by Plutarch (40–120 CE). He is the author of *Parallel Lives*, a collection of forty-four pairs of biographies in which he relates and compares the lives of important Greek figures of the Classical period with important Roman figures: for example, *Periclus and Fabius Maximus*, *Theseus and Romulus*, and *Lycurgus and Numa*. He also wrote biographies of the Caesars and several separate *Lives*, including, *Lives of Galba and Otho*, *Life of Artaxerxes*, and *Life of Aratos*. Plutarch emphasizes the virtues of these figures, while often leaving out their vices, aiming to encourage his reader to imitate these virtues. Additionally, Plutarch is the author of *Moralia*, a collection of about eighty treatises on moral issues, philosophy, religion, politics, science, history, and literature.[12]

As for the genre of rhetoric in the Roman period, worthy of mention is Dio of Prusa (ca. 40–110 CE), nicknamed Chrysostom or "golden mouth." Dio was one of the star orators of the time and the third-century Sophist Philostratus considered him to be part of the "Second Sophistic," a denomination for traveling orators with classical ideals. Additionally, there was Quintilian's *Institutio Oratoria*, a first-century CE twelve-volume handbook on the theory and practice of rhetoric. The book describes the rhetorical conventions of the time as well as prescribing how the elite ought to speak and perform in public. It relates not only to speech and spoken language but also to body language and performance more generally.

The Roman period is also known for the development of the genre of the novel. Of the five big novels of this period, only Chariton's *Chaereas and Callirhoe* can be dated as early as the first century CE. The Greek novel is primarily defined by its content: a love story. It is a work of fiction and not history, and it also shows analogies with drama.

As to the genre of history, the Roman period is largely concerned with the mythical past of Greece and its monuments. Apollodorus's *Library of Greek Mythology*, dated to around the end of the first century or the beginning of the second century CE, collects the traditional legends of Greece and carefully excludes a Roman influence (the legend of Aeneas). Other historians like Dionysius of Halicarnassus focused on Rome and sought to obtain a reconciliation between Rome and the people they had conquered. His *Roman Antiquities* comprises twenty books, of which only the first ten and most of the eleventh are extant. The first four books narrate the foundation of Rome and the reign of its kings. The following books are devoted to the history of the republic. Dionysius thus completed the work of Polybius, who had dealt with the later history of Rome. He was later imitated by the Jewish historian Flavius Josephus.[13]

Most prominent in the Roman period was the popular philosophy of the Stoics known to us through Musonius Rufus, Seneca, Plutarch, Epictetus, and Dio of Prusa. As in the Hellenistic period, the aim of their philosophy is "the good life." Their moral teaching was practical rather than theoretical in orientation, and knowing what to do and understanding one's responsibilities in social relations were its aims. Emotional self-control was their biggest concern. In this context, they developed their own methods to cultivate moral growth, which they considered to be a care of the soul or "psychagogy."[14]

Education and Curriculum

Roman education (or *paideia*) was primarily for the elite. It was centered on the trivium (grammar, rhetoric, and logic) and the quadrivium (arithmetic, geometry, music, and astronomy). Primary school (*ludus*) started around the age of seven. Basic reading, writing, and arithmetic were taught at this level. Afterward, students advanced to secondary education where the subjects of the trivium were introduced. Eloquence was of primary importance, and classical authors were read, especially Homer, Hesiod, and the lyric poets. After the trivium, students could proceed to higher studies in philosophy, law, and related fields. Stoic and Epicurean philosophies were popular in Rome, though many also studied philosophy outside of Rome.

The elementary stage of instruction in rhetorical education included the "preliminary exercises" or *progymnasmata*, which were very influential on Greco-Roman literature. The earliest ones known to us are those of Aelius Theon (first c. CE). The purpose of these exercises was to prepare students for composing public speeches and other texts.[15]

mythos or Fable
diēgēma or *narratio*
chreia or Anecdotal Apothegm
gnōmē or Maxim
anaskeuē and *kataskeuē* or Refutation and Confirmation
koinos topos or Commonplace
ēthopoiia or Speech Written in Character
ekfrasis or Description
thesis or General Question
nomou̜ eisfora or Introduction of a Law

Figure 5.8. *Progymnasmata.*

Digital Databases and Collections

All the writings and authors discussed above were influential in their own way and had a formative impact on the culture of the NT period. They can therefore all potentially be helpful for interpreting NT writings. They can also easily be consulted through digital databases and collections.

Databases	Collections
Thesaurus Linguae Graecae Thesaurus Linguae Latinae Perseus Digital Library Library of Latin Texts (Brepols)	Loeb Classical Library (also online) Collection Budé Bibliotheca Teubneriana Oxford Classical Texts Cambridge Classical Texts and Commentaries

Figure 5.9. Digital databases and collections.

TAKING A CLOSER LOOK: SOURCES

Sources from the World of the New Testament

Philodemus, *On Frank Criticism*

> And [having accomplished] nothing he will again employ [frankness] toward the same man. If, although he has erred, he [the student] did not heed the frank criticism, he [the teacher] will criticize frankly again. For although a doctor in the case of the same disease had accomplished nothing through a clyster, he would again purge [the patient]. And for this reason he will again criticize frankly, because before he accomplished nothing, and he will do this again and again, so that if not this time then another time... (Philodemus, *Lib.* fr. 64).
>
> And toward those stronger than the tender ones and those somewhat more in need of treatment, he intensifies [frankness], and toward the strong who will scarcely change [even] if they are shouted at, he will also employ the harsh form of frankness. (Philodemus, *Lib.* 7)[16]

The passages are taken from *On Frank Criticism*, a fragmentary writing from the Herculaneum library written by the Epicurean philosopher Philodemus. It is a compilation of lecture notes of his Epicurean teacher, Zeno of Sidon. Philodemus organized his material by first quoting a topic or question followed by his teacher's elaboration. In this fashion, he provides a philosophical reflection on the use of *parrhēsia* (frankness), its aim, and its pitfalls. The Greek term *parrhēsia* originally denoted the right of Athenian citizens to freely speak their minds and be heard in their political constitutions on matters of politics and government. In the context of the Epicurean community of Philodemus, the term *parrhēsia* relates to moral instruction and the ability of the members of the Epicurean community to reform the souls of one another: the psychagogic practice. Ideally, not only the teacher would use *parrhēsia*, but also the students would practice it among themselves by openly revealing their errors, so that they could mutually criticize one another. In this psychagogic practice, *parrhēsia* encompassed various forms of blame, reproach, criticism, and exhortation in the service of moral improvement and was often linked to terms signifying error and correction. In sum: It connotes the frank criticism of error.

In the first passage, Philodemus advises the use of *parrhēsia* in an experimental way, comparing it to the use of medicine, specifically a clyster and purging. Just as a doctor might misinterpret the signs of a disease, leading to ineffective treatment, a teacher can misinterpret the psychological state of a student, resulting in the student disregarding the criticism. The comparison with the use of medicine continues as Philodemus states that, just as the doctor would modify his approach after his failure and attempt purging again, the teacher will use *parrhēsia* again but adjust it to the circumstances and the psychological state of the student. He will continue to do so again and again until he is successful.

The second passage explains what this entails. The "tender ones" are the students that do not need a strong dose of *parrhēsia*. They can already learn based on mild criticism, which can be mixed with praise. The stronger ones, on the other hand, are students who are easily agitated and resist the *parrhēsia* of the teacher. In agreement with the pedagogy of his time, Philodemus recommends that they should be treated with a stronger dose of *parrhēsia*, meaning a harsh form of frankness involving strong reproach and severe criticism.

These prescriptions on the use of *parrhēsia* appear to be widespread in the Roman period. They can be found, with contextual differences, in the writings of Philo of Alexandria, the Cynic epistles, Plutarch, Dio Chrysostom, and Clement of Alexandria.[17] As for the New Testament, *On Frank Criticism*, has been successfully employed for interpreting and explaining the use of *parrhēsia* in deutero-Pauline writings as well as in the Gospel of John and the Johannine Epistles.[18]

Pseudo-Longinus, On the Sublime

> In writing to you, my dearest friend, at your advanced level of culture, I have practically no need to explain at length that sublimity is a supreme pre-eminence of language and that it is precisely this which has given

> the greatest poets and prose writers their paramount status and invested them with lasting fame. Exceptional writing induces in audiences not persuasion but ecstasy; what arouses intense wonder has a stunning impact and always outdoes what is merely persuasive and gratifying, since persuasion is largely under our control, whereas sublime effects exercise a mastery and irresistible force through which they impose themselves on every hearer. Moreover, we observe that adeptness in invention and the organization of subject matter reveal themselves not at separate points but gradually and in the entire fabric of discourse, whereas sublimity erupts at key moments, rips through the whole subject matter like a lightning bolt and instantly manifests the speaker's concentrated powers. (*Subl.* 1.3–4)[19]

The passage is taken from the beginning of the treatise *On the Sublime*, one of the most influential writings of rhetorical, literary, and aesthetic criticism. Its author is unknown and usually named "Longinus" or "Pseudo-Longinus" because the tenth-century *Parisinus graecus* 2036 manuscript, the most important attestation of the writing, mentions Dionysius or Longinus as the author. Unlike other theoretical writings on poetry and rhetoric, *On the Sublime* does not focus on the formal or structural features of poetic or rhetorical texts, but on one single category of thought and language: the sublime. Longinus is mostly interested in concentrated moments of expressive intensity in Greek literature, philosophy, and rhetoric. As we learn from our passage, Longinus writes his treatise for a good friend, who is introduced earlier in the work as Postumius Florus Terentianus. Surprisingly, throughout the treatise Longinus never directly answers the question what the sublime really is. Only in this passage, does he provide a somewhat vague definition: The sublime is "a supreme pre-eminence of language" belonging to all the greatest poets and prose writers. The original meaning of *hypsos*, the Greek word for sublimity, is "height." Longinus uses the vocabulary of height to refer to an excellence of discourse instead of a particular stylistic register. Longinus explains that the effect of the sublime goes beyond persuasion, because it has an ecstatic impact on the audience, stunning or overcoming their minds. It is an abundancy or excess, which like a volcano "erupts" at key moments and "rips through the subject matter like a lightning bolt." The sublime does not show itself in the totality of a work but manifests the concentrated powers of a speaker.

Recent scholarship has argued that the logic and concept of the sublime goes far beyond the treatise of Longinus and can be traced back as far as the pre-Socratic philosophers. It is one of the most important concepts for helping to understand the literary achievements of Greco-Roman culture.[20] Also NT scholars have recently discovered the benefits of the treatise for interpreting the use of imagery in Hebrews and the literary characterization of Jesus in the Gospel of John.[21]

Reading the New Testament

John 7:4–8, 26

> After this Jesus went about in Galilee. He did not wish to go about in Judea because the Jews were seeking to kill him. The Jewish feast of Tabernacles was near. So, his brothers said to him, "Leave here and go to Judea so that your disciples also may see the works you are doing; for no one who wants to be *en parrhēsiai* acts in secret. If you do these things, reveal yourself to the world." For his brothers did not believe in him. Jesus said to them, "My time [*kairos*] has not yet come, but your time [*kairos*] is always here. The world cannot hate you, but it hates me because I testify against it that its works are evil. Go to the festival yourselves. I am not going to this festival, for my time [*kairos*] has not yet fully come." . . . Now some of the people of Jerusalem were saying, ". . . And here he is speaking *parrhēsiai* and they say nothing to him! Can it be that the authorities really know that this is the Messiah?"[22]

The first difficulty of interpretation that we encounter in this passage is how to understand the request of Jesus's brothers for Jesus to be *en parrhēsiai*. Modern translators and commentators usually translate the Greek phrase with "in public," suggesting that the brothers urge Jesus to be in public so that everyone can witness his works. Yet, this translation and interpretation cannot explain why Jesus's being *en parrhēsiai* parallels the request of his brothers to reveal himself to the world. This request of revelation is not simply a matter of showing oneself in public, but of revealing his identity as the Christ. This is made clear in verse 26, when the Jerusalemites suggest that the authorities know that Jesus is the Christ because they allow him to speak with *parrhēsia*. The expectation of the Jerusalemites that the *parrhēsia* of Jesus would cause opposition among the authorities can be explained in light of Greco-Roman literature. As mentioned above, the term *parrhēsia* can refer to the psychagogic practice of the philosopher in the Roman period, who aims for the moral reform of his students. Apparently, John uses it in a similar fashion: to present Jesus as someone who is exhorting and criticizing people to convert them into faithful followers.

The second difficulty of interpretation in our passage is that Jesus initially claims that the time for his *parrhēsia* has not yet arrived and that he is not going to the feast, yet he eventually goes to Jerusalem, where the Jerusalemites observe him speaking with *parrhēsia*. How does one explain this narrative contradiction in the text? Again, Greco-Roman literature is a useful resource to explain this apparent aporia in the text. Unlike his brothers, the moment (or *kairos*)[23] of *parrhēsia* is not always present for Jesus but restricted to the specific hour of his death (John 16:25). Only at this time will Jesus effectively reproach the world through the Paraclete concerning its error or sin (16:8–9). Since this moment has not yet fully arrived, Jesus's claim that he will not go to the feast in Jerusalem to be *en parrhēsiai* makes sense. Why, then, does he go? The association of *parrhēsia* with *kairos* is common in popular philosophical Greco-Roman writings. As explained above, Philodemus considers *parrhēsia* to be an experimental teaching method that can only be effective at the critical moment (or the *kairos*). The idea of *parrhēsia* as a medicine that must be used repeatedly to approach its critical moment and be effective can also be found in Plutarch and Clement of Alexandria.[24] This idea helps to explain why Jesus repeatedly uses *parrhēsia* with his audience, even though he knows that its *kairos* is not yet fully there. The choice for Jesus's death as the *kairos* of his *parrhēsia* further aligns with the Greco-Roman convention that *parrhēsia* can only be effective when translated into actions. One cannot successfully criticize others if one's own conduct is full of errors or sins.[25] Jesus's death thus translates his teaching of the commandment of love into action (15:12–13), making it the moment when his *parrhēsia* becomes truly effective (see also 16:25).

Mark 3:22–27

> And the scribes who came down from Jerusalem said, "He [Jesus] has Beelzebul, and by the ruler of the demons he casts out demons." And he [Jesus] called them, and spoke to them in parables, "How can Satan cast out Satan? If a kingdom is divided against itself, that kingdom cannot stand. And if a house is divided against itself, that house will not be able to stand. And if Satan has risen up against himself and is divided, he cannot stand, but his end has come. But no one can enter a strong man's house and plunder his property without first tying up the strong man; then his house can be plundered."[26]

In this passage, the scribes accuse Jesus of being able to cast out demons only because he is collaborating with Beelzebul, the leader of the demons. The text does not elaborate further to help understand the logic of this argument but only mentions its refutation in the parables that follow. To understand the rhetorical function of these parables, Greco-Roman literature and rhetorical theory can be helpful. Aristotle observes that Socrates often used parables to correct and refute his opponents.[27] These parables employ arguments like the ones of the opponent to lead to an absurd conclusion, thereby prompting the listeners to recognize that there is something wrong in the opponent's reasoning.

The following example illustrates how this works. Zeno formulated the syllogism: "The rational is better than the irrational. But nothing is better than the universe. Therefore, the universe is rational."[28] To refute this syllogism, the dialectician Alexinus is said to have formulated the following parable: "The poetic is better than the non-poetical and the grammatical [is better] than the non-grammatical, and that wat is viewed according to the other arts is better than what is not; but nothing is better than the universe; therefore the universe is poetical and grammatical."[29] In this parable, Alexinus uses arguments similar to Zeno's. Instead of saying that the rational is better than the irrational, he claims that the poetic is better than the nonpoetic and the grammatical better than the nongrammatical. He replaces *rational* with *poetic* and *grammatical*, and *irrational* with *nonpoetic* and *nongrammatical*. The second premise of the syllogism, "but nothing is better than the universe," remains the same. By making these slight changes, he produces an obviously absurd conclusion: "the universe is poetical and grammatical." The parable, or comparison, shows that there is something flawed with Zeno's argumentation without explicitly saying what it is.

Jesus's parables in our passage seem to operate in a similar way. They employ arguments that are comparable to the arguments of the scribes to show that their argumentation is unacceptable. With his question, "How can Satan cast out Satan?" Jesus reformulates the claim of the scribes in comparable terms. He replaces "the ruler of the demons" and "demons" with "Satan." Satan can be compared with Beelzebul because Beelzebul is explicitly called a ruler and Satan is implicitly considered to be a king in the argument: "If a kingdom is divided against itself, that kingdom cannot stand." The comparison of Satan with demons is evidently also not far fetched. The implied logic of the verses that follow is as follows: Just as a kingdom or a house cannot be divided against itself without falling, Satan can also not rise against himself without coming to an end. In this indirect way, Jesus shows that there is something fundamentally wrong with the argumentation of the scribes. Since Satan cannot expel himself, "the ruler of the demons" can also not cast out "demons." It is therefore impossible that Jesus is collaborating with Beelzebul. Through his use of parables, Jesus refutes the scribes without explicitly saying what is wrong with their reasoning. The parables are comparisons that allow Jesus to refute the view that he casts out demons by the help of Beelzebul.

FURTHER READING

Fitzgerald, John. T. "Greco-Roman Context." In *Oxford Encyclopedia of Biblical Interpretation*. Vol. 1. *African American Interpretation—Materialist Criticism*, edited by Steven L. McKenzie. Oxford University Press, 2013.

Froelich, Margaret, Michael Kochenash, Thomas E. Phillips and Ilseo Park, eds. *Christian Origins and the New Testament in the Greco-Roman Context: Essays in Honor on Donald R. MacDonald.* Claremont Studies in New Testament & Christian Origins 1. Claremont School of Theology, 2016.

Montanari, Franco. *History of Ancient Greek Literature.* 2 vols. De Gruyter, 2022.

Porter, Stanley E. and Andrew W. Pitts, eds. *Christian Origins and Greco-Roman Culture: Social and Literary Contexts for the New Testament.* Vol. 1. Texts and Editions for New Testament Study 9/1. Brill, 2013.

Richardson, Peter. "Study of the Greco-Roman World." In *The Oxford Handbook of Biblical Studies,* edited by J.W. Rogerson and Judith M. Lieu. Oxford University Press, 2006.

Schnelle, Udo and Georg Strecker, eds. *Neuer Wettstein: Texte zum Neuen Testament aus Griechentum und Hellenismus.* 5 vols. De Gruyter, 1996–2013.

Walsh, Robyn Faith. *The Origins of Early Christian Literature: Contextualizing the New Testament Within Greco-Roman Literary Culture.* Cambridge University Press, 2021.

Notes

1 The overview is largely based on Suzanne Saïd and Monique Trédé, *A Short History of Greek Literature* (Routledge, 1999). Due to the broad historical range of this overview, the selection of authors and writings is necessarily limited. It is illustrative of traditions and genres rather than complete and exhaustive.

2 The hermeneutical priority of the first reader in historical study is a principle that is derived from Gadamer's *Wahrheit und Methode*: see Thomas Tops, "Transforming Historical Objectivism into Historical Hermeneutics: From 'Historical Illness' to Properly Lived Historicality," *Neue Zeitschrift fur Systematische Theologie und Religionsphilosophie* 61, no. 4 (2019): 490–515; Thomas Tops, *Paroimia and Parrēsia in the Gospel of John: A Historical-Hermeneutical Study*, Wissenschaftliche Untersuchungen zum Neuen Testament II/565 (Mohr Siebeck, 2022), 7–51.

3 *Respublica* 598d. For the use of Homer in the study of the NT, see Dennis R. MacDonald, *Christianizing Homer: The Odyssey, Plato, and The Acts of Andrew* (Oxford University Press, 1994); Dennis R. MacDonald, *The Homeric Epics and the Gospel of Mark* (Yale University Press, 2000); Dennis R. MacDonald, *Does the New Testament Imitate Homer?: Four Cases from the Acts of the Apostles* (Yale University Press, 2003).

4 See the Greek composition *Contest of Homer and Hesiod.*

5 Plato, *Theaetetus* 152a.

6 On the relevance of Euripides's writings for the interpretation of the Gospel of John, see Dennis R. MacDonald, *The Dionysian Gospel: The Fourth Gospel and Euripides* (Fortress, 2017).

7 On Plato and the interpretation of early Christian writings, see Ivan Miroshnikov, *The Gospel of Thomas and Plato: A Study of the Impact of Platonism on the "Fifth Gospel,"* Nag Hammadi and Manichaean Studies 93 (Brill, 2018); George Van Kooten, "The Johannine Christ, the 'Only-Begotten' Athena, and the Platonic Difference between 'Begotten' and 'Made': The Greek Mythological and Philosophical Background to

John's Gospel and the Nicene Creed," in *Perspektiven zur Präexistenz im Frühjudentum und frühen Christentum*, ed. Jörg Frey, Friederike Kunath, and Jens Schröter, Wissenschaftliche Untersuchungen zum Neuen Testament 457 (Mohr Siebeck, 2021), 209–45.

8 On the use of Aristotle to interpret the rhetoric of questions in the Gospel of John, see Thomas Tops, "Johannine Question-and-Answer Exchanges: A Historical-Rhetorical Study of John 2,18–22; 8,46–59; 10,30–36," *Biblica* 103, no. 4 (2022): 559–81.

9 For more detailed discussion, see the chapter on "Philosophical Schools and Ideas" by Johan Thom in the present volume.

10 On Epicureanism and the NT, see John Fitzgerald, Dirk Obbink, and Glenn Holland, eds., *Philodemus and the New Testament World*, Novum Testamentum, Supplements 111 (Brill, 2004); Fergus J. King, *Epicureanism and the Gospel of John: A Study of Their Compatibility*, Wissenschaftliche Untersuchungen zum Neuen Testament II/537 (Mohr Siebeck, 2020).

11 On Cynicism and the New Testament, see Francis Gerald Downing, *Christ and the Cynics: Jesus and Other Radical Preachers in First-Century Tradition* (Sheffield Academic, 1988); John Dominic Crossan, *The Historical Jesus: The Life of a Mediterranean Jewish Peasant* (T&T Clark, 1991); Bernhard Lang, *Jesus der Hund. Leben und Lehre eines jüdischen Kynikers* (C. H. Beck, 2010); Marie-Odile Goulet-Cazé, *Cynisme et christianisme dans l'Antiquité*, Textes et traditions 26 (Librairie philosophique J. Vrin, 2014).

12 On Plutarch in connection to the interpretation of NT writings, see Hans-Dietrich Betz, ed., *Plutarch's Theological Writings and Early Christian Literature*, Studia ad Corpus Hellenisticum Novi Testamenti3 (Brill, 1975);Rainer Hirsch-Luipold, ed., *Plutarch and the New Testament in Their Religio-Philosophical Contexts: Bridging Discourses in the World of the Early Roman Empire*, Plutarch Studies 9 (Brill, 2022).

13 Classical, Hellenistic, and Roman authors of historiography are often used to interpret Luke and Acts: see Clare K. Rothschild, *Luke-Acts and the Rhetoric of History: An Investigation of Early Christian Historiography*, Wissenschaftliche Untersuchungen zum Neuen Testament II/175 (Mohr Siebeck, 2004); Jörg Frey, Clare K. Rothschild and Jens Schröter, eds., *Die Apostelgeschichte im Kontext antiker und frühchristlicher Historiographie*, Beihefte zur Zeitschrift für die neutestamentliche Wissenschaft 162 (de Gruyter, 2009).

14 On Stoicism and the NT, see Troels Engberg-Pedersen, *Paul and the Stoics: An Essay in Interpretation* (T&T Clark, 2000); Tuomas Rasimus, Troels Engberg-Pedersen, and Ismo Dunderberg, eds., *Stoicism in Early Christianity* (Baker, 2010). On popular philosophy in general as a relevant category for the interpretation of the NT, see Johan C. Thom, "Popular Philosophy in the Hellenistic-Roman World," *Early Christianity* 3, no. 3 (2012): 279–95; Johan C. Thom, "Paul and Popular Philosophy," in *Paul's Greco-Roman Context*, ed. Cilliers Breytenbach, Bibliotheca Ephemeridum Theologicarum Lovaniensium 277 (Peeters, 2015), 47–74; Johan C. Thom, "Theology and Popular Philosophy," in *The Origins of New Testament Theology: A Dialogue with Hans Dieter Betz*, ed. Rainer Hirsch-Luipold and Robert M. Calhoun, Wissenschaftliche Untersuchungen zum Neuen Testament 440 (Mohr Siebeck, 2020), 119–26; Johan C.

Thom, "Cosmic Power in Pseudo-Aristotle's De Mundo and the New Testament," in *Power in the New Testament*, ed. Pieter G.R. de Villiers and Annette B. Merz, Contributions to Biblical Exegesis and Theology 107 (Peeters, 2021), 39–57; Johan C. Thom, "Pythagoreanism and Early Christian Identity," in *Paul, Christian Textuality, and the Hermeneutics of Late Antiquity: Essays in Honour of Margaret M. Mitchell*, ed. David P. Moessner et al., Supplements to Novum Testamentum 190 (Brill, 2023), 394–417.

15 On their influence on NT writings, see Michael Wade Martin and Mikeal C. Parsons, *Ancient Rhetoric and the New Testament: The Influence of Elementary Greek Composition* (Baylor University Press, 2018).

16 *Philodemus: On Frank Criticism. Introduction, Translation, and Notes*, trans. Davin Konstan et al., SBL Texts and Translations 43 Graeco-Roman 13 (Scholars Press, 1998), *Lib.* frag. 64; *Lib.* 7.

17 See Tops, *Paroimia*, 198–204, 211–28.

18 For deutero-Pauline writings, see Clarence E. Glad, *Paul and Philodemus: Adaptability in Epicurean and Early Christian Psychagogy*, Supplements to Novum Testamentum 81 (Brill, 1995); David E. Fredrickson, "ΠΑΡΡΗΣΙΑ in the Pauline Epistles," in *Friendship, Flattery, and Frankness of Speech: Studies on Friendship in the New Testament World*, ed. John T. Fitzgerald, Supplements to Novum Testamentum 82 (Brill, 1996), 163–83; Benjamin Fiore, "The Pastoral Epistles in the Light of Philodemus' 'On Frank Criticism,' " in Fitzgerald et al., *Philodemus New Testament World*, 271–93; J. Paul Sampley, "Paul's Frank Speech with the Galatians and the Corinthians," in Fitzgerald et al., *Philodemus New Testament World*, 295–321; Peter Lampe, "Can Words Be Violent or Do They Only Sound That Way? Second Corinthians: Verbal Warfare from Afar as a Complement to a Placid Personal Presence," in *Paul and Rhetoric*, ed. J. Paul Sampley and Peter Lampe (T&T Clark, 2010), 223–39. For the Gospel of John and the Johannine Epistles, see Tops, *Paroimia* and Connor Purcell Wood, "Epicurean Critical Praxis and Philonian Metaphor in Johannine *Parrhêsia*," *Journal for the Study of the New Testament* 45, no. 3 (2023): 330–47.

19 *Pseudo-Longinus: On the Sublime*, ed. and trans. Stephen Halliwell (Oxford University Press, 2022).

20 See James I. Porter, *The Sublime in Antiquity* (Cambridge University Press, 2016).

21 See Christopher T. Holmes, *The Function of Sublime Rhetoric in Hebrews: A Study in Hebrews 12:18–29*, Wissenschaftliche Untersuchungen zum Neuen Testament II/465 (Mohr Siebeck, 2018); Thomas Tops, "The Sublimity of the Language of Jesus in the Gospel of John: A Comparison with *De sublimitate*," *Biblische Zeitschrift* 69, no. 1 (2025) 51–72.

22 Author's translation.

23 On New Testament terminology about time (and especially the term *Kairos*) see Tobias Nicklas, "Kairos und Chronos: Variationen des Zeitdenkens im Neuen Testament," in *Neues Testament in der Koine. Semantische Fallstudien zu ausgewählten Schlüsselbegriffen*, ed. Stefan Alkier, Dominic Noichl and Thomas Schmitz, Beyond Historicism—New Testament Studies Today (Brill-Schöningh, forthcoming).

24 See Plutarch, *Adulator* 66b, 74d; Clement of Alexandria, *Paedagogus* 1.8.64.4–1.8.65.2; 1.9.83.3; 1.10.94.1. For my discussion of these texts, see Tops, *Paroimia*, 202–4.

25 See Philodemus, *Lib.* fr. 16:5–9; Plutarch, *Adulator* 71e–f; Lucian, *Piscator.* 31, 34.

According to Michel Foucault, this criterion of *parrhēsia* goes back to Plato's *Laches* in which only the courageous can teach effectively with *parrhēsia* about the virtue of courage; see Michel Foucault, *Le courage de la vérité: Le gouvernement de soi et des autres II. Cours au Collège de France (1983–1984)*, édition établie sous la direction de François Ewald et Alessandro Fontana, par Frédéric Gros, Hautes Études (Gallimard/Seuil, 2009), 156–57.

Additionally, moral philosophers often refer to the principle of conformity of words and deeds to justify their criticisms and exhortations: see the examples in Abraham J. Malherbe, *Moral Exhortation: A Greco-Roman Sourcebook*, Library of Early Christianity 4 (Westminster, 1986), 38–40.

26 Author'stranslation.

27 Aristotle, *Rhetoric* 1393b4.

28 Cicero, *Natura Deorum* 2.20, author's translation.

29 Sextus Empiricus, *Adversus mathematicos* 9.108, author's translation.

CHAPTER SIX

Archaeology

Nathaniel DesRosiers
(Stonehill College)

ARCHAEOLOGICAL REMAINS FROM the ancient Mediterranean have the ability to provide new and engaging contexts for interpreting and teaching the New Testament. For student and scholar alike, New Testament archaeology most obviously provides indispensable contexts for better understanding of countless biblical passages where ancient sites or manufactured objects are the key to a more holistic reading. As Titus Kennedy explained:

> Archaeological sites have been instrumental for furthering the understanding of ancient locations, geography, history, chronology, economics language, religion, and culture of the biblical world. Since early excavations in the 19th century, archaeology has revealed new information year by year and vastly increased our knowledge about the places where the Bible occurred.[1]

Ancient material finds not only allow the modern reader to access a more tangible ancient world, but they also humanize biblical figures and make them much more relatable. In short, material culture decreases the distance, demythologizes biblical narrative, and breathes new life into New Testament texts.

Sometimes these archaeological finds provide us with remarkably specific structures and artifacts, bringing new historical light to the biblical texts. For example, the discovery of inscriptions with the names of Roman officials, such as those found in Rome, Pisidian Antioch, and Cyprus mentioning Sergius Paulus corroborate that there was a Roman official by this name who was proconsul of Cyprus in the middle of the first century, just as Acts 13:6–12 relates.[2] Information like this, in turn, can help us to evaluate Acts as a whole: The text clearly is not just pious legend, but is based, at least in part, on historical information. Archaeology also can provide data that often is missing from the literary record. For instance, funerary monuments, inscriptions, and papyri[3] enlighten us about women's roles and occupations in the ancient world, providing needed perspective for the many named and unnamed women in the Gospels and Pauline

Epistles. Specifically, we can understand what may have attracted women to this movement, how they may have supported it financially, and what leadership roles they may have held in the early centuries.[4] Most often, archaeological finds provide us with broader contexts for studying the religion and culture of the New Testament era, aiding us in finding novel and more accurate interpretations. For example, Roman era coins can illuminate Jesus's words about paying taxes (Mark 12:22) or making temple offerings (Luke 21:1–4), oil lamps can better illustrate biblical metaphor (Matthew 5:15–16, 25:8–9), and the temples, synagogues, houses, and marketplaces of ancient cityscapes make the socioreligious lives of the earliest Christians more concrete and accessible.

Although there is great benefit to synthesizing text and artifact, it is important to note that archaeology and the New Testament is a fraught topic for a number of reasons. The first issue relates to the nature of the evidence itself. We have no material finds at all from first-century Christians, and early Christian symbols like fish, crosses, and anchors do not appear until the latter part of the second century CE. Overall, this should not be surprising since the early Jesus movement was small and many of the early adherents would have identified as Jewish. Therefore, any physical finds from the time of Jesus, the apostles, and the writing of the New Testament texts provide background for the Christian movement, but not direct proof of contemporary Christian art, ritual, or even communities. A second major issue is the rather dubious history of early biblical archaeology, which was plagued with confirmation bias, placing primary focus on proving the Bible to be true. This area of inquiry typically was more centered on the Hebrew Bible, but in the early days many scholars certainly did include a quest to prove the events of Jesus's life. This endeavor has largely failed and been discredited, as it relies on the belief that the Bible is historically accurate and divinely inspired. As such, it is unable to stand up against the proven findings of history and scientific archaeology.

Despite the significant issues related above, when employed properly, archaeology offers huge benefits for the study of the New Testament. What often is required to unlock these rewards is a change of mindset, since New Testament archaeology is not designed to prove or disprove the accuracy of these texts. Rather, archaeology can enlighten us about the lives and beliefs of the earliest Jesus followers and the world that shaped them. Put another way, Laura Nasrallah notes how when visiting ancient sites and museums, "theological and literary training in the New Testament seems to drain away" and people often are left with more basic questions about how these people lived, what they ate, and how they traveled. She posits that these *are* in fact questions about theology and the study of religion. Exploring the minutiae of daily social, economic, domestic, and political life helps us to access the raw materials that shaped ethical, religious, and philosophical thinking. We not only learn more about the historical contexts of the New Testament itself, but through material culture, we are better able to access the breadth of experiences and challenges of the earliest Christians.[5]

A Brief Sketch of New Testament Archaeology

It is first important to note that New Testament archaeology is not an academic field of its own, nor does it have unique methodology unto itself. Jodi Magness defines archaeology as "the study of the past as evidenced by human material culture."[6] What makes this field so important for the study of the New Testament are the types of sources considered. Historians and most biblical scholars rely primarily on literary sources, which usually were written by and for elites and relate their specific experiences. Alternatively, archaeology has the ability to uncover finds from across much broader economic and demographic spectrums.

In a sense, the earliest Christian pilgrims, among whom figures like Origen (ca. 185–253/54 CE) are of note, were the first to show interest in the physical locations and remains related to the New Testament writings. In more modern times, eighteenth and nineteenth century travelers and scholars fueled the movement that led to the development of the earliest excavations of Christian sites in Palestine. More systematic methods took place in the middle decades of the 1800s, with the rediscovery of several biblical sites by Edward Robinson and the land surveys of Israel by Charles Warren.[7] However, New Testament archaeology really begins with Adolf Deissmann, who in the early twentieth century, began searching for evidence—often in the form of inscriptions—to corroborate biblical accounts, especially related to the life of Paul.[8] Since the second half of the twentieth century the focus of New Testament archaeology has shifted, aiming to broaden our understanding of the Mediterranean world, rather than fixating on proving specific biblical events. By the 1970s, the field had largely adopted the methods, practices, and frameworks of broader fields such as classical archaeology, which focused on Greco-Roman sites, and Near Eastern archaeology, which primarily concerned itself with settlements in the Levant.[9]

The more recent "material turn" which has deepened our knowledge of the special characteristics and possibilities of material evidence, has also allowed scholars to consider how texts and objects may work together. For analyzing the matrixes of material culture and the Gospels, scholars often study three main types of remains from the land of Israel, including inscriptions, synagogues, and excavations in rural villages that yield pottery, ossuaries, lamps and other small finds to help us reconstruct the life of Galilean peasants. This approach considers more broadly the ways that non-Christian artifacts help us to see the world that influenced the earliest Christians. This is particularly enlightening for contemplating how Christians reinterpreted, adapted, and adopted existing socioreligious forms in the process of creating their own unique forms of expression and self-identity.[10] Some milestone works in this area include Gerd Theissen's 1982 book, *The Social Setting of Pauline Christianity: Essays on Corinth* and Wayne Meeks's *The First Urban Christians*, which both broadly consider the religious, social, and economic environments that shaped Paul's Corinthian correspondence. In recent decades, as archaeological fieldwork has shifted away from monumental buildings like palaces and temples, more focus has moved toward the domestic spaces of the common people. This is enlightening for New Testament scholars since we are more likely to find good evidence for reconstructing the lives and experiences of rank-and-file early Christians in houses and workshops.[11] This trend continues to influence contemporary works in New Testament archaeology. For example, from the 1990s to the 2020s, interdisciplinary work, bringing together archaeologists, epigraphers, biblical scholars, and classicists has developed into very much the norm. This includes volumes on Ephesus, Philippi, Pergamon, Corinth, and Thessaloniki.[12] In all cases, the general focus is to supplement our written sources so that we may cobble together the broadest possible portrait of the ancient Mediterranean world. In doing so we can have a window into the realia that shaped the everyday life during the time when the New Testament was written.

Material Discoveries and Their Significance for New Testament Study

Judaea, Samaria and Galilee in the Greco-Roman World

In the wake of Alexander the Great's conquest of the Levant, many cities were founded or rebuilt as Greek *poleis*, leading to a more cosmopolitan population and the spread of Greek education and language. While Hellenism often met opposition in Judea and the nearby regions, excavations have discovered bilingual inscriptions in Greek and Aramaic. By the second to first centuries BCE inscriptions written entirely in Greek demonstrate the inroads that Hellenistic culture had made in Judea, Samaria, and Galilee.[13] The influence of Greek urbanization is perhaps nowhere more evident than in Sepphoris (see fig. 6.1), which lies a mere six kilometers from Nazareth. Excavations have uncovered a theater, likely built by Herod Antipas, and many domestic buildings with rich Roman mosaic flooring. Furthermore, Sepphoris's proximity to Nazareth has led many scholars to speculate that Jesus may have worked there as a carpenter and encountered Hellenistic culture.[14]

In addition to Greco-Roman culture, archaeology also sheds light on the internal diversity of Judaism leading into the New Testament period. Most notable is the discovery of the Dead Sea Scrolls at Qumran in 1947, which included a collection of manuscripts dating to the first century BCE written in

Figure 6.1. Aerial view of Sepphoris. (AVRAMGR, Wikimedia Commons. Used under the Creative Commons Attribution-Share Alike 4.0 International license.)

Hebrew, Aramaic, and Greek.[15] This cache contains our oldest manuscripts of the Hebrew Bible and many other documents containing commentaries, rituals, and rules for the separatist community that produced them.[16] Excavations also have uncovered ancient synagogues in Italy, Greece, Asia Minor, and Syria as well as the land of Israel. Synagogues dating to the first century CE or earlier have been discovered in Gamla, Herodium, Jericho, Qiryat Sefer, and Masada, and recent excavations in Galilee have unearthed examples in Magdala and Khirbet Wadi Hamam. A consistent identifying feature of these Galilean synagogues is a tiered bench that runs along their walls, suggesting a few general interpretive opportunities. Benches around the perimeter of buildings clearly suggest a public function, as such an arrangement was common in all communal settings of the age.[17] These finds can provide useful contexts for considering the setting of Jesus's early ministry. In this regard, the Capernaum synagogue is perhaps the most noteworthy discovery due to its connections with the Gospels, but whether any part of the existing structure dates to the time of Jesus is disputed.[18]

Jesus, Galilee, and Jerusalem

Archaeology also corroborates the rural and Jewish character of the Galilee described in the Gospels. Consistently, stone cups and jars hand chiseled from local limestone are found throughout towns and villages from the Roman period. The use of stone vessels is important because these were understood to ensure the ritual purity of the contents inside. Likewise, *mikvaoth* or plastered, stepped pools for ritual bathing are also common, with over thirty excavated in public and domestic spaces, including Magdala, Gamla, Jericho, and Sepphoris to name a few. Evidence of animal butchering and kitchen deposits suggest a primary diet of kosher animals like sheep and goats, with little evidence of pork. Finally, burial practices reflected Jewish norms, using underground shaft tombs instead of cremation. These data indicate that Galilee was overwhelmingly Jewish in this period and that the Jewish law was of concern to the contemporary local population.[19] This evidence also provides sharper contrast to the debates between Jesus and the Pharisees over purity and kosher laws that took place in the Gospels throughout the towns and villages of Galilee (Mark 7:14–23; Matt 23:25–26).

First century CE finds from Jerusalem range from enlightening small artifacts to major sites that were the setting for significant events in the ministry of Jesus. Perhaps most important are the remains of Herod's Temple Mount. While

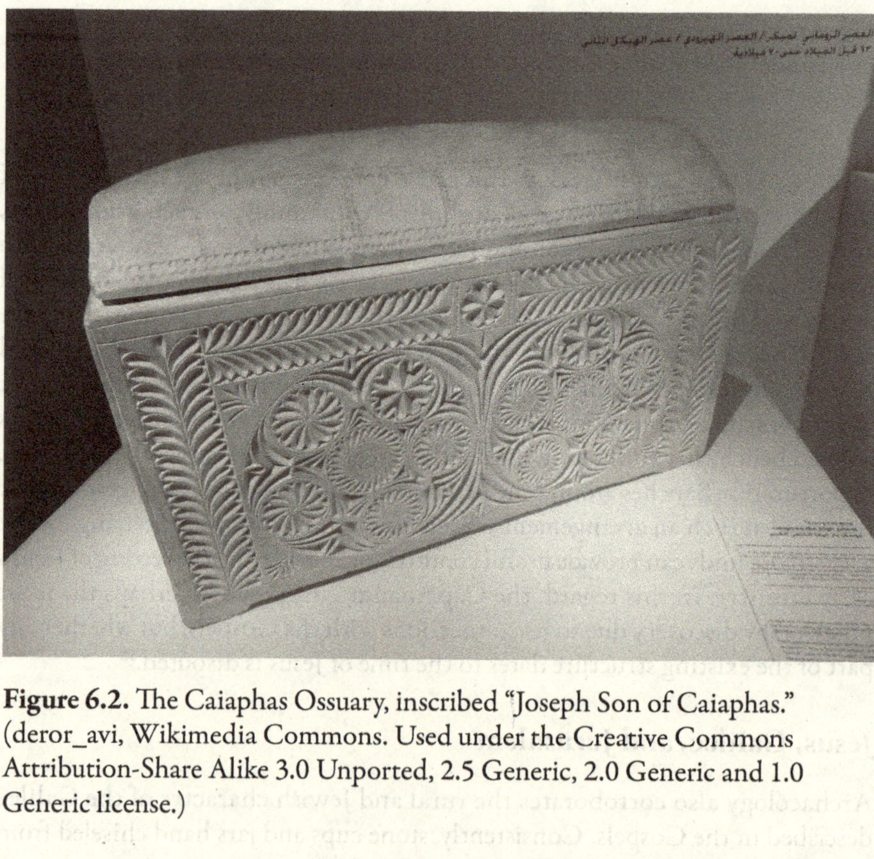

Figure 6.2. The Caiaphas Ossuary, inscribed "Joseph Son of Caiaphas." (deror_avi, Wikimedia Commons. Used under the Creative Commons Attribution-Share Alike 3.0 Unported, 2.5 Generic, 2.0 Generic and 1.0 Generic license.)

none of the temple itself survives, many of the gates and fragments of arches around the massive Temple Mount still relate the grandeur of the site.[20] Several ritual bathing pools have been unearthed in the vicinity of the temple, including the pools of Bethesda (John 5:2) and Siloam (John 9:7), both of which figure prominently in Jesus's ministry.[21] Likewise, the practice of secondary burial in shaft graves is also the standard around Jerusalem. One substantial difference in Jerusalem is the use of ossuaries for collecting the bones of the deceased after burial. Thousands of examples have been discovered ranging from plain to ornately carved boxes, which perhaps correlate with the economic status of the individual. One highly ornamental example includes the name Caiaphas and is believed to contain the remains of the high priest who served from 17–37 CE (Matt 26:3, 57; John 11:47–53; 18:12–28; see fig. 6.2).[22]

Paul and the Cities of Empire

Many of the cities of Asia Minor, Greece, and Italy have substantial archaeological remains that illuminate the everyday experiences and religious practices of life in the Roman Empire. Walking through the agora in Philippi, Ephesus, Athens, or Thessalonica, one can imagine the challenges for a Pauline Christ follower. The traces of ancient shops still are visible in these city centers, and they are surrounded by temples to the gods and emperors with evidence of cultic ritual throughout. Not only would early Christians frequent these markets, but traveling artisans like Paul the tentmaker may have plied their trade in a rented shop or warehouse.[23] In Corinth for example, these agora shops were ringed by temples dedicated to Apollo, Aphrodite, Asclepius, the Emperor Augustus, and many others, giving the modern reader better context and new resonance to Paul's warnings about idol worship in 1 Corinthians (8; 9:13; 10:14).[24]

These sites also have yielded several finds that correlate directly to specific events and structures in the New Testament. For example, inside of Corinth's agora is the *bema*, or speaker's platform, where according to Acts 18:12–17, Paul was tried before the Roman official Gallio. Additionally, over one hundred inscriptions dating to the New Testament period also have been unearthed in Corinth, including one located outside of the theater mentioning Erastus the aedile, whom many scholars believe is the same "Erastus the city treasurer" mentioned in Romans 16:23.[25] The great theater in Ephesus (fig. 6.3), which was remodeled and enlarged during Paul's time, also was the setting for the riot led by silversmiths who were protesting Paul's challenge to the cult of Artemis described in Acts 19:23–41.[26] While these artifacts do not prove that the events occurred as the biblical texts describe them, these remains do help us to understand the historical details and contexts of the accounts more accurately.

Figure 6.3. The Great Theater of Ephesus. (Nathaniel P. DesRosiers, used by permission.)

Perhaps the most useful finds for the study of earliest Christians are domestic spaces, and especially those in Pompeii, Herculaneum, and Ephesus. Since the earliest Christians did not have public meeting spaces, understanding how house churches may have functioned depends on the rediscovery of private dwellings. Excavations in urban centers like Ostia have demonstrated how cramped and squalid living conditions could be for the poor in large apartment blocks called *insulae*. Likely, Christian communities depended on wealthier members whose homes could accommodate the community. Accordingly, the study of larger Roman villas provides context for Pauline house churches (Phlm 1:2; Rom 16:5). Villas were often long, rectangular, and built around a central courtyard. The front part of the house was used by the paterfamilias to conduct business and meet with clients, with rooms near the entrance often used as shops. The back of the house was more private, with an outdoor peristyle courtyard leading to a large room, used for entertaining guests and dining.[27] These spaces often were richly decorated, relatively private, and naturally suited to sharing bread and wine (see fig. 6.4). The rediscovery of these spaces has enhanced our understanding of the development of the Christian ritual of communion, while also highlighting how social factions like those described in 1 Corinthians (1:10–17, 3:5–12, 6:1–8, 11:17–22) may have developed between wealthy homeowners hosting the church meeting and the poor of the community.

The many examples presented here demonstrate the value of bringing extrabiblical texts and especially artifacts into the analysis of New Testament texts. While these archaeological discoveries do not prove the New Testament accounts

Figure 6.4. A *triclinium* (dining room); House of the Cryptoporticus, Pompeii. (Nathaniel P. DesRosiers, used by permission.)

as historically reliable events, they does offer readers informative contexts for an interpretation. Modern methods of excavation and critically informed analysis of finds can sharpen our interpretive lens and open up greater engagement with the world of the New Testament. Specifically, these can add extra poignancy to the New Testament accounts by helping us to see the physical world that was familiar to ancient peoples.

TAKING A CLOSER LOOK: SOURCES

Sources from the World of the New Testament

The Galilean Boat

Excavations around the Sea of Galilee also have provided evidence that breathes interpretive insights into the Gospels. Archaeology has uncovered sixteen ancient harbors and the remains of moorings, ships' anchors, piers, and fishing weights. Most remarkably, a first-century CE fishing boat was unearthed buried in mud along the shores of the sea. It is estimated that it could fit up to fifteen people, allowing us to visualize the type of craft that could accommodate Jesus and the apostles as they crossed the Sea of Galilee (Mark 4:37–41; 6:1–24, and parallels). Furthermore, scholars have determined that the vessel was constructed out of

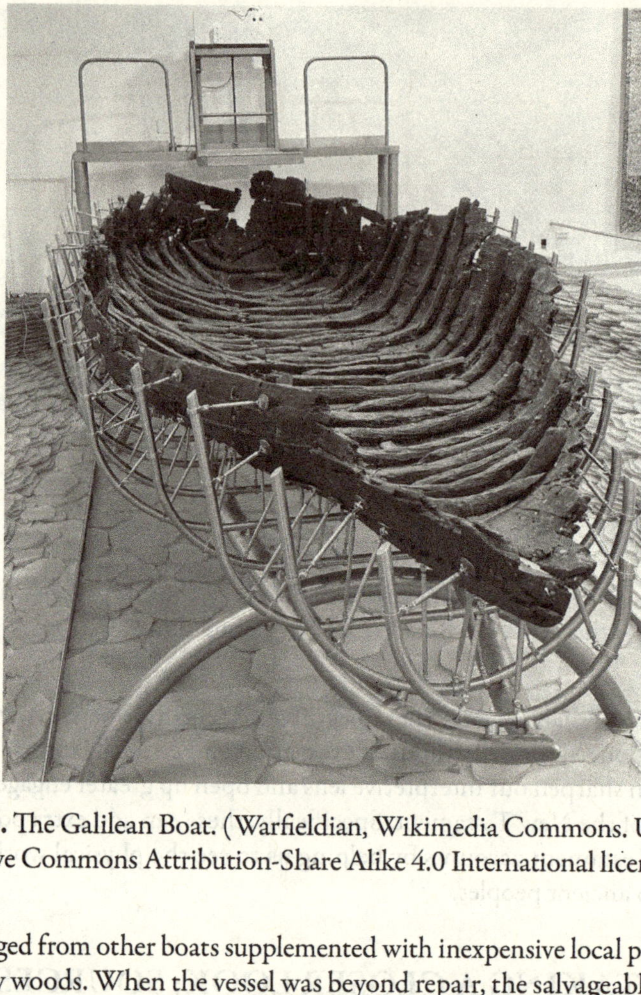

Figure 6.5. The Galilean Boat. (Warfieldian, Wikimedia Commons. Used under the Creative Commons Attribution-Share Alike 4.0 International license.)

parts salvaged from other boats supplemented with inexpensive local pine, jujube, and willow woods. When the vessel was beyond repair, the salvageable elements including the sail and nails were removed and the boat intentionally sunk.[28]

The manufacture and maintenance of this boat provides poignant testimony relating to the lives and economic conditions of the locals who labored around the Sea of Galilee. While some larger cities in the East experienced economic growth under the empire, it appears that rural Galilee largely remained left behind. For example, unlike the grand villas excavated in Pompeii, Herculaneum, Ephesus, and even Sepphoris in Israel, Galilean houses were typically small and constructed from unworked local fieldstone. Instead of plastered walls decorated with frescoes, these structures were typically sealed with mud, straw, and occasionally even dung for weatherproofing. No evidence of roof tiles is found in Galilee, as these probably were too expensive. Instead, archaeologists believe that roofing was constructed from local timber, thatched reeds, and mud.[29]

Figure 6.6. The Magdala Synagogue, Galilee. (AVRAM GRAICER, Wikimedia Commons. Used under the Creative Commons Attribution-Share Alike 3.0 Unported license.)

The Magdala Synagogue

As noted above, many first-century synagogues have been discovered in Israel, including several in Galilee. Overall, these structures are rather simple and typically lack inscriptions or symbols but are recognizable as synagogues through their apparent communal function. One location that stands out as distinctive is Magdala where the remains of three possible synagogues have been unearthed.[30] Of these, the most elaborate is a synagogue discovered in 2009, which is dated securely to the first century CE through small finds of limestone pottery, coins, and lamps. Like all first-century Galilean synagogues, the building featured stone benches along the walls in the main hall, verifying its use as a communal space. Beyond this, the structure is distinctive as it includes several novel features that are unusual for a synagogue of this period. Excavators unearthed colorful mosaics on the walls of the main hall as well as a rosette floor mosaic located in an adjacent smaller room. Most unique was the discovery of a large carved stone found on the floor of the main hall (see fig. 6.6). This artifact, known as the Magdala Stone features a relief of a seven-branched lampstand, making this stone one of the earliest known representations of the menorah in the Second Temple period. However, its precise function is unclear, as it has been variously interpreted as a low table for reading scrolls, a low *bema*, or the base of a lectern.[31]

While the Magdala synagogue still presents a lot of mystery, we also can gain some useful context for understanding the role and function of such buildings in Galilee during the time of Jesus. First, the arrangement of benches along the walls of these structures shows that these early synagogues had no orientation toward Jerusalem, indicating that they were not used for communal prayer but as a place of Torah reading and study.[32] The bench seating also suggests a level of equity within the community.[33] Extrapolating from this, one can imagine how a peasant carpenter such as Jesus would have the opportunity to speak in a synagogue and encounter pharisaic leaders (Mark 1:21–28; 6:1–6).[34]

Reading the New Testament Texts

Paul on the Agora

> While Paul was waiting for them in Athens, he was greatly distressed to see that the city was full of idols. So he argued in the synagogue with both Jews and God-fearing Greeks, as well as in the agora day by day with those who happened to be there. A group of Epicurean and Stoic philosophers began to debate with him. Some of them asked, "What is this babbler trying to say?" Others said, "He appears to be advocating foreign divinities." They said this because Paul was preaching the good news about Jesus and the resurrection. Then they took him and brought him to a meeting of the Areopagus, where they said to him, "May we know what this new teaching is that you are presenting? You are bringing some strange ideas to our ears, and we would like to know what they mean." (All the Athenians and the foreigners who lived there spent their time doing nothing but talking about and listening to the latest ideas.) Paul then stood up in the meeting of the Areopagus and said: "People of Athens! I see that in every way you are very religious. For as I walked around and looked carefully at your objects of worship, I even found an altar with this inscription: to an unknown god. So you do not even know that very thing that you proclaim to venerate among you—and this is what I am going to proclaim to you." (Acts 17:16–23)

First, we are told that Paul was in the agora, a location known to be frequented by Stoics and Epicureans who often were either teaching or seeking prospective students. As J. E. Atkinson has noted, one would feel a lot more Roman influence in the Athenian agora at this time, and philosophers likely were more defensive given how the emperor had prosecuted or banished philosophers in other cities, including Rome.[35] The specific charge in verse 18 that Paul was introducing *xenōn daimoniōn*, implies not only foreign gods, but also "lesser spirits" conveying a

Figure 6.7. Roman altar to the unknown gods, Palatine Hill. (Sailko, Wikimedia Commons. Used under the Creative Commons Attribution 3.0 Unported license.)

tone of Roman religious conservativism and superiority.[36] It makes sense then, that Paul was brought to the Areopagus, which was a court that tried serious matters, including homicide and religious infractions in Paul's time.[37] Whether or not an actual trial took place here is unknown, but the location and details give the account a sense of historicity and vividness.[38]

Archaeologically, the most important element of the story is the reference to the altar of the unknown god. While no such altar has ever been discovered in Athens, there are known examples from literature and other archaeological sites. The second-century CE geographer Pausanias mentions that such an altar did exist in Athenian territory, specifically in the port of Piraeus. "The Athenians have also another harbor, at Munychia. . . . Here there is also a temple of Athena Sciras, and one of Zeus some distance away, and altars of the gods named unknown, and of heroes, and of the children of Theseus and Phalerus."[39]

In addition to Pausanias's account, Philostratus, who also was writing in the century after Paul, mentions the existence of such altars in Athens: "For it is greater evidence of prudence and wisdom to speak well of the gods, especially at Athens, where altars are set up to unknown gods."[40]

Perhaps our most useful evidence comes, not from Athens, but from Rome, where an actual altar to the unknown gods was discovered in 1820 on the Palatine Hill (fig. 6.7).[41] The Latin inscription reads: "Consecrated to either god or goddess, Gaius Sextus Calvinus, son of Gaius praetor, restored this by assent of the senate," The inscription referencing Gaius Sextus Calvinus as praetor allows us to date the altar to the end of the second century BCE. This suggests that such altars were not only widespread but stood for at least a century before and after Paul. Therefore, while Acts is notoriously unreliable as a historical source, archaeological finds can provide numerous points of corroboration with the narrative. Literary and inscriptional evidence both substantiate that Stoics and Epicureans frequented the Athenian agora and that religious trials were handled by the Areopagus council. Most important, the discovery in Rome and elsewhere of altars to unknown gods as well as the accounts from Pausanias and Philostratus bring all the strands of this discussion together. Having textual and archaeological evidence for such altars from different times shows that this was not just a fictional object developed by Luke but an actual example of the diverse religious world out of which the New Testament developed. Furthermore, I would suggest that it highlights the potential challenges that early Christians faced as they developed their religious identity among Greco-Roman religious traditions.

Jesus in Caesarea Philippi

> When Jesus came to the region of Caesarea Philippi, he asked his disciples, "Who do people say the Son of Man is?" They replied, "Some say John the Baptist; others say Elijah; and still others, Jeremiah or one of the prophets." "But what about you?" he asked. "Who do you say I am?" Simon Peter answered, "You are the Messiah, the Son of the living God." Jesus replied, "Blessed are you, Simon son of Jonah, for this was not revealed to you by flesh and blood, but by my Father in heaven. And I tell you that you are Peter, and on this rock I will build my church, and the gates of Hades will not overcome it. I will give you the keys of the kingdom of heaven; whatever you bind on earth will be bound in heaven, and whatever you loose on earth will be loosed in heaven." Then he ordered his disciples not to tell anyone that he was the Messiah. (Matt 16:13–20)[42]

All three Synoptics preserve the identification of Jesus as the Christ by Peter, but only Mark and Matthew agree on the geographical setting in the gentile

Figure 6.8. Temples built into the front of the rocky grottos at the base of the mountain in Caesarea Philippi. (Bill Rice, Wikimedia Commons. Used under the Creative Commons Attribution 2.0 Generic license.)

territory of Caesarea Philippi.[43] While the first two Gospels preserve the location of the episode, the lengthy embellishments in Matthew 17–19 include several important and contentious additions, such as the first use of the term "church" in the Gospels, the description of Peter as the "rock," and the enigmatic statement about the "gates of Hades."[44] Interestingly, Matthew's additions to the account make a connection to the unique topography and history of Caesarea Philippi. Ancient readers would have recognized the significance of Matthew's creative allusions to the site, creating a powerful impact that is lost on most modern readers.

Historically, the mountain slopes in and around Caesarea Philippi were a place of cultic worship for the Canaanite god of weather and fertility, Baal, throughout much of the first millennium BCE.[45] Polybius mentions a major battle in 200 BCE during the Fifth Syrian War at "Panium," indicating that the area was already associated with the god Pan at this time.[46] Two centuries later, Josephus described the region as a wild area where Herod built a temple to Augustus and renovated the original shrine to Pan:

> And when Caesar had further bestowed upon him another territory, he built there also a temple of white marble, by the fountains of the

> Jordan: the place is called Panium, where there is a top of a mountain that is raised to an immense height, and at its side, underneath, or at its bottom, a dark cave opens itself; inside of which there is a terrible precipice, that descends quickly to great depth; it holds a massive quantity of water, which is still; and when anyone lets down anything to measure the depth of the earth beneath the water, no length of rope is enough to reach it. Now the fountains of Jordan rise at the floor of this cavity. (*J.W.* 1.404–6)[47]

Systematic excavations of the area beginning in the late 1980s have corroborated many elements of Josephus's accounts. Notably, the sanctuary of Pan was rediscovered, including evidence of a series of temples built in front of the rocky grottos perforating the base of the mountain (see fig. 6.8). Perhaps more important, inscriptions and small terracotta and glass vessels confirming the identification of the site and relating specifics about the cultic activities were unearthed.[48] Also useful is the discovery of several coins that were struck at the local mint between the first and third centuries CE. The earliest examples dating to the age of Herod the Great and his son Philip depict Augustus on the obverse and the imperial temple on the reverse, giving us some sense of the temple design. Later issues frequently depict the gods Pan, Zeus, and Tyche, with many coins also featuring the legend "Caesarea Sebastos, holy city of refuge, standing before the sanctuary of Pan," demonstrating its importance as a local Greco-Roman cultic site.[49]

These points also correlate well with Greek mythology and ritual practice, yielding even stronger contexts for deepening our understanding of Matthew's passage. In Greek religion, Pan was a god worshipped in caves and grottos, and he was associated the wild, woodlands, and often revelry and fertility.[50] It also is notable that Pan was a god with a dark side as he did have connections to chasms and the underworld. Both Josephus and archaeological evidence emphasize the great depths of the cave and springs, which in antiquity were seen as a gateway to Hades itself.

Putting all the archaeological and textual pieces together provides useful insight into Matthew's unique rendition of the pronouncement of Jesus as Messiah. As Davies and Allison have noted, the "mythological background to the imagery of the rock" should not be overlooked.[51] While Mark either omitted or did not know the full account that related the "rock" and "gates of Hades" references, Matthew's inclusion of them establishes links to the religious, social, and political significance of Caesarea Philippi for Jews and gentiles alike. Daniel Harrington emphasizes that the area around Caesarea Philippi had a long history as a place of revelation before Peter's messianic pronouncement especially in the Jewish tradition.[52] Others have found an intriguing analogy between Matthew 16:13–20's exchange between Jesus and Peter and God's oracle to David in 2 Samuel 2:4–16, where it is promised that David's descendants will rule Israel as the anointed, will build the temple, and that the kingdom will be forever. Furthermore, there was a tradition in Judaism that the rock that the temple in Jerusalem was founded upon also was the center of the world, linking "heaven and the underworld, being the gate to the former and the portal to Hades."[53] Thus, when Matthew's Jesus makes his declaration about Peter, the setting quite literally is the gates of Hades, and not just hyperbole.

The archaeological remains paint a much more vivid and highly symbolic picture of this event. Moreover, by incorporating the material remains into our analysis of Matthew 16:13–20, one could visualize a competition between old and new religious orders. Specifically, one could postulate that Matthew's rendering is intended to demonstrate how the eternal church will be founded on top of an earlier cultic site that Christians came to associate with dark and potentially evil underworld forces.[54]

FURTHER READING

Davis, Thomas W. "New Testament Archaeology beyond the Gospels." In *The Oxford Handbook of Early Christian Archaeology*, edited by William R Caraher and David K. Pettigrew. Oxford University Press, 2018.

Finegan, Jack. *The Archaeology of the New Testament: The Mediterranean World of the Early Christian Apostles*. Routledge, 2020.

Magness, Jodi. *The Archaeology of the Holy Land: From the Destruction of Solomon's Temple to the Muslim Conquest*. Cambridge University Press, 2012.

McRay, John. *Archaeology and the New Testament*. Baker Academic, 2008.

Nasrallah, Laura Salah. *Archaeology and the Letters of Paul*. Oxford University Press, 2018.

Price, J. Randall, and H. Wayne House. *Zondervan Handbook of Biblical Archaeology*. Zondervan Academic, 2017.

Strange, James Riley, and Luke Timothy Johnson. *Excavating the land of Jesus: How Archaeologists Study the People of the Gospels*. Eerdmans, 2023.

Notes

1 Titus Kennedy, *The Essential Archaeological Guide to Bible Lands* (Harvest House Publishers, 2023), 9.

2 *CIL* 41545. For discussion, see Jonathan L. Reed, *The Harper Collins Visual Guide to the New Testament: What Archaeology Reveals about the First Christians* (HarperOne, 2007), 12–14. For other inscriptions relating to Sergius Paulus, see W.M. Ramsay, "Colonia Caesarea (Pisidian Antioch) in the Augustan Age," *The Journal of Roman Studies* 6, no. 6 (1916): 83–134 (95–96).

3 See the chapter on "Documentary Sources" by Peter Arzt-Grabner in the present volume.

4 See Lynn Cohick, *Women in the World of the Earliest Christians: Illuminating Ancient Ways of Life* (Baker Academic, 2009); Carolyn Osiek and David L. Balch, *Families in the New Testament World: Households and House Churches* (Westminster John Knox, 1997); Ross S Kraemer and Mary Rose D'Angelo, *Women and Christian Origins* (Oxford University Press, 1999); Reed, *Harper Collins Visual Guide*, 24–27.

5 Laura Salah Nasrallah, *Archaeology and the Letters of Paul* (Oxford University Press, 2019), 5–7.

6 Jodi Magness, *The Archaeology of the Holy Land* (Cambridge University Press, 2012), 7.

7 James F. Strange, "Archaeology of the Gospels," in *The Oxford Handbook of Early Christian Archaeology*, ed. William R. Caraher and David K. Pettigrew (Oxford University Press, 2018), 31–33.

8 However, closer scrutiny of many of his sources and interpretations in recent years have called his conclusions into doubt. See, for example, William R. Caraher and David K. Pettigrew, "The Archaeology, History, Methods, and State of the Field," in *The Oxford Handbook of Early Christian Archaeology*, ed. William R Caraher and David K. Pettigrew (Oxford University Press, 2018), 1–30 (12–13); Nasrallah, *Archaeology and the Letters of Paul*, 27–29.

9 Caraher and Pettigrew, "Archaeology, History, Methods," 9.

10 See Nasrallah, *Christian Responses to Roman Art and Architecture* (Cambridge University Press, 2011).

11 L. Michael White, *The Social Origins of Christian Architecture*, 2 vols (Trinity, 1996); Osiek and Balch, *Families in New Testament*, 5–35; Olof Brandt, "The Archaeological Record, Problems of Interpretation," in *A Companion to Late Antiquity*, ed. Philip Rousseau (Wiley-Blackwell, 2012), 156–69.

12 Ephesus: Helmut Koester, *Ephesos Metropolis of Asia* (Harvard Theological Studies, 1995). Philippi: Helmut Koester and Charalambos Bakirtzis, *Philippi at the Time of Paul and After his Death* (Wipf and Stock, 1998). Pergamon: Helmut Koester, *Pergamon: Citadel of the Gods*, (Trinity International, 1998). Corinth: Dan Schowalter and Steve Friesen, *Urban Religion at Roman Corinth* (Harvard University Press, 2005); Steve Friesen, Dan Schowalter, and James Walters, *Corinth in Context* (Brill, 2010); Steve Friesen, Sarah James, Dan Schowalter, *Corinth in Contrast* (Brill, 2013). Thessaloniki: Laura Nasrallah, Charalambos Bakirtzis, and Steve Friesen, *From Roman to Early Christian Thessalonike* (Harvard Theological Studies, 2011).

13 See Reed, *Harper Collins Visual Guide*, 34–44.

14 John McRay, *Archaeology and the New Testament* (Baker Academic, 2009), 175–77; Alfred Hoerth and John McRay, *Bible Archaeology* (Baker Academic, 2006), 168–69.

15 See also the chapter on "Early Jewish Literature" by David Cielontko in the present volume.

16 See Jodi Magness, *The Archaeology of Qumran and the Dead Sea Scrolls* (Eerdmans, 2021).

17 Lee Levine, *The Ancient Synagogue: The First Thousand Years* (Yale University Press, 2000), 337–39.

18 Josephus related that there was a synagogue in Capernaum in the first century CE (*J.W.* 2.266–70, *Ant.* 20.173–78).

19 See Reed, *Harper Collins Visual Guide*, 60–64.

20 Kennedy, *Essential Archaeological Guide*, 153–57; Reed, *Harper Collins Visual Guide*, 86–89.

21 Magness, *Archaeology of Holy Land*, 230–43; Kennedy, *Essential Archaeological Guide*, 156–61; McRay, *Archaeology and the New Testament*, 106–8.

22 Reed, *Harper Collins Visual Guide*, 92–95.

23 Reed, *Harper Collins Visual Guide*, 111–12.

24 Kennedy, *Essential Archaeological Guide*, 432–33.

25 *IG IV Corinth* 8, 3 232. For discussion: Hoerth and McRay, *Bible Archaeology* 255–57.

26 Jerome Murphy-O'Connor, *St. Paul's Ephesus* (Liturgical Press, 2008), 183–200; McRay, *Archaeology and New Testament*, 258–61.

27 See Dennis E. Smith, *Symposium to Eucharist: The Banquet in the Early Christian World* (Augsburg-Fortress, 2003); Andrew McGowan, *Ancient Christian Worship* (Baker Academic, 2016; Andrew Wallace Hadrill, *Houses and Society in Pompeii and Herculaneum* (Princeton University Press, 1994), 17–37; Osiek and Balch, *Families in New Testament*, 5–35; Reed, *Harper Collins Visual Guide*, 109–14.

28 Hoerth and McRay, *Bible Archaeology*, 163; Randall Price, *Zondervan Handbook of Biblical Archaeology* (Zondervan, 2017), 262–63; Reed, *Harper Collins Visual Guide*, 68–69.

29 See Reed, *HarperCollins Visual Guide*, 67–69.

30 The first building, discovered in the early 1970s, was originally identified as a synagogue with a *mikveh*, but recent scholarship has questioned this identification and suggested that its function was a fountain house. See Levine, *The Ancient Synagogue*, 70. For arguments against synagogue identification, see Anders Runesson, David Binder, and Birger Olsson, eds. *The Ancient Synagogue from its Origins to 200 CE: A Sourcebook* (Brill, 2008), 55–56. The third building was discovered in 2021, and while findings are not fully published, identification of the site as a synagogue is not debated.

31 Lutz Doering, "The Synagogue at Magdala: Between Localized Practice and Reference to the Temple," in *Synagogues in the Hellenistic and Roman Periods: Archaeological Finds, New Methods, New Theories*, ed. Lutz Doering and Andrew Krause (Vandenhoeck and Ruprecht, 2020), 127–53.

32 Levine, *The Ancient Synagogue*, 55, 163–64.

33 Jodi Magness, *Ancient Synagogues in Palestine* (Oxford University Press, 2024); McRay, *Archaeology and New Testament*, 65–72.

34 See Magness, *Ancient Synagogues in Palestine*; Levine, *The Ancient Synagogue*; Nathaniel DesRosiers, "And They Were All Astonished? The Verb Ἐκπλήσσω, Competition, and Mark's Narrative." *Journal of Religious Competition in Antiquity* 3, no. 1 (2023): 25–46 (33–37); Eric Stewart, *Gathered around Jesus: An Alternative Spatial Practice in the Gospel of Mark* (Wipf and Stock, 2009), 189–94.

35 See J. E. Atkinson, "St. Paul's Encounter with the Athenian Stoics and Epicureans," *Akroterion* 61 (2016): 43–58, 51–53.

36 Cicero reflects the Roman attitude well: "We Romans are far superior in *religio*, by which I mean the worship of the gods." *De natura deorum*. 2.8. For discussion of the

inferiority of foreign or novel gods and practices, see Beard, North, and Price, *Roman Religion*, 211–44; Nathaniel DesRosiers, "Another Temple, Another Vessel," *Near Eastern Archaeology* 82, no. 3 (2019): 140–47 (142–44). All nonbiblical translations in this section are the author's unless marked otherwise

37 Douglas MacDowell, *The Law in Classical Athens* (Cornell University Press, 1978), 26–30.

38 Atkinson argues that such a hearing would not have taken place on the Areopagus in the Roman era, but within the agora at the Royal Stoa. Therefore, Luke is either referencing the council of the Areopagus and not the hill itself, or he is guilty of an embellishing anachronism. Atkinson "St. Paul's Encounter," 51–55.

39 Pausanias 1.1.4. Pausanias actually mentions another example at Olympia (5.14.8). Altars in Miletus, Pergamon, and Phrygia have also been rediscovered bearing inscriptions with dedications to unknown gods. For further examples and discussion, See Kennedy, *Essential Archaeological Guide*, 428–29; Albert Henricks, "Anonymity and Polarity: Unknown Gods and Nameless Altars at the Areopagus," *Illinois Classical Studies* 19 (1994): 27–58.

40 Philostratus, *Vita Apol* 6.3.

41 This altar is on display at the Palatine Museum in the Roman Forum and dates to the late second or first century BCE. The inscription has no catalogue number and has incomplete provenance beyond the fact that it was discovered near the Valabrum in the Southeastern part of the Forum. For discussion and further examples of such altars from other sites, see McRay, *Archaeology and New Testament*, 304–5. Lastly, at least two examples of "unknown god" altars were discovered as far away as Britain (*RIB* 1089, 1607).

42 Mark 8:27–30 and Luke 9:18–21 are parallels.

43 For the various theories relating to the origins of this passage and the possible relationship between Mark and Matthew's versions, see W. D. Davies and Dale C. Allison, *Matthew 8–18*, ICC (T&T Clark, 2004), 604–12; Craig S. Keener, *The Gospel of Matthew: A Socio-Rhetorical Commentary* (Eerdmans, 2009), 423–24; Daniel J. Harrington, *The Gospel of Matthew* (Liturgical Press, 1991), 249–51.

44 For discussion, see Davies and Allison, *Matthew 8–18*, 627–41.

45 For discussion of pre-Hellenistic cults, see John F. Wilson, *Caesarea Philippi Banias: The Lost City of Pan* (Palgrave, 2004), 1–18.

46 Polybius, *Histories* 16.18.

47 Josephus includes another similar account in *Ant.* 15.343–48.

48 Andrea Berlin, "The Archaeology of Ritual: The Sanctuary of Pan at Banias/Caesarea Philippi," *Bulletin of the American Schools of Oriental Research* 315 (1999): 27–45; Vassilios Tsaferis, "The Site," in *Rediscovering Caesarea Philippi: The Ancient City of Pan*, ed. John F. Wilson (Pepperdine University Press, 2001), 16–24.

49 Shoshana Israeli, "The Artifacts," in *Rediscovering Caesarea Philippi: The Ancient City of Pan*, ed. John F. Wilson (Pepperdine University Press, 2001), 46. Some believe that the site was originally a place of worship for the Semitic god Baal-Gad, who was worshiped as a god of fortune. In addition, the god Baal is often venerated as a god of fertility and in other places as a god of wind, rain, and thunder. This may explain why Pan, Zeus, and Tyche were venerated here after the Hellenistic period, since these

divinities are the Greek equivalents for Baal's many functions. See, Ryan Thomas, "The God Gad," *Journal of the American Oriental Society* 139, no. 2 (2019): 307–16.

50 Pan rarely was worshiped in a traditional temple sanctuary; rather, ritual activity often was in the high and rocky places, the most notable of which was on the slopes of the Acropolis in Athens at the Cave of Pan. See Herodotus, *Histories*, 6.102; Pausanias, *Description of Greece*, 1.24.4. For discussion: John Camp, *The Archaeology of Athens* (Yale University Press, 2001), 50, 119–20.

51 Davies and Allison, *Matthew 8–18*, 627.

52 Harrington, *Gospel of Matthew*, 250–51 includes several examples.

53 Davies and Allison, *Matthew 8–18*, 603–4.

54 In addition to the connection with Hades, ancients believed that, if angered or disturbed, Pan would send nightmares or even terror (literally *panic*) to transgressors. See Polybius, *Hist.* 20.6.12; cf. Davies and Allison, *Matthew 8–18*, 604.

CHAPTER SEVEN

Ancient Media Culture

Jan Heilmann
(Dresden University of Technology)

THE TERM "ANCIENT media culture" serves as a collective term for the complex interplay between communication, the dissemination and processing of information and messages, cultural practices, and media. This chapter provides a selective overview of ancient media culture based on key, primarily material media. The broad field of ancient visual media culture cannot be fully taken into account here. For a comprehensive contribution to ancient media culture, visual media must also be included—namely images found on a wide variety of media, such as walls, vases, wooden tablets, coins, statues, and sculptures, but also the architecture of private and public buildings and the architectural layout of cities or parts of cities, temples, and more. These media were also carriers of messages with which the vast majority of people in antiquity interacted, and which often stood in complex relationship with ancient texts. Such a broad and comprehensive treatment, however, lies beyond the scope of this chapter.

Orality and Literacy as Guiding Categories for Describing Ancient Media Culture

Some researchers have identified the great importance of oral communication and oral tradition in antiquity (especially in ancient Judaism and early Christianity)[1] as an essential feature of ancient media culture. This is seen as a central contrast to the importance of writing in modern times.[2] Ancient media culture differed from the print era primarily in terms of the quantity of written mass media. In addition, the medium of voice and the training of speech through rhetorical education were highly valued in ancient media culture. However, a binary distinction between orality and literacy—and the characterization of societies in the Greco-Roman world as dominated by orality—is too simplistic to offer a nuanced picture of ancient media culture.

To expand upon this, *graphic media carrying written texts*, for example, can be conceptualized as either written or oral. This is not a binary distinction; rather, the conception of a text should be understood as existing on a scale between the poles of oral and written.[3] While, for example, dialogues in symposium literature and, to a lesser extent, ancient letters[4] fall within to the conceptually oral category, ancient historiographical works and specialist books are conceptually written. Phonetic media can also be characterized on a scale between conceptually oral and conceptually written. For example, a spontaneous conversation among young people is clearly conceptually oral, but a scientific lecture is, according to convention, primarily conceptually written. The fact that the question of conceptuality is also relevant for antiquity is made clear several times in the sources: Speeches in antiquity were usually preconceptualized in writing,[5] ideally even written by hand,[6] and in some cases even written solely for publication and intended for a reading audience.[7] Augustus is a particularly telling example: According to Suetonius, he took written notes not only for his speeches, but also for his conversations with his wife.[8]

In ancient times, efficient mnemonic techniques were developed and taught.[9] Individual specialists were able to memorize large amounts of texts. However, the sources also reflect in many ways the advantages of rote learning based on written media, which is even attested to for the rhapsodes in classical Greece, and the great hurdles involved in retaining something purely through hearing.[10] In addition, people with high memory capacity were considered exceptional rather than the norm.[11]

Reading Literacy and Reading Practice

The question of the level of literacy in antiquity remains a matter of debate among researchers. The prevailing view, which is largely influenced by William V. Harris's monograph *Ancient Literacy*,[12] assumes that literacy rates were generally low in antiquity. From this perspective, the majority of the population, being illiterate, would have been relied on being read to, and even in early Christianity, texts would have been primarily experienced through hearing.

Recent studies examining the widespread use of writing in ancient material culture, on the other hand, assume higher literacy rates and more sophisticated reading skills. Harris is also criticized for his methodology, which fails to account for the factor of illiteracy in a quantitatively or mathematically rigorous way, based on the available sources. Even if Harris's estimates are taken as a baseline, the absolute numbers still amount to several million people who could read and write in the early imperial period.[13]

When it comes to ancient media culture, however, the question of participation is much more important than the question of the extent of illiteracy, because reading (literary) texts bore no interdependent relationship to the proportion of illiterate people in the population.

In other words, literature was inaccessible to the majority of the population not because they lacked the ability to read but because they did not have the time to read. Two aspects support this view: (1) From the perspective of economic history, it is clear that a large part of the population invested most of their time in securing their livelihood;[14] and (2) ancient sources explicitly mention time as an obstacle to reading. Lactantius, for example, states that women, slaves, workers, the poor, and people from the countryside had no time for reading—he does not mention a lack of literacy.[15] Similarly, the book of Sirach identifies time as a crucial prerequisite for reading as a means of attaining wisdom (see Sir 38–39).

These populations, occupied with work, were therefore hardly eligible as recipients of (literary) texts. If they could read themselves, which was necessary for some professional groups, they certainly came into direct contact with everyday documents. Others read important documents aloud to illiterate people, as is clear from documentary papyri.[16] For the New Testament and other early Christian writings, however, this means that these groups of the population cannot be considered the intended audience. The social context of the characters in the narrative world of the Gospels (fishermen, etc.) does not correspond to the social context of the audience of the New Testament texts.

In addition, hearing texts read aloud required a certain level of literary training for understanding complex content (such as the epistle to the Romans). This is certainly true if one assumes that the texts were intended to be understood by their listeners. Ancient media culture presented itself differently to a day laborer than it did to members of the elite and even to a significant number of people who lived above the subsistence level and could be expected to have adequate reading skills. The latter group included teachers, doctors, architects, craftsmen, merchants, officers, etc., who could afford to purchase books. The view of ancient books as luxury items is founded on a problematic calculation of book prices, derived from documented scribes' wages and material costs, which does not account for slave labor and must be rejected on the basis of sources from the early imperial period. This is because the documented market prices for books in literary and documentary sources show, in comparison with other products, that books were relatively accessible handcrafted products. A standard edition of the Gospel of Mark would have cost roughly as much as sixteen glasses of wine in a tavern in Pompeii, eight roof tiles, or a tunic.[17]

Ancient reading culture was characterized by great diversity, which was reflected in a wide variety of reading practices and social contexts, as well as access to a wide range of different written media. Contrary to what is often claimed, readers who were socialized in a writing system without spaces between words (*scriptio continua*) were able to read ancient texts without any problems. This is not only evident from the sources themselves but is also confirmed by cross-cultural cognitive scientific studies using modern writing systems that do not use spaces between words.[18] In addition, the *scriptio continua* writing system was not adopted in Latin until the second century CE, demonstrating that it was not a deficient writing system. The extremely diverse ancient terminology used to conceptualize reading metaphorically and metonymically is revealing for ancient reading culture. Greek and Latin have about one hundred lexemes that mark reading in ancient sources. These reading terms attest to very different approaches to ancient written media—especially nonvocalized individual reading, impressively expressed, for example, by verbs of visual perception (e.g., the motif of looking at a book in silence[19]). In addition, reading terminology from the source domain of searching and finding shows selective access to the ancient format of the scroll. Reading metaphors of movement, for example, "running through a text,"[20] impressively demonstrate that ancient readers were able to skim through texts at great speed to extract information. Other metaphors attest to immersive reading experiences, expressed through the motif of "leaning into a book" (Gk. *enkyptō*; Lat. *incumbo*).[21] Reflections by ancient authors on their readers also clearly show that they anticipated varied modes of reception. Impressive in this regard is a *proemium* in Polybius's *Histories*, which anticipates three types of readers: the intended reader, the casual reader who happens to come across the book, and the reader who seeks specific information.[22] These clearly represent three distinct types of individuals readers, each reading the text individually rather than having it read aloud to them in a group.[23] The diversity of ancient media culture can now be discussed in detail with an overview of various reading media.

Coins

Coins were not only a means of monetary exchange in the general sense, but also an important everyday medium in ancient times, combining writing and imagery.[24] Due to their great significance, they presumably reached the entire population of the Roman Empire.[25] The value of ancient coins varied considerably depending on the metal used. Gold coins certainly played no role for the majority of the population; silver coins were used for larger transactions, while bronze and copper coins were most commonly used in everyday life. In the Greek world, coinage was originally a matter for the *polis*; in the Roman Empire, there was a nationwide coinage system alongside various local coinages (which did not include gold or silver coins). Gold coins (*aureii*) and silver coins (*denarii*) were minted in central mints.

The iconography of local coinage was often characterized by local deities or mythical motifs that expressed the identity of the city. Since the Hellenistic period, coinage had also been an important means of communication for representing power. As the coin's sovereign, the king or *princeps* was depicted on the obverse and identified in the genitive case, while the reverse was used for a wide variety of motifs from the spheres of religion, mythology, or current political events.[26] However, it would be misleading to describe coins in the Roman Empire as a central instrument of propaganda. The seemingly systematic imagery of Roman coins in the early imperial period "resulted from the intertwining of the ruler's self-representation and the more or less spontaneous honors bestowed upon him, in a process that was largely self-perpetuating."[27] It is difficult to determine how much attention the images and texts on coins received from users in everyday life. The pericope about paying tax in the New Testament (Mark 12:13–17) suggests that the communicative messages on coins were at least not completely ignored in everyday life.

Inscriptions

Public spaces in Greek cities, but even more so in Roman cities, were characterized by inscriptions caved in stone. In view of the observable increase in the number of inscriptions during the Roman Empire, researchers even refer to an "epigraphic habit."[28] Inscriptions were used as a medium by the state, associations, and private individuals alike. The types of inscriptions range from decrees and laws, building inscriptions, honorary inscriptions, association statutes, literary texts, and dedicatory inscriptions to the widespread tomb inscriptions. Particularly noteworthy are the so-called graffiti, occasional inscriptions carved into stone or plaster by private individuals in their everyday lives, which show that a broader population was not only the recipient of inscriptions but also participated as a producer. We know of a large number of graffiti, more than eleven thousand, mainly from Pompeii, whose content ranges from vulgar everyday sayings to quotations from ancient high literature (such as Ovid, Propertius, and Virgil), suggesting that they were read by a wide audience.[29]

The ubiquity of inscriptions in ancient cities shows that their inhabitants almost inevitably came into contact with this written media. Numerous literary sources confirm that the inscriptions were actually noticed and read; primarily, reading terms related to sight were employed to describe the reception of ancient inscriptions.[30] The small inscriptions (*instrumenta domestica*) that have come to the fore in recent years illustrate that written forms of communication (some productive, but mainly receptive) were also used by broader sections of the population. Among the large number of finds, examples include the countless inscriptions and stamps on amphorae, but also inscriptions on wooden barrels,[31] and more specifically, the bilingual inscriptions of two enslaved female bricklayers from Pietrabbondante (100 BCE).[32] These examples suggest that estimates of very low literacy rates in the Roman Empire are probably too pessimistic.[33]

Wooden Tablets

Small wooden tablets (Gk. *pinax*, *deltos*, *deltion*; Lat. *tabula*, *tabella*, *pugillaris*) were another mass medium in the ancient Mediterranean world, used by a broad section of the population not only for recording information but also for creative purposes. Metal tablets were also used, for example, for military diplomas or as curse tablets (*defixiones*). There is evidence of both wooden tablets inscribed with ink and the well-known wax tablets (*tabulae ceratae* or simply *cera*), which were scratched with a stylus. A well-known find is the collection of wooden tablets from Vindolanda, which have been unearthed since the 1970s at the site of the Roman fort Vindolanda on Hadrian's Wall. Most of them are now in the British Museum and have been largely digitized.[34] The Vindolanda tablets consist of various everyday texts written in Roman cursive script from the late first and early second centuries CE and are fairly uniform in size (approximately 20 × 9 cm) with some even bound together into multilayered booklets. The wide range of texts, including military administration, private correspondence, receipts, etc., documents the spread of wooden tablets as an ancient mass medium and attests to the relatively high literacy rate even among those below the highest elites of the Roman Empire.[35] A letter from this corpus will be discussed later as an example.

During excavations beneath the Bloomberg building in London in the early 2010s, the remains of more than four hundred wax tablets as well as several dozens of styli were found. The text itself has not been preserved, but in some cases, the texts can be deciphered because the stylus had pressed through the wax into the wood. The find includes a wide variety of everyday documents written in Latin cursive script and dating from the second half of the first century, ranging from financial documents and legal correspondence to short letters and texts from the school sector.[36] A considerable number of wax tablets were also preserved by the eruption of Vesuvius in 79 CE. Measurements of the wax tablets have revealed a high degree of standardization. In addition, chemical analyses indicate that the wax tablets were not filled with liquid beeswax, but rather with premade sheets of artificial wax that pressed into the recesses of the tablets using standardized procedures. This made it possible to produce this mass writing medium manually, but on an industrial scale and therefore at a low cost.[37]

The small wooden tablets, which were written on with ink, were often whitewashed to make them easier to read. In more luxurious contexts, tablets made of ivory have also been found.[38] In addition to the smaller tablets, there were larger whitewashed boards (*leukóma; album*) that were written on with black ink and used primarily for public announcements and signage. The wax used on the wax tablets was typically black or sometimes colored red. The writing appeared light against the black background due to the reflective surface of the wax. The great advantage of wax tablets was that the written text could be erased by smoothing the wax with the flat end of the stylus, allowing for easy corrections and reuse.[39]

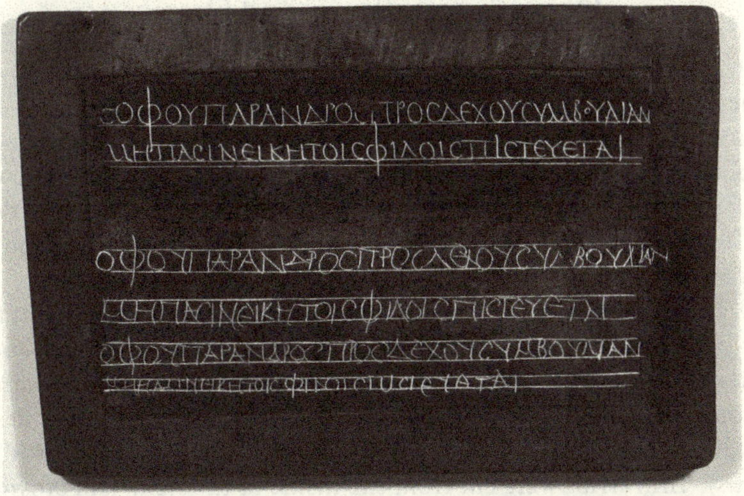

Figure. 7.1. Wax writing tablet. (British Library, Wikimedia Commons. Used under the Creative Commons CC0 1.0 Universal Public Domain Dedication.)

As an ancient mass medium, wooden tablets were used in single, double (*diptychon*), triple (*triptychon*; *triplex*), or multiple layers (*polyptychon*), bound together by thread, for a wide variety of ephemeral everyday texts. They were the basis for efficient administration in the Roman Empire and, as a medium for bookkeeping, were crucial to the Roman economy. In the field of literary production, they served as a medium for excerpts and as "draft paper."[40]

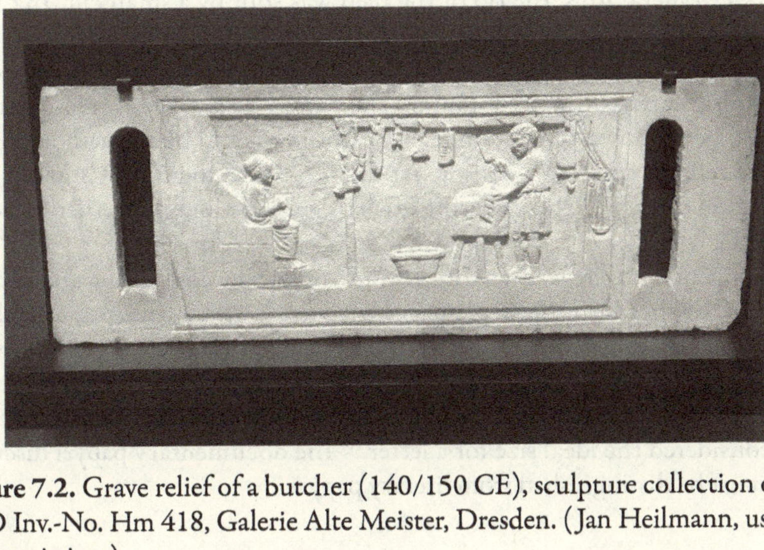

Figure 7.2. Grave relief of a butcher (140/150 CE), sculpture collection of the SKD Inv.-No. Hm 418, Galerie Alte Meister, Dresden. (Jan Heilmann, used by permission.)

Documentary Papyri and Ostraca

Ostraca and papyrus were among the other media used for everyday writing in ancient times, with the most surviving examples preserved in Egypt. Ostraca, which functions similarly to modern scrap paper, are fragments of clay pots that were no longer in use and were written on with ink or carved with letters.[41] The shards were used, for example, for notes, receipts, delivery slips, lists, short messages (mostly based on the ancient letter form), and school texts.[42]

While the cheaper writing material of ostraca was used for less formal everyday texts, papyrus was used for private and official correspondence, petitions to authorities, deeds, documents in commercial and administrative contexts, tax receipts, contracts, and wills. As Pliny the Elder describes in detail,[43] papyrus was made from the stem of the papyrus plant (*Cyperus papyrus*). Thin strips were cut from the inside of the stem, laid crosswise in two layers on a damp board, pressed, and dried in the sun. The papyrus sheets were then glued together to form a roll; the glued areas are called *kolleseis*. Papyrus was available in different quality standards, which were determined, among other things, by the degree of smoothing, the color, the fineness, and the density of the material.[44] Due to the method of manufacture, a papyrus roll had a front side (*recto*), on which writing was preferably done in the direction of the fibers; and a back side (*verso*), which was sometimes reused for secondary inscriptions.[45]

A reed pen (*kalamos*; *calamus*) was used for writing. It was sharpened at an angle with a knife and could be resharpened with a pumice stone. Similar to modern metal nibs, the tip of the reed was split by a small cut. Ink made from soot, water, and adhesives (Arabic gum, honey, oils, resins, fish glue) was used for writing. The ink could also be colored red with iron oxide–containing earths. The ink found on the papyri discovered in Herculaneum has also been shown to contain lead.[46] Soot ink could be washed off and the surface reused, creating a palimpsest.[47] In the Testament of Abraham from the second century,[48] these writing utensils are mentioned together in a court scene (12:7–8).

Longer texts were written directly onto preproduced scrolls available at the market. For shorter texts, single pages were used, which were presumably cut from scrolls in most cases, as can be seen from the glue marks (collations) on the surviving single pages.[49] Whether individual sheets of papyrus could also be purchased on the market is disputed. In ancient epistolography, a single page was considered the ideal size for a letter.[50] The documentary papyri discussed here must be distinguished from literary papyri.

Scrolls and Codices

The common format of ancient books (*biblion*; *liber*) was the scroll, which was made of papyrus or parchment, had a standard size of 20–30 cm, was approximately 10–11 m in length, and was usually written in columns on one side.[51] Scrolls that had writing on the back were usually reused.[52] Ancient scrolls were stored in collections in bookcases (*armarium*), bookshelves (*loculamentum*), or in book storage containers (*kistē* or *cista*, *capsa*, *scrinium*), which were also used for transport. Scrolls were read by unrolling the bundle in one hand and rolling it up in the other, such that the scroll had to be rolled back either before or after reading. The verbs used to describe how the scroll was handled are often also used as metonymic expressions for reading. Compared to the codex that developed later, the scroll should not be regarded as an inferior writing medium that was inherently more difficult to handle. Thus, the scroll remained the preferred writing medium for literary texts long after the introduction of the codex. Ancient reading terminology shows that ancient readers consulted texts in scroll format without any problems, regardless of their various reading interests (including selective, discontinuous, etc.), or, for example, engaged in intellectual pursuits by reading scrolls spread out on the floor around them.[53] In addition, special technical constructions known from Pompeii helped keep scrolls open at a specific point.[54] However, it must also be assumed that people from higher social classes were assisted by slaves when reading or working with texts.[55]

The codex, technically the precursor to the modern book, is a written medium that is likely developed from the practice of using multilayered tablets, which initially used parchment, and later papyrus. It is therefore assumed that the codex was initially used in a social milieu below the highest elites, who used multilayered writing tablets for their everyday professional activities. To make them, sheets of parchment, or papyrus cut from rolls, were folded in half, placed inside each other, and sewn together in one or more layers along the fold, allowing both sides of each leaf to be written on. Data from Egypt indicate that the codex only slowly gained acceptance as a medium for literary texts, replacing the scroll, which had long been the dominant form for literary books in high culture. However, it is striking that the codex dominated as a writing medium in early Christianity from the very beginning.[56] Martial, for instance, used the codex to publish his own works and praised its advantages as a special format for reading while traveling.[57] He also attests to the use of parchment codices for classical literary texts, which were quite extensive.[58] The extent to which the statistical findings regarding the ratio of codex to scroll usage in Egypt can be transferred to other provinces of the Roman Empire remains uncertain.

TAKING A CLOSER LOOK: SOURCES

Sources from the World of the New Testament

Cicero, *De oratore*

> But the chief thing is . . . to write as much as possible. The pen is the best and most eminent author and teacher of eloquence, and rightly so. For if an extempore and casual speech is easily beaten by one prepared and thought-out, this latter in turn will assuredly be surpassed by what has been written with care and diligence. The truth is that all the commonplaces, whether furnished by art or by individual talent and wisdom, at any rate such as appertain to the subject of our writing, appear and rush forward as we are searching out and surveying the matter with all our natural acuteness; and all the thoughts and expressions, which are the most brilliant in their several kinds, must needs flow up in succession to the point of our pen; then too the actual marshaling and arrangement of words is made perfect in the course of writing, in a rhythm and measure proper to oratory as distinct from poetry. These are the things which in good orators produce applause and admiration; and no man will attain these except by long and large practice in writing, however ardently he may have trained himself in those off-hand declamations; he too who approaches oratory by way of long practice in writing, brings this advantage to his task, that even if he is extemporizing, whatever he may say bears a likeness to the written word; and moreover if ever, during a speech, he has introduced a written note, the rest of his discourse, when he turns away from the writing, will proceed in unchanging style. Just as when a boat is moving at high speed, if the crew rest upon their oars, the craft herself still keeps her way and her run, though the driving force of the oars has ceased, so in an unbroken discourse, when written notes are exhausted, the rest of the speech still maintains a like progress, under the impulse given by the similarity and energy of the written word (1.33.149–55)[59].

In this excerpt from Cicero's foundational work on rhetoric (55 BCE), the character of Crassus explains the connection between writing and the conception and preparation of speeches. Crassus emphasizes the advantages of writing a speech in advance, in contrast to delivering spontaneous, unscripted speeches. Through his character of Crassus, Cicero clearly reflects here on the differences between conceptually oral and conceptually written speeches.

Tab. Vindol. II 310, 18.9 x 7cm, 103/104 CE

> Recto: Chrauttius to Veldeius, his old brother in arms and comrade, greetings. And I ask you, brother Veldeius—I am surprised that you have not written back to me for so long—whether you have heard anything from our ancestors, or in which unit Quotus is. And give him my regards in my words, as well as to the veterinarian Virilis! You will ask him to send the scissors he promised to sell me through one of our people. And I ask you, brother Viriis, to greet sister Thuttená for me. Write back and tell us how Velbuteius is doing. I hope you are very happy. Take care!
>
> Verso: In London (to be delivered to) Veldedeius, stable master of the governor, from comrade Chrauttius.[60]

This letter inscribed on a wooden tablet in the form of a diptych (*diptychos*; "double folded"), provides an exemplary window into the mediality (Ger. *Medialität*) and communication practices of the Roman military during the imperial period. The text reveals the typical structure of ancient letters: Following the greeting (*superscriptio*—Chrauttius; *adscriptio*—to Veldeius, his old brother in arms and comrade; and *salutatio*—many greetings), the body of the letter includes various communicative acts: a complaint about the lack of a reply, inquiries about the well-being of third parties, and attending to practical matters. The letter concludes with a standard greeting. The external address on the verso, directed to London, where the letter obviously never arrived, also corresponds to standard ancient letter-writing conventions of the time.[61]

The document, which attests to a communication network below the highest social classes, is of significant sociohistorical value. The text thus provides important insights into media practices, language usage, and social networking within provincial society. It attests to a developed written culture outside the urban centers of the empire, thereby challenging assumptions that ancient society was primarily characterized by oral communication.

Reading the New Testament Texts

The texts of the New Testament can be related to ancient media culture in two ways: through the media in which the texts were written at the time of their creation and through the history of the transmission of the texts's contents. Apart from the reference above to the great significance of the codex for early Christianity and for the history of the New Testament canon, the media composition of the texts is not considered in this article. Instead, a few passages from the New Testament are cited as examples.

John 19:20

> Many of the *Ioudaioi* (Jews and Judeans) read this inscription, because the place where Jesus was crucified was near the city; and it was written in Hebrew, in Latin, and in Greek. (NRSV, adapted)

The inscription affixed to Jesus's cross in the Gospel of John has several distinctive features compared to the Synoptic Gospels. Only here

- is Pilate named as author
- is the Latin loanword *titlos* used (in contrast to *epigraphē* in Mark 15:26 and Luke 23:38, and *aitia* in Matt 27:37)
- is it explicitly mentioned that many *Ioudaioi* read the *titulus* because it was close to the city
- is the trilingualism mentioned (but see the textual variant attested in Luke 23:38)
- is a discussion narrated between the high priests and Pilate about what has been written (John 19:21–22)

Drawing on his knowledge of media culture, an informed ancient reader would infer from this description that there is an inscription on a whitewashed wooden tablet. The trilingualism reflects the multilingual character of media culture in the Roman Empire. This is especially true in the East, where the local language, and Greek as the lingua franca that emerged from Hellenism, as well as Latin as the Roman administrative language coexisted.

Second Timothy 4:13

> When you come, bring the *phailonēn* that I left with Carpus at Troas, also the books (*biblia*), and above all the parchments (*membranas*). (NRSV, adapted)

At the end of 2 Timothy, Pseudo-Paul asks Timothy to bring him a few things from Troas in Asia Minor to Rome (2 Tim 1:17). These are primarily writing materials. The lexeme *biblion* most likely refers to scrolls. Presumably, the intended recipients are supposed to imagine scrolls containing Old Testament texts. Since *membrana* explicitly refers to parchment as a writing material, the recipients can infer papyrus scrolls. *Membrana* probably refers to parchment codices, which may be copies of the letters sent by Paul that were kept back. In connection with written media, it is worth considering whether the lexeme *phailonēs* refers not to an item of clothing but to a case—that is, a container for storing books. Understood in this way, Pseudo-Paul is simply explaining the contents of the container or requesting that the entire book container be brought along, but if this would be too much luggage for the journey, the parchment codices should be brought along.[62]

Mark 12:14–17

> And they came and said to him, "Teacher, we know that you are sincere and show deference to no one; for you do not regard people with partiality but teach the way of God in accordance with truth. Is it lawful to pay taxes to the emperor, or not? Should we pay them, or should we not?" But knowing their hypocrisy, he said to them, "Why are you putting me to the test? Bring me a denarius and let me see it." And they brought one. Then he said to them, "Whose head is this, and whose title?" They answered, "The emperor's." Jesus said to them, "Give to the emperor the things that are the emperor's, and to God the things that are God's." And they were utterly amazed at him.

From a reception-oriented perspective, it should also be assumed that the initial recipients associated the texts with their experience of the denarii as a familiar medium. Consequently, the images and inscriptions of the denarius from the second half of the first century should be considered in the analysis. Assuming that the recipients thought historically and associated the text with Augustus or Tiberius denarii still in circulation, then it is relevant to the interpretation of the text that the *princeps* was frequently refered to as *divi filius*—that is, as the son of the deified Caesar or Augustus, thus a designation that communicated the emperor's divine legitimacy. From the perspective of media history, the situation described presupposes that silver coins (in this case a Roman denarius) were part of everyday life, or at the very least, that their visual language and inscriptions were embedded in their cultural knowledge through contact with the coins. In response to a trick question posed to him by the Pharisees and scribes, Jesus uses a written and visual medium drawn from the narrated world: a coin bearing the image of the emperor on the one side, and an inscription on the other. Such a coin is completely plausible at the level of the narrated world, since the temple tax was paid in Tyrian shekels, which money changers could exchange for Roman denarii. For a long time, the prevailing view among researchers was that the text referred to a very specific, frequently minted Tiberius denarius from

Figure 7.3. Silver denarius of Tiberius, Lugdunum, dated to 14–37 CE. (American Numismatic Society, Public Domain.)

Lugdunum bearing the inscription *TI CAESAR DIVI—AUG F AUGUSTUS* (verso) *PONTIF MAXIM* (recto).[63] This standard identification assumes that the text recounts an event in the life of the historical Jesus. However, even on a historical level, other Augustus and Tiberius denarii would also be possible, as recent research has made clear.[64]

FURTHER READING

Bagnall, Roger S., ed. *The Oxford Handbook of Papyrology*. Oxford University Press, 2009.

Elder, Nicholas A. *Gospel Media. Reading, Writing and Circulating Jesus Traditions*. Eerdmans, 2024.

Heilmann, Jan. *Lesen in Antike und frühem Christentum. Kulturgeschichtliche, philologische sowie kognitionswissenschaftliche Perspektiven und deren Bedeutung für die neutestamentliche Exegese*. Texte und Arbeiten zum neutestamentlichen Zeitalter 66. Narr Francke Attempto Verlag, 2021.

Thatcher, Tom, Chris Keith, Raymond F. Person Jr., and Elsie R. Stern, eds. *The Dictionary of the Bible and Ancient Media*. Bloombsbury, 2017.

Notes

1 See Werner H. Kelber, *The Oral and the Written Gospel. The Hermeneutics of Speaking and Writing in the Synoptic Tradition, Mark, Paul, and Q*, 2nd ed. (Indiana University Press, 1997); Terence C. Mournet, *Oral Tradition and Literary Dependency. Variability and Stability in the Synoptic Tradition and Q*, Wissenschaftliche Untersuchungen zum Neuen Testament II/195 (Mohr Siebeck, 2005). For criticism of the thesis of oral

tradition in early Christianity, see Jan Heilmann, *Lesen in Antike und frühem Christentum. Kulturgeschichtliche, philologische sowie kognitionswissenschaftliche Perspektiven und deren Bedeutung für die neutestamentliche Exegese*, Texte und Arbeiten zum neutestamentlichen Zeitalter 66 (Narr Francke Attempto Verlag, 2021), 490–96. For criticism of the paradigm of orality as the basis for the Talmud, see Monika Amsler, *The Babylonian Talmud and Late Antique Book Culture* (Cambridge University Press, 2023).

2 Influence is Walter Jackson Ong, *Orality and Literacy. The Technologizing of the Word* (Routledge, 1982). For additional information on the problem, see Raymond F. Person, Jr. and Chris Keith, "Media Studies and Biblical Studies: An Introduction," in *The Dictionary of the Bible and Ancient Media*, ed. Tom Thatcher, Chris Keith, Raymond F. Person, Jr., and Elsie R. Stern (Bloomsbury, 2017), 1–15.

3 See Peter Koch and Wulf Oesterreicher, "Schriftlichkeit und kommunikative Distanz," *Zeitschrift für germanistische Linguistik* 35, no. 3 (2007): 346–75.

4 Impressive is Aristeas, *Apologia* 17.1. For further reading on the topic of ancient letters as a conversation see Heikki Koskenniemi, *Studien zur Idee und Phraseologie des griechischen Briefes bis 400 n. Chr.* (Suomalaisen Kirjallisuuden Kirjapaino, 1956), 172–86; Hans-Josef Klauck, *Die antike Briefliteratur und das Neue Testament. Ein Lehr- und Arbeitsbuch* (Schöningh, 1998), 149–56; Christina Hoegen-Rohls, *Zwischen Augenblickskorrespondenz und Ewigkeitstexten. Eine Einführung in die paulinische Epistolographie*, Biblisch-Theologische Studien 135 (Neukirchner Verlag, 2013), 19–39.

5 See Cicero, *De oratore* 1.33.149–1.34.159; Plutarch, *Life of Pompey* 79; Pseudo-Lucian, *Charidemus* 3; Lucian, *Symposium* 21; Quintilian, *Institutio oratoria* 10.3–5

6 Nicholas A. Elder, *Gospel Media. Reading, Writing and Circulating Jesus Traditions* (Eerdmans, 2024), 125–43.

7 Alcidamas, *On Sophists* 28; Menander Rhetor, *Epideictic Speeches* 2.386.29ff. See Heilmann, *Lesen in Antike*, 203.

8 Suetonius, *Divus Augustus* 84.

9 Jocelyn Penny Small, *Wax Tablets of the Mind. Cognitive Studies of Memory and Literacy in Classical Antiquity* (Routledge, 1997), 72–137.

10 See Xenophon, *Memorabilia* 10; Quintilian, *Inst.* 11.2.28–34; 11.2.28, 32; Aulus Gellius 19.1.13; Lactantius, *Divinae Institutiones* 3.25.9; Philo, *Spec.* 4.60. See also Dio Chrysostomus *Orationes* 18.19.

11 See Pliny, *Natura historia* 7.24.88–89.

12 William V. Harris, *Ancient Literacy* (Harvard University Press, 1989).

13 For more information, see Udo Schnelle, "Das frühe Christentum und die Bildung," *New Testament Studies* 61, no 2. (2015): 113–43; Heilmann, *Lesen in Antike*, 61–70.

14 See Helmut Krasser, "*'sine fine lecturias.'* Zu Leseszenen und literarischen Wahrnehmungsgewohnheiten zwischen Cicero und Gellius" (Habilitation thesis, Philologischen Seminar der Universität Tübingen 1996), 267–68; Kevin Künzl, "It's a Matter of Time: A Proposal on How to Approach the Question of Readers and Non-Readers in Antiquity," in *Economic Aspects of Reading in Antiquity*, ed. Jan Heilmann and Robyn Walsh (forthcoming).

15 *Institutio oratoria* 3.25.12. This source should not lead us to conclude that women in ancient times did not read. On the contrary, women reading are widely attested in iconographic, documentary, and literary sources from antiquity.

16 On documentary papyri, see also the chapter on "Documentary Sources" by Peter Artz-Grabner in the present volume.

17 See Jan Heilmann, "The Relevance of Book Prices and Markets for Ancient Reading Culture," in *Economic Aspects of Reading in Antiquity*, ed. Jan Heilmann and Robyn Walsh (forthcoming).

18 With further references to the research of Jan Heilmann, "Reading Early New Testament Manuscripts. *Scriptio continua*, 'Reading Aids,' and Other Characteristic Features," in *Material Aspects of Reading in Ancient and Medieval Cultures. Materiality, Presence and Performance*, ed. Anna Krauß, Jonas Leipziger, and Friederike Schücking-Jungblut, Materiale Textkulturen 26 (Berlin and Boston: de Gruyter, 2020), 177–96; Heilmann, *Lesen in Antike*, 215–69

19 See, Julian, *Epistles* 25.

20 See Seneca the Younger, *Epistulae* 2.2–6; Livy 9.8.12.

21 Achilles Tatius 1.6.6; Tertullian, *Exhortation to Chastity* 10.2; Aristides, *Apology* 16.4.

22 See Polybius 11 *proemium* 2. See also Diodorus Siculus, *Bib. hist.* 1.3; 2 Macc 2:24–25.

23 For more details, see Heilmann, *Lesen in Antike.*

24 See also the chapters on "Monetary Economy, Wealth, and Taxes" by Stefan Alkier and "Documentary Sources" by Peter Artz-Grabner in the present volume.

25 For further reading, see Benedikt Eckhardt and Katharina Martin, eds., *Geld als Medium in der Antike* (Verlag Antike, 2011).

26 For an introduction to numismatics, see Christopher Howgego, *Geld in der Antiken Welt. Eine Einführung*, 2nd ed. (WBG, 2011).

27 Paul Zanker, *Augustus und die Macht der Bilder*, 5th ed. (C. H. Beck, 2009), 13.

28 See Ramsay MacMullen, "The Epigraphic Habit in the Roman Empire," *The American Journal of Philology* 103, no 3. (1982): 233–46; Elizabeth A. Meyer, "Explaining the Epigraphic Habit in the Roman Empire: The Evidence of Epitaphs," *The Journal of Roman Studies* 80 (1990): 74–96; Erkki Sironen, "The Epigram Habit in Late Antique Greece," in *The Epigraphic Cultures of Late Antiquity*, ed. Katharina Bolle, Carlos Machado, and Christian Witschel (Franz Steiner Velag, 2017), 449–72.

29 See James L. Franklin, "Literacy and the Parietal Inscriptions of Pompeii," in *Literacy in the Roman World*, ed. Mary Beard, Alan K. Bowman, Mireille Corbier, et. al, Journal of Roman Archaeology Supplementary Series 3 (Journal of Roman Archaeology, 1991), 77–98; Kristina Milnor, *Graffiti and the Literary Landscape in Roman Pompeii* (Oxford University, 2014); Polly Lohmann, *Graffiti als Interaktionsform*, Materiale Textkulturen 16 (de Gruyter, 2018).

30 See Niall W. Slater, "Reading Inscription in the Ancient Novel," in *Readers and Writers in the Ancient Novel*, ed. Michael Paschalis, Stelios Panayotakis, and Gareth Schmeling, Ancient Narrative. Supplementum 12 (Barkhuis, 2009), 64–78; Heilmann, *Lesen in Antike*, 111–12, 146, 198–202.

31 See Regula Frei-Stolba, *Holzfässer. Studien zu den Holzfässern und ihren Inschriften im römischen Reich mit Neufunden und Neulesungen der Fassinschriften aus Oberwinterthur/Vitudurum Zürich* (Schwabe Verlag, 2017).

32 Helmut Rix, ed., *Sabellische Texte. Die Texte des Oskischen, Umbrischen und Südpikenischen* (Winter, 2002), Sa 35. I owe this reference to Candida Moss.

33 See Markus Scholz, "Tumbe Bauern? Zur Schriftlichkeit in ländlichen Siedlungen in den germanischen Provinzen und Raetien," in *Lesen und Schreiben in den Römischen Provinzen*, ed. Markus Scholz and Marietta Horster, RGZM-Tagungen 26 (Schneller & Steiner, 2015).

34 See Vindolanda Tablets Online, acessed May 14, 2025, http://vindolanda.csad.ox.ac.uk/.

35 See Alan K. Bowman, *The Roman Writing Tablets from Vindolanda* (British Museum Publications, 1983); Alan K. Bowman, "The Roman Imperial Army: Letters and Literacy on the Northern Frontier," in *Literacy and Power in the Ancient World*, ed. Alan K. Bowman (Cambridge University Press, 1994), 119–32; William S. Hanson and Richard Conolly, "Language and Literacy in Roman Britain. Some Archaeological Considerations," in *Becoming Roman, Writing Latin? Literacy and Epigraphy in the Roman West*, ed. Alison E. Cooley and Andrew Burnett, Journal of Roman Archaeology Supplementary Series 48 (Journal of Roman Archaeology, 2002), 151–64; Jacqueline Austin, "Letter Writing at Vindolanda (Northumberland, GB)," in *Lesen und Schreiben in den Römischen Provinzen*, ed. Markus Scholz and Marietta Horster, RGZM-Tagungen 26 (Schnell & Steiner, 2015), 15–25.

36 See Roger S. O. Tomlin, *Roman London's First Voices. Writing Tablets from Bloomberg Excavations, 2010–14*, MOLA Monograph 72 (Museum of London Archaeology, 2016).

37 Robert Fuchs, Ester Simoes B. Ferreira, and Michele Cammarosano, "Römische Wachstafeln aus Pompeji—Geschichte—Herstellung—Analysen," *Metalla: Sonderheft. Archäometrie und Denkmalpflege* 12 (2023): 45–47.

38 Donald J. Wiseman, "Assyrian Writing-Boards," *Iraq* 17, no. 1 (1955): 3–13; Margaret Howard, "Technical Description of the Ivory Writing-Boards from Nimrud," *Iraq* 17, no 1. (1955): 14–20.

39 See Victor Gardthausen, *Griechische Palaeographie* (Verlag der Wissenschaften, 1911), 182–202; Horst Blanck, *Das Buch in der Antike* (C. H. Beck, 1992), 65–66; Raffaella Cribiore, *Writing, Teachers, and Students in Graeco-Roman Egypt*, ASP 36 (Scholars Press, 1996); Small, *Wax Tablets*, 146; Rolf Hurschmann and Wolfgang Röllig, "Schreibmaterial," *Der Neue Pauly* 11 (2001): 226–30; Antonia Sarri, *Material Aspects of Letter Writing in the Graeco-Roman World. C. 500 BC–c. AD 300*, Materiale Textkulturen 12 (de Gruyter, 2017), 79–84.

40 See Dionysius Halicarnassus, *De compositione verborum* 25; Quintilian, *Inst.* 8.6.64; Diogenes Laertius 3.37; Ovid, *Epistulae ex Ponto* 4.2.24–33.

41 Cf. Monte Testaccio in Rome, an artificial mound in Rome composed almost entirely of broken oil amphorae from the time of the Roman Empire.

42 Sarri, *Aspects of Letter Writing*, 77–79.

43 *Naturalis historia* 13.71–89

44 Cf. Pliny, *Nat.* 13.78–81.

45 Sarri, *Aspects of Letter Writing*, 74–75.

46 See Emmanuel Brun, Marine Cotte, Jonathan Wright et al., "Revealing Metallic Ink in Herculaneum Papyri," *PNASUS* 113, no. 14 (2016): 3751–54.

47 Sarri, *Aspects of Letter Writing*, 76.

48 On the testamentary literature, see the chapter on "Early Jewish Literature" by David Cielontko in the present volume.
49 Sarri, *Aspects of Letter Writing.*
50 Cf. Seneca,Epistulae morales ad Lucilium 45.13; Cicero, *Epistulae ad familiares* 11.25.2.
51 It could also be written *transversa charta*, that is, across the fibers rather than parallel.
52 Adam Bülow-Jacobsen, "Writing Materials in the Ancient World," in *The Oxford Handbook of Papyrology*, ed. Roger S. Bagnall (Oxford University, 2009), 18–23.
53 Cicero, *Epistulae ad Atticum* 2.2.2; *De finibus* 3.7. Greek even has its own lexeme, *paranagignōskō*, to indicate comparative reading.
54 Susan Wood, "Literacy and Luxury in the Early Empire. A Papyrus-Roll Winder from Pompeii," *Memoirs of the American Academy in Rome* 46 (2001): 23–40; Brent Nongbri, "Another Question About Those Possible Stands for Holding Open Papyrus Rolls," *Variant Readings*, March 3, 2024, https://brentnongbri.com/2024/03/03/another-question-about-those-possible-stands-for-holding-open-papyrus-rolls/.
55 On this, see Candida R. Moss, *God's Ghostwriters. Enslaved Christians and the Making of the Bible* (Little, Brown and Company, 2024).
56 See Martin Wallraff, *Kodex und Kanon. Das Buch im frühen Christentum* (de Gruyter, 2013); Brent Nongbri, *God's Library. The Archaeology of the Earliest Christian Manuscripts* (Yale University Press, 2018).
57 Martial 1.2; 14.188. See also Julian, *Epistles* 29.
58 Martial 14.184–92.
59 Cicero. *De oratore III*, trans. E. W. Sutton, H. Rackham, LCL 348 (Harvard University Press, 1942).
60 Trans. Kramer, adapted by J. Cerone; cf. Johannes Kramer, ed., *Vulgärlateinische Alltagsdokumente auf Papyri, Ostraka, Täfelchen und Inschriften* (de Gruyter, 2007).
61 See Kramer, *Vulgärlateinische Alltagsdokumente auf Papyri, Ostraka, Täfelchen und Inschriften*, 47–58.
62 Joram Luttenberger, *Prophetenmantel oder Bücherfutteral? Die persönlichen Notizen in den Pastoralbriefen im Licht antiker Epistolographie und literarischer Pseudepigraphie*, Arbeiten zur Bibel und ihrer Geschichte 40 (Evangelische Verlagsanstalt, 2012), 323–65.
63 RIC Tib. 26.
64 Stefan Alkier, " 'Geld' im Neuen Testament: der Beitrag der Numismatik zu einer Enzyklopädie des frühen Christentums," in *Zeichen aus Text und Stein: Studien auf dem Weg zu einer Archäologie des Neuen Testaments: Studien auf dem Weg zu einer Archäologie des Neuen Testaments*, ed. Stefan Alkier and Jürgen Zangenberg, Texte und Arbeiten zum neutestamentlichen Zeitalter 42 (Francke, 2003), 308–35.

CHAPTER EIGHT

Social Status and Relations in Private Life

Michael Sommer, Isabel Kraus
(Goethe-Universität Frankfurt)

When examining family relationships and gender roles in the writings of the New Testament and early Christianity, one quickly realizes that the family structures depicted there do not differ significantly from those of its Hellenistic-Roman environment. This insight is of paramount importance for the study of the New Testament. It is essential to resist the idealization of early Christianity, a tendency that frequently characterized the twentieth-century scholarship. Indeed, the evidence suggests that the early followers of Jesus did not, in fact, bring about a revolution in ancient lifestyles in their private lives. Their life plans, including both social and private relationships, developed entirely within the context of Greco-Roman ideals. Writings such as the Pastoral Epistles (1–2 Timothy, Titus) or the First Epistle of Peter, as well as parts of the Pauline Epistles, present family and community models that are either based on, or correspond to, the structure of a typical Hellenistic-Roman household. In order to understand the manner in which these letters conceptualize an ideal community, it is imperative to examine the private life of a household. In ancient times, there existed specific ideals regarding the composition of a household. However, the family and household model in the Hellenistic-Roman world cannot be seen solely as a structure of order. For example, the world of thought of Dion of Prusa (also called Dion Chrysostomos), an ancient rhetorician and philosopher who lived around 40–120 CE, shows that it was seen not only as a principle of order anchored in nature, but also as a model according to which state structures could be organized. It is therefore not surprising that, at least in some parts of early Christianity, the model of an ideal household was seen as a model for the organizational structure of an ideal community.

Paterfamilias, Marriage and the Ideal of a Household

The ideal framework of the household (based on literary sources) was hierarchical and divided into public and nonpublic spaces. The father was the head of the household. Roman law established that the *paterfamilias* possessed *patria potestas*, which meant he could issue law-like regulations within the household that were binding for all family members.[1] The father also had the right to approve or reject children within his own household. Despite the fact that women in antiquity possessed at least some rights to act independently, ancient society remained fundamentally patriarchal. This is evidenced by the role of the *paterfamilias*. They exercised exclusive authority over the composition of their household, determining who belonged to it based on criteria that fell outside the purview of birth. Symbolically, accepting the newborn was done by taking the child in his arms after birth.[2] The *paterfamilias* also played an important role in *consensus* marriages, in which the bride and groom expressed their consent to the marriage (consensus), through the *patria potestas*. The authority was hereditary and usually passed to the eldest son, who became the head of the family when the father died. According to Roman law, there were two forms of marriage. The first form was contracted with *manus* (authority), while the second was contracted without *manus*. In the case of marriage with *manus*, the woman came under the legal authority (*manus*) of her husband or his family head. Without *manus*, according to Roman law, the bride could remain under the *patria potestas* of her father, but in a *manus* marriage she was usually moved to a new household and was under the *patria potestas* of her husband.[3]

Marriage law in the Roman Empire, however, was not uniform. In many provinces there were various kinds of legal forms for marriage depending on the citizenship of the bride and groom. This led to inconsistent rules and ideas in the ancient Mediterranean world. In addition, the majority of marriages were entered into informally, that is without a written contract or legal procedure. Nevertheless, household structures and ideals tended to follow similar patterns throughout the Roman Empire., People who could not legally marry lived together in a form of marriage known as concubinage, which closely resembled the structures of a household.[4] Following a year of unmarried cohabitation, the legal status of this union was recognized by law. An examination of matrimonial law reveals that people in ancient times held divergent perspectives on the concepts of childhood and adolescence than in modern times. This is particularly evident in light of the considerably lower life expectancy during that time, which resulted in the commencement of adulthood occurring much earlier than in contemporary times. According to Roman law, individuals were considered adults as soon as they reached puberty, at which point they could enter into legal matrimony. According to Roman law, boys could marry at the age of fourteen and girls at the age of twelve.[5]

From this age on, young men could also take over the management of a household. They could exercise the *patria potestas* and represent a family in public. The function of a household and the objective of private life were predicated on procreation. Offspring was of enormous importance to the ideal of a household. This notion was not merely a subject of discourse in ideal household descriptions; it was also a component of legal texts. The evolution of Roman law, inextricably linked to the transformation of social structures, also influenced the organization of private life within the domestic sphere. The legal framework for women with Roman citizenship also changed during the imperial period, when the *Lex Iulia et Papia* introduced the "three child law." The law was designed to establish incentives for families to procreate. Consequently, it naturally gave rise to budgetary ramifications, as it placed a premium on the ideal of the family. This law granted women with Roman citizenship certain special rights and business powers. This allowed them to manage their own legal and business affairs without a male guardian. Men with the *ius trium liberorum* were also able to rise more easily in the ranks of the Roman Empire. Families, likewise, were also granted special social rights.

The Augustan marriage laws also introduced the obligation for all Roman citizens to marry.[6] The *Lex Iulia de maritandis ordinibus* (18 BCE) and the *Lex Papia Poppaea* (CE 9) required unmarried women between the ages of twenty and fifty and unmarried men between the ages of twenty-five and sixty to remarry.[7] The period for remarriage, which was one year according to the *Lex Iulia*, was extended to two years by the *Lex Papia*. Suetonius also reports a relaxation of the law, suggesting a divergence between the legal norm, legal practice, and the reality of everyday private life. We can speculate whether the demands were realistic, but the pressures of the legal situation were also reflected in Hellenistic-Roman literature. The ideal of marriage was widespread in philosophy, literature, and historiography. Documentary papyri also attest to the abandonment of children to increase the chances of widowed women remarrying, although this was not solely due to the social pressure to remarry.[8] Infant abandonment was a common practice in the Roman Empire when offspring could threaten the economic survival of the family.[9] Such cases were so common that they became a legal practice in the Roman Empire. Infants taken from garbage dumps and brought into a new household were considered unfree and counted as slaves within that household.[10] Therefore, it is difficult to compare a household in the Roman Empire to the modern conception of the family. Rather, the Roman household was best understood as an economic network.[11]

Household Structures, Gender Roles and Roman Law

The subject of private life and household structures is inherently intertwined with the study of gender perceptions in ancient times. These perceptions were intricately woven into the very fabric of household structures, profoundly influencing their hierarchical organization of private life. Responsibilities in the household were divided according to gender. The man's role included representing the house in public and ensuring its stability. He was also responsible for managing the household's financial and legal affairs and representing the family in court.[12] Women, by contrast, were mainly responsible for the private, domestic sphere. Nevertheless, there were also opportunities for women to be active in public. However, the structures of a household touch on the legal regulations for the rights and duties of men and women. A thorough examination of the ideal household reveals that this subject is intricately linked with gender roles, as evidenced by its presence in Hellenistic literature and legal documents. These norms wielded such influence that they permeated the organizational framework of private life.

The legal framework also reflected the authority of the *patria potestas*, for under Roman law, women could not conduct business without the consent of their husband, a male relative, or a tutor. Accordingly, a woman required the authorization of the household's *patria potestas* or a representative, at least. However, the areas of law and everyday practice in the provinces differed in this respect, as different legal practices existed in parallel with the ancient Mediterranean. Women in the Egyptian province, for example, had more legal authority than women subject to Greek and Roman law. Documentary papyri on Egyptian law also suggest that women were able to conduct business independently in everyday life.[13] Even within Roman law itself, the function of the tutor seems to have been primarily a formality in many cases. However, this should not obscure the fundamentally patriarchal character of the Roman Empire and its provinces. Still, women certainly found ways to act within the legal framework of a patriarchal society. Under certain circumstances, they also had access to education, although the *paterfamilias* usually provided the framework for this. In Hellenistic-Roman literature, for example, the ideal that a woman should be educated but should exercise restraint and humility so as not to interfere with men's public activities is widespread.[14] The same is true of the ideal of beauty, which women should use with moderation and purpose. Both ideals are also found in biblical literature, especially in the Pastoral Epistles. In keeping with the division of roles between men and women in the ideal household, stereotypes of masculinity and femininity manifested themselves in the Hellenistic-Roman world. For example, women were seen as inherently weak, both physically and in their ability to manage their financial affairs. The ideal of male honor implied a man's obligation to stand up for the weaker and for women.[15] Such an understanding of roles can be found not only in household descriptions, but also in the formulaic language of Hellenistic-Roman administration. Official petitions to public officials often spoke of their benevolence and kindness, which was especially evident in their attention to weak and needy women. These were ideals that only partially corresponded to reality. Accordingly, the documentary papyri also contain evidence of strong and capable women who used the stereotype of the weak woman to their advantage in order to further their personal and business interests.

Slaves in Households

It is important to note that enslaved individuals were also members of households. At this juncture, it is imperative to acknowledge that slavery stands as one of the darkest chapters in human history. Even within the New Testament's perspectives on the social dynamics among Jesus followers, their role within households, and their private lives, it becomes evident that early Christianity did not contest the institution of slavery at all. It was accepted by early Christians as a norm because it was part of the prevailing culture. The fact that Christianity encompassed both Christian slaves and Christian slave owners is a testament to the pervasive nature of this institution. A critical examination reveals an absence of any discernible opposition to slavery within the corpus of ancient Christianity. From a contemporary perspective, this apparent acceptance of slavery must be regarded as a clear form of structural violence.

A thorough examination of the phenomenon of slavery is imperative for a comprehensive understanding of the ideal household structure within the context of the Roman Empire. The presence of slaves within households was indicative of affluence, as they were a valuable asset. However, it is important to note that not all households in the Roman Empire and its provinces possessed slaves. Instead, they were regarded as a luxury good. Their acquisition was costly, but if a family possessed the necessary resources, slaves belonged to their property. In the household, they were subject to the *paterfamilias*, but supervision of the unfree was the responsibility of the women of the house. According to Roman law, the slaves of the household were not considered people, but were treated as property belonging to the household. Their masters also owned their right to life.

The concept of *patria potestas* did not remain confined to familial relations. Instead, it was expanded to encompass the authority over the life and death of slaves. The legal framework of Roman law governing injuries to slaves explicitly acknowledges their status as property of the household, thereby underscoring the comprehensive nature of the *patria potestas*.[16]

Mistreatment of foreign slaves was considered by the courts to be damage to property of the household. Although documentary papyri and medical sources repeatedly report massive mistreatment of enslaved people, such behavior was considered only to be uneconomical, as slaves were considered a financial investment.[17] The ideal of a *paterfamilias* entailed the adept management of his household, ensuring the financial stability and well-being of his family. The ideal *paterfamilias* was expected to maintain his household in an economically good manner. Given the significant role of slaves within households, whether as laborers, educators, or primary domestic helpers, the infliction of excessive violence upon them was perceived as a sign of weakness on the part of the *paterfamilias*. Such actions were, in effect, self-destructive, as the *paterfamilias* was effectively damaging his own property. This perspective is particularly evident in Stoic literature. While these texts do not explicitly advocate for the gentle treatment of slaves, they do highlight the shortcomings of slaveholders who, from the perspective of Stoic philosophy,[18] are derelict in their paternal duties.

Of course, the question thus arises as to how enslaved individuals came to be present within households. Given the perception of slaves as property, their acquisition was facilitated through transactions at designated slave markets. An examination of ancient sales contracts reveals a clear delineation of this practice. These documents meticulously delineate the attributes of the enslaved individuals, enumerating their capabilities, physical state, and any perceived deficiencies. Failure to do so could result in claims for damages, which were codified in the Roman legal system. Individuals who had been captured in armed conflicts or were the victims of human trafficking often found themselves in the context of slave markets. However, from a historical perspective, a different route into slavery holds particular significance within the context of ancient households: Sexual reproduction within households led to the acquisition of new slaves. Roman law stipulated these cases in concise terms, thereby indicating that this was a prevalent practice within households in the Roman Empire. Owners had the right to regulate the sexual contacts of their unfree slaves. In fact, it was legally permissible for the *paterfamilias* to have offspring with female slaves who were born unfree and assigned to the household. In households, the offspring of the *paterfamilias* and slaves often grew up alongside the other children of the household, even if they were not considered free.[19] Texts such as the First Epistle of Peter show that household slaves could also be part of a Christian community. Although they usually belonged to the cult of their owner or *paterfamilias*, they were free to participate in Christian worship, given there is evidence found across a range of early Christian sources. Such sources include the correspondence between Pliny the Younger (ca. 61/62–113/15), then governor of the Roman province of Bithynia, and Emperor Trajan, revealing that slaves could take on roles beyond those strictly defined by their owner's household.[20]

TAKING A CLOSER LOOK: SOURCES

Sources from the World of the New Testament

Seneca's Critique of His Father

> If only the most exemplary of men, my father, less inclined to adhere to the traditions of his forefathers, had desired for you to be educated in accordance with the tenets of wisdom rather than merely initiated. It was no longer necessary to resist fate; rather, one had to act in

> accordance with it. As a result of the women who do not engage with science for the sake of wisdom but rather equip themselves with it for an elevated lifestyle, he has permitted you to devote only a limited amount of time to studies. (*Ad Helv.*, 17.4)[21]

In *Ad Helviam* 17.4, the Roman politician and Stoic philosopher Seneca (ca. 1–65 CE) offers a critique of his father's decision to deny his mother, Helvia, an extensive educational opportunity.[22] Seneca's argument for the education of women does not entail the abolition of existing gender roles. Rather, he views education as a fundamental necessity for women to be able to fulfill the roles in society that are traditionally associated with their gender. It is imperative that education not result in the arrogance of women. It is not the role of women to compete with men; rather, they should exemplify humility and restraint within the domestic sphere. Seneca assigns the decision regarding a woman's education to the man. In this way, he presents himself as the *paterfamilias*, the individual with the authority to determine the future of the woman. Musonius Rufus promotes a comparable stance to that of Seneca on this matter. Since men and women should cultivate the virtues that are characteristic of their gender in the same manner, and since education is a crucial precursor to this, he advocates for the provision of equal educational opportunities for both genders.[23] Additionally, he does not challenge the established norms.

Musonius on Female Education

> Above all, we ought to examine the doctrine which we think women who study philosophy ought to follow; we ought to see if the study which presents modesty as the greatest good can make them presumptuous, if the study which is a guide to the greatest self-restraint accustoms them to live heedlessly, if what sets forth intemperance as the greatest evil does not teach self-control, if what represents the management of a household as a virtue does not impel them to manage well their homes. Finally, the teachings of philosophy exhort the woman to be content with her lot and to work with her own hands. (*Discourses* 3)[24]

While Musonius, the Stoic philosopher, (ca. 30–101/102 CE) asserts that virtue for men consists in living as good citizens and acting in public, he maintains that women should fulfill their tasks in the private sphere within the framework of their household in an appropriate manner.[25] A clear gender-specific separation between a public and nonpublic sphere can be observed in Musonius's work. In alignment with the philosophical ideal of education, he confines the sphere of activity of women to the public domain of the household. Similarly, Musonius aligns with the conventional delineation of roles between men and women, thereby reinforcing the pervasive stereotypes associated with masculinity and femininity.[26] The Stoic is convinced that, given the fundamental strength of the male constitution in comparison to that of the female, "tasks should be assigned which are suited to the nature of each." This stereotypical view of femininity is reflected in numerous aspects of Roman legal norms. This also provides an explanation as to why women required the presence of a male representative when engaged in public duties. The source illustrates the tenuousness of the boundary between philosophical ideal and legal norm in the ancient Mediterranean. However, since all human tasks represent a common obligation and apply equally to both sexes, Musonius does not exclude the possibility that men may perform women's tasks and women may perform men's tasks if their physical constitution and the given circumstances so require. By referencing the human constitution, Musonius challenges the gender stereotypes embedded in the dominant gender roles to a certain extent.[27] In essence, the potential for women to engage in activities aligns with the evidence presented in documentary papyri, which often describe female endeavors in the nonpublic domain in conjunction with a specific skill. This illustrates that there were, at times, significant discrepancies between the ideal, the legal norm, and everyday practice. Nevertheless, it would be inaccurate to assume that Musonius questions or even relativizes gender-specific differences. In contrast, he elsewhere urges people to live in accordance with their gender when he censures men who shave their beards, which he regards as "nature's symbol of the male."[28]

Dion Chrysostom's Ideal Description of a Household as a Model for the Organization of a Polis

> We proceeded to enter the domicile and subsequently engaged in leisure activities for the remainder of the day. The men were situated on a raised platform of leaves and furs. The woman was situated in close proximity to her husband. A daughter provided us with service and poured us wine. The sons prepared the meat, which they then placed before us and consumed with us. I postulated that these individuals exhibited a greater degree of happiness than any other group with whom I had been acquainted. I had previously been a guest in the homes of affluent individuals, including those occupying positions of authority such as governors and kings. If they had seemed unhappy to me before, they seemed even more so now that I saw the poverty and independence of these people, that they lacked nothing in the joy of eating and drinking, indeed in this they were almost a little ahead of the rich. We were almost full when the brother arrived. He was followed by his son, a

> handsome boy with a hare in his hand. He blushed as he entered, and while his father greeted us, he kissed the girl and gave her the rabbit. The daughter stopped serving us and sat down next to her mother, and the boy replaced her. I asked our host if it was she from whom he had taken the skirt to give to the shipwrecked man. Laughing, he replied: "No, she's long married and has grown children with a wealthy man in the village."[29]

In his Euboean oration, the Cynic philosopher Dion Chrysostom, also known as Dion of Prusa (ca. 40–120 CE) offers a critique of the shortcomings of polis culture—that is, the culture of the ancient city—by delineating an idealized household. In this context, the women are tasked with managing the household. The huntsman is the primary authority figure within the family, responsible for maintaining a positive public image. This explains why he appears as the family's representative at the town meeting, while his wife and daughters remain at home. This distinction between the public and the domestic sphere is a defining feature of Mediterranean societies and is also mirrored in the legal system of the Roman Empire.

Dion also makes a remark regarding the role of women: The wife is positioned in the background, while the sons consume their food with the other men. The daughters subsequently enter the narrative and are obliged to serve the men. Dion states that the daughters are young and marriageable. In this way, he presents an idealized representation of women in Roman antiquity. Dion's portrayal reflects the typical characteristics of ideal womanhood in antiquity. As the narrative unfolds, we discover that one daughter is already married and has children; her husband is described as affluent. Dion suggests that a favorable marital union is one that produces progeny and provides sufficient livelihood. Within the household, a distinction can be made between its internal and external dimensions. The ideal husband is expected to fulfill three primary roles: representation, protection, and provision for the household. The ideal wife, in turn, provides progeny and stability within the domestic sphere. The other daughter will marry a man of limited financial means, but who is, however, proficient in hunting—thus, ensuring the continued well-being of the family unit.

Reading the New Testament Texts

Women and Silence

> As in all the churches of the saints, women should be silent in the churches. For they are not permitted to speak but should be subordinate,

> as the law also says. If there is something they want to learn, let them ask their husbands at home. For it is shameful for a woman to speak in church. (1 Cor 14:33–35)

Researchers debate whether this passage goes back to Paul or whether it is a post-Pauline interpolation.[30] However, if one assumes Pauline origins, it can be assumed that Paul is not formulating a general ban on women speaking here, but is merely trying to prevent disruptive questions from female members of the *ekklēsia* (that is, the Christian community) that would jeopardize the order of the meeting.[31] This could also be explained through the lens of ancient educational ideals and household norms, insofar as women should present their education in such a way that it did not challenge male authority in the public sphere. The fact that Paul did not intend a general ban on women speaking is suggested by 1 Corinthians 11:5, where he presupposes that women pray and prophesy publicly, and also by the list of greetings at the end of the Epistle to the Romans (Rom 16:1–6).[32] Paul's comments show that women were not only naturally part of the ecclesia but were also involved in missionary work and took on ecclesial leadership roles.[33] Paul therefore seems to have established a form of "female empowerment" that was unusual in the ancient world, particularly as a means of ensuring missionary work and the effective functioning of ecclesial life. Nevertheless, Paul continued to operate within the existing framework of ancient gender roles. Even if women were allowed to speak prophetically in the assembly and take on leadership functions, their fate remained, similarly to the ideas of the Stoics, in male hands.

The Ideal Household and the Limits of Pastoral Epistles

> Also that the women should dress themselves in moderate clothing with reverence and self-control, not with their hair braided or with gold, pearls, or expensive clothes, but with good works, as is proper for women who profess reverence for God. Let a woman learn in silence with full submission. I do not permit a woman to teach or to have authority over a man, she is to keep silent. For Adam was formed first, then Eve, and Adam was not deceived, but the woman was deceived and became a transgressor. Yet she will be saved through childbearing, provided they continue in faith and love and holiness, with self-control. (1 Tim 2:9–15)

The Pastoral Epistles aim to present the early Christian communities as an integral part of society, which should not stand out from the social environment.[34] This explains why the description of an ideal Christian community in 1 Timothy 2 begins with a prayer addressed not only to all men, but also explicitly to the political leaders whose authority has been acknowledged (1 Tim 2:1–2). The undertone is that a peaceful life is sought for the followers of Christ. 1 Timothy 2:8–15 goes on and describes the roles of men and women in the church. The text reflects both the distinction between the public and public realm found in Seneca, Musonius, Epictetus, and Dion of Prusa, as well as in the Stoic ideal of womanhood. Men are given the role of public speaking. According to 1 Timothy 2–3, men have the right to organize and lead the community. Women, however, are defined in relation to their husbands, as one can see in Dion's description of a household. On the one hand, women are expected to be modest in their outward dress and to refrain from wearing elaborate hairstyles and expensive jewelry. On the other hand, 1 Timothy 2:11–12 emphasizes that a woman is not allowed to teach in the church. In this regard, the Pastoral Epistles do not differ from gender ideals of the Mediterranean in antiquity. The middle Platonist philosopher, historian, and priest of Apollo Plutarch (ca. 45–125 CE) also describes the ideal woman as outwardly beautiful, but not provocative in public, so as not to disturb men in the performance of their duties. As with the Stoics, the ideal woman was to be educated, but without compromising her husband's role. The educational ideal of the imperial Stoics, that educated women should also exercise restraint, seems tacitly adopted here. The strategy of the Pastoral Epistles is one of adaptation rather than demarcation, which is why the ideals of the environment are taken up and mirrored. For this very reason, it can be assumed that the world behind the text had different realities than the ideals suggest. Presumably, the hierarchies depicted in 1 Timothy 2–3 were not as pronounced in reality as the text would have liked. A reading of 1 Timothy 2:11–12 leads to the conclusion that there must have been women in leadership positions in the churches otherwise the prohibitions in this text would be incomprehensible.

Household, Subordination, and Politics in 1 Peter

> Wives, in the same way, be subject to your husbands, so that, even if some of them do not obey the word, they may be won over without a word by their wives' conduct, when they see the purity and respect of your conduct. Do not adorn yourselves outwardly by braiding your hair and by wearing gold ornaments or fine clothing; rather, let your adornment be the inner self with the lasting beauty of a gentle and quiet spirit, which is very precious in God's sight. It was in this way long ago that the holy women who hoped in God used to adorn themselves by being subject to their husbands. Thus Sarah obeyed Abraham and called him lord. You have become her daughters as long as you do what is good and never let fears alarm you. Husbands, in the same way, show consideration for your wives in your life together, paying honor to the

> woman—though the weaker vessel, they are joint heirs of the gracious gift of life—so that nothing may hinder your prayers. (1 Peter 3:1–7)

The family model presented in 1 Peter is an essential component of the writer's political philosophy and strategy of adaptation and cultural integration. Similar to Dion's Euboean oration (see above), the First Epistle of Peter also interweaves perspectives on the cosmos, the natural order, and social structures with the idea of a household.[35] 1 Peter says that the structures of power in a Hellenistic-Roman city-state are divinely ordered (1 Pet 2:13–17). Submitting to these structures of *polis* and empire is described as freedom. Like the Stoic idea of freedom, 1 Peter's main idea of freedom is subordination, which the text demonstrates with many examples.[36] 1 Peter 2:18–25 refers to house slaves and 1 Peter 3:1–7 to marriage. The subordination of women in marriage shows that a Christian lifestyle aligns with Hellenistic-Roman ideals. As in 1 Timothy 2, there is a call for women to be modest. This reflects the broader ideal for women in Hellenistic-Roman literature. Dion also describes virtues like modesty, restraint, and humility in his account of the hunter's household, qualities that align with mentioned by authors such as a Stoic philosopher Epictetus (ca. 50–138 CE), Seneca, and Musonius. Similarly, 1 Peter 3:7 says that it is the role of men to protect, reflecting the broader Greco-Roman ideal. In this framework, traditional gender roles include not only female subordination but also consideration for women.

FURTHER READING

Hersch, Karen K. *The Roman Wedding: Ritual and Meaning in Antiquity*. Cambridge University Press, 2010.

Kreinecker, Christina. "Zum Alltagsleben von Frauen in neutestamentlicher Zeit anhand dokumentarischer Papyri." In *Frauen im antiken Judentum und frühen Christentum*, edited by Jörg Frey and Nicole Rupschus. Wissenschaftliche Untersuchungen zum Neuen Testament II/489. Mohr Siebeck, 2019.

Nussbaum, Martha C., and Juha Sihvola, eds. *The Sleep of Reason. Erotic Experience and Sexual Ethics in Ancient Greece and Rome*. University of Chicago Press, 2002.

Sommer, Michael. "Sharp Contrasts? 1 Timothy 5 and Roman-Hellenistic Stereotypes on Widows." In *Reading Women in the New Testament Letters*, edited by Korinna Zamfir and Uta Poplutz. The Bible and Women 2.2. SBL, 2024.

Notes

1 *Res Gestae Divi Augusti* 50.16; 195.2. Cf. Christina Urban, "Die Rollen der Familienmitglieder," in *Neues Testament und Antike Kultur. Band 2: Familie—Gesellschaft—Wirtschaft*, ed. Klaus Scherberich (Neukirchener Theologie, 2011), 17–21, (18).

2 Annika Backe-Dahmen, *Die Welt der Kinder in der Antike* (von Zabern, 2008), 23.

3 Arnold Angenendt, *Ehe, Liebe und Sexualität im Christentum* (Aschendorff Verlag, 2015), 42.

4 Angenendt, *Ehe, Liebe und Sexualität*, 45.

5 Cf. Angenendt, *Ehe, Liebe und Sexualität*, 43; Karen K. Hersch, *The Roman Wedding: Ritual and Meaning in Antiquity* (Cambridge University Press, 2010), 15–61.

6 Further, Anna McCullough, "One Wife, One Love: Coniugalis Amor, Grief and Masculinity in Statius' Silvae," in *Emotion, Genre and Gender in Classical Antiquity*, ed. Dana LaCourse Munteanu (Bloomsbury Publishing, 2011), 176–77. For more on the marriage laws, see Angelika Mette-Dittmann, *Die Ehegesetze des Augustus. Eine Untersuchung im Rahmen der Gesellschaftspolitik des Princeps* (Franz Steiner Verlag, 1991), 131–98.

7 *Tituli ex corpore Ulpiani* 16.1.

8 Cf. Michael Sommer, "Sharp Contrasts? 1 Timothy 5 and Roman-Hellenistic Stereotypes on Widows," in *Reading Women in the New Testament Letters*, ed. Korinna Zamfir and Uta Poplutz, The Bible and Women 2.2 (SBL, 2024), 179–98.

9 Cf. Sommer, "Sharp Contrasts," 184.

10 Cf. Josef Fischer, *Sklaverei* (wbg Academic, 2018), 119–20.

11 Cf. Urban, "Die Rollen der Familienmitglieder," 17.

12 Cf. Thomas Späth, "Performanz, Geschlecht—und die Antike," in *Das Geschlecht in der Antike: Zur Interdependenz von Antike und Geschlechterkonstruktionen von 1700 bis zur Gegenwart*, ed. Anna Heinze and Friederike Krippner (Wilhelm Fink, 2014), 19–40, 25.

13 For more details, Christina Kreinecker, "Zum Alltagsleben von Frauen in neutestamentlicher Zeit anhand dokumentarischer Papyri," in *Frauen im antiken Judentum und frühen Christentum*, ed. Jörg Frey and Nicole Rupschus, Wissenschaftliche Untersuchungen zum Neuen Testament II 489 (Mohr Siebeck, 2019), 129–50.

14 Cf. Katharina Greschat, *Gelehrte Frauen des frühen Christentums* (Hiersemann, 2015), 5.

15 Cf. Sommer, "Sharp Contrasts," 190–93.

16 Cf. Fischer, *Sklaverei*, 24–30.

17 Cf. Heinz Heinen, "Kindersklaven—Sklavenkinder im Rahmen des Mainzer Sklavereiprojekts. Forschungen, Themen, Texte," in *Kindersklaven—Sklavenkinder: Schicksale zwischen Zuneigung und Ausbeutung in der Antike und im interkulturellen Vergleich*, ed. Heinz Heinen, Forschungen zur antiken Sklaverei 39 (Franz Steiner Verlag, 2012), 1–42; Fischer, *Sklaverei*, 127.

18 See the chapter on "Philosophical Schools and Ideas" by Johan Thom in the present volume.

19 Cf. Fischer, *Sklaverei*, 116–20.

20 *Epistulae* 10.96.

21 Author's translation based on the Latin text of the edition of Manfred Rosenbach. Cf. Lucius Annaeus Seneca, *Philosophische Schriften. Lateinisch und Deutsch.* Zweiter Band: Dialoge VII–XII., ed. and trans. Manfred Rosenbach, 2nd ed. (WBG, 2011).

22 See also Franz Loretto, "Das Bild der Frau in Senecas philosophischen Schriften," *Ziva Antika* 27, no. 1 (1977): 119–28, here 125.

23 See Lisa Hill, "The First Wave of Feminism: Were the Stoics Feminists?" *History of Political Thought* 22, no. 1 (2001): 13–40 (19–20). In addition, see Martha C. Nussbaum, "The Incomplete Feminism of Musonius Rufus, Platonist, Stoic, and Roman," in *The Sleep of Reason: Erotic Experience and Sexual Ethics in Ancient Greece and Rome*, ed. Martha C. Nussbaum and Juha Sihvola (University of Chicago Press, 2002); Mercedes Mauch, *Seneca's Frauenbild in den philosophischen Schriften*, Studien zur klassischen Philologie 106 (Peter Lang, 1997), 17.

24 All quoted passages of Musonius follow the translation of Cora E. Lutz, "Musonius Rufus 'The Roman Socrates,'" in *Yale Classical Studies*, vol. 10 (Yale University Press, 1947).

25 *Disc.* 4.

26 For this, see the chapter on "Masculinity and Gender" by Lily C. Vuong in the present volume.

27 *Disc.* 4. See also Lothar Willms, "L'école des hommes: Geschlechter, Zeichen, Raum und Lehre bei Epiktet," *Wiener Studien* 124 (2011): 55–93 (89); Gretchen Reydams-Schils, *The Roman Stoics. Self, Responsibility, and Affection* (University of Chicago Press, 2005), 155.

28 *Disc.* 21. See Marcel Friesen, "Das lange Haar in 1 Kor 11,14–15a: Reevaluation der paulinischen Argumentation im Kontext antiker Haarmode und populärer Naturphilosophie," *Biblische Zeitschrift* 62, no. 2 (2018): 270–89 (279).

29 Dion, *Discourses*, 7.66–68. The translation of Dion is based on Winfried Ellinger, ed., *Dion Chrysostomos, Sämtliche Reden* (Artemis Verlag, 1967).

30 See, Armin D. Baum, "Paul's Conflicting Statements on Female Public Speaking (1 Cor. 11:5) and Silence (1 Cor. 14.34–35). A New Suggestion," *Tyndale Bulletin* 65, no. 2 (2014): 247–74, (248–51); Jill E. Marshall, *Women Praying and Prophesying in Corinth: Gender and Inspired Speech in First Corinthians*, Wissenschaftliche Untersuchungen zum Neuen Testament II/448 (Mohr Siebeck, 2017), 203–12.

31 Cf. Mira Stare, "'Der Prophezeiende aber erbaut die Gemeinde' (1 Kor 14,4b): Prophetisches Reden in der Gemeinde nach 1 Kor 11–14," *Protokolle zur Bibel*24, no. 2 (2015): 118–33 (131).

32 See Barbara Lumesberger-Loisl and Andrea Taschl-Erber, *Redeverbot für Frauen bei Paulus? Die Macht der Rezeption*, Wort-Schatz Bibel (Graz University Library Publishing, 2021), 10; Johanna Körner, *Sexualität und Geschlecht bei Paulus: Die Spannung zwischen „Inklusivität" und „Exklusivität" des paulinischen Ethos am Beispiel der Sexual- und Geschlechterrollenethik*, Wissenschaftliche Untersuchungen zum Neuen Testament II/512 (Mohr Siebeck, 2020), 278–87; Wayne A. Meeks, "The Image of the Androgyne: Some Uses of a Symbol in Earliest Christianity," *History of Religions* 13, no. 3 (1974): 197–98.

33 Cf. Sabine Bieberstein, "Die Frau rede in der Gemeinde! Frauen in der Jesusbewegung und in den frühen Gemeinden," *Bibel und Kirche* 4, no. 10 (2010): 202–3; Meeks, "Image of the Androgyne," 197–98; Lumesberger-Loisl and Taschl-Erber, *Redeverbot für Frauen*, 10.

34 Korinna Zamfir, *Men and Women in the Household of God: A Contextual Approach to Roles and Ministries in the Pastoral Epistles*, Novum Testamentum et Orbis Antiquus / Studien zur Umwelt des Neuen Testaments 103 (Vandenhoeck & Ruprecht, 2013).

35 For more detail, see Michael Sommer, "Fremde und Fremdheit im ersten Petrusbrief und bei Dion Chrysostomos, Gedanken eines Kynikers als Lektürehilfe für die Theologie von 1 Petrus," *Biblica* 104, no. 3 (2023): 426–48.

36 See Reinhard Feldmeier, "Basis des Kontakts unter Christen. Demut als Schlüsselbegriff der Ethik des Ersten Petrusbriefes," in *Bedrängnis und Identität. Studien zu Situation, Kommunikation und Theologie des 1. Petrusbriefes*, ed. David S. Du Toit, Beihefte zur Zeitschrift für die neutestamentliche Wissenschaft 200 (de Gruyter, 2013), 249–62.

CHAPTER NINE

Social Status and Relations in Civic Life

Susan Hylen
(Emory University)

AMONG THE FORCES that shaped ancient social life, the pursuit of status was one of the most important. Mediterranean cultures of the New Testament period were hierarchically structured and highly status conscious. In any social interaction, individuals sought to recognize status differences between those involved and to respond appropriately. Deference was due to those of higher status, and social norms created patterns of interaction that acknowledged and reinforced status.

Cities also competed with one another for honor. Rome was the most powerful city of the time, and its military success brought wealth and power. But cities across the Mediterranean sought to increase their relative standing by improving or adding to their temples and other monumental structures or by seeking the favor of the Roman authorities. Thus, both individuals and groups participated in competition for status.

Understanding how people of the time assigned value, and how these determinations shaped social interactions can be useful for the interpretation of New Testament texts. There are many ancient sources to which historians turn to better comprehend these dynamics. Literary sources (philosophical, historical, and narrative writings), largely authored by elite men, give a sense of the actions of the powerful, but they can also point us to values they assumed were widely shared.[1] Inscriptions, carved in stone to dedicate ancient buildings, statues, or burial sites, were themselves a tangible form of honor, contributing status to those named.[2] Papyrus fragments often give a sense of everyday life—receipts, legal documents, and so forth—and can help us understand the lives of nonelites.[3] Each kind of evidence provides a different angle of vision, but together they can help us see how social interactions were shaped by the pursuit of status.

Calculations of Status

Calculating a person's overall standing involved a complex combination of factors. One's family of origin, wealth, and gender were important, along with freeborn, freed, or enslaved status. Occupation, age, and perceived virtue also factored into the estimation of social rank. Being a citizen of an important city brought honor as well. Citizenship was granted to those born to citizen parents and was also bestowed upon enslaved people if they were manumitted. Rome honored individuals in distant cities by granting them Roman citizenship, often a reward for cooperation with Rome's interests.

People of the time were adept at picking up social cues, assessing the status of an individual they interacted with, and responding in appropriate ways. One's social status was always relative to that of other people, and so it was calculated in context, depending on who else was present. A young freeborn man, for example, might assert his authority over enslaved members of the household or freed men with whom he did business. Yet visiting a neighbor's dinner party, he might find himself to be of low status relative to other guests—perhaps because they were older than he, somewhat wealthier, or more prominent in business or politics. People moved fluidly between various contexts and altered their behavior in response to these considerations. Misreading the situation or responding as if one had greater status relative to the others involved when that was not the case brought dishonor.

Moreover, of the elements of social status listed above, no single factor was most important. Although as a general rule men had higher standing than women, a wealthy freeborn woman had greater status than a lower-class freeborn man, along with other freed and enslaved men.[4] Similarly, freeborn people had higher rank than freed or enslaved persons, but an enslaved man who was part of an elite household might have significant wealth and authority due to his position and could even rival in status other freeborn men and women. Someone from a prominent family whose wealth had declined might in some contexts be similar in status to a rich and well-connected freedman. The possibilities and variations were almost endless.

Thus, although cultures of the time clearly valued men over women, freeborn over enslaved, families of long-held status over the newly wealthy, and so forth, in practice the determination of rank was complicated. It was not the case that all men had authority over all women, for example, or that enslaved men and women never had greater standing than the freeborn. Other factors and the individual's rank relative to others in their immediate context meant that even those in a less valorized category might still operate with high standing in many situations.

The variability in these factors determining rank was also a reason that people of the time could change status during their lives. Some people's status increased over time: For example, an enslaved person might be manumitted; Freeborn women displayed "manly" virtues through their bold actions on behalf of others; Or one's family might become wealthier through new business ventures and connections. On the other hand, some people's standing decreased through loss of wealth or through behaviors deemed dishonorable. These were not simply changes in individual circumstances but had real effects on social interactions.

Although status changes were possible, they happened in specific, structured ways. It was not possible, for instance, for a freed person to become a freeborn person. The formerly enslaved were always tainted by slavery, and even their children born subsequently as freeborn people could always be deemed lesser than those born of freeborn parents. Some social mobility was possible, but the kinds of movement that happened reinforced the power of the elite and freeborn.

Nevertheless, compared to many premodern societies, there was considerable room for change in social rank during the New Testament period. The opportunity for change may be one of the reasons for the relative social and political stability of the period. Some families dropped out of the elite ranks, but social mechanisms existed by which they were replaced.

Political Roles

The highest-ranking citizens competed for political and military positions. In Rome, only members of the senatorial and equestrian classes were eligible to hold office. During the Republican period, these men wielded great authority and competed to achieve and retain the highest offices. By the New Testament period, however, power was concentrated in the hands of the emperor, who appointed elite men to carry out his wishes. Nevertheless, appointment to these posts brought great honor. And provincial governors still exercised political and judicial authority, even if their work was understood as an extension of the emperor's power, not their own.

Although Roman laws governed Roman citizens and its colonies (cities like Corinth and Philippi), in most of the empire, local customs and legal practices were left in place. Cities had their own leaders and court systems, and they oversaw local affairs.[5] They collected local taxes, repaired publicly owned buildings and city streets, and oversaw the marketplace. Thus, the Roman system of government left considerable room for a city's elites to manage regional affairs and shape the life of their city.

Judea was similar to other places Rome ruled in that there was a Roman layer of government alongside local courts and administration. The New Testament often references these varied roles: Roman governors (e.g., Pilate, Matt 15:1; Felix and Festus, Acts 24:27); local rulers (Herod [Antipas], Mark 6:14; Agrippa, Acts 25:13); local councils—in Jerusalem, the Sanhedrin (or council, Mark 15:1); and popular assemblies, called synagogues (John 9:22). (Synagogues were not simply places of worship but had judicial and administrative functions.)[6] The Greek cities to which Paul traveled had similar layers of government: a Roman governor in the provincial capital along with local leaders, assemblies, and courts.

There were democratic elements of city life, but status played an important role even within democratic institutions. Free male citizens were members of the assembly, which elected the city council. The council then oversaw expenditures, set the calendar of religious festivals, and made many other decisions about aspects of local life. But most members of the assembly were not eligible for the council. Local rules stipulated a certain level of wealth and other status markers needed to run for a seat. Town officials were typically chosen from the local elites.[7]

Magistrates and other officials were elected by the town council from the wealthiest ranks of the population. Magistrates had civic and judicial authority, and they presided over the town council and many civic events. This role also required significant personal expenditure. Thus, while it was a political office, it also shared elements of patronage, which are discussed in the next section.

Patronage

Although only a handful of people exercised political power, many individuals shaped the life of their city and gained status through patronage. Patron-client relationships structured many interactions in this period, and they signaled and reinforced the social hierarchy. A patron with higher status provided benefits to the lower-status client, who in turn gave honor to the patron. Patrons might offer loans to a client, provide business connections, or write letters of recommendation when the client traveled to another city. Clients honored patrons by visiting them, showing deference, and other signs of support. Becoming a patron or gaining clients brought honor to the patron and increased their status.

In addition to individual patron-client relationships, some people also served as patrons of cities or civic groups. Although roads and aqueducts were funded by Rome, most of the monumental architecture of the period was built and sustained by individual donors. Patrons erected and renovated theaters, baths, and temples, and paid for the games and festivals that took place there. Many of the advantages of city life were due to the actions of such benefactors. Cities competed for prestige through their temples, festivals, and games, and they sought to attract generous patrons to support civic life.

In return for such gifts, city councils often voted to erect a statue in the patron's honor. The accompanying inscription identified the individual's donations and leadership positions and became a visible recognition of their generosity. Civic honors like these added significantly to the patron's status and thus "repaid" the donation, albeit in a different currency. Many of these inscriptions still exist and are an important source for our understanding of ancient social relations.

Although many of the inscriptions identify very wealthy donors, some sources show that patron-client relations took place among those with lower status as well. In big cities, people often joined forces for a specific purpose by forming associations. Many were neighborhood groups, trade associations, or people devoted to a local deity.[8] Members usually paid dues to achieve the group's goals, but they often had a patron as well, usually someone of higher status than most of the association's members, though not necessarily one of the city's elites. Associations also had officers with titles who led the group. By serving in such roles, nonelites could accrue honor and increase their status.

Less wealthy individuals also contributed to the grand building projects of their city, only in smaller ways than the elites. Some inscriptions display a long list of donors who were credited for relatively small gifts that contributed to the improvement of a building—for example, the installation of a new mosaic floor. Thus, although the wealthiest members of society were honored in grand ways for large donations, those with lower stature also acted as patrons and were honored in similar ways. Social practices of patronage permeated every level of society.

Women served as patrons and competed for honor alongside men, often with the same titles.[9] When other social factors were equal, men had higher status than women simply by virtue of their gender. For this reason, men appear more frequently than women in inscriptions honoring patrons. Nevertheless, understanding that women patrons were not only common but also desirable, pursued by both cities and individuals, helps us better comprehend the social world of the New Testament period.

Patronage was an important form of leadership in Greek and Roman cultures. Cities sought out high status donors not only for monetary gifts but to guide aspects of civic life. Greek titles like *agōnothetēs* (director of the games), *gymnasiarchos* (head of the gymnasium), *stephanophoros* (magistrate), and *hieros* (priest) identified those who supported civic institutions financially but also led them for a period of time. Cities and groups sought out patrons who would contribute not only their money but also their stature, connections, and wisdom to these tasks.

Civic Virtue and Status

Why were people willing to undertake such large gifts, making financial sacrifices to beautify their city or support an association? Certainly, the likelihood of being honored publicly with an inscription was part of the story. But in addition to this, a web of social norms cultivated virtues that supported this kind of political activity and patronage. In addition to factors like wealth and citizenship, being acknowledged as a virtuous person brought honor. And many of the virtues emphasized the individual's willingness to forgo their own needs and act for the sake of their city and family.

A primary virtue of the time, and one that these social norms cluster around, was self-control (*sōphrosynē*). Broadly understood, self-control involved an ability to privilege the needs of one's family or of the wider community over one's own desires or whims. As taught in philosophical schools, it meant the capacity not to be driven by feelings like anger, greed, or sexual desire, but to restrain such desires in order to do what was wise.

As a political virtue, many philosophical teachings and popular stories lauded rulers who had acted on behalf of their people by restraining their desire for vengeance or by not displaying their power through violent action. In a time when great power was concentrated in the emperor, society praised the ruler who did not abuse such power but used it for the good of all.[10] The leader who treated others graciously would be honored by the people and remembered as a virtuous ruler.

Self-control was not only encouraged in the emperor, but in the population more broadly. Acts of civic benefaction were also related to self-control. A wealthy individual who spent lavishly on dinner parties and fancy clothes to display his status might have little left to use for the sake of his city. Curbing one's appetite for luxurious living was an important aspect of self-control, especially in this relatively prosperous era. Civic patronage was thus evidence of one's virtue because it suggested the donor had foregone self-indulgence to act on behalf of the city.

The same social norms supported the civic leadership of women. The Greek word *sōphrosynē* was also used to describe women. Although modern readers often imagine that the expectations of women's self-control created a restrictive environment that prevented them from exercising agency, the reality was more complicated than that.[11] There were certainly gendered aspects to self-control. For women, it could also mean sexual fidelity to one's husband or not adorning oneself with the finest jewels. Yet by acting in these ways, a woman demonstrated that she had the same desired capacity to control the passions and act with the greater good in mind. In doing so, she also displayed the qualifications of a good leader. Many inscriptions honored women for their leadership and for such virtues.

Many literary sources display how elite men jockeyed for status by using their rhetorical skills to praise or disparage the virtue of other men. Elite men might be criticized for sexual self-indulgence, for example, or for paying too much attention to their appearance. Conversely, they might be honored for sacrifices made for the city: monetary gifts but also enduring pain or even death during a military campaign. Whether told as stories of exemplary figures or as cautionary tales for the young of behaviors they should avoid, these writings reinforced agreed-upon social values.

Fewer sources exist to tell us about the social lives of the nonelite. But in Rome, for example, many freed men and women erected burial monuments and inscriptions, often stating their occupations and marital status.[12] These seem to have functioned as markers of respectability for a large group of people whose status would never match that of the elites, but who nevertheless valued the standing they were able to achieve and represented it publicly to others.

In summary, status, virtue, and patronage had a circular relationship. When a person's virtue was openly acknowledged, it brought honor, which increased their status. Having greater status brought additional opportunities for benefaction, and acting in these ways confirmed one's virtue, again increasing status. Similarly, a downward spiral might also ensue for those who lost status through various means. Many signals in the ancient evidence show the importance of status for ancient people and its effects on everyday life.

* * *

Social status and honor were foundational aspects of social and political life in Greek and Roman cities. Social structures encouraged civic-minded leaders and generous donors by repaying such individuals with honor, increasing their status. Playing roles as patrons allowed individuals to move up within the social hierarchy.

Early Christ followers had a new message to offer in their gospel of Jesus the Messiah. As they organized themselves to deliver that message, they drew on social forms that were familiar to them, establishing communities that resembled the local associations of Greek and Roman cities. They also encountered both acceptance and resistance from local power structures, and evidence of these encounters is found in the stories and letters of the New Testament. Recognizing the power of both the political structure and of individuals with higher status can help modern readers better understand many of the writings of the period.

TAKING A CLOSER LOOK: SOURCES

Sources from the World of the New Testament

A wide variety of sources attest to the social patterns described above. Literary sources include information about the governmental functions of elite men and their interactions with patrons and clients. Papyrus records provide glimpses into the official records, such as court and tax documents, of people from a range of class standings. Inscriptions show the public display of honor, and their wording helps us better understand the factors that contributed to social status. These sources reinforce the values that made possible the Roman social and political system.

Seneca the Elder on Political Influence

> Flamininus, when proconsul, was once asked a favor by a whore while dining. She said she had never seen a man's head being cut off. He had a condemned criminal killed. He is accused of lèse-majesté.
>
> ALBUCIUS SILUS: But if anyone, judges, wants me to tell of the praetor's cruelty, how many besides this man he slaughtered, how many innocent men he condemned, how many he shut up in prison, I promise that I shall satisfy such an enquirer: in one party I shall unroll the story of the accused and his praetorship: In his province he organizes a banquet. . . . A man is hauled from the prison and taken to the praetor's party; the whore smiles on the poor dazed wretch. Rods are produced, and the victim of sadism is slaughtered before the table and before the gods. Alas, you have made a game out of the terror inspired by the empire of Rome. In sadistic practices you have surpassed every tyrant! You alone find pleasure at dinner in the groans of the dying; this was the final touch to the feast.
>
> I see reclining together the love-sick praetor, and a whore greedy for a death; the whore rules the praetor, the praetor the province. They place there a man in chains; seeing the drooping eyes of that praetor and thinking that he is being released by his favor, he thanks him. Holding the table in both hands, he says: "May the immortal gods repay you the like!" Of those who sat in the same room, one wept floods of tears with bowed head, another averted his eyes from the cruel sight, a third laughed—to keep in with the whore. Here, amid these different expressions on the faces of the guests, the praetor orders room to be made, orders the wretched man to stand quietly and offer his neck to the blow. Meanwhile the pause is marked by cups of wine. A Roman citizen was killed—and by the hand of an executioner who was not even sober. I don't say that he should not be struck by the axe; but I do ask that he fall victim to the law rather than a prostitute. (*Controv.* 9.2.praef, 6–8)[13]

Many documents attest to the judicial functions of elite men, but the example selected here also addresses the social expectations of leadership. Seneca the Elder's *Controversiae* collected scenarios that elite men would comment upon as they practiced rhetorical skills. In this example, Flamininus, a proconsul, was accused of lèse-majesté, a violation of the dignity of the Roman people, understood as a form of treason.

Seneca's choice of this scenario and the oratorical responses to it (quoted here, one attributed to Albucius Silus) communicate a good deal about Roman norms of good government. As procurator (the Roman provincial governor), Flamininus had authority to sentence criminals to death and carry out their execution. There was no implication that the man he put to death was unjustly condemned. What was offensive to the Roman listener was the idea that Flamininus had exercised state authority to gratify desire—his own and that of a prostitute.

Many similar stories were told in antiquity of powerful men behaving badly at banquets (as an example, recall the biblical story of Esther, in which King Ahasuerus banishes Vashti for her refusal to appear at his banquet [Esth 1]). Banquets involved the display of status—especially for the host, whose lavish meal and entertainment were signs of his social standing. As such, banqueters often got drunk and indulged their sexual desires, and this created the potential for the abuse of power.

Flamininus's situation embodies these difficulties. His order of execution took place at a banquet, where he was imagined to be drunk. As another orator said, "it wasn't even a sober lictor who struck the blow."[14] Flamininus was accused of acting to display his power and thus reinforce his status—not simply to execute justice.

Because the request came from a prostitute, Flamininus was also assumed to be acting in ways controlled by his lust. In the quoted text, Albucius Silus commented that "the whore rules the praetor," suggesting that Flamininus's lust guided the events rather than his reason. Silus did not object to the person's execution but asked "that he fall victim to the law rather than a prostitute."[15] The idea that those in authority should be governed by reason and not by the whims of their passions was consistently stated by many sources of this period. The banquet and the prostitute in the scenario suggested to ancient readers that Flamininus was not in control of the situation but was led by the indulgence of his desires.

The low status of the prostitute was also an issue in the story. Prostitution was legal in the Roman world, but prostitutes occupied the lower ranks of society. An alternate version of the story in which the execution took place as a favor for a high-standing man would not likely have warranted extensive discussion, let alone criminal charges. The quoted paragraph indicates a problem with the prostitute wielding influence over political matters.

Inscription from Corinth Honoring Junia Theodora

> It was decreed by the federal assembly of the Lycians: since Junia Theodora, living in Corinth, a fine and honorable woman and devoted to the

> Lycian nation, has not ceased to show her zeal and generosity towards the nation and is full of good will to all travelers whether private individuals or ambassadors sent by the nation or by various cities, and has procured the gratitude of all of us by assuring the friendship of the authorities which she seeks to win by every means, and making well-disposed her heir Sextus Julius, a Roman, a good man also behaving with surpassing goodwill and with zeal towards our nation, imitating the devotion of Junia towards us which was mentioned above.[16]

This is a portion of one of five inscriptions that honored Junia Theodora for using her social power to assist her people in a time of need. The inscriptions focus on her devotion to her people, evidenced by the help she offered them in a time of need. Welcoming travelers was itself a form of patronage, but Junia went beyond simple hospitality to act as an advocate for the people, using her connections to assist them with a political agenda. In both formal and informal roles, wealthy and well-placed individuals asserted influence over political and judicial affairs.

On Patronage
Inscription from Chios Honoring Claudia Metrodora

Inscriptions honoring patrons are ubiquitous amid the ruins of ancient cities. These notices honored individuals for their leadership and bequests. For the most prominent benefactors, city councils voted to erect a statue and inscription in the town square, a monument that became an enduring sign of the recipient's standing in the community.

> For Claudia Metrodora, daughter of Skytheinos, head of the gymnasium four times who twice distributed oil to the city on the occasion of the festival of the Heraklea games; director three times of the games of the Heraklea Romaia and Kaisareia; queen of the thirteen cities of the Ionian federation, being desirous of glory for the city, a lover of her homeland and priest for life of the divine empress Aphrodite Livia, by reason of her excellence and admirable behavior towards it.[17]

This inscription displays many of the conventions of this honorific form. It first lists the recipient's offices. Claudia was unusual, not only in the large number of such positions she held, but also in the frequency with which she held them. She was director of the gymnasium, director of the games, led a regional body of cities in cooperation, and served as priest of a local temple. Such offices were appointed annually and were often held only once, but Claudia served in them multiple times and held a perpetual priesthood. All of this indicates her wealth and stature.

Also with conventional language, the inscription attributes honor to Claudia by describing her virtue: She was "desirous for the glory of the city" and "a lover of her homeland," as shown by her "excellence and admirable behavior toward it." This language identifies Claudia's actions as virtuous according to the standards of the time. Her generosity built up the city and its glory, and the city in turn acknowledged her importance to it.

Reading the New Testament Texts

The first readers of the New Testament shared this cultural background, and when they read these texts (or heard them being read aloud), they used their cultural knowledge to understand what was being said. When modern readers understand the importance of social rank and the assertion of status to influence affairs, we may notice the presence of these same social structures in the New Testament.

Consider the parable about a banquet told by Jesus in Luke 14:7–11. Jesus advised his hearers not to take one of the prominent seats at the table "in case someone more distinguished than you has been invited by your host" (Luke 14:8). It would be better to take a lower seat and be invited to move up: "Then you will be honored in the presence of all who sit at the table with you" (v. 10). Jesus's parable, which teaches listeners not to exalt themselves, draws on well-known social practices by which people at banquets ordered themselves according to rank.

On Political Influence and Power

> For Herod himself had sent men who arrested John, bound him, and put him in prison on account of Herodias, his brother Philip's wife, because Herod had married her. For John had been telling Herod, "It is not lawful for you to have your brother's wife." And Herodias had a grudge against him and wanted to kill him. But she could not, for Herod feared John, knowing that he was a righteous and holy man, and he protected him. When he heard him, he was greatly perplexed, and yet he liked to listen to him. But an opportunity came when Herod on his birthday gave a banquet for his courtiers and officers and for the leaders of Galilee. When his daughter Herodias came in and danced, she pleased Herod and his guests, and the king said to the girl, "Ask me for whatever you wish, and I will give it." And he swore to her, "Whatever you ask me, I will give you, even half of my kingdom." She

> went out and said to her mother, "What should I ask for?" She replied, "The head of John the baptizer." Immediately she rushed back to the king and requested, "I want you to give me at once the head of John the Baptist on a platter." The king was deeply grieved, yet out of regard for his oaths and for the guests, he did not want to refuse her. Immediately the king sent a soldier of the guard with orders to bring John's head. He went and beheaded him in the prison, brought his head on a platter, and gave it to the girl. Then the girl gave it to her mother. When his disciples heard about it, they came and took his body and laid it in a tomb. (Mark 6:17–29)

The power of Roman rulers enters into the New Testament at various points, including this story of the death of John the Baptist. The story centers on the events of a banquet that shares features of the one above: "Herod on his birthday gave a banquet for his courtiers and officers and for the leaders of Galilee" (Mark 6:21; cf. Matt 14:1–12). Pleased by Herodias's dancing, he made a rash promise: "Ask me for whatever you wish, and I will give it." Familiar with such scenarios, ancient readers would likely assume Herod's drunkenness and his desire to show off for his guests. Although John was not beheaded in the banquet hall, as in Flamininus's story, above, the scenario evokes a similar set of cultural values: Rulers who were unable to control their desires could be expected to act capriciously and violently.

The story of John's death also displays the informal social power of elite women. In this case, Herod's wife had a grudge against John, who had objected to her divorce of Herod's brother and remarriage to Herod (Mark 6:17–19). She sees her opportunity to strike back and seizes it. Although Herodias did not have official authority to put John to death, she had considerable influence and used it to her advantage. Readers of the time expected elite women to have and use such power for various purposes, for good as well as for ill.

Luke 8 on Patronage

Social practices of patronage also shaped the early Jesus movement. Signs in the Gospels as well as the letters of Paul suggest that, when forming groups of believers, the earliest followers adapted social practices of group organization that they were already familiar with from the culture at large. Patronage was a central feature of these practices.

> Soon afterward he went on through one town and village after another, proclaiming and bringing the good news of the kingdom of God. The twelve were with him, as well as some women who had been cured of

evil spirits and infirmities: Mary, called Magdalene, from whom seven demons had gone out, and Joanna, the wife of Herod's steward Chuza, and Susanna, and many others, who ministered to them out of their own resources. (Luke 8:1–3)

Luke's version of the gospel story recalls women who were patrons of Jesus's ministry (cf. Matt 27:55–56). Early readers would likely have understood that Jesus's traveling ministry was financially sustained by the benefactions of these women, the most prominent of whom are named. Joanna, the wife of Herod's steward, would likely have been a person of considerable influence, due to her family's proximity to Herod, even though she was not high born. It is impossible to say if Mary Magdalene's social standing in this group, demonstrated by her position in the list, stemmed from personal wealth or from the important role she came to play in the resurrection story. Both wealth and demonstrated virtue (through devotion to Jesus) would have brought status within the Jesus movement. The actions of these patrons would have given them influence within the emerging group of Christ followers.

Romans 16 on Patronage

I commend to you our sister Phoebe, a deacon of the church at Cenchreae, so that you may welcome her in the Lord, as is fitting for the saints, and help her in whatever she may require from you, for she has been a benefactor of many and of myself as well. Greet Prisca and Aquila, my coworkers in Christ Jesus, who risked their necks for my life, to whom not only I give thanks but also all the churches of the gentiles. Greet also the church in their house. (Rom 16:1–5)

In part, it is the genre of Paul's writing—letters—that makes patronage so visible in these texts. Letters established and confirmed relationships between people. By sending greetings to and from various individuals, Paul reinforces those connections and asserts the importance of those who are named. The closing of Paul's letter to the Roman assembly is full of personal greetings. Because Paul has not been to Rome, it may be more important for him to name his connections to prominent people there. The details he mentions provide some insight into these often-invisible leaders of the early churches.

Paul begins by introducing the letter carrier, Phoebe, indicating her status as "a deacon of the church at Cenchreae" and "a benefactor of many and of myself as well." Phoebe holds an office in the assembly in Cenchreae and has acted as a patron.[18] By introducing her to the Romans, Paul acts as a patron for her as well, using his connections and stature to assist her travel to another city:

"welcome her in the Lord, as is fitting for the saints, and help her in whatever she may require from you."

Early Christ followers drew upon the social structures that were familiar to them from associations as they organized themselves into groups. Scholars used to argue that church offices only developed at a later stage in the church's life, but the familiarity of associations makes it seem more likely that believers would have organized fairly quickly into groups with officers of some sort—although their titles and roles probably varied somewhat from place to place. In writing to the Philippians, Paul began, "To all the saints in Christ Jesus who are in Philippi with the bishops and deacons" (*syn episkopois kai diakonois*, Phil 1:1). Although there is no way to know what functions these officers fulfilled, Paul uses the words *bishop* (or *overseer*) and *deacon* (or *server*) as titles of acknowledged leaders of the fellowship. In order to fulfill the mission of the association, early Christ assemblies needed officers.

The author of 1 Timothy described the qualifications for such offices at some length, and the desired qualities cluster around self-control, that central virtue of leaders at that time. The author describes how bishops and male and female deacons should avoid excessive drinking, curb anger and greed, and control their tongues, varying the wording slightly for each group (1 Tim 3:1–13). Such virtues were familiar from literary works and inscriptions praising good leaders of the time. Not surprisingly, early Christ followers also wanted their leaders to show evidence of the same virtues that were commonly understood to foster strong social groups.

After the recommendation of Phoebe, Paul continues by greeting a long list of leaders in Rome whom he already knows. Leading off are Prisca and Aquila, coworkers from many stages of Paul's traveling ministry. In Corinth, Aquila and Prisca hosted Paul and became partners with him, later traveling with him to Ephesus (Acts 18:1–3, 18–19; 1 Cor 16:19). Having subsequently moved to Rome, Paul sends greetings to Prisca and Aquila and the church in their house. By hosting an assembly of believers in their home, Prisca and Aquila served as patrons. Paul's indication that they have "risked their necks for my life" underscores their virtue, for they are willing to risk for the greater good.

Paul's greetings bring honor to the people he lists. Readers would likely have expected that Paul began with the most prominent of his acquaintances and then moved on to those of lower status. However, all of the individuals named were important people, and their status was reinforced by Paul's inclusion in the letter.

FURTHER READING

Cupcea, George, and Rada Varga, eds. *Social Interactions and Status Markers in the Roman World*. Archaeopress Roman Archaeology 27. Archaeopress Publishing, 2018.

Hylen, Susan E. *Women in the New Testament World*. Oxford University Press, 2018.

Kuhn, Annika B., ed. *Social Status and Prestige in the Graeco-Roman World*. Franz Steiner Verlag, 2015.

Richardson, John. "Provincial Administration." In *The Oxford Handbook of Roman Law and Society*, edited by Paul J. du Plessis, Clifford Ando, and Kaius Tuori. Oxford University Press, 2016.

Roselaar, Saskia T. "Local Administration." In *The Oxford Handbook of Roman Law and Society*, edited by Paul J. du Plessis, Clifford Ando, and Kaius Tuori. Oxford University Press, 2016.

Notes

1 Literary sources are available in English translation in print or online. See for example the Loeb Classical Library, https://www.loebclassics.com/. For legal sources, see *The Digest of Justinian*, trans. Alan Watson, 4 vols. (University of Pennsylvania Press, 1985).

2 Inscriptions are published in a wide variety of forms, and they are not always translated. One useful collection is: John S. Kloppenborg, Richard S. Ascough, and Philip Harland, eds. *Greco-Roman Associations: Text, Translations, and Commentary*, 3 vols. (de Gruyter, 2011–20).

3 For examples, see Jane Rowlandson, ed., *Women and Society in Greek and Roman Egypt* (Cambridge University Press, 1998); Roger S. Bagnall and Raffaella Cribiore, *Women's Letters from Ancient Egypt: 300 BC-AD 800* (University of Michigan Press, 2015).

4 See Susan E. Hylen, *Women in the New Testament World* (Oxford University Press, 2018), 93–95.

5 For a discussion, see Saskia T. Roselaar, "Local Administration," in *The Oxford Handbook of Roman Law and Society*, ed. Paul J. du Plessis, Clifford Ando, and Kaius Tuori (Oxford University Press, 2016), 130–31.

6 See for example the discussion and sources cited by Wally V. Cirafesi, "Rethinking John and 'the Synagogue' in Light of Expulsion from Public Assemblies in Antiquity," *Journal of Biblical Literature* 142, no. 4 (2023): 667–75 (682–87).

7 See Roselaar, "Local Administration," 129–30.

8 For an introduction and examples, see Richard S. Ascough, Philip A. Harland and John S. Kloppenborg, *Associations in the Greco-Roman World: A Sourcebook* (Baylor University Press, 2012).

9 See Emily Hemelrijk, *Hidden Lives, Public Personae: Women and Civic Life in the Roman West* (Oxford University Press, 2015); Hylen, *Women in New Testament*, 100–107.

10 See Susan E. Hylen, "Femininity, Masculinity, and Sexuality," in *Cambridge History of Ancient Christianity*, ed. Bruce W. Longenecker and David E. Wilhite (Cambridge University Press, 2024), 565.

11 Hylen, "Femininity, Masculinity, and Sexuality," 570–72.

12 See Matthew J. Perry, *Gender Manumission, and the Roman Freedwoman* (Cambridge University Press, 2014), chap. 4.

13 Seneca the Elder, *Controversiae*, vol. 2, books 7–10, ed. and trans. Michael Winterbottom, Loeb Classical Library 464 (Harvard University Press, 1974), 9.2. praef, 6–8.

14 *Controv.* 9.2.3.

15 *Controv.* 9.2.8; cf. 9.2.11.

16 Demetrios I. Pallas et al., "Inscriptions Lyciennes trouvées à Solômos près de Corinthe," *Bulletin de correspondence héllenique* 83 (1959): 499. For the Greek text and translation, see Rosalinde A. Kearsley, "Women in Public Life in the Roman East: Iunia Theodora, Claudia Metrodora and Phoebe, Benefactress of Paul," *Tyndale Bulletin* 50, no. 2 (1999): 206.

17 Jeanne Robert and Louis Robert, "Bulletin épigraphique," *Revue des études grecques* 69 (1956): 152–53, no. 213. For the Greek text and translation, see Kearsley, "Women in Public Life," 208–9. I have slightly modified the translation.

18 For more details see Tobias Nicklas, "Phoebe: 'Patrona' des Paulus, Frau im Dienst des Evangeliums, Vorbild für Männer und Frauen," *Jahrbuch für Biblische Theologie* 33 (2018): 143–56.

CHAPTER TEN

Masculinity, Gender, and the New Testament World

Lily C. Vuong
(University of Oregon)

SINCE THE 1970S, studies in gender have recognized the complexity of the relationship between sex (physical anatomy) and gender (social construct) in our contemporary society. That is, *masculinity* and *femininity* are terms used not to describe the differences between men and women but rather to distinguish differing qualities among men and differing qualities among women. Recently, it has become more common to perceive sex as a social construct as many traditional ideas of gender have been challenged.[1] It has been increasingly clear that these same modern reflections could be applied to the ancient world and that doing so would uncover similar complexities.

In the ancient Mediterranean world, the concept of masculinity was deeply intertwined with social status, power, and honor. Within the New Testament context, ideas of what it meant to be a *man* or *manly* or *masculine* were shaped by cultural norms that were inextricably linked to one's authority, dominance, and public recognition. These cultural norms were heavily influenced by specifically Roman and Greek ideals of male virtue, which often placed great importance on military prowess, public success, and leadership in the household.[2] At the same time, the influence of traditional Jewish ideals of masculinity in the context of the family and Torah observance cannot be underestimated. There is no doubt that these complex dynamics and constructions contributed, shaped, and influenced the writings of the New Testament. While the New Testament offers a distinctive view of masculinity, on occasion challenging prevailing notions of power and authority through the teachings and example of Jesus, his followers, and Paul, it also adopted at times *hegemonic masculinity*,[3] a masculinity that necessitates the subordination of others, where the *other* is often femininities (what masculinity is not) and other masculinities.[4] By examining these ancient ideologies of masculinity (and by extension femininity) within the New Testament world, and exploring how early Christian communities responded to, subverted, or upheld such dominant cultural expectations, we can gain a deeper understanding of the complexities surrounding gender and power in the New Testament.

Greco-Roman Ideals of Masculinity

The complexity of ideal masculinities in the Greco-Roman world was perhaps inescapably complicated by the notions held about the fluidity of biological sex in antiquity. Unlike modern understanding, males and females were not considered opposite sex, but rather as differing degrees of a human whereby males were viewed as the ideal perfected human and females as incomplete humans because they lacked the necessary heat required in the womb to transform into males.[5] Greco-Roman medical and philosophical texts, including those of Galen[6] and Soranus of Ephesus[7] assert the sameness of male and female reproductive organs, distinguishable only in that female organs were incomplete and imperfect, which explained their position as inverted. The view of biological sex as a continuum whereby male and females were plotted as closer to perfection (male) or farther from perfection (female) naturally allowed for diverse plotting on the continuum and the confusion of sexes.[8] Since the body was viewed as unstable, masculine women were the result of an increase of heat whereas effeminate men were the result of a loss of that heat; both cases, however, were viewed as incomplete humans.

In the ancient Greco-Roman world, ideal masculinity was not automatically assumed simply because one was born with male genitalia and it is clear there was not one single way of being masculine.[9] Indeed, physical attributes could also determine masculinity and reveal personal traits and characteristics. Physiognomists believed that such bodily signs could distinguish not only between men and women, but also between masculine and effeminate men *and* masculine and feminine women.[10] Given that men were viewed as perfected and normative humans and women were viewed as imperfected beings, it is not surprising that stereotypical behavioral traits positioned themselves along this same continuum, so that "real men" were often aligned with virtues, and women with vices. Some stereotypes associated with males and females include the idea that real men were strong, brave, altruistic, rational, and most importantly had control, both over others and themselves. By contrast, women were weak, selfish, irrational, self-indulgent, deceptive, and lacked courage, self-control, and control over others.[11] Ironically, although women were viewed to naturally and biologically have these inherent vices, the expectation for women was to act against these natural inclinations and strive toward virtuous and masculine traits, as long as their behavior did not challenge other men or threaten their masculinity.[12] For instance, in his letter *To Helvia His Mother: On Consolation*, on living virtuously in the context of society's expectations, the philosopher Seneca argues that while women's vices (*muliebria vitia*) are antithetical to virtues (*virtus*), women should still strive for having virtues.[13] While these ideal belief systems seem to run counter to each other, they nevertheless were coexisting realities in the ancient world.

Of all the traits associated with masculinity in the ancient world, perhaps having control, both over others (esp. military strength) and oneself (esp. emotions), was the most important. The term *virtus*, derived from the Latin word for "man" (*vir*), and its Greek counterpart *aretē*, originally signified "manliness" or "manly behavior," reflecting the ideal conduct for men, particularly in martial contexts.[14] Roman men, in particular, prided themselves on their military and political accomplishments, consistently pictured themselves as soldiers, and frequently used military metaphors to illustrate their achievements. Militarism and manliness in the ancient world went hand in hand with *vita militaris* (a soldier's life) serving as a shorthand for the ideal manly life—one by which all men were measured.[15] Initially, *aretē* emphasized martial courage and bravery in battle, as seen in Plato's *Laches*, where courage is defined as standing firm in the face of danger. However, philosophers like Socrates broadened this definition, emphasizing qualities such as endurance through suffering, self-control, and the courage to face death.[16] Over time, self-control (*incontinentia*; *sōphrosynē*), initially meaning prudence, came to be regarded as the key masculine virtue, even above control over others, as it involved mastering emotions and passions. Eventually it would be adopted by followers of Jesus as the prime definition of Christian manliness.

By contrast, effeminacy was associated with a lack of self-control (*incontinentia; sōphrosynē*), particularly in the areas of food, drink, and sex.[17] Such traits were viewed as naturally feminine, thus when adopted by a man, made him effeminate. With regard to sexual matters, control and dominance by a man were viewed as important qualities alongside moderation and restraint. A *manly man* participated in sex for procreation alone and was expected to take an active and dominant role in sexual encounters.[18] In fact, the distinction between active and passive roles in sex was viewed as an important indicator for determining effeminacy, where passivity and being penetrated was seen as effeminate because it implied a lack of control.[19] Importantly, determining effeminacy was not necessarily linked to sexual orientation. In a same-sex sexual encounter, for instance, the active participant could still be seen as masculine, but it implied effeminacy for his partner who accepted the passive role. Men who sought to be penetrated, however, were always perceived as effeminate, regardless of their partner's gender, and were often labeled with derogatory terms like *cinaedus* or *pathicus*.[20]

Ideal Masculinity and Judaism

As a minor religious group that did not hold a dominant social or political position in the Greco-Roman world, Judaism had ideas on masculinity that were complex, being both resistant and tolerant of Greco-Roman ideals and expectations of masculinity.[21] Writings from the Hebrew Bible as well as early Jewish writings from the first few centuries CE, the period when the New Testament was written, illustrate the multifaceted and diverse ways in which Judaism understood and thought about masculinity.

In the Hebrew Bible, ideas on masculinity are typically expressed through important figures including Abraham, Isaac, and Jacob, who are depicted as exhibiting strength, leadership, and obedience to God. These patriarchs also demonstrate ideal masculinity through their engagement with society, responsibility to their families, and ensuring the foundations of the Israelite people are laid and continued.[22] These ideals, however, are sometimes complicated by the portrayal of the same patriarchs engaging in activities and expressing qualities traditionally seen as feminine by Greco-Roman standards. For instance, upon being given Joseph's bloody coat and believing his son to be dead, Jacob experiences intense grief over what he believes is the loss of his son and expresses a lack of control over his emotions (Gen 37:34–35).

Another important and popular expression of ideal masculinity in the Hebrew Bible can be found in military imagery and the depiction of warrior-like figures, of which King David is a prime, albeit complicated, example. David is described as witty and agile as well as a model for exemplary military strength, courage, and for his defense of country (Israel), a common expression of masculinity shared by Greco-Roman ideals but one that was also valued by many other cultures as well. David's successes include triumph over Goliath and the conquering of some 140,000 men in total, but he was also well known and praised for his political success through his verbal skills and ability to persuade, especially in his encounter with Saul. While these qualities align with Greco-Roman ideals of masculinity,[23] David's character is also deeply complicated by poor decision making and engagement in activities that were often viewed as against masculine norms. As Milena Kirova candidly notes, David is a frequent weeper. He weeps ("David wept the more" 1 Sam 20:41) when he must leave Jonathan upon finding out Saul's attempt on his life and is said to have wept at the deaths of Saul and his son Jonathan, and then again at Abner's (2 Sam 3:32–39) and his son Absalon's (2 Sam 18:33; 19:22) deaths. Although Kirova argues that David's crying serves to distinguish him as God's anointed and functions to highlight his ability to call on God,[24] and thus does not result in a loss of masculinity, David's repeated expression of passion and emotions runs counter to traditional Greco-Roman ideas on manly behavior.

To complicate the example of David further, his relationship with Saul's son, Jonathan, and his affair with Bathsheba, are of particular note. In the case of Jonathan, much has been made of their close friendship and deep love for each other. We are told that Jonathan's soul was bound to David's and that he loved David "as his own soul" (1 Sam 18:1), and that David kissed Jonathan at their final parting (1 Sam 20:41). Although an explicit sexual dimension to their relationship is never acknowledged, their close male bonding would have suggested it as a possibility and thus invited speculation about David's masculinity. As for David's affair with Bathsheba, his decisions in the matter highlight a lack of self-control, a failure to maintain authority, and an association with the feminine trait of passion.[25] The complex portrayal of masculinity demonstrated with the figure of David continues in other Jewish writings from the period contemporary to the New Testament.

In Jewish literature of the first century CE, ideas on masculinity were shaped by both cultural influences and one's devotion to God. While Greco-Roman ideas of strength, honor, and self-control continue to characterize ideal masculinity, these virtues were often reframed in terms of a commitment to the Jewish faith. In this way, early Jewish texts were at times more akin to early forms of Christian masculinities (discussed below), but at other times mirrored Greco-Roman beliefs, especially in their distinction between masculine and feminine traits. For instance, the view that masculinity and femininity stand in opposition to each other is supported in the writings of Philo of Alexandria. In his *On the Creation*, Philo associates masculinity with reason, divinity, and order; and femininity with irrationality, matter, and chaos.[26] The higher view of the masculine and lower view of the feminine continues in his discussion of the soul (see below). There he argues for two parts of the soul: the higher, rational, and masculine side, which strives toward divine perfection; and, the lower, irrational, and feminine side, which strives alternatively to the senses and passions.[27] Philo's works support the idea of a hierarchical dualism, aligning with Greco-Roman ideas that associate masculinity with being higher and spiritual, and femininity with being lower and material.

As a contemporary of Philo, Flavius Josephus, the Jewish historian, also provides important insights into Jewish ideals of masculinity. Apologetics, however, are detectable in his writings given that Josephus's relationship with the Romans was complicated: He initially opposed Rome in the Jewish Revolt but later defected and became a historian and adviser to the Roman emperor. In his musings on male biblical characters and in defense against accusations that Jewish men lacked masculine virtues, Josephus draws upon the masculine virtues of wisdom, bravery, resistance, temperance, justice, loyalty, and piety to make his case.[28] For instance, Josephus highlights Abraham and Moses (*Ant.* 1.154; 4.328)[29] as wise and skillful in the art of persuasion and praises Joshua, Saul, and David for their courage and military achievements in order to demonstrate their engagement in activities deemed masculine (*Ant.* 3.49; 6.54; 7.74, cf. 2 Sam 5:20).[30] On the virtues of modesty and self-control, Josephus points to the first three kings of Israel as important models.[31] For Josephus, Greco-Roman ideals of masculinity were not rejected but reframed in terms of the Jewish law and God.

Where one can detect more subverting of Greco-Roman ideas of ideal masculinity is in Jewish martyrdom texts of the first and second centuries, and the writings of the rabbis. In the case of the former, the martyrdom of the mother and her seven sons found in the writings of 4 Maccabees[32] serves as the key example of self-control and manly courage. The sons' gruesome deaths and the mother's witnessing of them are not only viewed as a model for manliness but evoke the idea of a vicarious death, a notion that would be exemplified and find its ultimate expression in the death of Jesus and serve as a playbook for many early Christian martyrs (see below).[33] Regarding the rabbis, although their works are much later than the writings of the New Testament and reflect a diverse range of views, some of their ideas on ideal masculinity provide a starker subverting of aggressive and violent masculinity, aligning more closely to the depiction of masculinity in the Gospels and in Pauline literature (see below). In particular, the Talmudic depiction of Roman masculinity as violent and cruel was seen in opposition to the ideal man, who was nonaggressive and focused on the study of Torah.[34] Although such activities would traditionally be viewed as feminine, the rabbis adopted and redefined them as expressions of ideal masculinity in their writings.

Masculinity and Early Christian Writings

Much like Greco-Roman and Jewish ideals, standards of masculinity for early Christians were diverse, complex, and reflected multiple cultural influences. The traditional Greco-Roman ideal of masculinity in terms of physical strength and bravery in military battle was influential in many early Christian martyrdom literatures where "manly courage" is used to depict the gumption needed to achieve martyrdom. While in the arena awaiting his death, Polycarp, the bishop of Smyrna, hears a voice from heaven encouraging him "to be strong . . . and have courage" (Mart. Pol. 9).[35] However, the irony is that, instead of viewing ideal masculinity as wielding physical strength against others, Christian masculinity became articulated in terms of enduring physical pain against one's own body; that is, enduring or submitting.[36] Indeed, the virtue of *patientia* (patience and submission) became the ultimate way to express masculinity by early Christians. This reversal of symbols naturally encompassed the virtue of self-control.[37] Polycarp's manliness is not only conveyed in terms of courage in the face of physical pain and endurance of persecution, but also through self-control akin to what Jesus exhibited during his own passion. This is portrayed in his unwavering and calm response to his executioners when he is threatened with being burned alive: "The fire you threaten me with burns merely for a time and is soon extinguished. It is clear you are ignorant of the fire of everlasting punishment and of the judgment that is to come, which awaits the impious. Why then do you hesitate. Come, do what you will" (Mart. Pol. 11).[38] After his death, the community also acknowledges his manliness in terms of the virtues of endurance and self-control: "He was not only a great teacher but also a conspicuous martyr, whose testimony, following the Gospel of Christ, everyone desires to imitate. By his perseverance he overcame the unjust governor and so won the crown of immortality." (Mart. Pol. 19).[39]

The influence of both kinds of manliness found in Polycarp's martyrdom story is a common feature in early Christian martyrdom narratives including those of female martyrs. In the Martyrdom of Perpetua and Felicitas, Perpetua is repeatedly described in terms of "manly courage" both by way of physical strength and power, but also, and more dominantly, in terms of having self-control. Regarding the former, while in the arena she is described as having "manly courage" when she must guide the trembling gladiator's sword toward her neck: [and she] "redirected the aimless hand of the inexperienced gladiator right at her neck. Perhaps such a great woman, who was feared even by an unclean spirit, could not have been killed unless she herself had wished it."[40] Indeed, even in preparation for the arena, Perpetua envisions herself as a physically powerful man who easily bests an Egyptian gladiator in battle, so that "He fell down flat on his face and I stepped on his head."[41] While Perpetua effectively demonstrates physical strength, it is the virtue of self-control that characterizes her throughout the narrative. Perpetua's deep emotional control during her trial is contrasted sharply with her father's effeminate response of tearing out his hair, weeping hysterically, and begging his daughter to reconsider. Perpetua's father is depicted as emotionally distressed: He says,

> "My daughter, have pity on me—look at my grey hair! Have pity on me—I am your father! Or don't I deserve the name any more? Didn't I bring you up with these hands, so that now you are in the flower of youth? Didn't I put you first, before all your brothers? Don't disgrace me in front of everyone."... Spoken like a dutiful father. Then he kissed my hands and threw himself at my feet and wept, and now he called me not "daughter" but "my lady."[42]

Perpetua's father's emotional vulnerability and fear highlight his weakness in the face of adversity, which contrasts sharply with his daughter's unwavering determination to embrace martyrdom.

The early Christian martyrs' reversal of symbols for the ideals of manliness, trading in the life of a soldier (*vita militaris*) for a soldier of Christ (*miles Christi*)—that is, a soldier who submits and suffers—is perhaps most perfectly modeled in the figure of Jesus whose vicarious death and crucified body came to symbolize not a violated, penetrated, and emasculated body, but one which embodied ideal Christian masculinity.[43] This alternative interpretation of Jesus's death required the acknowledgment of him as the Messiah, but not the kind of Messiah Jesus's disciples or followers expected. Instead of a strong military leader or warrior, qualities aligned with forms of masculinity expressed through control over others, Jesus is a Messiah that must suffer and die and it is in his willingness and embracing of his suffering and death that he becomes an exemplary figure. Ironically, this reconstruction of Jesus's death as a salvific death on behalf of humanity in contrast to an aggressive military manliness, likely had its roots in Greco-Roman noble death traditions.[44] Cicero, for instance, articulated the endurance of pain and a fearless death as important signs of masculinity especially for Stoic philosophers. The proper way to die—that is, a noble death—could demonstrate virtues especially when the death was on behalf of a noble cause like a war, a democratic ideal, for country, or in place of another worthy or good person.[45] For instance, Iphigenia's death in the myth of Agamemnon, and specifically, Euripides's retelling of the story, Iphigenia is presented as a willing victim for the sake and success of the Greek army during the Peloponnesian War. A similar situation occurs in Sophocles's *Antigone* in his account of the death of Creon's son, Menoceus. In Sophocles's portrayal, Menoceus's death becomes an act of vicarious sacrifice, when his life is forfeited to help the community and save Thebes.[46] Noteworthy is that vicarious deaths were not limited to men and that women too could equally participate in such noble acts. In such cases, the women were often praised for their bravery, which was primarily expressed in terms of manliness and could even become "honorary men" by demonstrating manly virtues but in womanly ways.[47] For both men and women who participated in a willing death for the sake of something greater, their acts of bravery and self-control were viewed as acts of manliness and exceptional character.

It should be noted, however, that although the ideal forms of masculinity articulated in the suffering and vicarious death of Jesus became the dominant form for Christians, it would be a mistake to assume early Christians simply rejected or overturned traditional Greco-Roman ideas of masculinity. The writings of Paul, for instance, demonstrate clearly the influence and value of athletic and martial ideas of masculinity. Paul often utilizes martial metaphors in his description and encouragement of the believers, calling them his "cosoldiers" (Epaphroditus in Phil 2:25; Archippus in Phlm 1:2) and encouraging them to wear the "breastplate of faith and love," "a helmet, the hope of salvation," (1 Thess 5:8) and "armor of light" (Rom 13:12), and to bear weapons of righteousness" (2 Cor 6:7).[48] The Gospels too participate in presenting Jesus's manliness in terms of power and authority. From calling upon his disciples to follow him (Mark 1:16–20; Matt 4:18–22) and commanding the attention of the people when he teaches (Mark 1:22; Luke 4:31–37; Matt 5–7) to controlling demons (Mark 1:27; Luke 4:31–37) and healing with authority (Mark 1:29–31; Luke 4:38–39), Jesus is presented in a decidedly masculine way by ancient standards. Even when Jesus is baptized by John the Baptist, a scenario that naturally questions Jesus's authority in relation to John, the Synoptic Gospels present Jesus as the commanding and authoritative figure. Where Mark and Luke have John the Baptist explicitly declare that Jesus is greater and more powerful than he, Matthew adds a scenario in which Jesus grants John specific permission to perform the baptism to underscore Jesus's authority even further. As such, the rhetoric of both Paul and the Gospels are shaped by the masculine metaphors of their culture, even as they consistently promote Jesus's vicarious death as a manly death.

While the letters of Paul and the Gospels utilize traditional Greco-Roman ideals of masculinity (Paul's use of athletic and martial metaphors, but also self-control), Christian ideals of manliness eventually and ironically became prominently expressed as the ability to bear pain, even in a humiliating experience such as crucifixion.[49] For Christians, the virtue of enduring pain and suffering and experiencing hardship became a virtue akin to endurance, conviction, and manliness. It is perhaps not surprising that in the transformation of Jesus's crucifixion from a humiliating to a vicarious and noble death that ideal Christian discipleship too transformed from a call to authority and power to a position of suffering and death as expressed both in the Gospels and the writings attributed to Paul. In this reconstructed view of endurance, weakness and passivity are revised as possible sources of power—that is, mastery and power over oneself. The evolving ideals of masculinity in early Christian thought reveal a complex interplay between Greco-Roman, Jewish, and emerging Christian values. What is clear, however, is the championing of Christian masculinity in terms of enduring and self-controlled suffering, of which Jesus's death on the cross was the original and ultimate example.

TAKING A CLOSER LOOK: SOURCES

Sources from the World of the New Testament

Greco-Roman Text on Physiognomy and Gender Stereotypes

> The physiognomist draws his data from movements, shapes and colours, and from habits appearing in the face, from the growth of hair, from the smoothness of the skin, from voice, from the condition of the flesh, from parts of the body, and from the general character of the body . . . The characteristics of the brave man are stiff hair, an erect carriage of body, bones, sides and extremities of the body strong and large, broad and flat belly; shoulder-blades broad and far apart, neither very tightly knit nor altogether slack; a strong neck but not very fleshy; a chest

> fleshy and broad, thigh flat, calves of the legs broad below; a bright eye, neither too wide opened nor half closed; the skin on the body is inclined to be dry; the forehead is sharp, straight, not large, and lean, neither very smooth nor very wrinkled. The signs of the coward are soft hair, a body of sedentary habit, not energetic; calves of the legs broad above; pallor about the face; eyes weak and blinking, the extremities of the body weak, small legs and long thin hands; thigh small and weak; the figure is constrained in movement; he is not eager but supine and nervous; the expression on his face is liable to rapid change and is cowed. . . . The marks of the shameless man are an eye wide-open and clear, eyelids bloodshot and thick; he is somewhat bowed; shoulders raised high; his figure is not erect but inclines to stoop forward, he is quick in his movements and reddish in body; his complexion is ruddy; he is round-faced with a high chest. These are the marks of the orderly man. He is deliberate in movement and in speech, his voice is husky and weak, he has a black lack-lustre eye, neither very wide open nor half closed, and it opens and closes slowly; for eyes that blink rapidly are signs either of the coward or of the hot-tempered. (Ps.-Aristotle, *Physiognomics* 806a–808a)[50]

Physiognomy is the practice of interpreting a person's character based on their physical features, particularly the face and body, but also from one's voice, hair growth, smoothness of skin, and pace of movement. In early Greek and Roman literature, physiognomy was also widely used to determine a person's perceived moral virtues and vices, as well as their personality and temperament.[51] Of particular note is the presentation of the material, which reports the observations in language similar to a medical document giving the impression that the physiognomist, akin to a doctor or scientist, is simply recording objective unbiased data. As the passage attributed to Pseudo-Aristotle above illustrates, certain physical features including a large and strong body, stiff hair, dry skin, and deliberate speech and movement are indicative of a "brave man" and an "orderly man." By contrast, a "coward" and a "shameless man" has a weak and disproportionate body, soft hair, a ruddy complexion, and quick in movement. As such, physiognomy was used in antiquity not only to differentiate between men and women but to reinforce a social and moral divide between men, sorting them along a continuum of ideal masculinity with "manly men" on one end of the spectrum and "effeminate men," on the other. These ideas would have resonated with New Testament audiences especially regarding references to Paul's bodily presence and speech (2 Cor 10:10; Acts 14:1, 12), as well as to Jesus's teachings on judging others superficially (John 7:24), albeit often in ways that subvert or push back against these physiognomic standards and norms.

Jewish Text on Virtues and Vices and the Nature of Men and Women

> This is the explanation commonly and widely stated, but I have heard another from highly gifted men who think that most of the contents of the law-book are outward symbols of hidden truths, expressing in words what has been left unsaid. This explanation was as follows. There is in the soul a male and female element just as there is in families, the male corresponding to the men, the female to the women. The male soul assigns itself to God alone as the Father and Maker of the Universe and the Cause of all things. The female clings to all that is born and perishes; it stretches out its faculties like a hand to catch blindly at what comes in its way, and gives the clasp of friendship to the world of created things with all its numberless changes and transmutations, instead of to the divine order, the immutable, the blessed, the thrice happy. Naturally therefore we are commanded in a symbol to cut off the hand which has taken hold of the "pair," not meaning that the body should be mutilated by the loss of a most essential member, but to bid us exscind from the soul the godless thoughts which take for their basis all that comes into being through birth; for the "pair" are a symbol of seed-sowing and birth. I will add another thought, following where the study of nature leads me. The monad is the image of the first cause, the dyad of matter passive and divisible. Therefore one who honours the dyad before the monad should not fail to know that he holds matter in higher esteem than God. It is for this reason that the law judged it right to cut off this tendency of the soul as if it were a hand, for there is no greater impiety than to ascribe to the passive element the power of the active principle. (Philo, *Spec.* III.178–80)[52]

Philo's writings offer an understanding of gender that reflects natural hierarchical structures, whereby men are naturally inclined toward active and superior roles in contrast to women who are associated with passive and inferior roles as a result of their "natural" proximity to God. As Philo writes, "the male soul aligns itself with God alone" and associates itself with the living and creation whereas "the female clings to all that is born and perishes." As with other Greco-Roman traditions and expectations, "real men" were viewed as strong, morally superior, rational, and were associated with self-control and the spiritual world. Women, on the other hand, were viewed as weak, morally deficient, simpleminded, submissive, fleshy, irrational, emotional, and were associated with the physical world and a lack of self-control, although they were often encouraged to resist these natural inclinations and vices. While early Christians both upheld[53] and subverted[54] these ideas, they were not immune to gender roles and expectations in the Greco-Roman world, which was hierarchical in structure and viewed men as superior, women as inferior, and effeminate men as problematic.

4 Maccabees on Jewish Martyrdom

> But sympathy for her children did not sway the mother of the young men; she was of the same mind as Abraham. (4 Macc. 14:20)
>
> O mother, tried now by more bitter pains than even the birth pangs you suffered for them! O woman, who alone gave birth to such perfect piety! Neither when the firstborn breathed his last, it did not turn you aside, nor when the second in torments looked at you piteously nor when the third expired, nor did you weep when you looked at the eyes of each one in his tortures gazing boldly at the same agonies and saw in their nostrils the signs of the approach of death. When you saw the flesh of children burned upon the flesh of other children, severed hands upon hands, scalped heads upon heads, and corpses fallen on other corpses, and when you saw the place filled with many spectators because of the children's torments, you did not shed tears. Neither the melodies of sirens nor the songs of swans attract the attention of their hearers as did the voices of the children in torture calling to their mother. How great and how many torments the mother then suffered as her sons were tortured on the wheel and with the hot irons! But pious reason, giving her heart a man's courage in the very midst of her passions, strengthened her to disregard, for the time, her parental love. (4 Macc. 15:16–23)
>
> O mother of the nation, vindicator of the law, and defender of piety who carried away the prize of the contest in your heart! O more noble than males in steadfastness and more courageous than men in endurance! Just as Noah's ark, carrying the world in the universal flood, stoutly endured the waves, so you, O guardian of the law, overwhelmed from every side by the flood of your passions and the violent winds—the torture of your sons—endured nobly and withstood the wintry storms raging on piety's account.
>
> If, then, a woman advanced in years and mother of seven sons endured seeing her children tortured to death, it must be admitted that pious reason is sovereign over the passions. Thus I have demonstrated not only that men have ruled over the passions but also that a woman has despised the fiercest tortures. The lions surrounding

> Daniel were not so savage nor was the raging fiery furnace of Mishael so intensely hot as was her innate parental love consuming her as she saw her seven sons tortured in such varied ways. But the mother quenched so many and such great passions by pious reason. (4 Macc. 15:29–16:4)

The story of the mother and her seven sons from 4 Maccabees above (see also the parallel in 2 Macc 7) offers a fascinating depiction of a mother who embodies a number of virtues often associated with both Greco-Roman and some Jewish ideas about the masculine: courage, endurance, and most impressively, self-control. What elevates her suffering and death even above other martyrdoms is her role as a witness to the torture and deaths of her seven sons. Here, the mother's piety and steadfast love for God takes precedence over the deep motherly love for her children, and she is specifically praised for having "a man's courage," resisting her natural disposition to respond with great passion and overwhelming emotion. Indeed, the narrator emphasizes her strength and endurance by exalting her for displaying greater steadfastness, courage, and endurance in her suffering than that of men.

Noteworthy is that the mother is not praised for having physical strength or power over others, but for her moral determination and spiritual resilience, qualities expected of real men, but which were encouraged of women even if it went against their perceived nature. Additionally, the narrative compares the mother to important biblical figures, asserting she was of the same mind of Abraham and of the same courage as Noah.

The martyrdom of the mother and her seven sons was an important model for early Christian martyrdoms, which, in turn, have their roots in the martyrdoms recorded in the New Testament,[55] the most important and climactic example being the martyrdom of Jesus himself (Mark 15; cf. Matt 27 and John 19). The story of the mother both subverts the traditional expectations of women but also articulates and frames the praise in terms of ideal masculinity.

Reading the New Testament Texts

Jesus on Ideals of Masculinity

> He called the crowd with his disciples and said to them, "If any wish to come after me, let them deny themselves and take up their cross and follow me. For those who want to save their life will lose it, and those who lose their life for my sake, and for the sake of the gospel, will save it. For what will it profit them to gain the whole world and forfeit their life? Indeed, what can they give in return for their life? Those who are

> ashamed of me and of my words in this adulterous and sinful generation, of them the Son of Man will also be ashamed when he comes in the glory of his Father with the holy angels."
>
> And he said to them, "Truly I tell you, there are some standing here who will not taste death until they see that the kingdom of God has come with power." (Mark 8:34–9:1)

> "I am sending you out like sheep into the midst of wolves, so be wise as serpents and innocent as doves. Beware of them, for they will hand you over to councils and flog you in their synagogues, and you will be dragged before governors and kings because of me, as a testimony to them and the gentiles. When they hand you over, do not worry about how you are to speak or what you are to say, for what you are to say will be given to you at that time, for it is not you who speak, but the Spirit of your Father speaking through you. Sibling will betray sibling to death and a father his child, and children will rise against parents and have them put to death, and you will be hated by all because of my name. But the one who endures to the end will be saved. When they persecute you in this town, flee to the next, for truly I tell you, you will not have finished going through all the towns of Israel before the Son of Man comes." (Matt 10:16–23)

Jesus's teachings on discipleship found in the two passages cited above demonstrate a shift in ideals of masculinity. Instead of viewing masculinity in terms of miliary power and domination, Jesus instead promotes a model of discipleship rooted in suffering, self-denial, and endurance. As the ideal man, Jesus taught that to "take up the cross and follow" him (Mark 8:34) was a path that did not lead to traditional power, authority, or conquest, but rather to deep suffering and possibly, death. Glory for Jesus and those who follow him in discipleship is not achieved through inflicting violence on others, but by allowing, through courage, patience, and endurance, others to inflict pain, violence, and even death on oneself for the sake of the gospel. Here, the ideal forms of Greco-Roman masculinity are not outright rejected but rather are reinvented so that the direction and location of violence are reversed.

In Matthew 10:16–23, a similar idea is promoted by Jesus when he sends his disciples out "as sheep among wolves" and instructs them to embrace and endure suffering rather than resist with force and violence. While Jesus's teaching does not align with Greco-Roman ideas of masculinity in terms of outward physical power and strength, it does, however, reflect shared values such as self-control and the noble death, where masculinity could also be achieved not by overpowering enemies, but by enduring suffering with restraint and self-control. As the ultimate model for discipleship, Jesus redefined expectations of masculine honor not by rejecting violence but by reframing it in terms enduring persecution.[56]

Betrayals of Peter and Judas

> Now Peter was sitting outside in the courtyard. A female servant came to him and said, "You also were with Jesus the Galilean." But he denied it before all of them, saying, "I do not know what you are talking about." When he went out to the porch, another female servant saw him, and she said to the bystanders, "This man was with Jesus the Nazarene." Again he denied it with an oath, "I do not know the man." After a little while the bystanders came up and said to Peter, "Certainly you are also one of them, for your accent betrays you." Then he began to curse, and he swore an oath, "I do not know the man!" At that moment the cock crowed. Then Peter remembered what Jesus had said: "Before the cock crows, you will deny me three times." And he went out and wept bitterly. (Matt 26:69–75)

> When Judas, his betrayer, saw that Jesus was condemned, he repented and brought back the thirty pieces of silver to the chief priests and the elders. He said, "I have sinned by betraying innocent blood." But they said, "What is that to us? See to it yourself." Throwing down the pieces of silver in the temple, he departed, and he went and hanged himself. (Matt 27:3–5)

The passages above describe two separate accounts of the betrayal of Jesus by his disciples, Peter and Judas, respectively. While Peter is described as the "first" of Jesus's disciples in Matthew 10:2, is also the only one to confess Jesus's identity, and displays a genuine desire to follow Jesus, he nevertheless misunderstands Jesus's messiahship—Peter's expectation of a powerful, prestigious, and military messiahship is dismissed and sharply corrected as a messiahship of suffering, humiliation, and death. More so than the Gospel of Mark, Matthew intensifies Peter's culpability in his thrice denial of Jesus. The fact that Peter's first and second denial of knowing Jesus is initiated by a female servant—a doubly marginalized figure—underscores Peter's weakness and failure to keep his promise even to those who pose little social or political threat. Matthew's version is also heightened because Peter's denial is declared "before all of them" and because it is followed by two oaths, a condemnable and prohibited act according to Jesus (Matt 5:33–37). It is only after the cock's crow that Peter is reminded of Jesus's prediction and must confront his lack of masculine courage and loyalty that he boasted earlier of having. Peter's bitter weeping is a display of uncontrolled emotions, but it also aligns with the culturally irresolute and unmasculine responses to his accusers.

The second passage directly identifies Judas as Jesus's betrayer. Although Judas is able to acknowledge and lament with deep despair over his traitorous acts against Jesus, the circumstances surrounding his decision to hang himself would have been viewed as contrary to expectations of both Greco-Roman and emerging Christian ideals of masculinity. While suicide was deemed honorable and socially acceptable in cases involving altruistic or self-sacrificing motives because it allowed one to regain honor, Judas's hanging lacked both the redemptive and socially acceptable conditions required for it to be viewed positively. Honorable suicides that were viewed positively include, for instance, Samson's intentional destruction of the temple pillar resulting in his death and the lives of some 3,000 Philistines (Judg 16:23–30); Lucrezia's suicide after the loss of her chastity);[57] and Emperor Marcus Otho's suicide to prevent further conflict among the Romans.[58] By contrast, Judas's hanging was viewed as an act of weakness since it neither reversed his shameful status nor did it serve as a morally righteous act of valor. Instead, it was predicated on a private emotional crisis akin to the negative view held of Mark Antony's suicide, which was based on romantic love rather than for virtuous reasons.

FURTHER READING

Asikainen, Susanna. *Jesus and Other Men: Ideal Masculinities in the Synoptic Gospels*. Brill, 2018.

Conway, Colleen M. *Behold the Man: Jesus and Greco-Roman Masculinity*. Oxford University Press, 2008.

Gleason, Maud W. *Making Men: Sophists and Self-Presentation in Ancient Rome*. Princeton University Press, 1995.

Haddox, Susan E. "Masculinity Studies of the Hebrew Bible: The First Two Decades." *Currents in Biblical Research* 14, no. 2 (2016): 176–206. https://doi.org/10.1177/1476993X15575496.

Hylen, Susan E. "Masculinity, Femininity, and Sexuality." In *The Cambridge History of Christianity*, edited by Bruce W. Longenecker and David E. Wilhite. Cambridge University Press, 2024.

Kuefler, Mathew. *The Manly Eunuch: Masculinity, Gender Ambiguity, and Christian Ideology in Late Antiquity*. University of Chicago Press, 2001.

Moore, Stephen D. and Janice Capel Anderson, eds. *New Testament Masculinities*. Society of Biblical Literature Press, 2003.

Notes

1 Suzanne J. Kessler and Wendy McKenna, *Gender: An Ethnomethodological Approach* (University of Chicago Press, 1985).

2 Susan Hylen, "Masculinity, Femininity, and Sexuality" in *The Cambridge History of Christianity*, ed. Bruce W. Longenecker and David E. Wilhite (Cambridge University Press, 2024).

3 The term "hegemonic masculinity," introduced by Tim Carrigan, et al. is commonly used in discussions about masculinity. This concept suggests that there was a main or dominant form of masculinity that functioned as the ideal way to express or embody masculinity in cultural and political power structures. As an ideal, this form of masculinity necessitated that not all men could live up to such standards of masculinity but was something for which many men still strived. Carrigan argued that hegemonic masculinity is not a fixed concept and was constantly being challenged by alternative expressions of masculinity. These competing forms are often referred to as "marginalized masculinities," which represent groups who are pushed to the margins due to their lack of dominance in areas like race, religion, or social status; Tim Carrigan, Bob Connell, John Lee, and Peter F Murphy, "Toward a New Sociology of Masculinity," in *Feminism and Masculinities* (Oxford University Press, 2004). See also Susanna Asikainen's study, *Jesus and Other Men: Ideal Masculinities in the Synoptic Gospels* (Brill, 2018), 5–6.

4 Colleen M. Conway, *Behold the Man: Jesus and Greco-Roman Masculinity* (Oxford University Press, 2008), 9.

5 Asikainen, *Jesus and Other Men*, 20–21.

6 See Galen, *On the Usefulness of the Parts of the Body*, trans. Margaret Tallmadge May, in Lefkowitz, Mary R, and Maureen B Fant. *Women's Life in Greece & Rome: A Source Book in Translation*, 2nd ed. (Johns Hopkins University Press, 1992), 14.6–7.

7 See *Soranus' Gynecology*, trans. Owsei Temkin (Johns Hopkins University Press, 1991), 14, 31; see also 10n6, where Temkin notes that the word for tube is also penis. On Soranus and Galen's views of women's bodies as the imperfect, inverted, and colder version of male bodies, see Laqueur, Thomas Walter, *Making Sex: Body and Gender from the Greeks to Freud* (Harvard University Press, 1990), 25–35. For a survey of ancient Greek physicians and their view on the female body, see Bonnard, Jean-Baptiste, "Male and Female Bodies According to Ancient Greek Physicians." *Clio (English Ed. En Ligne)*, no. 37 (2014), https://doi.org/10.4000/cliowgh.339.

8 Conway, *Behold the Man*, 16–18; Asikainen, *Jesus and Other Men*, 20–22.

9 Maud W. Gleason, *Making Men: Sophists and Self-Presentation in Ancient Rome* (Princeton University Press, 1995), 59.

10 Conway, *Behold the Man*, 19–20; Asikainen, *Jesus and Other Men*, 23–24.

11 Hylen, "Masculinity, Femininity, and Sexuality," 563–64. For instance, in Simonides of Amorgos's *Types of Women*, the Greek poet compares different types of women to animals and other negative metaphors, for example, some women are compared to foxes (deceptive and sly), others to pigs (dirty and greedy), and some to weasels (loathsome

and sex crazed). The poem portrays women as unreliable, driven by primitive desires, and prone to various moral failings. The only recommended woman is likened to a bee since she is hardworking and graceful; Diane Arnson Svarlien, "Semonides of Amorgos' Women (Poem 7)," in *The Greek Poets: Homer to the Present*, ed. Peter Constantine and Robert Hass (W.W. Norton, 2010), 78–81.

12 Asikainen, *Jesus and Other Men*, 20–22; Hylen, "Masculinity, Femininity, and Sexuality," 564.

13 *Helv.*, in *Moral Essays: In Three Volumes*, ed. and trans. John W. Basore (Harvard University Press, 1979), 416–90; Asikainen, *Jesus and Other Men*, 30; Hylen, "Masculinity, Femininity, and Sexuality," 564.

14 Hylen, "Masculinity, Femininity, and Sexuality," 561; Asikainen, *Jesus and Other Men*, 30.

15 Mathew Kuefler, *The Manly Eunuch: Masculinity, Gender Ambiguity, and Christian Ideology in Late Antiquity* (University of Chicago Press, 2001), 37–38.

16 *Laches*, in *Plato: Laches, Protagoras, Meno*, trans. and ed. William R. M. Lamb, Loeb Classical Library 36 (Harvard University Press, 1924), 221–22; Asikainen, *Jesus and Other Men*, 31–32.

17 Asikainen, *Jesus and Other Men*, 24.

18 See Karen Torjesen, "The Penetrator and the Penetrated" in *When Women Were Priests: Women's Leadership in the Early Church and the Scandal of Their Subordination in the Rise of Christianity*, ed. Karen Torjesen (HarperOne, 1995), 179–202.

19 Torjesen, "Penetrator and Penetrated," 179–202.

20 Asikainen, *Jesus and Other Men*, 33–34.

21 See Ovidiu Creangă, *Men and Masculinity in the Hebrew Bible and Beyond* (Sheffield Phoenix Press, 2010).

22 Susan E. Haddox, "Masculinity Studies of the Hebrew Bible: The First Two Decades," *Currents in Biblical Research* 14, no. 2 (2016): 176–206, https://doi.org/10.1177/1476993X15575496.

23 On David's various expressions of masculinity, see David J. A. Clines, "David the Man: The Construction of Masculinity in the Hebrew Bible," in *Interested Parties: The Ideology of Writers and Readers of the Hebrew Bible*, ed. David J. A. Clines, Journal for the Study of the Old Testament Supplement Series 205 (Sheffield Academic Press): 212–43.

24 Milena Kirova, "When Real Men Cry: The Symbolism of Weeping in the Torah and the Deuteronomistic History," in *Biblical Masculinities Foregrounded*, ed. Ovidiu Creangă and Peter-Ben Smit (Sheffield Phoenix, 2014), 35–50.

25 Clines, "David the Man," 228–31; Haddox, "Masculinity Studies," 189.

26 Philo, *On the Creation* (*De Opificio Mundi*), in *Philo: Complete Works*, trans. and ed. Francis H. Colson, Loeb Classical Library 226 (Harvard University Press, 1900), 130–31.

27 See Philo, *On the Special Laws* (*De Specialibus Legibus*), in *Philo: Complete Works*, trans. and ed. Francis H. Colson, Loeb Classical Library 226 (Harvard University Press), 587–88, where Philo continues this gendered division, associating virtue and wisdom

with male figures in biblical texts, while female figures are depicted as embodying more emotional or chaotic traits.

28 Asikainen, *Jesus and Other Men*, 40.

29 See William Whiston, trans. and ed., *Josephus, Complete Works* (Kregel Publications, 1987), 38 and 125.

30 Asikainen, *Jesus and Other Men*, 41n144.

31 Saul (*Ant.* 6.63); and David (*Ant.* 7.391), and Solomon (*Ant.* 7.362).

32 For this writing see also the chapter on "Early Jewish Literature" by David Cielontko in the present volume.

33 Stephen D. Moore and Janice Capel Anderson, "Taking It like a Man: Masculinity in 4 Maccabees," *Journal of Biblical Literature* 117, no. 2 (1998): 249–73; Johannes N. Vorster, "Re-membering the mother of the seven in 4 Maccabees," *Studia Historiae Ecclesiasticae* 41, no. 3 (2015): 23–43.

34 Daniel Boyarin, *Unheroic Conduct: The Rise of Heterosexuality and the Invention of the Jewish Man* (University of California Press, 1997), 1–6.

35 Translation from Herbert Musurillo, *The Acts of the Christian Martyrs* (Clarendon Press, 1972), 9.

36 Kuefler, *Manly Eunuch*, 109.

37 Kuefler, *Manly Eunuch*, 111–17.

38 Musurillo, *Christian Martyrs*, 11.

39 Musurillo, *Christian Martyrs*, 17.

40 Joseph Farrell and Craig Williams, trans. and ed., "The Passion of Saints Perpetua and Felicity," in Perpetua's passions: *Multidisciplinary Approaches to the Passio Perpetuae et Felicitatis*, ed. Jan N. Bremmer and Marco Formisano (Oxford University Press, 2012), 23.

41 Farrell and Williams, "Perpetua and Felicity," 19.

42 Farrell and Williams, "Perpetua and Felicity," 16–17.

43 Kuefler, *Manly Eunuch*, 111–17.

44 See further, Arthur J. Droge and James D. Tabor, *A Noble Death: Suicide and Martyrdom among Christians and Jews in Antiquity* (Harper Collins, 1992).

45 Conway, *Behold the Man*, 70–71.

46 Conway, *Behold the Man*, 70.

47 Conway, *Behold the Man*, 71–72.

48 Conway, *Behold the Man*, 69.

49 Conway, *Behold the Man*, 96–104.

50 *Minor Works: On Colours. On Things Heard. Physiognomics. On Plants. On Marvellous Things Heard. Mechanical Problems. On Indivisible Lines. The Situations and Names of Winds. On Melissus, Xenophanes, Gorgias*, trans. W. S. Hett (Harvard University Press, 1936), 92–93, 99–101.

51 Gleason, "The Semiotics of Gender: Physiognomy and Self-Fashioning in the Second Century CE," in *Before Sexuality: The Construction of Erotic Experience in the Ancient World*, ed. David M. Halperin, John J. Winkler, and Froma I. Zeitlin (Princeton University Press, 1990), 389–415.

52 *On the Decalogue. On the Special Laws, Books 1-3*, trans. F. H. Colson, Loeb Classical Library 320 (Harvard University Press, 1937), 586–589.

53 For example, 1 Cor 11:2–16; 14:34–35; 1 Tim 2:11–15; Titus 2:3–5, etc.

54 For example, Acts 18:2–3; Mark 16:1–8; Gal 3:28.

55 For example, Stephen in Acts 6:8–7:60; John the Baptist in Matt 14:1–2, cf. Mark 6:14–29, Luke 9:9; James in Acts 12:1–2, etc.

56 Asikainen, *Jesus and Other Men*, 158–60.

57 Livy, *History of Rome* 1.58.

58 Suetonius, *Otho* 11–12.

CHAPTER ELEVEN

The Spatial Context of the Ancient Mediterranean

Cavan W. Concannon
(University of Southern California)

The study of the New Testament and other early Christian literature has been dominated by philological approaches. The dominance of philology as the primary mode through which ancient Christian texts are historicized owes a great deal to the origins of the study of ancient Christianity outside the theological faculty of the early modern university.[1] As a result, biblical scholarship has largely followed the study of words as they appear within literary sources. While philology is necessary for studying ancient literature, like that found in the New Testament, it is equally important to remember that ancient literature was produced within, evoked images of, and was directed toward lived spaces. Biblical scholars need to take into account the spatial context of the ancient world when engaging with their primary texts.[2]

The Mediterranean Context of Early Christianity

Before considering the civic context of early Christ groups represented in New Testament texts, we must start with the wider landscape in which the cities of the ancient world were situated. The ancient Mediterranean and its hinterlands represent the initial frame for thinking about the development of various forms of Christ devotion.

The Mediterranean world at the time of the earliest Christians was politically unified by the conquests of the Romans over the previous centuries. This violent imposition of Roman rule organized what had been true for centuries: that the Mediterranean basin and its hinterlands had been knit together by human work. The Mediterranean, as a geographic entity, is made up of innumerable microregions, each with their own specific geographies and climates. Climatic and geographic diversity played important roles in the forces that drove the Mediterranean together over the many millennia in which humans have inhabited its shores.

Because the region has so many microclimates in proximity to each other, the human experience of the Mediterranean is one of irregular but proximate scarcity. One valley might get enough rainfall to grow crops one year, while a region a few miles away might not get enough. This periodic scarcity pushed humans to connect across different microregions, creating connections that forged cultural and social relationships. In other words, there is cultural and social unity in connecting across geographic and climatic diversity, and it is humans who do the work of forging those connections.

In general, the sea was a major facilitator of connectivity, though not through the kinds of fixed trade routes that dominate the contemporary seascape. Waterborne trade and regional connectivity were forged through cabotage, sea travel that moved along short distances, with boats usually traveling routes that kept them within sight of land. Trade generally followed these short distances before arriving at major hubs. Emporium cities like Antioch and Corinth saw the arrival of goods from nearby regions and thus served as nodal points within ancient networks. It is these complex trading networks that would have facilitated the movement of cults, like the cult of Christ, throughout the Mediterranean world.

The earliest Christ groups were clustered in cities tied to the sea and to heavily trafficked overland trade routes. Paying attention to how people moved between these cities, crossing a complex and often dangerous geography, helps us to better understand the ways in which networks of early Christ groups came together and fell apart.

The Civic Context of Early Christianity

The Roman Empire was dominated by cities, which served as the main structural nodes in Roman trade, imperial management, and communication, as well as the major population, cultural, and economic centers. The city was also the main unit of political participation and socialization, since politics and social formation were tied to civic institutions. Political life was shaped by participation in voting and deliberation, at least for free, propertied males. Cities were also the medium through which Roman officials dealt with provincial matters, often working through local civic elites when implementing policy, collecting taxes, and otherwise managing imperial affairs. They were also the main drivers of economic production, whether that be through the production of commercial goods, the growing of foodstuffs in the city's hinterlands, or the management of trading concerns, including the movement of building materials. In other words, the city was a crucial unit in Roman imperial society.

The Greco-Roman city, taken generally and not specifically (no one city was the same as another!), originated in the tenth century BCE, as a result of demographic, political, and military changes. Over time, the *polis* model of urbanization would spread out from Greece, particularly in the wake of Alexander's conquests, and later would be integrated into the Roman imperial administrative apparatus. The literature on ancient cities is vast and thus it is impossible here to do justice to the plurality of issues related to the spatial arrangement and cultural and political meanings of space within Greek and Roman cities.[3] In the remainder of this section, I will briefly summarize some of the important spaces that one might find in Greek and Roman cities, recognizing that for every city there were different configurations of these spaces and their functions.

Most Greek and Roman cities, when they had the means to engage in centralized urban planning, organized civic space around a grid model, with streets running at right angles and enclosed within a network of walls or natural barriers (such as an acropolis or shoreline). The urban grid created a series of rectangular blocks (*insulae*) that comprised space for both private and public buildings. Along the streets, one would find shops, taverns, and businesses, connected to residential spaces. In Roman cities, *insulae* could include apartment-style buildings that rose to as many as five stories in height.

The civic limits were often set by rituals that constructed city space as sacred. Romans would ritually delimit civic space through the ritual plowing of the *pomerium*, while the sacrality of civic space was manifested in the built environment at the *prytaneion*, the site of the city's sacred hearth. The sacred limits to civic space marked the division between the city (*astȳ*; *urbs*) and the land it controlled in its immediate vicinity (*chora*; *ager*; *territorium*). It also marked the boundary between the living and the dead, as corpses could not be buried within the limits of the city. Many citizens would live and work outside the city in its hinterlands, where settlement patterns (such as villages, large estates, or scattered farmsteads) differed from the dense organization of the city.

Greek cities typically were governed by a council (*boule*) and the voting assembly of citizens (*demos*). This is paralleled in the famous Latin phrase *senatus populusque romanus* (the Senate and the people of Rome). These were the main deliberative bodies, and each had a specific place to meet within the city. For the council or the Senate there was usually a meeting place in the city's agora (forum). This structure might be called a *boulèterion* or a *curia*. In Greek cities, the council often managed the flow of concerns that would be presented for deliberation by the people's assembly, while in Roman cities and colonies the council tended to manage civic affairs directly. When called to deliberate, Greek citizens would come together as an assembly (*ekklēsia*),[4] which usually met in the city's theater. Assembly meetings involved speeches and debates on issues as well as the election of officers to manage civic administrative affairs. Roman citizens voted in tribes and primarily focused on the election of officers. Thus, in Roman cities, voting did not always take place in the theater but often occurred in open spaces where the voting tribes could assemble.

The local council's meeting place was usually erected in the center of the city on the agora, or forum. These central squares were common features of ancient cities and could include a range of structures. In planned Roman cities, the forum would be located at the intersection of the two main roads (the *cardo* and *decumanus*); however, each civic landscape had to balance standardization with what was available in terms of topography and existing structures when making any choices around urban planning. In the agora, one might find important civic cults, each of which would have received approval from the council and the assembly for construction; offices of civic administration; businesses and shops; markets; imperial cult sites; the sacred hearth (*prytaneion*); and civic monuments to famous citizens or events. Roman cities and colonies usually made arrangements for the erection of a *Capitolium* near the forum. These temples were dedicated to the Capitoline triad (Jupiter, Juno, and Minerva) and mimicked the temple on the Capitoline Hill in Rome. While state-sponsored cults were often located along the agora, in some cities the major cult site could be found outside the city limits and not in the civic center (as was the case with the Temple of Artemis in Ephesos).

Ancient cities also included spaces that served the general public. Public entertainment could be found in the city's theater or stadium. Cities in the Roman West often built amphitheaters to house games and other forms of spectacle entertainment. Many of these entertainment spaces, much like modern cultural and sport arenas, had seating arrangements that segregated attendees by status or class, making them not only sites of spectacle entertainment but spaces the made visible the orders of the civic hierarchy. Other public amenities found in ancient cities included spaces like *gymnasia* and bath complexes. *Gymnasia* were multiuse spaces, where one might find places to exercise but also gatherings of men to discuss civic affairs or philosophy. Often students would attend school in the porticos of the city's gymnasium. Bath complexes were a Roman introduction to civic space, offering affordable access to things like baths, saunas, and recreational activities. Though many wealthy families would build bath facilities in their sumptuous homes, the civic baths were often donated to the city by an emperor or local elite as a benefaction to the city and its residents.

Recent biblical scholarship that has rediscovered the importance of local spaces for the study of ancient literature has often turned to city-based analyses, drawing on archaeological research to situate early Christian texts within local civic contexts.[5] This approach has borne much fruit in the field and remains an active avenue for research. One methodological caution, however, is in order. Analyzing texts within a local civic context often proceeds from an assumption that a local city (say, the Roman colony of Philippi in Macedonia) was known to both the author and the first readers of a text (to continue the example: Paul's letter to the Philippians) and that the local civic context played a role in the shaping and reception of the text in question. While this may have been the case, it cannot be assumed. It is not clear, for example, that Paul's letter to the Ephesians was written to Ephesos or by someone familiar with the city and its local conditions. Thus, the degree to which textual interpretation can benefit from attention to specific civic locales is dependent on our confidence in the provenance of our source material. With that caveat in mind, it is worth attending to both the wider patterns of civic life in the Roman world alongside attention to local contexts where appropriate when studying ancient Christian texts.

TAKING A CLOSER LOOK: SOURCES

Sources from the World of the New Testament

In this section, I look in depth at two examples of how ancient voluntary associations navigated the institutional and geographic landscapes of ancient cities. These examples will help us think not only about the ancient civic landscape but will also serve as comparanda for thinking about how the earliest Christ groups negotiated their place within and between ancient cities.

Thracians in Athens

> Whereas, the People of Athens granted to the Thracians, alone of all of the immigrant groups [*ethnê*], the right to own property [*enktēsis*] and to build a sanctuary in accordance with the oracle of Dodona and to have a procession from the hearth of the building of the civic presidency [*prytaneion*]. Now those who have been chosen to build a sanctuary in the Asty think that both groups should be favorably disposed to each other, so that the sacrificing associates [*orgeōnes*] may also be seen to be obedient to the law of the city, which orders the Thracians to have their procession continue to the Piraeus, and being favorably disposed towards the sacrificing associates who are in the Asty. . . . When the sacrifices occur, the priest and the priestess shall pray—in addition to the prayers that they normally pray and in the same way—for the sacrificing associates who are in the Asty, so that when these things take place and the entire immigrant group [*ethnos*] lives in concord, the sacrifices and other rites shall be made to the gods, in accordance with both the ancestral customs of the Thracians and the laws of the city. So that it will turn out well and in a manner reflecting piety for the entire immigrant group [*ethnos*] in matters concerning the gods. (GRA I 23)[6]

In 240/39 BCE, the Thracian association of Bendis in Piraeus erected an inscribed stele commemorating the unification of the Thracian Bendis associations in Athens and Piraeus.[7] The occasion for their reconnection was the passage of a grant by the Athenian Thracians for the erection of a new temple to Bendis in the Asty. To mark the occasion, the Athenian Thracians had asked for the right to participate in the festival of the Bendideia with a procession from the Athenian *prytaneion* to the shrine of Bendis in Piraeus, alongside the Thracians from Piraeus. The inscription notes that the two Thracian groups would arrange themselves separately and walk together from the city to the port. Upon arrival, the supervisors of the Piraeus group would "supply sponges in the Nymphaion and cups and water and wreaths and a breakfast in the temple, just as they prepare for themselves." During the sacrifices, the priests were to pray for both groups in the same way and, furthermore, members of each group could access the other's association and even switch membership without a fee.

Thracian immigrants to Athens were granted the right to build a shrine to Bendis in the fifth century BCE and their festival of the Bendideia was also sanctioned around the same time. The Thracians claim, probably based on an earlier inscription, that "they alone of all of the *ethnē*" had been granted *enktēsis*, the right to own property and build a temple and make their procession from the *prytaneion*. The place of the Thracian cult in the city (both its temples and its processions) was thus contingent on successfully negotiating with the Athenian civic administration.

According to the inscription, the Bendideia marks Thracianness, even though it was an Athenian state festival. The civic group wants both groups to be favorably disposed to each other, but only insofar as that presents a favorable display to Athenian observers. They want their members to be "seen to be obedient to the law of the city," which prescribes that the Thracians (represented as a singular ethnic group and not two different ones) make their procession to the Piraeus. The rationale is rooted in what Athenian citizens (and presumably other viewers) will perceive when witnessing the Thracians processing. The hope is that the two groups will be seen as unified representatives of Thracianness.

This is further emphasized with the instructions for the sacrifices that take place at the end of the procession. The priests will do the same things for both groups "so that when these things take place and the entire *ethnos* lives in concord, the sacrifices and other rites shall be made to the gods, in accordance both with the ancestral customs of the Thracians and the laws of the city and so that it will go well and piously for the entire *ethnos* in matters concerning the gods."[8]

The festival is thus not merely a civic event, but an opportunity to make Thracianness itself an event. While the inscription presents the alignment of the two cult groups as in keeping with the law, a chance to create intergroup friendship, and placate the gods, it is also staking a claim to represent Thracianness in Athens. The inscription shows how institutional groups used cultic practice to position themselves as arbiters of Thracianness. What it meant to be Thracian was constructed in the complicated negotiation over space to build and to walk in the *polis*.

Tyrians in Puteoli

> To the civic leaders [*archontes*], Council and People of their sovereign homeland, from those settled in Puteoli [*hoi en Potiolois katoikountes*], greetings. Because of the gods and the fortune of our lord, the emperor, if there are any other stations in Puteoli, our station [*statiōn*] is better than the others both in adornment and in size, as most of you know. In the past, this was cared for by the Tyrians settled in Puteoli, who were numerous and wealthy. But now our number has dwindled to a few and, since we pay the expenses for the sacrifices and services to our ancestral gods established here in temples, we do not have the means to pay the station's annual payment of 250 denarii, especially as the expenses for the bull sacrifice at the games in Puteoli have been imposed on us. We therefore beg you to provide for the station's continued existence. Now it will continue if you make provision for annual payment of 250 denarii. For we took care of the other expenses and those incurred in the restoration of the station for the sacred day of our lord, the emperor, so as not to burden the city [i.e., Tyre]. We also remind you that no income accrues either from shippers [*nauklēroi*] or from merchants [*emporoi*] to our station, as is the case with the station in royal Rome. We therefore beg you to make provision in this circumstance. Written in Puteoli, July 23, during the consulship of Gallus and Flaccus Cornelianus. (IG XIV 830)[9]

Another example of how space and distance played a role in shaping ancient civic life comes from the port city of Puteoli in the second century CE, with an inscription by the *statio* of the Tyrians at Puteoli.[10] The inscription, dated to 174 CE, records an embassy to Tyre in Phoenicia sent by Tyrian merchants living in Puteoli. The leader of the embassy was a certain Laches, whose goal was to get the city of Tyre to pay 250 denarii per year for the upkeep (*misthos*) of the Tyrian station in Puteoli. The argument presented by the embassy is that they needed this extra help for several reasons: Their numbers had diminished and they lacked sufficient funds to pay for the traditional rites and sacrifices that they were already obligated to provide. They noted that up to the point of the embassy, the merchants had themselves paid for these costs on their own.

After recording the embassy's request to the Tyrian assembly, the inscription then records the *acta* of the assembly meeting in Tyre. What follows is a fractious debate about whether to grant the station the money requested. A Tyrian council member named Philokles, son of Diodoros, argues against the request and offers a counter proposal, namely that the Puteolian station be merged with and put under the control of another station of Tyrian merchants in Rome. The *acta* then record exclamations from members of the assembly, some in favor of the request ("Justly do those in Puteoli ask") and some opposed ("Philokles speaks well"). Laches finally resolves the debate by reading from a tablet recording an earlier decision by the Tyrian assembly concerning the two stations at Rome and Puteoli. Unfortunately, the text breaks off at this point, so we do not know exactly how the debate was resolved; however, the fact that the inscription at Puteoli exists shows that Laches's mission was considered a success by the local group. It seems likely that the two groups remained distinct, though under an official charter from the Tyrian assembly, and that the assembly agreed to provide the 250 denarii to support the Puteolian *statio*.

This fascinating inscription offers us access to debates within a single city about how to manage their trade representatives in two other cities, halfway across the Mediterranean. The Tyrians in Puteoli had seen their once wealthy group diminish due to trade shifts but also remained tightly connected to Tyre. The Roman *statio* clearly also maintained tight connections with Tyre, since they had a supporter in Philokles, who advocated strongly on their behalf in the assembly. The Puteolian letter asked for a small amount of yearly assistance, but Philokles saw this as a chance to make the Roman *statio* into the sole chartered Tyrian group serving Roman trade interests. Thus, both *stationes* maintained strong civic connections between their respective *stationes* and the home city, referred to in the inscription as both a mother city and a fatherland.

The Tyrian assembly projected its civic control over Tyrian interests abroad by creating the *stationes* in Puteoli and Ostia. These organizations were the face of Tyrianness in each port as it related to economic concerns, but also in cultic festivals where the *stationarii* displayed Tyrian integration into their adopted home. In their letter, the Puteolians emphasize the "splendor and greatness" of their *statio*, such that it surpasses other *stationes* in the port. They also make a point of mentioning that, as their finances dwindled, they continued to pay for the sacrifices and rites to their ancestral Tyrian gods, a bull sacrifice at the city's games, and the outfitting of the *statio* during the sacred days venerating the imperial family. The *stationarii* thus present themselves to the Tyrian assembly as faithful representatives of the city's interest, having fulfilled their remit of representing Tyrianness in Puteoli. In addition, the inscription's existence indicates that the Tyrians in Puteoli wanted local audiences to witness their commitment to civic and cultic participation. One could be from Tyre, venerate one's local deities, and still participate in the civic life of a new place or home.

Reading the New Testament Texts

An Assembly in Corinth

> For I, though absent in body, am present in spirit, and as if present I have already pronounced judgment in the name of the Lord Jesus on the man who has done such a thing. When you are assembled and my spirit is present with the power of our Lord Jesus, you are to hand this man over to Satan for the destruction of the flesh, so that the spirit may be saved in the day of the Lord.
>
> When any of you has a grievance against another, do you dare to take it to court before the unrighteous, instead of taking it before the saints? Do you not know that the saints will judge the world? And if the world is to be judged by you, are you incompetent to try trivial cases?
>
> Judge for yourselves. (1 Cor 5:3–5; 6:1–2; 11:13)

The Tyrian *statio* in Puteoli offers an example for thinking about the early Christ group in Corinth. There has long been an unresolved debate about the demographics, structure, and size of the Christ group(s) here during the time of Paul.[11] What we can note, however, is that the Christ group in Corinth was presented by Paul as an *ekklēsia*. This term frames the Christ group as a democratic voting assembly, like that described in the Tyrian inscription, in which discernment and debate would have taken place.[12]

It is clear that the Christ group in Corinth did engage in some sort of democratic debate. Throughout the Corinthian correspondence, Paul suggests that the Corinthians ought to engage in a communal form of judgment in regard to a number of issues: the man sleeping with his stepmother (1 Cor 5:1–13, esp. 12–13), the settling of legal disputes within the community (1 Cor 6:6–11), the dangers of idolatry (1 Cor 10:15), the appropriateness of female head coverings (11:13), the proper way to celebrate the Lord's Supper (1 Cor 11:28–32), the interpretation of spiritual gifts (1 Cor 14:26, 28–33a), and the evaluation of Paul's authority with regard to the "super apostles" (2 Cor 10:7). Paul's discussion of the process of expelling the man sleeping with his stepmother includes Paul casting his own vote (1 Cor 5:3), which suggests that some sort of voting procedure was involved in communal decision making. These examples show that Paul's letters contended with and were directed toward an actively discerning community that could be persuaded but would ultimately pass its own judgments on issues that came to the group's attention. One might imagine, like in the Tyrian inscription, members shouting, "Stephanas speaks well!" and "Paul's opinion is not wanted!" as part of a process of collective discernment.

If the Christ group's meetings were conceptualized as akin to the assembly that met in the city's theater, they would have seen their gathering not merely as a place for debate, but as a site for accountability. The Tyrian assembly met to discuss the accounting books of its *stationes* overseas and to discuss how best to organize and manage them. The Corinthian letters also show evidence for similar processes. In 1 Corinthians 4:1–5, Paul suggests that the Corinthians have begun to investigate him in some fashion. Paul's response is to shift the question of judgment from the sphere of the Corinthians to the sphere of the pneumatic (*pneumatikos*) and the divine. Having labeled the Corinthians as fleshly (*sarkikos*) in 3:1–4 as a result of their factions (here described as jealousy and infighting [*zēlos kai eris*]), Paul suggests that they do not have the ability to pass judgment on him. As a servant of Christ and an enslaved manager of the mysteries of God (*hōs hypēretas Christou kai oikonomous mystēriōn theou* [4:1]), Paul is to be judged by God alone (4:4–5). Paul thus tries to undermine the efficacy of the Corinthians' communal discernment in regard to the evaluation of his own ministry. Paul faces continued examination by the Corinthians, when the group there begins to question his credentials and asks for letters of recommendation. Rather than suggesting that the Corinthians are unable to evaluate him, that his gospel is somehow "veiled" (1 Cor 4:3), Paul stresses the transparency of his motives and dealings with the Corinthians (2 Cor 2:17; 3:12–13; 4:2). Paul presents himself as a frank speaker whose motivations and actions are transparent and honest. For him a *yes* is a yes and a *no* a no (2 Cor 1:17–20). While Paul is anxious to defend himself as an authority over the Corinthians in matters of debate, his arguments only underscore the sense that the Corinthians are actively involved in making their own decisions about how to evaluate and view him.

The Corinthian *ekklēsia* thus seems to have modeled its activities around the civic assemblies in Greek cities, where members debated issues, voted, discussed rules and procedures, and managed finances. While a Christ group meeting in a house or rented space would hardly look like the civic assemblies that met in Greek theaters, it seems that some aspects of this institutional component of civic life influenced the practices of early Christ groups.

Traveling with Paul

> During the night Paul had a vision: there stood a man of Macedonia pleading with him and saying, "Come over to Macedonia and help us." When he had seen the vision, we immediately tried to cross over to

> Macedonia, being convinced that God had called us to proclaim the good news to them. (Acts 16:9–10).

The ancient Mediterranean was knit together by forging connections across small distances.[13] For its inhabitants the Mediterranean was a cultural zone connected by the sea. Ancient literature is often preoccupied with travel and movement, from Odysseus's travels in the *Odyssey* to Hesiod's anxiety about boat travel[14] to Lucius's wanderings as an ass in Apuleius's *Metamorphoses*. Early Christ followers also made their way around the Mediterranean, clustering initially in urban environments along trade routes. Later generations of Christians "remembered" these early travels by narrating legendary stories about founding figures who traveled the roads and the seas in service of spreading the Christ cult.

The most famous of these travelogues is the canonical Acts of the Apostles. Written well into the second century, Acts looks back on the founding generation of "the Way" (9:2; 19:9, 23; 22:4; 24:14, 22) and crafts fantastical stories about their travels. Its author was likely from the North Aegean region, perhaps from Macedonia or Ephesos, since he has a better understanding of the terrain, cities, and routes in this region than elsewhere. In this case study, I focus on how Acts narrates Paul's travels to and through Macedonia (Acts 16:1–17:15), treating the text not as a historical source for actual historical events but as evidence for how second-century Christians constructed the connections between cities in the Roman province as cultural memories of the founding generation of Christians.[15]

Acts 16 finds Paul with Timothy in Troas. While in Phrygia and Galatia the two are forbidden by the Holy Spirit to go to the province of Asia Minor and so eventually find themselves in the port city of Troas (16:6–8). While there Paul has a vision of a "man of Macedonia" who pleads with him to "come over to Macedonia and help us" (16:9). They sail from Troas to Samothrace and then to Neapolis and then move over land to Philippi. They start a group there in the home of Lydia, a purple cloth dealer from Thyatira, and eventually run afoul of the local authorities when Paul casts a "spirit of divination" out of a local slave. Paul and his colleague Silas are beaten in the marketplace before the magistrates and cast into prison. They are eventually cleared of the vague charges and are then asked to leave the city.

Traveling along the Via Egnatia they pass through Amphipolis and Apollonia before coming to Thessaloniki. Paul preaches in the local synagogue and builds a local following of Jews, Greeks, and "not a few of the leading women" (17:1–4). The local Jews become upset by this and create a riot in the city, which leads to a search for Paul and Silas, who escape that evening from the city and make their way to Beroea (17:10). Here the apostle has more success in the local synagogue, until Jews from Thessaloniki arrive and cause trouble. Paul leaves for Athens and Silas and Timothy remain behind.

Paul's travels through Macedonia in Acts do not speak of the landscape between cities, but of a series of interconnected civic spaces. Unlike in other ancient travel tales, Paul does not meet danger in the country outside the city. There are no bandits on the roads or other dangers. Even the Jews who track Paul from Thessaloniki to Beroea hear news of his arrival quickly and traverse the landscape with seemingly no difficulties along the way (17:13). The landscape is traversed without note; the real dangers lie in the city. In the cities of Philippi, Thessaloniki, and Beroea, Paul and his compatriots meet persecution but also find allies. Paul gets into trouble in Philippi when he exorcises a fortune-telling spirit from an enslaved woman, costing her owner an income. This leads to Paul and Silas being dragged before the magistrates, beaten, and then imprisoned. Though Paul and Silas suffer beating and imprisonment, they are released the next day by the magistrates "in peace," after which Paul reveals that he and Silas are Roman citizens, which causes the magistrates to come and apologize for their treatment of the apostles. In Thessaloniki, the apostles are persecuted by the local Jewish community, from which Paul draws converts. The unbelieving Jews then spark mob riots in the city that lead to a convert named Jason being dragged before the civic authorities.

In each locale, the civic landscape, both figuratively and literally, becomes a part of the apostolic journey. In Philippi, an earthquake strikes the city while Paul and Silas are in prison. Even though all the doors of the prison are thrust open by the quake, Paul and Silas remain in their cell, much to the jailer's great surprise. In Thessaloniki, the mob that drags Jason before the magistrates accuses him of entertaining as guests "these people who have been turning the world upside down" (17:6).

In Acts, Macedonia is treated as a string of civic set pieces. Entrance to the province is dictated by the will of God, and once entered, the heralds of the Christ cult confront and experience persecution, which offers the apostles and believers the opportunity to demonstrate their virtue to an audience of other believers. Acts offers a linear layout of the province as Paul moves from one entry point to one exit point in a straight line. As an exercise in Christian cultural memory production, Acts treats civic spaces as sites of Christian miracles that also showcase the brave virtues of founding Christian figures. Moving along short distances, Paul, Timothy, and Silas knit together cities into a network of memory, offering etiological accounts of how the Christ cult moved miraculously and with divine aid through the cities of Roman Macedonia. The memories draw on the author's understanding of civic space to present origin stories that feature the kind of travel that made the

Mediterranean, and in the case of Acts, the movement known as "the Way," into a unified cultural whole.

FURTHER READING

Aldrete, Gregory S. *Daily Life in the Roman City: Rome, Pompeii, and Ostia*. University of Oklahoma Press, 2009.

Concannon, Cavan. *Assembling Early Christianity: Trade, Networks, and the Letters of Dionysios of Corinth*. Cambridge University Press, 2017.

Harrison, James R. and L. L. Welborn, eds. *The First Urban Churches*. 7 vols. SBL, 2015–22.

Horden, Peregrine and Nicholas Purcell. *The Corrupting Sea: A Study of Mediterranean History*. Blackwell, 2000.

Ma, John. *Polis: A New History of the Ancient Greek City-State from the Early Iron Age to the End of Antiquity*. Princeton University Press, 2024.

Notes

1 See Stephen D. Moore and Yvonne Sherwood, *The Invention of the Biblical Scholar: A Critical Manifesto* (Fortress, 2011).

2 See Laura Nasrallah, "Spatial Perspectives: Space and Archaeology in Roman Philippi" in *Studying Paul's Letters: Contemporary Perspectives and Methods*, ed. Joseph Marchal (Fortress, 2012).

3 For a general introduction to space in ancient cities, see Arjan Zuiderhoek, *The Ancient City* (Cambridge University Press, 2016).

4 This Greek term is used also by Pauline Christians to describe their communities and is sometimes anachronistically translated as "churches."

5 For an overview of the history of biblical studies' engagement with archaeological research, see Cavan Concannon, "The Archaeology of the Pauline Mission," in *All Things to All Cultures: Paul among Jews, Greeks, and Romans*, ed. Mark Harding and Alanna Nobbs (Eerdmans, 2013), 57–83.

6 For a critical edition, translation, and commentary, see John S. Kloppenborg and Richard S. Ascough, *Greco-Roman Associations: Texts, Translations, and Commentary. I. Attica, Central Greece, Macedonia, Thrace* (de Gruyter, 2011), 125–32, no. 23.

7 *IG* II^2 1283.

8 Kloppenborg and Ascough, *Greco-Roman Associations*, no. 23, ll.20–26.

9 Translation from Richard S. Ascough, Philip A. Harland, and John S. Kloppenborg, eds., *Associations in the Greco-Roman World: A Sourcebook* (Baylor University Press, 2012), no. 317.

10 On the inscription, its reconstruction, and the historical context that it describes, see Joshua D. Sosin, "Tyrian Stationarii at Puteoli," *Tyche* 14 (1999): 275–84.

11 For a summary, see Steven J. Friesen, "Prospects for a Demography of the Pauline Mission: Corinth among the Churches," in *Urban Religion in Roman Corinth:*

Interdisciplinary Approaches, ed. Daniel N. Schowalter and Steven J. Friesen (Harvard Theological Studies; Distributed by Harvard University Press, 2005).

12 On democratic discourse in 1 Corinthians and in Roman Greece more broadly, see Anna C. Miller, *Corinthian Democracy: Democratic Discourse in 1 Corinthians*. Princeton Theological Monographs (Pickwick, 2015).

13 See also the chapter on "Travel, Migration, and Exchange" by Susanne Luther in the present volume.

14 *Works and Days* ll. 643–94.

15 For a similar approach to Acts, see Melanie Johnson-Debaufre and Laura Nasrallah, "Beyond the Heroic Paul: Toward a Feminist and Decolonizing Approach to the Letters of Paul," in *The Colonized Apostle: Paul Through Postcolonial Eyes*, ed. Christopher D. Stanley (Fortress, 2011).

CHAPTER TWELVE

Temporalities in the Ancient Mediterranean

Kylie Crabbe
(Australian Catholic University)

THERE IS A clock tower at Harris Manchester College in Oxford with words set into the stone on different sides. Approaching from one side, all that can be seen to begin with are the words "It's later than you think." This might be rather an alarming message, or perhaps a viewer might find the warning motivating. (The emotional valance of the inscriptions might be even more salient when one is aware that this is a college with a particular focus on mature students!) Approaching from a different angle, however, one sees the words "But it's never too late."[1] This clock tower holds together multiple kinds of tensions about time. As a clock tower, it marks the passing of time in regular, measurable units, with each passing minute and hour. But alongside this it sets the viewer's present moment in the context of a wider claim: Time itself is moving on. This is not simply a comment on a student running late for a particular class, as the second inscription clarifies. This is a claim about time itself, about some kind of approaching deadline, whether the personal limits of an individual's lifespan or something more global and eschatological (even climate related?), alongside an invitation or challenge to make the most of the time remaining. After all—the clock tower preaches—it is never too late.

On the surface, talking about temporalities—that is, different ways of understanding time—might not seem all that relevant to understanding the worlds of the New Testament texts. What do we need to know about time itself in order to understand biblical texts?

And yet, when we delve into this further, we find not only that questions of temporality permeate the New Testament but that the worlds in which it was formed likewise have their own strong traditions about time. We have histories that organize their material according to the reigns of different emperors, revolutionary groups who strike new images onto coins to show the beginning of a new era, storytelling traditions that rework familiar myths in new ways to show how they are being lived out again in slightly different ways in the author's current events, and much more.

This chapter will provide some examples of the ways that different texts play with time and consider how traditions in the worlds of New Testament writers shape their politics, accounts of hope, claims about divine activity and the nature of the created world, and more.

Marking Time

Days, Weeks, and Years

Among the rich varieties of Jewish practices, Greek and Roman traditions, and the approaches that would emerge in earliest Christianity—and the intermingling between any and all of these—communities observed regular patterns of life and celebrated festivals. Sometimes the festivals of different traditions intersected with one another, and for some groups, polemics emerged over, for example, the use of calendars that deliberately differed from the calendars of other groups.

Such patterns include daily, weekly, and annual periodization, along with variations within them. Each day was divided into sections. In Roman tradition, the night is divided into periods of the night watch, and both Roman and Hebrew law specify more severe punishments for crimes committed during the nighttime (Twelve Tables 8.16; Exod 22:2). Sabbath practices designate particular days with a different quality, recounted through connections to divine activity in creation (Exod 20:11) and in rescue from slavery in the Exodus (Deut 5:15). Communities across antiquity celebrated harvest festivals and other annual moments, tying celebrations to particular deities. And annual traditions among Jewish communities, such as that of Passover, not only remembered particular events of the past but reinterpreted their significance for life in the present and future.

In early Christian traditions, including the worlds of the New Testament texts, these ways of marking time remained important, even as elements were also reworked. In New Testament texts we see Jesus and his followers observing regular patterns in time, celebrating festivals (John 7:10; Acts 2:1, and many others), and as in other Second Temple Jewish traditions, reinterpreting those traditions for new settings. Understanding the emotions and theological commitments of such temporal patterns helps readers of New Testament texts to make better sense of what they are reading. For instance, the Synoptic Gospels each recount Jesus celebrating Passover with his friends on the night before his death. But in John's Gospel, Passover is the day on which Jesus dies; John uses the tradition and its message of sacrifice and divine rescue to recast Jesus as the paschal lamb (something readers may have suspected since John the Baptist described Jesus as the lamb of God back in 1:29). Thus New Testament temporalities, like those in its wider world, include regular community patterns. But there are also broader temporal elements at work across diverse ancient literatures.

If we want to understand what the New Testament (and other Greek texts of the Hellenistic and early Roman periods) mean when they speak of "time," we need to recognize that the Greek language uses several distinct terms to express different aspects of temporality.[2] In any case, we must not assume that when modern translations use the term *time*, they always correspond exactly to what we typically understand as clearly measurable sequences of time. The Greek terms can mean a given *duration* of time, or a particularly important *moment* or *season*. While there is overlap in the ways the terms are used by the time of the Greek of the New Testament, here are some examples that show differences.

The Greek word *chronos* is often used in a way that corresponds most closely to our modern concept of a measurable span of time. It is generally used to express a not-too-short period of time that passes evenly. Mark 2:19 is typical in this regard—a text which assumes that Jesus will only remain with his disciples for a certain period of time. Particularly interesting is the use of *chronos* in the Apocalypse of John, which can make one imagine that the (remaining) *chronos* will be brief (Rev 6:11; 20:3) or even that there will no longer be any *chronos* in the new creation (Rev 10:16).

Even more intriguing is the Greek term *kairos*, whose meaning can differ from *chronos*. *Kairos* can denote a (very) short period of time, but in many cases its meaning is deeper: It denotes a critical (and sometimes particularly fateful) moment—a decisive point in time that cannot be measured quantitatively. This is particularly important for Mark 1:15, the basic summary of Jesus's message in that Gospel: Jesus speaks here of the fullness of the *Kairos*—that is, the singular and very special moment in which God's reign has *already* come within reach and is within reach *at all times*. The Apocalypse of John can be read in a similar way: The text is framed by the announcement that the *kairos* is close at hand (Rev 1:3; 22:10). Such statements do not mean that chronological time is coming to an end, but rather that the *all-decisive moment* of the final encounter with God is immediately present.

These words, used in a variety of different ways, show how important temporality is in our Greek sources. And, indeed, sometimes *kairos* and *chronos* can be used together, as when Daniel interprets Nebuchadnezzar's dream about the *kairoi* and *chronoi* (Dan 2:21, Greek), or when Jesus responds to the disciples by saying it is "not for you to know the *chronoi* and *kairoi* that the Father has set" (Acts 1:7), communicating a temporal awareness that spans both the political periods of historical time and eschatological realities.

Finally, the word *aiōn* is often rendered as "eternity." However, it is perhaps better understood as a particular duration of time, which can have a special quality of time—a world age (*saeculum*, in Latin) or an epoch (immeasurable for human judgment). When used for eternity, this is often used as literally "into the age(s)" (plural in Luke 1:33, or singular in John 6:51). It can also be associated with the special quality of God's time. A key example is Matt 28:20, where the resurrected Christ promises his apostles that he will be "with them" throughout the entire age to come.

Figure 12.1. Terminology of "time."

Marking Time Through the Passage of History

In addition to dividing days, weeks, and years, texts also move outside of these recurrent or remembered patterns into ways of thinking about an overarching passage of time, often linear in shape. For some, this means recording history through chronological events which cover measurable periods of years, whether that is an Olympiad or *age* (*aiōn*) or the reigns of different emperors. Linear movements through time may also be marked by decline or progress.[3] Or linear time might even be ruptured by events that, writers claim, make the present moment utterly *un*like those periods that have gone before—whether that rupturing event is the fall of the Jerusalem temple; the rise of the Roman Empire; or the life, death, and resurrection of Jesus. The following sections explore examples of each of these kinds of texts.

Measuring and Moving Through Time

Some kinds of texts in antiquity communicate a striking time*lessness*. For instance, proverbs and other texts of popular morality often deliberately play on a timeless quality.[4] Here the point is that whatever wisdom or ethical instruction is communicated through a proverb applies to people in any time or place. But for a wide variety of writers, the passage of time plays at least some role in their writing, and for texts written in genres like history or apocalypse, this is especially important.

Ancient and Hellenistic historians often introduce their works by setting out the scope their histories will cover. They might suggest a year or occasion that is particularly fitting to set the scene of the events they wish to recount, or which makes sense as a break in time because of, for instance, a change of ruler or a given battle that reshapes geography or political realities. It is also common for a historian to present themselves as the continuer of an earlier historian by taking up their narrative at the point at which their predecessor left off, as for example, the second-century BCE Greek historian Polybius claims to do with the histories of Aratus and Timaeus. In the New Testament, Luke appears to be doing something similar, presenting his history as a continuation of the story of God's activity as recorded in the Septuagint. Knowing that other ancient writers employed this practice invites us to consider how we read Luke and Acts.

These texts generally also suggest, either explicitly or implicitly, some kind of divine role in shaping or guiding the events of such histories. In the earliest Greek histories or epics, like Herodotus's *Histories* or Homer's *Iliad*, personified gods play this role. In histories closer to the time of the New Testament writers, non-Jewish Greek and Latin historians seem to have removed these personified gods from being characters in the story. In their place, however, we find various divine forces, such as fate (*heimarmenē*; *fatum*), providence (*pronoia*; *providentia*), fortune (*tychē*; *fortuna*), and necessity (*ananke*; *necessitas*). These forces can be found as deities themselves, such as the goddess Fortuna, who is identified with Rome and especially the fortune of the Flavian emperors, beginning with Vespasian and Titus (around the time the Second Temple was destroyed and the Gospels were written). However it is conceived, divine guidance of history intersects importantly with a writer's account of time. For instance, is the divine agent causing decline in human experience as a form of punishment? Might the text at the same time promise some improvement through repentance—a pattern famously found in the histories of the Hebrew Bible/Old Testament? Or is the divinity involved in drawing human history to a particular end point? Or are they perhaps returning human experience to an idyllic picture of its beginnings?[5]

A writer's relationship to the past can be an important part of how they tell their narrative about their own time. Second-century Roman historian Tacitus (ca. 58–120 CE) has difficulty keeping his nostalgia for the Roman Republic at bay as he describes decline in the successive reigns of emperors in his histories. He is clear that things are much worse now and uses his attitude to the past to highlight the downward trajectory of Rome over time. By contrast, Polybius (ca. 200–120 BCE) explains from the outset of his *Histories* that his account of events provides evidence of the guidance of *tychē* (fortune) in bringing Rome to power. The rise of Rome receives significant acclaim in Polybius's narrative, showing the positive progress that he argues history has made in reaching this time.

Importantly, however, even these histories can also contain subtle signs of discontent. Toward the end of Polybius's forty-book history, when recounting the fall of Carthage, he sows seeds of the end even of Rome's magnificent reign. Polybius shows a Roman military leader, Scipio, grief-stricken by the realization that Rome, too, will one day fall.[6] Here Polybius perhaps draws on his own Greek background to offer some subtle resistance, despite his apparent focus on how terrific the Roman Empire is. Likewise, Josephus, the foremost Jewish historian of the first century and especially of the Jewish-Roman War, uses the idea of changing regimes to subtly undermine Rome's power. He seems to celebrate the Roman victory and Vespasian, but he does so by claiming such power can only come from divine power. He suggests that this Roman dominance is part of God's punishment of the Jewish people and that Rome will, in turn, be overcome as the rule moves to the next regime (*J.W.* 5.367).

Political regimes are an important feature of the periodization of time seen in apocalypses as well as in histories and other works. The idea of a succession of kingdoms is found across a great range of literature. It might be simply pragmatic, in that one regime always follows another (which could evoke hope or anxiety in a reader, depending on their view of the current regime's reign), or it might be part of a dramatic, all-encompassing paradigm within a periodized progression of time. In Hesiod's *Works and Days*, which is a very old Greek text (dated to the seventh century BCE), history is divided into five "generations": the golden, silver, bronze, heroes, and iron generations. The generations named after metals show marked decline, as they descend into greater violence and so on (the heroes generation shows a temporary improvement). The writer says that they live in the time of the iron generation, a period marked by extreme hardship. Other writers also play with this idea of metallic generations (without the heroes generation), with examples ranging from Ovid (Latin, early first century) to the book of Daniel, 4 Ezra, the New Testament book of Revelation, the early second-century Epistle of Barnabas and so on. In many of these works, the four kingdoms are applied to specific historical political regimes. In Jewish and Christian traditions, however, the paradigm is extended with an additional kingdom following the traditional fourth. The fourth kingdom (aligned with the present time and certainly the worst of the progression) is succeeded by a final, unending divine reign. We can already begin to see how this pattern includes the idea of a significant future change in history, which we will revisit below. But first, it will be helpful to examine a few more elements of diverse treatments of the past.

Reinterpreted Past

As noted above, a writer's attitude to the past plays an important role in the effect of their text's temporalities. The past can be important for more than showing whether history is declining or progressing positively. Often it plays a role in interpreting the significance of the present moment and may even offer some insight into the future. Indeed, many Jewish and Christian texts use claims about the past to reassure readers about divine action that was not only effective in the past but can also inspire confidence in divine faithfulness to fulfill promises made about the future. The result is a text that seeks to address the concerns of readers in their own times.

Writers reinterpret the past to address the present using a variety of techniques. Some texts show a close relationship between the present and past by appropriating stories or symbols from the past into a text about the present time. For instance, in the late first century BCE, Virgil's Latin epic the *Aeneid* tells the story of Aeneus as he leaves the destroyed Troy, foreshadowing the founding of Rome. The poem in twelve Books draws heavily on Homer's Greek epics the *Iliad* and *Odyssey* and reinterprets those founding texts for a new and different audience in Augustan Rome. Knowing the connections between these texts helps readers to notice how Virgil is reimagining these traditions, values, and hopes. Imperial Rome is presented as subsuming but also superseding these events of the Greek past.

The writers of the apocalypses 4 Ezra and 2 Baruch (both Jewish apocalypses from around the end of the first century CE) also play with time in their texts by setting their stories within the past. Here the heartache of the Roman destruction of the *Second* Temple in the writers' context is communicated by writing a text set in the time of the Babylonian destruction of the *First* Temple. Each author uses protagonists from the Babylonian exile (Ezra and Baruch), not only drawing on all the emotions associated with the exile but, in a sense, collapsing the time between these events as though they represent a single experience of hostility from others and punishment for failings in their own communities. At the same time, this approach might enable not only lament but also hope for future rebuilding.

Second Temple Jewish texts also reinterpret the past by engagement or reengagement with founding stories. Ari Mermelstein observes that during the Babylonian exile, many Jewish texts begin their stories of divine faithfulness by going back all the way to creation, rather than to Sinai.[7] He suggests that, in the context of the temple's destruction and exile, it may appear as though the close relationship between Israel and Yahweh has come to an end, implying that Israel's period of favor was simply one in a succession of political empires and that Yahweh has now moved on to a new covenant partner. Mermelstein argues that, by tracing the story back to earlier origins, many Second Temple texts emphasize that Yahweh established the relationship even earlier and, just as there was a period before the Mosaic covenant, so shall there also be a continuing relationship beyond the exile. By contrast, in her discussion of the Second Temple's destruction, Hindy Najman speaks about a "reboot" of Torah practice in 4 Ezra as a way of reenlivening Israel's founding story and providing hope and instruction for readers.[8]

The New Testament likewise includes retellings that leverage emotions and beliefs about past events when describing new events in the New Testament writer's own time. For instance, in addition to Luke's use of the Septuagint as the starting point for his own history, as noted above, he also uses typologies that align elements of that story with his own. The miraculous births in Luke's infancy narratives (Luke 1–2) draw directly on (and extend) the narratives of women who struggle to become pregnant in the Hebrew Bible. Elizabeth is described in terms reminiscent of Sarah, Rebekah, Rachel, and Hannah, while Mary's Song (the Magnificat—i.e., Luke 1:46–55) reinterprets the song offered by Hannah. In terms of temporalities and divine guidance over time, the typology taps into both the sadness and joy of the matriarchs, emphasizing divine action that can achieve the seemingly impossible. This use of time shows that God's activity is entirely consistent over time and yet, with the miraculous story of Mary's conception of Jesus, an even more extreme version of this pattern shows that something new and ultimate is at work as well.

In a similar way, Matthew uses typology from Moses in his presentation of Jesus—from the infancy escape to Egypt and murder of infants, to Jesus's proclamation from the mountain.[9] Again this enables him to draw on the story of the divinely-sustained, faithful leadership of Moses in the past to show continuity with Jesus's ministry, while also extending his story into something more in this new time. Likewise, echoing Mermelstein's observations of other texts, the prologue of John's Gospel goes back even earlier to ground the story of Jesus in an account of creation.

These efforts create new eras that are embedded strongly in the old. Such an approach affirms a kind of theological continuity, even where some adaptation is also included in the reworking—something that the above demonstrates is present not only in early Christian literature but Jewish literature as well. The approach also shows that, just as God has been faithful throughout these past events, the reader may likewise find hope for the future within their lives now.

Ruptured Time

While writers deploy numerous ways of communicating the passage of time and various continuities in human experience or divine faithfulness over time, they can also show significant events doing something entirely new. Such events might create a sense of *rupture* in time.[10] In fact, key events can be so significant to a writer that they seem to reshape the importance of every other time in their temporal schema. You might have heard people speak of a fundamental shift in time after, for instance, a wrenching bereavement. Time stops and can now be measured as time before or after the bereavement. The bereavement itself might make one see past events in a new light. (This could be similar to how time is measured before and after, for instance, the onset of the COVID-19 pandemic, the birth of a child, or war.)

Writers in antiquity identified a range of dramatic events which they presented as altering history. It might be the violence of Antiochus IV Epiphanes's Seleucid reign, the fall of Carthage, or founding of the Roman Empire, the time of the Teacher of Righteousness's ministry in some Dead Sea Scrolls texts (Pesher Habakkuk), or the fall of the first or Second Temple as noted above—or an anticipated cataclysmic end to all through installation of divine reign. Even the texts that are so focused on continuity of divine faithfulness, such as the Animal Apocalypse's treatment of creation and promise of a kind of return to Eden, or 4 Ezra's emphasis on a return to Torah practice, emphasize this precisely because they are concerned about a possible appearance of rupture.

Dynamic portrayals of successive political regimes are common in both Jewish and non-Jewish Greek and Roman literature. The pattern communicates continuity, with the successive regimes, but also *dis*continuity, with a genuine shift between each kingdom. For instance, as already noted, even Polybius, who considers Rome's rise an utterly new achievement performed by Fortune, ultimately presents Rome as one in a series of empires—even if this is a particularly impressive one. But it is primarily in Jewish literature that the idea of a complete, rupturing end to this pattern with the installation of an eternal divine regime is found.

Using the archetypal, five-kingdom model that many later texts draw on explicitly, Daniel 2 and 7 each present metaphorical accounts of four political kingdoms—the first in the imagery of a statue made of different materials and the second with imagery of different fantastical animals who dominate one after another. As noted above, each kingdom becomes worse than the preceding, with the author identifying the writer's present time as the fourth kingdom, the worst of all. However, an abrupt shift in time is promised in the near future. Asserting divine control over the shift in regimes, the writer promises an imminent end to this fourth, oppressive regime and installation of a divine kingdom. This does more than offer the next kingdom in turn; it brings an end to the pattern of revolving regimes altogether.

In a text closer to the New Testament period, Josephus (see above) uses interpretation of Daniel to promise an imminent end to the current regime, though subtly. A bit like Polybius's political context, Josephus is in a slightly tricky political situation of his own, as he works under the benefaction of the emperor Vespasian despite having previously been a general in the Jewish army. Nonetheless, Josephus's prediction of the end of Rome is clear for readers who understand his instructions about how the *final* divine reign will arrive at a time secretly coded within Daniel's text (*Ant.* 10.210, 276).

For some, the cataclysmic event that reshapes time relates to the fall of the temple. In 4 Ezra, the fall of the temple causes a crisis for the character Ezra, prompting a rethinking of the relationship between God and God's people and, as noted above, a "reboot" of Torah practices. However, this is not yet the final turning point in history, which the text continues to expect. In its apocalyptic visions, 4 Ezra reinterprets the promises of Daniel, just like Josephus did, offering a coded message that God will soon bring an end to the Roman Empire and install a divine kingdom (as symbolized by the messianic lion promising the destruction of an eagle, commonly used to represent Rome, 12:31–34).

Continuity and rupture in time play out in different ways across the texts of the New Testament's wider context. Already it is clear that some rupturing events discussed by ancient writers lie in the writers' past and some are still in the future. The founding of the Roman Empire or ministry of the Teacher of Righteousness lay in the past. The fall of the Second Temple might make communities rethink their theology, but it is an event in the past for those writers that discuss it, though in each case, the ongoing effect and what happens next are still open questions.

When it comes to the effect of the life, death, and resurrection of Jesus, we find something potentially even more complicated. Clearly these events are also already in the past for the New Testament writers—they have inspired the authors to tell Jesus's story and believers to live in communities formed in response to Christ. But a key question of temporalities that runs throughout the New Testament is whether the past events have already utterly reshaped human history, or whether there is something anticipated that is still to come: a parousia or second coming of Jesus. This is often described as the "already-not yet" tension within New Testament texts. On the one hand, for writers across the New Testament, Jesus's life, death, and resurrection have ruptured history. These events have ensured that the experience of the New Testament readers, living after this time, is utterly unlike that which came before. According to some New Testament texts, the power of sin has already been broken. This concept is often referred to as "realized eschatology." On the other hand, New Testament texts reflect to varying degrees on the ways in which present experience remains imperfect. Governing authorities do not seem to enact the will of God and may even persecute members of the Jesus movement who seek to do so. Death persists in human experience, and sin and the power of evil still appear to be present in the world (though some texts suggest they may already be constrained or in their final throes).

As such, we see that temporalities play a crucial role in some fundamental theological questions in the biblical text. Understanding how these temporalities are similar to, or different from, the wider world in which the New Testament texts were written will enhance our understanding of how first readers may have encountered the texts that became the New Testament.

Why Does Temporality Matter?

However the past and future are presented in diverse texts from antiquity, in so many ways writers remain focused on their own present time. Tacitus's nostalgia for the time of the Roman Republic (which he sees as the pinnacle social moment) is a commentary on the declining standards he perceives in life under the Roman Empire. Temporalities across antique texts make for significant political differences for the readers' present time. For instance, Virgil retells origin stories to emphasize that history has in fact reached its ideal endpoint in the glorious Roman Empire under Augustus. By contrast, Polybius celebrates Rome's rise but makes a political claim that this too will end. In these different temporalities we encounter what Karl Mannheim describes as the difference between "ideology" and "utopia."[11] Virgil's version proclaims the present as the ideal and looks for no further political shift. Polybius, however (like Josephus and most other early Christian and Jewish texts), still looks for a shift beyond the current time. This may be simply the movement onto a new regime, as for Polybius, or it may be a utopian final change that is anticipated.

The focus on the present also sees writers that play with earlier texts recalibrating predictions so that they remain focused on the new time of their readers. This is particularly powerful in relation to prophecies about the end of oppression, where writers recalibrate to ensure that the promised end remains imminently expected. For instance, Jeremiah 25:11–12 calculates that the divine action to end the suffering of the exile will take place after seventy years. Daniel 9 draws on this tradition but describes it as seventy *weeks* of years. Even later, 4 Ezra explicitly claims that the eagle in its vision is the fourth kingdom "that appeared in a vision to your brother Daniel," while noting that it was not explained then as it is explained by Uriel now (12:11–12). In this way, 4 Ezra moves the penultimate regime from the Greek to Roman. In fact, as shown in the texts below, 4 Ezra gives instructions on how to measure the nearness of divine action on the basis of other events unfolding in the readers' present time.

Temporality in the New Testament is likewise focused on the experience of the present time. These texts are written for early Christian audiences, grappling with the challenges of making sense of the Christ event. They are trying to discern how God's activity through the story of Israel might have led to the new claims about Jesus (coming up with different answers to this question of continuity and discontinuity along the way). Moreover, these writers are considering what all this means for how people should live now, in a world where things do not yet seem to be perfectly under God's control, while still finding hope in what might yet come.

Thus, we see a variety of ways in which temporalities from texts in the surrounding context might inform our readings of the New Testament. This is true not only in how, for instance, the book of Revelation considers changes in political regimes in apocalyptic visions, but also in more diverse or subtle considerations. Paul writes lists of virtues and vices that might seem like the "timeless" ethical instruction of popular proverbs, but in fact are given an eschatological framework that shifts the urgency and consequences of these behaviors to be quite different from those other texts (1 Cor 6:9–11). He also talks about divine activity in covenant with Abraham (Rom 4:9–25) or by analogy to Hagar (Gal 4:21–31), and in overcoming the groaning of creation (Rom 8:19–23). Luke tells his infancy narratives with explicit reference to what is happening in the imperial setting (the time of Quirinius as governor and so on) and even sets up direct comparison between Jesus and Augustus. Some early New Testament letters proclaim expectation of Jesus's imminent return "like a thief in the night" (1 Thess 5:2) and encourage all wherever possible to remain single given the imminent end (1 Cor 7:8), while other later texts deal with continuing realities, such as the importance of having children (as is the social context of the controversial statement in 1 Tim 2:15).

Time runs throughout the New Testament texts and the worlds in which they were written. It shapes theology, discipleship, politics—from the everyday to the final culmination of all things. Our familiarity with the temporal dynamics from the surrounding world will help us as rigorous readers of the New Testament to see the many similar and different ways in which New Testament writers explore the past, consider the future, and provide comfort and challenge to their readers in the present.

TAKING A CLOSER LOOK: SOURCES

Sources from the World of the New Testament

Time in Polybius, *The Histories*

For what gives my work its peculiar quality, and what is most remarkable in the present age, is this. Fortune has guided almost all the affairs of the world in one direction and has forced them to incline toward one and the same end; a historian should likewise bring before their readers under one synoptical view the operations by which she has accomplished her general purpose. Indeed it was this chiefly that invited and encouraged me to undertake my task; and secondarily the fact that none of my contemporaries have undertaken to write a general history, in which case I should have been much less eager to take this in hand. As it is, I observe that while several modern writers deal with particular wars and certain matters connected with them, no one, as far as I am aware, has even attempted to inquire critically when and whence the general and comprehensive scheme of events originated and how it led up to the end. I therefore thought it quite necessary not to leave unnoticed or allow to pass into oblivion this, the achievement of Fortune most excellent and profitable to contemplate. For though she is ever producing something new and ever playing a part in the lives of humans, she has not in a single instance ever accomplished such a work, ever achieved such a triumph, as in our own times. We can no more hope to perceive this from histories dealing with particular events than to get at once a notion of the form of the whole world, its disposition and order, by visiting, each in turn, the most famous cities, or indeed by looking at separate pictures of each: a result by no means likely. For we can get some idea of a whole from a part, but never knowledge or exact opinion. Special histories therefore contribute very little to the knowledge of the whole and conviction of its truth. It is only indeed by study of the interconnection of all the particulars, their resemblances and differences, that we are enabled at least to make a general survey and thus derive both benefit and pleasure from history. (1.4.1.–7, 9–11, adjusted for inclusive language)[12]

Polybius is a Greek historian of the second century BCE. This excerpt from early in his forty-book *Histories* demonstrates both Polybius's celebration of Rome and his claims about the superiority of his approach to "general" or "universal" history. Polybius contrasts his own work with that of historians of individual cities or battles, claiming that the most important thing a history should do is to make clear large movements over time—which, he says, is only possible if the historian gives an overview of both time and geography. (We can set aside whether Polybius actually achieves this in his still rather limited focus.) Notice how Polybius refers to the present time. *Tychē* (*fortuna*), though always doing new things, has done something completely unprecedented now, he claims. How might Polybius's cursory references to the past and claims about the present shape how a reader approaches the rest of his history?

The Signs of the End in 4 Ezra

Then I answered and said, "O Lord, you have already shown me a great number of the signs that you will do in the last times, but you have not shown me when you will do them."

He answered me and said, "Measure carefully in your mind, and when you see that some of the predicted signs have occurred, then you will know that it is the very time when the Most High is about to visit the world that he has made. So when there shall appear in the world earthquakes, tumult of peoples, intrigues of nations, wavering of leaders, confusion of princes, then you will know that it was of these that the Most High spoke from the days that were of old, from the beginning. For just as with everything that has occurred in the world, the beginning is evident, and the end manifest; so also are the times of the Most High: the beginnings are manifest in wonders and mighty works, and the end in penalties and in signs.

"It shall be that all who will be saved and will be able to escape on account of their works, or on account of the faith by which they have believed, will survive the dangers that have been predicted, and will see my salvation in my land and within my borders, which I have sanctified for myself from the beginning. Then those who have now abused my ways shall be amazed, and those who have rejected them with contempt shall live in torments. For as many as did not acknowledge me in their lifetime, though they received my benefits, and as many as scorned my law while they still had freedom, and did not understand but despised it

> while an opportunity of repentance was still open to them, these must in torment acknowledge it after death. Therefore, do not continue to be curious about how the ungodly will be punished; but inquire how the righteous will be saved, those to whom the age belongs and for whose sake the age was made." (4 Ezra 8:62b–9:13)

4 Ezra is a Jewish apocalypse written around the end of the first century CE. It comprises seven episodes, the first three of which are dialogues between the human protagonist, Ezra, and an angel, Uriel. This passage comes as part of the third dialogue. The dialogues are rigorous and at times heated, as Ezra continues to challenge the angel over the suffering and injustice in the world. Here only a section of the dialogue is provided and although the excerpt ends with a comment from Uriel, note that it is not necessarily the case that his view prevails. See the full text of 4 Ezra to consider the relationship between the views of Ezra and Uriel and what view(s) the text itself seeks to persuade its reader to adopt.

In this passage, the angel Uriel explains to Ezra how to recognize when the time of final divine action is approaching. Many texts from antiquity prophesy events unfolding in a step-by-step list, including events from both the writer's past and future. Scholars refer to this type of prophecy as a "*vaticinium ex eventu*"—that is, a prophecy after the event. The texts are set at an earlier time and "foretell" a series of "future" events; some of these, however, are events that have already taken place before the writing (ensuring the writer has a good grasp of the details of those events), whereas others remain predictions about future events. By using this technique, writers seek to establish the credibility of the prophecy through the accurate "prediction" of past events, thereby building the reader's confidence that future events really will happen. This instruction from Uriel provides a clear example of an ancient text explaining how to read such prophecies. Modern scholars also use this technique in reading such texts, identifying the concrete historical events named in the prophecy to identify the likely time of writing. How might a reader of 4 Ezra, approximately three decades after the fall of the Second Temple, respond to Uriel's instruction? Does such temporality and future anticipation engender hope, fear, challenge—or perhaps a combination of all three?

Coins of the Bar Kokhba Revolt

In the second Jewish revolt against Rome, 132–35 CE, the revolutionary groups created new coins for themselves, beginning again from year one. Here is an image of both sides of a small bronze coin. One side (the obverse) shows a palm tree with the words (in Hebrew) "Eleazar the priest," and the other side

Figure 12.2. Coin from Bar Kokhba Revolt, dated to first year of the revolt.[13] (CNG, Wikimedia Commons. Used under the Creative Commons Attribution-Share Alike 3.0 Unported license.)

(the reverse) shows three bunches of grapes with the words "Year one of the redemption of Israel." Given what you have read above about periodization under different political regimes, what might such new coins indicate about the hopes and beliefs of those who were part of this revolt?

Reading the New Testament Texts

Romans 13

> Besides this, you know what time it is, how it is now the moment for you to wake from sleep. For salvation is nearer to us now than when we became believers; the night is far gone, the day is near. Let us then lay aside the works of darkness and put on the armor of light; let us live honorably as in the day, not in reveling and drunkenness, not in debauchery and licentiousness, not in quarrelling and jealousy. Instead, put on the Lord Jesus Christ, and make no provision for the flesh, to gratify its desires. (Rom 13:11–14)

In his letter to the Christian communities in Rome, Paul uses evocative imagery to encourage faithfulness, and perhaps to exhort his readers not to worry too much about the current political circumstances because they are about to come to an end. Paul draws on the emotional valence of day and night, and of light and dark, by using this imagery. Rather than portray God's final activity as delayed and irrelevant, Paul heightens the urgency by suggesting that salvation (dawn) is closer than ever. Perhaps akin to the "earth clock" that climate scientists use to demonstrate where the present time fits within the broader context of history since the universe began, and when, without drastic climate action, it will end, Paul maps the larger eschatological message onto the temporal scope of a single day. How might this imagery feel to readers in a context where night has some additional qualities, for instance, as noted above, during which the same crimes attract greater punishment? Alternatively, how might the "day" feel for Paul's readers? Are his readers among those who might fear the coming "day" to which Paul refers, or does the letter suggest that the readers belong to a discipleship community that approaches the dawning salvation with greater confidence?

Luke 21

> When some were speaking about the temple, how it was adorned with beautiful stones and gifts dedicated to God, he said, "As for these things that you see, the days will come when not one stone will be left upon another; all will be thrown down."
>
> They asked him, "Teacher, when will this be, and what will be the sign that this is about to take place?"
>
> And he said, "Beware that you are not led astray; for many will come in my name and say, 'I am he!' and, 'The time is near!' Do not go after them.
>
> "When you hear of wars and insurrections, do not be terrified; for these things must take place first, but the end will not follow immediately."
>
> Then he said to them, "Nation will rise against nation, and kingdom against kingdom; there will be great earthquakes, and in various places famines and plagues; and there will be dreadful portents and great signs from heaven.
>
> "But before all this occurs, they will arrest you and persecute you; they will hand you over to synagogues and prisons, and you will be brought before kings and governors because of my name. This will give you an opportunity to testify. So make up your minds not to prepare your defense in advance; for I will give you words and a wisdom that none of your opponents will be able to withstand or contradict. You will be betrayed even by parents and brothers, by relatives and friends; and they will put some of you to death. You will be hated by all because of my name. But not a hair of your head will perish. By your endurance you will gain your souls.
>
> "When you see Jerusalem surrounded by armies, then know that its desolation has come near. Then those in Judea must flee to the mountains, and those inside the city must leave it, and those out in the country

must not enter it; for these are days of vengeance, as a fulfilment of all that is written. Woe to those who are pregnant and to those who are nursing infants in those days! For there will be great distress on the earth and wrath against this people; they will fall by the edge of the sword and be taken away as captives among all nations; and Jerusalem will be trampled on by the Gentiles, until the times of the Gentiles are fulfilled.

"There will be signs in the sun, the moon, and the stars, and on the earth distress among nations confused by the roaring of the sea and the waves. People will faint from fear and foreboding of what is coming upon the world, for the powers of the heavens will be shaken. Then they will see 'the Son of Man coming in a cloud' with power and great glory. Now when these things begin to take place, stand up and raise your heads, because your redemption is drawing near." (Luke 21:5–28)

This long interaction between Jesus and his disciples in Luke's Gospel takes place in Jerusalem, as Jesus's death draws nearer. It is a passage with which scholars have often wrestled, wondering if Luke's descriptions of political events suggest that he is no longer looking to a seemingly-delayed future parousia (or second coming of Christ), but is instead focusing on identifying God's activity with events within history. In light of the discussion above about rupture in history and 4 Ezra's insight about how to read a *vaticinium ex eventu*, how would you read the temporalities and prophesied events here in Luke's text? (Does Luke list the events in a linear order?) If Luke is providing a *vaticinium ex eventu* here, then the historical events may be providing the context and evidence for his readers to discern their own historical time and, importantly, when the final events might take place (thereby responding to the various questions about "when" these things will occur—v. 7). How might such temporalities shape how readers approach the rest of Luke's Gospel (and possibly Acts) as they read in the years following the fall of the temple?

FURTHER READING

Barr, John. *Biblical Words for Time*. 2nd rev. ed. Studies in Biblical Theology 33 (SCM, 1969).

Becker, Eve-Marie. *The Birth of Christian History: Memory and Time from Mark to Luke-Acts*. Anchor Yale Bible Reference Library (Yale University Press, 2017).

Collins, John J. "Temporality and Politics in Jewish Apocalyptic Literature." In *Apocalyptic in History and Tradition*, edited by Christopher Rowland and John Barton. Journal for the Study of the Pseudepigrapha: Supplement series 43 (Sheffield Academic, 2002).

Crabbe, Kylie. *Luke/Acts and the End of History*. Beihefte zur Zeitschrift für die neutestamentliche Wissenschaft 238 (de Gruyter, 2019).

Cullmann, Oscar. *Christ and Time: The Primitive Christian Conception of Time and History*. Translated by Floyd V. Filson. Rev. ed. (SCM, 1962).

Mermelstein, Ari. *Creation, Covenant, and the Beginnings of Judaism: Reconceiving Historical Time in the Second Temple Period*. Supplements to the Journal for the Study of Judaism 168 (Brill, 2014).

Najman, Hindy. *Losing the Temple and Recovering the Future: An Analysis of 4 Ezra*. Cambridge University Press, 2014.

Nicklas, Tobias. "Kairos und Chronos: Variationen des Zeitdenkens im Neuen Testament." In *Neues Testament in der Koine. Semantische Fallstudien zu ausgewählten Schlüsselbegriffen*, ed. Stefan Alkier, Dominic Noichl, and Thomas Schmitz. Beyond Historicism—New Testament Studies Today. Brill Deutschland, 2026 (forthcoming).

Stuckenbruck, Loren T. "How Much Evil Does the Christ Event Solve? Jesus and Paul in Relation to Jewish 'Apocalyptic' Thought." In *Evil in Second Temple Judaism and Early Christianity*, edited by Chris Keith and Loren T. Stuckenbruck. Wissenschaftliche Untersuchungen zum Neuen Testament 2/417. Mohr Siebeck, 2016.

Notes

1 This clocktower was designed by Yiangou Architects and built in 2014. Images of the inscriptions are available at "Oxford Inscriptions: Harris Manchester College," History on the Streets of Oxford, Stephanie Jenkins, accessed July 7, 2025, http://www.oxfordhistory.org.uk/streets/inscriptions/central/harris_manchester.html.

2 For more detailed discussion, see Kylie Crabbe, *Luke/Acts and the End of History*, Beihefte zur Zeitschrift für die neutestamentliche Wissenschaft 238 (de Gruyter, 2019); Tobias Nicklas, "Kairos und Chronos: Variationen des Zeitdenkens im Neuen Testament," in *Neues Testament in der Koine. Semantische Fallstudien zu ausgewählten Schlüsselbegriffen*, ed. Stefan Alkier, Dominic Noichl, and Thomas Schmitz, Beyond Historicism—New Testament Studies Today (Brill-Schöningh, 2026, forthcoming).

3 Crabbe, *Luke/Acts* (de Gruyter, 2019), 57–63.

4 Teresa Morgan, *Popular Morality in the Early Roman Empire* (Cambridge University Press, 2007), 242.

5 This might be communicated in the Animal Apocalypse (1 En. 85–90) by the similarity between its picture of creation and the end. For this text, see the chapter on "Early Jewish Literature" by David Cielontko in the present volume.

6 Polyb. *Histories* 38.21–22.

7 Ari Mermelstein, *Creation, Covenant, and the Beginnings of Judaism: Reconceiving Historical Time in the Second Temple Period* (Brill, 2014).

8 Hindy Najman, *Losing the Temple and Recovering the Future: An Analysis of 4 Ezra* (Cambridge University Press, 2014).

9 Dale Allison, *A New Moses: A Matthean Typology* (Fortress, 1993).

10 Crabbe, *Luke/Acts*, 61.

11 Karl Mannheim, *Ideology and Utopia: An Introduction to the Sociology of Knowledge* (Routledge & Kegan Paul, 1960), 36. See application to biblical studies in John Collins, "Temporality and Politics in Jewish Apocalyptic literature," in *Apocalyptic in History and Tradition*, ed. Christopher Rowland and John Barton (Sheffield Academic, 2002).

12 Polybius. *The Histories, Volume I: Books 1-2*, trans. W. R. Paton, rev. F. W. Walbank and Christian Habicht, Loeb Classical Library 128 (Harvard University Press, 2010).

13 See Ya'akov Meshorer, *A Treasury of Jewish Coins from the Persian Period to Bar Kokhba* (Yad ben-Zvi, 2001), 246.

CHAPTER THIRTEEN

Monetary Economy, Wealth, Taxes

Stefan Alkier
(Goethe-Universität Frankfurt)

IN ANTIQUITY, RELIGION, politics, economics, and law formed an interwoven network of beliefs, power structures, economic practices, legal norms, and social customs. Coins functioned not only as a means of payment but also as a means of conveying religious and political messages. Political rulers not only had secular power but also fulfilled priestly roles and were even considered divine beings. Temples served as religious places of worship but also as important economic institutions and places of justice. Religious beliefs were expressed not only in worship but in food production, the design of tools and living spaces, and, last but not least, played a significant role in political decisions. When this interconnection is recognized without modern prejudices and presuppositions, a better understanding of biblical texts can be achieved.

Ancient Economy

The multicultural Greco-Roman world consisted mainly of developed agrarian societies, as observed and articulated by G. E. Lenski.[1] The majority of the workforce was invested in agriculture and the processing of agricultural products. Land ownership was the decisive factor in determining wealth and power. Economic life—the production and distribution of goods and services—was determined by supraregional and regional factors, the interaction of which gave rise to various and sometimes complex forms of production and distribution. Although the economies of the state, polis, temple, and private *oikos* were interconnected, they represented distinct forms of economic organization, each with their own scope of action. There was, however, no economic policy in the modern sense. Instead, economic conditions developed primarily as a result of the politics of power on the one hand, and the necessity to satisfy the basic needs of the population on the other. There was no strict separation between religion and politics, and consequently, no strict separation between religious and economic institutions.

Basic Features of the Hellenistic Economy

The triumph of Alexander the Great, king of Macedonia, had far-reaching consequences, not only in terms of politics of power and intellectual history, but also because of the considerable economic changes it brought—developments which Michael Rostovtzeff describes in detail in his still unrivaled work, *The Social and Economic History of the Hellenistic World*. Alexander's army, which Rostovtzeff characterizes as a mobile city, was itself a significant economic factor and played an important role in the intensification of the monetary economy and the construction of roads. Of particular economic importance were the key role of the monarch in economic life, the intensive expansion of the monetary economy, and the growth of urban centers.

An important aspect of the charismatic kingship of Alexander and his successors in the Hellenistic Diadochi empires was the belief that the king owned the land he ruled. However, the limitation of communication and agricultural technology available to ancient societies prevented the royal family from directly cultivating all the land. Instead, through various forms of land tenure, a privileged upper class oversaw the further exploitation of the land. Cities, and in some cases temples, such as the Temple of Artemis in Ephesus, enjoyed a degree of autonomy, and in some cases also had considerable amounts of land at their disposal.[2] A complex tax system ensured that a large portion of the revenue was returned to the royal court. In addition to the direct use of the royal land and the indirect management through the granting of rights of use, monopolization became a significant source of income for the Hellenistic kings. This practice was particularly pronounced in the Ptolemaic Empire, with Egypt as its heartland. There, the king held monopolies on salt, beer, spices, coinage, and banking.

Overall, the Hellenistic kings promoted an economic mindset focused on profit maximization. Although the supply of essential goods to the population was largely secured, it was no longer the primary focus of the royal and aristocratic cultivation of land. A decisive instrument of this economic shift was the expansion of the monetary economy, as it allowed not only for greater state control but was also more conducive to the accumulation of available wealth. Alexander had the Persian state treasure he had captured minted into coins and used them to pay his soldiers, among other things. With this new coinage, he intended to establish a uniform currency and thereby promote trade across regions. However, regional coins retained their value, resulting in several coinage systems circulating simultaneously. Alexander's successors in the Diadochi empires continued this policy with varying degrees of intensity and focus, as did the Romans later on. The Ptolemies were particularly keen to enforce a single currency as the basis for a flourishing economy through the aforementioned monopolization. While Alexander and the Seleucids based their coinage on the

Attic standard, the Ptolemies initially followed the Rhodian but later adopted the Tyrian coinage. These differences led to two different economic zones in the Hellenistic world.

Alexander, who was highly educated, was not only a military leader but also personally designed much of his city, Alexandria. His successors likewise devoted time and money to building new cities, expanding older ones, and developing trade routes. The ancient metropolis is a product of Hellenism, with Pergamon (over one hundred thousand inhabitants), Seleucia (over two hundred thousand), and Alexandria (a good five hundred thousand) standing out as particularly noteworthy examples. The construction projects themselves were an innovative boost to the Hellenistic economy. At the same time, the emergence of new metropolitan lifestyles also created new economic opportunities and markets. New business and service opportunities arose in the large cities. However, they also brought with them considerable social problems.

In contrast to the Persian administrative system, the Diadochi empires reduced the size of their administrative areas. In this context, a number of new cities emerged, and many older settlements grew into smaller cities due to their newly acquired administrative functions.

Basic Features of the Economy in the Roman Empire

While the Hellenistic states were kingdoms and remained so until their respective ends, Rome began its history as a city-state and later became a republic. It was not until the time of Augustus that the imperial era began, which initially retained a republican character, but gradually evolved, despite occasional attempts at reform, into a system increasingly open to military dictatorship. These political changes went hand in hand with the processes of economic transformation. While the economy of early Rome and even that of the early republic was primarily geared toward regional self-sufficiency through agriculture, Rome's expansion from the third century BCE onward marked its emergence as an international economic power clearly focused on profit maximization. Although Rome had abundant salt deposits near Ostia, it was otherwise poor in natural resources. After Carthage, Rome's fiercest trading rival, was finally defeated, and the Roman Empire expanded eastward and took over the legacy of the Hellenistic monarchies, it reached a size unprecedented in world history. Material goods such as food, luxury goods, money, gold, and natural resources, but also thousands upon thousands of enslaved people from the conquered territories, were brought to Rome. Slavery played a far greater role in the economy of an expanding Rome than it did in the Hellenistic kingdoms.

While Rome followed in Greece's cultural footsteps, it made a distinctive contribution through its continuous development of a professionalized legal system, which also regulated the administration of the empire and large parts of economic life through complex systems of taxation.

Although Rome did not mint its own coins until the end of the fourth century BCE, the monetary economy soon came to play an even greater role than in the Hellenistic monarchies. The exploitation of the provinces, some of which were far away, was greatly promoted and facilitated by the use of money, even though taxes continued to be levied in kind.

The supply of provisions to the city of Rome was an economic factor in its own right. During the Republic, grain (and at times other staple foods) was occasionally distributed free of charge to citizens in need. It was part of Augustus's politics of power to win the favor of the masses as a benefactor. He therefore introduced a permanent supply of grain and, in some cases, even meat, olive oil, and wine in the city of Rome. The imperial province of Egypt became Rome's breadbasket, as the province of Africa had been before. The provinces not only had to provide the necessary grain free of charge but were also responsible for organizing and financing its transport. Nevertheless, it is also true of the Roman Empire that there was no economic policy in the modern sense. Rather, the preservation of Rome's power, or, from Augustus onward, that of the emperor, was at primary consideration in economic decisions. The provinces served primarily as a source for exploitation. Nevertheless, there was some room for maneuver and large regional differences, which were handled differently by the individual governors. Most of them had come to the office at great expense and were often in debt. They now had to recoup this money in the provinces, which often led to unbearable burdens for the provincial population, as evidenced by a quote from Tiberius in a letter to the provincial governors, which has been handed down by Suetonius: "To the governors who recommended burdensome taxes for his provinces, he wrote in answer that it was the part of a good shepherd to shear his flock, not skin it."[3]

The wealth from the provinces enabled numerous cities to be expanded and important trade and military roads to be built and maintained. At its peak, the city of Rome had a population of around one million. As already noted in connection with the Hellenistic cities, this also led to the emergence of new markets and services. Precious luxury goods from all provinces found their way to the capital. Overall, the Romans intensified the Hellenistic policy of urbanization.

Despite Rome's immense wealth, there was also great poverty in the heartland. The members of the senatorial, equestrian, and decurionic classes became particularly wealthy, but together they made up less than 1 percent of the population. The power of Augustus had an economic foundation. The distinction he introduced between imperial and senatorial provinces meant that income from Egypt, for example, flowed directly into his personal coffers. The charity of Augustus toward the citizens of Rome was largely paid for by the inhabitants of the imperial provinces. No one could match the wealth of Augustus.

Basic Features of the Economy in Roman Palestine

Due to its strategic geographical location as a link between Asia and Africa, the economy of the Levant has always participated in intercontinental trade, albeit with some striking regional differences. The Phoenician cities on the Mediterranean, especially Tyre, maintained intensive trade relations by sea with Carthage, Asia Minor, Greece, and Sicily. It was not Alexander and his successors, but rather the Phoenicians before them who must be regarded as cultural mediators, precisely because of their economic and intercontinental relations between East and West. The Levant has always been a multicultural entity with considerable geographical, cultural, and economic differences, and this remained the case during the time of the Roman province of Palestine. Archaeological finds indicate that Galilee was far more involved in these international and intercultural trade relations than Judea.

Tyrian money, which served as a stable currency throughout the Levant well into Roman times, played a significant economic role across the region. For a long time, only the Tyrian shekel was accepted as payment for temple taxes in Jerusalem. The good reputation of Tyrian money persisted even long after it ceased to be minted. In the second half of the first century CE, Tyrian money became a metaphor for solid currencies.

After Alexander's conquest, not much changed at first for the former Persian satrapy of Jehud. In the course of the Diadochi wars, the country fell to the Ptolemies and enjoyed relative stability in the third century BCE. The Ptolemies reduced the size of the administrative units for better control. This led, among other things, to the urbanization of various areas. At the beginning of the second century BCE, the Seleucids conquered the Levant. The Judeans were thus successively integrated into both Hellenistic economic spheres, and their assessment of the Ptolemies and Seleucids was by no means uniform. The influential Judean family of the Tobiads emerged as general tenants, who initially had to pay the required revenues to the Ptolemies, and from 198 BCE to the Seleucids, but compensated themselves in the process. The revealing letters of the Ptolemaic administrator Zenon from the middle of the third century BCE provide insight into the extent of the economic activities of such tenants.

After the Maccabean revolts and the establishment of the Hasmonean monarchy, the Judeans regained state autonomy for just under a century. At times, the Hasmonean Empire was larger than it had been in Solomon's time. Although the Maccabean revolt was directed against excessive Hellenization, the Hasmonean monarchy became a Hellenistic variant in terms of economic policies and politics of power. There were even cases of forced Judaization in conquered areas. During the disputes over the succession to the throne, the Roman general Pompey was called in as an arbitrator by both Judean parties. He took advantage of the situation and entered Jerusalem in 63 BCE without significant resistance. The nearly seven-hundred-year Roman rule over the Judeans began.

These turbulent and decisive political events had economic consequences, with the Judean economy remaining tied to the respective political power. Under Hellenistic and then Roman rule, the Judean economy also became largely profit oriented in order to generate the necessary taxes. However, urbanization also brought about some changes comparable to the phenomena described above, and ultimately, Hellenization also increased the importance of the monetary economy for the structure of the Judean economy. Other important factors for the Judean economy during the period described in the New Testament included the reign of Herod the Great and the economic function of the temple in Jerusalem.

Herod the Great, an Idumean, was a peculiar product of the cultural diversity and political complexity of the Levant. He was all at once, a ruthless Hellenistic power politician, an admirer of Rome, and a promoter of the Judean temple cult. Economically, his enormous building program was of great significance. He built fortifications and entire cities, and, not least, in agreement with the initially suspicious Jerusalem leadership, he had the temple in Jerusalem rebuilt on a scale and with a splendor that is also admired in the New Testament (Mark 13:1). These extensive construction activities created jobs and greatly promoted the Judean construction industry.

Even more important than Herod is the economic function of the temple in Jerusalem. The temple was at once a house of worship, a place of ritual, a treasury, and a "stock exchange," and as such was the largest employer in Judea, with the latter three functions all having enormous economic significance. The cult at the temple in Jerusalem was primarily a sacrificial cult. The countless animals sacrificed there were mostly supplied by Judean livestock farmers. Pilgrims from the diaspora did not usually bring their own sacrificial animals with them but bought them at the temple in Jerusalem. The sacrificial animals and all other expenses for the operation of the temple, such as the remuneration of craftsmen, money changers, suppliers of all kinds, etc., were taken from the temple treasury, which in turn consisted primarily of the income from the temple tax.[4] The temple tax was paid with the Tyrian shekel. The exchange rates were set by the high priest and his council and served as the reference rate for all currency exchange transactions. The Samaritan temple complex on Mount Gerizim also had supraregional economic significance until its destruction by the Judean Hasmoneans.[5]

Money

Coins are a form of money. The worldwide spread of money and the diversity of its forms, as well as the constant endeavor to make forms of money more manageable and borderless, can be explained in particular by its transportability, durability, the pleasure derived from its open possibilities, and, last but not least, the logic of comparability.

The Triumph of Coins—A Brief Historical Sketch

Coins have been documented since the sixth century BCE. "A coin is a piece of money made of metal which conforms to a standard and bears a design"[6] The Lydian coinage system was adopted and modified by the Persians, while Greek coinage spread rapidly throughout the Greek world under the hegemony of Athens.

Rome entered the history of coinage relatively late. The Romans initially minted their own city coins, but after gaining supremacy in central Italy, they followed the Etruscan coinage tradition. It was not until the introduction of the denarius at the beginning of the third century BCE that a separate Roman coinage system emerged. Over the course of the second and first centuries BCE, this Roman system overtook the Lydian-Persian system, which itself had already collapsed following the defeat of the Persians by Alexander the Great's Greek-Macedonian army. The Greek-Hellenistic coinage system, which had become most widespread under Alexander and the Diadochi empires, was gradually supplanted as well. Due to Augustus's decree equating the denarius and the drachma—"by reducing the weight of the Attic tetradrachma from about 17 g to just under 15 g"[7]—they circulated side by side for a long time, although in the Levant, Roman imperial coinage with Latin inscriptions was significantly less widespread than the Greek coinage tradition until the second century CE.

Coins in the Geographical Area of the New Testament Writings

If one reads the New Testament writings with the question "money in the New Testament" in mind, the high number of hits is astonishing, but the terminology is confusing.

Figure 13.1. Tyrian half-shekel, 102–101 BCE. (Unknown author, Wikimedia Commons. Used under the Creative Commons CC0 1.0 Universal Public Domain Dedication.)

The variety of coins in circulation stems from the fact that ancient coinage was more analogous to our postage stamps than to our modern coins. The new designs on stamps and ancient coins did not generally replace the older ones but rather were added alongside them. The value system was not affected by new designs.

The terminology for money in the New Testament is also confusing because it mixes units of weight and actual coins. A talent (Matt 18:24; Rev 16:21; cf. Exod 38:25), for example, is no more a coin than a "mina" (Luke 19:13; cf. Ezek 45:12) or a "litra" (John 12:3; 19:39). Rather, currency systems mix units of weight and specific coins. This is related to the emergence of coinage, when weighed precious metals were used as premonetary forms of money.

The major powers dealt with the various weight and coinage systems in different ways. It was not until Alexander and the Diadochi empires, and with even greater consistency the Romans, that attempts were made to standardize the system across the empire, and these attempts were largely successful. The Ptolemies showed Athenian zeal in this regard, while the Seleucids tended to follow the more liberal Persian tradition. However, even the Romans, who sought uniformity, did not achieve their goal until the third century CE.

The money changers mentioned in the Gospels did not have an easy task. Due to all the different currencies with different weights and, above all, different proportions of precious metal, it is understandable why the temple tax was paid primarily with the Tyrian shekel. This coin was considered particularly stable in value until the First Jewish-Roman War, which resulted in the destruction of the temple.

The coins mentioned in the New Testament[8] therefore belong to the following coinage systems,[9] and I have marked with a superscripted ° the terms that refer purely to weight and are not coins:

Greek:

1 talent (°) = 60 minas (°)

minah (°) = 25 staters (°)

1 stater (°) = 1 tetradrachma

1 tetradrachma = 2 didrachmas (silver)

1 didrachma = 2 drachmas (silver)

1 drachma = 6 obols (copper)

1 obol = 2 hemiobols (copper)

1 hemiobol = 4 chalkoi (copper)

1 chalkoi = 3 lepta (copper)

In addition:

Decadrachma (silver) = 10 drachmas

Hemidrachma (silver) = half-drachma

Roman:

1 aureus (Golden denar) = 25 (silver)denars

1 denar = 4 sesterce (brass)

1 sestertius = 2 dupondian (brass)

1 dupondius = 2 asses (copper)

1 ass = 2 Semis (brass)

1 semis = 2 quadrants (copper)

Tyrian:

Shekel (silver) corresponds to the tetradrachma

The half-shekel (silver) corresponds to the double drachma

Figure 13.2. Values of Greek, Roman, and Tyrian coins.

It is striking that the regional bronze coins, such as those of the Herodians, are not mentioned in the New Testament. Meshorer,[10] for example, lists:

1 hadris = 2 hanzin

1 hanzin = 2 shamin

1 shamin = 2 prutot

Such regional bronze coins played a much greater role in everyday life than the denarius, the drachma, or the Tyrian silver shekel.

Taxes

The collection of taxes, customs duties, and levies was a fundamental part of Roman political rule, but the Romans proved particularly effective in taxation through their systematic compilation of tax lists. This enabled them to calculate how much tax revenue could be expected annually whenever an area passed from indirect Roman rule under a local client ruler to direct administration as a Roman province. Of course, the inhabitants of Judea, Galilee, and Samaria had to pay taxes, customs duties, and levies even before that, but these went to the local rulers and the temple in Jerusalem. What was new was the direct payment of taxes to Rome, which was gradually introduced in the Palestinian region with the Roman administration. Local customs duties and the temple tax were not affected by this at first; they continued to be paid separately.

The Lukan account of the tax assessment therefore has a historical basis in the administrative transformation of Judea into a subregion of the Roman province of Syria. As the emperor's governor (legate), Quirinius was also responsible for organizing and supervising the collection of Roman taxes. Not everyone was taxed in 6 CE, only the inhabitants of Judea. But it was not only the small and relatively insignificant Judea that had to pay taxes to the Roman Empire, but all Roman provinces, which since Augustus had been divided into senatorial and imperial provinces. Indirectly, however, the inhabitants of dependent client kingdoms also paid taxes to Rome, as the client rulers had to pay "gifts" to Rome in order to fulfill their obligations as "friends of Rome," as was the case in Galilee at the time of Jesus. They collected the necessary funds from their own people in addition to the taxes levied for their own needs.

When Jesus traveled from Galilee to Judea, he not only changed locations, but also moved between different forms of government and their associated administrative systems. Taxes and duties were levied more or less moderately across the regions relevant to the New Testament writings, though some cities enjoyed complete exemption from taxation due to imperial privileges.

Judeans in and outside Judea paid the temple tax for the temple in Jerusalem in addition to their other taxes and duties. The revenue from this was initially used for the elaborate cult. Thousands of priests were needed to perform the daily sacrificial service and observe all the purity regulations. The money changers at the temple were not independent bankers, but mostly priests, who worked on behalf of the temple. Craftsmen were also often priests of the temple to ensure that all repair and construction work could be carried out in accordance with cultic requirements. The temple tax was used to finance these expenses, as well as smaller local construction projects. Until the end of the Jewish-Roman War (70 CE), it served, together with the consecration gifts, as a kind of state treasury, which at least guaranteed the High Council of Jerusalem a degree of independence even during the Roman occupation. The temple tax was levied on every Jewish man in Tyrian coin, the half-shekel, or in a currency comparable to the value of the Tyrian shekel, for example, the Greek double drachma, which in turn corresponded to the value of two denarii.

Although the temple in Jerusalem was largely destroyed after the catastrophic defeat in the Jewish-Roman War, the Jewish temple tax continued to be collected. It was no longer paid to Jerusalem but was redirected into a fund in Rome, created specifically for this purpose by Emperor Vespasian, known as the *fiscus Iudaicus*. Whereas previously only twenty-to-fifty-year-olds had to pay the temple tax, it was now also demanded from children in the same amount of two denarii, which led to a considerable additional burden on the approximately five million Jews in the Roman Empire. It is estimated that up to ten million denarii flowed into the *fiscus Iudaicus* each year, a considerable amount of money and a serious redistribution of economic capital. It is difficult to imagine the humiliation that must have been felt by the Jews when their tax, intended for the central Jewish cult, was appropriated by the Romans for their own ends.

In addition to the general imperial taxes and duties mentioned above, there were others specific to particular economic sectors: Local taxes and customs duties on goods, roads, fishing rights, etc. were levied by private tax collectors. The indirect taxes collected by these financial companies were paid by everyone who participated in public trade. The privatization of the tax revenue collection dates back to the Ptolemies in the third century BCE and the beginnings of Roman provincial administration. Smaller or larger financial companies purchased the rights to collect levies and taxes from the relevant administrative authority. For the administration, which was usually poorly staffed, this procedure had the advantage that it did not have to collect the taxes itself and could count on predictable income thanks to the lease payments set in advance.

Many of these tax collectors had a bad reputation because they were allowed to set the amount of taxes at their own discretion, provided there was no unrest. Time and again, money collectors succumbed to the temptation to demand excessive customs duties or taxes in order to increase their profits. However, tax collection was initially a socially accepted, fiscally desirable, and familiar activity.

The taxes paid to Rome were in the form of natural produce and goods, as well as coinage. Egypt, for example, was considered Rome's breadbasket. In this case, the logistics of transport were part of the taxes. Only the distribution in Rome was organized by the Roman authorities under the aegis of the emperor.

The Roman Senate, in cooperation with the imperial administration, determined the appropriate taxes and duties for each province with a fair degree of discretion. The basis for this was provided by the tax lists of the respective provinces mentioned above. The annual poll tax (*tributum capitis*) was levied on all those who did not have Roman citizenship—that is, men, women, and children aged twelve and above, regardless of their income. This poll tax was extended to be an income tax for wealthier provincials. A tax assessment, such as that carried out by Quirinius in Judea in 6 CE, was therefore simultaneously a census and an assessment of wealth with a view to levying the poll tax, as well as clarifying property ownership in order to estimate the land tax (*tributum soli*), which affected all land and property owners who did not have Roman citizenship.

During the imperial period, tax revenues essentially flowed into two different coffers: the *aerarium populi Romani*, which was the monetary state treasury that had been kept in the Temple of Saturn since Republican times, and the *fiscus Caesaris*, where the emperor's revenues were collected. In reality, however, the emperor increasingly controlled the *aerarium* through his political power and influence in the Senate. When the various direct and indirect, regional and imperial, state and cult taxes, levies, and customs duties were added together, they accounted for approximately 30 to 50 percent of the cost of living for a private household. If, in addition, particularly greedy officials or private tax collectors wreaked havoc, this could lead to additional burdens that were almost impossible to compensate for and sometimes even led to unrest. One of the causes of the zealot revolts in Judea in 66 CE, which then led to the Jewish-Roman War, was the increasingly excessive tax demand of the local Roman administration in Judea.

Tax revenues were of enormous importance to economic life in antiquity, not least because they also benefited the inhabitants of the provinces. Not only did they promote a relatively efficient bureaucracy and the administrative structures it organized, as well as the legalization of property and trade relations, but they also contributed significantly to the expansion of local, regional, and imperial infrastructure. Ports, road systems, protection from bands of robbers and pirates, and the expansion of cities and supraregional communication structures were all funded by tax revenue, so that despite exploitation by Rome, prosperity increased noticeably in most provinces in the first century CE. Thus, the cult of the emperor in Asia Minor was not a propaganda measure imposed by Rome, but rather a ritualized expression of gratitude for the increase in security and general prosperity.[11]

TAKING A CLOSER LOOK: SOURCES

There are now several highly recommended monographs available for those who wish to familiarize themselves with economic and historical issues related to the monetary economy of the ancient Mediterranean world. The works of Hans Kloft,[12] Sitta von Reden,[13] and Hans-Joachim Drexhage, Heinrich Konen, and Kai Ruffing[14] offer a good overview. The future of the research, however, lies in detailed regional studies. Notable examples include the early and still indispensable studies by Séan Freyne on Galilee and K. C. Hanson and Douglas E. Oakman on Palestine. With their indexes, these works also provide quick access to ancient sources. Students interested in economic history will certainly start by reading ancient works by Marcus Terentius Varro, Marcus Porcius Cato, or

Caijus Plinius Secundus, for example. In principle, however, almost all surviving texts from antiquity can be examined with a focus on economic issues. Biblical texts play a major role here, as they are not primarily testimonies of the economic elite, but rather provide insights into the perspectives of the middle class by talking about free craftsmen, farmers, and fishermen. They do not take the perspective of day laborers or slaves. They talk about them, but not with them. Thus, Jesus's closest circle of disciples included the sons of fishing entrepreneurs and tax collectors, but no slaves or day laborers.

Intensive archaeological research has also made it clear that, in order to gain an adequate picture of antiquity, it is necessary to interpret not only texts but also material artifacts.[15] For this reason, I have placed great emphasis on insights from numismatics in the above remarks in the first section . However, the findings of landscape archaeology and, in particular, scientific research into rubbish dumps and waste must also be taken into account, as these can sometimes reveal what was actually on the menu in many villages.

Sources from the World of the New Testament

Aristophanes, *Plutus*

The comedy *Plutus* deals with the unjust distribution of wealth and, in an almost cynical manner, blames the gods for this—above all Plutus, the god of wealth, who is symbolically depicted as blind. Chremylos, the righteous human protagonist of the story, has Plutus healed in the Temple of Asclepius. The god, now able to see, redistributes wealth, but this does not lead to a more just world. The goddess Penia, the goddess of poverty, appears as his antagonist and praises poverty because it leads to modesty and humility and therefore contributes far more to a pious and livable society than the redistribution of wealth.

The distinction between the Greek words *penēs* (poor) and *ptōchos* (destitute) is particularly interesting in terms of social and economic history. The goddess Penia is therefore the goddess of poverty, but not of destitution. Let us examine this distinction in the dialogue between the human chorus and the goddess Penia in Aristophanes's comedy, "Wealth," performed in Athens around 388 BCE:

> CHREMYLUS: Well, we do say, don't we, that Poverty is the sister of Destitution?
>
> POVERTY: Yes, you do, and you also say that Dionysius is no different from Thrasybulus! My kind of life doesn't involve that sort of thing, by Zeus, and it never could. The life of the destitute, which is what you're talking about, is to have to live on nothing. The life of a poor man is to

live economically and keep at one's work, not having any surplus but not having a shortfall either. (548–554)[16]

The destitute have no daily income and do not know at the beginning of the week whether they will be able to feed themselves and their families at the end of the week. Day laborers, who live from hand to mouth, are therefore considered destitute. Most slaves were better off economically than free day laborers or the chronically ill, who had no land and had to rely on the compassion of their fellow human beings. On the other hand, anyone who worked hard and was able to feed themselves and their families, even if they had to live like Chremylos's slaves and could hardly save anything from their earnings, was considered poor.

However, wealth is by no means described as elite or extraordinary, so that it would only be attainable by a privileged few. Even the coveted wealth in Aristophanes is not associated with fantasies of power in the style of an Elon Musk, but with secure and luxurious prosperity within one's own home, as described by Karion, the slave of Chremylos:

> Our meal-tub is full of white barley groats, our jars full of dark wine with a beautiful bouquet. Every container is miraculously filled with gold and silver coin. Our well is full of olive oil; our flasks are overflowing with perfume, our upstairs room with dried figs. Every vinegar-cruet and bowl and pot has turned to bronze; those rotten cleaning-boards that stank of fish, you can see they're all silver; and all of a sudden we've got an ivory kitchen! (806–815)[17]

Josephus, *Jewish War*

Although taxation and the levying of duties are almost as old as the establishment of state structures themselves, and although this method of financing collective tasks has become established worldwide to this day, there is probably no text on the subject of taxes that has become as famous as the episode of the tax assessment recounted by Luke (Luke 2:1–2). In fact, this episode recalls a dramatic change in the form of government and administration in the region of Judea in the year 6 CE. This incorporation into the Roman provincial and tax system is probably also the historical background to the tax question of whether it was permissible to pay taxes to the emperor, which we will discuss later.

The equally political, legal, and religious significance of this question is evident in an episode recounted by Josephus in his historical work *Jewish War*. After the death of Herod the Great in 4 BCE, his kingdom was divided among three of his sons: Herod Archelaus received Judea and Samaria, Herod Antipas received Galilee and Perea, and Herod Philip received some territories in the Northeast. However, following vehement complaints from Judea and Samaria in 6 CE, Augustus deposed and exiled Archelaus due to his lawless administration.

During Coponius's term of office, the first Roman prefect after the deposition of Herod's son Archelaus in Judea and the conversion of Judea into an administrative district of the Roman province of Syria (cf. Luke 2:1–2), the following episode occurred:

> A certain Galilean, whose name was Judas, prevailed with his countrymen to revolt; and said they were cowards if they would endure to pay a tax to the Romans, and would, after God, submit to mortal men as their lords. (Josephus, *J.W.* 2.117)[18]

According to Josephus, this Judas was the founder of the zealot movement, which Josephus ultimately holds responsible for the Jewish-Roman War (66–70 CE). Historically, this probably refers to a radical group of Pharisees whose zeal for the Torah did not allow for any compromises with prevailing balance of power and who sought to follow in the footsteps of the Maccabees (cf. 1 Macc 2). The popular uprising led by Judas around 6 CE is also mentioned in Acts 5:37 with the note of his death, indicating that this historical episode was engraved in the collective memory of both Jews and Christians in the first century.

The tax issue was by no means solely about the power and social policy dimensions of the exploitation of the Judean population by the Roman occupiers and their allied client rulers. The tax coin—the Roman denarius—contained political and religious significance through its imagery and inscriptions. Augustus had deliberately used coinage as a means of propaganda and, with its help, proclaimed the good news, the "Gospel of the Romans about the Golden Age," which was linked both politically and religiously to the reign of Augustus. Not only did many Jews in Judea and Galilee anticipate the dawn of a new era, but many Romans were also firmly convinced that a new Saturnian age full of happiness, peace, and prosperity was about to begin. When the appearance of a comet was announced for the year 17 BCE, it was interpreted as a divine sign from heaven, and Augustus declared that the Golden Age (*Aurea Aetas*) had arrived. It was celebrated with a state festival lasting several days, the *Saecularia*, from May 30 to June 3, 17 BCE. In various cult ceremonies, Augustus himself said prayers and also offered sacrifices with his own hands. This sacrificial scene was also recorded on a coin.

The refusal to pay taxes to the Roman occupying power in 6 CE, which was due in no small part to religious zeal, clearly took the emperor's Roman self-portrayal as a divine being and supreme priest of the Roman state religion at face value and refused to follow this religious counterforce.

Reading the New Testament Texts

Give to Caesar What Is Caesar's

> Then they sent to him some Pharisees and some Herodians to trap him in what he said. And they came and said to him, "Teacher, we know that you are sincere and show deference to no one, for you do not regard people with partiality but teach the way of God in accordance with truth. Is it lawful to pay taxes to Caesar or not? Should we pay them, or should we not?" But knowing their hypocrisy, he said to them, "Why are you putting me to the test? Bring me a denarius and let me see it." And they brought one. Then he said to them, "Whose head is this and whose title?" They answered, "Caesar's." Jesus said to them, "Give to Caesar the things that are Caesar's and to God the things that are God's." And they were utterly amazed at him. (Mark 12:13–17)

The narrative strategy of the text consists in proving Jesus to be truly what the hypocritical *captatio benevolentiae* of his opponents simultaneously attributes to him and denies him. Verses 15–17 stage Jesus's response, in which he proves himself to be a teacher, truthful, and the one whose teaching can distinguish between God and man, and therefore truly teaches the way of God.

In the story, Jesus lets his opponents know that he has seen through them. He then begins his strategy with an instruction: "Bring me a denarius, so that I may see." He tells them what to do, and by following his instruction, they implicitly accept his authority as a teacher. However, the wording of the instruction also makes it clear that Jesus does not have a denarius, but his opponents do. The immediate willingness of his opponents, in turn, shows that they possess Roman denarii.

The second phase of Jesus's counterstrategy argues with the coin's design. He asks his opponents about the image and the inscription. Jesus does not draw on his knowledge to identify the coin. He does not look at the faces of the people, thereby transforming the hypocritical distinction made in verse 14 into a truly accurate one. His opponents look at the image on the coin and give the brief answer: "the emperor's."

Jesus's response in verse 17 works in the same way as the third feigned appreciation in verse 14, with one difference: emperor vs. God. This opposition strips the emperor of all semantic characteristics of the divine and places him in the opposition from verse 14: man vs. God. Even toward the emperor, Jesus thus remains on the path of God and thereby proves that he truly does not look at the face of men, even if it is that of the emperor.

Through the narrative strategy of the text, Jesus emerges as the clear winner of this debate. Readers can conclude that the accolades hypocritically bestowed upon him in verse 14 are in fact accurate.

Let us now bring numismatic knowledge into play. What does the text's mention of a denarius mean at the time of the narrative, around the year 30 CE? At the text-immanent level of the discourse universe of the text, we learn that the denarius is a means of payment for the tax payable to the emperor. And that it bears the image and inscription of the emperor.

When the dispute took place, Tiberius was emperor. The Roman historian Suetonius reports on the reign of Tiberius, "That even such acts as these were regarded as capital crimes: to beat a slave near a statue of Augustus, or to change one's clothes there; to carry a ring or coin stamped with his image into a privy or a brothel, or to criticize any word or act of his."[19]

In other words, it is not known whether carrying a coin with Augustus on it to the toilet or into a brothel actually led to a court case for lèse-majésté.[20] Nevertheless, this law, whose historicity is undisputed and which can be classified among the laws on *maiestas minuta* (offenses against the majesty), a group of laws that had existed since republican times, shows that coins, with their images and inscriptions, were more than mere means of payment. Rather, they had a special symbolic power.

The coin in Mark 12:15 must be accounted for as a second layer of context and analyzed intermedially alongside the written text, because the imagery and inscriptions on coins can be read as ideograms with specific political and religious messages.

Since F. W. Madden's *History of Jewish Coinage and of Money in the Old and New Testament*,[21] the view has prevailed that the denarius mentioned in Mark 12:15 can be identified with certainty. According to this view, it is the denarius of Tiberius, which Berhard Overbeck describes as follows:

> Denarius, silver, minted in Lugdunum, 14/17 CE—Obverse: Head of Tiberius facing right with laurel wreath; inscription TI CAESAR DIVI—AVG F AVGVSTVS. Reverse: Concordia seated on the right with a scepter in her raised right hand and a branch in her left, PONTIF—MAXIM. This seated female figure has been interpreted as Livia Drusilla or Pax. It is now certain that this coin refers to the events of the year 10 CE, when Tiberius received a series of honors. On January 16 of that year, he dedicated the Temple of Concordia in his name and that of his deceased brother Drusus. This deity, perhaps even her statue, is depicted here.[22]

H. St J. Hart's criticism was justified, not in terms of the possibility of identification, but rather in questioning the exclusivity of that identification. According to Hart, any denarius bearing an image of Augustus or Tiberius could potentially fit the description. In support of the identification with the Tiberius denarius described above, it is repeatedly pointed out that this denarius was minted frequently. However, this ignores the archaeological finding that, according to Hart, only four examples of this denarius have been found in Palestine.

How should this numismatic-archaeological finding be evaluated? First of all, skepticism is warranted against hasty and unequivocal identifications, and it is advisable to consider other possibilities, namely the denarii of Augustus, especially since they were more widely distributed throughout the Levant around 30 CE. This means, however, that the iconography of Augustus, which Paul Zanker reconstructed in his outstanding study *Augustus und die Macht der Bilder*, must also be taken into account here.

There is another point that needs to be addressed. The Roman denarius was not the most widely circulated coin in the Levant, and certainly not in Judea.[23] The conclusion drawn from the pericope on paying taxes—that the historical Jesus did not possess any silver coins[24] or even any money at all—is based on the overlooking of the circulation of coins in antiquity. In the absence of Jewish silver or even gold coins, it was not the Roman denarius but the Tyrian shekel and the Hellenistic drachma that were the most common currencies in Galilee, Samaria, and Judea, with regional bronze coins used for everyday needs. If Jesus did not carry a denarius with him in the story, this would not be unusual. Rather, what is surprising is that the Pharisees and Herodians who question him are immediately able to produce a denarius. The narrator thus marks them as being in league with the Roman occupying power from the outset, and their question appears to have been decided long ago. The immediate presentation of this coin, which was not very common in Judea, visually and tangibly exposes the hypocrisy of Jesus's opponents in the story.[25]

But let us tentatively consider the encyclopedic possibility that the Tiberius coin described here is the one intended. The inscription on the front with the head of Tiberius reads: TI CAESAR DIVI—AVG F AVGVSTVS. This can be translated as: "Tiberius Caesar, son of the divine Augustus, Augustus." The reverse side with the goddess Concordia bears the inscription PONTIF—MAXIM, meaning "high priest," an office held by Tiberius since 15 CE. If we establish an intermedial relationship between the text of Mark and this Tiberius coin, we see a competition between sons of God and the sons of god. The Gospel of Mark narrates the gradual recognition of Jesus Christ as the Son of God, while the coin proclaims Tiberius as the son of the god Augustus. The Pharisees and Herodians in the narrative have proven themselves to be disconnected from Jesus Christ, the Son of God, through their intention to convict him of a state crime and through their hypocrisy. Meanwhile, their possession of the coin visually and haptically connects them to the Roman son of god. Jesus's demand must then be understood as a call to sever ties with the rival Roman son of god and to see him merely as a human political leader. This means, however, that the entire pericope is a profound critique of the political and religious message of the Tiberius coin.

FURTHER READING

Alkier, Stefan, ed., with the assistance of Dominic Blauth. *Konstellationen antiker Tempelwirtschaft. Neue Perspektiven auf den Tempel am Garizim, den Jerusalemer Tempel und das Artemision in Ephesos.* Beyond Historicism—New Testament Studies Today 2. Brill, 2022.

Alkier, Stefan, Rainer Kessler, and Michael Rydryck. *Wirtschaft und Geld. Lebenswelten der Bibel.* Gütersloher Verlag, 2016.

Hanson, K. C. and Douglas E. Oakman. *Palestine in the Time of Jesus. Social Structures and Social Conflicts.* Fortress, 1998.

Howgego, Christopher. *Ancient History from Coins.* Routledge, 1995.

Kloft, Hans. *Die Wirtschaft der Griechisch-Römischen Welt. Eine Einführung.* WBG, 1992.

von Reden, Sitta. "Antike Wirtschaft." In *Enzyklopädie der griechisch-römischen Antike.* Vol. 10. De Gruyter, 2015.

Reiser, M. "Numismatik und Neues Testament." *Biblica* 81, no. 4 (2000): 457–88.

Rostovtzeff, Michael. *The Social and Economic History of the Hellenistic World.* 2nd ed. Clarendon, 1953.

Weiser, Wolfram, and Hannah H. Cotton. " 'Gebt dem Kaiser, was des Kaisers ist . . .' Die Geldwährungen der Griechen, Juden, Nabatäer und Römer im syrisch-nabatäischen Raum unter besonderer Berücksichtigung des Kurses von Sela'/Melaina und Lepton nach der Annexion des Königreiches der Nabatäer durch Rom." *Zeitschrift für Papyrologie und Epigraphik* 114 (1996): 237–87.

Weiser, Wolfram and Hannah H. Cotton. "Neues zum 'Tyrischen Silbergeld' herodianischer und römischer Zeit." *Zeitschrift für Papyrologie und Epigraphik* 139 (2002): 235–50.

Notes

1 G. E. Lenski, *Power and Privilege. A Theory of Social Stratification*, 2nd ed. (University of North Carolina Press, 1984).

2 On this, see Stefan Alkier, ed., with the assistance of Dominic Blauth, *Konstellationen antiker Tempelwirtschaft. Neue Perspektiven auf den Tempel am Garizim, den Jerusalemer Tempel und das Artemision in Ephesos*, Beyond Historicism—New Testament Studies Today 2 (Brill, 2022).

3 *Tiberius*, in *Lives of the Caesars, Volume I: Julius. Augustus. Tiberius. Gaius Caligula*, trans. J. C. Rolfe, with an introduction by K. R. Bradley, Loeb Classical Library 31 (Harvard University Press, 1914), 32.2.

4 Alkier, *Konstellationen antiker Tempelwirtschaft*, 147–248.

5 Alkier *Konstellationen antiker Tempelwirtschaft*, 21–144. See the chapter on "Samaritans" by József Zsengellér in the present volume.

6 Christopher Howgego, *Ancient History from Coins* (Routledge, 2015), 1.

7 Marius Reiser, "Numismatik und Neues Testament," *Biblica* 81, no. 4 (2000): 457–88 (460).

8 Informative overviews are provided in Augustus Spijkerman, "Coins Mentioned in the New Testament," *Studii biblici Franciscani liber annuus* 6 (1955/56): 285–98; Ruprecht Ziegler, "Münzen, Münzsysteme und Münzumlauf im Palästina der frühen

Römischen Kaiserzeit," in *Neues Testament und Antike Kultur I*, ed. Kurt Erlemann (Neukichen Verlag, 2004), 130–36.

9 An outstanding contribution to the complexity of coinage systems is provided by Wolfram Weiser and Hannah M. Cotton, " 'Gebt dem Kaiser, was des Kaisers ist . . .' Die Geldwährungen der Griechen, Juden, Nabatäer und Römer im syrisch-nabatäischen Raum unter besonderer Berücksichtigung des Kurses von Sela'/Melaina und Lepton nach der Annexion des Königreiches der Nabatäer durch Rom," *Zeitschrift für Papyrologie und Epigraphik* 114 (1996): 237–87.

10 Ya'akov Meshorer, *Ancient Jewish Coinage*, 2 vols. (Amphora Books, 1982), 2:14.

11 See Michael Mann, *Geschichte der Macht*, vol. 2, *Vom Römischen Reich bis zum Vorabend der Industrialisierung*, Theorie und Gesellschaft 20 (Campus 1994), 33–45.

12 H. Kloft, *Die Wirtschaft der Griechisch-Römischen Welt. Eine Einführung* (WBG, 1992).

13 Sitta von Reden, "Antike Wirtschaft," in *Eznzyklopädie der griechisch-römischen Antike* 10 (de Gruyter, 2015).

14 Hans-Joachim Drexhage, *Heinrich Konen, Kai Ruffing, Die Wirtschaft des Römischen Reiches (1.–3-Jahrhundert). Eine Einführung* (de Gruyter, 2002).

15 S. Alkier and J. Zangenberg, eds., with the assistance of V. Kristina Dronsch and Michael Schneider, *Zeichen aus Text und Stein. Studien auf dem Weg zu einer Archäologie des Neuen Testaments*, Texte und Arbeiten zum neutestamentlichen Zeitalter 42 (Francke, 2003).

16 Aristophanes, *Wealth, the comedies of Aristophanes*, edited with translation and commentary by Alan H. Sommerstein, vol. 11 (Warminster, 2001), 548–54.

17 Aristophanes, *Wealth*, 806–15.

18 Flavius Josephus and William Whiston, *The Works of Josephus: Complete and Unabridged* (Hendrickson, 1987), 605.

19 Suetonius, *Lives of the Caesars, Volume I: Julius. Augustus. Tiberius. Gaius Caligula*, trans. J. C. Rolfe, introduction by K. R. Bradley, Loeb Classical Library 31 (Harvard University Press, 1914), liber III Tiberius, 58.

20 Zvi Yavetz, *Tiberius. Der traurige Kaiser*, trans. D. Ajchenrand (Beck, 2002), 93.

21 Bernard Quaritch, 1864.

22 J. P. C. Kent, B. Overbeck, and A. U. Stylow, *Die Römische Münze, Aufnahmen von Max und Albert Hirmer* (Hirmer, 1973), 97. The coin is depicted in plate 40, no. 151.

23 Reiser, "Numismatik und Neues Testament," 575–76, also confirms the limited circulation of the denarius "in the eastern Roman Empire in the first century."

24 For example, Ernst Hähnchen, *Der Weg Jesu. Eine Erklärung des Markusevangeliums und der kanonischen Parallelen* (de Gruyter, 1966), 406: "Jesus asks to be shown a denarius—he himself did not possess any silver coins."

25 This is impressively pointed out by Reinhard Breymeier, "Zur Pragmatik des Bildes. Semiotische Betrachtungen zum Streitgespräch Mk 12, 13–17 ('Der Zinsgroschen') unter Berücksichtigung der Spieltheorie," *LingBib* 13/14 (1972): 19–51.

CHAPTER FOURTEEN

Travel, Migration, and Exchange

Susanne Luther
(Georg-August-Universität Göttingen)

THE TEXTS OF early Christianity bear witness to extensive, unceasing traveling. The Gospels report that Jesus and his disciples had no fixed abode but were constantly on the move. The letters of Paul and the Acts of the Apostles reveal that Paul traveled through large parts of the Roman Empire as part of his work as a missionary and planter of Christian communities. There are stories about Paul's journeys on the extensive Roman system of roads as well as by sea and of the hardships and dangers of travel as well as of customary ports of call for Jewish and Christian travelers such as the synagogue communities or early Christian house communities. The Apocryphal Acts of the Apostles continue the tradition of such reports when they narrate the apostles' missionary journeys, which extended far beyond the Roman Empire. This chapter aims to contextualize these narratives of astonishingly extensive early Christian travels.

Perspectives on Traveling in the Ancient World

Movement in the Globalized World of the Roman Empire

For the ancient Mediterranean region, there is ample evidence of a high level of connectivity and mobility of people, goods, and ideas.[1] This was due to the good economic, social, and communicative infrastructure in the Roman Empire, resulting from the predominantly peaceful political conditions, but also due to the well-developed road system and the advances in seafaring,[2] which—despite the considerable dangers of travel and transportation, such as bandits, pirates, accidents, storms, and shipwrecks[3]—provided convenient travel routes and the possibility of rapid communication.[4]

People traveled on foot, with mount or pack animals; used wagons or carts; and traveled overland or by sea. They were guided by the seasonal weather, the developed system of roads, the nature of the terrain, and the existence of stables and inns along the imperial roads where one could rest. On foot, it was possible to cover only about twenty miles (roughly 30 km) per day, and using a means of transportation would increase the distance covered to about fifty or sixty miles (roughly 80–90 km) per day. By regularly changing the means of transportation, the speed of travel could be greatly accelerated; messengers on horseback were able cover up to about two hundred miles (roughly 320 km) per day.[5]

Travel made up an inherent part of life—especially in elite circles: People traveled to explore the world; traveled as merchants[6] and as tourists; traveled to religious events, to healing sanctuaries, and to pilgrimage sites;[7] and embarked on journeys to visit family or to gain knowledge by studying with renowned rhetors and teachers in cities such as Athens or Rome.[8] But travel was also essential in warfare and diplomacy. It is therefore appropriate to speak of a "traveling culture" in the first and second centuries CE, which developed as a result of the close and diverse interconnections around the Mediterranean and generated a perception of the *oikoumenē* (the inhabited world) of the time as a globalized world—a perception also shared by ancient Judaism and early Christianity.

A primary reason for travel was profit. Overseas merchants often formed syndicates of countrymen and lived abroad for extended periods of time to trade their goods, thus forming "trade diasporas," which were "communities of merchants living among aliens in associated networks."[9] Trade diasporas operated as autonomous groups within the communities in which they lived, they kept internal order and enforced discipline on members who deviated from established economic practices or shared moral and cultural values. Trade diasporas were a major impetus for the dispersal of minorities throughout the Roman Empire.[10] Early Christian communities like the Pauline congregations or the addressees of the Epistle of James, can be considered diaspora communities.

The early Roman Empire (27 BCE–68 CE) has been termed an "age of migration."[11] Due to the centralization of the Roman provinces toward the capital, migrants from all over the Mediterranean were attracted to the city of Rome, and due to the intense interconnectedness of the empire through the constant movement of people and goods, migrants were able to leave their local contexts and travel to the capital, where their own culture and identity came into contact and interacted with the dominant Roman context.[12] In recent years, the impact that these migrants from Hellenized provinces had on Rome has increasingly become a focus of scholarship, as their writings—such as the works of Strabo of Amasia, Dionysius of Halicarnassus, Antipater of Thessalonica, Nicolaus of Damascus, and Philo of Alexandria—are "migrant literature." These authors referred "to themselves as 'traveler by ship' (*emporos*) or 'away from home' (*apoikos*); they write about their 'traveling' (*poreia*) and 'being away from home' (*apodēmein*). But they could also refer to their 'displacement' (*metanastasis*) and to their 'change of abode' (*metoikia*), terms that come close to the connotations of the modern term 'migration,' " but also to exile.[13] Drawing on postcolonial studies, early imperial Greek literature has been described as characterized by in-betweenness, ambivalence, and polyphony, as "the experience of migration to Rome had a fundamental impact on their literary writing: It transformed their intellectual outlook. This was reflected in their writing, which voices fascinating responses to Rome and sophisticated reflections on the interaction between Greek, Roman, and local cultures."[14] This is relevant to our focus on traveling, since Paul of Tarsus also should be understood as an author of "migrant literature."

Theory on Globalization and Networks

Travel, migration, and exchange all take place under certain conditions. These can be elucidated through the analysis of network and globalization theories. *Network theory* and analysis are helpful tools in describing and evaluating the interconnectivity and exchange in the ancient Mediterranean and in particular the relationship between social networks and the dissemination of religious ideas in early Christianity. It has been argued that the success of the early Christ movement was based on Paul's reliance on so-called weak ties for the spread of the gospel: "Since Paul moved about so much, he was prevented from maintaining many strong social links, but it enabled him to develop a great number of weak ties with individuals in a variety of geographical and social locations. Such a position could be best described as that of a *between-group broker* . . . that is, he connects members of various communities who possibly never met each other."[15] In addition to the importance of the weak ties for Paul's missionary strategy, its success was also sustained by strong ties that is, the relationships between Paul and his local congregations as well as the relationships between the members of those congregations.[16]

Globalization theory can also be applied fruitfully to the analysis of early Christianity in the era of the Roman Empire.[17] In general terms, "globalization can be described as processes by which localities and people become increasingly interconnected and interdependent."[18] It is "the trend of growing worldwide interconnectedness."[19] Moreover, globalization has been defined as "processes of increasing connectivities that unfold and manifest as social awareness of those connectivities."[20] As has already been indicated above, recent research on mobility, migrations, and the travel of knowledge and wisdom has shown that "with regard to mobility, the Roman world breaks with stereotypical representations of the past as immobile, fragmented, segmented, sheltered, closed off."[21] It can be stated that "from the period of 200 BCE onwards, therefore, the whole *oikoumenē* is one 'hyper-network,' which we should call "global" to better indicate the degree of connectivity and time-space compression we are talking about."[22]

The applicability of the concept of globalization to the Roman world has, of course, been challenged. From a geographical perspective, for instance, the

Roman Empire was never "global"—in the sense of world spanning—in its expanse, and while Roman imperialism may have increased connectivity by reducing the costs of traveling and transportation and providing more security and information, innovations in Roman transport and communication do not testify to a noticeable time-space compression as we experience it in the modern globalized world.[23] This means, that with a view to the Roman Empire, the focus for globalization has to be "on social relationships, cultural practices and above all individual subjectivities," rather than on "physical structures and processes."[24] What is "globalized" in the Roman world is the "imaginative construction," the ideology of the Roman Empire as a "global" structure. What can be detected, therefore, is the shift in perception among individuals and groups within the Roman Empire, who experience themselves as being part of a globalized world and react by constructing identities for themselves as members of this globalized world, not only of their own community, region, or nation.[25] Paul's idea of extending his mission to Rome and then as far as Spain matches this mindset.

What is of particular significance with regard to early Christianity is the impact of globalization on cultures. The focus here is, on the one hand, on the homogenization that occurs, and, on the other hand, on the heterogeneity that arises. Both are encompassed by the term *glocalization*, which describes the tendency toward global localization. The concept of glocalization helps to emphasize how the homogenizing elements of global culture (from institutions and commodities to social practices and ideas) are differentially incorporated into local cultures, which are in turn altered in the process.[26] Glocalization is thus an effect of the interconnectedness and interchange of the ancient globalized world. It describes "the ways in which broadly shared ideas, goods, and practices are modified and adapted locally to accord with local practice, customs, habits, and beliefs,"[27] for "as those globally common practices reverberate through a cultural group—in the form of new shapes, styles, or goods—social practices within that group evolve to build upon the initial thread that facilitated global-level understanding in the first place. Often, such evolutions are adapted in a way that speaks directly and explicitly to that group, which increases their appeal locally. This is the idea of glocalization, or the local adaptation of those widely shared practices and values, which appears in the convergence most popularly associated with globalization."[28] The concept of glocalization can help to explain the adaptation of early Christian teachings to different cultural contexts.

Thus, the application of globalization theory encourages the identification and appreciation of networks based on the Roman imperial infrastructure beyond the physical level. The Roman Empire was perceived as an "integrated, well-connected and, as it were, 'global' oikoumene"[29] and this led to the experience of living in a globalized world. This perception is primarily founded on the strong connectivity through interregional as well as global networks, which emerged all over the Roman Empire with a view to religion, trade, or migration.[30] Moreover, the perspective of globalization "has the potential to provide detailed insights into degrees of global consciousness, participation and exclusion from aspects of global culture, and the general experiences of living in the Roman world for all social groups, especially non-elites."[31] This approach therefore takes the "world consciousness" of individuals and groups and their experience of cosmopolitanism within the ancient "globalized world" into account. In this way, the approach allows for a bigger picture as the intense inter- and intracultural as well as inter- and intraregional connectivities and pluriform "global" interactions are applied to illuminate our understanding of the flow of people, ideas, and objects in the world we focus on when we read the New Testament texts. Early Christianity with its intense travel and migration activities has to be perceived as an active agent within this cultural, social, religious, and intellectual hypernetwork of the ancient Mediterranean. Traveling and migration within the ancient global *oikoumenē* can be considered as one of the practices that triggered globalization.

TAKING A CLOSER LOOK: SOURCES

Sources from the World of the New Testament

Ancient literature refers to traveling in a wide variety of genres. The works of, for example, Pausanias, Galen, and Pliny the Elder contain journeys of discovery and descriptions of geographical regions. Ancient novels use travel as a means of shaping the plot. Texts of different genres refer to traveling for different reasons—pilgrimage, business, diplomacy, education, attending sporting events, visiting important sites, or family visits, but also deportations of slaves and troop deployment in the context of war or migration. In the following, the focus will be on only two aspects of travel selected from this wealth of material.

Movement for Migration and Politics

Flavius Josephus—a Jewish author writing in Rome and addressing a Roman audience with an apologetic focus—is increasingly recognized as a migrant writer. His knowledge of Roman discourse, the Roman characteristics of his Judaism, and his Roman citizenship have been highlighted, and his importance as a Roman historian with a broad network among Roman intellectuals has been brought to light.[32] According to the *Jewish War*, Josephus served as a military commander against the Romans during the First Jewish War, but was taken prisoner, prophesied that Vespasian would become emperor, and—when this came to pass as predicted—rose to honor in Rome.[33] At the end of *Life*, he describes his life in Rome after the Jewish War:

> When Titus had brought an end to the disturbances in Judea, figuring that the properties I held in the environs of Jerusalem would become unprofitable to me on account of the Roman patrol that was about to go into quarters here, he gave me a different area in the plain. And when he was about to depart from Rome, he welcomed me as his sailing companion, assigning me every honor. When we came to Rome, I met with every provision from Vespasian. He even gave me lodging in the house that was his before the *imperium*. He honored me with Roman citizenship. He gave me a stipend for supplies, and continued [these] honors until his departure from life, taking back nothing of his goodness toward me—which brought me into danger on account of envy. For a certain Judean by the name of Ionathes, having fomented sedition in Cyrene and helped to persuade 2000 of the natives [to join in], became with them an agent of destruction. He was put in chains by the one governing the region and then, when he was sent to the imperator, he insisted that I had sent weapons and supplies to him. Lying certainly did not escape Vespasian's notice, but he passed a sentence of death and, having been handed over, he [Ionathes] was put to death. After these things, those who were envious of my success often fabricated charges against me, but I escaped by the provision of God. And I received from Vespasian a gift of considerable land in Judea. . . . After these things I took for myself a woman who, though she had settled in Crete, was by ancestry a Judean, of parents who were the most noble and most distinguished in that region. In character she excelled many women, as her subsequent life demonstrated. From this wife two children were born to me: the older one Iustus and after him Simonides, who was surnamed Agrippa. These are my household affairs. The things given by the *imperators* remained much the same. When Vespasian died and Titus succeeded him in the rule, he preserved the same sort of honor towards me as his father and, though I was often accused, he did not credit [the charges]. When Domitian had succeeded Titus, he further increased the honors towards me. For example, he disciplined the Judeans who had accused me, and he ordered that a eunuch slave and tutor of my son who had accused me be disciplined. He also gave me tax exemption for my territory in Judea, which is the greatest honor for the recipient. Domitia, the wife of Caesar, continued benefiting me in many ways. These are the things that occurred throughout my entire life; from them let others judge my character as they might wish.[34]

This text by Josephus offers insights into the life of a renegade who is intent on assimilating into the Roman upper class and who enjoys the patronage of the Roman rulers, but, at the same time, runs into conflict with his own compatriots. In his *Life*, written for a Roman audience, Josephus records in detail the generosity and kindness that the *imperators* showed him, emphasizing their understanding of his situation and status, and portraying himself as being on the side of the Romans.

A different picture of the relationship between Rome and the Jewish community is presented by Philo of Alexandria, writing one generation earlier than Josephus. In his treatise *Legatio ad Gaium*, he reports on his journey to Rome around 40 CE[35] as part of a Jewish delegation, which sought to address the anti-Jewish violence and persecution of Jews in Alexandria that resulted from riots due to the emperor's attempt to place statues in Jewish synagogues and to prevent the emperor from erecting his statue in the Jerusalem temple:

> We sailed in midst of the stormy winter, not knowing how great a storm was awaiting us, a land storm far more dangerous than that of the sea. For that is the work of nature who divides the annual seasons, and nature is a preserver. But the other is the work of a man whose thoughts are not those of a man, a youth with the recklessness of youth, invested with irresponsible dominion over all. And youth coupled with absolute authority is subject to unrestrainable impulses, a formidable power for evil. Shall we be allowed to come near him and open our mouths in defense of the houses of prayer to the destroyer of the all-holy place?[36]

This text is particularly interesting since Philo refers to seasonal traveling as a historical reference *and* as a metaphorical characterization of their mission. The delegation set sail during a stormy winter, but they are also prepared for the "far more dangerous" stormy encounter with the emperor. In Rome, the delegation is granted an audience with the Emperor Gaius Caligula (37–41 CE), but Philo describes the mission as a failure, since the emperor remained indifferent to Jewish concerns.[37] Nevertheless, Philo's journey to Rome had a fundamental impact on the intellectual life of this "Mediterranean thinker."[38] It has been argued that whereas his earlier works engage in an inner-Jewish discourse, Philo's later treatises are overtly apologetic.[39]

Movement for Education and Wisdom

Philo of Alexandria describes those who seek to attain wisdom as travelers. He states that just as merchants travel far across land and sea for the sake of gain, letting no person, adverse circumstances, or hazards prevent them from traveling, so should those who want to gain wisdom, travel far and wide for the sake of gaining this most desirable of all possessions. Philo describes them as explorers—curious, investigative, and insatiable for the gain of knowledge:

> Love of learning is by nature curious and inquisitive, not hesitating to bend its steps in all directions, prying into everything, reluctant to leave anything that exists unexplored, whether material or immaterial. It has an extraordinary appetite for all that there is to be seen and heard, and, not content with what it finds in its own country, it is bent on seeking what is in foreign parts and separated by great distances. We are reminded that merchants and traders for the sake of trifling profits cross the seas, and compass the wide world, letting stand in their way no summer heat nor winter cold, no tempestuous or contrary winds, neither youth nor age, no sickness of body, neither the daily intercourse with friends nor the pleasure too great for words which we take in wife and children and in all else that is our own, nor the enjoyment of our fatherland and of all the gracious amenities of civic life, nor the safe use of money and property and abundance of other good things, nor in a word anything else either great or small. If so, it is monstrous, such speakers urge, when we stand to gain a thing most fair, worth all men's striving for, the special prerogative of the human race, namely wisdom, to refrain from crossing every sea, from exploring earth's every recess, in the joy of finding out whether there is in any place aught that is fair to see or hear and from following the quest of it with utmost zest and keenness, until we can come to the enjoyment of the things that we are seeking and longing for. (*Migr.* 216–18)[40]

The motives for setting out on a journey are diverse, but mostly focus on gain, whether expressed in the intention to make profit as traders or in the desire to acquire wisdom and knowledge for one's own pleasure or in order to benefit one's home community (cf. *Abr.* 65).[41] The close correlation of searching for wisdom and traveling coincides with the ancient perception of travel as an educational experience. In the text quoted above, Philo uses travel as an allegory of spiritual travel.[42] The Book of Sirach, on the other hand, draws on the experience of travel when it acknowledges the intrinsic value of travel and states in chapter 34,

> Since a man roamed [*anēr peplanēmenos*], he knew many things, and he who is experienced will tell with understanding. He who had no experience knows few things, but he who has roamed [*peplanēmenos*] will increase cleverness [*panourgian*]. I have seen many things in my wandering [*en tē apoplanēsei mou*], and more than my words is my

> understanding. Frequently I was in danger of death, and I was saved because of these things. (Sir 34:9–13, [NETS])[43]

The traveler thus gains knowledge and wisdom, although he "may not be traveling primarily for the sake of wisdom . . . the travel motif is linked with his capability to distinguish good from bad. This implies that the traveler is expected to deliberate, making observations and judgements on what he encounters away from home."[44] And, according to Ben Sira, his travels gain him *panourgia*, the trait that also characterizes the "cunning" Odysseus.[45]

Reading the New Testament Texts

The Acts of the Apostles

The canonical Acts of the Apostles provides an account of the early Christian movement, focusing on the spread of the mission after Jesus's resurrection and ascension throughout the Roman Empire, until it reaches the city of Rome. Acts uses the term "the Way" (*hodos*; Acts 9:2; 19:9, 23; 22:4; 24:14, 22; cf. Isa 40:3) to describe the early Christian movement, referring both to a spiritual and a physical journey. The followers of Jesus are portrayed as being "on the move," and spreading the message across the Roman world. This mobility, however, is not simply about geographical expansion, it also includes the ideological adaptation of Christian beliefs in different cultural contexts:[46]

> the book of Acts, written in the late 1st or early 2nd century CE, uses motion as a topos to describe the early Jesus movement as a global, or supra-ethnic, group in which Judaeans and non-Judaeans come together. Through its description of how this movement spread beyond Roman Palestine and eventually reached Rome, Acts characterizes the Jesus movement as a glocal (!) movement: that is, a movement that incorporates a wide range of local cultures and traditions—which Acts' protagonists encounter on their journeys—within a global whole—the ascended Jesus and his teachings.[47]

While the early Christian movement spread in a globalized world, Acts presents early Christianity as a *glocal* phenomenon, meaning that it adapts global (universal) phenomena to local conditions. This dynamic is evident in the way the Christian message is tailored to different audiences even as it maintains its core identity. The apostles, particularly Paul, encounter various cultural and religious groups, and their message evolves in response to these encounters. For example, when in a Jewish context, Acts presents the Jesus movement as the fulfillment of Jewish eschatological hopes; when addressing the Roman official Cornelius, Paul uses vocabulary that associates the peace Jesus brings with the Pax Romana (Acts 10:36); and in Paul's speech at the Areopagus in Athens (Acts 17), he engages with Greek philosophical ideas to make Christianity more accessible to a Hellenistic audience.[48] Moreover, Acts positions Christianity as both an extension of Jewish tradition and as a movement that is promoted by early Christians who are portrayed as travelers, preachers, or even Roman citizens, engaging with the broader Roman imperial context. Christianity is thus presented as a movement that transcends ethnic and national boundaries and derives its identity from its interaction with different cultures. That is to say, it is a movement that is adaptable, inclusive, and mobile, negotiating between local traditions and a universal Christian message.

The Epistle of James

The Epistle of James is addressed to "the twelve tribes scattered among the nations" (Jas 1:1), and formulates some advice to merchant travelers in James 4:13–15:

> Come now, you who say, "Today or tomorrow we will go [*poreusometha*] to such and such a city and spend a year there and engage in business [*emporeusometha*] and make profit [*kerdēsomen*]" yet you do not know what will be tomorrow, what your life will be like; for you are mist that appears for a little while and then vanishes. Instead, you should say, "If the Lord wills, we will live and do this or that."

The verb used for the merchants' planned actions, *emporeuomai* (Jas 4:13), refers to their manner of trading, for it describes the work of wholesalers (*emporoi*) who traded goods overseas, who may have been ship owners, or may have been businessmen traveling on merchant ships. The goods—wine, oil, grain, spices, precious metals, wood, pottery, textiles, and so forth—were then sold locally either by the *emporoi* themselves or by local retail merchants (*kapēloi*).[49] Although the two terms, *emporoi* and *kapēloi*, came to be used increasingly interchangeably in the Roman imperial period, the terminology used in James, in conjunction with its argumentative context, suggests that the author does not have itinerant craftsmen or small retailers in mind, but rather merchants on a larger scale who engaged in long-distance, overseas commerce and spent extended periods of time in a foreign place, for example, for wintering purposes.[50] This provides grounds for assuming that the addressees were widely connected and integrated into the networks of the Roman Empire, that they were involved in transporting goods as well as knowledge, ideas, and wisdom, and that they were probably included in networks of merchant travelers and established their own Jewish-Christian networks within the ancient world.

This passage portrays merchants whose self-confidence in making travel plans is exposed as presumptuous and insolent toward God. The criticism, however, is not focusing on travel plans or even the pursuit of profit per se. Rather, the letter cautions against reckoning one's ambitious and presumptuous plans, especially concerning such dangerous and unpredictable undertakings as long-distance travel, as being within one's own sphere of influence instead of in the hands of the Lord who governs all things. It is precisely the experience of traveling that should teach merchants to be prudent and God-fearing in their planning, and it is wisdom literature, a tradition of great importance to the Epistle of James, that reinforces the awareness of the uncertainty of human plans for the future (cf. Prov 16:9; Sir 11:18–19).

FURTHER READING

Barclay, John M. G. *Jews in the Mediterranean Diaspora from Alexander to Trajan (323 BCE–117 CE).* T&T Clark, 1999.

Collar, Anna. *Religious Networks in the Roman Empire: The Spread of New Ideas.* Cambridge University Press, 2013.

Gruen, Erich S. *Diaspora: Jews amidst Greeks and Romans.* Harvard University Press, 2002.

Hezser, Catherine. *Jewish Travel in Antiquity.* Texts and Studies in Ancient Judaism 144. Mohr Siebeck, 2011.

Jennings, Justin. *Globalizations and the Ancient World.* Cambridge University Press, 2011.

Niehoff, Maren R., ed. *Journeys in the Roman East: Imagined and Real.* Culture, Religion, and Politics in the Greco-Roman World 1. Mohr Siebeck, 2017.

Pitts, Martin and Miguel John Versluys. *Globalisation and the Roman World: World History, Connectivity and Material Culture.* Cambridge University Press, 2014.

Online resources

ORBIS—The Stanford Geospatial Network Model of the Roman World (interactive maps of the Roman road network): https://orbis.stanford.edu/

Pleiades—The Ancient World Mapping Center and the Institute for the Study of the Ancient World at the University of North Carolina at Chapel Hill (interactive maps of Greek and Roman World): https://pleiades.stoa.org/home

Notes

1 For perspectives on traveling in the ancient world see Susanne Luther, "'Today or tomorrow we will go to such and such a city. . .' (Jas 4:13): The Experience of Interconnectivity and the Mobility of Norms in the Ancient Globalized World," in *Jewish, Christian and Muslim Travel Experiences. 3rd century BCE–8th century CE*, ed.

Susanne Luther, Pieter B. Hartog, and Clare E. Wilde, Judaism, Christianity, and Islam - Tension, Transmission, Transformation 16 (de Gruyter, 2023).

2 Cf. Laura Nasrallah, "Imposing Travellers: An Inscription from Galatia and the Journeys of the Earliest Christians," in *Journeys in the Roman East: Imagined and Real*, ed. Maren R. Niehoff, Culture, Religion, and Politics in the Greco-Roman World 1 (Mohr Siebeck, 2017), 274–75, on the Roman road system.

3 Cf. Ryan S. Schellenberg, " 'Danger in the Wilderness, Danger at Sea': Paul and the Perils of Travel," in *Travel and Religion in Antiquity*, ed. Philip Harland, Studies in Christianity and Judaism 21 (Wilfrid Laurier University Press, 2011).

4 On Jewish travel in antiquity, see Catherine Hezser, *Jewish Travel in Antiquity*, Texts and Studies in Ancient Judaism 144 (Mohr Siebeck, 2011); see also Wayne O. McCready, "Pilgrimage, Place, and Meaning Making by Jews in Greco-Roman Egypt," in Harland, *Travel and Religion in Antiquity*.

5 Cf. the Stanford ORBIS tool: ORBIS, The Stanford Geospatial Network Model of the Roman World, Stanford University Libraries, https://orbis.stanford.edu/ (last accessed 4 April 2025) or Pleiades, Ancient World Mapping Center and Institute for the Study of the Ancient World, https://pleiades.stoa.org/home (last accessed 4 April 2025).

6 Cf. Kenn Hirth, *The Organization of Ancient Economies: A Global Perspective* (Cambridge University Press, 2020), 194–235; for the ancient merchant diaspora, see Hirth, *Organization of Ancient Economies*, 218–25.

7 Cf. Jás Elsner and Ian Rutherford, eds., *Pilgrimage in Graeco-Roman and Early Christian Antiquity: Seeing the Gods* (Oxford University Press, 2005); Steven Muir, "Religion on the Road in Ancient Greece and Rome," in Harland, *Travel and Religion in Antiquity*, 29–47; René Bloch, "Show and Tell: Myth, Tourism, and Jewish Hellenism," in *Ancient Jewish Diaspora: Essays on Hellenism*, ed. René Bloch, Supplements to the Journal for the Study of Judaism 206 (Brill, 2022), 101–27.

8 Marie Pretzler, "Greek Intellectuals on the Move: Travel and Paideia in the Roman Empire," in *Travel, Geography and Culture in Ancient Greece, Egypt and the Near East*, ed. Colin Adams and Jim Roy (Oxbow, 2007), 123–38; on the parody of such educational journeys cf. Maren R. Niehoff, "Parodies of Educational Journeys in Josephus, Justin Martyr, and Lucian," in *Journeys in the Roman East*, 203–24.

9 Philip Curtin, *Cross-Cultural Trade in World History* (Cambridge University Press, 1984), 3.

10 Hirth, *Organization of Ancient Economies*, 219–20.

11 Casper C. de Jonge, "Greek Migrant Literature in the Early Roman Empire," *Mnemosyne* 75, no. 1 (2022): 10–36 (10); cf. Laurens E. Tacoma, *Moving Romans. Migration to Rome in the Principate* (Oxford University Press, 2016).

12 Cf. Irmgard Männlein-Robert, "Move Your Self: Mobility and Migration of Greek Intellectuals to Rome," in *Self, Self-Fashioning, and Individuality in Late Antiquity New Perspectives*, ed. Maren R. Niehoff and Joshua Levinson (Mohr Siebeck, 2019), 331–52.

13 Cf. De Jonge, "Greek Migrant Literature," 17.

14 Cf. De Jonge, "Greek Migrant Literature," 14.

15 István Czachesz, "Women, Charity and Mobility in Early Christianity: Weak Links and the Historical Transformation of Religions," in *Changing Minds: Religion and Cognition Through the Ages*, ed. István Czachesz and Tamás Biró, Groningen Studies in Cultural Change 42 (Peeters, 2011), 143; cf. Anna Collar, *Religious Networks in the Roman Empire: The Spread of New Ideas* (Cambridge University Press, 2013).

16 Cf. Dennis C. Duling, "Paul's Aegean Network: The Strength of Strong Ties," *BTB* 43, no. 3 (2013): 135–54.

17 Cf. Martin Pitts and Miguel John Versluys, "Globalisation and the Roman World: Perspectives and Opportunities," in *Globalisation and the Roman World: World History, Connectivity and Material Culture*, ed. Martin Pitts and Miguel John Versluys (Cambridge University Press, 2014); Justin Jennings, *Globalizations and the Ancient World* (Cambridge University Press, 2011).

18 Pitts and Versluys, "Globalisation the Roman World," 11.

19 Jan Nederveen Pieterse, "Ancient Rome and Globalisation: Decentring Rome," in *Globalisation and the Roman World: World History, Connectivity and Material Culture*, ed. Martin Pitts and Miguel John Versluys (Cambridge University Press, 2014), 235.

20 Tamar Hodos, "Globalization: Some Basics: An Introduction to The Routledge Handbook of Archaeology and Globalization," in *Routledge Handbook of Archaeology and Globalization*, ed. Tamar Hodos (Routledge, 2016), 4.

21 Nederveen Pieterse, "Ancient Rome and Globalisation," 231.

22 Miguel John Versluys, "Roman Visual Material Culture as Globalising *Koine*," in Pitts and Versluys, *Globalisation the Roman World*, 163.

23 Cf. Neville Morley, "Globalisation and the Roman Economy," in Pitts and Versluys, *Globalisation the Roman World*, 49–68.

24 Morley, "Globalisation and Roman Economy," 59.

25 Morley, "Globalisation and Roman Economy," 59; cf. Jan Nederveen Pieterse, *Ethnicities and Global Multiculture: Pants for an Octopus* (Rowman & Littlefield, 2007), 9: "King Herod, who was appointed King of Judea by the Romans, was 'by birth an Idumean (i.e. Edomite), by profession a Jew, by necessity a Roman, by culture and by choice a Greek.' Multiple and intersecting cultural layers and overlapping jurisdictions, then as now, generate multiple identities."

26 Pitts and Versluys, *Globalisation the Roman World*, 14. The central elements to be identified and analyzed in this approach are therefore power, resources, and identity, which determine the process of global intermingling of cultures.

27 Hodos, "Globalization: Some Basics," 6.

28 Hodos, "Globalization: Some Basics," 6.

29 Michael Sommer, "OIKOYMENH: Longue Durée Perspectives on Ancient Mediterranean 'Globality,' " in Pitts and Versluys, *Globalisation the Roman World*, 176, who gives an overview over ancient perceptions of globalization, for example, by Aelius Aristides in Arist. 26.101–2.

30 For the effect of globalization on everyday life on a local and regional level through research into mass consumption in the Roman empire, cf. Martin Pitts, "Globalisation, Circulation and Mass Consumption in the Roman World," in Pitts and Versluys, *Globalisation the Roman World*.

31 Pitts, "Globalisation, Circulation and Consumption," 93.

32 Cf. Eelco Glas, *Flavius Josephus' Self-Characterisation in First Century Rome. A Historiographical Analysis of Autobiographical Discourse in the Judaean War*, Historiography of Rome and Its Empire 19 (Brill, 2024).

33 On the problems arising from the deviating representation in *Life*, cf. Steve Mason, *Josephus and the New Testament* (Handrickson, 1992).

34 Steve Mason, *Flavius Josephus: Translation and Commentary*, vol. 9, *Life of Josephus* (Brill, 2011), 422–30.

35 Niehoff dates Philo's arrival in Rome to the autumn of 38 AD, cf. Maren Niehoff, *Philo of Alexandria. An Intellectual Biography* (Yale University Press, 2018), 17.

36 *On the Embassy to Gaius. General Indexes*, trans. F. H. Colson, index by J. W. Earp, Loeb Classical Library 379 (Harvard University Press, 1962), 190–91.

37 Cf. Pieter B. Hartog, "Space and Travel in Philo's *Legatio ad Gaium*," *SPhiloA* 30 (2018): 71–92; Pieter B. Hartog, "Contesting *Oikoumenē*: Resistance and Locality in Philo's *Legatio ad Gaium*," in *Intolerance, Polemics, and Debate in Antiquity. Politico-Cultural, Philosophical, and Religious Forms of Critical Conversation*, ed. George van Kooten and Jacques van Ruiten (Brill, 2019), 205–31.

38 Maren R. Niehoff, "Wie wird man ein mediterraner Denker? Der Fall Philon von Alexandria," in *Ein pluriverses Universum. Zivilisationen und Religionen im antiken Mittelmeerraum*, ed. Richard Faber and Achim Lichtenberger, Mittelmeerstudien 7 (Schöningh, 2015), 355–67.

39 Niehoff, *Philo of Alexandria*, 19.

40 *On the Confusion of Tongues. On the Migration of Abraham. Who Is the Heir of Divine Things? On Mating with the Preliminary Studies*, trans. F. H. Colson and G. H. Whitaker, Loeb Classical Library 261, (Harvard University Press, 1932).

41 Cf. for Philo Elisa Uusimäki, "Itinerant Sages: The Evidence of Sirach in its Ancient Mediterranean Context," *JSOT* 44, no. 3 (2020): 315–36 (325).

42 Cf. Sean Adams, "Movement and Travel in Philo's Migration of Abraham: The Adaptation of Genesis and the Introduction of a Metaphor," *SPhiloA* 30 (2018): 47–70.

43 Cf. Sir 8:15; 26:12; 33:2; 36:31; 42:3. For the translator of Ben Sira as traveler from Israel to Egypt cf. Elisa Uusimäki, "The Formation of a Sage according to Ben Sira," in *Second Temple Jewish 'Paideia' in Context*, ed. Jason M. Zurawski and Gabriele Boccaccini, Beihefte zur Zeitschrift für die neutestamentliche Wissenschaft 228 (de Gruyter, 2017), 59–69; Elisa Uusimäki, "The Rise of the Sage in Greek and Jewish Antiquity," *JSJ* 49, no. 1 (2018): 1–29.

44 Uusimäki, "Itinerant Sages," 319.

45 Cf. Burkard M. Zapff, "Normenbegründung vor gewandeltem Hintergrund: Jesus Sirach als Vermittler zwischen traditionellem jüdischem Glauben und hellenistischem Geist," in *Athen, Rom, Jerusalem: Normentransfers in der antiken Welt*, ed. Gian Franco Chiai, Eichstätter Studien Neue Folge 66 (Pustet, 2012), 36.

46 Cf. Peter B. Hartog, "Reading Acts in Motion: Movement and Glocalisation in the Acts of the Apostles," in *Mediterranean Flows: People, Ideas and Objects in Motion*, ed. Anna Usacheva and Emilia Mataix Ferrándiz, Contexts of Ancient and Medieval Anthropology 3 (Brill Schöningh, 2023), 100–102.

47 Hartog, "Reading Acts in Motion," 99.

48 Cf. Hartog, "Reading Acts in Motion," 104–10.

49 Cf. Wiard Popkes, *Der Brief des Jakobus*, Theologischer Kommentar zum Neuen Testament 14 (Evangelische Verlagsanstalt, 2001), 288–90. On marketplaces and the structure of the ancient economy, see Hirth, *Organization of Ancient Economies*. For Roman seafaring and laws relating to Roman maritime commerce, see Peter Candy and Emilia Mataix Ferrandis, eds., *Roman Law and Maritime Commerce* (Edinburgh University Press, 2022).

50 Cf. Rainer Metzner, *Der Brief des Jakobus*, Theologischer Kommentar zum Neuen Testament 14 (Evangelische Verlagsanstalt, 2017), 244–46.

CHAPTER FIFTEEN

Philosophical Schools and Ideas

Johan C. Thom
(Stellenbosch University)

From a very early period, Christian authors already viewed ancient philosophy as a natural *comparandum* for early Christianity. In 1 Corinthians 1:22–23, Paul contrasts the gospel proclaimed by him to the wisdom (*sophia*) sought after by the Greeks. The author of Acts depicts Stoic and Epicurean philosophers as Paul's conversation partners in Athens (Acts 17:18–34), while in Colossians 2:8 the teaching of Christ is contrasted with philosophy (*philosophia*) based on human tradition. Apologists of the second century like Justin Martyr, Theophilus of Antioch, and Tatian, all similarly compared and contrasted Christianity with philosophy. It is clear that they considered Christianity and philosophy similar enough to compete within the same social and cultural contexts.

According to tradition, the term *philosophy* can be traced back to Pythagoras (sixth to fifth century BCE), who defined it as the desire or search for wisdom. Philosophy was understood as the continual pursuit of wisdom, and wisdom itself was viewed as the ability to live wisely and to achieve a good and happy life. Philosophy provided practical guidance on how to live and thus shaped the whole of a philosopher's life. A philosophical life required a radical change from the normal, everyday way of life practiced by nonphilosophers and demanded a life-long commitment. Because the change involved the whole person and not just a part of one's being or behavior, it was inherently spiritual—a transformation of all one's views, principles, actions, habits, etc. There were therefore many implicit connections between philosophy and early Christian thought, making philosophy an important aspect of the cultural context of early Christianity. Few people in the world of the New Testament would have had detailed and technical knowledge of individual philosophical schools, but they were nevertheless aware of important philosophical ideas and concepts circulating as part of popular philosophy, which formed part of the broader cultural and intellectual context.

Major Philosophical Traditions

Influential philosophical movements in the New Testament period include Platonism, Aristotelianism, Stoicism, Cynicism, Epicureanism, Skepticism, and

Pythagoreanism. Here we will concentrate on the most significant characteristics of the various traditions.[1]

Platonism

The Platonist movement originated with Plato (ca. 427–348 BCE). His work was foundational for the development of the Western tradition of philosophy, and his dialogues remained the basis of Platonist philosophy throughout antiquity. A dialogue of special interest for the study of the New Testament is the *Timaeus*, in which the creation and composition of the world is discussed. Plato founded a school called the Academy which continued his teaching after his death. In antiquity, four periods of Platonism may be distinguished: the Old Academy (347–267 BCE), the "New" (Skeptical) Academy (267–ca. 80 BCE), Middle Platonism (ca. 80 BCE–250 CE), and Neoplatonism (ca. 250 CE).

Already in the Old Academy, three branches of philosophy were distinguished: physics, ethics, and logic. This period also produced a synthesis of Platonic doctrines which formed the basis of a system still influential in the time of early Christianity. Its main features included (1) a distinction between two levels of reality, the intelligible world (consisting of God and the Ideas, which are transcendent models or forms of which the things of this world are images), and the world of sense perception; (2) a belief in the immortality of the soul in reincarnation; (3) a moderate asceticism aiming to separate the soul as far as possible from bodily influences; and (4) a preference for the processes of pure reason over the evidence of the senses.

By the time of the New Testament, Platonism had incorporated ideas from other traditions such as Aristotelianism and Stoicism; this phase of the Platonist tradition is typically referred to as Middle Platonism. Important figures of Middle Platonism are Philo of Alexandria (ca. 15 BCE–ca. 50 CE) and Plutarch of Chaeronea (ca. 45–before 125 CE). Philo took over the Stoic concept of the Logos as the active, immanent aspect of god in the world. Plutarch continued this development, emphasizing a dualistic view of the world.

The Platonist goal is perhaps best encapsulated in the phrase *homoiōsis theō*, "likeness to god," that is, becoming like god. This concept entails one escaping from the bonds of bodily existence in order for the soul to be purified and become more and more like god. In later Platonists, the ultimate goal is the mystical vision of, and union with god, an ascent attained through graded levels of knowledge and contemplation.

Aristotelianism

Plato's most influential student was Aristotle (384–322 BCE), who founded his own school, the so-called Peripatos. Aristotle differed from his teacher Plato through his engagement in a wide range of scientific studies. This included, among other subjects, metaphysics, cosmology, meteorology, logic and syllogistics, literary theory, rhetoric, political theory, and ethics. He wrote numerous works, some aimed at the general public (his exoteric writings), and others for use by his students (his esoteric writings). Most of the former have been lost or are extant only as fragments. Among the latter, his *Nicomachean Ethics* and his *On Rhetoric* are of particular interest to students of the New Testament. Andronicus of Rhodes collected and edited Aristotle's works in the first century BCE, providing a solid foundation for the commentaries on Aristotle that were produced in the imperial period.

Aristotle's research was continued, expanded, and systematized by his students, who added investigations into areas such as botany, geography, music theory, and biography. Later, important pseudepigraphical writings, that is, texts falsely attributed to Aristotle, such as *On the Cosmos* and *On Virtues and Vices*, were produced in Aristotle's name in response to contemporary philosophical developments.

For Aristotelians, the philosophical life was a life devoted to *theōria*—that is, study and contemplation—a life devoted to the activity of the intellect. Such a life was not purely theoretical but also required the concrete implementation of intellectual ideals—that is, the actualization of the divine in the human.

Stoicism

In the time after Plato and Aristotle, several traditions developed that are usually collectively referred to as Hellenistic philosophy. Stoicism was one of the major Hellenistic philosophies and perhaps also the most influential in the New Testament period (cf. Acts 17:18). The school was founded by Zeno of Citium (335–263 BCE), who taught in the "Painted Colonnade" (Stoa) in Athens, from which the movement derived its name. Zeno was succeeded as head of the Stoic school by Cleanthes of Assos (331–230 BCE), best known for his religious interpretation of Stoic ideas (exemplified by his *Hymn to Zeus*) and his uncompromising ethics. The third head of the school, Chrysippus of Soli (ca. 280–207 BCE), reestablished Stoic orthodoxy and is often considered the second founder of Stoicism. During the late Hellenistic period, Stoics like Posidonius incorporated Platonic and Aristotelian ideas into their teaching. In the early imperial period, Stoic philosophers such as Musonius Rufus (died before 101 CE), Seneca (ca. 4 BCE–65 CE), Epictetus (mid-first century–second century CE), and the Roman Emperor Marcus Aurelius (121–80 CE) focused on Stoicism as a way of life rather than a system of philosophy.

Stoicism's aim was to teach people to attain happiness by taking control of their lives, emphasizing virtue as the only true good worth striving for, with all other things considered indifferent. Its strength lay in offering to its adherents a systematic and all-comprehensive worldview, based on material pantheism. Students were exhorted to live in accordance with nature, which was variously identified with god, the divine principle of order, fate, and providence.

Stoic theology may be described as a monistic and materialistic pantheism, in which god permeates all of nature, from the cosmos as a whole down to the lowliest physical object. God, as the active principle, or reason (Logos), acts upon the passive principle, matter, but both principles have a bodily existence. Nothing exists outside the world and its material principles. God as ordering and creative principle is physically present in all things as a fine, fiery substance, called the "designing fire" or *pneuma* (*breath* or *spirit*, a fiery form of air), which gives everything its form and internal cohesion. Since he is present throughout the whole universe and gives everything within its character, god is in a sense identical with the universe.

For the Stoic, happiness consists in attaining one's goal (*telos*) as a human being, which is "to live in agreement with nature"; that is, in agreement with our own rational nature, as well as in agreement with the nature of the universe of which we are part. Virtue is the only true good essential for happiness. Our happiness does not depend on acquiring external goods such as health or wealth, but rather on making the right choices and attempting to put them into effect. Happiness therefore depends on what is within our power (making rational choices) and not on things beyond our control (attaining wealth or being healthy). The latter are thus "indifferent" (*adiaphora*) with respect to happiness.

Emotions such as fear or grief are false judgments about the world for the Stoic. Rather than fearing or grieving over what lies beyond our control, one should accept it as part of nature's plan and resist giving in to such emotions. The Stoics thus advocated for the goal of *apatheia*—"being without passions." Because everything in nature is rationally and providentially arranged, the wise person accepts their fate willingly because it is the divine will.

Cynicism

Important early Cynics are Antisthenes (died ca. 365 BCE), Diogenes of Sinope (412/403–324/321 BCE), and Crates of Thebes (died 270 BCE). They left no writings, but anecdotes about their actions and sayings attributed to them were very influential throughout antiquity. In the early imperial period popular philosophers like Dio Chrysostom (ca. 40–after 112 CE) conveyed Cynic ideas in public speeches in the so-called *diatribe* style. From this time, we also have pseudepigraphical letters attributed to well-known Cynics.

The name *Cynic* (*kynikos*) probably derives from *kyōn*, the Greek word for *dog*. This refers to the Cynics' "shamelessness" and shocking disregard for the conventions of social behavior.

Cynics rejected many of the intellectual disciplines taught in other schools, focusing solely on ethics. The Cynics' way of life was itself meant to teach: to challenge all values and opinions, and to live instead according to nature. They advocated for a simple life focusing on basic and natural needs, free from societal expectations and social conventions. Like the Stoics, they thought that happiness lay in living in agreement with nature. Their aim was self-sufficiency and independence, achieved through self-mastery, which enables one to live happily even in difficult circumstances.

Epicureanism

Epicurus (342/341–271/270 BCE) founded another major Hellenistic school of philosophy called "The Garden" (*kēpos*) in Athens. He wrote extensively, but only a few of his writings have survived: a letter to Herodotus, a summary of his physics; a letter to Pythocles, a summary of astronomical and meteorological teachings; a letter to Menoeceus, an introduction to his ethics; a collection of sayings called *Kyriai Doxai* (Principal Doctrines); another collection called "Vatican Sayings"; and some fragmentary papyri.

Epicurus's ethics are rooted in his teachings on physics, which is based on a form of atomism. According to this view, the universe consists of the void (an infinite empty space), and an infinite number of invisible and indivisible bodies—atoms. The atoms move rapidly and as they collide, they form bigger complexes, the largest of which is a complete world system. The universe contains an infinite number of worlds, which are constantly being created and destroyed. Only the universe as a whole, with its atoms, and the gods are indestructible and everlasting.

Epicurus taught that gods exist because there is a universal concept of them among all people. Like everything else in the universe, the gods consist of atoms. However, they do not belong to a specific world, but rather live in the space between worlds. They do not interact with the world and do not concern themselves with human beings, enjoying a perfectly happy life by themselves. As such, they need not be feared; instead they provide humans with an example of perfect happiness. Epicurus wanted to free humans not only from their fear of the gods, but also from their fear of death. Since a human is made up of body atoms and soul atoms, when a person dies, the soul dissolves along with the body. Therefore, there is no afterlife with a reward or punishment.

For Epicureans, pleasure is the ultimate good and goal of life, but their hedonism is qualified in several respects. It is not a life of dissipation, but freedom from physical pain and mental disturbance. Pleasures that cause discomfort are to be avoided, and some pains are to be endured when they are followed by a greater and long-lasting pleasure. Self-sufficiency is considered a great good because it enables one to take pleasure in even the simplest things, such as being healthy without being dependent on luxuries. For such a life prudence—knowing what to choose and what to avoid—is essential; it gives rise to all the other virtues. A pleasurable life is, indeed, inseparable from a life of virtue. A truly happy life is a quiet life characterized by freedom of mental disturbance, that is, tranquility and enjoying the simple joy of existing.

Skepticism

Skepticism was another school of thought that originated in the Hellenistic period. Skeptics did not accept any opinion as the truth, but rather continually subjected all opinions to examination (the ancient term "skeptic," *skeptikos*, derives from *skeptesthai*, "to investigate, examine"). There were two strands of Skeptics: (1) the Academics; and (2) the Pyrrhonians, of which Sextus Empiricus (second century CE) was the most prominent. The Pyrrhonians were the most extreme, teaching a life without any opinions whatsoever, while the Academics were more moderate, teaching that it was permitted to form an opinion on any matter as long as such an opinion was not mistaken for knowledge. The Roman author Cicero (106–43 BCE) was an adherent of the latter view.

The goal of Skeptics was freedom of mental disturbance in matters of opinion and moderation of emotions in response to unavoidable circumstances. This means that the Skeptics tried to suspend judgment on any matter about which there could be a difference of opinion—particularly about whether anything is by nature good or bad (for example, whether death or illness are great evils). In practice, this entailed suspending judgment about everything; that is, refraining from committing to any conclusions. Since total inactivity is impossible, even while suspending judgment, the Skeptic would still act in accordance with what is natural or customary, but without any commitment to the rightness or truth of those actions.

Pythagoreanism

The origins of the Pythagorean tradition can be traced back to Pythagoras (sixth or fifth century BCE). Although he did not leave any writings, he is traditionally credited with teachings on the immortality and the transmigration of the soul, the eternal cyclic recurrence of events, and the kinship of all living things. According to later tradition, Pythagoras was interested in both mathematical sciences (including astronomy and music) and religion. Oral tradition played an important role in the preservation and transmission of Pythagorean teachings.

The Pythagorean community was famous in later antiquity for its communal living and shared possessions. Within the movement, a distinction was made, however, between esoteric and exoteric members: The former fully embraced the Pythagorean life, and devoted themselves to study, while the latter observed less stringent ritual and dietary rules and were less involved in the esoteric doctrines of the sect. Ancient authors like Josephus (*Ant.* 15.10.4) drew parallels between the Pythagorean way of life and that of the Essenes, a Jewish sect living in the region of the Dead Sea.

Early Pythagoreanism largely disappeared by the fourth century BCE, but a large collection of pseudepigraphical writings ascribed to Pythagoras and ancient Pythagoreans was produced in the Hellenistic and early imperial periods. From the first century BCE onward, there was a revival of interest in Pythagoreanism, known as neo-Pythagoreanism. This movement included philosophers interested in the numerical and mathematical aspects of the Pythagorean tradition, philosophers focusing on the Pythagorean way of life, and miracle workers like Apollonius of Tyana (first century CE).

The basic features of neo-Pythagoreanism included an interest in arithmology, a belief in the transmigration of souls, and an emphasis on the need for the purification of the soul, which was accomplished through ascetic and theurgic practices. The early Pythagorean ideal expressed by the maxim *hepou theō*, "follow god," became synonymous with the Platonic ideal of "becoming like god."

Psychagogy or Moral Formation

Philosophers of most schools developed a program of psychagogy (the moral and spiritual formation of the soul) to prepare their students for a philosophical way of life.[2] Psychagogy started with an exhortation to embrace a philosophical life, which demanded a radical break from the normal everyday life practiced by non-philosophers and a life-long commitment to its philosophy. Because this transformation involved the whole person, and not simply an aspect of one's being or behavior, it was inherently spiritual: a reorientation of all one's views, thinking, attitudes, principles, goals, actions, customs, etc. In fact, it constituted a form of conversion. Such exhortations to the philosophical life formed the contents of popular speeches delivered in public or in popular texts. The training that followed involved learning foundational principles for ethical behavior, as well as exercises and practices designed to inculcate and reinforce these principles in daily life.

The Stoics and Epicureans, in particular, systematized their teachings into a concise set of principles that were logically coherent, psychologically persuasive, and easier to memorize. This ensured that the principles remained always "available" enabling the student to recall and apply them as circumstances required and to orient themselves in the world with philosophical clarity. These principles were usually expressed in the form of maxims. A well-known example is the Epicurean *tetrapharmakos* (fourfold remedy): "God presents no fears, death no worries. And while good is readily attainable, evil is readily endurable."[3]

In order to inculcate and reinforce the principles and put them into practice, there were exercises the student was required to accomplish on a regular basis.[4] These exercises strengthened self-awareness, a consciousness of one's position in the world, and insight into the moral implications of one's actions. In modern terms, we could say that they encouraged mindfulness. Examples of such exercises include: the contemplation of one's mortality (*meditare mortem*), in order to constantly remind ourselves that death is inevitable; the contemplation of future evils (*praemeditatio malorum*) so that we may prepare ourselves for unexpected circumstances like poverty, suffering, or the loss of loved ones; deliberation before action, in order to carefully consider what the action entails and what its consequences might be; self-examination and reflection, often practiced at the end of the day, as to reflect on any mistakes made during the day and to assess progress toward a virtuous and happy life. These exercises are all forms of meditation. Meditation involves the regular contemplation of the various philosophical principles and their application to one's life. This includes memorizing appropriate maxims and aphorisms, as well as reading and studying appropriate texts that provide further material for meditation and reflection.

Although personal independence and self-sufficiency were emphasized by all philosophical traditions, this does not mean that spiritual transformation took place in a vacuum. The social context played an important role in supporting moral progress and development. Philosophical traditions consistently agreed that good friendships were essential for a happy life. A true friend should not only provide advice and support, but also frank criticism when necessary. The Epicureans, in particular, elevated the practice of honest criticism into a refined discipline. They lived in communities of friendship aimed at promoting a happy and virtuous life. According to the Epicurean handbook *On Frank Criticism* by Philodemus (first century BCE), teachers within such a community were expected to apply frank criticism carefully and with discrimination, adapting their approach to the specific situation and character of the person.

TAKING A CLOSER LOOK: SOURCES

Sources from the World of the New Testament

Cleanthes's Hymn to Zeus

Noblest of immortals, many-named, always all-powerful
Zeus, first cause and ruler of nature, governing everything
with your law,
greetings! For it is right for all mortals to address you:
for we have our origin in you, bearing a likeness to God,
we, alone of all that live and move as mortals on earth.

Therefore I shall praise you constantly; indeed I always sing of your rule.
This whole universe, spinning around the earth, truly
obeys you wherever you lead, and is readily ruled by you;
such a servant do you have between your unconquerable hands,
the two-edged, fiery, ever-living thunderbolt.
For by its stroke all works of nature <are guided>.
With it you direct the universal reason, which permeates
everything, mingling with the great and the small lights.
Because of this you are so great, the highest king for ever.
Not a single deed takes place on earth without you, God,
nor in the divine celestial sphere nor in the sea,
except what bad people do in their folly.
But you know how to make the uneven even
and to put into order the disorderly; even the unloved is dear to you.
For you have thus joined everything into one, the good with the bad,
that there comes to be one ever-existing rational order for everything.
This all mortals that are bad flee and avoid,
the wretched, who though always desiring to acquire good things,
neither see nor hear God's universal law,
obeying which they could have a good life with understanding.
But they on the contrary rush without regard to the good, each after different things,
some with a belligerent eagerness for glory,
others without discipline intent on profits,
others yet on indulgence and the pleasurable actions of the body.
<They desire the good,> but they are borne now to this, then to that,
while striving eagerly that the complete opposite of these things happen.
But all-bountiful Zeus, cloud-wrapped ruler of the thunderbolt,
deliver human beings from their destructive ignorance;
disperse it, Father, from their souls; grant that they obtain
the insight on which you rely when governing everything with justice

so that we, having been honoured, may honour you in return,
constantly praising your works, as befits
one who is mortal. For there is no other greater privilege for mortals
or for gods than always to praise the universal law in justice.

Cleanthes's *Hymn to Zeus* was written in the Hellenistic period, probably during the first half of the third century BCE.[5] Although Cleanthes was one of the leading Stoic philosophers, the poem contains very few overtly Stoic elements and was clearly intended for a wider audience beyond students of Stoicism. Its basic message is that moral evil is due to the irrational behavior of humans, which in turn disrupts the cosmic order; though this disturbance can be remedied with god's help.

The *Hymn to Zeus* (*HZ*) is a hexameter poem with a typical threefold hymnic structure—that is, with an "Invocation" (*HZ* 1–6), "Argument" (*HZ* 7–31), and "Prayer" (*HZ* 32–39). The "Invocation" addresses the all-powerful Zeus, chief of the gods, who rules everything with his law (*HZ* 1–3a). In Stoicism, Zeus often represents the divine rational principle in the universe. Human beings have a special relationship with Zeus because they can trace their origin to Zeus and because they bear his likeness (i.e., share in his rationality) (*HZ* 4–5).

The "Argument" section starts with a description of Zeus's orderly rule throughout nature (*HZ* 7–14). The whole cosmos responds with willing obedience to the guidance Zeus provides by means of his thunderbolt, the iconographic symbol representing the ever-active, inexhaustible, fiery force always at Zeus's command (*HZ* 7–11). The thunderbolt alludes to the Stoic concept of the fiery *pneuma*, the material mode of God's creative activity in matter. As such it also acts as the medium through which divine intelligence (Logos) permeates matter (*HZ* 12–13). After emphasizing that nothing happens anywhere in the world without his involvement (*HZ* 15–16), the next verse comes as a shock: There is something that evades God's order—namely, the foolish actions of "bad people" (*kakoi*) (*HZ* 17). This marks a thematic shift: The point of the hymn is not simply to praise Zeus's orderly rule, but to reflect on the moral disorder caused by bad people. Yet in the following verse, Zeus himself provides the solution to the problem created by the *kakoi*: He is able to transform disorder into order (*HZ* 18–19) and has structured the world in such a way that the end result will be rational order (Logos) (*HZ* 20–21).

The final subsection of the "Argument" describes, in fairly traditional terms, the refusal of the bad people to accept god's rational order (the universal Logos and *nomos*) and its consequences, remaining blind and deaf to the true good—obedience to god's law (*HZ* 22–25). Instead, they pursue conventional worldly goals such as honor, wealth, and pleasure (*HZ* 26–29), only to find themselves in a state of chaos and incoherence, the complete opposite of the good life they seek (*HZ* 30–31).

Against the background developed in the "Argument" (that Zeus's rule finds a positive response in nature, but is rejected by bad human beings, and that Zeus is able to restore his order), the hymn moves to its climax: the "Prayer" (*HZ* 32–39). Cleanthes petitions Zeus to deliver human beings from the ignorance destroying their lives and to grant them insight (*gnōmē*), the same principle upon which Zeus's own rule is based (*HZ* 33–35). With such understanding, humans will then be able to reciprocate by praising Zeus's works continuously (*HZ* 36–39). By helping them to understand his world order (*HZ* 34–35), Zeus enables people to participate in the just praise of this order (*HZ* 36–39), thus restoring the disorder created by the *kakoi* (cf. *HZ* 18–19).

The *Hymn to Zeus* is one of the most important examples of philosophical hymns in antiquity and thus offers a valuable point of comparison for the hymnic material found in the New Testament, especially in John 1:1–18 and in various letters (Phil 2:6–11; Col 1:15–20; Heb 1:3–4).

Strikingly, the worldview reflected in the *Hymn to Zeus* also shares significant common ground with that of New Testament texts. Both affirm a world order established and maintained by god, which may be perceived in the regularity of nature (*HZ* 7–16). Both also acknowledge the privileged relationship between human beings and the divine (*HZ* 3–5; cf. *HZ* 36), and both recognize the tendency for humans to disregard or even reject god's order in their selfish pursuit of short-term goals (*HZ* 17, 22–31). Humans can only be saved from the destructive consequences of their actions by divine assistance (*HZ* 32–35), as only god can restore the order disrupted by human actions (*HZ* 18–21). The ultimate goal is one in which all humans, alongside the heavenly beings, live in conformity with god's will, singing in continuous praise of god's order (*HZ* 36–39; cf. *HZ* 3, 6).

Pseudo-Aristotle, *On the Cosmos*

> It now remains to speak in summary fashion about the cause holding the universe together. . . . There is indeed an ancient account, native to all people, that all things have come into existence from God and because of God, and that no thing by itself is self-sufficient, if deprived of the preservation deriving from him. Therefore, some of the ancients were also led to say that all these things that appear to us through the eyes and hearing and every sensation are full of gods, presenting an idea appropriate to the divine power, not however to the divine essence. For God is really the preserver of all things and the begetter of everything however it is brought about in this cosmos, without indeed enduring the hardship of a creature hard at work for itself, but by making use of an untiring power, by means of which he prevails even over things that seem to be far away. He has been allotted the highest and first place,

> and is therefore called Supreme, established according to the poet "on the highest peak" of the whole heaven.[6]
>
> This one should also think about God, who is strongest in power, fairest in beauty, immortal in life, outstanding in excellence; because though he cannot be seen by any mortal being, he is seen from the works themselves. For it could truly be said that all that take place in the air and on land and in water are the works of God who has power over the cosmos. (Ps.-Aristotle, Cosmic Order, 6, 399b19–22)

The treatise *On the Cosmos* (*De mundo*) is ascribed to Aristotle, but a majority of scholars agree that it deviates in several respects from Aristotle's teaching and that it could only have been written much later, sometime between ca. 200 BCE and the second century CE. It was also likely intended for an audience with a general education rather than for those with specialized scientific or philosophical training.

The treatise contains an extensive description of the cosmos, including sections on the cosmos in general,[7] geography,[8] and meteorology.[9] The focus is not, however, on the individual phenomena as such, but rather on the diversity and the tensions that characterize the cosmos. This description provides the backdrop for discussing the central question, namely how the cosmos is preserved despite the conflicting and mutually destructive forces active within the cosmos. The author maintains that the cause holding the universe together is ultimately god. However, he is not directly involved in the workings of the cosmos; instead, he influences the cosmos indirectly by means of his power (*dynamis*). While god is located at the highest point of the cosmos, his power permeates the entire universe, extending even to its lowest levels.[10]

In this way, *On the Cosmos* provides a peripatetic solution to the question of the relationship between god and the world; that is, how can god be active in the world while still maintaining his transcendence.

Reading New Testament Texts

The Prologue to John

> In the beginning was the Word, and the Word was with God, and the Word was God. He was in the beginning with God. All things came into being through him, and without him not one thing came into being. What has come into being in him was life, and the life was the light of all people. The light shines in the darkness, and the darkness did not overtake it. . . . He was in the world, and the world came into being through him, yet the world did not know him. He came to what was his own, and his own people did not accept him. But to all who

> received him, who believed in his name, he gave power to become children of God, who were born, not of blood or of the will of the flesh or of the will of man, but of God. And the Word became flesh and lived among us, and we have seen his glory, the glory as of a father's only son, full of grace and truth. . . . No one has ever seen God. It is the only Son, himself God, who is close to the Father's heart, who has made him known (John 1:1–18).

The origin of the concept of the Logos, translated here as *Word*, in the prologue to John (John 1:1–18) remains a subject of considerable scholarly debate. Proposed sources include the pre-Socratic philosopher Heraclitus, Plato, Stoicism, Philo of Alexandria, Gnosticism, the Hermetic writings, and Jewish wisdom traditions.[11] The *Hymn to Zeus* provides a valuable Stoic perspective.[12] Although there is a significant difference between the impersonal Logos of the *Hymn to Zeus* and the Word that became flesh of John, there are also some notable similarities. In both texts, the Logos is closely related to god (John 1:1–2, 14, 18; *HZ* 12–14, 20–21), intimately involved with the creation and ordering of the world (John 1:3, 10; *HZ* 12–13, 20–21), and identified with true life and understanding (John 1:4–5, 14, 17–18; *HZ* 25, 35). Furthermore, we find in both texts the irony that this very Logos, through whom the world came into existence and on whom human beings' true life depends, is not recognized and is even rejected by humanity (John 1:5, 10–11; *HZ* 22, 24). Finally, in both texts the "solution" lies in the acceptance of the Logos, an acceptance which can only be mediated and accomplished by god.

From a Middle Platonic and neo-Pythagorean perspective, the Logos in the prologue of John represents a "second divine principle." There is a tendency in Platonic and neo-Pythagorean texts of the early imperial period to split the demiurge (creator) god into two (or more) principles: a fully transcendent god, and a lower principle on which the demiurgic functions devolved. This principle is variously identified as the world soul, the cosmic intellect, a second or third demiurge, etc. The distinction made in these texts between the different divine principles serves to maintain the transcendence of the supreme god, who was considered too pure to engage directly with the material world, but at the same time, actively engaged in creation. As we have seen, an early example of this tendency is already present in Pseudo-Aristotle's *On the Cosmos*, where the transcendent god acts on the world through his *dynamis*.[13]

Paul's Areopagus Speech

> While Paul was waiting for them in Athens, he was deeply distressed to see that the city was full of idols. So he argued in the synagogue with the Jews and the devout persons and also in the marketplace every day

> with those who happened to be there. Also some Epicurean and Stoic philosophers debated with him. Some said, "What does this pretentious babbler want to say?" Others said, "He seems to be a proclaimer of foreign divinities." . . . So they took him and brought him to the Areopagus and asked him, "May we know what this new teaching is that you are presenting? . . ."
>
> Then Paul stood in front of the Areopagus and said, "Athenians, I see how extremely spiritual you are in every way. For as I went through the city and looked carefully at the objects of your worship, I found among them an altar with the inscription, 'To an unknown god.' What therefore you worship as unknown, this I proclaim to you.
>
> "The God who made the world and everything in it, he who is Lord of heaven and earth, does not live in shrines made by human hands, nor is he served by human hands, as though he needed anything, since he himself gives to all mortals life and breath and all things. From one ancestor he made all peoples to inhabit the whole earth, and he allotted the times of their existence and the boundaries of the places where they would live, so that they would search for God and perhaps fumble about for him and find him—though indeed he is not far from each one of us. For 'In him we live and move and have our being'; as even some of your own poets have said, 'For we, too, are his offspring.'
>
> "Since we are God's offspring, we ought not to think that the deity is like gold or silver or stone, an image formed by the art and imagination of mortals. While God has overlooked the times of human ignorance, now he commands all people everywhere to repent." (Acts 17:16–32)

In Acts 17:16–32, the author narrates an encounter between the apostle Paul and Stoic and Epicurean philosophers in Athens, culminating in a speech Paul delivers in response to the philosophers' questions.[14] The setting of the speech contains several motifs reminiscent of the ancient Athenian philosopher and Plato's teacher Socrates. Like Socrates, Paul is critical of what he sees is happening in Athens (17:16), engages in conversations with people he encounters in the marketplace (17:17), is criticized for talking nonsense and accused of introducing foreign gods (17:18), and has to defend himself in a place known for hearings on religious matters (17:19), just as Socrates had to defend himself against similar charges in front of the Athenian jury. In the speech itself, Paul employs two well-known Socratic techniques: irony (in praising the Athenians for being "very religious"; 17:22), and the exposure of people's ignorance (17:29–30).

Paul makes use of several popular philosophical ideas in the speech. The speech begins with the question of how the Creator God should rightly be worshipped (17:24–25), the one who created and ordered everything in nature

(17:26), so that human beings "would search for God and perhaps fumble about for him and find him—though indeed he is not far from each one of us" (17:27). This reflects a standard motif of natural theology: Human beings should be able to recognize God from the order existing in nature (cf. below, Rom 1:19–20). A similar idea is expressed in Pseudo-Aristotle, *On the Cosmos*:

> Though he [god] cannot be seen by any mortal being, he is seen from the works themselves. For it could truly be said that all that take place in the air and on land and in water are the works of God who has power over the cosmos.[15]

The fact that humans are unable to recognize God and that they have to search for God, is due to *agnoia*, ignorance (17:23, 30). This ignorance prevents proper worship (17:24–25, 29), despite the fact that God is near (17:27b)—both because he is visible through his acts in nature and history (17:24–26), and because human beings owe their very existence to him (17:28a). Paul underscores this relationship by stating "For we are in fact his offspring" (*genos*) (17:28b). The inability or unwillingness of human beings to comprehend God's works is another popular philosophical motif. In Cleanthes's *Hymn to Zeus*, the cause of human deviation from the true worship of god is folly and ignorance (*HZ* 17, 26, 33). Humans reject the order god established in nature (*HZ* 21–22) and cannot recognize his universal law which would have provided the foundation for a happy life (*HZ* 23–25).[16]

The quotation "For we are his offspring" (17:28c) comes from the Stoic poet Aratus's *Phaenomena* 5 and was perhaps taken from an anthology used in an educational context. A strikingly similar idea is found in *Hymn to Zeus* 4, "For we have our origin in you, bearing a likeness to god." In a Stoic context, both texts could have featured in the same anthology given that they imply a kinship based on shared rationality between humans and the divine. The irony, from Paul's perspective, is that despite the intimate connection humans share with God, they continue to worship God in inanimate, material objects (17:29).

Romans

> For the wrath of God is revealed from heaven against all ungodliness and injustice of those who by their injustice suppress the truth. For what can be known about God is plain to them, because God has made it plain to them. For his invisible attributes, that is, his eternal power and divinity, are clearly seen from the world as creation, because through his works they are perceived by the mind. So they are without excuse, for though they knew God, they did not honor him as God or give thanks

> to him, but they became futile in their thinking, and their senseless hearts were darkened. Claiming to be wise, they became fools. . . .
>
> Therefore God gave them over in the desires of their hearts to impurity, to the dishonoring of their bodies among themselves. They exchanged the truth about God for a lie and worshiped and served the creature rather than the Creator, who is blessed forever! Amen. . . .
>
> And since they did not see fit to acknowledge God, God gave them over to an unfit mind and to do things that should not be done. (Rom 1:18–28 NRSVue, slightly adapted)

Several of the popular philosophical motifs found in *On the Cosmos* and in the *Hymn to Zeus* also appear in Paul's accusations of idolatry and moral corruption in Romans 1:18–28.[17] According to Paul, ignorance of God leads not only to false worship but also immoral behavior. Although God is invisible, Paul insists that does not mean he is unknowable, for God has revealed to humans what can be known (1:19). Paul substantiates this statement with a remarkable formulation in 1:20 that God's invisible attributes, his eternal power, and divinity, are clearly seen from creation.[18] That is, while God cannot be perceived by the senses, he can become "visible" to the rational mind through the order of the world. Human beings, as rational creatures, not only have the ability but also the responsibility to interpret God's works correctly; they are therefore without excuse (1:20). Failure to do so is caused by faulty reasoning (1:21). Although they consider themselves to be wise, they become foolish (1:22), exchanging the truth about God for a lie (1:25). Because they do not give due recognition to God, their minds become worthless (1:28). The result is that they are driven by their desires (1:24), doing what should not be done (1:28).

Paul's assertions in Romans 1:20 share close parallels with *On the Cosmos* 399b21–22: "Though he [god] cannot be seen by any mortal being, he is seen from the works themselves." A little earlier, Pseudo-Aristotle refers to god as "the leader and begetter of all things, being invisible except to the power of reason."[19] In both cases, knowledge of God depends not on seeing God, but on the rational reflection on the structure and order of the cosmos. Humanity's failure to recognize God is thus a failure of reason.

Cleanthes's *Hymn to Zeus* also provides a parallel to Paul's condemnation of human folly. Foolish bad humans ignore God's universal order because they cannot see or hear it (*HZ* 17, 22, 24). As a result, they pursue worthless and destructive goals, resulting in incoherent, disruptive, and unfulfilled lives (*HZ* 26–31). We find in the hymn also an awareness of the irony and even tragedy of the human condition (cf. *HZ* 23): Humans, who of all creatures on earth are closest to God in nature because they share in his rationality (*HZ* 4–5), are the only beings who in their ignorance reject and distort God's order (cf. *HZ* 7–17).

As the discussion above illustrates, to gain insight into the philosophical context of the New Testament, texts like the *Hymn to Zeus* and *On the Cosmos* should be carefully studied in their own right, and not merely as collections of "parallels" to New Testament texts. Only in this manner will the real differences and similarities between such philosophical and New Testament texts become apparent and the philosophical context of the New Testament gain depth and specificity.

FURTHER READING

Algra, Keimpe, Jonathan Barnes, Jaap Mansfeld, and Malcolm Schofield, eds. *The Cambridge History of Hellenistic Philosophy*. Cambridge University Press, 1999.

Dillon, John. *The Middle Platonists: 80 B.C. to A.D. 220*. Cornell University Press, 1977.

Engberg-Pedersen, Troels. *Cosmology and Self in the Apostle Paul: The Material Spirit*. Oxford University Press, 2010.

Goulet-Cazé, Marie-Odile. *Cynicism and Christianity in Antiquity*. Eerdmans, 2019.

Hadot, Pierre. *What is Ancient Philosophy?* Translated by Michael Chase. Harvard University Press; Belknap, 2002.

Hirsch-Luipold, Rainer, ed. *Plutarch and the New Testament in Their Religio-Philosophical Contexts: Bridging Discourses in the World of the Early Roman Empire*. Brill's Plutarch Studies 9. Brill, 2022.

Long, A. A. *Epictetus: A Stoic and Socratic Guide to Life*. Clarendon, 2002.

Long, A. A. *Hellenistic Philosophy: Stoics, Epicureans, Sceptics*. 2nd ed. University of California Press, 1986.

Long, A. A., and D. N. Sedley. *The Hellenistic Philosophers*. 2 vols. Cambridge University Press, 1987.

Malherbe, Abraham J. *Paul and the Popular Philosophers*. Fortress, 1989.

Notes

1 For more detailed discussions of the different traditions treated below, see articles in *The Anchor Bible Dictionary*, ed. David N. Freedman, 6. vols. (Doubleday, 1992): "Platonism," "Cynics," "Stoics, Stoicism," "Epicureanism," "Pythagoreanism." See also, in *Brill's New Pauly*, ed. Hubert Cancik, 22 vols. (Brill, 2002–11): "Aristotelianism," "Scepticism,"; *Dictionary of New Testament Background*, ed. Craig A. Evans and Stanley E. Porter (IVP, 2000), under "Stoicism."

2 See Johan C. Thom, "Spiritual Transformation in Graeco-Roman Philosophy," in *Spiritual Transformation in the New Testament and Related Literature*, ed. Albert L. A. Hogeterp, D. Francois Tolmie, and Jan G. van der Watt, Wissenschaftliche Untersuchungen zum Neuen Testament 522 (Mohr Siebeck, 2024), 57–72.

3 Philodemus, *Against the Sophists* 4.9–14 in *The Hellenistic Philosophers*, trans. Anthony A. Long and David N. Sedley (Cambridge University Press, 1987), 1:156.

4 For an overview of such exercises, see Pierre Hadot, *Philosophy as a Way of Life: Spiritual Exercises from Socrates to Foucault*, ed. Arnold I. Davidson, trans. Michael Chase (Blackwell, 1995), 81–125; Ilsetraut Hadot, "The Spiritual Guide," in *Classical Mediterranean Spirituality: Egyptian, Greek, Roman*, ed. Arthur H. Armstrong, World Spirituality 15 (Crossroad, 1986), 450–55.

5 For an introduction, text and translation, and detailed commentary, see Johan C. Thom, *Cleanthes'* Hymn to Zeus: *Text, Translation, and Commentary*, Studien und Texte zu Antike und Christentum 33 (Mohr Siebeck, 2005). For what follows, see also Johan C. Thom, "Cleanthes' *Hymn to Zeus* and Early Christian Literature," in *Antiquity and Humanity: Essays on Ancient Religion and Philosophy Presented to Hans Dieter Betz on His 70th Birthday*, ed. Adela Yarbro Collins and Margaret M. Mitchell (Mohr Siebeck, 2001).

6 *Cosmic Order and Divine Power: Pseudo-Aristotle* On the Cosmos, ed. Johan C. Thom, introduction, text, translation, and interpretative essays by Johan C. Thom, Renate Burri, Clive Chandler, Hans Daiber, Jill Kraye, Andrew Smith, Hidemi Takahashi, and Anna Tzvetkova-Glaser, Scripta Antiquitatis Posterioris ad Ethicam Religionemque Pertinentia 23 (Mohr Siebeck, 2014), 6, 397b9–27.

7 *Cosmic Order*, 391b9–393a8.

8 *Cosmic Order*, 393a9–394a6.

9 *Cosmic Order*, 394a7–396a32.

10 *Cosmic Order*, 397b9–27.

11 See Jörg Frey, "Between Torah and Stoa: How Could Readers Have Understood the Johannine Logos?" in *The Prologue of the Gospel of John: Its Literary, Theological, and Philosophical Contexts: Papers Read at the Colloquium Iohanneum 2013*, ed. Jan G. van der Watt, R. Alan Culpepper, and Udo Schnelle, Wissenschaftliche Untersuchungen zum Neuen Testament 359 (Mohr Siebeck, 2016).

12 See Thom, "Cleanthes' *Hymn to Zeus*," 495–97.

13 *Cosmic Order*, 397b20–24. Elsewhere in the New Testament, the second, demiurgic principle is Christ as the "image of God" in 2 Cor 4:4 (cf. Col 1:15); and the Son in Heb 1:3, "who is the radiance of the glory of God and the exact imprint of his essence, who upholds the universe by the word of his power"; cf. the role of Wisdom in Wis 7:24–27; 8:1.

14 For a more detailed discussion, see Thom, "Cleanthes' *Hymn*," 497–99.

15 *Cosmic Order*, 399b21–25.

16 This motif also occurs in John 1:10–11; Rom 1:19–21.

17 For a more detailed discussion, see Johan C. Thom, "Paul and Popular Philosophy," in *Paul's Graeco-Roman Context*, ed. Cilliers Breytenbach, Bibliotheca Ephemeridum Theologicarum Lovaniensium 277 (Peeters, 2015).

18 For this translation, reading *apo* not as indication "time from which" (*Greek-English Lexicon of the New Testament and Other Early Christian Literature*, 3rd ed, under 2bα) but as "source of perception" (*Greek-English Lexicon*, under 3d); cf. *On the Cosmos*, in *Cosmic Order*, 399b22; Wis 13:4, 5.

19 *Cosmic Order*, 399a30–35.

CHAPTER SIXTEEN

Greek and Roman Religion

Christoph Auffarth
(Universität Bremen)

Hellenistic Culture in the Mediterranean World

THE PEOPLE WHO adhered to Christ and worshipped him were surrounded by a culture that was Hellenistic in character—and of which they themselves were a part. Encounters with the Hellenistic religion were part of their everyday lives. A civilization with Greek characteristics had spread or adapted its elements across the entire Mediterranean world. On the one hand, this cultural system was defined by a shared way of life organized around an urban structure known as a *polis* (city-state is an inaccurate translation). This term referred to communities ranging from a few hundred people to large cities, but which still bore traits of face-to-face societies. Only a small proportion of the population held the rights of citizenship: men who could take up arms against external rivals but did not carry weapons in the *polis*. These men were also entitled to take part in political decisions, to have disputes heard in courts, and then to issue judgments. By some counts, the number of *poleis* around the Mediterranean was as high as 1,035.[1] Aristotle claimed that humans could only survive as "political" beings (*zōon politikon*). Politically, these *poleis* were organized as monarchies, aristocracies (the families of the elites decided who ruled among themselves), or as democracies that decided everything in the plenary assembly (*ekklēsia*)—often swayed by populist leaders.

The Romans initially formed such a *polis*, but through warfare, they acquired more and more rivals. In 168 BCE they defeated the Macedonians (Alexander the Great's successors), and in 146 BCE they destroyed the two greatest powers in the region: Greek Corinth and the Phoenician Carthage, thus rising to become a world power. Their empire had two sides: Many of the subjugated embraced its more attractive features and were able to invest in business and the beautification of their city, especially now that they were no longer burdened with any military expenses. They paid their taxes and enjoyed the Pax Romana (Roman peace). Others, however, opposed the Roman rule (seeing them as oppressors), but were ultimately humiliated and crushed by Rome's military power. With Roman rule came Hellenistic culture, which the Romans had also adopted. The Roman poet

Horatius (also known as Horace, 65–8 BCE), writing two generations before Jesus, summarized the tension between power and culture with the famous sentence: "Greece was conquered, but it conquered the victor by introducing its culture into uncivilized [Rome and its region] Latium" (*Graecia capta ferum victorem cepit et artes intulit agresti Latio*).[2] Hellenistic culture meant large public squares with shaded halls, open-air theaters, freedom of speech, and festivals for the gods. Labor was primarily performed by noncitizens: women, children, and slaves. The Romans also brought bathing halls and gladiator games, and sometimes even free staple food—*panem et circenses* (bread and games). What they did not bring, however, was Roman religion.

When the Romans had conquered the entire Mediterranean world, the Greek historian Polybios, who had experienced the Roman power firsthand as a prisoner in 167 BCE, asked what had made Rome so strong. After giving several reasons, he states,

> But the quality in which the Roman commonwealth is most distinctly superior is in my opinion the nature of their religious convictions. I believe that it is the very thing which among other peoples is an object of reproach, I mean superstition [*deisidaimonia*],[3] which maintains the cohesion of the Roman state. These matters are clothed in such pomp and introduced to such an extent into their public and private life that nothing could exceed it, a fact which will surprise many.[4]

For the Greek, religion was primarily a festival: a performance of dance, music, sport, joy, a shared meal, and a sense of the sublime. By contrast, what Polybius observes in Rome is a religion marked by fear of the gods and an almost embarrassing concern for the correctness of ritual. By this, he refers to a specific part of Roman religion: the *religio Romana*.

The "Religious Cosmos" in the Diversity of Cities

The Romans did not use their religion as a means for implementing power. Rather, it can be understood on four distinct levels: First, the *religio Romana* was practiced by representatives of Roman authority when seeking the approval of the gods before a political event and requesting divine consent for a favorable outcome. The precise execution of the ritual was crucial; if it did not promise good results, the ritual had to be repeated. This level of religion was restricted to the city of Rome, though it was also performed on official occasions in the provinces, but not by non-Romans.[5]

Second, the *religio Romana* offered little for personal religion and piety; For this, there was the *ritus graecus* (Greek rite). This term is understood to mean

> In contrast to other cultures, Hellenistic culture only tolerates a concept of god in the shape of a human being. In Egypt, the god Apis was worshipped in the form (and with the magnificent powers) of a bull. When the Greek-Egyptian kings of Hellenism installed their god for worship outside Egypt, they combined Apis with Osiris to form Serapis. As an image, he was now likened to the supreme Greek god Zeus, as depicted by the artist Phidias in Olympia: a powerful man, full-haired like a king sitting on a throne with a sceptre. This god was known to many athletes and spectators who visited the Olympic Games from all over the world. A god in the form of an animal was unthinkable for the Greeks.[6]

Figure 16.1. The anthropomorphic image of god.

not only Greek religion, but also a wide range of cults that had been aesthetically adapted to Hellenistic culture (see fig. 16.1). A *polis* typically had several temples for the gods that it had accepted into the city as its own—a local pantheon that was limited in number. From among these goddesses and gods, people in the city would choose a personal deity. They made offerings to them, and ate meat sacrificed at the altar with their family and friends. This practice required financial means, but it also brought joy, companionship, and a sense of belonging.

Third, migrants brought their ethnic religion with them, but these had to be adapted to Hellenistic culture. By the next generation "the old gods in the new homeland" were also worshipped by others. In this way, ethnic religion became simply another urban cult. Whether more exotic or more assimilated, these new religions fit into the city's existing ensemble of gods. They were not viewed as foreign or "oriental" religions in the way later scholarship at times implied. Even the mystery religions were only gradually seen as different, not fundamentally different.

Finally, below the level of the city gods (*polis* religion), there were religious specialists who offered resources for their clients when official prayers to the gods failed. These specialists offered help in the areas of health, wealth, love, and children's blessings. However, they could also be hired to inflict harm on competitors or enemies.

Thus, a religion of the empire emerges, not simply as a conglomerate, but as a "religious cosmos." Religions from the globalized world of the empire rarely gathered in cities through organized mission but mostly as "religion in luggage." However, they fit into the *polis* according to Hellenistic norms and formed an order (*kosmos*). Fundamental to the functioning of religious pluralism is the deliberate confusion in which no distinction is made between Isis, Aphrodite, and Venus (*Interpretatio Romana*). Monotheism can also be practiced in this religious cosmos because the cult is always directed at *one* deity (henotheism, megatheism).[7]

In order to avoid the term "Roman religion" in the narrower sense of *religio Romana*, some scholars chose the plural Religions of Rome, while renown scholar Jörg Rüpke uses *Religion of the Romans.*[8] Others even prefer to skip the term "religion" as being "postcolonial." As a hermeneutical tool, however, the term opens the other dimensions of religion, focusing not only rituals, but also the intellectual (faith, literature), social (priests, community), institutional, aesthetic (images of goddesses, temples, hymns), emotional (coping with diseases, the end of life and world), and moral dimensions.[9]

Figure 16.2. Roman religion.

Imperial Cult

The older narrative saw two major innovations in the religious history of the imperial era, which replaced the god cults that had become meaningless: imported "Oriental religions" and the imperial cult. As will be shown in the following section, Religion in Transition, the traditional cults of the Hellenistic religion were not discarded but instead were given new meaning and significance. The so-called oriental cults had long been part of the religious cosmos of the globalized Roman Empire. For a long time, the imperial cult was understood as a means for religiously legitimizing the power of the Romans—that is, a coercive cult that declared the emperor to be the supreme god and demanded from subjects a symbolic act of submission and loyalty.

The case of the Christians in Bithynia (northern Asia Minor) seems to confirm this assessment: Around 110 CE, the governor of the province, Pliny, received a complaint from the farmers that they could no longer sell the animals they had fattened for sacrifices. The reason was the Christians, who were no longer commissioning sacrificial offerings. Pliny asked the emperor whether his measures were appropriate. He interrogated the people accused—often anonymously—as to whether they were Christian. Apparently, mere membership of the criminal conspiracy ("the name alone") was enough to constitute a crime, even without any specific act. He had also received a whole list of names anonymously. If the accused denied being Christians, or no longer claimed to be Christians, he demanded them to prove it by cursing Christ, honoring the image of the emperor with incense (alongside other images of the gods), and offering him a consecration of wine. Those who refused to do this were executed.[10] This rare case should not be understood as representative of the general relationship between Roman rule and the Christians.[11] The later Christian martyr ideology elevated such instances into the ideal: choosing confession and death as the birth into heavenly life. But many Christians did not behave so heroically. After the last persecutions of Christians (Emperor Decius, ca. 250; Diocletian, ca. 300 CE, which were the first to be organized *throughout* the empire), a dispute arose as to whether the "fallen" Christians should be excluded from the community. The more lenient position, supported by the great majority, ultimately prevailed.[12] Like many others, Christians lived relatively secure lives and enjoyed the more pleasant aspects of the Pax Romana. Even if occasionally hostile, Roman law, in fact, protected and made possible the spread of Christianity from the distant province of Judaea to the imperial capital of Rome.

The imperial cult, however, was not the enforced cult that Roman rule imposed on its subjects. On the contrary, it was often the provincials themselves who benefited from Roman rule, and who wanted to show their gratitude. As emperors rarely traveled to the provinces, Roman sympathizers in the provinces demanded that they be allowed to erect not only images and statues of the emperor and his family but also to build temples in their honor. The first emperors were cautious about this and refused many such requests since emperors were not to receive divine honors during their lifetime, but only after death. Even after the apotheosis during cremation, they were not referred to as *deus* (god), but as *divus* (deified). In addition, they did not receive animal sacrifices like the traditional gods. One way around this tradition was to place the image of the emperor in the temple of a deity and worship it "as a roommate." When a priest in rural Greece rededicated the altar of Zeus to "Zeus Nero," this was considered inappropriate since Emperor Nero had not yet been deified, and his name was later chiseled out.[13]

Religious Knowledge

Priests and Specialists

The *religio Romana* required the utmost precision in the performance of the ritual and thus, this necessity required the presence of specialists. The Roman priests led the ritual but had no formal training. Like their Greek counterparts, the Roman priesthood was more of a political appointment rather than a religious specialism. There was no "*Rituale Romanum*" to ensure the accuracy of a ritual by meticulously prescribing the order of the service and the position of the participants. Instead, slaves in the sanctuary instructed the priests beforehand on how and when to carry out each action. The interpretation of the sacrifice or the interpretation of the will of the gods from the entrails of the sacrificed animals or the flight of the birds (*augurium*), required actual training and knowledge. The specialists learned the *disciplina etrusca* "precision of the Etruscans" (a civilization neighboring the city of Rome with a distinct language, script, and ritual system). Roman priests viewed the dependence on non-Roman science with suspicion, especially since it allowed for the possible manipulation of the results in moments when divine favor was sought; that is, before a Senate meeting or battle.

There was a lot of freedom in the personal piety of Hellenistic religion; there was little that one could do wrong. Some cults, especially the mysteries, required a hierophant (one who explained the sacred) and priests who performed the ritual based on observation and experience.[14] In addition to these "official" and "social" cults, there were also people who made a living from religion, such as: exegetes (oracle poets), wreath weavers, cattle breeders, artists and architects, philosophers for public lectures, and their teachers. These were people whom we should not too quickly dismiss as charlatans (as is sometimes done in theological discussion)—even Paul could be understood as such a religious "freelance expert."

Holy Books

Holy books—something like the Bible for the Jews and Christians—did not exist in Hellenistic religion. To be sure, there were certainly hymns (analogous to the psalms), prayers, collections of sayings of wisdom, laws and commandments (such as Plato's *Nomoi* or Cicero's *De legibus*), historical narratives of religiously significant events, (polemical) comparisons with other religions (as in Herodotus's *historiai*, Caesar's *de bello Gallico*, Tacitus's *Germania*), as well as "letters," apocalyptic prophecies, and public dramas in which religious themes were discussed and debated. But there was no "doctrine of the church" or creed. In other words, there was no institution that defined and controlled the knowledge of religion and trained experts for it. Instead, religious knowledge was open to artistic creation. Religion increasingly became a topic of literature, especially in the era in which the many books, letters and apocalypses were written, from which the New Testament was then selected (see below in the section on religion in transition).

A special case is the *Sibylline Books*. The Sibyls were later depicted as Roman counterparts to the Hebrew prophets (for example, in the Sistine Chapel, early sixteenth century). These books were kept in the Temple of Jupiter and only brought out in extreme crises to consult about the future of Rome and respond appropriately. The *Oracula Sibyllina*, a later, publicly circulated collection, included sayings that offered Jewish and Christian prophecies about the downfall of Rome. To prevent the influence of these prophesies, Augustus ordered the collecting and burning of thousands. Nevertheless, new ones were constantly being written.

Religion in Transition

Greco-Roman religions had changed over the course of more than a thousand years of history. As noted above, Hellenistic religion had already emerged as part of a mixture of cultures since the time of Alexander the Great. For the purposes of this chapter, the primary focus is the religious landscape of the early Roman Empire. However, this does not mean that there was a single, unified religion with a common center;[15] "Greco-Roman religion" could share common features across the empire but at the same time could remain diverse in practice.

For the period around the "birth of Christ"(a date that was not declared *the* turning point in world history until the sixth century CE), the first emperor, Augustus (31 BCE–14 CE), implemented religious and cultural reform. He claimed a return to the good old days of Roman religion and society. This image was designed to be a contrast to his rival Mark Antony, whose love for Egypt and its queen Cleopatra were prioritized over Rome. While Mark Antony had a pyramid built for himself as a tomb, Augustus had his tomb designed in the style of the ancient Roman kings. Augustus chose to live near the hut of Romulus and Remus (the mythological founders of the city of Rome) while also linking his house architecturally to a temple of Apollo—his chosen personal god.

Augustus's reforms encouraged a return to tradition across all walks of cultural life. He made it a point to discourage Romans from wearing sporty Greek clothing and promoted the donning of the Roman toga instead. Marriage laws returned to a focus on monogamy, making divorces more difficult to attain. These reforms attempted to signal a renewal after a period of intense civil conflict. Octavian, as he was known before—he was given the honorary name Augustus—as Caesar's adopted son, came to power during turbulent times marked by civil wars and unrest. Octavian's own rise to power was also characterized by violence: At Perugia in 40 BCE, he had three hundred prisoners of war "slaughtered" at Caesar's altar as sacrifices.[16] Following Julius Caesar's elevation to divine status, Augustus was now allowed to call himself "son of the divine Caesar." After his victory over Antony (at Actium 31 BCE), he disarmed the army and declared peace. On Augustus's birthday, the hand of the sundial pointed directly to the steps of the Ara Pacis, the "altar (of the goddess) Peace." Peace had indeed arrived, thanks to Augustus. With it came the dawn of a new "golden age"—the *saeculum Augustum*—which Augustus lavishly celebrated in a festival in Rome during the secular celebration in 17 BCE.[17]

Religion thus elevated Augustus's rule, despite its bloody beginnings, into a superhuman sphere, shielding it from human criticism. The emperor and his successors were viewed as being under the favor of the gods. The *euangelion* (good news) was proclaimed throughout the empire as a divinely ordained "peace on earth." But what did the "old Roman religion" that Augustus sought to restore actually look like? This ideal came up against a new perception of religion that had emerged a generation earlier through thinkers like Varro and Cicero and was now being glorified by the poets and historians of Augustus's time in their works. Accordingly, the task of this theology was not left to priests or scholars at universities. Rather, the meaning of public rituals was provided by poets in "great narratives."

In his extensive work, the historian Livy reconstructed the history of Rome "from the founding of the city" and emphasized the importance of religion from the earliest times alongside the military campaigns. After many perils, this history ultimately led to the happy times of Augustus. The empire that the Romans had conquered by force was depicted as the fulfillment of divine will.

Similarly, Virgil (P. Vergilius Maro) was able to bring two things from the past into the present time of Augustus in his inspiring verses of the famous epic *Aeneid*. The founding of the Roman Empire is presented as the result of divine intervention, when Jupiter drove Aeneas and his followers from Troy. Later, Aeneas fathered a son, Julus, with the goddess Venus (Aphrodite in Greek), who became the progenitor of the imperial family of Gaius Julius Caesar. Even Aeneas's love for the Queen of Carthage, Dido, could not distract him from fulfilling his destiny. In the midst of a storm at sea, which could have ended his journey, Jupiter promises Aeneas world domination: "I appoint to these neither period nor boundary of empire: I have given them dominion without end."[18] And later, the order to the Romans reads: "But thou, O Roman, learn with sovereign sway to rule the nations. Thy great art shall be to keep the world in lasting peace, to spare humbled foe, and crush to earth the proud."[19] In book 6 of the *Aeneid*, Aeneas is led into the underworld, where he sees the past and future. The heroes of Roman history are already waiting to be born there, including Iulus, the founder of the family. One of Iulus's descendants is Augustus, the last in the line. Jupiter has predestined everything, and Virgil serves the role of the prophet (*vates*).

In a poem of epic proportions, Ovid describes the meaning of the feast days of the Roman year, or the festival calendar known as the *fasti*. He gives meaning to each festival, explains its name, and includes references.

Finally, there is Horace, who wrote the poem performed by twenty-seven girls and twenty-seven boys at the secular celebration in honor of Apollo in 17 BCE. His personal piety is particularly interesting. He chose Mercurius (Greek Hermes) as his personal god.[20] However, the same Horace calls himself "a hog from Epicurus's herd" (*Epicuri de grege porcum*).[21] Epicurus, however, had declared religion irrelevant because, in his view, the gods were not interested in people at all—neither protecting nor punishing them. His name even became an equivalent to *atheist*. However, in his individual religiosity, Horace can do both: challenge the gods and talk to his god.

The "old Roman religion" that Augustus sought to reintroduce as an invented tradition was constructed by the historians and poets such as Livy, Virgil, Ovid, and Horace. The festivals, which had previously been celebrated as rituals, were now reinterpreted through art and infused with meanings that made Augustus's reign appear as a divine gift. Only at this point does Roman religion begin to develop into something akin to a theology. However, not through an institution of priests and experts, but through artists, all of whom, incidentally, were not from Rome itself. Their non-Roman provenance made them uniquely qualified to offer unreserved praise and admiration for the city.

At the same time, a broader process began, which saw a gradual decline of public rituals and an increase emphasis on "rituals in ink." Bloody animal sacrifice, in particular, came to be viewed as an abomination, and thus was practiced less and less, even before it would eventually be banned by Christian emperors. This mutation of religious practice runs through all religious traditions: Religion increasingly becomes a way of life rather than a theatrical performance in a sacred place.[22]

TAKING A CLOSER LOOK: SOURCES

Sources from the World of the New Testament

Euangelion

A New Era Begins with Savior

> [I. Order of the Roman Governor] Blessed was the day of the birth of the most divine Caesar /Emperor, . . . which we consider as if it were equal to the day of creation. . . . But even if everything had fallen apart and the attitude of mankind had become unfortunate, he restored everything and gave the whole world a new outlook, most welcome for those who had already accepted the downfall. Caesar was born as a stroke of luck for the whole of humanity.
>
> [II. Resolution of the Cities of the Province] Providence, which divinely orders our lives, in its effort and generosity has adorned life with the perfect good by bringing us Augustus. She did us the favor of humanity: she gave us and our fellow human beings the perfect power, the [Savior (*sōtēr*)]: He ended war, orders peace. The Caesar/emperor revealed what everyone had hoped for [and expected as *euangelia*], he not only surpassed all the benefactors before him, but he also gave those to come no chance to surpass him. From the day of his birth as God, good news (*euangelia*) began for the world through him. (*Priene inscription*, 9 BCE)[23]

The inscription, found in Priene, Asia Minor and dated to 9 BCE, consists of eighty-four lines. In part II (lines 30–84), the cities of the province of Asia adopt the decree of the proconsul Paullus Fabius Maximus (part I of the inscription). The Greek calendar was synchronized with the Roman calendar by aligning the year with the birthday of the Emperor Augustus on the 23rd of September (lines 50–80). Gaps in the text can be reconstructed through parallels with similar texts commemorating the same event.

A few details stand out: It mentions the name *Caesar*, but this does not refer to Julius Caesar; it already functions as a title referring to Augustus. The text does not use biblical terminology for *creation* but instead reads "the beginning of everything." This cosmological framing follows closely the Hellenistic worldview. It also contains the word *sōtēr*, which means *savior* in Greek and was often used as a title for the gods. This is directly tied to Augustus's role in ending wars and establishing peace. The practice of using this title began with the Ptolemaic and Seleucid kings, who increasingly adopted it for themselves. Notably, it is also applied to Jesus in the New Testament (Luke 2:11; John 4:42) and in many second-century Christian writings.

The inscription also contains the word *euangelion* (good news), which the New Testament uses for the gospel concerning Jesus of Nazareth, the Messiah and Son of God (see Mark 1:1). Here, it is used in the plural form in the context of the imperial cult. The accession of a new emperor is announced throughout all provinces and reinforced by the gift of "freedom" (tax-free year). The reference to the benefaction of *providence* (*pronoia*), is now tied to Caesar Augustus as the benefactor (*euergetēs*). Cities typically honored those who sponsored festivals, buildings, or communal meals with this title. The title is associated with reciprocal generosity and the hope of receiving further benefactions in the future.

The language used to speak about Jesus in the New Testament, with terms such as *sōtēr* or *euangelion*—even connected to the inauguration of a new era—is therefore not an isolated theological language of Christians but rather has important connotations in the broader cultural context.

A Private Religious Entrepreneur
Lucian, The Death of Peregrinus

> At this time, he [Peregrinos] learned the astonishing wisdom of the Christians and he met in Palestine their priests and teachers. I can tell you, he pretty soon let them look like pupils; he became their prophet, leader of the community, ruler of the congregation—all in one person; he expounded their books, commented on them, wrote books himself. They venerated him like a God, asked him for new laws, and declared him their patron in the same manner as they, to this day, worship a man, who was crucified in Palestine, because he introduced a new cult. Well, the end of it was that Proteus was arrested and thrown into prison. This was the very thing to lend an air to his favorite arts of claptrap and wonder-working; he was now a self-made man. The Christians . . . brought elegant dinners to the prisoner; their sacred

> writings were read; and our old friend Peregrinos . . . became for them "the new Socrates." . . . The Christians, these unfortunate people, are convinced that they are immortal and will live forever, which explains their contempt of death and voluntary self-devotion by many of them. Further, their original lawgiver taught them that they are all siblings to each other as soon as they affiliate and deny the gods of the Greeks, and venerate the crucified sage, and live after his laws. They despise all worldly goods alike, regarding them merely as common property; all this they take bona fide without a voucher of receipt. Whenever a shaman or a crafty person comes to them and seizes the situation with energy, he immediately becomes rich in a short time making a fool of this simple folk. (Lucian, *De mort. Peregr.* 11–13)[24]

Peregrinus is portrayed by Lucian as one of the many religious entrepreneurs traveling across the Mediterranean and offering religious teachings and rituals. This short episode describes his short Christian career. This is preceded and followed by his other religious endeavors.

Lucian gives him the name *Proteus*, evoking the mythic figure who has the ability to transform himself—a fitting symbol for someone who is able to repeatedly reinvent himself in different religious contexts. There are a few points in his presentation of Peregrinus and the Christians that are worth noting.

Lucian refers to Christian gatherings as a *thiasos*, a term more commonly associated with Dionysian cults, rather than the Christians who preferred *ekklēsia*. He also uses *synagōgē* for their community, a designation rarely applied to Christians except for a unique instance in James 2:2. Peregrinus is presented as an "expounder," that is someone who explains the meaning of oracles. His authority was further solidified by his position as president (*prostatēs*) of the community.

Lucian's mention of books is interesting because it shows that even at this early stage, the Christian movement was characterized by book production, even though the educated elite viewed them as low literature. The parallel with Socrates is also noteworthy. In his *Phaedo*, Plato describes how friends visited Socrates in prison and listened to his final words before he died by suicide, to which the trial had sentenced him. Regarding Christians, he writes that they worship "a man who was crucified in Palestine," referring to Jesus, who is also referred to as the crucified "sage" or "Sophist" (*ho aneskolopismenos sophistēs*).

An Amulet with a New Protector

On a blue glass gem dating from the first to the fourth century CE, discovered near Kenchreai (the eastern port of Corinth), Aphrodite is depicted on one side, emerging naked from the sea and casting a dress over her body.[25] On the reverse

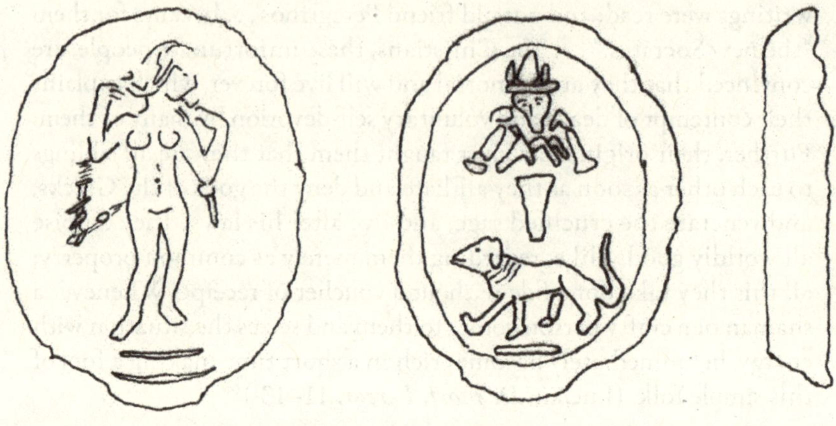

Figure 16.3. An Amulet with a new protector. (Christoph Auffarth, used by permission.)

side, Osiris appears as a mummy with the royal scepter atop a striding lion. Together, these two gods symbolize beauty and life after death. The lion beneath Osiris symbolizes protection, warding off any danger or threat. Interestingly, the inscription on the rim, written in Greek as a permanent prayer, does not invoke either god, but appeals instead to the Jewish God:

> JAO (YHWH) GIVE STRENGTH AND CHARM TO THE ONE WHO WEARS THIS! The competencies of attractiveness and strength (also against death) are now expected by the wearer of the same symbols from YHWH.[26]

This amulet is a rare witness for someone who bought or inherited a piece of Greco-Egyptian divine protection but hoped that his Jewish God would avert evil incidents. Jewish monotheism as represented in this amulet does not exclude different divine powers. Modern scholars call mingling different creeds "syncretism."

Reading the New Testament Texts

Room for yet Another God

Paul's Address to the Members of the Areopagus

> Then Paul stood in front of the Areopagus and said, "Athenians, I see how extremely spiritual you are in every way. For as I went through the city and looked carefully at the objects of your worship, I found among

> them an altar with the inscription, 'To an unknown god.' What therefore you worship as unknown, this I proclaim to you.
>
> "The God who made the world and everything in it, he who is Lord of heaven and earth, does not live in shrines made by human hands, nor is he served by human hands, as though he needed anything, since he himself gives to all mortals life and breath and all things. From one ancestor he made all peoples to inhabit the whole earth, and he allotted the times of their existence and the boundaries of the places where they would live, so that they would search for God and perhaps fumble about for him and find him—though indeed he is not far from each one of us. For 'In him we live and move and have our being'; as even some of your own poets have said, 'For we, too, are his offspring.'
>
> "Since we are God's offspring, we ought not to think that the deity is like gold or silver or stone, an image formed by the art and imagination of mortals. While God has overlooked the times of human ignorance, now he commands all people everywhere to repent, because he has fixed a day on which he will have the world judged in righteousness by a man whom he has appointed, and of this he has given assurance to all by raising him from the dead."
>
> When they heard of the resurrection of the dead, some scoffed, but others said, "We will hear you again about this." At that point Paul left them. But some of them joined him and became believers, including Dionysius the Areopagite and a woman named Damaris and others with them. (Acts 17:22–34)

In Acts, Luke has Paul deliver a speech to the highly educated members of the elite club of Athens in order to introduce his religion. Noting an altar dedicated to an unknown god, Paul uses it as a way proclaim the monotheistic God. His arguments are reminiscent of philosophical discourses about god, as was customary among the Greeks: god as the beginning of all things, a being who cannot be imprisoned in temples, does not need gifts from people, and is not represented by images.[27] Even the characterization of god as judge is aligned with Plato's ideas regarding the judgment of the dead. However, when Paul speaks of the resurrection of the body and not the soul, some reject him, while others want to hear more.

Gods Visit Men in Human Disguise
Paul and Barnabas at Lystra

> In Lystra there sat a man who was lame. He had been that way from birth and had never walked. He listened to Paul as he was speaking.

> Paul looked directly at him, saw that he had faith to be healed and called out, "Stand up on your feet!" At that, the man jumped up and began to walk. When the crowd saw what Paul had done, they shouted in the Lycaonian language, "The gods have come down to us in human form!" Barnabas they called Zeus, and Paul they called Hermes because he was the chief speaker. The priest of Zeus, whose temple was just outside the city, brought bulls and wreaths to the city gates because he and the crowd wanted to offer sacrifices to them. But when the apostles Barnabas and Paul heard of this, they tore their clothes and rushed out into the crowd, shouting: "Friends, why are you doing this? We too are only human, like you. We are bringing you good news, telling you to turn from these worthless things to the living God, who made the heavens and the earth and the sea and everything in them. In the past, he let all nations go their own way. Yet he has not left himself without testimony: He has shown kindness by giving you rain from heaven and crops in their seasons; he provides you with plenty of food and fills your hearts with joy." Even with these words, they had difficulty keeping the crowd from sacrificing to them. Then some Jews came from Antioch and Iconium and won the crowd over. They stoned Paul and dragged him outside the city, thinking he was dead. (Acts 14:8–19)

Greco-Roman literature contains many narratives of gods visiting humans in disguise. The miracle done for the crippled man evokes the impression of the people of Lystra that this deed could only be accomplished by gods. Though the people of Lystra speak their own language, which the Christian missionaries do not understand, they practice the common Greco-Roman religion, in which Hermes is honored as the interpreter of the gods. Zeus, meanwhile, is considered the mightiest of the gods. Because of this, Paul and Barnabas are seen as Hermes and Zeus. The most expensive ritual offered to the gods is the sacrifice of a bull, which is considered the best gift by which people can show their gratitude. However, Paul and Barnabas refused to accept a sacrifice made to them as gods. Instead, they refer to the "living God," who is the source of all the benefits that human beings enjoy. By contrast, Emperor Vespasian accepted the fact that he was celebrated as a miracle worker, which provided him with authority.[28]

In the past, God had permitted different "ways" for nations to practice their religions. But that was in past generations; Paul and Barnabas are bringing "good news" (*euangelion*) to turn people away from "worthless things" toward the "living God," who is different to mythical gods Zeus and Hermes.

FURTHER READING

Auffarth, Christoph. *Opfer. Eine Europäische Religionsgeschichte.* Vandenhoeck & Ruprecht, 2023.

Auffarth, Christoph. "With the Grain Came the Gods from the Orient to Rome: The Example of Serapis and Some Systematic Reflections." In *Religions and Trade. Religious Formation, Transformation and Cross-Cultural Exchange between East and West*, edited by Peter Wick and Volker Rabens. Leiden, 2013.

Beard, Mary, John North, and Simon Price. *Religions of Rome.* 2 vols. Cambridge University Press, 1998.

Bremmer, Jan N. "Early Christians in Corinth (A.D. 50–200): Religious Insiders or Outsiders?" *Annali di storia dell' exegesi* 37, no. 1 (2020): 181–202.

Bremmer, Jan N. *Greek Religion.* 2nd ed. Cambridge: Cambridge University Press, 2021.

Bremmer, Jan N. "Peregrinus' Christian Career," In *Maidens, Magic and Martyrs in Early Christianity: Collected Essays 1.* Wissenschaftliche Untersuchungen zum Neuen Testament 379. Mohr Siebeck, 2017, 65–79.

Gordon, Richard and Georgia Petridou, eds. *Beyond Priesthood: Religious Entrepreneurs and Innovators in the Roman Empire.* De Gruyter, 2017.

Leppin, Hartmut. *The Early Christians: from the Beginnings to Constantine.* Oxford University Press, 2023.

Merkt, Andreas, *Die religiöse Verwandlung der Welt. Die Anfänge ‚moderner' Religion in der Spätantike.* Herder, 2024.

Price, Simon R. F. *Rituals and Power: The Roman Imperial Cult in Asia Minor.* Cambridge University Press, 1984.

Rives, James B. *Animal Sacrifice in the Roman Empire 31 BCE–395 CE: Power, Communication, and Cultural Transformation.* Oxford University Press, 2024.

Rüpke, Jörg. *Religion of the Romans.* Polity, 2007.

Rüpke, Jörg and Greg Woolf, eds. *Religion in the Roman Empire.* Kohlhammer, 2021.

Wendt, Heidi. *At the Temple's Gate: The Religion of Freelance Experts in the Roman Empire.* Oxford University Press, 2016.

Notes

1 Mogens Herman Hansen and Thomas Heine Nielsen, eds., *An Inventory of Archaic and Classical Poleis* (Oxford University Press, 2004).

2 Horatius, *Epistulae* 2.1.156f, author's translation.

3 "Fear of the gods," scrupulous in religion, overacting piety (in Greek view), superstition.

4 *The Histories, Volume III: Books 5-8*, trans. W. R. Paton, rev. F. W. Walbank and Christian Habicht, Loeb Classical Library 138 (Harvard University Press, 2011) 6.56.6–8; see also 12.24.5.

5 Dirk Koßmann, "Zur Anwesenheit römischer Stadthalter der Kaiserzeit bei einheimischen Kultfeiern und Festen im Osten des Reiches," In *Religion und*

Epigraphik: Kleinasien, der griechische Osten und die Mittelmeerwelt, ed. Dagmar Hofmann et al., Asia Minor Studien 102 (Habelt, 2023).

6 Christoph Auffarth, "With the Grain Came the Gods from the Orient to Rome: The Example of Serapis and Some Systematic Reflections," in *Religions and Trade. Religious Formation, Transformation and Cross-Cultural Exchange between East and West*, ed. Peter Wick and Volker Rabens (Brill, 2014).

7 For exclusive monotheism, see Tertullian, *Adversus Hermogenem*. On the other hand, monotheism in the context of pluralism appears in Philo, *Legatio ad Gaium* and 1 Cor 8:1–6.

8 See Mary Beard, John North, and Simon Price, eds., *Religions of Rome*, 2 vols (Cambridge University Press, 1998); Jörg Rüpke, *Die Religion der Römer. Eine Einführung* (C. H. Beck, 2001).

9 For Postcolonial criticism, see Brent Nongbri, *Before Religion: A History of a Modern Concept* (Yale University Press, 2013). This was, however, criticized by Ilinca Tanaseanu-Döbler, "Introduction," in *Libraries, Handbooks, Encyclopedias. Ancient and Early Medieval Repositories of Knowledge and their Religious Aspects*, ed. Ilinca Tanaseanu-Döbler (Mohr Siebeck 2024).

10 See Pliny the Younger, *Epistulae* 10, 96.

11 Acts 11:26. See Jan N. Bremmer, "Why Did Jesus' Followers Call Themselves 'Christians'?" in *Maidens, Magic and Martyrs in Early Christianity: Collected Essays I*, Wissenschaftliche Untersuchungen zum Neuen Testament I/379 (Mohr Siebeck, 2017). Again, in Roman terms *Ioudaioi* is not the same as "Jews" but denotes only those who lived in or are coming from the province of Judaea. See Benedikt Eckhardt, "Rom und die Juden—ein Kategorienfehler?," in *Religio licita? Rom und die Juden*, ed. Görge Hasselhoff and Meret Strothmann (de Gruyter, 2017).

12 Cyprian, *de lapsis*.

13 Wilhelm Dittenberger, ed., *Sylloge Inscriptionum Graecarum*, vol. 3 (S. Hirzel, 1915–24). See also Christoph Auffarth, "Herrscherkult und Christuskult, " in *Die Praxis der Herrscherverehrung in Rom und seinen Provinzen*, ed. Hubert Cancik and Konrad Hitzl (Mohr Siebeck, 2003); Tassilo Schmidt, "Kaiserliche Kreativität Nero in Korinth," in *Corinth II: Das römische Korinth*, ed. Christoph Auffarth and Stefan Krauter, Civitatum Orbis MEditerranei Studia 7 (Mohr Siebeck, 2024), 97–99, 101.

14 Christoph Auffarth, "Religious Education in Classical Greece," in *Religious Education in Pre-Modern Europe*, ed. Ilinca Tanaseanu-Döbler and Marvin Döbler (Brill, 2012).

15 The same applies to the local Christian communities: ,They were networked with each other without any local center, just as the Jews were after destruction of the Jerusalem temple. Christian communities used letters to communicate, along with personal visits, such as Phoebe's in Rom 16:1, and traveling missionaries.

16 Suetonius, *Divus Augustus* 15.

17 Bärbel Schnegg, *Die Inschriften zu den Ludi saeculares* (de Gruyter, 2020).

18 *The Aeneid of Virgil*, trans. T. C. Williams (Houghton Mifflin, 1910) 1.278–79.

19 *Aeneid of Virgil*, 6.851–54.

20 Horace, *Odes* 2.7, lines 9f.

21 *The Epistles of Horace*, trans. Christopher Smart (Bell and Daldy, 1863), 1.4.

22 Christoph Auffarth, *Opfer. Eine Europäische Religionsgeschichte*, Theologische Bibliothek 8 (Vandernhoeck & Ruprecht, 2023); Andreas Merkt, *Die religiöse Verwandlung der Welt. Die Anfänge "moderner" Religion in der Spätantike* (Herder, 2024).

23 *IK Priene* 14. For edition, see in Reinhold Merkelbach and Wolfgang Blümel, eds., *Inschriften der Städte Kleinasiens*, vol. 69 (Habelt, 2014). Translation from Robert K. Sherk, ed., *Rome and the Greek East to the Death of Augustus* (Cambridge University Press, 1984), 124–27.

24 Author's translation.

25 See Christopher A. Faraone, "A Blue-Glass Amulet with Aphrodite, Osiris, and Jahweh," in *On the Edge of a Roman Port: Excavations at Koutsongila, Kenchreai, 2007-2014*, ed. Elena Korka and Joseph L. Rife (American Sschool of Classical Studies, 2022), 1045–50.

26 Author's translation.

27 Cf. Christoph Auffarth, "The Materiality of God's Image: Olympian Zeus and the Ancient Christology," in *The Gods of Ancient Greece: Identities and Transformation*, ed. Jan N. Bremmer and Andrew Erskine, Edinburgh Leventis Studies 5 (Edinburgh University Press, 2010), 465–80.

28 Suetonius, *Life of Vespasian* 7.2–3.

CHAPTER SEVENTEEN

Magic, Miracles, and Healing

Janet E. Spittler
(University of Virginia)

WHAT ROLE DID miracles play in early Christianity? Is there a difference between *miracle* and *magic*? How did early Christians understand miracles and magic? How did their pagan neighbors understand miracles and magic? And how have contemporary scholars made sense of Christian miracle accounts within the broader cultural and literary context of Greco-Roman miracles and magic? With respect to extant Christian literature from the first few centuries CE (both canonical and noncanonical), the answer to our first question is clear: *Miracles played a central role in early Christianity*, as evidenced by their frequent inclusion in both New Testament and apocryphal narratives. But the answers to the other questions are complex and vary over time. To put it simply: *It depends on who you ask*. This chapter offers a brief survey of the "miraculous landscape" of the first few centuries CE, with particular attention to miraculous healings (as these are so prominent in early Christian works); attention is also paid to how miraculous claims and accusations of sorcery were used and abused by both Christians and pagans in antiquity. We are fortunate to have rich source material—particularly from the first and second centuries CE—illustrating the situation.

Miracles, Exorcism

Miracles recounted in the canonical New Testament have often been divided into three distinct categories: (1) healing miracles, in which Jesus or his apostles cure bodily illnesses (up to and including death); (2) exorcisms, in which Jesus or his apostles cast out demons; and (3) nature miracles, in which Jesus or his apostles defy the laws of nature by, for example, miraculously multiplying food or controlling the weather. To these we might add (4): miracles involving bodily form, in which the physical appearance of Jesus or his apostles is miraculously changed (as with Jesus at the transfiguration) or their bodies miraculously appear and disappear (as Jesus does in John 20:19 and 20:26).

Scholars of early Christianity have occasionally suggested that the Christian vocabulary of the miraculous (that is, the specific Greek terms used to describe miracles) differs from pagan usage; some have gone so far as to argue that Christian authors explicitly avoided pagan terms like *thaumasia* or *paradoxa*, instead adopting terms like *dynameis*, *semeia*, and *terata* in an intentional effort to distinguish divine miracles from mere "wonders."[1] This view is, however, not supported by the evidence.[2] While New Testament texts do often use the hendiadys *semeia kai terata* as a calcified phrase referring to the miracles of the Hebrew Bible (in LXX translation), vocabulary usage does not differentiate Christian from non-Christian miracle accounts in ancient sources. To the contrary, Christian and pagan sources share a basic vocabulary of the miraculous that includes both terms with positive, neutral, and negative valence (with, to name just one example, *goēs* used almost exclusively in the imperial period to negatively characterize a "sorcerer").

Early Christian accounts of miracles performed by Jesus and the apostles do not appear out of nothing in the first century CE. In the first place, there are parallels in the Hebrew Bible and Septuagint. One might compare, for example, Jesus's resurrection of the widow's son at Nain (Luke 7:11–17) and Peter's resurrection of Tabitha (Acts 9:36–43) with Elijah's resurrection of a widow's son in Zarepthah (1 Kgs 17:17–24) or Elisha's resurrection of the Shunnamite woman's son (2 Kgs 4:18–37). Likewise, one might compare Jesus's multiplication of loaves and fishes in the Synoptic Gospels (Mark 6:30–44; 8:1–10.) with Elisha's multiplication of oil (2 Kgs 4:1–7), Elijah's multiplication of oil and meal (1 Kgs 17:8–16), or the miraculous provision of meat and bread (or manna) after the Israelites' exodus from Egypt (Exod 16). But in addition to these narratives from Jewish scripture—and more temporally proximate to early Christianity—there are many accounts in Greco-Roman literature of miraculous occurrences and miracle workers.

Healing Miracles

With respect to miraculous healings—perhaps Jesus's most prominent miraculous activity in the canonical Gospels—the most obvious comparisons are the miraculous healings attributed to Asclepius. Generally understood as the deified son of the Greek god Apollo and a human mother, Asclepius was worshipped for centuries at multiple cult sites across the Mediterranean, above all at Epidaurus. Worshippers with illnesses and injuries could visit Epidaurus (or other Asclepius temples) and request healing from the god. While the specific practices varied across time and location, ailing individuals would often sleep at the temple, reporting their dreams to the priests of Asclepius, who would then devise medical treatments based on the information conveyed in the dreams. Recipients of miraculous healings might express their gratitude to the god in the form of a dedicatory plaque or inscription, many of which are extant today, providing invaluable evidence of these cult sites. On a stele at Epidaurus from the second half of the fourth century BCE, for instance, an inscription testifies to Asclepius's healing of a blind man by using his finger to open his eyes:

> Alcetas of Halieis. This blind man saw a dream. It seemed to him that the god came up to him and with his fingers opened his eyes, and that he first saw the trees in the sanctuary. At daybreak he walked out sound.[3]

From these sources, we learn that Asclepius was believed to have miraculously healed a wide range of injuries and diseases, including many that Jesus is also reported to have healed (blindness, deafness, muteness, and various forms of paralysis). One well-known story about Asclepius (recorded, for example, by Apollodorus) recounts that his miraculous healing extended to raising the dead: Zeus, fearing that Asclepius might share this knowledge and ability with human beings, struck him down with a thunderbolt. While Asclepius was surely the most well known and widely venerated healing deity in Greco-Roman religion, there were many others—including, for example, Amphiaraus, a hero whose cult site is at Oropos in Greece.

In addition to (or instead of) traveling to healing sites, individuals in need of healing might turn to various ritual devices (such as amulets) or to ritual practitioners (essentially contemporary miracle workers). Evidence of amulets made to heal and protect those who wore them abound in the ancient Mediterranean, particularly in Egypt, where, in addition to amulets made of gemstones and metals, the climate and sands have even preserved amulets made of papyrus. While many are identifiable as explicitly Jewish, Christian, or pagan, others are not so easily classified—either because they bear no explicit references to Jewish, Christian, or pagan gods, because their divine referents are ambiguous, or because they refer to multiple gods across these three categories. Particularly interesting is evidence from the "Greek magical papyri" (often referred to as the "PGM" from Latin *Papyri Graecae Magicae*)—that is, collections of magical spells, hymns, and rituals preserved on papyrus—material that, in some instances, is virtually a recipe book for ancient magical practice. Here we find, for example, instructions on how to construct healing amulets and ingredient lists for healing potions.

Evidence of the presence of miracle workers is similarly plentiful; reports—both skeptical and credulous—of individuals with the power to heal are found in multiple literary sources, particularly from the Roman imperial period. Indeed,

Roman emperors themselves were occasionally thought to have the power to miraculously heal the sick. Tacitus, for example, reports that the emperor Vespasian healed a blind man and cured another man's withered hand.

> Vespasian at first ridiculed these appeals and treated them with scorn; then, when the men persisted . . . believing that his good fortune was capable of anything and that nothing was any longer incredible, with a smiling countenance, and amid intense excitement on the part of the bystanders, did as he was asked to do. The hand was instantly restored to use, and the day again shone for the blind man.[4]

Here, Vespasian's ability to miraculously heal the blind and restore withered limbs is an interesting point of comparison for early Christian miracle accounts since these are precisely the sorts of maladies that Jesus is depicted as healing and are similar to many healing episodes in the canonical Gospels. Of particular note is the emperor's use of his own spittle to heal the blind man—this element calls to mind gospel episodes (including Mark 8, below) in which Jesus uses his own spittle in healing.

Exorcisms

Within the New Testament canon, exorcisms are, after healing, the second-most common miraculous activity—although accounts of exorcisms are conspicuously absent from the Gospel of John. But even within the canonical texts, the exorcism of demons is not quite limited to Jesus and his disciples. In Acts 19, we find the fascinating story of the "sons of Sceva," men who are identified by the narrator as "Jewish exorcists" (*Ioudaioi exorkistai*) and attempt to cast out demons using the name "Lord Jesus." The episode depicts them as failures: The demons hear them and respond, but do not obey. Particularly interesting, however, is the correspondence between what these men are quoted as saying ("I adjure you by the Jesus whom Paul proclaims!"), actual exorcistic amulets from antiquity and, in the PGM, instructions for conducting exorcistic rituals. This suggests that the author of Acts is drawing upon exorcistic formulations that would have been familiar to his early readers. Notably, traveling exorcists seem to have been particularly associated with Syria-Palestine, as evidenced in Lucian of Samosata's *Philopseudes*, a dialogue on the topic of telling lies and fanciful tales; there, among multiple accounts of wonder workers, is a reference to a famous Syrian who routinely casts out demons after first asking the demons where they came from and how they entered the afflicted person's body:

> When he stands beside them as they lie there and asks: "Whence came you into his body?" the patient himself is silent, but the spirit answers in Greek or in the language of whatever foreign country he comes from, telling how and whence he entered into the man; whereupon, by adjuring the spirit and if he does not obey, threatening him, he drives him out. Indeed, I actually saw one coming out, black and smoky in color.[5]

Of particular note are the symptoms of demon possession, which include "fall[ing] down in the light of the moon," the "roll[ing of] their eyes," and the "foaming at the mouth" that, along with the description of the exorcist questioning the demon and the demon responding in Greek, are also found in early Christian exorcism stories (cf. Mark 5:9). Lucian, who seems to regard exorcists as shameless grifters, includes reference to the high fees charged for exorcisms—an observation that provides useful context for understanding the insistence in many early Christian narratives that Jesus healed and cast out demons for free.

Another figure reported to have exorcised demons is Apollonius of Tyana, whose life is narrated in extraordinary detail in a biography by Philostratus of Athens. Multiple points of contact make this work a fascinating source for understanding how Jesus (and the apostles) are depicted in Christian literature and how those depictions were received by both Christians and pagans. Apollonius was a historical figure, who lived in the first century CE; his biography, seemingly commissioned by the Roman Empress Julia Domna in the early third century CE, is the longest that survives from antiquity, presenting Apollonius as a Pythagorean sage who traveled through India, Arabia, Ethiopia, and to Rome; along the way, he delivers wisdom, reforms religious practice, performs miracles, and enters conflict with the Roman authorities—first the emperor Nero, then later, the emperor Domitian, before whom he faces trial (and miraculously escapes). Several miracles performed by Apollonius, as recounted by Philostratus (particularly the exorcism of a demon from a young man and the resurrection of a young woman both quoted below), are remarkably similar to miracles performed by Jesus, as recounted by the canonical Gospels, as well as miracles performed by the apostles in canonical and apocryphal Acts. Beyond Julia Domna's apparent interest, there is evidence of Apollonius's veneration—whether as god or sage or something in between—by Caracalla, Alexander Severus, and the wider public.

Most interesting, however, is the fact that the potential for comparison of Jesus and Apollonius was already recognized and discussed *in antiquity* by both pagans and Christians. In the early fourth century, an official from Diocletian's empire named Sossianus Hierocles wrote an anti-Christian pamphlet titled *Lover of Truth*, in which he, in part, compared Jesus and Apollonius, criticizing the credulity of Christians. This pamphlet is extant only in quotations of it in a response written by Eusebius, *Reply to Hierocles* (much as Celsus's *The True Doctrine* is extant only in Origen's quotations in his *Against Celsus*). Granted that our only access to Hierocles's writing is mediated by a rather indignant Eusebius, reading both Philostratus's biography of Apollonius and Eusebius's *Reply to Hierocles* (and perhaps Lucian's scathing *Alexander the False Prophet*) offers the contemporary scholar remarkable access to how at least *some* ancient people were thinking about miracles, magic, and healing with respect to Jesus and other historical figures. The reader of this volume would surely benefit from encountering this material on their own, but in short: accusations of magic, sorcery and trickery were lobbed by Christians against pagans *and* by pagans against Christians, with each group mocking the perceived credulity of the other.

Nature Miracles

The "nature miracles" of Jesus and his apostles also have parallels in Mediterranean antiquity. A miraculous multiplication of food, for example, seems to be attributed to the Roman king Numa in his biography by Plutarch. Likewise, Iamblichus, in his biography of Pythogoras, reports that the philosopher stilled a storm to protect his own disciples and demonstrated control over other elements of nature, including "infallible predictions of earthquakes, rapid expulsions of pestilences and hurricanes, instantaneous cessations of hail, and tranquilizations of the waves of rivers and seas." These divine abilities are typical among other lists of Pythagoras's miraculous capacities, as they are for other famous sages (for example, Abaris, also mentioned in Iamblichus's account). In addition to his power over nature, Iamblichus reports that Pythagoras "during the same day . . . was present in Metapontum in Italy, and at Tauromenium in Sicily, discoursing with his disciples in both places, although these cities are separated, both by land and sea, by many stadia, the traveling over which consumes many days."[6] The report that Pythagoras appeared on the same day in two far-flung locations seems at first to be an instance of bilocation; alternatively, the reader may be meant to understand this as miraculously swift travel. In either case, the miraculous capacity might be compared with Jesus's postresurrection appearances, particularly in some of the later acts of the apostles.

The other "nature miracles" commonly attributed to Pythagoras and other Greco-Roman wonder workers, including the prediction of earthquakes and the discovery of the causes of epidemics, are *not* reported of Jesus. Polymorphy (that is, the ability to change one's physical appearance so as to be unrecognizable to human beings, including one's own disciples or devotees) is a basic facet of Greco-Roman divinity: Numerous myths and stories are founded on an understanding of the gods' ability to disguise themselves. While polymorphy can be found in the canonical New Testament (in Jesus's transfiguration and his resurrection appearances to Mary Magdalene in the Gospel of John and on the road to Emmaus in the Gospel of Luke), it is much more prominent in Christian narratives of the second century and beyond, the "shape-shifting" Jesus of the Acts of John being a classic example.

TAKING A CLOSER LOOK: SOURCES

Sources from the World of the New Testament

Exorcistic Magical Formula

Excellent rite for driving out daimons: *Formula* to be spoken over his head: Place olive branches before him, and stand behind him and say:

"Hail, God of Abraham; hail, God of Isaac; hail, God of Jacob; Jesus Chrestos, the Holy Spirit, the Son of the Father, who is above the Seven, who is within the Seven. Bring Iao Sabaoth; may your power issue forth from him, NN, until you drive away this unclean daimon Satan, who is in him. I conjure [*exorkizō*] you, daimon, whoever you are, by this god, SABARBARBATHIŌTH SABARBARBATHIOUTH SABARBARBATHIŌNĒTH SABARBARBAPHAI. Come out, daimon, whoever you are, and stay away from him, NN, now, now, immediately, immediately. Come out, daimon, since I bind you with unbreakable adamantine fetters, and I deliver you into the black chaos in perdition."

Preparation: take seven olive branches; for six of them tie together the two ends of each one, but for the remaining one use it like a whip as you utter the conjuration. Keep it secret; it is proven.

After driving out the daimon, hang around him, NN, a phylactery, which the patient puts on after the expulsion of the daimon—a phylactery with these things [written] on a tin metal leaf: "BŌR PHŌR PHORBA PHOR PHORBA BES CHARIN BAUBŌ TE PHŌR BŌRPHORBA PHORBABOR BAPHORBA PHABRAIĒ PHŌRBA PHARBA PHŌRPHŌR PHORBA "BŌPHOR PHORBA PHORPHOR PHORBA BŌBORBORBA PAMPHORBA PHŌRPHŌR PHŌRBA, protect him, NN." But ***another version*** has a phylactery on which this sign occurs: 8. (PGM, IV.1227–64)[7]

This magical spell, written in a combination of Greek and Coptic, is preserved in a codex that likely dates to the fourth century CE. Its two parts instruct the reader on the ritual formula to be said as well as the materials (here, a phylactery of inscribed tin) to be made; the afflicted individual is here referred to in Greek as *deina* (that is, "so-and-so," represented in translations as "NN"). It is rich with *voces magicae*, or "magical words" (typically printed in all caps) that are incomprehensible. There is much to be said about this fascinating text; a few brief observations must suffice. Here, the power to perform the exorcism seems to reside in knowing what to say and do—and that power is thus available, apparently, to anyone with access to these instructions. This contrasts with miracle accounts in the canonical New Testament, in which the power to exorcise seems to reside with God and Jesus, and secondarily with Jesus's disciples. As is clear in Acts 19, simply knowing the words to say or which gods to call upon only gets you so far. How should we classify this exorcistic formula? Is it Christian? Or is it precisely the type of magical text that is burned in Acts 19:19? Or could it be both?

Apollonius Casts Out a Demon and Resurrects a Young Woman

> Once he was lecturing on the subject of libations, and there happened to be present at the talk a foppish youth with such a reputation for shamelessness that he had once been the subject of bawdy songs. Corcyra was his place of origin, and he claimed descent from Alcinous, Odysseus's host on Phaeacia. Apollonius was explaining how to pour libations, and advising not to drink from this kind of cup, but to keep it for the gods, undefiled and untouched by human lips. He also advised that the cup should have handles, and that one should pour libations over the handle, the part from which humans are least likely to drink. The youth greeted his remark with a loud, licentious laugh, at which Apollonius looked up at him and said, "It is not you that are committing this outrage, but the demon who controls you without your knowledge."
>
> In fact, without knowing it the youth was possessed by a demon. He laughed at things that nobody else did and went over to weeping without any reason, and he talked and sang to himself. Most people thought that the exuberance of youth produced these effects, but he was being prompted by the demon and only seemed to be playing the tricks that were being played on him. When Apollonius looked at the spirit, it uttered sounds of fear and fury, such as people being burned alive or tortured do, and it swore to keep away from the youth and not enter into any human. But Apollonius spoke to it as

> an angry householder does to a slave who is wily, crafty, shameless, and so on, and told it to give a proof of its departure. It replied, "I will knock that statue over," indicating one of the statues around the Royal Colonnade, where all this was taking place. When the statue first moved slightly, then fell, the outcry at this and the way people clapped in amazement were past description. The youth, as if waking up, rubbed his eyes, looked at the sun's beams, and won the respect of all the people gazing at him. From then on he no longer seemed dissolute, or had an unsteady gaze, but returned to his own nature no worse off than if he had taken a course of medicine. He got rid of his capes, cloaks, and other fripperies, and fell in love with deprivation and the philosopher's cloak and stripped down to Apollonius's style. (Philostratus, *Apollonius* 4.20)[8]

> Apollonius performed another miracle. There was a girl who appeared to have died just at the time of her wedding. The betrothed followed the bier, with all the lamentations of an unconsummated marriage, and Rome mourned with him, since the girl belonged to a consular family. Meeting with this scene of sorrow, Apollonius said, "Put the bier down, for I will end your crying over the girl." At the same time he asked her name, which made most people think he was going to declaim a speech of the kind delivered at funerals to raise lamentation. But Apollonius, after merely touching her and saying something secretly, woke the bride from her apparent death. The girl spoke and went back to her father's house like Alcestis revived by Heracles. Her kinsmen wanted to give Apollonius a hundred and fifty thousand drachmas, but he said he gave it as an extra dowry for the girl. He may have seen a spark of life in her which the doctors had not noticed, since apparently the sky was drizzling and steam was coming from her face, or he may have revived and restored her life when it was extinguished, but the explanation of this has proved unfathomable, not just to me but to the bystanders. (4.45)[9]

This episode surely calls to mind Jesus's resurrection of the widow's son at Nain (Luke 7:11–17). In both passages, the miracle worker has a chance encounter with the funeral procession of a beloved family member that has died too young; in both, the miracle worker interrupts the procession and approaches the bier, speaks to the deceased, and thereby raises them from the dead. While early Christian works often emphasize that Jesus heals and raises the dead without expecting or accepting payment, here it is Apollonius who refuses payment, redirecting the funds to the young woman's dowry. Note that Philostratus offers an alternative, less miraculous, explanation for what happened, but ultimately concludes that the event cannot be explained away.

Selections from Eusebius's Response to Hierocles

> Expressing his admiration and approval of Apollonius, [Hierocles] says that "he performed his miracles through some divine, ineffable wisdom, not by the tricks of sorcery," believing and insisting without proof that somehow or other these things really occurred. Just listen to what he says in his own words: "They talk of Jesus up hill and down dale, revering him for giving sight to the blind and doing some such miracles as these." Then some sentences later he says, "Well, let us consider how much better and more intelligent we are in our understanding of such matters, and in the opinion we form of men of virtue." (Treatise of Euesebius, 2.1)[10]
>
> Then he catalogs his remarkable deeds, beginning with the first, before saying the following in these very words: "Why then have I mentioned all this? So that the reader can compare our careful and sober judgment in respect to each with the gullibility of the Christians. We do not think a man who performed such deeds to have been a god, but only a man pleasing to the gods; while they are led by a few illusions to declare Jesus a god." After this he continues: "The following too should be taken into account. While the deeds of Jesus have been exaggerated by Peter, Paul, and people of their stripe—liars, yokels, sorcerers—, the deeds of Apollonius have been recorded by Maximus of Aegae, Damis the philosopher who studied with him, and Philostratus of Athens. All of these reached a very high level of culture and honored truth, and from motives of humanity did not wish the acts of a virtuous man, a friend of the gods, to go unknown." These are the very words of Hierocles, who entitled his attack on us The Lover of Truth." (Treatise of Euesebius, 2.2)[11]
>
> The author says that, after returning from India to Greece, Apollonius was pronounced a peer of the gods by the gods themselves. They sent the sick to him to be cured, and in fact, as if bringing Apollonius back for us from Arabs, Magi, and Indians as someone extraordinary and divine, he begins extraordinary stories from this point on. Yet one might reasonably say that, if he had a nature more divine than human, then he should have begun his miraculous deeds long ago and not now, before participating in those of other people. The vast learning of Arabs, Magi, and Indians would have been unnecessary for him to

> acquire if he had already possessed it, as the basic premise supposed; but lo and behold, it is only now, after his study with all these teachers, according to the "truth-loving" author, that Apollonius parades his wisdom. (Treatise of Euesebius, 26.1)[12]
>
> As for the girl whom he later brings to life again after her death in the city of Rome, the story seems quite incredible even to Philostratus himself, so that we can pass it by. However, in his uncertainty he wonders whether some spark of life had remained in the girl that her doctors had not noticed, since, so he says, "apparently the sky was drizzling and steam was coming from her face." In fact, if Apollonius had really done something of the sort in Rome, it would not have escaped the emperor first of all, and after him all his officials, but particularly the philosopher Euphrates, who was visiting just at that time and staying in Rome. It was he, so it is recorded, who later engineered a charge of sorcery against Apollonius, and if this too had really happened, the accuser would certainly have included it in the charges against him. (Treatise of Euesebius, 30.2)[13]

Assuming that Eusebius quotes him fairly accurately, it is clear in section 2.1 that Hierocles recognizes similarities between the miraculous deeds reportedly accomplished by Jesus and those of Apollonius—the difference being that, in Hierocles's opinion, Apollonius's miracles were performed via "divine ineffable wisdom," as opposed to the "tricks of sorcery" he presumes Jesus employed. Eusebius's position is, of course, exactly the opposite—though he would likely attribute Jesus's miracles to his divine identity, rather than wisdom. In the quotations of Hierocles in section 2.2, again assuming Eusebius represents his views accurately, it is clear that one basis for his critique is his low opinion of the sources: Peter and Paul, to whom Hierocles attributes reports of Jesus's activities, are "liars, yokels, sorcerers," whereas the sources of information about Apollonius are well respected philosophers and authors. Eusebius's critique of Hierocles is, in fact, primarily a critique of Philostratus's biography; Philostratus is "the author" referred to in sections 26.1 and 30.2. In some instances, Eusebius pokes holes in Philostratus's logic, suggesting in section 26.1 that, if Apollonius truly had a divine nature, he would not have had to acquire learning in his travels abroad. Elsewhere, Eusebius casts doubt on the reports, pointing out in section 30.2 that Philostratus himself seems to question whether the girl Apollonius raised was actually truly dead. The distinction drawn here between true resurrection and what we might call mere resuscitation is important context for understanding the depiction of the resurrection of Lazarus in the Gospel of John, in which the dead man is quite explicitly described as a stinking corpse.

Reading the New Testament Texts

Jesus Heals a Blind Man at Bethsaida

> They came to Bethsaida. Some people brought a blind man to him and begged him to touch him. He took the blind man by the hand and led him out of the village, and when he had put saliva on his eyes and laid his hands on him, he asked him, "Can you see anything?" And the man looked up and said, "I can see people, but they look like trees, walking." Then Jesus laid his hands on his eyes again, and he looked intently, and his sight was restored, and he saw everything clearly. Then he sent him away to his home, saying, "Do not even go into the village." (Mark 8:22–26)

This is a particularly interesting healing story, inasmuch as it seems to take place in two steps, with Jesus pausing to gauge its success, then continuing when the man's still imperfect vision indicates more miraculous action is necessary. Moreover, the man's exceedingly apt description of his intermediate state ("I can see people, but they look like trees, walking") strikes a chord with those of us afflicted by myopia. Also notable is Jesus's use of spittle—an element that we find again in John 9:6. As seen in the passage from Tacitus quoted above, spittle—often, though not exclusively, as a bodily fluid from a significant individual—was a fairly common medical and magical substance used in healing.

Jesus Casts an Unclean Spirit Out of a Boy

> When they came to the disciples, they saw a great crowd around them and some scribes arguing with them. When the whole crowd saw him, they were immediately overcome with awe, and they ran forward to greet him. He asked them, "What are you arguing about with them?" Someone from the crowd answered him, "Teacher, I brought you my son; he has a spirit that makes him unable to speak, and whenever it seizes him, it dashes him down, and he foams and grinds his teeth and becomes rigid, and I asked your disciples to cast it out, but they could not do so." He answered them, "You faithless generation, how much longer must I be with you? How much longer must I put up with you? Bring him to me." And they brought the boy to him. When the spirit saw him, immediately it convulsed the boy, and he fell on the ground and rolled about, foaming at the mouth. Jesus asked the father, "How long has this been happening to him?" And he said,

> "From childhood. It has often cast him into the fire and into the water, to destroy him; but if you are able to do anything, help us! Have compassion on us!" Jesus said to him, "If you are able! All things can be done for the one who believes." Immediately the father of the child cried out, "I believe; help my unbelief!" When Jesus saw that a crowd came running together, he rebuked the unclean spirit, saying to it, "You spirit that keeps this boy from speaking and hearing, I command you, come out of him, and never enter him again!" After crying out and convulsing him terribly, it came out, and the boy was like a corpse, so that most of them said, "He is dead." But Jesus took him by the hand and lifted him up, and he was able to stand. When he had entered the house, his disciples asked him privately, "Why could we not cast it out?" He said to them, "This kind can come out only through prayer." (Mark 9:14–29)

The similarities between this account and the two non-Christian accounts quoted above are quite clear: The symptoms of demon possession are quite similar across all three passages, as is the basic method of exorcism: commanding the demon to come out of the person. Interesting here, and with limited parallels in non-Christian sources, is the implication that the belief of the miracle's beneficiary is a prerequisite for its success.

Jewish Exorcists Attempt to Cast Out a Demon

> God did extraordinary miracles through Paul, so that when the handkerchiefs or aprons that had touched his skin were brought to the sick, their diseases left them, and the evil spirits came out of them. Then some itinerant Jewish exorcists tried to use the name of the Lord Jesus over those who had evil spirits, saying, "I adjure you by the Jesus whom Paul proclaims." Seven sons of a Jewish high priest named Sceva were doing this. But the evil spirit said to them in reply, "Jesus I know, and Paul I know, but who are you?" Then the man with the evil spirit leaped on them, mastered them all, and so overpowered them that they fled out of the house naked and wounded. When this became known to all residents of Ephesus, both Jews and Greeks, everyone was awestruck, and the name of the Lord Jesus was praised. Also many of those who became believers confessed and disclosed their practices. A number of those who practiced magic collected their books and burned them publicly; when the value of these books was calculated, it was found to come to fifty thousand silver coins. So the word of the Lord grew mightily and prevailed. (Acts 19:11–20)

As noted above, the exorcistic language of this passage ("I adjure you," *horkizō*, or, in some papyri and manuscripts, "we cast you out" *exorkizomen*) has close a parallel in the ritual instructions for casting out demons quoted above (PGM IV.1227–64).[14] But just as interesting as the attempted exorcism is the material that accompanies it in this passage. It begins with a reference to the miraculous power of objects that touched Paul's body, the implication being that his power is so great that it literally exudes from his skin and can be captured and stored in cloth for later use. The passage ends with Christian believers confessing their former magical practice and burning the magical books. Taken as a whole, this short episode is a prime illustration of how difficult it is to disentangle Christian "miracles" from pagan "magic."

FURTHER READING

Betz, Hans Dieter, ed. *The Greek Magical Papyri in Translation*. University of Chicago Press, 1986.

Edelstein, Emma J., and Ludwig Edelstein. *Asclepius Collection and Interpretation of the Testimonies*. 2 vols. Johns Hopkins University Press, 1945; repr., 1998.

Grant, Robert M. *Miracle and Natural Law in Greco-Roman and Early Christian Thought*. North Holland, 1952.

Harmon, Austin M. *Lucian*. Vol. 4. Loeb Classical Library 162. Harvard University Press, 1925.

Jones, Christopher P. *Philostratus. Apollonius of Tyana*. 3 vols. Loeb Classical Library 16, 17, and 458. Harvard University Press, 2005–6.

Paget, James Carleton. "Miracles in Early Christianity." In *The Cambridge Companion to Miracles*, edited by Graham H. Twelftree. Cambridge University Press, 2011.

Zimmermann, Ruben, ed. *Kompendium der frühchristlichen Wundererzählungen, Band 1 und 2*. Gütersloher Verlagshaus, 2013 and 2017.

Notes

1 See, for example, Charles F. D. Moule, "Excursus I: The Vocabulary of Miracle," in *Miracles: Cambridge Studies in their Philosophy and History*, ed. Charles F. D. Moule (Mowbray, 1965).

2 See, for example, Harold Remus, "Does Terminology Distinguish Early Christian from Pagan Miracles," *Journal of Biblical Literature* 101, no. 4 (1982): 531–51.

3 Inscriptiones Graecae, IV^2, 1, nos. 121–22, 18; Translation from Emma J. J. Edelstein and Ludwig Edelstein, *Asclepius: Collection and Interpretation of the Testimonies* (John Hopkins University Press, 1998), 423.

4 *Histories, Books 4-5. Annals: Books 1-3*, trans. Clifford H. Moore and John Jackson, Loeb Classical Library 249 (Harvard University Press, 1931) 4.81.

5 *The Dead Come to Life or The Fisherman. The Double Indictment or Trials by Jury. On Sacrifices. The Ignorant Book Collector. The Dream or Lucian's Career. The Parasite. The Lover of Lies. The Judgement of the Goddesses. On Salaried Posts in Great Houses*, trans. A. M. Harmon, Loeb Classical Library 130 (Harvard University Press, 1921), 345.

6 *The Life of Pythagoras*, trans. Kenneth Sylvan Guthrie (Platonist, 1919), 28.

7 *The Greek Magical Papyri in Translation*, trans. Hans Dieter Betz (University of Chicago Press, 1986), 62.

8 *Apollonius of Tyana, Volume I: Life of Apollonius of Tyana, Books 1-4*, ed. and trans. Christopher P. Jones, Loeb Classical Library 16 (Harvard University Press, 2005).

9 Philostratus, *Apollonius of Tyana*.

10 *Apollonius of Tyana, Volume III: Letters of Apollonius. Ancient Testimonia. Eusebius's Reply to Hierocles*, ed. and trans. Christopher P. Jones, Loeb Classical Library 458 (Harvard University Press, 2006).

11 *Apollonius of Tyana, Volume III.*

12 *Apollonius of Tyana, Volume III.*

13 *Apollonius of Tyana, Volume III.*

14 *The Greek Magical Papyri in Translation*, ed. Hans Dieter Betz (University of Chicago Press, 1986), 62.

CHAPTER EIGHTEEN

Living as a Jew in Judea and Galilee

Lutz Doering
(University of Münster)

BEING JEWISH IN antiquity meant adherence to a specific lifestyle oriented toward the Torah. Contrary to claims by earlier Christian, particularly Protestant, scholars, such a lifestyle is not an expression of "work righteousness" but a form of response to the covenant offered by God to Israel, and thus needs to be seen within the framework of "covenantal nomism."[1] Summarizing this concept, Sanders writes,

> The "pattern" or "structure" of covenantal nomism is this: (1) God has chosen Israel and (2) given the law. The law implies both (3) God's promise to maintain the election and (4) the requirement to obey. (5) God rewards obedience and punishes transgression. (6) The law provides for means of atonement, and atonement results in (7) maintenance or re-establishment of the covenantal relationship. (8) All those who are maintained in the covenant by obedience, atonement and God's mercy belong to the group which will be saved.[2]

Sanders later complemented this suggestion by the notion of "common Judaism," a concept according to which all Jews in antiquity shared certain practices and beliefs.[3] In a later summary, Sanders writes of this:

> Whatever their differences, they shared several practices and beliefs. Common Judaism is defined by a "laundry list" of beliefs and practices running from monotheism through Sabbath observance to sacrifice in the temple in Jerusalem (while it still stood).[4]

Both suggestions have received some criticism. As to the former, covenantal nomism, numerous ancient Jewish texts still know of a judgment according to works, so even with the possibility of atonement, some transgressions might remain unatoned.[5] As to the second, common Judaism, it seems as if Sanders has leveled the variation within Second Temple Judaism too much, underestimating the differences in halachic approach and Torah practice among Jews. A more appropriate approach would therefore describe the *dialectic* between commonality and diversification in Second Temple Judaism.[6] Nevertheless, a covenantal understanding of Torah praxis seems apposite and is adopted in what follows, nuanced by reference to the different varieties of practice. These pertain also to differences between Jewish life in the historic land of Israel and Jewish life in the diaspora; I shall indicate where such distinctions are relevant.

Areas Inhabited by Judeans in the Land of Israel

Before going into the details, it is necessary to look at the main areas of the land of Israel in which Jews lived in the late Second Temple period. Continuing the Jewish presence as extended by the Hasmoneans, Jews lived, roughly speaking, in Judea and the Galilee. Following the conquest by John Hyrcanus I after 112 BCE, Judea included Idumea, whose native population (as far as they remained in the land) adopted a Jewish lifestyle and were henceforth widely regarded as Jews. Later, Judea also included an area in northern Transjordan, the so-called Perea (in the area of the former Gilead). In contrast, the cities of the coastal plain were largely dominated by non-Jewish populations, and the area north of Judea called Samaria was inhabited by a competing Israelite group, the Samaritans, whose relationship with the Jews became increasingly hostile, especially after Hyrcanus destroyed their temple on Mount Gerizim. Nevertheless, the Samaritans also had a version of the Torah and practiced its laws according to their own legal tradition. The other main area inhabited by Jews was the Galilee in the north; it was conquered and attached to the Hasmonean state by King Aristobulus I in 104/3 BCE, after which many Jews moved there from Judea. Subsequently, Jews also settled in parts of the Golan (e.g., Gamla, founded by King Alexander Jannaeus in ca. 81 BCE). By the time of Jesus of Nazareth, Judea was under direct Roman rule, while Galilee and Perea were ruled by Herod Antipas, and the Golan as well as northern areas (inhabited mainly by non-Jews) were under the rule of his brother Philip. Only briefly (41–44 CE) were all these territories reunited under King Agrippa I; after his death, they were once again made a Roman province, now including the Galilee. A group of ten cities, the Decapolis, situated south and east of the Sea of Galilee, remained a center for non-Jewish life and culture throughout the period.

Dietary Laws

What were the defining characteristics of the lifestyle of a Jew in Judea or the Galilee—for ease of terminology, we shall refer to such a person as a "Judean"—at the end of the Second Temple period? Let us begin with food, an important and socially significant part of daily life. The Pentateuch contains numerous dietary laws. The most important ones are bans on consuming certain kinds of animals, fish, birds, and insects found in Leviticus 11:1–23, 41–47 and Deuteronomy 14:3–20. Quadrupeds permitted for consumption include only those that have divided hooves, are cleft-footed, and chew the cud. This excludes specifically the camel, the hyrax (rock badger), and the hare because they do not have divided hooves, and the pig because it does not chew the cud. Among the aquatic animals, only fish that have both fins and scales are permitted. A number of birds are also forbidden, as are any "creeping things," such as reptiles and insects, except for four species of locusts. Edible animals that die on their own or are torn by predators are not permitted for consumption (Exod 22:30; Lev 22:8; Deut 14:21). One must neither eat the blood (Gen 9:4; Lev 17:10–14) nor the fat of animals (Lev 3:17; 7:23–27). The thigh muscle near the hip is also forbidden as Jacob is said to have been injured at this point (Gen 32:33).

What do we know about adherence to such laws? Literary sources from the Hellenistic and Roman periods mention Jewish dietary preferences, particularly the abstention from pork, not only for Judeans in Judea and Galilee but also in the diaspora. The Damascus Document specifies the prohibition of crawling things, including the larvae of bees, and requires beyond Pentateuchal law that fish be torn so that their blood is drained and that locusts must be placed alive in fire or water before consumption "because this is the ordinance of their creation" (CD 12:11–15). The New Testament mentions the (permitted) consumption of locusts for John the Baptist (Mark 1:6) and Peter's revulsion to slaughtering creeping things (Acts 10:9–14). The Apostolic Decree issued by the community of Judean Christ followers in Jerusalem reflects a concern, inter alia, for dietary laws by calling on the gentile Christ followers of Antioch, Syria, and Cilicia to abstain from blood and from what is strangled, as well as from idol meat and fornication (Acts 15:29). Flavius Josephus refers to a variety of dietary laws, probably reflecting the practical knowledge of a Judean of priestly descent. We should also note that halachic rules for dietary laws were still developing in the late Second Temple period. Thus, the separation of meat from dairy products, central for observant Jews until this very day, was unknown in prerabbinic Judaism: An interpretation of the prohibition of "cooking a kid in its mother's milk" (cf. Exod 23:19; 34:26; Deut 14:21), as referring to mixing meat and milk, is nowhere attested in Second Temple sources.[7]

From the archaeological records, we see that in the Hellenistic and particularly the Roman period, Judeans refrained more consistently from pork than their non-Jewish neighbors. The evidence is similar for scaleless fish (sharks and catfish), although there is some *limited* evidence for its consumption even in Judean sites in Hellenistic and Roman times.[8] It is a reasonable assumption that the heightened reluctance by Judeans in the Hellenistic and Roman periods corresponds with the Pentateuchal food prohibitions.

"Household Judaism"
Common Tableware, Stepped Pools

Closely related to dietary choices is the use of a common domestic environment in which to live and to eat. Archaeologists have discovered that Judeans across Judea and Galilee, and up to the Golan, preferred a similar type of locally made tableware from the first century CE onward, instead of importing vessels from Greek territories, such as wine amphorae from Rhodes, decorated red-slip dishes from Mediterranean potters, decorated oil lamps, or terracotta figurines, which had been characteristic before the Hasmoneans came to power. Also, in the first century BCE, we find the emergence of stepped pools across the areas inhabited by Judeans in the land of Israel (including the Perea), which arguably were used for ritual purification by immersion (see below). Andrea Berlin has labeled this emerging uniform Judean culture *household Judaism*. "With its practice, Judeans live as one people—no matter where they actually reside within the Hasmonean kingdom."[9]

Nonfigural Art and Decoration

In addition, most Judeans living in Judea or the Galilee during the late Second Temple period would have refrained from using depictions of humans and animals in their residences, preferring instead floral or geometrical decorations. This can be seen as an attempt to live by the command to make no "graven images" (Exod 20:4–5; Deut 5:8–9; cf. Deut 4:15–19). Such an implementation is first materially attested by the Hasmoneans who refrained from displaying humans and animals on their coins, beginning with John Hyrcanus I.[10] There were exceptions to this restraint, mainly by cosmopolitan members of the elite, such as Herod I, who had his bathhouse and royal theater box at Upper Herodium decorated with depictions of fowls, other animals, and even human beings. However, there are also a few traces of faunal decoration from private mansions in the Upper City of Jerusalem.[11] Nevertheless, in his buildings oriented toward the Judean population (the Jerusalem temple, the palaces at Masada), even Herod I did without offensive decorations, similarly in his coinage (except for one coin series showing an eagle). This was continued by Herod's sons Archelaus and Antipas, who ruled over areas with a largely "Judean" population, in contrast to Philip, who primarily reigned over non-Jewish territories, which may explain the deployment of his portrait on some of the coins. King Agrippa

I had imageless coins minted in Jerusalem but elsewhere commissioned coins with his image or that of the emperor. In view of the absence of images on coins issued by Judean rulers in Judean territories, both the Tyrian shekel used as coin for the temple tax (containing the image of Melkart-Heracles on one side and an eagle on the other),[12] and the Roman tax coin carrying the portrait of the emperor (Mark 12:13–17), would have exerted the tolerance of Judeans around the turn of the era. Some scholars have proposed that Jesus's overturning of the money changers' tables might have been caused by his opposition to the presence of Tyrian shekels in the temple precinct.[13]

Chalk Vessels

From the latter first century BCE onward, archaeological records attest to the increased use of chalk vessels. In the first century CE they become a ubiquitous sight at places inhabited by Judeans—and *only* in those places—that is, in Judea, the Galilee, the Golan, and the Perea. Chalk vessels are absent from the coastal plain, western Galilee, Samaria, the Decapolis, and the far south of Israel. Neither are they normally in use in the Jewish diaspora. In the New Testament, we find a reference to them in John 2:6, in the narrative of the Wedding at Cana: "Now standing there were six stone water jars in accordance with the purification [laws] of the Judeans." Why were chalk vessels—made of a porous material that posed challenges for practical use—produced by Judeans, and *only* by Judeans? The reason is that they were deemed insusceptible to ritual defilement. While the most widespread vessels, those made from clay, had to be broken if defiled (Lev 11:33; 15:12), there was nothing to be feared with chalk vessels since they did not carry the same risk.[14]

Purity Laws

This brings us to the larger framework of purity laws, which had a significant impact on the life of Judeans in the land of Israel. One important category relevant for purity laws is *ritual impurity*; such impurity is generated, to a large degree inevitably, by certain events in the human life cycle: childbirth, genital discharges, various kinds of skin disease, and death, as well as contact with animal carcasses, spots on clothes or the walls of a house, and the ashes of a red heifer. According to Pentateuchal law, ritual impurity is caused by the following persons or objects: a woman after childbirth (Lev 12:1–8); a person with a specified skin disease (Lev 13:1–46); cloth or leather showing certain spots (Lev 13:47–59); walls of a house showing certain spots (Lev 14:33–57); a man with abnormal genital discharge (Lev 15:1–15); human semen (Lev 15:16–18); a woman with menstrual bleeding (Lev 15:19–24); a woman with abnormal genital discharge or bleeding (Lev 15:33); a human corpse, bone, or grave (Num 19:11–22); carcasses of animals forbidden for consumption (Lev 11:8, 11, 24–33); carcasses of animals permitted for consumption that died on their own (*nevelah*) or were torn apart (*ṭerefah*) (Lev 11:39–40); those who slaughter and burn the red heifer, collect its ashes, or sprinkle or touch "purification water" containing these ashes (Num 19:1–10, 21)—which is used for the purification of those who have come in contact with a human corpse, bone, or grave.

The impurity issuing from these persons or objects can be transmitted in various ways, depending on the source of impurity; for example, by touching or sitting on the source of impurity, entering the impure house or coming under the same roof as a corpse, or in the case of *nevelah* or *ṭerefah*, consuming it. The transmission of impurity follows a graded system, in which contact with a certain source of impurity renders a person impure, but to a lesser degree. Ritual impurity can usually be removed by appropriate means: full immersion for human beings, washing for cloth or leather. In the case of a person defiled by a corpse, sprinkling on the third and seventh day with the "water of purification" is required, in addition to immersion. An impure clay vessel must be broken, and an impure house must be destroyed. People undergoing purification often needed to bring a concluding sacrifice and await sunset before they could fully regain their purity. There were debates among various Jewish groups about what tasks someone who had "immersed during the day" (*ṭevul yom*) could already resume before sunset.

There is also evidence from Qumran texts, Josephus, and the New Testament that purity laws attracted considerable attention in the late Second Temple period. One area of relevance was access to the temple and participation in sacrifices. Only the ritually pure were allowed to do so. Therefore, Judeans visiting the temple had to arrange for the appropriate means of purification in advance. But even apart from the temple, in remote villages throughout Judea and the Galilee, Judeans wished to become pure after impurities incurred through sex, birth, contact with a corpse, or defiling illnesses. The most important facilities that helped them in this respect were stepped pools, which allowed for full-body immersion. These pools start to appear in the late second or early first century BCE and are frequent at Judean sites in the first century CE and beyond. They served for *ritual*, not hygienic purification. Many pools would have been filled in the rainy season of the winter months, with the water standing, diminishing, and attracting algae and insects over the long summer months—nevertheless, they continued to be frequented by Judeans eager to purify themselves. While the spread of stepped pools (called *miqwa'ot* by a later, rabbinic name) suggests a similar approach to purification all over Judea and the Galilee, there were nevertheless disputes and differences in matters of purity. In addition to the debate about the *ṭevul yom* mentioned above, we note that handwashing before meals (Mark 7:1–4) was a stringency apparently innovated by the Pharisees. It is mentioned neither in the Hebrew Bible nor in the texts from Qumran.

Tithes

Another topic of the Torah that had significant impact on the lives of Judeans was tithing. This was only relevant in the land of Israel. According to Pentateuchal law, tithes—the tenth of all produced—are to be given from grain and fruit trees (Lev 27:30) as well as wine and oil (Num 18:27; Deut 12:17; 14:22–23). Numbers 18:21–28 directs that this "first" tithe be given to the Levites, who then shall give a tenth of it to the priests. This was apparently the prevailing (and ideal) practice during the Second Temple period (cf. Neh 10:38–40; Tob 1:7 (G^{II}); 11QT^{a} 60:6–7; Philo, *Spec.* 1.156–57; *Mut.* 191; Josephus, *Ant.* 4.240). However, there were also other opinions that suggested the "first" tithe be given directly to the priests (cf. Jub. 13:25–27; Jdt 11:13). In addition, according to Leviticus 27:32, every tenth cattle and sheep from the herd or flock is "holy to the Lord." Again, it was debated among Second Temple Judeans whether this "cattle tithe" was to be given to the priests[15] or more broadly to "the priests and Levites" (see 2 Chr 31:4–6). Moreover, in line with Deuteronomy 14:22–27, which requires the spending of the tithe in Jerusalem, a second tithe developed, in which a tenth of the produce of grain, wine, and oil was sold, and the proceeds were spent by the owners in Jerusalem (cf. Jub. 32:10–14; Tob 1:7 G^{II}). However, in every third year the tithe was to be deposited locally and made available to *personae miserae* (cf. Deut 14:28–29; 26:12–13; Tob 1:8 G^{II}; Josephus, *Ant.* 4.240; Tg. Ps.-J. Deut 26:12).[16] This system was complex and demanding as well as economically challenging for many peasants. Hence, suspicion lingered that tithes were not properly separated. This was particularly relevant for the consumption of grain, fruit, wine, and oil, which was allowed only if correctly tithed. It seems that the Pharisees were particularly scrupulous with tithing (cf. Luke 18:12b). Moreover, the polemic in Matthew 23:23–24 charges "the scribes and Pharisees" with extending the separation of tithes even to herbs such as mint, dill, and cumin, claiming that they disregarded "the weightier things of the law." A similar extension to herbs is later found in the Mishnah: "Whatever is food, and is kept, and grows from the earth, is liable for tithes" (m. Maʿaś. 1:1), with discussion of dill (m. Maʿaś. 4:5) and cumin (m. Demai 2:1). In sum, we see that tithing was an issue under debate in ancient Judaism.

The Sabbath

Both forms of the Decalogue contain a commandment to "sanctify" the Sabbath day and to abstain from "labor" on this day, which applies also to children, slaves, and cattle (Exod 20:8–11; Deut 5:12–15). However, it is not specified what "labor" is, and further texts from the Hebrew Bible provide limited examples for what is precisely forbidden: various agricultural works (Exod 34:21; Neh 13:15), kindling fire (Exod 35:3), gathering wood (Num 15:32–36), carrying loads (Jer 17:19–27; cf. Neh 13:15), pursuing one's business, selling goods (Isa 58:13; Neh 10:32; 13:16; cf. Amos 8:5), going one's ways, leaving one's place (Isa 58:13; Exod 16:29), "saying a word" (Isa 58:13); also, one should "prepare" meals before the Sabbath (cf. Exod 16:5).

In the Second Temple period, the list of prohibited labors was extended and later differentiated. There were also differences in emphasis between the various Jewish groups. The oldest lists come from Jubilees, perhaps written in the 150s BCE.[17] In Jubilees 2:29–30 and 50:8, 12, we find the following activities prohibited: preparing food and drink; drawing water; transporting objects into and out of a house; sexual intercourse; talking about work, a journey, or selling and buying; walking a distance; cultivating a field; kindling fire; riding; going on a trip by boat; beating and killing a living being; slaughtering cattle or birds; catching game, birds, or fish; fasting; and making war.[18] Some prohibitions are striking, such as the interdicts of sexual intercourse or making war, both of which were not generally accepted by Second Temple Judeans. The former was due to a particular understanding of "sanctifying" the Sabbath, which deemed sex (and probably the ritual defilement inevitably associated with it) as inappropriate for encountering the holy (cf. Exod 19:14–15). This view is possibly attested in texts from Qumran (see below) and among other groups, such as the Samaritans. In contrast, the rabbis later encouraged sexual relations on the Sabbath (euphemistically referred to as "eating garlic"; see m. Ned. 3:10; y. Meg. 4:1, 75a; b. B. Qam. 82a). Regarding the prohibition against waging war on the Sabbath, the Maccabees are said to have permitted self-defense to avoid total destruction (1 Macc 2:29–41). In the first century CE, Josephus limits Jewish warfare on the Sabbath strictly to self-defense (*J.W.* 1:146; *Ant.* 12:277; 14:63; *Life* 159, 161).

In the Qumran texts, we find further prohibitions lists, but with some differentiation. The Damascus Document contains an extensive section of Sabbath laws (CD 10:14–11:18),[19] including the prohibitions of: business talk and lending; inspecting a field; commissioning a foreigner with labor; wearing soiled clothes; "intermingling voluntarily" (perhaps including sexual intercourse); carrying objects into, or out of, a house; opening a sealed vessel; carrying medicines on the body; lifting rock or soil in a house; carrying an infant in or out; "urging" a slave or a hired laborer (to do work); helping cattle in distress; spending the Sabbath close to gentiles; desecrating the Sabbath on account of property and gain; using implements when rescuing a human being; and urging that only sacrifices appropriate for the Sabbath be brought on this day. In addition, walking up to one thousand cubits is permitted, or up to two thousand cubits when pasturing an animal. Fragments of texts from Qumran Cave 4 provide several additional laws on: forbidden and permitted talk, the use of one's garment when rescuing a human being from a water source (see below), ritual purification before the Sabbath, and the prohibition of private reading of scripture, as well as polemics against the waving of the *ʿomer* sheaf on the Sabbath.[20] The latter was debated among various Jewish groups in the Second Temple period. While the Pharisees, along with other Jews, interpreted Leviticus 23:11 ("on the morrow of the Sabbath") to refer to the cutting and waving of the first barley sheaf *on the day after the first Passover holiday*—thus permitting these activities even if they occurred on a Sabbath (see m. Menaḥ. 10:3; cf. Lev 23:11 LXX; Philo, *Spec.* 2.162; Josephus, *Ant.* 3.250)—the Boethusians, Sadducees, and the Qumran *yaḥad* rejected this position. Nevertheless, the general determination to save a human life on the Sabbath was upheld across various groups. However, whereas the Qumran texts prohibited the use of implements forbidden to carry on the Sabbath for this purpose, the rabbis (and probably the Pharisees before them) knew no such restrictions.

Synagogue Assemblies

One activity that is actively encouraged on the Sabbath is assembling for the study of Torah. This is similar for Jews in the diaspora and in the land of Israel. In fact, we hear more on Sabbatical synagogue (or *proseuchē*) assemblies from the diaspora (see Philo, *Hypoth.* 7.12–13; *Somn.* 2.127; *Contempl.* 30–31; Josephus, *Ant.* 16.43; *Ag. Ap.* 2.175), but there is some textual evidence for Judea as well.[21] The Theodotus inscription[22] attests to a synagogue of Greek-speaking Jews in Jerusalem. Archaeological evidence for synagogues in Judea goes back to the late second or early first century BCE—such as Umm el-Umdan in the Shephelah—and becomes broadly attested by the first century CE. For instance, synagogues have been identified at Qiryat Sefer in the Judean Shephelah, Masada, and Herodium (these last two were adapted for synagogue use in the First Judean War, and for Herodium, possibly even in the Second War), Gamla (and perhaps Khirbet Majduliya) in the Golan, Magdala (where two synagogues have been discovered, the first one in 2009 [see figure 5] the second one only in 2021) and Khirbet Qana in the Galilee (the latter perhaps from the second century CE). Potential additional candidates include Khirbet Diab and Khirbet aṭ-Ṭawani in the Judean Mountains.[23] All of these buildings are characterized by benches on three or four sides around a rectangular room, with columns at the corners supporting the roof; there is no recognizable orientation for these buildings. It is questionable whether they were perceived as extensions of the Jerusalem temple.[24] As Matthew 6:5 shows, Jewish prayer in the first century CE could be conducted in either synagogues or street corners; thus, the synagogue was not yet the place of statuary prayer.

The Temple as Experienced by the Judean People

Sacrifices and Festivals

The Jerusalem temple was a remarkable building for any visitor. Herod I had begun to extend the temple compound in grand style in 22 BCE (cf. Josephus, *J.W.* 5.184–227), although the work would not be completed for another eighty years (cf. Josephus, *Ant.* 20.219). Along the interior walls of the temple square were colonnades, the largest of which was the royal colonnade on the south side. The temple itself was situated amid a series of concentrical courtyards: the "Court of the Gentiles," bounded by a barrier with stone tablets warning non-Jews against entering the inner district under threat of death; the Court of the Women; the Court of the Israelites; and the Court of the Priests. Sacrifices were offered in the Court of the Priests, which featured the burnt offering altar, the slaughtering block, and the water basin. In the front hall of the temple stood the seven-branched candelabrum (*menorah*), the showbread table, and the incense altar. Behind a curtain was the holy of holies, empty at that time (cf. Josephus, *J.W.* 5.219); supposedly, only the high priest entered it once a year on the Day of Atonement.

The main activity in the temple was the sacrifice, although prayers and the recitation of Torah sections by the priests, as well as the singing of hymns and

Figure 18.1. Herod's Temple in Jerusalem. (David Cielontko, used by permission.)

the blowing of trumpets, took place at designated times. The priests were organized into twenty-four divisions, each serving in the temple for one week at a time in rotation. The Levites supported them as gatekeepers and temple singers. Among the communal sacrifices were the daily burnt offering (*tamid*)—that is, one lamb each in the morning and in the afternoon—as well as the Sabbath burnt offering and the additional sacrifices for new moons, annual festivals, and the Day of Atonement. Among the sacrifices to be brought by individuals according to Pentateuchal law were sin offerings for unintentional transgressions (cf. Lev 4) and for the purification of a leper (cf. Lev 14), and guilt offerings for certain offenses (cf. Lev 5), as well as *shelamim* offerings ("sacrifice of well-being"), whose meat the owner consumed communally (cf. Lev 3). In addition to cattle and small livestock, some types of sacrifice required a pair of turtledoves or pigeons (cf. Lev 15:14–15, 29–30), which could also be used to replace other sacrificial animals when the owner was poor (cf. Lev 12:8). Grain and drink offerings also accompanied the animal sacrifices. Some but not all sacrifices served the purpose of atonement; further offerings were gifts or tokens of gratitude to God, while others completed purification rites.

According to Pentateuchal law (Exod 23:17; 34:23; Deut 16:16), male Israelites were "to appear before the Lord" three times a year during the pilgrimage festivals of Passover (*Pesach*), Weeks (*Shavuot*), and Tabernacles (*Sukkot*). In practice, the closer Judeans lived to Jerusalem the more likely were they able to come for pilgrimage; women and children also attended, although some groups attempted to limit certain rites to men. In the afternoon of 14 Nisan, the heads of dining parties comprising of roughly ten to fifteen people, slaughtered a Passover animal (a lamb or a kid) in the Court of the Israelites, while the priests assisted in the removal of the blood. The animals were then roasted and eaten in the residential areas of Jerusalem, with pilgrims offered temporary lodging for the celebration (cf. Mark 14:12–16).[25] By the Second Temple period, Passover had been merged with Massot (Deut 16:1–18; Lev 23:5–8), a seven-day festival during which leaven was not permitted for consumption or storage. After the end of the first holiday of Passover-Massot (15 Nisan) or alternatively after the end of the Sabbath following the Passover-Massot week (for the controversy, see n 27), a sheaf (*'omer*) of barley was harvested and waved in the temple. This marked the beginning of a fifty-day period until the Festival of Weeks, when two wheat loaves were brought to the temple. The festival of Tabernacles in autumn was celebrated for eight days (15–22 Tishri) by dwelling in huts (*sukkot*), taking and shaking the festival bundle (a *lulav* of palm leaves, willows, and myrtles in addition to an *etrog*, a citrus fruit) in the temple compound, nocturnal celebrations in the temple courts accompanied by music and dance, a ceremony with willow branches, and a water libation by the high priest that heralded the rainy season. The Sadducees rejected the water libation, however, and argued that the willow branch ceremony does not override the Sabbath (t. Sukkah 3:1, 16). In addition, the Day of Atonement on 10 Tishri was characterized by communal atonement and fasting. The high priest carried out a complex ritual in accordance with Leviticus 16, which included slaughtering a ram for a sin offering, entering the holy of holies, uttering the divine name, sprinkling the blood of the sin offering inside the holy of holies, and sending another ram, the "scapegoat," into the desert for the sins of the community as well as offering concluding sacrifices.

TAKING A CLOSER LOOK: SOURCES

Sources from the World of the New Testament

The Theodotus Inscription

This synagogue building inscription, dated between the first century BCE and the first century CE, attests to the erection of a synagogue in Jerusalem by a Greek-speaking Jewish family. It also gives some details on the activities connected with this synagogue. The inscription was found in a cistern at the Ophel, south of the Temple Mount (the current Haram esh-Sharif).

> Theodotos son of Vettenos, priest and archisynagogos, son of an archisynagogos, grandson of an archisynagogos, built the synagogue for

Figure 18.2. The Theodotus inscription. (Andrey Zeigarnik, Wikimedia Commons. Used under Creative Commons Attribution-Share Alike 2.0 Generic License.)

> the reading of the Law and teaching of the commandments [*ōkodomēse tēn synagōgēn eis anagnōsin nomou kai eis didachēn entolōn*], and the guest-house and the (other) rooms and water installations(?) [*ta chrēstēria tōn hydatōn*] for the lodging of those who are in need of it from abroad, which [the synagogue] his forefathers, the elders and Simonides founded [*ethemeliōsan*]. (*CIIP* 9)[26]

The inscription, with its context and dating shows, first, that the synagogue referred to was in Jerusalem when the temple still stood (cf. Acts 6:9; 24:12); second, that it was "built" by a Greek-speaking Jew whose father's name was of Latin origin,[27] and that his ancestors and others had "founded" the synagogue, which suggests that this might have been intended for a Jewish congregation originating in the diaspora and resettling in Jerusalem. The inscriptions states, third, that the synagogue was built "for the reading of the Law and teaching of the commandments," the two predominant activities in Second Temple synagogues observed above, while no mention is made of regular, fixed prayer. The term *chrēstēria tōn hydatōn* might refer to water installations, and hence probably facilities for ritual purification. It seems that the synagogue particularly served the needs of Jewish visitors from abroad, including providing them with accommodation.

Life Saving

Human Beings and Beasts in Danger on the Sabbath

The following passages from the Damascus Document (CD and 4Q parallels) and 4Q265, both belonging to the Dead Sea Scrolls and dated to ca. 100, and somewhere in the first century BCE, respectively, discuss cases in which either a beast or a human being is in danger on the Sabbath. Similar discussions can be found in some sections from Tosefta Shabbat, a rabbinic text redacted around 300 CE. Which actions do these texts permit and which ones do they prohibit as part of proper Sabbath rest in such cases?

> Let no one assist a beast to give birth on the Sabbath day. *vacat* And if it falls into a cistern or a pit, he may not lift it up on the Sabbath. *vacat* Let no one spend the Sabbath in a place close to Gentiles on the Sabbath. *vacat* Let no one profane the Sabbath for wealth and gain on the Sabbath. *vacat* And anyone who falls into a place of water, *or into a pool* let no one bring him up with a ladder, a rope, or a utensil. (CD 10:13–17a, italics added)

According to the Damascus Document, a beast giving birth may not be assisted, nor a beast fallen into a cistern be lifted out on the Sabbath. As for a human being, this text focuses on the prohibition against using implements that are banned from being carried on the Sabbath. Does this mean that a human being cannot be rescued from a cistern on the Sabbath? Here, 4Q265 provides the following regulations:

> Let no one raise up a beast which has fallen into the water on the Sabbath day. But if it is a living person who has fallen into the water [on] the Sabbath [day,] one shall extend his garment to him to raise him up with it, but he may not carry an implement. (4Q265 6 5–7)

We see a similarly negative stance regarding a beast. However, with respect to a human being, 4Q265 provides a "creative" solution in allowing the use of one's garment, rolled together, while again excluding the use of any instrument. Hence, this Dead Sea scroll shows concern for human beings in distress but does *not* advocate breaching Sabbath rules for their rescue.

The accents and details are different in the rabbinic texts. Tosefta Shabbat 14[15]:3 (end) reads: "And if a beast falls into a cistern, they shall put food before it in its place so that it will not die." Here, we see a concern with the survival of the animal; however, rather than lifting the beast up, food should be put in front of the beast, as permitted on the Sabbath. This is different in the case of a human being in danger. As Tosefta Shabbat 15[16]:11, 13–15 shows, danger to life, and even the suspicion of such danger (*safeq nefashot*) allows for life saving (*piqquaḥ nefesh*), for which the Sabbath regulations *may be set aside.* The rabbis encourage Jews to act accordingly:

> One is concerned because of the suspicion of danger to life, and the zealous one—lo, he is to be praised; and one does not need to ask permission from the court. How so? If a person falls into the sea and cannot resurface, if someone's ship sank in the sea and does not resurface, one may go down and bring him up from there; and one does not need to ask permission from the court. . . . If a man falls into a well and cannot climb back up, they may break down its side and bring him up from there; and they need not ask permission of the court. If an infant went into a house and cannot come out again, then one may break the doors of the house for him, even if they are made of stone, lift him up and get him out from there; and one does not need to ask permission from the court. One may extinguish and stop a fire on the Sabbath, and the zealous—lo, he is to be praised; and one does not need to ask permission from the court. If someone has been bitten by a snake, one may call a doctor from a (different) place and slaughter a hen and cut

off some leeks for him, and one does not need to tithe—(these are) the words of Rabbi (Judah the Prince). R. Shim'on ben El'azar says: It is necessary to tithe. One may prepare hot water for a sick person on the Sabbath, whether to give him to drink or to heal him, and one does not say: Wait with him, in case he might stay alive, but his suspected case sets aside the Sabbath (rules). (t. Šabb. 15[16]:11, 13–15)

As some of these examples show, there was a wide understanding of danger to life (or the suspicion of such danger), including caring for a sick person, for whom hot water may be prepared, if it was intended to have healing effects. Such actions would have involved stirring coals or even lighting a fire, activities otherwise clearly forbidden on the Sabbath (cf. Exod 35:3). It is unclear whether all of these traditions were already in place in the first century CE, but they are certainly relevant for the discussion of the Sabbath pericopes in the Gospels.

Reading the New Testament Texts

Jesus and the Sabbath

One sabbath he was going through the grain fields; and as they made their way his disciples began to pluck heads of grain. The Pharisees said to him, "Look, why are they doing what is not lawful on the Sabbath?" And he said to them, "Have you never read what David did when he and his companions were hungry and in need of food, how he entered the house of God, when Abiathar was high priest, and ate the bread of the Presence, which it is not lawful for any but the priests to eat, and he gave some to his companions?" Then he said to them, "The Sabbath was made for humankind, and not humankind for the Sabbath; so the Son of Man is lord even of the Sabbath." (Mark 2:23–28 NRSVue, modified)

Again he entered the synagogue, and a man was there who had a withered hand. They watched him to see whether he would cure him on the Sabbath, so that they might accuse him. And he said to the man who had the withered hand, "Come forward." Then he said to them, "Is it lawful to do good or to do harm on the Sabbath, to save life or to kill?" But they were silent. He looked around at them with anger; he was grieved at their hardness of heart and said to the man, "Stretch out your hand." He stretched it out, and his hand was restored. (Mark 3:1–5 NRSVue, modified)

> He said to them, "Suppose one of you has only one sheep and it falls into a pit on the Sabbath; will you not lay hold of it and lift it up? How much more valuable is a human being than a sheep! So it is lawful to do good on the Sabbath." (Matt 12:11–12 NRSVue, modified)
>
> Then he said to them, "If one of you has a child or an ox that has fallen into a well, will you not immediately pull it up on a Sabbath day?" (Luke 14:5 NRSVue, modified).

One consistent feature of Jesus's conduct on the Sabbath, according to the Gospels, is his healing of chronically sick persons on this day. In Mark 3:4 Jesus seems to refer to the notion of *piqquaḥ nefesh*, grounding it in the principle of doing good and contrasting it with killing: "Is it lawful to do good or to do harm on the sabbath, to save life (*psychēn sōsai*) or to kill?" When he then heals a man with a withered hand, this probably reflects a wider understanding of "danger to life" than some of his contemporaries would have held, certainly those adhering to the rules of the Damascus Document, and perhaps even the predecessors of the rabbis. There is no evidence that healing was generally permitted in the first century CE, nor that healing by words, as in Jesus's case, was seen as exempt from Sabbath restrictions.[28] One possible explanation for Jesus's wide understanding was his view that "the Sabbath was made (*egeneto*) for humankind, not humankind for the Sabbath" (Mark 2:27), evoking the primordial function of the Sabbath as intended for human benefit. In Matthew and Luke's Sabbath pericopes, Jesus further appeals to the example of animals fallen into water. In Matthew 12:11–12, Jesus asks rhetorically, "Suppose one of you has only one sheep and it falls into a pit on the Sabbath; will you not lay hold of it and lift it up?" Very likely, this practice of small peasants (see the "one" sheep) is more lenient than what we observed in the Tosefta (and certainly in the Damascus Document). Again, Jesus uses this argumentation for justifying his healing of a human being. Similarly, in Luke 14:5, he states that anyone would be prepared to pull out one's "son or ox" fallen into a well on the Sabbath (even though, as seen earlier, some might be more hesitant about the ox). In sum, when we view the gospel texts in their Jewish context, it becomes clear that Jesus does *not* intend to abrogate the Sabbath commandment ("Lord of the Sabbath" in Mark 2:28 does not imply abolishing Sabbath law). Rather, he takes part in a contemporary Jewish discourse about the Sabbath, adopting a lenient stance, with a broad notion of *piqquaḥ nefesh*, restoring chronically sick people to health and enabling them to experience the Sabbath as a good and joyous day.[29]

Synagogue Assemblies

> They went to Capernaum, and when the Sabbath came, he entered the synagogue and taught. (Mark 1:21)

> When he came to Nazareth, where he had been brought up, he went to the synagogue on the Sabbath day, as was his custom. He stood up to read, and the scroll of the prophet Isaiah was given to him. He unrolled the scroll and found the place where it was written: "The Spirit of the Lord is upon me, because he has anointed me to bring good news to the poor. He has sent me to proclaim release to the captives and recovery of sight to the blind, to set free those who are oppressed, to proclaim the year of the Lord's favor." And he rolled up the scroll, gave it back to the attendant, and sat down. The eyes of all in the synagogue were fixed on him. Then he began to say to them, "Today this scripture has been fulfilled in your hearing." (Luke 4:16–21)

> Now he was teaching in one of the synagogues on the Sabbath. And just then there appeared a woman with a spirit that had crippled her for eighteen years. She was bent over and was quite unable to stand up straight. (Luke 13:10–11).

In light of the archaeological, epigraphic, and literary evidence for synagogues in the land of Israel during the Second Temple period, we are better equipped to understand references to synagogue assemblies in the Gospels. To be sure, the redacted Gospels, in particular Mark and Luke, were not written in the land of Israel, and as we shall see, they retain certain peculiarities. Nevertheless, there is no reason to question their accounts in general. When Jesus enters a synagogue on the Sabbath, we find the Judean population of the given locality assembled there including women (Luke 13:11).[30] Jesus appears there to be teaching (Mark 1:21; Luke 13:10) his interpretation of the Torah and Jewish scriptures more widely. While synagogues in the land of Israel might have functioned as *optional* places of prayer (cf. Matt 6:5), they had not yet become the site for the thrice-daily, statutory prayer going on in synagogues, as we find it later. Rather, their main focus was on reading and interpreting the Torah; that Luke 4:16–21 mentions a reading from the Prophets and its interpretation, may reflect a particular custom or concern.[31] A text like Acts 3:1 shows that Judeans in Jerusalem would find it attractive to go to the temple "at the hour of prayer, around the ninth hour," which means that they prayed when the priests brought the afternoon *tamid* offering. That is, different actions took place in different localities when the temple still stood, as we were able to gauge from the evidence of the Theodotus inscription.

FURTHER READING

Adler, Yonatan. *The Origins of Judaism: An Archaeological-Historical Reappraisal*. The Anchor Yale Bible Reference Library. Yale University Press, 2022.

Berlin, Andrea M. "Manifest Identity: From *Ioudaios* to Jew. Household Judaism as Anti-Hellenization in the Late Hasmonean Era." In *Between Cooperation and Hostility: Multiple Identities in Ancient Judaism and the Interaction with Foreign Powers*, ed. Rainer Albertz and Jakob Wöhrle. Journal of Ancient Judaism Supplements 11. Vandenhoeck & Ruprecht, 2013.

Doering, Lutz. "Judaism at the Turn of the Era." In *The Biblical World*. 2nd ed., ed. Katharine J. Dell. Routledge, 2022.

Doering, Lutz. *Schabbat: Sabbathalacha und -praxis im antiken Judentum und Urchristentum*. Texts and Studies in Ancient Judaism 78. Mohr Siebeck, 1999.

Doering, Lutz, and Andrew R. Krause, eds. *Synagogues in the Hellenistic and Roman Periods: New Finds, New Theories, New Methods*. Ioudaioi 11. Vandenhoeck & Ruprecht, 2020.

Doering, Lutz, Jörg Frey, and Laura von Bartenwerffer, eds. *Purity in Ancient Judaism: Texts, Contexts, and Concepts*. Wissenschaftliche Untersuchungen zum Neuen Testament 528. Mohr Siebeck, 2025.

Fine, Steven. *Art and Judaism in the Greco-Roman World: Toward a New Jewish Archaeology*. Cambridge University Press, 2005.

Sanders, Ed P. *Judaism: Practice and Belief, 63 BCE–66 CE*. SCM, 1992.

Notes

1 See Ed P. Sanders, *Paul and Palestinian Judaism: A Comparison of Patterns of Religion* (Fortress, 1977).

2 Sanders, *Paul and Palestinian Judaism*, 422.

3 This is comprehensively developed in Ed P. Sanders, *Judaism: Practice and Belief, 63 BCE–66 CE* (SCM, 1992), 45–314.

4 Ed P. Sanders, "Comparing Judaism and Christianity: An Academic Biography," in *Redefining First-Century Jewish and Christian Identities: Essays in Honor of Ed Parish Sanders*, ed. Fabian E. Udo (University of Notre Dame Press, 2008), 23.

5 For evaluation, see Donald A. Carson, Peter T. O'Brien, and Mark A. Seifrid, eds., *Justification and Variegated Nomism*, vol. 1, *The Complexities of Second Temple Judaism*, Wissenschaftliche Untersuchungen zum Neuen Testament II/140 (Mohr Siebeck, 2001).

6 For an initial outline, see Lutz Doering, "Judaism at the Turn of the Era," in *The Biblical World*, ed. Katharine J. Dell, 2nd ed. (Routledge, 2022), 681–704. I am currently preparing a book-length discussion of Jewish religion in the Greco-Roman period along these lines.

7 It is first attested in the Mishnah; see m. Ḥul. 8:1–4.

8 See Yonatan Adler, *The Origins of Judaism: An Archaeological-Historical Reappraisal*, The Anchor Yale Bible Reference Library (Yale University Press, 2022), 31–49.

9 See Andrea M. Berlin, "Manifest Identity: From *Ioudaios* to Jew. Household Judaism as Anti-Hellenization in the Late Hasmonean Era," in *Between Cooperation and Hostility: Multiple Identities in Ancient Judaism and the Interaction with Foreign Powers*, ed. Rainer Albertz and Jakob Wöhrle, Journal of Ancient Judaism Supplements 11 (Vandenhoeck & Ruprecht, 2013), 170.

10 See Adler, *Origins of Judaism*, 87–112.

11 The evidence has been summarized in Lutz Doering, "Das Bilderverbot im hellenistisch-frührömischen und rabbinischen Judentum," in *Bilder, Heilige und Reliquien: Beiträge zur Christentumsgeschichte und zur Religionsgeschichte*, ed. Mariano Delgado and Volker Leppin (Schwabe; Kohlhammer, 2020).

12 See Steven Fine, *Art and Judaism in the Greco-Roman World: Toward a New Jewish Archaeology* (Cambridge University Press, 2005), 71–73.

13 See Adela Yarbro Collins, *Mark: A Commentary*, Hermeneia (Fortress, 2007), 528.

14 See Adler, *Origins of Judaism*, 66–71. For significant archaeological finds, cf. Yitzhak Magen, *The Stone Vessel Industry in the Second Temple Period: Excavations at Ḥizma and the Jerusalem Temple Mount* (Israel Exploration Society, 2002); Yonatan Adler and Dennis Mizzi, "A Roman-Era Chalk Quarry and Chalk-Vessel Workshop at 'Einot Amitai in the Lower Galilee: A Preliminary Report," *Israel Exploration Journal* 72, no. 1 (2022): 113–32.

15 This is evidenced in a number of sources, for example, Jub. 32:15; 4QMMT B63–64; 4Q270 (4QD^{e}) 2 ii 6–8; Tob 1:6–7 (G^{II}).

16 Rabbinically called "pauper's tithe."

17 James C. VanderKam, *The Book of Jubilees: A Commentary on the Book of Jubilees*, 2 vols., Hermeneia (Fortress, 2018), 37–38.

18 These are discussed in detail in Lutz Doering, *Schabbat: Sabbathalacha und -praxis im antiken Judentum und Urchristentum*, Texts and Studies in Ancient Judaism 78 (Mohr Siebeck, 1999), 71–108.

19 The regulations are discussed in detail in Doering, *Schabbat*, 133–215.

20 See discussion in Doering, *Schabbat*, 224–55.

21 See Philo, *Prob.* 81–83 about the Essenes; probably 4Q251 1–2 5; 4Q264a 1 5; cf. Jesus's visits to, and teaching in, synagogues on the Sabbath, Mark 1:21; 3:1; Luke 4:16–21.

22 *Corpus Inscriptionum Iudaeae/Palaestinae* 9.

23 See Lutz Doering and Andrew R. Krause, "Introduction: Synagogues in the Hellenistic and Roman Periods," in *Synagogues in the Hellenistic and Roman Periods: New Finds, New Theories, New Methods*, ed. Lutz Doering and Andrew R. Krause, Ioudaioi 11 (Vandenhoeck & Ruprecht, 2020).

24 See, however, Donald D. Binder, *Into the Temple Courts: The Place of Synagogues in the Second Temple Period*, The Society of Biblical Literature Dissertation Series 169 (Society of Biblical Literature, 1999).

25 Some texts, such as Jub. 49:17; 11QT^{a} 17:8–9; 4Q265 3 3, wished to exclude women (for discussion, see VanderKam, *Jubilees*, 1184–5) and minors from partaking of the Passover meal, but this was not generally realized.

26 *Corpus Inscriptionum Iudaeae/Palaestinae*, vol. 1, *Jerusalem*, Part 1, *1–704*, inscription no. 9.

27 This might be too little to suggest provenance specifically from the city of Rome.

28 See Lutz Doering, "Much Ado about Nothing? Jesus' Sabbath Healings and their Halakhic Implications Revisited," in *Judaistik und Neutestamentliche Wissenschaft: Standorte—Grenzen—Beziehungen*, ed. Lutz Doering, Hans Günther Waubke, and Florian Wilk, Forschungen zur Religion und Literatur des Alten und Neuen Testaments 226 (Vandenhoeck & Ruprecht, 2008).

29 See my analyses in Doering, *Schabbat*, 408–67; and Lutz Doering, "Sabbath Laws in the New Testament Gospels," in *The New Testament and Rabbinic Literature*, ed. Raimund Bieringer et al., Supplements to the Journal for the Study of Judaism 136 (Brill, 2010).

30 There were no women's galleries in Second-Temple or Roman period synagogues.

31 Cf. also Acts 13:27. In general, clear evidence for the reading from the Prophets (*haftara*), in addition to the Torah, is only found in later periods.

CHAPTER NINETEEN

Living as a Jew in the Diaspora

Ruben A. Bühner
(University of Zurich)

Short History of Ancient Jewish Diaspora

DURING THE TIME of the New Testament, a significant number of Jews—likely the majority—lived outside of their homeland, dispersed across various regions in what is referred to as the diaspora. While concrete numbers are elusive, it is essential to recognize that this phenomenon of diaspora Judaism cannot be devalued as secondary in comparison to Jews residing in the land of Israel. The distinctive living conditions experienced by Jews in the diaspora had a formative influence on Jewish life, necessitating a separate examination of Jewish identity in these regions compared to their counterparts in the motherland.

The diaspora Jewish communities were concentrated in various geographical areas, including Egypt and Rome, as well as places in Asia Minor and Greece. Additionally, there were many Jews residing in Mesopotamia, although our knowledge of them during the time of the New Testament is limited compared to the Mediterranean diaspora. Ancient sources provide scant information about the precise origins of the Jewish diaspora in Asia Minor and Rome. However, Roman historian Valerius Maximus (writing in the first half of the first century CE) speaks as though Jews were already established by the second half of the second century BCE, suggesting that they must have arrived earlier.[1] It is conceivable that Jews initially arrived in Asia Minor during the Seleucid rule and may have subsequently been brought to Rome as slaves following the Roman victories against Antioch III in the early second century BCE.[2] This hypothesis aligns with the account provided by Philo of Alexandria, a first-century CE writer, who reports that most Jews in Rome obtained Roman citizenship after being freed from slavery (*Legat.* 155). Fortunately, the hot and humid climate in Egypt has preserved numerous papyri, providing us with better insights into the beginnings of the Jewish diaspora in that region. Egypt served as a potential place of refuge for Jews from Palestine since at least the Babylonian conquest of Jerusalem in the sixth century BCE as evidence from the Old Testament attests. Aramaic papyri and potsherds found in Elephantine indicate that Jews were already serving in the Egyptian military during this time.[3] Alexander the Great's conquest of Egypt likely triggered larger migration movements to Egypt. The Letter of Aristeas reports that Ptolemy I (305–282 BCE) deported numerous Jews from Judea to Egypt, subjecting them to enslavement.[4] Similar events likely occurred during the subsequent military conflicts between the Seleucids and Ptolemies over Syria in the third century BCE, resulting in the presence of Jews not only in the newly established city of Alexandria but also in various rural areas of Egypt.

What sets the Jewish diaspora in Egypt and Alexandria apart from other Mediterranean regions is the fact that Jews here were more often part of the educated elite. This can be seen not only in the numerous works that have survived from Philo, but also in the fact that the gradual translation of the Hebrew scriptures into Greek, later known as the Septuagint, originated in Egypt. Moreover, there is evidence of a surprising and rare occurrence of political and legal autonomy for Jews living in Egypt during the early Roman period. They had their own legal and political institutions and offices, showcasing not simply their population size and broader influence, but also their strong sense of communal Jewish identity.

In general, Roman authorities did not specifically target Jews, and there is only sporadic evidence of Jewish persecution. Rather, according to the accounts of Josephus (*Ant.* 14; 16; 19), there were various political, religious, and civic privileges accorded to Jewish communities. One fundamental right granted to Jews was the autonomy to make decisions concerning their own affairs (*Ant.* 14.235, 260). Furthermore, they enjoyed the right to gather and have their own spaces for assembly (*Ant.* 14.214–16, 227, 235, 257–61), to observe the Sabbath (*Ant.* 14.226, 242, 245, 258, 263–64.), and to celebrate Jewish festivals (*Ant.* 14.213–16, 257). Additionally, they were allowed to live according to their ancestral traditions and were exempted from military service (*Ant.* 14.223–40). They were also permitted freedom from participating in the cult of emperor worship (*Ant.* 19.280–85).

However, it is worth noting that Jews were sometimes implicated in Roman actions against various foreign cults, primarily to solidify the ruler's image as the protector of ancient Roman traditions (such as during the reign of Tiberius in 19 CE and under Claudius in 49 CE). An exception to this general tolerance occurred in the Alexandrian pogrom against Jews in 38 CE. The Roman governor of Egypt, Flaccus, facing a politically unstable situation, allowed parts of the Greek population to violently attack and kill Jews in Alexandria. The primary motivation for these actions against the Jews was likely the local Greeks' resentment over the loss of their own political and social status following the annexation of Egypt by Octavian in 30 BCE, leading to animosity toward the Jews and their privileges.

Already the actions in 38 CE diminished Jewish autonomy and opportunities for social advancement in Egypt. However, it was the Jewish uprising in Cyrenaica, Egypt, and Cyprus between 115 and 117 CE that marked a crucial turning point in the history of diaspora Jewish communities in these regions. The events unfolded in a series of brutal clashes that led to the demise of the once-thriving Jewish communities in northern Africa and Cyprus. In contrast, Jewish communities in other locations, such as Rome, seem not to have been affected directly by these events. Rather, during the Jewish War in 66–74 CE, a significant number of slaves were captured, which resulted in the influx of more Jews into the Roman capital and other cities.

Synagogues

The Greek word "synagogue" (*synagōgē*; "gathering") originally referred to a group of people assembling together. However, it could probably also be used to describe a Jewish building already in the first century CE (see the Theodotos inscription). In addition to being referred to by the originally nonreligious term "synagogue," these buildings were also called proseuche (*proseuchē*; "[house of] prayer"), particularly in Egypt. Regardless of the terminology employed, synagogues played a significant role as gathering spaces for diverse civil and religious functions. The existence of these Jewish gathering places is attested by numerous literary and archaeological sources, both in Israel and throughout the diaspora. While the destruction of the temple in 70 CE likely contributed to an increase in their numbers, it is evident that synagogues already existed well before that time.

The historical origins of synagogues remain a subject of debate. The earliest known archaeological evidence of synagogues in the diaspora can be found on the Greek island of Delos, with Jewish usage dating back to the first century BCE, as well as a synagogue in Ostia, dating to the mid-first century CE. It is worth noting that synagogue architecture during the period of the rise of the Jesus movement did not adhere to a standardized format. These structures were versatile, serving a variety of purposes including gatherings, prayer meetings, educational activities, as locations for manumission of slaves, and administrative functions. Philo in particular, writing from an Alexandrian perspective and interested in presenting it to his readers as a philosophical school, depicts the synagogue as a space dedicated to the study of scripture and the dissemination of knowledge (*Somn.* 2.127). Some synagogues even included facilities such as kitchens and dining rooms. Thus, synagogues were also utilized as community centers in a broader sense.[5]

Artistic depictions, whether of biblical motifs or other figures, become more prevalent in later synagogues, as seen in the famous synagogue of Dura Europos.

Similarly, Torah shrines, which are characteristic of later synagogue architecture, are rarely found during the period of our interest. An exception to this is the first-century synagogue at Ostia. The scarcity of archaeological evidence in the diaspora compared to the wealth of textual sources regarding Jewish existence during this period, may suggest that many Jewish communities either did not have dedicated synagogue buildings or utilized private homes that cannot be archaeologically identified as synagogues.

The legal categorization of Jewish communities within cities like Rome as *collegia* or as *thiasoi* (i.e., clubs of individuals with shared interests), is a subject of debate among scholars with the prevailing view contending that Jewish synagogues should be classified as such associations according to Roman law. However, there is no definitive evidence to suggest that Jews were officially recognized or self-identified as *collegia* or *thiasoi*.[6] That said, there are certainly common aspects that might bring a Greek or Roman observer to interpret a Jewish community as another form of cult association: initiation rituals, regular meetings for exchange and communal dining, commemoration of a deity, gatherings in private homes or dedicated club buildings, the use of a group-specific name, collective concern for burial, and the maintenance of certain ethical standards. Yet it is also important to note that there are notable distinctions between Jewish communities and other religious associations in the Roman world. This distinction arises from the fact that being Jewish was not determined solely by voluntary affiliation, but rather by one's ethnic background. Despite this distinction, it remains plausible that synagogues or Jewish communities may have been perceived or presented externally as *collegia* or *thiasoi*.

Integration into Majority Societies

Jews in the diaspora certainly differed in many ways among each other. This diversity is also true with respect to their integration into the larger society. Whereas Jews were nowhere totally isolated from their environment, we find different levels of integration and assimilation with respect to various parts of ancient life.[7] Numerous inscriptions and papyri provide evidence of the presence of diaspora Jews in various social strata, including slaves, citizens, and in ethnically mixed marriages. Likewise, evidence proves their involvement in diverse professions. They served, for example, as soldiers, councillors, officials, and merchants.

This inner-Jewish diversity can be exemplified, for instance, with respect to Jewish participation in Greek educational institutions such as the gymnasium (a center for the education and training of young athletes). On the one hand, a critical position is prominent in some literary sources such as 1 Maccabees 1:11–15 and 2 Maccabees 4:7–14 relating to the construction of a Greek gymnasium in

Jerusalem during the reign of Antioch III. On the other hand, we find a multilayered picture regarding the evaluation of the Hellenistic educational institution and Jewish participation in it as attested by Josephus, Philo, and even more so in the extant documentary sources. In *Jewish Antiquities* 12.119–20, Jews in Antioch receive a pecuniary compensation from the gymnasium teachers instead of oil, which presupposes the participation of Jews in the institution. Similarly, Philo portrays Moses as having been instructed in the seven liberal arts (*Mos.* 1.23–24) and mentions Hellenes as Moses's teacher. Even more so, the active participation of at least some diaspora Jewish circles in the Hellenistic educational institutions is indicated by the presence of highly educated Jews such as Philo or the unknown translators of the Septuagint.

Numerous archaeological and epigraphic sources, along with papyri, indicate that Jews participated in Hellenistic gymnasiums. This is evidenced by the presence of Jewish names in lists of ephebes. The most significant archaeological evidence linking a Jewish synagogue to a Hellenistic gymnasium can be found in the synagogue of Sardis. This synagogue was an integral part of a larger complex, which includes a bath and gymnasium. However, it is known to have existed only from the fourth century CE onwards.[8]

Similar forms of Jewish integration into the broader society can also be seen with respect to various athletic competitions, either as athletes or spectators. Notably, the most extensive ancient account of sports can be found in the writings of Philo of Alexandria. Philo provides detailed reports on a range of Hellenistic sports such as boxing, running, and long jump, suggesting that he likely witnessed these events firsthand (cf. *Agr.* 25, 111–27, 121; *Spec.* 1.7, 38; *Deus* 16, 75; *Abr.* 30, 166; *Fug.* 18, 97–98; *Cher.* 14, 80–81; *Somn.* 1.21, 129).

Various degrees of integration can be seen also in relation to the participation of Jews as soldiers in foreign armies. Josephus mentions certain privileges that allowed Jews to be exempted from military service (*Ant.* 14.234–40). However, these privileges likely only applied to Jews with Roman citizenship and Josephus's accounts are limited to specific provinces, predominantly in the 50s BCE. In contrast, Ptolemaic papyri provide evidence of Jews without Roman citizenship serving in auxiliary troops, both in large numbers and across various military roles, including infantry, cavalry, and even as officers or paymasters.[9] Despite the privileges mentioned by Josephus, there is no doubt that some Jews did indeed serve in the Ptolemaic armies in Egypt during this period. Additional support comes from the Letter of Aristeas, which suggests that Ptolemy I (305–282 BCE) forcibly conscripted a significant number of Jewish prisoners of war for military service, numbering around one hundred thousand individuals.[10] Although these figures may be exaggerated, they align with the practice of relying on subjugated peoples to form the Ptolemaic standing army.[11] All these exemplary aspects of ancient social life suggest that Jews in the diaspora integrated into their local societies to varying degrees, rather than living in isolation from non-Jews.

Jewish Halacha in the Diaspora

The majority of Jewish laws and regulations found in the Hebrew Bible pertain specifically to the land of Israel and the Israelites residing there. Many of these rules are not applicable outside of the homeland or without a direct connection to the temple. For example, the regulations concerning tithes and first fruits are explicitly limited to the produce of the land of Israel. Moreover, the Hebrew Bible does not explicitly address guidelines for interaction with non-Israelites in non-Jewish contexts, nor does it provide explicit instructions on implementing related restrictions. Therefore, the application of Jewish halachic thought and practice in the diaspora depends on individual religious interpretation, determining how these rules can be observed or substituted in modified form. As a result, Jewish halachic life in the first century CE in the diaspora had a significantly different character compared to that which could be derived from the Torah for Jews living in the land of Israel. In other words, the majority of Jews during this period had to shape their Jewish life within a predominantly non-Jewish context outside the homeland, thus creating a completely different situation compared to the framework envisioned by most of the Torah's regulations.[12]

While one might be tempted to label diaspora Jews as less halachic oriented in general, there are indications that it is precisely in a foreign country that the awareness of one's own halachic traditions is further sharpened. This can be observed, for instance, in the case of Josephus. In his work *Jewish War*, written shortly after his arrival in Rome, Josephus still exhibits a strong Palestinian influence, giving prominence to the (already destroyed) temple and the cult in Jerusalem. However, in his later work *Jewish Antiquities*, the relevance of the temple diminishes, and the focus shifts toward the Torah and its associated narratives and figures.[13]

Of particular significance in relation to Jewish Halacha in non-Jewish environments are the so-called diaspora novels, Daniel, Judith, Esther, Joseph and Aseneth, and Tobit. Each of these narratives revolves around Jewish figures, mostly young, who live in a foreign country outside the land of Israel and must grapple with the challenges of maintaining their Jewish identity and way of life under adverse conditions. These sources present diverse Jewish perspectives regarding the possibility of interactions with non-Jews, such as forms of table fellowship.

There are texts that express a more stringent viewpoint, advocating for refraining from consuming any food of distinctly non-Jewish origin. For example, the story of Tobit mentions that other Jews abandon the Jewish law, but Tobit himself does not partake in eating the food of the gentiles (Tob 1:10–11). This possibly excludes any food prepared or processed by non-Jews. The book of Judith presents a more nuanced perspective. While table fellowship with non-Jews seems unproblematic, any form of table fellowship involving food and drink produced in a non-Jewish kitchen appears to be contrary to the Torah. Thus, Judith can eat her food alongside her non-Jewish host, but she rejects the food offered to her and instead brings her own (cf. Jdt 10:5; 12:1–2, 19). The narrative of Joseph and Aseneth takes a different approach. While forms of table fellowship are assumed in the narrative without further remarks or specifications, Joseph refuses to eat at the same table as his gentile host, the priest Pentephres, in the latter's house (Jos. Asen. 7:1). However, Joseph has no issue consuming the same food as his gentile host.[14] A different halachic view is evident in the various ancient versions of Esther. While the Masoretic text does not indicate any reservations about eating and drinking together with gentiles, the Septuagint version of the Esther narrative contains numerous shifts suggesting a rejection of participation in eating at the gentile table as a matter of principle (Esth 28c LXX). Daniel presents yet another halachic viewpoint. On the one hand, sitting at the common table with gentiles and accepting food from them seems unproblematic according to the narrative (Dan 1:12–15). On the other hand, Daniel rejects the food originally offered to him without specifying the type of food he rejects (Dan 1:8) and requesting instead a different kind in its place. Josephus, in his *Life* 14, recounts Jewish priests limiting themselves to figs and nuts during their imprisonment in Rome, representing another halachic perspective.

It becomes apparent that there was no single (halachic) Jewish way of life with respect to interaction with non-Jews. Rather, the interaction between Jews and non-Jews in religious and cultural terms was highly variable. Participation in many aspects of social and cultural life in the diaspora was not possible for Jews without developing situational coping strategies to preserve their Jewish identity. It is important to emphasize that these sources, despite their diversity, do not indicate a fundamental arbitrariness or pragmatism on the part of diaspora Jews regarding relevant dietary laws or related regulations. They do not question the fundamental orientation toward traditional norms of Jewish life. On the contrary, the literary texts demonstrate an intensive and serious halachic struggle, even and especially in the diaspora, precisely because of the complex treatment of the subject matter. Regulations that were intended for Jewish life in Israel, and thus in a Jewish majority society, needed to be adapted in various ways for life in different circumstances. Therefore, diversity is not a sign of indifference, but rather an expression of the multilayered living conditions experienced by Jews in the diaspora.

Contact with Jerusalem and the "Mother Land"

Jews in the diaspora only rarely constructed or identified themselves as a diaspora population. In his work, In Flaccum, Philo describes the relationship between Jews in the diaspora and their host countries. While the diaspora Jews consider their host country to be their "father[land]" (*patris*), Jerusalem is seen as their center or mother city (*mētropolis*). Most Jews in the diaspora maintained a self-perception of being part of the Jewish *ethnos*, thereby establishing a connection to Jerusalem and to Jews residing in the homeland. This understanding is exemplified by their practice of paying an annual tithe to the temple in Jerusalem, a tradition that probably originated during Hasmonean times. The collection of this tax was likely carried out by Jewish communities on a city-by-city basis and was prevalent throughout the Mediterranean region. Consequently, significant amounts of money were transferred to Jerusalem, a fact that did not escape the notice of the Roman authorities (cf. Josephus, *Ant.* 14.110; 18.312–13; *J.W.* 7.45). These authorities repeatedly intervened to suppress this practice, likely motivated by economic reasons. However, their attempts were met with fierce and successful protests by the Jewish community.[15] Following the destruction of the temple, the Romans transformed this tithe into a Roman tax collected from Jews for the cult of Jupiter Capitolinus.

In addition to this financial devotion to Jerusalem, diaspora Jews also undertook pilgrimages to the temple. This was particularly evident during festivals, which attracted Jews from all corners of the ancient world (cf. Philo, *Spec.* 1.69; Josephus, *J.W.* 2.280; Acts 2:1–11). The Theodotos inscription from Jerusalem suggests that synagogues provided some kind of infrastructure for such pilgrims. However, it is impossible to ascertain the exact number and frequency of these pilgrimages.

This orientation toward the "motherland" does not exclude the possibility that Jews could also connect their residing place with their inherited traditions and narratives. A vivid example of this can be found in the Sibylline Oracles and their references to the flood in Genesis 5–9. In Sibylline Oracles 1:196–98 and 261–62, the land Phrygia, from which the author presumably originates, is referred to as the land that first emerged from the waters after the flood, and it is said that the mountain of Ararat is located there. This local tradition is also depicted on contemporary coins, which feature images of Noah and the Ark.

The cessation of the diaspora situation and the gathering of the scattered Jews in the land of Israel was not so much an event actively pursued by diaspora Jews, but rather an eschatological hope, the fulfillment of which was expected entirely from God (cf. Isa 11; 27:12–13; Mic 4:6–7; Joel 4:1–2; Zeph 3:9–20; Dan 9:24–27; Pss. Sol. 17:31).

Antagonism and Attraction Toward Jews

The notes provided by Greek authors regarding Jews and their interactions with non-Jews are predominantly brief but carry a consistent and overwhelmingly negative sentiment, as perceived by the authors. For instance, Diodorus references the Greek historian Hecataeus, who claims that Moses had allegedly imparted rules and customs to his people that not only differed completely from those of other nations but also led to an "inhuman and xenophobic way of life."[16] Diodorus further characterizes the Jews as a people who refuse to associate with individuals from other communities and view them as enemies. This includes the accusation that Jews never partake in meals with non-Jews.[17] Josephus also quotes a polemic against Jews, labeling them as "inhuman" (*Ag. Ap.* 1.239; 2.148). In the third century, Cassius Dio provides a general description of Jews as distinct from all others in terms of their dietary practices.[18] These negative assessments of the Jews' reluctance to engage with non-Jews can also be found in strikingly similar accusations made by Latin authors. For instance, Tacitus, in his well-known digression *On the Jews*, asserts that while "the" Jews are always willing to show compassion toward their fellow Jews, they harbor only hatred and enmity toward all other peoples. Tacitus adds that Jews separate themselves during meals, sleep apart, and abstain from relationships with non-Jewish women.[19] Additionally, the Roman satirist Juvenal claims that Jews, following certain commandments of Moses, would even refuse to provide directions to non-Jews when asked.[20]

These and similar characterizations, as presented by Greek and Roman authors, are not only largely negative but also remarkably consistent. However, it is important to recognize that these accounts primarily serve as anti-Jewish polemics and stereotypes, offering only a limited reflection of actual events. All the sources mentioned exhibit a tendency to distort, focusing on caricaturing specific characteristics of certain Jewish groups rather than presenting a comprehensive portrayal of Jewish life. The high degree of agreement in the negative judgments is more likely indicative of a widespread stereotype and gossip. It is possible that the polemical testimonies of these pagan authors may apply to some extent to certain Jews in the diaspora and their behaviors. Nevertheless, as generalized statements, they are historically unreliable.

In contrast, we have ample evidence of non-Jews being attracted to Jewish synagogues, Jewish piety, and various aspects of the Jewish way of life (cf. Josephus, *Ag. Ap.*, 2.282).[21] Such instances of "judaizing" (i.e., the adoption of

Jewish customs without full conversion) should be distinguished from the act of converting to Judaism including formal circumcision. An inscription at Aphrodisias provides evidence that, in the ancient Jewish community, there were distinct groups of members within the synagogue community, including Judaeans, proselytes, and God fearers.[22] There are also records of non-Jews serving as sponsors for synagogues or supporting Jewish writers like Josephus.

There is no evidence to suggest that Jews actively engaged in missionary activities. However, it is documented that some non-Jews, known as proselytes, did formally convert to Judaism through circumcision, leading to conflicts with their families and other members of their original ethnic group. It is plausible that the anti-Jewish polemics from certain Greco-Roman authors originated from their disapproval of proselytism.

TAKING A CLOSER LOOK: SOURCES

Sources from the World of the New Testament

Philo on Jews in Rome

> Most of them [i.e., the Jews in Rome] were Roman citizens, having been emancipated; for, having been brought as captives into Italy, they were manumitted by those who had bought them for slaves, without being forced to abandon the customs of their fathers. (*Leg.* 155)[23]

This section of Philo's account detailing his involvement in the Jewish embassy from Alexandria to Emperor Gaius in Rome provides valuable evidence of the diverse experiences and social dynamics that characterized the Jewish diaspora in the Roman Empire. First, it sheds light on the initial presence of Jews in Rome, indicating that many of them were likely brought as prisoners of war. Additionally, it suggests that by the time of Philo, in the mid-first century CE, a significant number of Jews had already acquired Roman citizenship, implying that at least some members of the Jewish community had achieved a certain level of social advancement.

Of particular interest is Philo's mention that these Jews were not forced to abandon their ancestral customs. It highlights the fact that Jews managed to maintain their religious and cultural practices within the Roman context. Yet this statement should be understood from Philo's own perspective, as he himself was an exceptionally assimilated Jew. Contrary to Philo's portrayal, it is evident that being a slave had a detrimental impact on certain aspects of Jewish life, such as observing the Sabbath, undertaking pilgrimages, or finding suitable food. Consequently, Philo's depiction also highlights the diverse experiences of Jews in the diaspora.

Josephus on the Availability of Food for Jews

> The senate and people have decreed to permit them [the Jews] to assemble together on the days formerly appointed, and to act according to their own laws; and that such a place be set apart for them by the praetors, for the building and inhabiting the same, as they shall esteem fit for that purpose: and that those that take care of the provisions for the city, shall take care that such sorts of food as they esteem fit for their eating, may be imported into the city. (*Ant.* 14.261)

The text is part of a longer passage in which Josephus recounts various privileges granted to Jews in different cities. This passage focuses on the city of Sardis. It reveals both the generally benevolent attitude of Roman authorities and the practical challenges of maintaining a Jewish life in the diaspora. Of particular interest is the Senate's directive to market officials in the city to ensure the availability of food suitable for Jews. In the immediate context of other aspects of state care for the Jewish population and their needs, this likely refers to food specifically required for a Jewish way of life. Thus, it becomes apparent that the availability of such suitable food was not always a given for Jews, even in large cities like Sardis. The option to obtain assistance from local authorities is just one of several methods available to navigate these challenges.

Inscription in the Palaestra at Hypaepa

> ΙΟΥΔΑ[Ι]ΩΝ ΝΕΩΤΕΡΩΝ
>
> of the Jewish *neoteroi*.[24]

An inscription from Hypaepa (second–third century CE), potentially serving as a seating designation in the palaestra of Hypaepa, a town to the south of Sardis, mentions the group *Ioudaiōn neōterōn*, "of the Jewish *neoteroi*." Here, *neoi* probably signifies the specific status of a group of youths after their training as ephebes in the Greek gymnasium. Hence, *Ioudaiōn neōterōn* is presumably the designation of a distinct Jewish collegium of such *neoi*. This designation suggests a potential means of reconciling integration into the broader society with the preservation of one's distinct Jewish identity. Through building their own and ethnically distinct subgroup, the member could probably more easily maintain certain forms of Jewish life but still participate in the Hellenistic gymnasium where the presence of cult statues, common meals in honor of some deities, and other habits which might portray challenges for some Jews, were commonplace.[25]

Reading the New Testament Texts

Paul on the Food Sold at the Market

> Eat whatever is sold in the meat market without raising any question on the ground of conscience, for "the earth and its fullness are the Lord's." If an unbeliever invites you to a meal and you are disposed to go, eat whatever is set before you without raising any question on the ground of conscience. But if someone says to you, "This has been offered in sacrifice," then do not eat it, out of consideration for the one who informed you and for the sake of conscience. (1 Cor 10:25–28)

In his letter to the Corinthians, Paul addresses in a rather long discussion (1 Cor 8–10) the question of whether his addressees should eat food that had been previously used in cultic ceremonies. The issue arises because the non-Jewish Christ followers in Corinth were used to eating food offered to idols before they turned to Christ, and because meat in particular was often used in cultic ceremonies before it was sold in the marketplace.

Probably, Paul's casuistic and detailed response reflects a typical diaspora Jewish perspective on how to navigate life in a non-Jewish environment. He advises a balanced approach, avoiding excessive questioning while also respecting the sensitivities of others. It is evident that Paul's own background as a diaspora Jew from Tarsus influenced his halachic views on Jewish interaction with non-Jews. Therefore, when interpreting Paul's letters, it is important to recognize that he was already familiar with the challenges of coexistence between Jews and non-Jews, allowing him to draw upon existing strategies.

Acts on Synagogues and Godfearers in Asia Minor

> After Paul and Silas had passed through Amphipolis and Apollonia, they came to Thessalonica, where there was a Jewish synagogue. And Paul went in, as was his custom, and on three Sabbath days argued with them from the scriptures, explaining and proving that it was necessary for the Messiah to suffer and to rise from the dead and saying, "This is the Messiah, Jesus whom I am proclaiming to you." Some of them were persuaded and joined Paul and Silas, as did a

> great many of the devout Greeks and not a few of the leading women. (Acts 17:1–4)

The book of Acts assumes here, as in other instances, the presence of local synagogues in various cities of Greece and Asia Minor where Paul could visit and spread the message of the gospel. It is intriguing to note that Paul, as a traveling Jew, was able to identify and participate in these synagogues, suggesting some form of public visibility and a shared sense of Jewish identity that surpassed regional boundaries. Caring for fellow Jews passing through was probably one of the usual activities of a Jewish community.

Notably, the narrative in Acts 17 suggests that the synagogue in Thessaloniki not only had Jewish members but also included God-fearing non-Jews who were attracted to Judaism but had not formally converted or undergone circumcision. Thus, not only did Jews integrate into the majority society, but conversely, they also had an attractive influence on non-Jews.

Acts on the Diaspora Jew Paul

> Paul replied, "I am a Jew from Tarsus in Cilicia, a citizen of an important city; I beg you, let me speak to the people." (Acts 21:39)

According to the Acts, Paul was born in Tarsus into a Jewish family (Acts 9:11; 21:39; 22:3) and maintained connections to the region even after turning to Christ (Acts 9:30; 11:25). Growing up in his hometown of Tarsus, it is likely that Paul was exposed to the Greek language, the Septuagint scriptures, and the non-Jewish culture and environment just as other diaspora Jews were. While little is known about his upbringing, it can be assumed that Paul faced the same everyday challenges of living a Jewish life outside of the homeland, as is typical for the diaspora. These challenges would include acquiring suitable food, navigating the prevalent foreign cults, and coexisting with non-Jews. If we assume that the mention of his occupation as a "tentmaker" (*skēnopoios*) is historically accurate (Acts 18:3; 1 Cor 9:12–18; 1 Thess 2:9) and that he learned this trade in Tarsus, it suggests that he had significant interaction with non-Jews.

If it is true that Paul possessed Tarsian and Roman citizenship from birth (Acts 21:39; 22:25, 28), this further suggests that he came from a Jewish family that had close ties to the majority society. The Pauline Epistles demonstrate a high level of education, a rhetorically trained Koine Greek style, and the use of metaphors and imagery drawn from the Hellenistic world as well as popular philosophical techniques and motifs. This makes it at least possible that in his early years Paul underwent formal education.

FURTHER READING

Barclay, John M. G. *Jews in the Mediterranean Diaspora. From Alexander to Trajan (323 BCE–117 CE)*. University of California Press, 1996.

Bühner, Ruben A. *Paulus im Kontext des Diasporajudentums. Judenchristliche Lebensweise nach den paulinischen Briefen und die Debatten um "Paul within Judaism."* Wissenschaftliche Untersuchungen zum Neuen Testament 511. Mohr Siebeck, 2023.

Gruen, Erich S. *Diaspora. Jews amidst Greeks and Romans*. Harvard University Press, 2022.

Williams, Margaret H. *The Jews among the Greeks & Romans. A Diaspora Sourcebook*. Johns Hopkins University Press, 1998.

Notes

1 The text by Valerius Maximus (1.3.2) has only come down to us in later excerpts from the fourth or fifth century. For a recent discussion see Eugene N. Lane, "Sabazius and the Jews in Valerius Maximus: a Re-examination," in *Journal of Roman Studies* 69 (1979): 35–38.

2 On the spread of Jews in the Mediterranean world, see Erich S. Gruen, *Diaspora: Jews amidst Greeks and Romans* (Harvard University Press 2022), 15–21.

3 See CPJ I 18–32; cf. Josephus, *Ag. Ap.* 2.49–56.

4 See Aristeas 12–13.

5 For a broader discussion of the available evidence, see Anders Runesson, Donald D. Binder, and Birger Olsson, eds., *The Ancient Synagogue from its Origins to 200 C.E.: A Source Book*, Ancient Judaism and Early Christianity 72 (Brill, 2007).

6 The only elusive evidence might be Josephus, *Ant.* 14.215–16.

7 For an overview, see John M. G. Barclay, *Jews in the Mediterranean Diaspora: From Alexander to Trajan (323 BCE–117 CE)* (University of California Press, 1996).

8 For a broader discussion, see Ruben A. Bühner, *Negotiating Jewishness: Paul's Ethnicity between Continuity and Discontinuity* (Baylor University Press, forthcoming 2025), 43–51.

9 CPJ I 18–32.

10 Aristeas 12–13.

11 The survey of Raúl González-Salinero, *Military Service and the Integration of Jews into the Roman Empire*, BRLJ 72 (Brill, 2022), provides a helpful analysis of (often voluntary) Jewish service in the imperial army, especially as a means to attain citizenship.

12 For a broader discussion of the available evidence, see Ruben A. Bühner, *Paulus im Kontext des Diasporajudentums: Judenchristliche Lebensweise nach den paulinischen Briefen und die Debatten um "Paul within Judaism,"* Wissenschaftliche Untersuchungen zum Neuen Testament 511 (Mohr Siebeck, 2023).

13 On this see Michael Tuval, *From Jerusalem Priest to Roman Jew*, Wissenschaftliche Untersuchungen zum Neuen Testament 357 (Mohr Siebeck, 2013).

14 See Ruben A. Bühner, "Interaktion mit dem Fremden: Grenzen und Möglichkeiten der Tischgemeinschaft anhand von Daniel und Ester," *Zeitschrift für die Alttestamentliche Wissenschaft* 133.3 (2021): 329–45; idem, "Zwischen Abgrenzung und Annäherung:

Essens- und Tischgemeinschaft von Juden und Nichtjuden anhand der Diasporanovellen Judith sowie Josef und Asenet," *Zeitschrift für die Neutestamentliche Wissenschaft* 113.2 (2022): 284–302.

15 Cf. Cicero, *Pro Flacco* 66–68; Josephus, *Ant.* 16.28; 16.45.

16 Diodorus Siculus, *Bibliotheca historica.* 40.3.4.

17 Diodorus Siculus, *Bibliotheca historica.* 34.1.1–3.

18 Cassius Dio, *Roman History* 37.17.2.

19 Cassius Dio, *Roman History* 5.5.1–2.

20 Juvenal, *Satires* 14.103–104.

21 See also Arrian, *Discourses* 2.9.19–20.

22 IJO 14.

23 For a helpful collection of important primary sources of Jews in the diaspora, see Margaret H. Williams, ed., *The Jews among the Greeks and Romans: A Diasporan Sourcebook* (Johns Hopkins University Press, 1998).

24 CIJ II, 755.

25 For further on the inscription and its interpretation, see Paul R. Trebilco, *Jewish Communities in Asia Minor*, Society for New Testament Studies Monograph Series 69 (Cambridge University Press, 1991), 177.

CHAPTER TWENTY

Apocalypticism

Jörg Frey
(University of Zurich)

IN MODERN LANGUAGES, *apocalyptic* is used to describe doomsday, the end of the world, and related catastrophes. But this is far too superficial and one-sided. Related texts, including the biblical book of Revelation, offer much more: visions of heavenly scenes and salvation, and hope for the defeat of evil and ultimate justice. Apocalypticism is not only an important tradition in Second Temple Judaism, but also a crucial background for understanding the early Jesus movement and New Testament texts.

Jewish Apocalypticism

Apocalyptic is a research term coined in the early nineteenth century,[1] in reference to the heading and beginning of the book of Revelation (*apokalypsis*), used to describe literature similar to the biblical books of Daniel and Revelation. At the time, only a few such books were known: 4 Ezra, the Sibylline Oracles, and 1 Enoch, freshly discovered by travelers to Ethiopia. Further textual discoveries have greatly increased the number of similar writings. In particular, the Qumran texts have significantly altered our knowledge of the origin, date, and characteristics of early Jewish apocalypticism.[2] Terminologically, three dimensions can be distinguished:

a) The term *apocalypse* describes a genre of literature, including various subgenres (visionary accounts, tours of heaven or hell, "prophetic" accounts of history, etc.). The classical definition was provided by John J. Collins:

> "Apocalypse" is a genre of revelatory literature with a narrative framework, in which revelation is mediated by an otherworldly being to a human recipient, disclosing a transcendent reality which is both temporal, insofar as it envisages eschatological salvation, and spatial, insofar as it involves another, supernatural world.[3]

Apocalypses can also be embedded within other texts (e.g., Mark 13 within a gospel; 1 Thess 4:16–17 within a letter, etc.), just as other genres can be embedded within texts of the genre apocalypse.

b) The adjective *apocalyptic* refers to terms, themes, and motifs closely related to or first developed in apocalypses, but also appearing in the context of other genres and texts (e.g., "kingdom of God" in Jesus's parables, judgment language in Paul's letters, etc.).

c) The noun *apocalypticism* denotes a line of tradition, an intellectual current, or a movement that produces apocalyptic literature or cherishes apocalyptic thought. There is continuity (with fluid boundaries) from Jewish to early Christian apocalypticism. Apocalyptic thought and the production of new apocalypses continue through church history into the modern era, sometimes drawing on "canonized" apocalyptic motifs (from Revelation and other texts), but often creatively combining different motifs and responding to new challenges and crises.[4]

Origins, Function, and Themes

Within the Hebrew Bible, topics such as the resurrection of the dead, the final judgment, or the future of the universe do not appear until relatively late in the postexilic period. The only full-fledged "apocalyptic" book is Daniel (especially chapters 7–12), the last book of the Hebrew Bible, dated to the Maccabean period (ca. 165 BCE). Some other texts resemble the imagery and contain motifs of later apocalypticism, such as Isaiah 24–27, parts of Isaiah 56–66, some visions of Ezekiel, and Zechariah 8–14. Thus, scholars have assumed that apocalypticism is a continuation of biblical prophecy or, according to some, a form of its decline in the postprophetic age. An important piece of evidence for this connection is the transformation of the seventy years in Jeremiah 25:11 into seventy weeks of years (490 years) in Daniel 9:24–27. This means that, in Daniel, the unfulfilled prophecy of Jeremiah is stretched and rephrased into a new kind of "prophecy" of end-time events. Thus, apocalyptic thought was seen as the product of unfulfilled hopes or illusory wishful thinking. This led to a negative view of apocalypticism as a speculative form of religious thought presented in pseudonymous writings that could not be considered truthful by modern readers. In the face of such a negative judgment, Christian theologians often tried to distance Jesus and the apostles from these Jewish traditions and to show that their message was essentially different from the colorful apocalyptic speculations and fictitious predictions of end-time history.[5]

Other scholars have instead suggested that apocalypticism is rooted in wisdom traditions.[6] Major figures in apocalyptic writings, such as Daniel and Ezra, are considered wise men, and central themes of biblical wisdom, such as the correlation between deeds and fate and the contrast between the righteous and the wicked, are adopted in apocalyptic texts.

There was a fundamental shift in apocalyptic studies with the discovery of the Dead Sea Scrolls: Among the Qumran finds were numerous Aramaic manuscripts of portions of the Book of Enoch, some of which had been written in the pre-Maccabean period (early second or third century BCE), predating Daniel.[7] Thus, the rise of apocalypticism had to be dated earlier, before the Maccabean crisis, within the Enochic tradition. Since the earliest sections of 1 Enoch focus on calendrical and cosmological wisdom, the roots of apocalypticism can now be better explained against the background of sapiential traditions from learned scribal circles rather than from disappointed lower-class circles.

These insights fundamentally changed the view of the objectives and themes of apocalypticism. The primary perspective of apocalypticism was not the expectation of the end times but, as the early Enochic tradition demonstrates, the basic idea of an original cosmic order, the experience of a world thoroughly permeated by evil (i.e., violence, disease, demons), and the question of the origin of evil and its ultimate overcoming. The key question posed was whether and how God's cosmic order remained in force, even as the world continued to be under foreign rulers and evil powers. Early apocalyptic thought aims at theodicy—it draws on a tradition of cosmological and calendrical wisdom, develops a view of the world influenced by intermediary figures (angels and demons), and focuses on the spatial dimension of otherworldly places rather than the temporal dimension of end-time history. It also envisages a final judgment and a restitution of the slain or, later, a resurrection of (some, but not all) dead in the question of the final removal of evil.

If the rise of apocalypticism is not a result of the Maccabean crisis, it cannot be characterized as a mere reaction to a political and religious crisis. At the very least, the crisis may be an internal crisis, perceived only by some, caused by the cultural experience of Hellenistic foreign rule and the experience of violence, godlessness, and even apostasy within Israel. With the division between the godly and the ungodly within Israel, the connection between nation and religion was severed: The Israelite history of salvation and the covenant could no longer ensure salvation. Only a new and final intervention of God and the defeat of evil powers could purify creation and bring about salvation. Thus, the apocalyptic perspective is no longer merely Israelite but universal and cosmic. Apocalyptic imagery should not be seen as a pseudoscientific speculation about the future but rather as an effective imaginary world, a counterreality created to help its recipients maintain their trust in the power of God and the validity of his decrees, and to endure the tensions and hardships of their own situation.

Jewish Apocalypticism Between Daniel and the Destruction of the Temple

Obviously, the experiences of the Maccabean period led to an intensification of apocalyptic thought. This can be seen in the composition and rapid dissemination of the book of Daniel, but also in the composition of other "historical" apocalypses from the same period. The Animal Apocalypse (1 En 85–90) and the Apocalypse of the Ten Weeks (1 En 93:1–10; 91:11–17) are of particular note in the growth of the Enochic traditions and in the dissemination of apocalyptic thought in Daniel as well as numerous other texts (e.g., in the Qumran Corpus).[8]

In Daniel 11, we find the clearest example of a "prophetic" description of the history written in retrospect (*vaticinium ex eventu*), a literary device often used in later apocalyptic texts. Up until Dan 11:39, the history of the Ptolemaic and Seleucid rulers is "foretold" from the narrative perspective of Daniel, an exile figure, as the events actually unfolded. However, in 11:40, with the phrase "and in the time of the end" the actual "prophecy" begins, but we know from other sources that history did not unfold as anticipated in these verses. This allows critical scholars to determine the author's point of view and when the text was likely written. The description of the end times continues with the expectation of the final rise of Michael (Dan 12:1), a time of final tribulation for the godly, and the resurrection of many (but not all) of the dead, some to "everlasting life" (*zoē aiōnios*) and others to eternal shame and perdition (Dan 12:2–3). The idea of a double resurrection appears here for the first time, but only in relation to those who have fallen short on earth (the martyrs), and who will now experience a bodily restitution, while the wicked must at least awaken in order to acknowledge that they were wrong and are condemned. Daniel and related texts forward the expectation of the establishment of God's reign (Dan 7). While some texts conceptualize a salvific future in earthly and still nationally Israelite terms (cf. Jub 23), other texts adopt a broader, universal, and cosmic perspective with the final defeat of all evil powers and a multistep sequence of judgments (Apocalypse of the Weeks). The world is so steeped in evil that salvation cannot be achieved through human efforts, such as better education or observance of the law; rather, it can only be obtained through a new, divine intervention. Furthermore, in view of the bodily suffering and martyrdom of the pious, salvation cannot be understood merely as a "transcendent," spiritual, postmortal existence. It is conceived in bodily terms, as a corporeal and thus "real" resurrection "from the dead" or from the grave.

In the late second and first centuries BCE, the ideas of the coming kingdom of God, the resurrection of the dead, and the final judgment became widespread in many circles of Palestinian Judaism, especially in the Pharisaic movement, which accepted not only the Torah (as the Sadducees did) but also the prophets and the writings, including Daniel. New apocalypses were also written, such as the Apocalypse of Moses (the Greek version of the Life of Adam and Eve), which not only provides extended details of Adam and Eve's fall in paradise but also develops a more elaborate image of the devil and introduces the ideas about the final redemption of Adam and his descendants. Another example is the Testament of Moses (Assumption of Moses), which offers an extensive *ex eventu* "prophecy" recounting the history of Israel up to the time of Herod, along with a vivid picture of the horrors of the Last Days.

Later Developments

The destruction of the Jerusalem temple in 70 CE greatly stimulated the change and development of Jewish thought, eventually leading to the rabbinic renewal of Judaism with its emphasis on the Hebrew traditions. The catastrophe of the Jewish War had also demonstrated the dangers of certain forms of eschatological enthusiasm or "revolutionary" zealotry. But even though the rabbis did not include more apocalyptic writings in the developing Hebrew canon, the destruction of the temple stimulated the production of new apocalypses, such as 4 Ezra and 2 Baruch, which reflect and explain the catastrophe without any reference to eschatological adversaries, but with sole reference to God as the Most High. Both apocalypses develop views close to later rabbinic ideas. They also provide numerous parallels to eschatological ideas in the New Testament, in the writings of Paul, and especially in Revelation.

Apocalyptic ideas were transmitted and renewed in numerous new apocalypses (and other genres) throughout the Jewish tradition of late antiquity,[9] and also within the growing Christian tradition (e.g., Apocalypse of Peter, Apocalypse of Paul, Lactantius, etc.).[10] Images of the final salvation and even more so of the judgment and the netherworld continued to fascinate believers. Even if the hope of the imminent return of Christ (as shared by Paul and his contemporaries) had to be considered false, this did not lead to a collapse of apocalyptic expectations but rather to a constant process of reinterpretation and adaptation, partly in response to external and internal crises, but also in interpretation of the canonical apocalypses, Daniel and Revelation.

Apocalypticism in the New Testament

The imaginative world of Jewish apocalypticism is the fundamental source of many concepts and themes of the early Jesus movement, such as the *kingdom of God*, the *Son of Man*, the *resurrection of the dead*, and the *last judgment*. It is also central to the understanding of salvation (*sōtēria*) as deliverance from (eschatological) death and to any notion of postmortal life (eternal life), whether envisioned on a renewed earth, in the new Jerusalem, or in a heavenly realm. Apocalypticism has even be called the "mother of Christian theology"[11], for without the concept of the collective (end-time) resurrection of the dead, which was widespread in Palestinian Judaism from the Maccabean period on, Jesus's disciples would not have been able to interpret the visions and experiences after his death as resurrection. What had happened to the crucified Jesus could now be interpreted as the beginning of the end-time events of the resurrection of the dead. The Easter events showed not only the individual revivification of a single righteous man, but also the beginning of the collective resurrection of the dead—indeed, the beginning of the end times. In the awareness that God's eschatological and salvific acts had begun with Jesus, the mission of the church could grow. Thus, apocalypticism provided the foundational conceptual framework at the very beginning of the church.

John the Baptist and Jesus

John the Baptist was "an eschatological prophet tinged with some apocalyptic motifs."[12] His proclamation of judgment (Matt 3:7–10, 12; Luke 3:7–9, 17) was characterized by the coming wrath, the axe laid to the root of the trees, and by the judgment of fire. For him, the judgment on Israel was imminent, and the appeal to Abraham or the covenant could no longer save. Salvation could only come through the judgment, the purifying fire. The water of his immersion rite was to replace the fire and save those who repented from judgment.

Historically, the earthly Jesus of Nazareth can also be classified as an apocalyptic prophet.[13] His message had some ideas in common with the baptist, especially the expectation of sudden judgment that would cause division within Israel (Luke 17:34–5), with the implication of a reversal of circumstances in favor of the last (Mark 10:31), the poor, the hungry, and the weeping (Luke 6:20–22). Despite the significant differences between Jesus and the baptizer, there is a strong apocalyptic tone in Jesus's central preaching, the proclamation of the kingdom of God. The manifestation of God's kingdom was anticipated in prophetic and apocalyptic texts (Isa 52:7; Ezek 20:33; Isa 24;21–23; Zeph 3:15; Zech 14:9, 16–7; and esp. Dan 2:44; 7:14, 27), in the (Pharisaic) Psalms of Solomon 17:21–46, in Testament of Moses 10:1–10, and in numerous other postbiblical Jewish texts. The specific idea that this kingdom was already present in Jesus's exorcisms and healings was not a reduction but rather an intensification of apocalyptic thought. Jesus's teachings about the Son of Man (cf. Dan 7:13) acting in judgment in the company of the heavenly angels (Luke 12:8), his words about judgment (Luke 10:13–15; 11:31–2), the heavenly banquet (Mark 14:25; Luke 13:28–9), and in the woe on Capernaum (Matt 11:23; Luke 10:15), the reference to Hades as the place of eschatological punishment (cf. 1 En 103:7–8), all draw on apocalyptic ideas and themes.[14] The gospel of salvation could only be formulated on the basis of the assumption that human beings are fundamentally lost and doomed to face the last judgment.

Paul

Paul's letters contain numerous apocalyptic motifs and traces of apocalyptic thinking, with which the apostle was familiar due to his Pharisaic background and education. In 1 Thessalonians 4:16–7 (cf. 1 Cor 15:51–52), he adopts a scenario of Christ's parousia, the resurrection of the dead, and the transformation of the living (see below). In 1 Corinthians 15:23–8, Paul adopts another apocalyptic scenario in which, as in 4 Ezra 7 and Revelations 20–21, the reign of the Messiah, the destruction of all enemies, and eternal salvation ("God all in all") appear in a single sequence. According to 1 Thessalonians 3:13, Christ comes "with his saints that is, his [angels]," which corresponds to 1 Enoch 1:8–9. Paul speaks of the "day of the Lord" (1 Cor 1:8; 5:5; 2 Cor 2:14) or "of Christ" (Phil 1:6, 10), which comes as a thief (1 Thess 5:2), as well as the "day of wrath" (Rom 2:5) and the "revelation of judgment." In 1 Corinthians 3:13, he links the "day" with the fire of judgment.[15]

Most significant is Paul's imminent expectation of the end. In 1 Thessalonians 4:17 and 1 Corinthians 15:52–3, he seems to expect the parousia of Christ during his lifetime. This is linked to an understanding of time that can only be explained by Palestinian-Jewish apocalypticism: the form of this world is passing away (1 Cor 7:31), the church is approaching its "salvation" (Rom 13:11–2), but it is in the "birth pangs of the end time" (Rom 8:18–30). The present age is the end time (1 Cor 10:11), it is compressed (1 Cor 7:29), full of turmoil, but it also confirms the hope of imminent deliverance and salvation. These motifs have close correspondences in apocalyptic texts such as 4 Ezra: The pattern of the two ages (eons, from Greek *aiōnes*) which is fully developed in 4 Ezra and the rabbis is also partly found in Paul: This (evil) eon (Gal 1:4; cf. Rom 12:2; 1 Cor 5:10), in which "rulers" (1 Cor 2:6) or even Satan (2 Cor 4:4) reign, is passing away (1 Cor 7:31); and at another time, the "kingdom of God" (1 Cor 15:50) will come. Parousia and judgment are linked to the apocalyptic hope of the elimination of evil (Rom 16:20), which Paul understands in personal terms as Satan (1 Cor 5:5; 7:5; 2 Cor 2:11; 11:14; 12:7), "the god of this age" (2 Cor 4:4). He knows the idea of Satan as an angel of light and thus the tradition of Satan's primordial fall (2 Cor 11:14). Paul also mentions the experience of a journey to heaven or the rapture to the "third heaven" (2 Cor 12:2), which demonstrated his familiarity with visionary experiences.

Some apocalyptic motifs are also significantly transformed. Paul uses the motif of the "new creation" (Isa 65:17; Jub 4:26; etc.), but he relates it, not to an imminent future, but to the life of faith in the present (2 Cor 5:17; Gal 6:15). Apocalyptic modes of thought are characteristically modified here. Additionally, when Paul speaks about eternal life it is sometimes understood as a future gift (Rom 2:7; 5:21; 6:22–3; Gal 6:8; cf. Dan 12:2), while in other places, the life of believers is seen as a gift already present through faith through the death of Jesus (Gal 2:20; 5:25; Rom 6:8; 8:2, 6, 10; 2 Cor 4:10–12). Yet such modification and even the formulation of a present-oriented eschatology (cf. Rom 5:1; 8:1 etc.) is not a reduction of apocalyptic thinking but an intensification.

Johannine Tradition

This is also true for the Johannine tradition. Here, scholars have often sought to find a marked distance from apocalypticism, especially in its present-oriented eschatology and in the absence of certain eschatological discourses (such as Mark 13). Yet the Johannine epistles give evidence of apocalyptic traditions that were vividly taught in the Johannine communities,[16] and some of these traditions can also be found in the background of the Gospel. For example, 1 John 2:18 and 4:3 state that the addressees have heard "that the Antichrist is coming," and this situation has now come to pass with the appearance of the false teachers (1 John 2:18: "many antichrists"). Here, an apocalyptic teaching about the final appearance of an adversary—an end-time tyrant or a tempter, already couched in Christian terms—was well known in the congregations. Similar expectations can be found in Mark 13, 2 Thessalonians 2:3–13, Revelations 13:1–11, and Didache 16:4, but their background lies in early Jewish traditions about an end-time tyrant developed in Daniel 7–8 with reference to Antiochus IV Epiphanes and then later applied to other political or religious figures, particularly Nero.[17]

A such, the tradition of the Johannine school was shaped by apocalyptic views, including end-time events, a temptation and trial of the believers (1 John 2:19), and the passing of the world (1 John 2:17), which was ruled by "the evil one" (1 John 5:19). Community teaching included instruction about the "day of judgment" (1 John 4:17), the parousia of Christ (1 John 2:28), and the transfiguration of the believers (1 John 3:2). It is only plausible that such traditions were known to the first readers of the Gospel. Mention should also be made of the Johannine use of the term *Son of Man* in John 5:27, where the scene from Daniel 7:13 is alluded to, and of the eschatological scenario of Jesus's return in John 14:2–3 (cf. 16:16–19; 21:22–3). Traditions about the resurrection of the dead and the eschatological judgment were well known, although the evangelist relates both to the presence of Jesus and of his word, since Jesus is the eschatological agent who has been given the authority to give life and to judge (John 5:21–27). This, however, is not a critique of apocalypticism, as modern scholarship suggests,[18] but rather an intensification with a focus on the present authority of Jesus.

Revelation

The most important apocalyptic text in the New Testament is, of course, Revelation. Wrapped in an epistolary frame, the book is a dense visionary account in which the seer is led around by an angel (cf. Rev 4:1). Thus, the book fits well with John Collins's definition of the apocalyptic genre cited above. But in its adoption of prophetic texts from Zechariah, Ezekiel, Daniel, and others, Revelation could also be considered a prophetic book, the sum total of biblical prophecy. Thus, its genre is as unprecedented as its opening term *apokalypsis*.

Structurally, Revelation is strongly shaped by a series of seven (letters, seals, trumpets, bowls), which show the influence of the heptadic chronological structuring, for example, in the Apocalypse of the Weeks or Jubilees. It adopts the medium of a visionary revelation and the narrative of a cosmic journey as well as the motifs of the plagues of the exodus period, but it is linked with later prophetic traditions on the "day of the Lord."[19] In Revelation 13, the four beasts of Daniel 7:1–8 are united into one beast with seven heads and ten horns, symbolic of the Roman Empire. In Revelation 17, Rome is represented as a woman, the goddess Roma, called the harlot Babylon, which, with its economy and culture, seduces all nations into idolatrous worship. But the final expectation is that this Babylon (Rome) must fall, so that the kingdom of God can be revealed. The final chapters, Revelation 20–22, are patterned after the end of the book of Ezekiel (36–48), featuring the reign of the Messiah, the battles against Gog and Magog, and the vision of the new Jerusalem, a heavenly city of gigantic proportions, not just a square (as in Ezekiel 40–48) but a cube, 2000 km in length, width, and height. Here, Revelation expands older images into a surreal and utopian, yet impressionistic, form.

Revelation has often been considered a reaction to an external crisis or persecution, under the emperor Domitian. However, as there is no evidence of a systematic persecution during that time, it is likely that Revelation is responding to a "perceived crisis,"[20] instead of an actual external one. Rather than being a book of comfort, it serves as an exhortation to remain steadfast and pure. With its strong anti-Roman stance and heightened sensitivity to the idolatrous nature of the Roman society in Roman Asia Minor, Revelation stands as the most critical voice in the Bible against human rulers and earthly powers. It is a political book, as it refuses to separate earthly rule and the kingdom of God (cf. John

18:36) or to adapt to the surrounding society; instead, it calls for distance from the majority society, strongly demanding earthly obedience and advocating for an earthly and realistic understanding of salvation.[21]

The visionary account of Revelation gives the impression that a coherent sequence of external events is prophesized here. But this would be a misinterpretation that ignores the literary composition and structure of the book, which is not a simple realistic visionary account.[22] Various traditional images are combined and modified in an act of literary art, and all attempts to relate the sequence to any period of church history or to construct an eschatological timetable are bound to fail. The main idea is that when Babylon (Rome) falls, the eternal kingdom will arrive. With its expectation of an earthly millennium, Revelation has influenced both church and political history, and with its final image of the new Jerusalem (Rev 21:1–22:5) it has shaped the ultimate image of Christian hope.

TAKING A CLOSER LOOK: SOURCES

Sources from the World of the New Testament

The Vision of God on a Heavenly Throne

1 Enoch 14:8–25, presents an impressive vision of God on a heavenly throne, described in colorful images, expressing fear and splendor. This text influenced not only Reveleation 4–5 but also any further throne visions and throne mysticism:

> And in (the) vision it was shown to me thus: Behold, clouds in the vision were summoning me, and mists were crying out to me; and shooting stars and lightning flashes were hastening me and speeding me along; and winds in my vision made me fly up and lifted me upward and brought me to heaven. And I went in until I drew near to a wall built of hailstones; and tongues of fire were encircling them all around; and they began to frighten me. And I went into the tongues of fire, and I drew near to a great house built of hail stones; and the walls of the house were like stone slabs, and they were all of snow, and the floor was of snow. And the ceiling was like shooting stars and lightning flashes; and among them were fiery cherubim, and their heaven was water; and a flaming fire encircled all their walls, and the doors blazed with fire. And I went into that house—a hot as fire and cold as snow; and no delights of life was in it. Fear enveloped me, and trembling seized me; and I was quaking and trembling, and I fell upon my face. And I saw

> in my vision, and behold, another open door before me: and a house greater than the former one; and it was all built of tongues of fire. And all of it so excelled in glory and splendor and majesty that I am unable to describe for you its glory and majesty. Its floor was of fire; and its upper part was flashes of lightning and shooting stars; and its ceiling was a flaming fire. And I was looking, and I saw a lofty throne; and its appearance was like ice; and its wheels were like the shining sun; and its <guardians> were cherubim; and from beneath the throne issued streams of flaming fire. And I was unable to see. And the Great Glory sat upon it; his raiment was like the appearance of the sun and whiter than much snow. And no angel could enter into this house and behold his face because of the splendor and glory; and no flesh could behold him. Flaming fire encircled him, and a great fire stood by him, and none of those about him approached him. Ten thousand times ten thousand stood before him; but he needed no counselor; his every word was deed; and the holy ones of the watchers who approached him did not depart by night, nor <by day> did they leave him. And I had been until now on my face, prostrate and trembling. And the Lord called me with his mouth and said to me, "Come here, Enoch, and hear my word(s)." And one of the holy ones came to me and raised me up and stood me (on my feet) and brought me up to the door. But I had my face bowed down. (1 Enoch 14:8–25 [Nickelsburg])[23]

The five-part corpus of 1 Enoch is a rich text for understanding the apocalyptic tradition. It is fully preserved only in the Ethiopic canon, but also in a fragmentary Greek version and now in Aramaic fragments from Qumran. Notably, 1 Enoch 1:8–9 is quoted in the NT as a prophet in Jude 14. 1 Enoch developed during the fourth and third centuries BCE (astronomical books, 1 En. 72–82; then the Book of the Watchers, 1 En. 1–36) to the late first century BCE (Book of Parables, 1 En. 37–71). In the Book of the Watchers, we find the myth of the fall of the Watchers (1 En. 6–12), which offers the earliest Jewish explanation for the origins of evil. It also contains the first testimony of the concept of a final judgment and the preservation of sinners for judgment (1 En. 10:12–14), as well as Enoch's throne vision (1 En. 14), and his journeys to the places of punishment and salvation (1 En. 17–36). Most important is the Book of Parables, where we find a heavenly figure called the "Righteous One," "Elect One," "Anointed One" (Messiah!), or "Son of Man." Other texts of the Enochic tradition that did not become part of 1 Enoch, include the Book of the Giants (attested in Aramaic in Qumran), Jubilees (found in Hebrew in Qumran), and Slavonic or 2 Enoch, (composed in Greek but preserved only in Slavonic), which provides a lengthy account of Enoch's ascent to the seventh heaven. Later traditions in Hebrew

(3 Enoch, Sefer Hekalot; fourth–sixth century CE) are examples of Jewish mysticism, reflecting the heavenly temple and chariot.

The Birth of the New Age

> For behold, the time will come, when the signs which I have foretold to you will come to pass, that the city which now is not seen shall appear, and the land which now is hidden shall be disclosed. And every one who has been delivered from the evils that I have foretold shall see my wonders. For my son the Messiah shall be revealed with those who are with him, and those who remain shall rejoice four hundred years. And after these years my son the Messiah shall die, and all who draw human breath. And the world shall be turned back to primeval silence for seven days, as it was at the first beginnings; so that no one shall be left. And after seven days the world, which is not yet awake, shall be roused, and that which is corruptible shall perish. And the earth shall give up those who are asleep in it, and the dust those who dwell silently in it; and the chambers shall give up the souls which have been committed to them. And the Most High shall be revealed upon the seat of judgment, and compassion shall pass away, and patience shall be withdrawn; but only judgment shall remain, truth shall stand, and faithfulness shall grow strong. And recompense shall follow, and the reward shall be manifested; righteous deeds shall awake, and unrighteous deeds shall not sleep. Then the pit of torment shall appear, and opposite it shall be the place of rest; and the furnace of hell shall be disclosed, and opposite it the paradise of delight. (4 Ezra 7:26–44 RSV)

A characteristic example of later Jewish apocalypticism is 4 Ezra, probably written in Hebrew around 100 CE, but preserved in Latin in the Vulgate tradition (as 2 Esdras or 4 Esdras). In the manuscript tradition, the Jewish book of 4 Ezra is 4 Ezra 3–14, while chapters 15–16 are the later Christian text now called 5 Ezra, with chapters 1–2 assigned as 6 Ezra, an even later Christian text. The book responds to the destruction of the temple in 70 CE by the Romans. It contains a dialogue between Ezra and the archangel Uriel, structured in seven visions. Ezra laments and questions the angel and receives explanations. While the first three visions reflect the destruction of the temple, visions four to seven provide eschatological instructions. In the fourth vision, Zion is depicted as a woman in mourning and lamentation, but is then transformed into a glorious city, the new Jerusalem (4 Ezra 10:25–27; cf. Rev 21:1–8). In 4 Ezra 7:26–26 we find a description of the end-time events, including a messianic kingdom of four hundred years (cf. Rev 20:1–6), the end of the old age, the rise of the new age, and finally the revelation of the final judgment with the resurrection of the dead.

Reading the New Testament Texts

Paul's Comforting Adoption of an Apocalyptic Scenario

> But we do not want you to be uninformed, brothers and sisters, about those who have died, so that you may not grieve as others do who have no hope. For since we believe that Jesus died and rose again, even so, through Jesus, God will bring with him those who have died. For this we declare to you by the word of the Lord, that we who are alive, who are left until the coming of the Lord, will by no means precede those who have died. For the Lord himself, with a cry of command, with the archangel's call and with the sound of God's trumpet, will descend from heaven, and the dead in Christ will rise first. Then we who are alive, who are left, will be caught up in the clouds together with them to meet the Lord in the air, and so we will be with the Lord forever. Therefore encourage one another with these words. (1 Thess 4:13–18)

In his earliest surviving letter, Paul responds to the deaths of some believers in Christ in Thessalonica, which troubled the church. Perhaps they feared that the dead would not participate in Christ's coming, his parousia. It is unclear whether Paul had not taught about the resurrection of the dead or if the believers simply had forgotten his teachings, but Paul writes the letter to comfort them and give them hope (v. 13; 18). He affirms the hope of the resurrection of the dead as a consequence of the resurrection of Jesus (v. 14) and quotes as a "word of the Lord" (v. 15) an apocalyptic scenario with colorful motifs (the descent of the Lord, the voice, the archangel, the trumpet) and a sequence of events (the resurrection of the dead, the rapture of the living, including Paul himself, so that both will meet the Lord). But the entire phrase focuses on the idea that: "we will always be with the Lord." Thus, Paul is not emphasizing the details of the dramatic scenario but highlighting the final state of unquestioned fellowship with Christ. The aim is not to speculate or teach about the details of the rapture or the details of spaces in the air, but to comfort the addressees. The apocalyptic elements are functionalized here, with the details becoming less important as the emphasis shifts elsewhere.

The Last Image of the Bible

The Appearance of the New Jerusalem

> Then I saw a new heaven and a new earth, for the first heaven and the first earth had passed away, and the sea was no more. And I saw the holy city, the new Jerusalem, coming down out of heaven from God, prepared as a bride adorned for her husband. And I heard a loud voice from the throne saying, "See, the home of God is among mortals. He will dwell

> with them; they will be his peoples, and God himself will be with them and be their God; he will wipe every tear from their eyes. Death will be no more; mourning and crying and pain will be no more, for the first things have passed away." And the one who was seated on the throne said, "See, I am making all things new." Also, he said, "Write this, for these words are trustworthy and true." (Rev 21:1–5)

The final and most impressive image in the Bible is the descent of the new Jerusalem in Revelation 21, presented first in a vision (21:1–5[–8]), and then in a cosmic journey in which the seer is guided by an angel and shown the heavenly city's architecture, colors, and dimensions, drawn from Ezekiel 40–48 and other texts. As in 4 Ezra 10, the new Jerusalem is presented as a female figure, the "bride" of Christ (v. 2). As in 4 Ezra 7 (see above), there is a gap between the old and the new eon: The first world has passed away (v. 1) before the new world appears. It is not a restoration, but a "new" world. As in 1 Enoch 14 and Revelation 4, God is seated on a high throne from which he speaks. The final perspective is God's dwelling among people, drawing on elements of biblical and postbiblical shekinah theology,[24] which is here linked with a form of the "covenant formula" (v. 3). The promise is that God will remove all suffering and tears and create universal shalom ("all things new"). This is an impressive combination of motifs from biblical prophecy but also from postbiblical traditions. Rather than being a realistic prophecy of some future event, the scene presents a vivid counterreality that has inspired generations to maintain hope in the midst of tribulation. Although this image does not teach doctrines or represent future historical events, its truth may lie in the fact that its vivid imagery has proven effective in inspiring and moving recipients through the ages.

FURTHER READING

Collins, John J. *The Apocalyptic Imagination*. 2nd ed. Eerdmans, 1998.

Collins, John. J., ed. *The Oxford Handbook of Apocalyptic Literature*. Oxford University Press, 2014.

Frey, Jörg. "The Qumran Discoveries and the Understanding of Apocalypticism." In *Qumran, Early Judaism, and New Testament Studies*, ed. Jacob N Cerone. Wissenschaftliche Untersuchungen zum Neuen Testament 424. Mohr Siebeck, 2019.

Reddish, Mitchell G., ed. *Apocalyptic Literature: A Reader*. Hendricksen, 1990.

Tilly, Michael. *Apokalyptik*. Uni-Taschenbücher. Francke, 2012.

Notes

1 The first scholar to use it widely was Friedrich Lücke in his introduction to Revelation: Friedrich Lücke, *Versuch einer vollständigen Einleitung in die Offenbarung Johannis*

und in die gesammte apokalyptische Litteratur (Weber, 1832). On the history of scholarship, see Johann M. Schmidt, *Die jüdische Apokalyptik. Die Geschichte ihrer Erforschung von den Anfängen bis zu den Textfunden von Qumran* (Neukirchener, 1969).

2 See Jörg Frey, "The Qumran Discoveries and the Understanding of Apocalypticism," in *Qumran, Early Judaism, and New Testament Interpretation*. Kleine Schriften 3, ed. Jacob N. Cerone, Wissenschaftliche Untersuchungen zum Neuen Testament 407 (Mohr Siebeck 2019), 195–205.

3 John J. Collins, "Introduction: Towards the Morphology of a Genre," in *Apocalypse: The Morphology of a Genre*, ed. John J. Collins, Semeia 14 (Scholars, 1979), 9.

4 See the *Encyclopedia of Apocalypticism*, ed. Bernard McGinn, John J. Collins, and Stephen J. Stein, 3 vols. (Continuum, 2000).

5 Among the scholars who held a very negative view of apocalypticism are the OT scholar Julius Wellhausen and also the most influential NT scholar of the 20th century, Rudolf Bultmann. Cf. Werner Zager, *Begriff und Wertung der Apokalyptik in der neutestamentlichen Forschung*, Europäische Hochschulschriften 358 (Lang, 1989), and Jörg Frey, "Jesus und die Apokalyptik," in *Von Jesus zur neutestamentlichen Theologie. Kleine Schriften 2*, ed. Benjamin Schliesser, Wissenschaftliche Untersuchungen zum Neuen Testament 368 (Mohr Siebeck, 2016), https://www.mohrsiebeck.com/buch/von-jesus-zur-neutestamentlichen-theologie-9783161550164/.

6 See Gerhard von Rad, *Theologie des Alten Testaments*, 2 vols. (Kaiser, 1957–67), 2:316–23.

7 See 4Q208; 4Q201; see also J. T. Milik, *The Books of Enoch: The Aramaic Fragments from Qumran* (Oxford University Press, 1976), 7, 140, and 273.

8 Apart from numerous manuscripts of Enoch and also Daniel, the Qumran Corpus produced a large number of previously unknown apocalyptic texts—for example, a description of the last war between the Sons of Darkness under Belial (a "devilish" figure) and the Sons of Light led by Michael (the War Scroll, 1QM), and a scripture-oriented Midrash about Melchizedek as a heavenly, angelic redeemer figure proclaiming a new year of God's redemption (11QMelch) in relation to Isa 61. The congregation saw itself actually living in the "end of the days," the end-time period. There are dualistic reflections about the struggle between good and evil in history (in the Treatise on the Two Spirits 1QS III 13–IV 26 and the War Scroll, 1QM), various concepts of eschatological opponents and also various concepts of royal, prophetic, priestly, or even angelic Messianic figures.

9 On later Jewish apocalypses, see Gerbern S. Oegema, *Zwischen Hoffnung und Gericht. Untersuchungen zur Rezeption der Apokalyptik im frühen Christentum und Judentum*, Wissenschaftliche Monographien zum Alten und Neuen Testament 82 (Neukirchener, 1999).

10 Cf. Jörg Frey, "Apocalypses in the Second Century," in *Second Century Christianity: A Comprehensive Guide to its Sources*, ed. Scott Harrower and Michael F. Bird (Baylor University Press, forthcoming).

11 Ernst Käsemann, "The Beginnings of Christian Theology," in *New Testament Questions for Today*, trans. W. J. Montague (SCM, 1969), 102. Originally published as "Die Anfänge christlicher Theologie," *ZTK* 57 (1960): 162–85.

12 John P. Meier, *A Marginal Jew. Rethinking the Historical Jesus*, vol. 2 (Yale University Press, 1994), 31.

13 Cecilia Wassen, *Jesus the Apocalyptic Prophet* (Bloomsbury, 2021); Dale C. Allison, *Jesus of Nazareth, Milleniarian Prophet* (Fortress, 1998).

14 See Frey, "Jesus und die Apokalyptik,"147–8.

15 See Jörg Frey, "Heil. Neutestamentliche Perspektiven," in *Von Jesus zur neutestamentlichen Theologie: Kleine Schriften 2*, ed. Benjamin Schliesser, Wissenschaftliche Untersuchungen zum Neuen Testament 386 (Mohr Siebeck, 2016), 550–68, https://www.mohrsiebeck.com/buch/von-jesus-zur-neutestamentlichen-theologie-9783161550164/.

16 Jörg Frey, "Eschatology in the Johannine Circle," in *Die Herrlichkeit des Gekreuzigten. Studien zu den johanneischen Schriften 1*, ed. Juliane Schlegel, Wissenschaftliche Untersuchungen zum Neuen Testament 307 (Mohr Siebeck, 2013), https://www.mohrsiebeck.com/buch/die-herrlichkeit-des-gekreuzigten-9783161527968/.

17 See Bert Jan Lietaert-Peerbolte, *The Antecedents of the Antichrist* (Brill, 1993); Gregory C. Jenks, *The Origins an Early Development of the Antichrist Myth*, Beihefte zur Zeitschrift für die neutestamentliche Wissenschaft 59 (de Gruyter, 1991).

18 As argued, for example, in the Bultmann's school.

19 See Michael Sommer, *Der Tag der Plagen*, Wissenschaftliche Untersuchungen zum Neuen Testament II/387 (Mohr Siebeck, 2015).

20 Thus, Adela Yarbro Collins, *Crisis and Catharsis: The Power of the Apocalypse* (Fortress, 1984), 84–110.

21 This was the reason why it was criticized by many later interpreters, starting with Origen and the Platonists.

22 Cf. Jörg Frey, "Was erwartet die Johannesapokalypse: Zur Eschatologie des letzten Buchs der Bibel," in *Die Johannesapokalypse. Kontexte, Konzepte, Wirkungen*, ed. Jörg Frey, James A. Kelhoffer, and Franz Tóth, Wissenschaftliche Untersuchungen zum Neuen Testament 287 (Mohr Siebeck, 2012).

23 George W. E. Nickelsburg, *1 Enoch 1*, Hermeneia (Fortress, 2001), 257, 267. Cf. Jörg Frey, " 'Mystical' Traditions in an Apocalyptic Text? The Throne Vision of Revelation 4 within the Context of Enochic and Merkavah Texts," in *Apocalypticism and Mysticism in Ancient Judaism and Early Christianity*, ed. John J. Collins, Pieter G. R. de Villiers, and Adela Yarbro Collins, Ekstasis 7 (de Gruyter, 2018) 111–20.

24 The shekinah is the tradition about God's dwelling in the sanctuary, that is adopted in later times (a) in sapiential forms (Sir 24; cf. John 1:14) and (b) in eschatological expectations; cf. Zech 2:14–15; Joel 4:17; Jub 1:17 (based on Ezek 3:26–28) and 11QTemp 29:7–8a. See Jörg Frey, "God's Dwelling on Earth: '*Shekhina*-Theology' in Revelation 21 and in the Gospel of John," in *John's Gospel and Intimations of Apocalyptic*, ed. Christopher Rowland and Catrin Williams (Bloomsbury T&T Clark, 2013).

CHAPTER TWENTY-ONE

Early Jewish Messianism

Thomas R. Hatina
(Trinity Western University)

THE MOST DISTINGUISHING feature of the Christian religion is its claim and belief that Jesus of Nazareth was and is the Messiah, or Christ, who was sent by God to save the world. The term *messiah*, which refers to an anointed person in Jewish contexts, is a Hebrew transliteration of *māšîaḥ* and an Aramaic transliteration of *mešîḥā*. In antiquity, the term was translated as *christos* in the Greek and *christus* in the Latin. While it is uncertain if Jesus himself ever ascribed the title and role to himself or if it was ascribed to him during his lifetime, it is certain that all of the earliest groups that followed Jesus after his death, as represented in the NT writings, ascribed the title to him despite their varied interpretations.[1] The origin of this ascription has generated much discussion and continues to remain unresolved because the portrayals of Jesus as Messiah in the earliest Christian writings differ from Jewish conceptions of messiah found in the early Jewish writings. During his ministry, Jesus does not accomplish the eschatological tasks that were commonly associated with the coming of messiah. Nevertheless, for the early Jesus followers the title was predominantly connected with Jesus's death and resurrection, which were central in shaping new ways to think about the restoration of the world. The term *christos* appears approximately 350 times in the NT, usually with reference to Jesus. In ascribing the title to Jesus, the earliest followers, who were predominantly Jewish, faced an unprecedented problem. They had to make sense of a crucified messiah at the hands of Israel's gentile occupiers, which differed drastically from popular Jewish expectations of a messiah who would be victorious over Rome and its collaborators by putting an end to the present age and bringing about a new one. Expressions of the disconnect appear in the NT (and beyond) on occasion (Mark 12:35; 15:32; John 4:25; Acts 9:22; 18:5, 28), but the most explicit summary is Paul's contention that a crucified Christ is a "stumbling block for the Jews" (1 Cor 1:23). In reinventing and reinterpreting the meaning of messiah, often in relation to other titles (Lord, Son of God, Son of Man), the earliest Jesus followers attempted to justify their claim by appropriating the Jewish scriptures and traditions, which provided the perception of fulfilled expectations and continuity with Israel's past.[2] A study of early Jewish messianic conceptions not only brings the uniqueness of the early Christian conceptions into sharp relief, but it also (1) unveils the sociopolitical conditions in which earliest Christianity emerged; and (2) provides insights into how a new religious movement might begin. The focus of this chapter is on the Jewish conceptions of messiah(s) during the latter part of the Second Temple period which extends roughly from 200 BCE to 70 CE.

Religious and Historical Foundations

For much of Israelite and Jewish history, the conception of messiah did not figure prominently in its ethnic or national identity or its eschatological hopes. Yet it is foundational for understanding conceptions of messiah in early Judaism and Christianity since it contains implicit and explicit references to the anointing of leaders who affected the political and religious life of Israel. According to OT references, anointing was usually conferred by means of a ritual in which oil was smeared on the recipient. Most commonly, language of anointing was applied to kings (e.g., Saul, David, Solomon, Jehu, Joash, Jehoahaz, Cyrus) who were viewed as divinely appointed defenders, overseers, and liberators of Israel, yet at the same time represented God's reign over the world and other deities. In some cases, the "spirit of the Lord" was imparted to the anointed for what appears to be the duration of the reign as conveyance of blessing, authority, and the word of God. Kings, however, were not the only anointed figures. On occasion, anointing was extended to priests (e.g., Aaron, Zadok) and prophets (Elisha) who were chosen successors of divinely sanctioned offices. Unlike the broader use of the verb for anointing, the noun *māšîaḥ* (anointed one) was limited to persons in the service of Israel and its relationship to God.[3]

Since many of the NT writings quote or allude to the Jewish scriptures to demonstrate that Jesus fulfilled ancient prophecies and typologically embodied prominent figures and events from Israel's past, it can give the impression of messianic continuity. The Jewish scriptures, however, do not contain a consistent, long-standing prediction of a royal messiah.[4] Instead, they contain sporadic and situational prophecies of rulers who are often connected with the Davidic dynasty. The usual role of the anticipated divine agent was to deliver Israel from her enemies and usher in a time of national peace, justice, and righteousness as a demonstration of Yahweh's superiority over the other gods.

Conditions in the Late Second Temple Period

Similar uses of messianic terminology appear in the nonbiblical Jewish writings from the latter part of the Second Temple period. It is during this time that specific messianic conceptions begin to emerge, though isolating their origin has been difficult. Some scholars argue that the hope of a messianic deliverer may have originated during the Maccabean wars against the Seleucids, as can be implied by texts like Daniel 7:13–14 that speak of the coming of the Son of Man who will liberate Israel. Others trace the origins to the latter years of the Hasmonean rule when the royal claim of Alexander Jannaeus was dashed by the Romans.[5] On a broader societal level, the proclivity toward anointed agents during the latter part of the Second Temple period, particularly after the Roman subjugation of Palestine (63 BCE), cannot be reduced to ideological reasons. It is better correlated with political and economic factors. Internal political corruption was generally associated with the elite class, and more particularly with the Jewish temple establishment that collaborated with the Roman administration. The Jewish elite class contributed to the problem as it was impugned for both its levels of taxation, which created harsh economic conditions, and its enforcement of externally imposed social and legal conditions. Grass root reactions occasionally generated social fervor that included anticipations of a messianic agent(s) who would liberate the righteous of Israel (self-proclaimed practitioners of select laws) from both internal corruption and external oppression. Unfortunately, historians have very little information about the breadth of these anticipations.

The hope of divine justice and restoration is found in the literature of both apocalyptic and nonapocalyptic groups. While these groups differed on the process of how history will unfold, sometimes not even including a divine agent, but God acting alone (Sir 36:1–17), both had a common expectation: that history will change radically and permanently in Israel's favor.[6] Numerous figures are mentioned in the sources from this period who allegedly will contribute to the unfolding change in history that will result in the end of the present age and the beginning of the new age.

As is the case in the earliest Jesus movements, conceptions of messianic figures in early Judaism were influenced by the Jewish scriptures which provided at least three key antecedents within the cultural memory that could explain the unfolding of difficult situations and their remedy. First, they provided the prophetic material which allowed for multiple fulfillment options that could address each new circumstance. Second, the scriptures contained a reservoir of titles like "Chosen One" (Ps 89:4; Isa 42:1), "my [God's] son" (Ps 2:7), and "prince" (Ezek 34:24; Dan 9:25–26), that were reapplied and newly anticipated in a related sense and were capable of being used messianically (1 En. 37–71). Third, they provided the opportunity for early Jewish writers to typologically link notable events and figures from Israel's remembered past (particularly Moses and David) with contemporary or imminently expected successors. In antiquity, cultural memory provided a past that was not very far away and could be utilized anytime that the present situation required explanation. Since the future was already embedded in narrations about the messiah, the past was always capable of being recycled.[7]

Messianic Identities and Activities

Messianic identity and activity during the latter part of the Second Temple period was far from being uniform or ubiquitous. It must be reiterated that not all Jewish people at this time were expecting a messiah. Some scholars even claim that most were not. On occasion, when social conditions deteriorated, messianic hopes escalated. While the definite title "the messiah" is sparse in much of the Second Temple literature, it does appear with some regularity during the Roman period. Most of the references to a messianic agent(s) who assists God in the final restoration of the present age are diverse, using titles like *Chosen One*, *Son of David*, *Son of Man*, or *Righteous Branch*. Where the term *messiah* does appear, it is predominantly used in relation to three kinds of figures—namely, kingly messiahs, prophetic messiahs, and priestly messiahs. Each kind can be organized into two broad categories: the unrealized messianic agents who were the objects of expectations, and the realized messianic agents who were deemed the fulfillments of expectations.[8]

Royal Messiahs

Most common is the kingly or royal messiah who is often tied to a Davidic ideal.[9] This is not surprising since Jewish cultural memory seamlessly led to reimagining reconstitutions of a Davidic dynasty that would ultimately be theocratic. This kingly messiah is sometimes comfortably asserted alongside the widespread affirmation of God's eternal kingship. While the kingly messiah is appointed by God and appears to be human in most texts, his origins vary. He often comes from the line of David, which can sometimes refer to Israel, but on occasion his origins are supernatural. For example, in 4 Ezra 13 the writer has a dream that the messiah rises out of the sea and rides on the clouds. Another supernatural explanation is that the messiah, who is identified as the Son of Man, is hidden from before creation, which may refer to his preexistence (1 En. 48:2–3). This is similar to the postmortem preservation of Melchizedek, Enoch, and Elijah for eschatological tasks.

In some apocalyptic texts, like 1 Enoch, which is discussed below, the visions of a divinely appointed agent(s) who will be instrumental in defeating Israel's oppressors and in bringing about the end of the age are often militant. A more violent expectation is provided, for example, in 2 Baruch 72–76 which pronounces that the "time of my messiah" will have global implications, leading to the annihilation of all nations that have ruled over Israel. The resultant new age, when pain and death are irradicated, is envisioned as a utopian harmony enjoyed by people and even animals. The prophecy compares the pending judgment and restoration to the exodus from Egypt.

The same kind of militant urgency and function of the kingly messiah was anticipated by the Qumran community, which is believed to have composed the Dead Sea Scrolls (see below). Despite the widespread anticipations of the imminent final battle, the documents contain only a few references to a Davidic messiah. The clearer texts use a variety of titles, such as the *messiah of righteousness* who redrafts a royal covenant (4Q252), the *shoot of David* (4Q174), or the *prince* who wields a scepter against the unrighteous (CD 7:18–21). While the details of events vary in the Scrolls, which is understandable given that they represent many generations of the sectarian community, the kingly messiah is clearly a military leader who will engaged in the final battle, even if at times he appears to be subordinate to prophetic and priestly messianic offices (1QSa 2:14–15).

Not all unrealized messiahs, however, are depicted in militant ways. Both apocalyptic writings, like 4 Ezra and nonapocalyptic writings, like the Psalms of Solomon (discussed below), refer to a hidden messianic figure who is only known to God until the day of his revelation. Yet both writings disclose that he will be a descendant of David and God's Son. Instead of using the weapons of warfare, the messiah will accomplish his task of destroying the unlawful nations and restoring the righteous by simply declaring them into being (4 Ezra 13; Pss. Sol. 17). In 4 Ezra we find an unusual extension of the prophecy. His revealing appears to launch a messianic age that will last four hundred years, culminating in his death (which is given no significance), followed by the inauguration of the new age (7:26–30). The messianic kingdom is lengthy, but temporary, which differs from those expectations that envision an eternal kingdom (e.g., 1 En. 38:5–6; 2 Bar. 73:3).

In many of the references to an expected kingly messiah, he is instrumental in the events that lead to the end of the age, but there is less consistency concerning his involvement in the new age. For instance, the distinction between the messianic age and the new age in 4 Ezra 7 leaves no room for the messiah's inauguration of the latter. The messiah's role in the resurrection of the righteous is also inconsistent. Some clearly expected that the messiah's function was inaugural (2 Bar. 30:1), but this idea remains ambiguous. Others expected the *branch of David* to rise at the end of the age (4Q161). Still others expected the resurrection of the righteous and unrighteous to occur after the messiah's death (4 Ezra 7:27–32) when all are raised for the final judgment. Nowhere, however, do we find the messiah raising the dead. The messiah's role in judgment is also varied. The final judgment of the sinners appears to occur after the messiah's death, which differs from other predictions where he is directly involved (e.g., Pss. Sol. 17:33; 4 Ezra 12:31–33).

In addition to awaited or unrealized messiahs, there is a concentration of figures in the writings of the Jewish historian Josephus that scholars often identify as messianic claimants or aspirants. As a client (Lat. *cliens*) of the Roman emperor writing after 70 CE, Josephus's depictions of messianic claimants are understandably hostile since they are viewed as disrupters of the Pax Romana. For Josephus, they were no more than brigands (*Ant.* 17.285). Nevertheless, he provides an inventory of revolts and revolutionaries who were probably attributed royal status by their supporters. Kingship often assumed anointing. Though, Josephus never refers to any of them as *messiah*. All were military leaders who were focused on overthrowing the Roman occupation and may have viewed their campaigns eschatologically, even aspiring to rule Israel. None proved victorious. All were subdued by Roman forces. Josephus lists seven leaders of uprisings from the end of Herod's reign in 4 BCE to the destruction of the temple in 70 CE These include Judas son of Hezekiah,[10] Simon of Perea,[11] Athronges the Shepherd of Judea,[12] Judas the Galilean,[13] Menahem (grand)son of Judas the Galilean,[14] John of Gischala,[15] and Simon bar Giora of Gerasa.[16] Josephus mentions two other messianic figures that incited revolts, namely Lukuas of Cyrene (ca. 114 CE) and more importantly Simon ben Kosiba (bar Kokhba) who led the rebellion in 132–35 CE. What is unusual about these realized messianic figures is that they are identified by name and not the typical titles we find attributed to the unrealized messiahs. The closest parallels to identifying a messianic figure by name, whose followers awaited revolt, are found in the naming of Jesus as the Christ in the NT.

Priestly Messiahs

Some segments of early Judaism expected the coming of a priestly messiah alongside a royal one. At Qumran there is a handful of texts that can be read this way. In 1QS 9:11–12, for instance, the community awaits the coming of the "prophet and the messiahs of Aaron and Israel." Here two messiahs are awaited, with the priestly one serving a prominent role. In a related Qumran text (CD 14:19), the community awaits "the messiah of Aaron and Israel," which probably refers to a single priestly messiah, whose role is more militant. The blending of a priest and king is not unprecedented in biblical accounts, most notably those about Saul (1 Sam 14:35), David (2 Sam 6:12–19), and Solomon (1 Kgs 3:15). Parallels are also found in the Testaments of the Twelve Patriarchs, which anticipates a priestly and kingly ruler. Although this is a second-century CE document, it may preserve early anti-Hasmonean sentiment. The early dating of the Community

Rule and the Damascus Document is more certain as they may reflect a reaction to the alleged corruption of the Hasmonean priests in Jerusalem, some of whom may have regarded themselves to be kings (Josephus, *J.W.* 1.70; *Ant.* 13.320). Scholars have speculated that the Essene faction at Qumran may have originally consisted of disgruntled priests who awaited a divine regime change in the operations of the Jerusalem temple. It is probable that the earliest conceptions of messiah by this group were primarily priestly, which may have been amended after Rome's occupation. By contrast, there is almost no mention of realized priestly messiahs in the Jewish writings from this period.[17]

Prophetic Messiahs

References to unrealized messianic prophets pale by comparison. An example of one expectation of a messiah, who is probably the widely awaited prophet (cf. Deut 18:15–18) we find in other Jewish writings, is found in the Qumran document 4Q521. Here the messianic age is described as a time when "his [God's] Messiah" will rule. It is prophesied that in those days, the prisoners will be freed, the blind will see, the sick will be healed, and the dead will rise. The miracles, which are probably influenced by Isaiah 35:5, are prophetically relayed, but will be performed by the Lord and not the messiah. This text has received considerable attention over the years since it parallels Jesus's response to the Baptist in Luke 7:22. While it is doubtful that Luke knew this scroll, both may be reflecting a broader eschatological belief.[18]

As a second example, one of the most unusual references to an anointed prophet anywhere in the Jewish literature appears in a short document from Qumran, called 11Q13, which is largely about the return of Melchizedek (the priest-king of Salem in Gen 14:18 and Ps 110:4). In this medley of biblical citations, Melchizedek is presented as a divine agent who will exercise the customs of the jubilee year by atoning for the sins of the righteous and judging the wicked, activities usually reserved for God. He will also transfer the control of the world from Satan to the Sons of Light. Remarkably, a second figure appears who brings God's message about the course of history to the followers of Melchizedek (citing Isa 52:7). This messenger, who is presented as a prophetic figure, is identified as the "anointed of the spirit." Like the fate of the royal messiah in 4 Ezra, he dies, which somehow initiates the last days (citing Dan 9:26 and Isa 61:2).

Josephus makes mention of several Jewish figures during the first century (up to 70 CE) who claimed to be prophets. Like the kingly aspirants, the prophetic ones were focused on the liberation of Israel and were not shy in advocating militant action against the Romans. The traditions of Moses commonly functioned as a pattern for their own agendas. Although Josephus often calls them impostors, false prophets, or madmen, and never attributes to them the title *messiah*. Their eschatologically symbolic actions—like the promise of signs and apparitions, the summoning of followers into the wilderness, and the promise to part the Jordan River—can be associated with the expectation of the prophet-like Moses at the end of the age. For this reason, some scholars have placed this group of realized prophets into a messianic camp. Josephus gives attention to the Anonymous Samaritan, Theudas (also mentioned in Acts 5:36), the Anonymous Egyptian, the Anonymous Impostor, and Jonathan the Refugee.

* * *

In summary, messianic conceptions during the Second Temple period are far from consistent. There was no monolithic Jewish messianism or a single definition of messiah. And there is no evidence to suggest that all Jews shared in these expectations despite the pervasive anticipation of the end of the age. For many Jews, God was the eternal king and liberator. References to messiah(s) are infrequent, allow for an array of chronologies, and provide very little information about the tasks for which the messiah(s) is responsible. Most scholars agree that there are no Jewish texts dated prior to the second century BCE that refer to the coming of a messianic leader who would fulfill God's plan for the end of the age. While this chapter focuses on references that include some component of the term *anointing* or *anointed one*, messianism was not limited to specific terminology.

A measure of consistency, however, does appear in placing the messiah(s) at the end of the present age and in ascribing to them a prominent role that will lead to political and societal change in the service of Israel and God. Since expectations share a view of time that is divinely fixed and all-encompassing, where the future is fused into the narratives, as opposed to a linear set of events leading to an unknown, the coming of messiah(s) was not simply a remedy for temporal or situational problems, but part of discourses about the *telos* of history and Jewish identity.

TAKING A CLOSER LOOK: SOURCES

Almost everything we know about Jewish messianism before the destruction of the temple in 70 CE comes from written sources, many of which have already been briefly mentioned. However, the sources do not, in and of themselves, penetrate the ancient mind. They are only a residue of how some people engaged in various discourses about messianism. They neither lead to a formal definition of messiah nor should they be used to validate an overarching Christian ideal or precursor. Furthermore, as modern research has borne out, the selection, prioritization and organization of the specific texts affect how scholars construct ancient messianism.[19]

Sources from the World of the New Testament

For students approaching this field of study, familiarity with primary sources is necessary. In addition to the late biblical writing of Daniel, the main primary sources which contain references to messiah(s) are found in three groupings of early Jewish writings.[20] The first is the Old Testament Pseudepigrapha, which is a designation given to an unstructured collection of over fifty diverse Jewish writings that mainly span from 200 BCE to 200 CE. These writings contain a handful of texts that refer to messianic figures and acts of anointing, most of which appear in the apocalyptic texts of 1 Enoch, 4 Ezra, and 2 Baruch, and the nonapocalyptic texts of the Psalms of Solomon and book 3 of the Sibylline Oracles.

The second grouping is the Dead Sea Scrolls, which is a modern designation given to a collection of writings that began to be discovered in 1947 near the western shore of the Dead Sea adjacent to a wadi (dry riverbed) called Qumran. Most scholars have associated these writings, which range in genres that include biblical writings, with a faction of the Essenes that established communities in the wilderness in anticipation of the imminent coming of God. The discovery of these writings has revealed a treasure trove of sectarian Jewish beliefs, customs, interpretive practices, and rituals that have enriched our understanding of early Judaism and the earliest Christianity. The most significant messianic texts are found in the community's foundational documents, called the Rule of the Community (1QS), and the Damascus Document (CD), dated to the early first century BCE.

The final grouping is the writings of the Jewish historian Josephus. His two primary writings that describe the rise of would-be kings in Judea are *Jewish War* and *Antiquities of the Jews*, dated respectively in the 70s and 90s CE This is perhaps the most contentious grouping, since the term *messiah* is never attributed to the so-called messianic aspirants. Other Jewish texts can also be useful, such as early rabbinic writings and the early targumim (Aramaic paraphrases of the Jewish scriptures), especially their comparisons of Moses with messiah and David, but their late dating make reconstructions of messianic figures and claimants during the first century challenging. By contrast there is no mention of a messiah figure in the numerous writings of the first-century CE Jewish philosopher Philo of Alexandria (apart from a reference in *Praem.* 95 to an oracle that predicts the coming of a powerful man who will subdue nations) or by the unknown writer designated as Pseudo-Philo to whom is attributed Liber antiquitatum biblicarum (LAB), which is a creative first-century CE rewriting of select scriptural stories. Since many more documents circulated and since orality was the primary medium of communication in popular culture (and can no longer be retrieved), our information is limited.

The concluding portion of this chapter offers a closer look at four sample texts that are frequently cited in studies of early Jewish messianism and early Christology. The first two are taken from the OT Pseudepigrapha—one apocalyptic and the other nonapocalyptic—and the last two are from the Gospel of Mark.

Messiah in the Parables of Enoch

The sample apocalyptic text comes from 1 Enoch (also known as the Ethiopic Apocalypse of Enoch) which is attributed to the seventh descendant of Adam and Eve, who in Genesis 5:24 disappeared because "God took him." In modern scholarship, 1 Enoch is commonly viewed as a composite of five major sections, each stemming from different sources ranging from approximately 200 BCE to 100 CE More specifically, the messianic text provided here comes from the section called the Similitudes, or Parables of Enoch (1 En. 37–71), dated usually to the first century BCE Reference to messiah in the Similitudes may well be among the earliest in the Pseudepigraphal literature. Selections from this section are often cited in studies of early Jewish and Christian messianism because its central figure is ascribed lofty messianic titles that are also used of Jesus in the NT (e.g., Mark 13:26). In 1 Enoch 46:1–4, one of these titles, the *Son of Man*, which is most likely derived from the apocalyptic vision in Daniel 7:13–14, takes on a prominent role.

> There I saw one who had a head of days, and his head was like white wool. And with him was another, whose face was like the appearance of a man; and his face was full of graciousness like one of the holy angels. And I asked the angel of peace, who went with me and showed me all the hidden things, about that son of man—who he was and whence he was (and) why he went with the Head of Days. And he answered me and said to me, "This is the son of man who has righteousness, and righteousness dwells with him. and all the treasuries of what is hidden he will reveal; For the Lord of Spirits has chosen him, and his lot has prevailed through truth in the presence of the Lord of Spirits forever. And this son of man whom you have seen—he will raise the kings and the mighty from their couches, and the strong from their thrones. He will loosen the reins of the strong, and he will crush the teeth of the sinners." (1 En. 46:1–4 [Nickelsburg and VanderKam])[21]

While the term *messiah* is only used twice in the Similitudes (48:10; 52:4), which may have been influenced by Ps 2:2, the titles *Son of Man* and *Chosen One* are used more often. Despite the interchanging titles, this heavenly redeemer who accompanies God from creation (48:3, 6) to the end of age, will judge the deeds of humanity, destroy the unrighteous, and establish a community of elect ones who will live with him forever. Why are the unrighteous destroyed? Most notably, it is because they did not "praise the name of the Lord of the Spirits" (1 En. 46:6). In the broader context of the Similitudes, the writer explains certain heavenly mysteries, paradise, the resurrection of the righteous, and the fate of the fallen angels. Though, the messiah's involvement in the resurrection is contentious given the ambiguous reference to a certain "he" who chooses the righteous among the dead (1 En. 51:1–2). The pronoun might refer to God, the Lord of the Spirits, or to messiah who is given authority to make all things happen (1 En. 52:4). Elsewhere, the function of the messiah is opaque. The end of the Similitudes which arguably may not have represented the author's intended ending, has the Son of Man being removed from the world to live in heaven (70–71).

The Son of David in Psalms of Solomon

The second sample text is from the nonapocalyptic writing Psalms of Solomon (esp. 17–18), which is often thought to be a hostile response to the corruption of the latter Hasmonean rulers who attributed kingly titles to themselves. In this writing, which also contains one of the earliest uses of messiah in the Pseudepigrapha (first century BCE), the author anticipates a Davidic king who will liberate Israel and reign forever, but apart from these vague aims, the messiah's job description is sparse. He is judge, destroyer, and restorer. Heavily indebted to select OT psalms and prophecies, the author reminds God of his ancient promises that Israel will have an enduring progeny as "the firstborn son, an only child." The reminder invokes not only the promise to Abraham, but also to David, whose reign functions as a model for a new king and a kingdom that will have no end. The author implores God to hastily appoint a king who will permanently rule over Israel. Psalms of Solomon 17:21–23 captures the author's urgency during seemingly dire social conditions. The author prays,

> See, Lord, and raise up for them their king,
> the son of David, to rule over your servant Israel
> in the time known to you, O God.
> Undergird him with the strength to destroy the unrighteous
> rulers,
> to purge Jerusalem from gentiles
> who trample her to destruction;

in wisdom and in righteousness to drive out
the sinners from the inheritance;
to smash the arrogance of sinners
like a potter's jar. (Pss. Sol. 17:21–23 [Wright])[22]

In the subsequent sections, the foreseen king is designated as *christos kyrios* (either "Lord Anointed" or "Lord's Anointed") in 17:32 and 18:7, and as "his [God's] Anointed" in 18:5. These do not seem to be titles, but rather terms of function. The provenance of the designations is debated, with some scholars arguing for their later Christian derivation. Nonetheless, this king is not only portrayed militarily, politically, and as a judge, but also ethically and spiritually. His righteousness, wisdom, and compassion for Israel form the basis of his divine agency. The main reason for the destruction of the "unrighteous rulers" is that they have ruled over Israel, which is divinely reserved for the descendant of David, who is identified as "the Lord Messiah" (17:32). Jerusalem will be purged in the process but eventually will be restored to a state of holiness. The destruction of Jerusalem, however, is not a common theme associated with the coming of messiah, which allows for the possibility of other nations being spared.

Reading the New Testament Texts

Turning to the Christological texts in the NT, the earliest attributions of Christ to Jesus are found in the undisputed letters of Paul. His conception is nuanced and not fully developed, but the general idea that emerges from the numerous references is that *Christ* is not a name, but an honorific title (intersecting with other titles, like *Son of God*) referring to his obedience (suffering and death) and vindication (resurrection and exaltation) through which God reconciled the world to himself. His followers received a new identity as a people "in Christ," which consisted of Jews and gentiles who awaited the imminent return of Jesus and the general resurrection. The canonical Gospels, which are the earliest narrations about Jesus's ministry and make up a considerable portion of the NT, are surprisingly much less overt in ascribing the title *Christ* to him. Two sample texts are offered from Mark, our first and foundational Gospel, to show how affirmations of Christ in the story can be subtle, vague, ironic, and even secretive. Although the reader knows from the opening line and the closing scenes that Jesus is the Christ, in the story the focus of Jesus's preaching is not the coming of the messiah, but the coming of God's kingdom.

Jesus, the Son of God

In Mark, Jesus's identity and ministry are launched by John's baptism for the forgiveness of sins (1:4, 9). The magnitude of the baptism is conveyed in Mark 1 which reads,

> And just as he was coming up out of the water, he saw the heavens torn apart and the Spirit descending like a dove upon him. And a voice came from the heavens, "You are my Son, the Beloved; with you I am well pleased." (Mark 1:10–11).

The heavenly proclamation that calls Jesus a beloved Son has endured much debate about its possible scriptural influence. Three prominent candidates have emerged as probable echoes—namely, Isaiah 42:1, Genesis 22:2, and Psalms 2:7. Although the general tendency among scholars has tended to be reductionistic in the attempt to arrive at *the* echo, the inclusion of all three candidates is a viable option, especially when the exegesis of each is traced within the Jewish context, resulting in vagueness.

In the attempt to establish the precise echoes of the heavenly voice's affirmation that Jesus is God's Son, the Hebrew Masoretic Text (which uses the word *servant*) and the Greek Septuagint (which uses a word that can mean both *son* and *servant*) are often identified as influences. Scripture, however, did not circulate in a vacuum. Texts were mired in meanings. When the exegetical traditions of these texts are traced in Judaism, clearer echoes begin to be heard. With respect to Isaiah 42:1, which identifies the Son as the servant of Second Isaiah whose mission is to establish justice and righteousness on the earth (42:1–4) and to be a light to the nations (vv. 5–9), some similarities to Mark appear. They are considerably strengthened, however, when certain Aramaic targumic traditions of Isaiah, which may have circulated orally in Jewish liturgical associations during the first century, are examined, particularly related servant texts in Tg. Isa. 41:8–9; 43:10:

> **Isaiah 41:8–9:**
>
> *Aramaic*—"You, Israel, my servant, Jacob, in whom I am well pleased. . . . I said to you, you are my servant, I am well pleased with you."
>
> *Hebrew/Greek*—"You, Israel, my servant, Jacob, whom I chose . . . I said to you, you are my servant, I chose you."
>
> **Isaiah 43:10:**
>
> *Aramaic*—"My servant the messiah in whom I am well pleased."
>
> *Hebrew/Greek*—"And my servant whom I chose."

In addition to the clause "in whom I am well pleased," the Targum is closest to Mark in its use of direct address (41:8, 9), the giving of the Spirit (42:1), and the messianic reference (43:10).

The story of the binding of Isaac (especially Gen 22:2, 12, 16 LXX) coheres quite well with Mark's "heavenly voice" on strict dictional grounds, but there is very little in the way of thematic parallels. However, when later receptions of this story are considered—in (1) the Testament of Levi 18:6–7, where the story of the binding of Isaac appears in a passage that is quite similar to the baptism of Jesus; (2) the Targum Neofiti Genesis 22:10, which portrays Isaac as the essence of obedience and even a "servant of Yahweh" (Tg. Job 3:18); and (3) rabbinic literature which contains several texts linking Isaac's willingness to die with atonement and the paschal lamb (Mek. on Exod 12:11–14 [Tractate *Pisha* 7])—closer alignment with Mark can be argued.

The echo from Psalms 2:7 has also been enhanced by the study of its exegetical traditions. Once thought by some to have no relevance to Mark 1:11 due to its nonmessianic quality, it has emerged as a prime candidate on the basis of Qumran exegesis which associated God's Son with the messianic prince from the line of David who will bring rule and restoration to Israel (4Q174 1:10–13). If all three scripture texts play a role in Mark's portrayal of Jesus as the Christ, it demonstrates in one example the complexity of early Christian constructs of the Christ. In further reflection, it is interesting to chronologically trace when Jesus becomes God's Son in the NT. For example, in Paul, it is at his exaltation (and possibly in the general resurrection). In Mark, it is at his baptism. In Matthew and Luke, it is at conception. And in John, he always was God's Son (as the Logos).

The Son of Man in Mark

> But he was silent and did not answer. Again the high priest asked him, "Are you the Messiah, the Son of the Blessed One?" Jesus said, "I am, and 'you will see the Son of Man seated at the right hand of the Power' and 'coming with the clouds of heaven.' " (Mark 14:61–62)

The second text extends the ambiguity in a different direction. When Jesus is directly asked at his trial in Mark 14:61–62 if he is the messiah, he affirms "I am" and then proceeds to identify with the future coming of the Son of Man (cf. 8:38; 13:26), echoing the anticipated figure occasionally mentioned in some apocalyptic Jewish writings (e.g., 1 En., Dan). Jesus's bold affirmation is the only one of its kind in the NT. As a result, it figures prominently for those who question if Jesus viewed himself as the Messiah. The affirmation as it stands in modern translations, however, is not certain for several reasons. First, some manuscripts do not read "I am," but "you say so," which removes the certitude. Second, in the parallel passages, Jesus says, "you say so" (Matt 26:64) and "if I tell you, you will not believe" (Luke 22:67), both of which requiring explanation if Mark's "I am" was redacted. Third, when Peter hails Jesus as the Christ in Mark 8:30, Jesus neither affirms nor denies the title, but quickly transitions to predicting the suffering of the Son of Man. When Peter rebukes this idea, Jesus flings a terrible accusation at him, "Get behind me Satan." Finally, when Jesus stands before Pilate and is asked, "Are you the king of the Jews?" (which is messianic language to Romans), he responds "you say so" (Mark 15:2), as Matthew and Luke likewise report. Pilate's response is muted, though in Luke 23:4 he says, "I find no crime in him." In John, he also does not affirm messiahship but instead tells Pilate that his kingdom is not of this world (18:33–38). The ambiguity in these exchanges may suggest at the very least that (1) Jesus did not like the designation *messiah*, preferring *Son of Man*, (2) the uncertainty was intentional, or (3) reinterpretation of the title was necessary.

The relationship between messianism and Christology remains perplexing, intriguing, and important. While Jewish messianism and many of its underlying assumptions were clearly influential—such as the ascription of titles like *Son of Man* and *Son of God*, and placing his coming at the end of the age—early Christological receptions of them were far from dependent, continuous, and consistent.

FURTHER READING

Charlesworth, James H., ed. *The Messiah: Developments in Earliest Judaism and Christianity.* Fortress, 1992.

Collins, John J. *The Scepter and the Star: Messianism in Light of the Dead Sea Scrolls.* Anchor Bible Reference Library. Doubleday, 1995.

Elgvin, Torleif. *Warrior, King, Savior: Messianism in the Hebrew Bible and Early Jewish Texts.* Eerdmans, 2022.

Horsley, Richard A., and John S. Hanson. *Bandits, Prophets, and Messiahs: Popular Movements at the Time of Jesus.* HarperCollins, 1985.

Novenson, Matthew V. *The Grammar of Messianism: An Ancient Jewish Political Idiom and Its Users.* Oxford University Press, 2017.

Notes

1 See the discussion in Dale C. Allison Jr., *Jesus of Nazareth: Millenarian Prophet* (Fortress, 1998).

2 This longstanding observation, which is pivotal for the earliest formations of Christian identity and theology, is often rooted in the work of David Friedrich Strauss (1808–74), especially his *Das Leben Jesu, kritisch bearbeitet*, 2 vols (C. F. Osiander, 1835–36), later translated into English as *The Life of Jesus: Critically Examined*, 2 vols (Calvin Blanchard, 1860).

3 See the comprehensive treatment in Torleif Elgvin, *Warrior, King, Savior: Messianism in the Hebrew Bible and Early Jewish Texts* (Eerdmans, 2022).

4 See, for example, Matthew's Christological uses of Isaiah in Richard Beaton, *Isaiah's Christ in Matthew's Gospel*, Society for New Testament Studies Monograph Series 123 (Cambridge University Press, 2002).

5 James H. Charlesworth, "From Messianology to Christology: Problems and Prospects," in *The Messiah: Developments in Earliest Judaism and Christianity*, ed. James H. Charlesworth (Fortress, 1992).
6 See also the chapter on "Apocalypticism" by Jörg Frey in the present volume.
7 For accessible treatments of the political and social conditions, see Shaye J. D. Cohen, *From Maccabees to the Mishnah* (Westminster, 1987); Richard A. Horsley and John S. Hanson, *Bandits, Prophets, and Messiahs: Popular Movements at the Time of Jesus* (HarperCollins, 1985).
8 On varied messianic activities and identities, see Richard A. Horsley, *Jesus and the Spiral of Violence: Popular Jewish Resistance in Roman Palestine* (Fortress, 1993).
9 See especially, Matthew V. Novenson, *The Grammar of Messianism: An Ancient Jewish Political Idiom and Its Users* (Oxford University Press, 2017). For an accessible treatment, see John J. Collins and Adela Yarbro Collins, eds., *King and Messiah as Son of God: Divine, Human, and Angelic Messianic Figures in Biblical and Related Literature* (Eerdmans, 2008); James C. VanderKam, "Messianism and Apocalypticism," in *The Encyclopedia of Apocalypticism*, ed. John J. Collins, vol. 1, *The Origins of Apocalypticism in Judaism and Christianity* (Continuum, 2000).
10 Active in 4 BCE; *Ant.* 17.271–98; *J.W.* 2.56, 66–79.
11 Active in 4 BCE; *Ant.* 17.273–76; *J.W.* 2.57–59; Tacitus *Historiae.* 5.9.
12 Active in 4–2 BCE; *Ant.* 17.278–84; *J.W.* 2.60–65.
13 Active in 6 CE; *Ant.* 18.4; 20.102; Acts 5:37.
14 Active in 66–70 CE; *J.W.* 2.433–48.
15 Active in 66–70 CE; *J.W.* 4.121–46, 147–50, 393–94.
16 Active in 66–70 CE; *J.W.* 4.508–10.
17 For an accessible treatment of messiah in the Scrolls, see John J. Collins, *The Scepter and the Star: Messianism in Light of the Dead Sea Scrolls* (Doubleday, 1995).
18 Michael Wise, Martin Abegg Jr., and Edward Cook, *The Dead Sea Scrolls: A New Translation* (HarperCollins, 1996), 420–21.
19 See the essays on various sources in James H. Charlesworth, ed., *The Messiah: Developments in Earliest Judaism and Christianity* (Fortress, 1992).
20 For more information, see the chapter on "Early Jewish Literature" by David Cielontko in the present volume.
21 George W. E. Nickelsburg and James C. VanderKam, *1 Enoch: The Hermeneia Translation* (Fortress, 2012).
22 Robert B. Wright, ed., *The Psalms of Solomon: A Critical Edition of the Greek Text*, Jewish and Christian Texts in Contexts and Related Studies 1 (Bloomsbury: 2007).

CHAPTER TWENTY-TWO

Afterlife Expectations in Early Judaism

Michael Scott Robertson
(Universität Regensburg)

DEATH IS A universal human experience, and throughout history, people have pondered what, if anything, lies beyond it. In this regard, early Israelites, Jews, and Christians are not unique. However, their views of the afterlife developed in distinct ways, shaped by specific social and historical circumstances. Given the long history of Judaism and its various geographic contexts, it should be no surprise that many competing, conflicting, and contradictory views emerged regarding the ultimate fate of the departed. Do the dead simply cease to exist? Do they continue to live in a different form of existence? Will the dead come back to life? Ancient Israelites, Jews, and Christians grappled with these questions, offering a wide range of answers. A natural starting point for exploring these views is the Hebrew Bible.

Hebrew Bible

The Hebrew Bible is a diverse collection of texts that were composed, redacted, and edited over the span of several centuries. Despite this diversity, these texts deal with the question of death and the afterlife very sparingly. The relative lack of discussion of the afterlife in the Hebrew Bible, though surprising, is likely due to the outlook found throughout most of this corpus that focuses on the whole of Israel rather than the individual. However, a few texts do present perspectives on individual death. The most common view among these texts is that death is the final destiny of all people, with the clear exception of Daniel 12:1–3 to which we will return below.[1] Death as the end can also be seen in Qoheleth (Ecclesiastes): "The living know that they will die, but the dead know nothing; they have no more reward, and even the memory of them is lost. Their love and their hate and their envy have already perished; never again will they have any share in all that happens under the sun" (Eccl 9:5–6). Here, any meaningful human existence ceases upon the individual's passing.

The abode of the dead in the Hebrew Bible is called Sheol (*šəʾôl*), a term which is often used synonymously with the grave. In addition to this proper name, the location of the dead person may also be called Destruction (*ʾăbaddôn*) or the Pit (*bôr*; *šaḥat*).[2] Sheol is described as a shadowy place, where all who dwell are cut off from all else (Job 10:21; Ps 88:12; Eccl 9:5–10). Existence in Sheol is characterized by silence and stillness (Ps 94:17; Ezek 32:21), and it is the end of human existence.[3] However, it is unlikely that this represents the full spectrum of afterlife beliefs in this period. In addition to the text of the Hebrew Bible, there is archaeological evidence, such as burials that contained food, amulets, jewelry, etc., that point toward a more varied and multifaceted set of beliefs about the afterlife existing in ancient Israel and Judah than what has come down to us in the textual tradition.[4]

Origins of the Belief in Resurrection

The exact origins of the belief in resurrection in Judaism remain a topic of debate—did it arise from external influences, such as from Zoroastrianism, or was it an internal development through reflection, elaboration, and creative rearticulation of Israelite theology in response to changing circumstances?[5] The nuances of this debate need not be repeated in detail here, but it is important to acknowledge that these views are not mutually exclusive, and the truth may lie somewhere between these two poles.[6] An important element in the discussion of the origins of the belief in resurrection is its development in light of persecution and martyrdom during the Maccabean revolt under the Seleucid ruler Antiochus IV Epiphanes in the middle of the second century BCE. Although, as will be seen below, texts expressing views of resurrection did seem to proliferate in response to these events, the Book of the Watchers shows that the belief in resurrection can be dated to at least a century prior to the Maccabean revolt.[7] Because of this situation, the exact origins of belief in resurrection in early Judaism are unclear.

Resurrection Beliefs

The earliest extant Jewish text that references resurrection and has extensive descriptions of the afterlife is the Book of the Watchers (1 En. 1–36). This text dates to the third century BCE and is therefore older than the canonical book of Daniel, which dates to the mid-second century.[8] In the Book of the Watchers, Enoch ascends to heaven and is taken on a guided tour. During his travels, an angel showed him "to the west a great and high mountain of hard rock" (1 En. 22:1).[9] This mountain contained four hollow places where the spirits of the dead would be held in separate containers until the day of judgment (22:3–4). About one of these hollow places, the angel Raphael says, "And this was created for the spirits of the people who will not be pious, but sinners, who were godless, and they were companions with the lawless. And their spirits will not be punished on the day of judgment, nor will they be raised from there" (22:13). Although it is phrased in the negative, the idea that the spirits will not be raised is a hint at the idea of resurrection. If resurrection was not a conceptual category at this time, there would be no need to deny that one of the four groups would receive it. The implication is that others will be resurrected.

In Daniel 12:1–3, there is a more explicit reference to resurrection. Daniel 12:2 says, "Many of those who sleep in the dust of the earth shall awake, some to everlasting life, and some to shame and everlasting contempt." Here, it is clearly stated that those who are asleep, a metaphor for those who are dead, shall wake up.[10] It is important to note here, however, that neither in Daniel nor in the Book of the Watchers, as seen above, is resurrection said to be *bodily*.[11] Instead, the wise "shall shine like the brightness of the sky, and those who lead many to righteousness, like the stars forever and ever" (Dan 12:3). In Daniel 8:10, angels are described as stars, and so it is likely that for Daniel, resurrection of the righteous entails a transformation into angelic beings.[12] Resurrection in this text, however, is not reserved solely for the righteous, but is the destiny for all. The text distinguishes between those who will have everlasting life and those who will have shame and contempt, but this differentiation occurs after resurrection.

In roughly the same period as Daniel, 2 Maccabees also shows evidence of belief in resurrection. 2 Maccabees was written between the late second century BCE and the middle of the first century BCE,[13] and it tells the story of the Maccabean revolt that occurred in the middle of the second century BCE. In this text is an account of the martyrdom of a mother and her seven sons (7:1–42). These individuals were killed during the reign of Antiochus for their faithfulness to God's law (7:9). With his last breath, the second brother says, "the King of the universe will raise us up to an everlasting renewal of life, because we have died for his laws" (7:9b). Here, the text unambiguously references resurrection from the dead. However, it goes beyond the Book of the Watchers and Daniel in that it also affirms a *bodily* resurrection. After the torturers demanded the third brother stretch out his hands, the brother said, "I got these from Heaven, and because of his laws I disdain them, and from him I hope to get them back again" (7:11). In his hope to get his hands back, the brother affirms his expectation of a corporeal existence after his resurrection. In this way, resurrection, for 2 Maccabees, is a consequence of God's creative power. In other words, because God is all-powerful, and thus able to re-create limbs, he is also, by extension, able to re-create the whole person, thereby resurrecting the dead. However, resurrection is only for the righteous, as it emphatically declares that sinners will not be raised but instead be judged and receive punishment (7:14, 35–36).[14]

In the New Testament period, the Pharisees are a group that believed in resurrection, as Acts 23:8 says. Further, Josephus mentions that Pharisees believed that the righteous will be resurrected, but the unrighteous will not (*Ant.*

18.14). If Josephus is correct, the Pharisees, then, did not see resurrection as the common lot of all humanity. It was a reward only for the righteous.

With these texts, a variety of views on resurrection is apparent. There are a number of separate components that can be separated out: resurrection of the righteous; resurrection of sinners; resurrection of the body; resurrection (or afterlife) of the soul or spirit; angelic transformation of the righteous; and punishment of the sinners. These ideas can be combined to form several different views on the fate of individuals after death.[15]

No Afterlife

In addition to the view that (some) individuals are resurrected after death, a number of texts present a completely opposite approach to the afterlife—that there is no afterlife. One of the clearest depictions of this view is found in the book of Sirach (also called Ben Sira and Ecclesiasticus). This wisdom text was originally written in Hebrew ca. 200 BCE and translated into Greek by the author's grandson in Egypt after 132 BCE.[16] This dating places the time of the original writing before the Maccabean revolt, but its translation after, which means that the ideas contained in this text are from roughly the same period as the texts discussed above.

Sirach emphatically denies the possibility of resurrection. In speaking of the dead, he says, "Do not forget, there is no coming back; you do the dead no good, and you injure yourself" (38:21). The only hope of an "afterlife" that Sirach gives is the remembrance of one's name postmortem (30:4–5; 41:3). Punishment for sinners is that the Lord will make the final hours of life before death so miserable that any former delight will be forgotten (11:26–27), and their names will be forgotten (41:7–10).

A similar view of death is present in 1 Maccabees. Much like 2 Maccabees, 1 Maccabees recounts the story of the Maccabean revolt, but from a different perspective, and it is roughly contemporaneous with 2 Maccabees. 1 Maccabees presents death as an end with the ultimate hope for the deceased being the remembrance of one's name forever. This comes to the fore in the death of Eleazar, who ran ahead in battle to stab an elephant from underneath. When the elephant died, it fell on Eleazar, killing him. The text says of his death, "he gave his life to save his people and to win for himself an everlasting name" (6:44). There is no mention of any postmortem destiny apart from an "everlasting name."

A similar view of death is held by at least one group of Jews during the time of the New Testament. Acts 23:8 says, "The Sadducees say that there is no resurrection, or angel, or spirit." Josephus puts it this way, "The Sadducees hold that the soul perishes along with the body" (*Ant.* 18.16).[17] In this way, the Sadducees seem to be the heirs of the view found in ancient Israelite religion.

Immortality of the Soul

A further view of the afterlife is the immortality of the soul. This view is distinct from the idea of resurrection in that existence as a postmortem, disembodied soul or spirit is the final form of existence. Cielontko helpfully clarifies the distinction:

> Unlike in the tradition represented in the Book of the Watchers and similar texts, the Jewish conception of the immortality of the soul does not consider the soul's posthumous existence to merely be a temporary form awaiting a final judgment, resurrection, and an ensuing transfiguration. Rather, it is a final form, although it may also be associated with a subsequent transformation into a heavenly being.[18]

The Wisdom of Solomon, written in Egypt in the first century BCE (or maybe even later), is representative of this view. This text envisages an eternal life for the righteous who have died:

> But the souls of the righteous are in the hand of God, and no torment will ever touch them. In the eyes of the foolish they seemed to have died, and their departure was thought to be a disaster, and their going from us to be their destruction; but they are at peace. For though in the sight of others they were punished, their hope is full of immortality. (3:1–4)

However, elsewhere it is clear that this eternal existence is not in the body, as it says, "a perishable body weighs down the soul" (9:15a). The wicked, however, will be judged and suffer punishment (4:18–20).

An important witness to this view is 4 Maccabees, a philosophical work written toward the end of first or beginning of the second century CE. This text reflects upon the martyrdoms of Eleazar and the mother and seven sons in 2 Maccabees 6–7 but does not present their ultimate hope as resurrection. In reflecting upon the effect of these martyrdoms, the text says, "for on that day virtue gave the awards and tested them for their endurance. The prize was immortality in endless life" (17:12), and "The tyrant himself and all his council marveled at their endurance, because of which they now stand before the divine throne and live the life of eternal blessedness" (17:17–18). Thus, the text reflects a view that righteous individuals have everlasting life after they have died. However, there is no resurrection. Instead, the text indicates that this is their final state as these individuals stand before God's throne for eternity. The Jewish view of the immortal soul is that it is the reward of the righteous, by which it stands in contrast to the Greek, Platonic belief where immortality is a universal experience of all souls.

Realized Immortality

Realized immortality is a view of the afterlife wherein the living community currently experiences immortalization and communion with the angels even prior to death. The primary representative of this view is the Qumran community, an ascetic Jewish community that existed on the shore of the Dead Sea and who are connected with the texts commonly called the Dead Sea Scrolls. The clearest statement of such an idea is found in a collection of thanksgiving hymns, known as the Hodayot. The most complete manuscript of this text dates to the second half of the first century BCE, however, it is clear that the text itself is older.[19] The text says,

> I thank you, Lord, because you saved my life from the pit, and from Sheol and Abaddon you have lifted me up to an everlasting height, so that I can walk on a boundless plain. And I know that there is hope for someone you fashioned out of clay to be an everlasting community. The corrupt spirit you have purified from the great sin so that he can take his place with the host of the holy ones and can enter in communion with the congregation of the sons of heaven. (1QH[a] 11:19–23 [Martínez])[20]

Becoming part of the community brought the individual into a new existence where they are now "saved" from the pit, Sheol, and Abbadon. More than that, the individual now has a place beside and enjoys communion with the angels. In this way, the living members of the community need not wait until their deaths for full participation in the "afterlife," but partake in it alongside the heavenly beings.

The idea of a realized immortality is not confined to the Qumran community. Joseph and Aseneth was written ca. 100 BCE–115 CE,[21] and it expands upon the short statement in Genesis 41:45 that Joseph married Aseneth, the daughter of an Egyptian priest. In this text, Aseneth converts to Judaism, and an angel says to her,

> Behold, from today, you will be renewed and formed anew and made alive again, and you will eat blessed bread of life, and drink a blessed cup of immortality, and anoint yourself with blessed ointment of incorruptibility. Courage, Aseneth, chaste virgin. Behold, I have given you today to Joseph for a bride, and he himself will be your bridegroom for ever (and) ever. (Jos. Asen. 15:5–6)[22]

Aseneth is described as being made alive again and having immortality while alive. In this way, her afterlife has already been inaugurated through her conversion to Judaism. Much as seen in Hodayot, Aseneth need not wait to enjoy blessings associated with the afterlife because she has already participated in this realm.

Angelic or Astral Transformation

The idea of individuals being transformed into angelic beings was briefly discussed above in relation to resurrection in Daniel. Transfiguration into a heavenly being is also present in other texts that describe resurrection, such as the Epistle of Enoch, Jubilees, the Animal Apocalypse, the Parables of Enoch, 4 Ezra, 2 Baruch, and the Sibylline Oracles.[23] However, this type of transformation is not restricted to those who believe in resurrection, but instead, it cuts across different views of the afterlife.

The Wisdom of Solomon, as discussed above, demonstrates a belief in the immortality of the soul as the final form of the deceased with no view of resurrection. This text also evinces a belief in transmogrification into angels. In 5:5, it says, "Why have they been numbered among the children of God? And why is their lot among the saints?" Here, the "children of God" is likely a reference to angelic beings, and the souls of the departed being numbered among them indicates that these souls have become like them.[24]

Similarly, the Qumran community also had texts that indicate that they believed in the transformation of the dead into angels. In the Songs of the Sage, the following appears: "God makes [some] holy for himself like an everlasting sanctuary, and there will be purity amongst those purified. And they shall be priests, his holy people, his army and his servants, the angels of his glory" (4Q511 35 3–4).[25] In this text, God will make some of the holy people into angels. For the Qumran community, then, the idea of realized immortality was compatible with the belief that (at least some) individuals will become angels.

In some texts, it seems that individuals may be transformed into stars or some sort of astral being. An example of this type of postmortem existence may be found in 2 Baruch, an apocalypse written ca. 70 CE–135 CE that deals with the aftermath of the destruction of the temple. In 51:10, the text says, "For they will dwell in the heights of that world, and they will be made like angels. And they will be made equal to stars, and they will be changed into any form they desire; from beauty into loveliness, and from light into the splendor of glory."[26] The dead here are said to be like angels and equal to the stars, indicating that they may not be actual angels or stars, but some other heavenly or astral being.

The Testament of Moses, a text from the first century CE,[27] also describes an astral existence in the afterlife. We find this in 10:9, "And God will raise you to the heights. Yea, he will fix you firmly in the heaven of the stars, in the place of their habitations."[28] In this text, the dead are said to be put in the astral heaven, which may mean that they themselves will become stars.

From the texts above, the idea of persons transformed into angels can be combined with a number of different views of the afterlife, from resurrection to the immortality of the soul, to realized immortality. This adds to the diversity of views on the afterlife attested in early Judaism in the environment in which the New Testament was written.

TAKING A CLOSER LOOK: SOURCES

Sources from the World of the New Testament

The Resurrection in the Book of Parables

> In those days, the earth will give back what has been entrusted to it, and Sheol will give back what has been entrusted to it, and destruction will restore what it owes. For in those days, my Chosen One will arise and choose the righteous and holy from among them, for the day on which they will be saved has drawn near. And the Chosen One, in those days, will sit upon my throne, and all the secrets of wisdom will go forth from the counsel of his mouth, for the Lord of Spirits has given (them) to him and glorified him. In those days the mountains will leap like rams, and the hills will skip like lambs satisfied with milk; and the faces of all the angels in heaven will be radiant with joy, and the earth will rejoice, and the righteous will dwell on it, and the chosen will go upon it. (1 Enoch 51:1–5 [Nickelsburg])[29]

This passage is found in the Enochic Book of Parables, which, although now part of what is known as 1 Enoch, is considerably later than the earlier sections of the Enochic corpus, such as the Book of the Watchers cited above. Although there has been considerable debate over the dating of the Book of Parables, it is most likely that it was written in the late first century BCE or early first century CE.[30] The Book of Parables, then, was written close to much of the New Testament and represents Jewish ideas that were circulating at the time of birth of the early Jesus movement.

In the passage cited above, the text envisions the resurrection of all—righteous and unrighteous alike. However, these two groups are distinguished by "the Chosen One" who will take the righteous out for their salvation. In this way, the Book of Parables stands in the tradition of the Book of the Watchers and Daniel in presenting an idea of the dead being resurrected in the future. Further, it appears to agree with Daniel that resurrection will be experienced by both the righteous and sinners.

Philo of Alexandria on Immortality

> So too, when Abraham left this mortal life, "he is added to the people of God," in that he inherited incorruption and became equal to the angels, for angels—those unbodied and blessed souls—are the host and people of God. In the same way again the Practiser Jacob, we read, is added to something better, when he left the worse. Once more there is Isaac to whom was granted the higher gift of self-learnt knowledge. He too abandoned all such bodily elements as had been interwoven with the soul. (Philo, *Sacr.* 5–6)[31]

Philo of Alexandria lived ca. 20 BCE–50CE and authored a large number of texts that have survived to the present. His thought is deeply immersed in Greek Philosophy, particularly Middle Platonism.[32] Nowhere in his writings does he advocate for the idea of resurrection. Philo viewed the body as mortal and a tomb for the soul, which was immortal. This contrast between bodily mortality and immortality of the soul comes through in the above quote. Abraham's death is described as leaving this "mortal life" and inheriting "incorruption." Gaining this incorruption makes Abraham "like the angels" who have no bodies but instead are "blessed souls." Philo also shows that he finds the disembodied existence better than that in the body when he notes that Jacob left something worse for something better, with the worse indicating life in the body and the better being life without the body. In this way, Philo evinces belief in the immortality of the soul as the final form of existence, placing him in the tradition of the Wisdom of Solomon and 4 Maccabees.

This text also displays Philo's belief that humans become angels. As noted above, this view can be found in representatives of most other views of the afterlife in early Judaism. Philo describes Abraham as becoming equal to the angels and then describes these angels as the people of God. This description of the angels likely shows that Philo views Abraham as becoming an angel himself.[33] Thus, the idea of the immortality of the soul coupled with angelic transformation was extant during the early years of the nascent Jesus movement.

Reading the New Testament Texts

Jesus and the Sadducees in Mark (and Parallels)

> Some Sadducees, who say there is no resurrection, came to him and asked him a question, saying, "Teacher, Moses wrote for us that if a man's brother dies, leaving a wife but no child, the man shall marry the widow and raise up children for his brother. There were seven brothers; the first married and, when he died, left no children, and the second

> married the widow and died, leaving no children, and the third likewise; none of the seven left children. Last of all the woman herself died. In the resurrection, when they rise, whose wife will she be? For all seven had married her."
>
> Jesus said to them, "Is not this the reason you are wrong, that you know neither the scriptures nor the power of God? For when people rise from the dead, they neither marry nor are given in marriage but are like angels in heaven. And as for the dead being raised, have you not read in the book of Moses, in the story about the bush, how God said to him, 'I am the God of Abraham, the God of Isaac, and the God of Jacob'? He is God not of the dead but of the living; you are quite wrong." (Mark 12:18–27).

This passage is from the Gospel of Mark, probably the earliest of all the Gospels. It is also found in Matthew 22:23–32 and Luke 20:33–38. Here, Jesus is questioned by some Sadducees regarding the nature of the resurrection. They pose Jesus with a hypothetical scenario about a woman who was married seven times and ask about which of those husbands she will be married to in the resurrection. Jesus's response is that she will be married to none of these men. Instead, they will be like the angels. There is no affirmation of the resurrection of the body, but individuals will be resurrected and transformed into angels.[34] 1 Enoch 15:1–11 explains that because angels are immortal, they have no need of women for reproduction. Humans, however, because they are mortal, must procreate with women to continue humanity beyond the death of the individual. It seems that Jesus, in the passage above, uses similar logic—that because individuals are transformed into immortal angels in the resurrection, they need not marry and procreate. It must be noted, however, that in this passage, Jesus only quotes from the Pentateuch for his argument. He does not refer to Jewish writings that present a similar view of resurrection as his own to buttress his case. Instead, Jesus grounds his argument in God's power and the idea that God is the God of life. This passage, then, portrays Jesus's view of the afterlife in the same vein as that of Daniel or 2 Baruch.

The Resurrected Bodies in 1 Corinthians

> So it is with the resurrection of the dead. What is sown is perishable; what is raised is imperishable. It is sown in dishonor; it is raised in glory. It is sown in weakness; it is raised in power. It is sown a physical body; it is raised a spiritual body. If there is a physical body, there is also a spiritual body. Thus it is written, "The first man, Adam, became a living being"; the last Adam became a life-giving spirit. But it is not the spiritual that is first but the physical and then the spiritual. The first man was

> from the earth, made of dust; the second man is from heaven. As one of dust, so are those who are of the dust, and as one of heaven, so are those who are of heaven. Just as we have borne the image of the one of dust, we will also bear the image of the one of heaven. What I am saying, brothers and sisters, is this: flesh and blood cannot inherit the kingdom of God, nor does the perishable inherit the imperishable. Look, I will tell you a mystery! We will not all die, but we will all be changed, in a moment, in the twinkling of an eye, at the last trumpet. For the trumpet will sound, and the dead will be raised imperishable, and we will be changed. For this perishable body must put on imperishability, and this mortal body must put on immortality. (1 Cor 15:42–53).

This passage comes from Paul's first letter to the Corinthians, written in the 50s CE, making it among the earliest New Testament writings. Here, Paul describes his belief in the resurrection of individuals at the eschaton. He describes a distinction between a physical and spiritual body, and this distinction has led to considerable debate over Paul's conception of the resurrection body ever since.[35] The issues in this debate are complex and cannot be adequately adjudicated here. It is important given the above discussion, however, that Paul is clear the resurrection will be bodily, even if he is not clear as to the nature of that body. 2 Baruch 49:1–51:10 shows a similar interest in the form of the resurrected body. It emphasizes that there is a need for bodies to be transformed, the righteous into glorious angelic bodies, and the unrighteous into horrifying forms. In contrast, Paul focuses only on the bodies of the righteous.

These two passages from the New Testament represent differing ideas concerning the resurrection of individuals. However, both have precedent in earlier and contemporaneous Judaism.

FURTHER READING

Cielontko, David. "Resurrection in Early Judaism within the Context of Existing Beliefs about the Afterlife." In *Bible, Christianity, and Culture. Essays in Honor of Professor Petr Pokorný*, edited by Pavol Bargar. Karolinum, 2023.

Collins, John J. "The Afterlife in Apocalyptic Literature." In *Apocalypse, Prophecy, and Pseudepigraphy: On Jewish Apocalyptic Literature*. Eerdmans, 2015.

Elledge, Casey D. *Resurrection of the Dead in Early Judaism*. Oxford University Press, 2017.

Finney, Mark T. *Resurrection, Hell and the Afterlife: Body and Soul in Antiquity, Judaism and Early Christianity*. 1st ed. Routledge, 2016.

Neusner, Jacob, and Alan J. Avery-Peck, eds. *Judaism in Late Antiquity. Part Four. Death, Life-after-Death, Resurrection and the World-to-Come in the Judaisms of Antiquity*. Brill, 2000.

Nickelsburg, George W. E. *Resurrection, Immortality, And Eternal Life in Intertestamental Judaism and Early Christianity*. Harvard University Press, 1972.

Nicklas, Tobias, Friedrich V. Reiterer, and Joseph Verheyden, eds. *The Human Body in Death and Resurrection*. Deuterocanonical and Cognate Literature Yearbook 2009. De Gruyter, 2009.

Sigvartsen, Jan Age. *Afterlife and Resurrection Beliefs in the Apocrypha and Apocalyptic Literature*. T&T Clark, 2019.

Notes

1 Some scholars also consider Isaiah 24–27, Ezekiel 37, and Hosea 6:1–3 to be exceptions, but these texts use resurrection as a metaphor to describe the renewal of Israel as a people rather than as a description of the fate of individuals. See David Cielontko, "Resurrection in Early Judaism within the Context of Existing Beliefs about the Afterlife," in *Bible, Christianity, and Culture. Essays in Honor of Professor Petr Pokorný*, ed. Pavol Bargar (Karolinum, 2023), 32.

2 John Goldingay, "Death and Afterlife in the Psalms," in *Judaism in Late Antiquity. Part Four. Death, Life-after-Death, Resurrection and the World-to-Come in the Judaisms of Antiquity*, ed. Jacob Neusner and Alan J. Avery-Peck, Handbuch Der Orientalistik (Brill, 2000), 63.

3 See Mark T. Finney, *Resurrection, Hell and the Afterlife: Body and Soul in Antiquity, Judaism and Early Christianity*, 1st ed. (Routledge, 2016), 27.

4 See Richard Elliott Friedman and Shawna Dolansky Overton, "Death and Afterlife: The Biblical Silence," in *Judaism in Late Antiquity. Part Four. Death, Life-after-Death, Resurrection and the World-to-Come in the Judaisms of Antiquity*, ed. Jacob Neusner and Alan J. Avery-Peck, Handbuch Der Orientalistik (Brill, 2000).

5 Cielontko, "Resurrection in Early Judaism," 35–36.

6 Casey D. Elledge, *Resurrection of the Dead in Early Judaism* (Oxford University Press, 2017), 44–65.

7 Cielontko, "Resurrection in Early Judaism," 44.

8 On dating the book of Daniel, see John J. Collins, *The Apocalyptic Imagination: An Introduction to Jewish Apocalyptic Literature* (Eerdmans, 2016), 110–13.

9 All translations of 1 Enoch are from George W. E. Nickelsburg and James C. VanderKam, eds., *1 Enoch: A New Translation: Based on the Hermeneia Commentary* (Fortress, 2004).

10 This metaphor is known throughout the ancient world, see Thomas H. McAlpine, *Sleep, Divine and Human in the Old Testament*, Supplements to the Journal for the Study of the Old Testament 38 (JSOT, 1987), 135–49.

11 See Cielontko, "Resurrection in Early Judaism," 39–40.

12 Finney, *Resurrection, Hell and Afterlife*, 67; John J. Collins, *Daniel: A Commentary*, Hermeneia (Fortress, 1993), 392–94

13 Friedrich Avemarie, Jan Willem van Henten, and Yair Furstenberg, *Jewish Martyrdom in Antiquity: From the Books of Maccabees to the Babylonian Talmud*, Compendia Rerum Iudaicarum ad Novum Testamentum 17 (Brill, 2023), 76.

14 See George W. E. Nickelsburg, *Resurrection, Immortality, and Eternal Life in Intertestamental Judaism and Early Christianity* (Harvard University Press, 1972), 119–38.

15 For a helpful and concise overview, see the chart in Cielontko, "Resurrection in Early Judaism," 64.

16 See Roland E. Murphy, "Death and Afterlife in the Wisdom Literature," in *Judaism in Late Antiquity. Part Four. Death, Life-after-Death, Resurrection and the World-to-Come in the Judaisms of Antiquity*, ed. Jacob Neusner and Alan J. Avery-Peck, Handbuch Der Orientalistik (Brill, 2000), 110.

17 *Jewish Antiquities, Volume VIII: Books 18-19*, trans. Louis H. Feldman, Loeb Classical Library 433 (Harvard University Press, 1965); See also *J.W.* 2.165.

18 Cielontko, "Resurrection in Early Judaism," 56.

19 John J. Collins, *Apocalypticism in the Dead Sea Scrolls* (Routledge, 1997), 119.

20 Florentino García Martínez, ed., *The Dead Sea Scrolls Translated: The Qumran Texts in English*, trans. Wilfred G. E. Watson, 2nd ed. (Brill, 1996), 332.

21 Susan Docherty, "Joseph and Aseneth: Rewritten Bible or Narrative Expansion?" *Journal for the Study of Judaism*35, no. 1 (2004): 27–48 (31).

22 Christoph Burchard, "Joseph and Aseneth," in *The Old Testament Pseudepigrapha*, ed. James H. Charlesworth, 1st ed. (Doubleday & Company, 1983), 2:226.

23 See, Cielontko, "Resurrection in Early Judaism," 64.

24 See, David Winston, *The Wisdom of Solomon: A New Translation with Introduction and Commentary*, Anchor Yale Bible Commentaries 43 (Doubleday, 1979), 147.

25 García Martínez, *Dead Sea Scrolls Translated*, 374.

26 Daniel M. Gurtner, ed., *Second Baruch: a critical edition of the Syriac text: with Greek and Latin Fragments, English Translation, Introduction, and Concordances*, Jewish and Christian Texts 5 (T&T Clark, 2009), 91.

27 Marek Parchem, "The Apocalyptic Character of the Testament of Moses," *Biblical Annals* 14, no. 3 (2024): 461–80 (462).

28 John Priest, "Testament of Moses," in *The Old Testament Pseudepigrapha*, ed. James H. Charlesworth, 1st ed. (Doubleday, 1983), 2:932.

29 Nickelsburg and VanderKam, *1 Enoch: A New Translation*.

30 See James H. Charlesworth, "The Date and Provenience of the Parables of Enoch," in *Parables of Enoch: A Paradigm Shift*, ed. James H Charlesworth and Darrell Bock, Jewish and Christian Texts 11 (Bloomsbury, 2013).

31 Philo, *On the Cherubim. The Sacrifices of Abel and Cain. The Worse Attacks the Better. On the Posterity and Exile of Cain. On the Giants*, trans. F. H. Colson and G. H. Whitaker, Loeb Classical Library 227 (Harvard University Press, 1929), 97–99.

32 See Lester L. Grabbe, "Eschatology in Philo and Josephus," in *Judaism in Late Antiquity. Part Four. Death, Life-after-Death, Resurrection and the World-to-Come in the Judaisms of Antiquity*, ed. Jacob Neusner and Alan J. Avery-Peck, Handbuch Der Orientalistik (Brill, 2000), 164.

33 Cielontko, "Resurrection in Early Judaism," 58–59.

34 See Adela Yarbro Collins, *Mark: A Commentary*, Hermeneia (Fortress, 2008), 561–62.

35 See James Ware, "Paul's Understanding of the Resurrection in 1 Corinthians 15:36–54," *Journal of Biblical Literature* 133, no. 4 (2014): 809–35.

CHAPTER TWENTY-THREE

Samaritans

József Zsengellér
(Jewish Theological Seminary, Budapest)

The Origins

THE TERM *SAMARITANS* (*samareitai*) is derived from the Greek word for the area surrounding the city of Samaria in northern Israel and is also used to referred to the inhabitants of the area in the Hellenistic-Roman period, akin to the naming of Romans after the city of Rome. From a certain time, the designation has been used also or especially for the members of a certain Yahwistic religious group who had its cultic center on Mount Gerizim next to the ancient city of Shechem, present-day Nablus. In the New Testament time, the Greek city Sychar was located near by the ruins of Shechem. Between the two settlements there is a well traditionally called "Jacob's well" referring to the stay of the patriarch next to Shechem in Genesis 33:18–35:4. This is also the place where Jesus met the Samaritan women according to John 4. In the Old Testament, Gerizim was the Mountain of Blessings as attested in Deuteronomy 11:29–30; 27:12–13, and in Joshua 8:30–35, but its area was also called the "navel of the Earth" in Judges 9:37. As such, its religious importance was recognized from ancient times on.

The Samaritans claim that they represent true Israel, having preserved (*shomrim*) the traditional customs and Mosaic Torah in its original form at the sole center of God's earthly presence, Mount Gerizim. In accordance with Samaritan tradition, a schism occurred during the tenure of the high priest Uzzi, who was the elder brother of Eli, known from the book of Samuel (1 Sam 1–4). Eli sought to become high priest and gained the support of half of the Israelites by presenting a replica of the holy ark, the holy tent, and its vessels. He relocated his people from Mount Gerizim to Shilo, which became their new religious center. The true Israel, the *shomrim* stayed on Mount Gerizim and went on to honor God there, but Uzzi hid the holy tent, the ark with its vessels in a cave until the coming of the true prophet who will reveal it. This marked the end of the period of divine blessing (*rahuta*) and the beginning of the period of divine disgrace (*phanhuta*). The survived Samaritan historiography originates from the Islamic period, after the twelfth century.

Figure 23.1. Samaritan tradition on the schism with the Jews.

The two distinct Yahwistic kingdoms, Israel and Judah, each had their own designated religious centers, namely Bethel and Dan for Israel and Jerusalem for Judah. This resulted in the manifestation of slightly disparate religious practices. Following the conquest of Samaria in 722 BCE by the Assyrian king Sargon II, the former northern kingdom of Israel ceased to exist (2 Kgs 17; Nimrud prism IV:25–41)[1]. While many were taken captive by the Assyrians and a sizable foreign population was settled in the region, the remaining Israelites continued to practice their religion under the Assyrian provincial administration based in Samaria,[2] with Mount Gerizim becoming an increasingly important center for religious activities. The kingdom of Judah, with Jerusalem as its capital and religious center, retained its independence and maintained an alliance with the Assyrian Empire. After the Babylonian occupation of the region and the fall of Jerusalem in 587 BCE (2 Kgs 25), the province of Samerina exercised control over the Judeans who had not been displaced. In addition to repatriating the previously displaced Yahwistic population, the Persian Cyrus facilitated the reconstruction of their temples (Ezra 1; Cyrus cylinder 30–36).[3] Archaeological evidence indicates that a temple of YHWH was constructed on Mount Gerizim in approximate parallel with the temple reconstruction in Jerusalem described in the books of Ezra and Nehemiah in the late sixth to early fifth century BCE.[4] The religiosity of the Judeans returning from captivity and the local population in the region of former Israel and Judah exhibited some differences due to the effects of more than half a century of exile. Notwithstanding the geographical separation of the two temples, situated in the distinct Persian provinces of Samerin and Yehud, where the Yahwistic population practiced their religion separately,[5] their scribes collaborated in the joint compilation of their defining religious document—the five books of Moses, the Torah.[6] Despite this common basic theological work, further theological differences between the two Yahwistic groups intensified toward the end of the Persian period.[7]

Hellenistic Period

The advent of the Hellenistic period saw not only a change in the use of language with the introduction of Greek, but also a transformation in imperial administration.[8] The Ptolemies incorporated the high priests into the tax collection system of the provinces (*hyparchies*), while the Seleucids appointed direct imperial inspectors to oversee the temples as attested in the Hefzibah and Heliodoros inscriptions.[9] During the reign of Antiochus IV, the supervision had already included confiscating the temple treasures and renaming the temples, both in Jerusalem and on Mount Gerizim (2 Macc 5–6). Subsequently, the entire practice of Yahwistic religion was outlawed, the Torah was prohibited, and those who resisted were persecuted. The temple in Jerusalem was desecrated and partly destroyed (1 Macc 1:10–64; 2 Macc 5:11–6:11). The fate of the temple on Mount Gerizim and the Samarian Yahwists remains uncertain. They do not appear to be involved in the rebellion of the Judean Yahwists, which is known as the Maccabean revolt.[10] In addition to reoccupying and rededicating the Jerusalem temple—which is still commemorated on *Hanukkah* (1 Macc 4:36–59; 2 Macc 10:1–9; *J.W.* 1.39–40; *Ant.* 12.316–26)[11]—the Maccabeans redefined their religion as Judaism, thereby positioning the Jerusalem temple as the sole center of Yahwism.[12] Additionally, they also began the recapture of former Israelite (Judean and Samarian) territories from the Seleucid Empire.

In approximately 108 BCE, the Maccabean ruler, John Hyrcanos, conquered Shechem and destroyed the temple on Mount Gerizim (*J.W.* 1.62–63; *Ant.* 13.254–56) due to the Samarian Yahwists' refusal to join Judaism.[13] This date marks a significant turning point in the history of the Yahwist groups, marking the beginning of a distinct Samaritan identity. At this time begins the theological exaltation of Mount Gerizim in Samaritan theology as well as the production of anti-Samaritan writings among Judeans.[14] The schism also resulted in modifications to the text of the Torah. For example, in Deuteronomy 27:4, the Jews replaced Gerizim with Ebal,[15] while the Samaritans inserted the veneration of Gerizim into the Ten Commandments.[16] The Samaritans utilized the ancient paleo-Hebrew script to transcribe the Torah, whereas the Jews adopted the square script.[17]

The situation was further complicated by the demographic composition of Samaria: The western part of the province was inhabited by gentiles, while the Samaritans resided on the eastern part. This non-Jewish Samaria separated Judea and Galilee, provinces which were inhabited by Jews; consequently, the shortest way from Galilee to Jerusalem required travel through Shechem. Separate Samaritan diaspora can be detected since the second century BCE in Greek-speaking islands such as Delos, and in Egypt.[18] Additionally, Jews and Samaritans began to differentiate themselves from one another, a process that culminated in a type of excommunication as expressed in rabbinical writings (t. Ter. 4:12, 14; b. Ḥul. 6a).

As with the Jews, the Samaritan community underwent numerous linguistic transformations, resulting in the emergence of Greek and Aramaic translations of the Hebrew text of the Samaritan Pentateuch. The Greek translation, known as the *Samarieitikon*, has survived only in allusions and fragments found in other works. It is assumed that some of the Old Testament quotations in the New Testament are not from the Septuagint, but from the *Samareitikon*. The Aramaic language, along with the Aramaic translation (the Samaritan Targum), remained in use until the 600s CE, when it was replaced by Arabic.

The Samaritans accepted only the Torah as a holy book (perhaps accepting even the Book of Joshua for a brief period),[19] and they observed its tenets in full,

The Jewish tradition regarding the origin of the Samaritans is based on their interpretation of 2 Kings 17:24–36, where the Assyrians settled the inhabitants of various eastern regions, including *Kutah*, in the territory of Samaria. The text was subsequently amended to include the term *Samaritans* (*shomronim*) to denote these people. The essence of the narrative is that these foreigners introduced their idolatrous customs, but God sent ferocious lions to kill them for this reason, so they converted to Yahwism. However, they retained some elements of their former faith in their religious practice. The Samaritans, therefore, represent an alien ethnic group who practice a kind of syncretistic Yahwism, which is contrary to God's will. The Septuagint translated *shomronim* as *samareitai*, which became the term used to refer to the Samaritans in the New Testament. Another designation of the Samaritans originates from this story: *kutim* (people of Kutha), which was found in a text from the Dead Sea Scrolls (4Q550^{d} iv.5), and later appears in rabbinic literature, as well as in the works of Josephus Flavius (*khutaioi*). At times the Talmud (e.g., y. Git. 43c; b. Qidd. 75a–76b; b. Sanh. 85b) refers to them as lion proselytes (*gere ariyot*), based on the same story from 2 Kings 17. Josephus is the first source to equate all three expressions.

Figure 23.2. Jewish tradition on the origin of the Samaritans.

with greater rigor than the Jews, given that they did not cultivate the practice of eruvim (b. ʽErub. 31a).

Despite the destruction of their temple, the practice of the Pesach sacrifice on Mount Gerizim is still observed by the community to this day. Additionally, synagogues were constructed, with written references to them emerging from the Hellenistic period. However, archaeological evidence only exists from the second and third centuries CE, in various settlements, including Gerizim.[20] The practice of religion beyond the High Holidays was concentrated in synagogues. During festivals, pilgrims gathered on Mount Gerizim, where a large flat rock was commemorated as the site of Isaac's sacrifice (Gen 22), and twelve stones were venerated as memorial as those erected by Joshua (Josh 4).

Roman Period

The Roman invasion of Palestine in 63 BCE brought an end to the Jewish domination over the Samaritans and established them as equals among the other non-Roman inhabitants of the provinces. Some Samaritans relocated to larger, predominantly gentile settlements and cities, such as Sebaste and Caesarea, which were constructed by Herod. One of Herod's wives is still regarded as a Samaritan, despite the lack of evidence to support this claim.[21] However, neither Herod nor his sons exhibited any particular degree of bias toward the

Matt 10:5	Jesus forbids his disciples to go to any town of the Samaritans with the gospel.
Luke 9:52–55	The disciples want to call down fire from heaven to burn a Samaritan village that refused to accept Jesus, but Jesus prevents them from doing so.
Luke 10:30–37	The parable of the Good Samaritan.
Luke 17:11	Jesus makes his way from Galilee to Jerusalem, passing through Samaria along the way.
Luke 17:12–19	Jesus heals ten lepers, and only one of them, a Samaritan, returns to express gratitude.
John 4:4–42	Jesus meets and talks to a Samaritan woman at Jacob's well and the Samaritans acknowledge him as the Savior.
John 8:48	After Jesus publicly disowns his Jewish audience as children of Abraham, some of them claim that he is a Samaritan.
Acts 7:15–16	Stephen mentions a Samaritan tradition in his speech before the Sanhedrin.
Acts 8:5–25	Philip baptizes many Samaritans. Peter and John preach the gospel in many Samaritan villages.

Figure 23.3. New Testament texts connected to the Samaritans.

Samaritans as they were neither more friendly nor hostile toward them than they were of the Jews.[22]

In the period covered by the New Testament, the Samaritans constituted a religious group who resided primarily in the Samaritan highlands, situated between Galilee and Judea. The New Testament makes no direct reference to the origins of the Samaritans, but it offers a few indirect references to their ethnic status. In Matthew 10:5b, a threefold distinction is made between the gentiles, the Samaritans, and the "lost sheep of the house of Israel." This latter expression refers to those Jews who, for various reasons, do not belong to the community of Israel, regardless of whether they reside in its territory or in the diaspora. If the Samaritans are excluded from this category, they are therefore not considered Israelites, namely Jews. This assertion is corroborated by the term "foreigner" (*allogenēs*) in Luke 17:18. Thus, the Samaritans are depicted in at least in two Gospels as non-Jewish, alien people, though distinct from the gentiles of the period. At the same time, other passages in Luke introduce further nuance, complicating the picture.[23]

The growing divergence between Samaritans and mainstream Judaism prompted a continual reexamination of their shared heritage and the nature of their relationship. In this context, it is noteworthy that in Luke, Jesus refers to the Samaritans as exemplary figures, especially given the increasingly distinct theological and social foundations on which the two groups were based. The Samaritans appear not only as protagonists in a parable but are also featured in a healing narrative. In the parable of the Good Samaritan (Luke 10:30), a parallel is drawn between the Samaritan and two other figures: a priest and a Levite. The latter two characters are distinguished from the Samaritan by their adherence to rigorous Jewish ritual purity standards. The narrative presents two interpretative pathways, but both lead to the same moral teaching. On the one hand, if the Samaritan is identified as unclean and effectively a gentile, a distinction is drawn between his moral action over the Jews who adhere to the ritual purity laws. Conversely, on the other hand, if the Samaritan is defined as a member of a rejected Yahwistic religious group known for its extremely precise observance of the law—then the contrast is even more pointed. Either way, the Samaritan is not simply a protagonist in the parable; he also serves as a moral exemplar and a model of neighborly love for the Jews and followers of Jesus (i.e., Christians). The same dynamic is also found in the narrative of the healing of the ten lepers (Luke 17:11–19), in which only one returns to the healer to give thanks. The one who returns to expresses gratitude to God and prostrates himself at Jesus's feet is a Samaritan, identified explicitly as a foreigner. Jesus expresses displeasure at the failure of the other individuals to return, shifting the positive-negative ratio from one out of three to one out of ten—thus, underscoring the Samaritan's gratitude in contrast to the ingratitude of the Jews.

The Pauline letters, written some decades earlier, do not make reference to the Samaritans. However, Paul's deliberate use of terms such as Israel, Israelites, Hebrews, and seeds of Abraham, rather than simply "Jews," may suggest a broader theological framework that could include Samaritans, since they were also circumcised and followed the Mosaic law (e.g., Rom 2:9–10; 10:12; 1Cor 9:20–21; Gal 2:7–10; 3:28; Phil 3:1b–11).[24] In any case, as evidenced in Acts 8:4–25, and subsequently reiterated by the Church Fathers, the post-Easter Christian mission among the Samaritans proved to be a fruitful endeavor.

During the Roman era, Samaritan pilgrimage to Gerizim was repeatedly prohibited, and those who defied the decree were subject to severe consequences. Josephus reports that a figure claiming to be a messiah led a large crowd up the mountain, but under the order of the Roman procurator, Pilate, they were massacred. Pilate was denounced to the emperor and removed from his post (*Ant.* 18.85–89). Based on Deuteronomy 18:15–19, the Samaritans held a messianic expectation based on prophetic figure whom they later called Taheb.[25] Additionally, a messianically inclined minority group called Dositheans emerged from the Samaritan tradition.[26]

TAKING A CLOSER LOOK: SOURCES

Sources from the World of the New Testament

Delos Inscriptions

In the vicinity of a Jewish synagogue on the Greek island of Delos, two Greek inscriptions have been unearthed. Through paleographic analysis, these texts have been dated to the early second century BCE and the mid-first century BCE, respectively. While the names and circumstances of the two texts differ, there is a notable degree of similarity between them:

> No 1: The Israelites on Delos who make offerings/contributions to the temple of Mount Gerizim [*Argarizein*] crown, with a gold crown, Sarapion, son of Jason, of Knossos, for his benefactions toward them.
>
> No 2: The Israelites who make offerings/contribution to the holy temple of Mount Gerizim [*Argarizein*] honor Menippos, son of Artemidoros, of Heraklion, both himself and his descendants, for constructing and dedicating, out of his own funds, to the synagogue [*proseuchē*] of Go[d] the . . . and the walls and the . . . with a gold cro[w]n.[27]

The term *Argarizein* (Mount Gerizim), which is written in one word[28], makes it evident that the inscription was created by members of the Gerizim Yahwist community, later called Samaritans. Additionally, it demonstrates that the term *Israelites* (*Israeleitai*) is not a unique term for this group. Given that chapters 3 and 7 of 1 Maccabees repeatedly employ "sons of Israel" to refer to the Jerusalemite Yahwists, "Israelites" can be interpreted as a general designation for the Yahwists of this period. The term *offerings* in the inscription can be interpreted not only as a food offering but also as a temple tax. For members of the diaspora, the remitting a monetary tax would have been more convenient and beneficial than sending perishable food.

The two inscriptions indicate that the Greek archipelago diaspora of the Gerizim Yahwists was already established at the time of the temple's operation. Furthermore, they demonstrate that this diaspora even constructed their own synagogue.[29] The people living in distant locations provided the community and the cult with sacrificial food and financial contributions. At the same time, the evidence suggests that they had a positive relationship with the Judean Yahwists given the close proximity of their synagogues. Additionally, they shared a common identity with the other Yahwist group, as indicated by their common "Israelite" designation, despite their distinct cultic centers.

Pseudo-Eupolemos on Shechem

In a fragment by an unknown Hellenistic-Jewish writer of the end of second century BCE called "Pseudo-Eupolemos," the story of Abraham is retold. At the conclusion of the treatment of Genesis 14, the following is presented:

> He was also received as a guest by the city at the temple of Mount Gerizim [*Argarizin*], which is interpreted as the "mountain of the Most High [*horos hypsistou*]." He also received gifts from Melchizedek who was a priest of God and a king as well.[30]

This text is not a part of the Torah, but rather a historical paraphrase of the Abraham story, which interprets the meeting of Abraham and Melchizedek as an encounter that takes place on Mount Gerizim. The pairing of city and temple on Mount Gerizim indicates that the author was familiar with the pre-Hyrcanian status of Mount Gerizim, where a temple-city existed.[31] For this reason, Pseudo-Eupolemos is typically regarded as a Samaritan writer.

Jewish Interpretation of Genesis 34

The biblical narrative of Genesis 34, in which Simeon and Levi perpetrate violent retribution for their sister's rape, despite a covenant with the Shechemites, and are ultimately cursed by their father (Gen 49:5–7), is reinterpreted or rewritten in numerous Jewish texts. In the writings from the late second to the early first centuries BCE, the epic Jewish poet Theodotus, in a passage from his *On the Jews*, discusses the divine plague on Shechem as punishment for the city's wickedness.[32] The Book of Jubilees, which is also found in excerpts at Qumran, states that Simeon and Levi were acting under divine command and that the people of Shechem were pagans. The Aramaic Testament of Levi suggests that all of Jacob's sons participated in the massacre, which is portrayed as the result of God's wrath and ultimately leads to the brothers inheriting the territory of Shechem.

> God disabled the inhabitants of Shechem, for they did not honor whoever came to them, the low, not even the noble; neither did they dispense justice nor enforce laws throughout the city. Their deadly deeds were their chief concern. (Theodotus, 9.22.9)[33]

> Therefore, I command you, saying, "Proclaim this testimony to Israel:" See how it was for the Shechemites and their sons, how they were given into the hand of the two children of Jacob and they killed them painfully. And it was a righteousness for them and it was written down for them for righteousness. (Jub. 30:17 [Wintermute])[34]

> From this day forward, Shechem shall be called "City of Fools" because as one mocks a fool, so we mocked them, because defiling our sister they indeed committed folly in Israel." (T. Levi 7:2–3 [De Jonge])[35]

The three alternative versions of Genesis 34 present the conquest of Shechem by Simeon and Levi in a favorable light, and moreover, implicitly depict John Hyrcanus's assault on Shechem and the temple of Gerizim as divinely legitimized.[36] In these retellings, the Samaritan Yahwists, who are identified with the Shechemites, are subjected to a sustained campaign of character assassination: They are labeled pagans, unclean, erased from the tables of life, and fools. The line is continued later by the book of Judith (Jdt 9:2–4), 4Q371–72, and Josephus.[37] However, in these three texts, which were probably written in the time of Hyrcanus, a strong propagandistic tendency is discernible.

Reading the New Testament Texts

Jesus and a Samaritan Woman in John

> So he left Judea and went back once more to Galilee. Now he had to go through Samaria. So he came to a town in Samaria called Sychar, near the plot of ground Jacob had given to his son Joseph. Jacob's well was there, and Jesus, tired as he was from the journey, sat down by the well. It was about noon. When a Samaritan woman came to draw water, Jesus said to her, "Will you give me a drink?" (His disciples had gone into the town to buy food.) The Samaritan woman said to him, "You are a Jew and I am a Samaritan woman. How can you ask me for a drink?" (For Jews do not associate with Samaritans.) (4:3–9)

> Our ancestors worshiped on this mountain, but you Jews claim that the place where we must worship is in Jerusalem." "Woman," Jesus replied, "believe me, a time is coming when you will worship the Father neither on this mountain nor in Jerusalem. You Samaritans worship what you do not know; we worship what we do know, for salvation is from the Jews. Yet a time is coming and has now come when the true worshipers will worship the Father in the Spirit and in truth, for they are the kind of worshipers the Father seeks. God is spirit, and his worshipers must worship in the Spirit and in truth." The woman said, "I know that Messiah" (called Christ) "is coming. When he comes, he will explain everything to us." Then Jesus declared, "I, the one speaking to you—I am he." (20–26)

> Many of the Samaritans from that town believed in him because of the woman's testimony, "He told me everything I ever did." So when

the Samaritans came to him, they urged him to stay with them, and he stayed two days. And because of his words many more became believers. They said to the woman, "We no longer believe just because of what you said; now we have heard for ourselves, and we know that this man really is the Savior of the world." (39–42)

John 4 provides the most comprehensive account of Jesus's encounter with a Samaritan. The fundamental circumstances are analogous to those depicted in Luke 9:51–56, which speaks about Samaritans who do not want to host Jesus because he is on the way to Jerusalem—but the outcome is different. Several core issues of Samaritan theology are dealt with here.

In the initial portion of verse 9, the Samaritan woman expresses astonishment at Jesus's request for a drink from her, given that he is a Jew, and she is a Samaritan and a woman. This sentence alone indicates the existence of certain tensions between the two groups. It can be assumed that this tension was rooted in religious differences, as the woman's astonishment appears to extend beyond mere social norms around gender interactions. It is also plausible that her reaction was influenced by his request of a drink from her—namely, that a Jew would be willing to drink from a vessel handled by a Samaritan, something that would have been deemed unusual or even taboo. The second sentence of the verse, which elucidates the woman's astonishment and is absent in a number of significant manuscripts,[38] remains the subject of scholarly debate.[39] Earlier translations (e.g., KJV and RSV) state, "for the Jews have no dealings with the Samaritans." This version implies a total rupture between the two groups, a notion that is not corroborated by the remainder of the New Testament or the narrative itself, since the disciples, for instance, entered the city Sychar, where the majority of the population were Samaritans (Luke 9:51–56; 17:11–19). A more nuanced translation (e.g., in the NEB) reads: "Since the Jews and Samaritans did not share common vessels." Even if the sentence is a later insertion, this translation lends support to the assumption that religious, specifically halachic concerns about purity standards were at stake. However, the ambiguity of this clause makes it difficult to conclude definitely that the use of shared vessels was the main issue.[40] An alternative hypothesis is that the impurity of the Samaritan woman herself would have presented a greater problem for a Jew than the communal use of the vessel. This idea is supported in verse 27, as the disciples are taken aback by the fact that he is "speaking with a [Samaritan] woman."

The Samaritan woman's reference to "this mountain" (v. 20)—Gerizim—as a legitimate place of worship for God, in contrast to Jerusalem, reflects her awareness of the importance of the location of worship in the context of Jewish-Samaritan relations.[41] Furthermore, her use of the phrase *our ancestors* and *you* (instead of *we*) indicate a perceived divergence in lineage or heritage. These ancestors (*pateres*) could be the Samaritan leaders and priests of the period, but the aorist verb (*prosekynēsan*) suggests a more distant past. Thus, the phrase, "our father Jacob" may subtly imply that the Samaritans regarded themselves, and not the Jews, as the descendants and heirs of Jacob. Third, the Greek text employs the word *god* in the singular, without qualification or distinction between the God of the Jews and the God of the Samaritans. This usage indicates that the Samaritan woman assumes a shared belief in the same deity as the Jews.

As counterpart to the Samaritan's woman's previous statement, Jesus's response in vv. 21–24 establishes a connection between the Samaritans and the Jews, by emphasizing their shared relationship to the same divine entity, whom he names *Father*. While distinguishing between *us* (Jews) and *you* (Samaritans), and associating the origin of salvation with Judaism in contrast to the Samaritans, Jesus reorients the conversation away from the boundaries between Jews and Samaritans, and toward a distinctly Christian theological perspective.[42] In this move, Jesus asserts that worship of the Father is not confined to a particular location, whether on Mount Gerizim or in Jerusalem, but is instead "in spirit and in truth."

Verse 25 indicates that the Samaritans at that time held beliefs pertaining to a specific "messiah"[43] who would "come and explain everything to us." If the pronoun *to us* (*hēmin*) indeed refers to the Samaritans, which seems probable, it is unlikely that this messiah would be imagined as a shared Jewish figure. By contrast, in verse 26, Jesus identifies himself with this anticipated messiah expected by the Samaritans, marking a turning point in the dynamics of the story.[44] The theological world constructed around Jesus, previously framed in Jewish terms, now erases the tension between Jews and Samaritans. Jesus not only arbitrates the two rival cultic sites, but supersedes both by presenting himself as a third "site" for the worship of God, and also as a third *messiah* who fulfills the anticipation of the other two. From this standpoint, it can be argued that the Samaritans, if they are consistent with their own messianic expectations, must recognize Jesus, and align themselves with his followers, the Christians. The second half of the story describes this very process: Jesus is no longer a rejected dissenter (as in Luke 9:53) but is welcomed like an invited guest (v. 40); he is no longer a strange Jew who engages in conversation even with a Samaritan woman but "the savior of the world" (v. 42). This conversion was effective[45] and anticipates the successful Samaritan mission depicted in Acts 8.[46] As such, the Samaritans in the Gospel of John serve as a good example for converts whether Jew or pagan.[47]

Jacob Tradition in Acts

> Then Jacob went down to Egypt, where he and our ancestors died.
> Their bodies were brought back to Shechem and placed in the tomb

> that Abraham had bought from the sons of Hamor at Shechem for a certain sum of money. (Acts 7:15–16)

In Acts 7:1–53, Stephen's defense speech before the Sanhedrin recalls the history of Israel largely grounded in the Torah, but verse 16 contains a specific contradiction concerning Shechem. Neither the Masoretic text nor the Samaritan Pentateuch makes a connection between Jacob's death and Shechem as Stephen does.[48] Moreover, this verse indicates that Abraham purchased a piece of land in the vicinity of Shechem from Hamor, which is inconsistent with the accounts in both versions of the text, which attribute this action to Jacob. The only viable solution to this contradiction is to assume that Stephen was engaging a contemporaneous Samaritan theological tradition.[49] Following the destruction of the Samaritan temple in 108 BCE by Hyrcanus, Samaritan theology discourse (but not the Samaritan Pentateuch itself) began to associate some pivotal events in the lives of the patriarchs with Shechem and its environs. This coincidence does not necessarily imply that Stephen himself was a Samaritan, although this is not an impossibility. In the remainder of his speech, Old Testament prophets are quoted, who are not recognized by Samaritans. In any case, the author of the speech—probably not the historical Stephen—was aware of this tradition and must have identified with it, as evidenced by the confessional nature of his speech. Consequently, the author of this speech (or the tradition behind it) may have been either a Jew who was raised in a Samaritan environment or a Samaritan who converted to Christianity.

FURTHER READING

Alkier, Stefan. *Konstellationen antiker Tempelwirtschaft: Neue Perspektiven auf den Tempel am Garizim, den Jerusalemer Tempel und das Artemision in Ephesos*. Beyond Historicism—New Testament Studies Today 2. Brill and Schöningh, 2022.

Böhm, Martina. "Samaritans in the New Testament." *Religions* 11, no. 3 (2020): 1–16. doi:10.3390/rel11030147.

Crown, Aalan D., ed. *The Samaritans*. Mohr Siebeck, 1989.

Knoppers, Gary N., *Judah and Samaria in Postmonarchic Times*. Forschungen zum Alten Testament 129. Mohr Siebeck, 2019.

Magen, Yitzhak. *The Samaritans and the Good Samaritan*. Judea and Samaria Publications 7. Civil Administration of Judea and Samarian and Israel Antiquities Authority, 2008.

Meier, John P. "The Historical Jesus and the Historical Samaritans: What can be Said?" *Biblica* 81 (2000): 202–32.

Schapdick, Stefan. *Auf dem Weg in der Konflikt: Exegetische Studien zum theologischen Profil der Erzählung vom Aufenthalt Jesu in Samarien (Joh 4,4–42) im Kontext des Johannesevangeliums*. Bonner biblische Beiträge 126. Philo, 2000.

Schattner-Rieser, Ursula. "Jesus in den Samaritanischen Chroniken." In *Die Samaritaner und die Bibel: Historische und literarische Wechselwirkungen zwischen biblischen und samaritanischen Traditionen* [The Samaritans and the Bible historical and literary interactions between biblical and Samaritan traditions], edited by Jörg Frey, Ursula Schattner-Rieser, and Konrad Schmid. Studia Samaritana 7. De Gruyter, 2012.

Zangenberg, Jürgen. *Frühes Christentum in Samarien: Topographische und traditionsgeschichtliche Studien zu den Samarientexte im Johannesevangelium*. Texte und Arbeiten zum neutestamentlichen Zeitalter 27. Francke, 1998.

Notes

1 *The Royal Inscriptions of Sargon II. King of Assyria (721–714 BC)*, ed. Grant Fram, The Royal Inscriptions of the Neo-Assyrian Period 2 (Eisenbrauns, 2021).

2 Nadav Na'aman and Ran Zadok, "Assyrian Deportations to the Province of Samerina in the Light of Two Cuniform Tablets from Tel Hadid," *Tel Aviv* 27, no. 2 (2000): 159–88.

3 *The Cyrus Cylinder. The King of Persia's Proclamation from Ancient Babylon*, ed. Irving Finkel (Tauris, 2013).

4 See Yitzhak Magen, *Mount Gerizim Excavations Volume II. The Temple City*, Judea and Samaria Publications 8 (Israel Antiquities Authority, Civil Administration of Judea and Samaria, 2008).

5 See Christian Frevel, *Geschichte Israels*, 2nd rev. ed. (Kohlhammer, 2018).

6 See Benedikt Hensel, *Juda und Samaria. Zum Verhältnis zweier nach-exilischer Jahwismen*, Forschungen zum Alten Testament 110 (Mohr Siebeck, 2016); the papers in Benedikt Hensel et al., eds., *Yahwistic Diversity and the Hebrew Bible: Tracing Perspectives of Group Identity from Judah, Samaria, and the Diaspora in Biblical Traditions*, Forschungen zum Alten Testament 120 (Mohr Siebeck, 2021). The various forms of the text of the Torah are evidenced in the dissimilar manuscripts of the Dead Sea Scrolls, for example, the so-called pre-Samaritan texts. Cf. Sydnie White Crawford, "The Pentateuch as Found in the Pre-Samaritan Texts and 4QRewritten Pentateuch," in *Changes in Scripture: Rewriting and Interpreting Authoritative Traditions in the Second Temple Period*, ed. Hanne von Weissenberg et al., Beihefte zur Zeitschrift für die alttestamentliche Wissenschaft 419 (de Gruyter, 2011).

7 See Gary N. Knoppers, *Jews and Samaritans. The Origins and History of Their Early Relations* (Oxford University Press, 2013); Raik Heckl, "The Composition of Ezra–Nehemiah as a Testimony for the Competition Between the Temples in Jerusalem and on Mt. Gerizim in the Early Years of the Seleucid Rule over Judah," in *The Bible, Qumran, and the Samaritans*, ed. Magnar Kartveit and Gary N. Knoppers, Studia Samaritana 10 (de Gruyter, 20018).

8 See Jan Dušek, *Aramaic and Hebrew Inscriptions from Mt. Gerizim and Samaria between Antiochus III and Antiochus IV Epiphanes*, Culture and History of the Ancient Near East 54 (Brill, 2012).

9 See Yohanan H. Landau, "A Greek Inscription Found Near Hefzibah," *Israel Exploration Journal* 16, no. 1 (1966): 54–70; Lester L. Grabbe, "Hyparchs, Oikonomoi and

Mafiosi: The Goverment of Judah in the Ptolemaid," in *Judah Between East and West, The Transition from Persian to Greek Rule (ca. 400–200 BCE)*, ed. Lester L. Grabbe and Oded Lipschits (Bloombury, 2013); Hanna M. Cotton and Michael Wörrle, "Seleukos IV to Heliodoros: a New Dossier of Royal Correspondence from Israel," *Zeitschrift für Papyrologie und Epigraphik* 159 (2007): 191–205.

10 See Menahem Mor, "Samaritan *History* I, The Persian, Hellenistic and Hasmonean Period," in *The Samaritans*, ed. Alan D. Crown (J.C.B. Mohr Paul Siebeck, 1989).

11 See Doron Mendel, *The Rise and Fall of Jewish Nationalism, Jewish and Christian Ethnicity in Ancient Palestine* (Eerdmans, 1992).

12 See Robert Doran, *Temple Propaganda: The Purpose and Character of 2 Maccabees* (The Catholic Biblical Association of America, 1981); József Zsengellér, "Maccabees and Temple Propaganda," in *The Books of the Maccabees. History, Theology, Ideology*, ed. Géza Xeravits and József Zsengellér, Supplements to the Journal for the Study of Judaism 118 (Brill, 2007).

13 See Jonathan Bourgel, "The Destruction of the Samaritan Temple by John Hyrcanus: A Reconsideration," *Journal of Biblical Literature* 135, no. 3 (2016): 499–517; József Zsengellér, "Samaritan Persecution in the Hellenistic Period According to Josephus Flavius," in *Passion, Persecution and Epiphany in Early Jewish Literature*, ed. Nicholas P. L. Allen, Pierre Jordan, and József Zsengellér (Routledge, 2020).

14 See Magnar Kartveit, *Origin of the Samaritans*, Vetus Testamentum, Supplements 128 (Brill, 2009); Hensel, *Juda und Samaria*.

15 See James H. Charlesworth, "What Is a Variant? Announcing a Dead Sea Scrolls Fragment of Deuteronomy," *Maarav* 16, no. 2 (2009): 201–12, 273–74; Adrian Schenker, "Textgeschichtliches zum Samaritanischen Pentateuch und Samareitikon," in *Samaritans: Past and Present: Current Studies*, ed. Menachem Mor and Friedrich V. Reiterer, Studia Samaritana 5 (de Gruyter, 2010).

16 See Stefan Schorch, "The So-Called Gerizim-Commandment in the Samaritan Pentateuch," in *The Samaritan Pentateuch and the Dead Sea Scrolls*, ed. Michael Langlois, Contributions to Biblical Exegesis & Theology 94 (Peeters, 2019); Gary N. Knoppers, "The Samaritan Tenth Commandment: Origins, Content and Context," in *Judah and Samaria in Postmonarchic Times*, Forschungen zum Alten Testament 129 (Mohr Siebeck, 2009), 275–99.

17 See Reinhard Pummer, *The Samaritans: A Profile* (Eerdmans, 2016).

18 See József Zsengellér, "The Samaritan Diaspora in Antiquity," *Acta Antiqua Academiae Scientiarum Hungaricae* 56, no. 2 (2016): 157–75.

19 See József Zsengellér, "Canon and the Samaritans," in *Canonization and Decanonization. Papers Presented to the International Conference of the Leiden Institute for the Studies of Religion (LISOR), Held at Leiden 9–10 January 1997*, ed. Arie van der Kooij and Karel van der Toorn, Numen Book Series 82 (Brill, 1998).

20 See Reinhard Pummer, "Samaritan Synagogues and Jewish Synagogues. Similarities and Differences," in *Jews, Christians, and Polytheists in the Ancient Synagogue*, ed. Steven Fine (Routledge, 1999).

21 See Daniel R. Schwartz, "Malthace, Archelaus and Antipas: Between Genealogy and Typology," in *Sources and Interpretation in Ancient Judaism: Studies for Tal Ilan at*

Sixty, ed. Meron M. Piotrkowski et al., Ancient Judaism and Early Christianity 104 (Brill, 2018).

22 Josephus reports on Archelaus's brutality against Jews as well as Samaritans: *Ant.* 17.342; *J.W.* 2.111.

23 See Jörg Frey, " 'Gute' Samaritaner? Das neutestamentliche Bild der Samaritaner zwischen Juden und Paganen," in *Die Samaritaner und die Bibel: Historische und literarische Wechselwirkungen zwischen biblischen und samaritanischen Traditionen*, ed. Jörg Frey et al., Studia Samaritana 7 (de Gruyter, 2012); Martina Böhm, *Samariern und die Samaritai bei Lukas. Eine Studie zum religionshistorischen und traditionsgeschichtlichen Hintergrund der lukanischen Samarientexte und zu deren topographischer Verhaftung*, Wissenschaftliche Untersuchungen zum Neuen Testament 111 (Mohr Siebeck, 2012), 194–202.

24 See Martina Böhm, "Wer gehörte in hellenistisch-römischer Zeit zu 'Israel'? Historische Voraussetzungen für eine veränderte Perspektive auf neutestamentliche Texte," in *Die Samaritaner und die Bibel: Historische und literarische Wechselwirkungen zwischen biblischen und samaritanischen Traditionen*, ed. Jörg Frey et al., Studia Samaritana 7 (de Gruyter, 2012), 181–202.

25 See Ferdinan Dexinger, *Der Taheb. Ein "messianischer" Heilsbringer der Samaritaner*, Kairos Religionswissenschaftliche Studien 3 (Otto Müller, 1986).

26 Stanley J. Isser, *The Dositheans: A Samaritan Sect in Late Antiquity*, Studies in Judaism in Late Antiquity 17 (Brill, 1976).

27 See Philippe Bruneau, "Les Israelites de Délos et la juiverie délienne," *Bulletin de Correspondance Hellénique* 106 (1982): 465–504; A. Thomas Kraabel, "New Evidence of the Samaritan Diaspora has been Found on Delos," *The Biblical Archaeologist* 55, no. 1 (1984): 44–46.

28 In the Samaritan tradition, the name of Mount Gerizim (*Har Garizim*) is written in one word: *Hargarizim* in Hebrew and *Argarizein* in Greek.

29 Zsengellér, "Samaritan Diaspora in Antiquity."

30 Cited in Eusebius, *Preparatio evangelica*, 9.17.5–6. Translation in *Fragments from Hellenistic Jewish Authors*, trans. Carl R. Holladay, vol. 1, *Historians*, SBL Text and Translations 20 (Scholar Press, 1983).

31 Holladay, *Fragments*, 182. Halladay and others postulated that the city was in fact Shechem. See also Kartveit, *Origin of the Samaritans*, 243–56.

32 See also the chapter on "Early Jewish Literature" by David Cielontko in the present volume.

33 Eusebius, *Praeparatio evangelica*, in *Fragments from Hellenistic Jewish Authors*, trans. Carl R. Holladay, vol. 2, *Poets*, SBL Text and Translations 12 (Scholar Press, 1989).

34 O. S. Wintermute, "Jubilees," in *The Old Testament Pseudepigrapha*, ed. James H. Charlesworth, vol. 2, *Expansions of the "Old Testament" and Legends, Wisdom and Philosophical Literature, Prayers, Psalms, and Odes, Fragments of Lost Judeo-Hellenistic Works* (Doubleday, 1983), 2:35–144.

35 Michael De Jonge, *The Testaments of the Twelve Patriarchs. A Critical Edition of the Greek Text*, Pseudepigrapha Veteries Testamenti Graece 1 (Brill, 1978).

36 See John J. Collins, *Between Athens and Jerusalem: Jewish Identity in the Hellenistic Diaspora*, (Eerdmans, 2000).

37 József Zsengellér, *Gerizim as Israel: The Northern Tradition of the Old Testament and the Early History of the Samaritans*, Utrechtse theologische reeks38 (Rijksuniversiteit Utrecht, 1998); Kartveit, *Origin of the Samaritans*, 109–202.

38 The sentence is not present in *Codex Sinaiticus* and *Codex Bezae Cantabrigiensis*. Cf. the critical apparatus of the latest Nestle-Aland edition.

39 Raymond E. Brown, *The Gospel According to John (I–XII)*, Anchor Bible Commentary 29 (Yale University Press, 1984).

40 Alan D. Crown, "Redating the Schism between the Judeans and the Samaritans," *Jewish Quarterly Review* 82, no. 1/2 (1991): 17–50.

41 In Tractate Kutim, a minor tractate of the Talmud, a strong Jewish position is recorded: "When do we take them back? If they deny Mount Gerizim and believe in Jerusalem and in the resurrection of dead." (2:8).

42 Cf. Hartwig Thyen, *Das Johannesevangelium*, Handbuch zum Neuen Testament 6 (Mohr Siebeck, 2005).

43 Dexinger, *Der Taheb*.

44 Ingrid Hjelm, *The Samaritans and Early Judaism. A Literary Analysis*, Journal for the Study of the Old Testament. Supplement Series 303 (Sheffield University Press, 2000).

45 Due to the orientation of the passage, many have postulated the existence of a Samaritan editorial influence or a Samaritan target audience in the Gospel of John. Cf. Edwin D. Freed, "Samaritan Influence in the Gospel of John," *The Catholic Biblical Quarterly*30, no. 4 (1968): 580–657; Edwin D. Freed, "Did John Write his Gospel Partly to Win Samaritan Converts?" *Novum Testamentum* 12, no. 3 (1970): 241–56; John Bowman, "The Fourth Gospel and the Samaritans," *Bulletin of the John Rylands Library* 40 (1958): 298–308.

46 Cf. Böhm, *Samarien und die Samaritai*, 279–308.

47 Frey, " 'Gute' Samaritaner?," 230–31.

48 Reinhard Pummer, "The Samaritan Pentateuch and the New Testament," *New Testament Studies* 22, no. 4 (1975–76): 441–43.

49 William F. Albright and C. S.Mann, "Stephen's Samaritan Background," in *The Acts of the Apostles*, ed. Johannes Munck, Anchor Bible Commentary 31 (Yale University Press, 1958).